THE
MEDAL
YEARBOOK
2012

Edited by
John W. Mussell, FRGS
and
the Editorial Team of MEDAL NEWS

ISBN: 978 1 870 192.46 0
Hardback edition ISBN: 978 1 870 192 51 4

Published by
TOKEN PUBLISHING LIMITED

Orchard House, Duchy Road, Heathpark, Honiton, Devon EX14 1YD, UK
Telephone: 01404 46972   Fax: 01404 44788
e-mail: info@tokenpublishing.com   Website: www.tokenpublishing.com

USA distributor: Jeffery Stone, 2000 Bloomingdale Road, Suite 200, Glendale Heights, IL 60139
Canadian distributor: Eugene G. Ursual, PO Box 788, Kemptville, Ontario, Canada, KOG 1JO

Front cover illustration: Coronation Medal, 1902 (bronze), Delhi Durbar Medal, 1911,
Silver Jubilee Medal, 1935 and Coronation Medal, 1937 to
Sir George Townsend Boag, K.C.I.E., C.S.I. (1884-1969)

Printed in

D1343248

Worcestershire Medal Service Ltd

Medals Mounted for Wear and Display

We carry one of the most comprehensive stocks of ribbon from the UK and Commonwealth together with a large selection of world ribbons. Sashes, both full size and evening dress are manufactured to order.

Miniature & Full Size Medals

We have large stocks of miniature medals from the UK and other countries around the world, particularly where UK service personnel serve on attachment such as Oman and Brunei. We also provide miniatures of awards such as the Russian 40th Anniversary of WW2 and the Malta 50th Anniversary of the GC which have been granted permission to wear.

Medal Manufacture

Our manufacturing division produces bespoke items as well as Orders and Medals from around the world. We also produce UK awards under license from the MoD

We are always prepared to discuss your requirements and offer advice and information on medals and medal mounting, please contact a member of our staff by phone, fax or email or visit our secure on-line web site.

56 Broad Street, Sidemoor, Bromsgrove, B61 8LL Tel: +44(0)1527 835375 Fax: +44(0)1527 576798
Email wms@worcmedals.com   www.worcmedals.com   MoD License D/IPR/1X/E/0019/02

GLADMAN & NORMAN

51-53 Tenby Street North, Birmingham, B1 3EG
Tel: +44 (0)121 236 5752, Fax +44 (0)121 233 4539
Information@gladman-norman.co.uk   www.gladman-norman.co.uk

Specialist Craftsmen in Metals and enamels - Established 1910

Manufacturers of High Quality Insignia and bespoke Jewels and Regalia.

Our highly skilled team offer the finest quality manufacture incorporating vitreous enamelling and fine quality hand painting.

We can supply quantities from a single piece to large quantity runs in base metal or precious metals. Our team pride themselves on delivering high quality, to our customers exacting standards.

In addition we are always willing to undertake repairs of historic pieces.

Contact us to discuss your personal requirements.

The Elizabeth Cross, instituted by HM The Queen on 1st July 2009 Designed & Manufactured by Gladman & Norman Ltd

Contents

Foreword 9
Market highlights—a review of the auctions 15
Guide to prices paid when buying at auction 24
Operational honours 30
Wearing awards 36
The Order of Wear 38
Collecting medal ribbons 45
Miniature medals and decorations 47
Orders of Knighthood .... ◆ 49
Decorations .... ◆ 75
Mentions and commendation 107
Campaign medals .... ◆ 108
Long and Meritorious Service medals .... ◆ 209
Coronation and Jubilee medals .... ◆ 265
Miscellaneous medals .... ◆ 289
Medals for saving life .... ◇ 317
Foreign medals found in British groups .... ◇ 349
Medals of the Irish Republic (Eire) .... ◆ 361
Awards of the British Commonwealth
    Australia .... ◆ 374
    Canada .... ◆ 409
    New Zealand .... ◆ 439
    South Africa .... ◇ 459
Unofficial medals 489
Abbreviations and initials 507
Current regiments 511
Researching your medals/Books for the medal collector 515
Societies for medal collectors 523
Professional directory
    Auctioneers 524
    Dealers 526
    Booksellers 530
    Fairs 533
Museums and collections 534
Medal ribbons in colour 543
Index of medals 573

INDEX TO ADVERTISERS

Aberdeen Medals....................... 170
Ackley Unlimited....................... 263
Award Productions Ltd.............. 488
Baldwin's Auctions 11
Louis Bannon 106
Bonham's............. Inside front cover
Bosleys ....Inside back cover
Bostock Militaria 12
Britannia Medal Fair 506
British Medals 70
A. F. Brock & Co Ltd 2
Jim Bullock Militaria 80
Philip Burman 41
Chelsea Military Antiques............ 73
City Coins 264
C. J. Medals................................371
Colonial Coins and Medals 26
Cultman Collectables................. 105
Thomas Del Mar Ltd................... 43
DNW.............. 25, 141, 155, 335, 360
C. J. & A. J. Dixon Ltd. 6

ELM Singapore 37
Emedals.ca................................. 50
First Light Militaria....................... 42
Bill Friar Medals........................ 125
A. D. Hamilton........................... 106
Intramark Ltd............................. 28
Jäger Medals & Militaria 111
Jeffrey Hoare Auctions Inc............. 8
Alec Kaplan & Son...................... 80
George Kidner............................ 23
Künker....................................... 77
L.S.A.R.S................................... 316
Lockdales.................................... 77
Medal Tracker........................... 315
Morton & Eden............................ 13
Peter Morris............................. 162
Peter Nichols Cabinet Makers...... 80
OMRS....................................... 163
OMRS Miniature Branch 46
OMRS Ribbon Branch 44
Q & C Militaria.......................... 264

R & M International 48
Recherché................................... 27
S. A. Militaria............................ 471
S. E. Sewell.............................. 145
Scotmint 105
Spink & Son Ltd...Outside back cover
The Medal Centre 106
The Treasure Bunker.................. 77
Thomson, Roddick & Medcalf 29
Toye, Kenning & Spencer Ltd 3
Ulric of England 131
Eugene Ursual........................... 74
Wakefield Medal Fair................. 106
Wallis & Wallis 14
Warwick & Warwick.................... 78
Stephen Wheeler 162
Howard Williamson 264
Worcestershire Medal Service Ltd. 5
World Wide Militaria Exchange Inc.4
York Coin & Stamp Centre 105

Foreword

IT IS with some incredulity that I realise I am writing the foreword to the 2012 edition—2012 is such a futuristic date; if Hollywood is to be believed it is the year the world nearly ends—again, and when it was announced that the Olympic Games were coming to Britain this year it was a time that seemed impossibly far away. Of course time is the one thing we are unable to control and not only is this the 2012 edition but it is also the eighteenth that Token Publishing have produced and that in itself seems an incredible statistic. It seems impossible to believe that we have produced 18 of these tomes, yet if you compare this latest incarnation with that from 1994 you will realise that it hasn't been a straightforward rehashing of the same old material each year with just a new cover stuck on the front. The YEARBOOK now is far more of a comprehensive volume than ever the early issues were and now it is far and away the most broad ranging publication of its type. Of course where there is breadth depth may well be lacking, but the YEARBOOK was never meant to be an in-depth encyclopaedia of medals—it is simply a guide to as many medals that we collectors may come across, it is a handbook to the hobby and will, hopefully, lead on to further research with the plethora of books and websites that are out there to help. Another avenue of research that goes far beyond the scope of the YEARBOOK is, of course MEDAL NEWS magazine, our regular publication dedicated to medals and battles. Many readers of the YEARBOOK are already MEDAL NEWS readers but if you aren't do please take a look—you will, I am sure, be pleasantly surprised with the wealth of information it contains. Normally the MEDAL YEARBOOK contains a cumulative index to the magazine in the famed "blue pages" but this year we have made the decision to remove them in order to keep the book at a manageable pagination. However, the index will still be available but as a pdf download from our website www.tokenpublishing.com, and it may reappear in future in hardcopy form—do please let us know your thoughts on that.

One of the key areas of the YEARBOOK that sets it apart from other more specialised works is the inclusion of prices, the value of the medals and we are often asked both how we come to these prices and whether they are values for selling or buying. To arrive at the prices we enlist the help of a number of dealers/collectors/associations and take an average of their prices, along with those on other selected dealers' lists and an average of those fetched at auction (although auction prices are notoriously difficult to factor in because a single sale where two bidders are fighting for a particular medal may skew the final figures and may not be a true reflection of market prices, so they have to be examined very carefully. This is particularly true with on-line auction prices where true market values often have no influence on the bidding). All prices quoted in this book are what you would expect to pay a dealer/at auction and are based on the medals being awarded, unless otherwise stated, to an "ordinary" ranked recipient, e.g. a Private soldier, in a "standard" line regiment (or equivalent), i.e. not one involved in a particular action for which the regiment is famous (for example the Light Brigade at Balaclava, the 24th Foot at Isandlwana or the "Glorious Glosters" at Imjin River). That recipient will be male unless the medal is usually awarded to women and will not be a casualty (wounded or killed)—all of these factors having an effect (usually upward) on the price. We don't include different price points for different "grades" of medal, as generally speaking condition doesn't affect value overmuch as whilst there are some who will only collect "mint condition" medals others actively welcome polished or worn awards as they show they were worn with pride by the recipient themselves—all adding to the story.

We are sometimes asked why we don't value groups in the same way as "singles". We do value the more commonly found groups such as the World War I Trio—but to go further would be to open up a can of worms (we would inevitably omit some that collectors considered "common" whilst including others considered rare) and, with the vast permutations available, it would prove nigh on impossible to include everything. Valuing medals is never easy but every year we endeavour to do our best, however it must be remembered that we are reflecting the market, not leading it—we are not trying to increase the value of medals for the sake of it, so if you find from one year to the next prices for some medals haven't changed overmuch please do not immediately think it is because we haven't bothered to review them, rather it is a simple case of the current economic climate ensuring that prices are kept at reasonable levels rather than soaring away as they did a few years ago. The cost of medals is always a sore point amongst collectors, many bemoaning the current upward trend (particularly in "quality" items as quality will always sell), as they are no longer able to buy to add to their collections as once they were. But conversely no-one actually wants to see the price of medals fall. Many of us have put a large amount of money into our collections and whilst few have done it purely as a vehicle for investment no-one wants to lose money! At the moment, with the world still in a state of economic flux, medals are actually holding their own very well, there have been no huge advances in prices but neither are they coming down. One downside of the current conditions is the increase in the cost of precious metals: items like the Kaiser-I-Hind have gone up in value simply because gold has gone up and whilst it is unlikely such a medal as that will be scrapped as it is relatively rare, something like the British War Medal may well be suffering the same fate as it did in the late 1970s when thousands were melted down for scrap leaving us with the tragedy of broken groups. Already we are experiencing sellers on-line offering BWMs at scrap price (some even being pictured on scales to show their weight) and so whilst a collector might be unwilling to pay more than the "standard" £15–18 for such a medal, we have had to increase its value in the YEARBOOK to reflect the price others are prepared to pay. Sadly it is an uncomfortable fact of life that if we as medal collectors are not prepared to buy items at on or above their scrap value they will be bought by others, melted down and lost forever, which is something we should all consider. Luckily most medals are still valued as items of history and so sell well above their scrap value. Let us hope that remains the case.

As mentioned prices on the whole have been fairly sedate in the past year. However, there are a number of new medals that have been brought to our attention since the 2011 YEARBOOK was published and we are indebted to a number of people both for helping ensure our prices are realistic and for providing us with information on the new medals, as well as images for some of the existing ones. These people include the various members of the on-line British Medal Forum who are always most helpful and eager to see the book go from strength to strength, and a large number of others. There are too many to mention individually although Samuel Alfred, Jack Boddington, Colin Bruce II, Philip Burman, Howard Chamberlain, Peter Digby, Chris Dixon, Ken Fowler, Colin Hole, John Millensted, Thomas Mitchell, Michael O'Brien, Malcolm Rouse and Steve Verralls have all contributed greatly to making this edition the best ever. In addition, we are also delighted that the relevant government departments of Canada and New Zealand have thoroughly updated their sections, ensuring that they remain a valuable and accurate reference. We are also indebted to the many auction houses who have allowed us to illustrate medals from their archives.

We are always happy to hear from readers with any queries, additions and amendments—and remember, our website tokenpublishing.com is constantly being up-dated with news and other valuable information.

MARKET HIGHLIGHTS

In the period from July 2010 to the time of going to press *Medal News* has reported, in its "Market Scene" feature, on public auctions in the UK run by the well-known houses: DNW, Spink, Bonhams, Bosleys, Lockdales, Morton & Eden, Warwick & Warwick, etc. Occasionally results from other auctioneers have appeared in our news pages when particular items of interest to medal collectors have been sold by their respective firms, such as Wallis & Wallis, Kidner, and Dreweatts. This review pulls together some of the highlights of the sales that have appeared in "Market Scene" in the period under review, but unfortunately we have space for only relatively few of the exceptional lots that have passed through the auction rooms. All prices quoted here include the buyer's premium levied by the respective auction houses.

Inevitably, the choice of the "highlights" is personal and subjective, but some items choose themselves, and gallantry groups above all, which generally sell for more than anything else, cannot be ignored. Good examples of the phenomenon this year were the seven Victoria Crosses sold at **Spink**. The first was the group awarded to (Admiral of the Fleet) Sir Nowell Salmon (Lucknow), which made £228,000 on **July 22, 2010**. Again, on **November 25, 2010**, there were no fewer than four VCs on offer: (Major-General) Robert Montresor Rogers (44th Foot, China 1860), which sold for £216,000; Lance-Sergeant Thomas Neeley (King's Own Royal Lancaster Regiment, Flesquieres), £132,000; (Major-General) George Alexander Renny (Bengal Horse Artillery, Delhi), £156,000; Second Lieutenant Donald Simpson Bell (Yorkshire Regiment, Somme 1916), £252,000. And yet again, on **April 21, 2011,** two more VCs were sold: Sir Christopher Charles Teesdale (RA, Crimea 1855) for £260,000, and (Colonel) Charles John William Grant (Indian Staff Corps, Manipur 1891) for £230,000.

ORDERS AND DECORATIONS

In the sale at **DNW, July 7–8, 2010**, the highest price in the auction was paid for the Korea Military Medal group to James Arthur Walter Robson (1921–2003), Gloucestershire Regiment, a machine gunner during the infamous Imjin River battle in April 1951. His group consisted of the MM (EIIR), 1939-45/Burma Stars, Defence & War Medals, Queen's and UN Korea Medals, and it made £66,000.

At **Spink, July 22, 2010** a Distinguished Flying Cross group to (Squadron Leader) Bryan Vincent Draper RAFVR (1916–45) was sold, comprising DFC (GVI) dated 1940 and engraved "B V Draper 74 (F) Squadron", 1939–45/Air Crew Europe/Burma Stars, Defence & War Medals. Draper was a hero of the Battle of Dunkirk and the Battle of Britain flying Spitfires, and shot down three enemy aircraft in one combat mission. This achieved £36,000.

At **Warwick & Warwick, August 11, 2010,** the Distinguished Service Order group including China 1900 Medal, 1914–15 Star Trio (MiD), Belgium Order of the Crown, Belgium Croix de Guerre (three palms), Monaco Order of St Charles, to (Captain) Geoffrey Basil Spicer-Simson, RN (1876–1947), who commanded the expedition that captured the German ship *Kingani* on Lake Tanganyika, was bid up to £40,250.

The Conspicuous Gallantry Cross (for Afghanistan) to Paul Darren Willmott, 2/Mercian, was the pick of the sale at **Bosleys, September 1, 2010**. Willmott's citation showed

James Robson's Imjin River, Korea, MM group which realised £66,000 at DNW.

DNW achieved £72,000 for the stunning DCM group to John Vincent Byrne.

an incredible disregard for his own safety in recovering the dead body of his section leader, and the lot sold for £48,300.

DNW, September 16–17, 2010, sold the Order of the Bath, Royal Guelphic Cross, Waterloo Medal, Russian Order of St Vladimir, to Joseph Muter (he added the name Straton from 1816), Colonel of the Inniskilling Dragoons. It realised £32,400. An outstanding World War II group to Eric Frank Knowles Campling comprised DSO (GVI), DFC (1942), 1939–45/Air Crew Europe Stars, Defence & War Medals. He was awarded the DFC for a daring low-level attack on the *Scharnhorst*, and the group was knocked down for £18,000. A truly awe-inspiring group (above) awarded to John Vincent Byrne comprised Distinguished Conduct Medal (GVI), 1939-45/Africa/France & Germany Stars, Defence & War Medals, General Service Medal 1918 clasp *Malaya*, Africa General Service Medal clasp *Kenya*. Byrne was a founder member of the SAS; he was captured in 1943, but eventually escaped to Sweden (DCM). After the war he joined the Kenya Police before volunteering for Malaya. The lot achieved £72,000.

At **Lockdales, September 19, 2010**, the MM (11/Suffolks), 1914 Star & Bar Trio (2/Suffolks), and Silver War Badge to Arthur Cuthbert, who came from Hintlesham (a Suffolk village) ticked all the local boxes and was bid up to £1,525.

The prize lot at **Bonhams, September 29, 2010**, was the group to the late Thomas Palmer, SAS, one of the team which stormed the Iranian Embassy in 1980: Queen's Gallantry Medal, GSM 1962 clasps *Northern Ireland, Dhofar,* South Atlantic Medal (rosette). The lot included a wealth of material relevant to Palmer, and achieved £99, 875. A superb, and rare, World War II DCM and Bar, 1939–45/Burma Stars, Defence & War Medals, was awarded to (Colour Sergeant) G. M. Boyle, Lincolnshire Regiment. The lot included photographs and documents relating to the recipient's bravery, both citations being for Burma; it sold for £15,863.

A stunning group to (Lieutenant-Colonel) Frederick George Lawrence, South Wales Borderers, comprised DSO (V), Officer of the Order of the British Empire (GV), Queen's South Africa Medal clasps *Cape Colony, Orange Free State, Transvaal,* King's South Africa Medal two clasps, 1914 Star & Bar Trio (MiD), and two foreign awards; Lawrence received his DSO for services in South Africa. Unsurprisingly the lot was bid up to £5,400 at **Dreweatts 1759, October 26, 2010.**

As well as the four VCs at **Spink, November 25, 2010**, an impressive gallantry group was offered consisting of DSO (GVI), DFC and bar (both awards for 1940), 1939–45/Air Crew Europe/Burma Stars, Defence & War Medals, GSM 1918 clasp *Canal Zone*, Coronation 1953 to (Wing Commander) Robert Francis Thomas Doe, RAF, the third most successful fighter pilot of World War II; extremely well researched, it was bid up to £222,000. A unique group to (RSM) George Thomas Armstrong (1910–79), Grenadier Guards, comprised DCM (GVI), 1939–45/Africa/Italy Stars, Defence & War Medals, GSM 1918 clasps *Palestine 1945–48, Malaya,* Coronation 1937, Coronation 1953, Long Service Medal (GVI), Meritorious Service Medal (GVI), Army Best Shot Medal clasps *1951, 1955*. His DCM was awarded for Anzio, and he became a Yeoman Warder in 1964. For this wonderful group the successful buyer paid £15,600.

The DCM (V), South Africa 1877 Medal clasp *1879*, Long Service Medal (V) to (Colour Sergeant) Samuel Smith, 90th Foot was sold at **Bosleys, December 1, 2010**; Smith rallied his company during an attack by Zulus on the Tutu Plateau in April 1878. This was knocked down for £7,820. Another DCM group was awarded to (WO II) George A. Walker, 8th Hussars: DCM (GV), QSA clasps *Orange Free State, Transvaal, South Africa 1901, South Africa 1902*, 1914 Star Trio, GSM 1918 clasp *Iraq*, Long Service Medal (GV), Meritorious Service Medal (GV). The DCM citation recorded his bravery, walking along the top of the trench in the open, encouraging his men under bombardment. The successful bidder had to pay £4,025. A fascinating Distinguished Flying Medal, 1914–15 Star Trio, French Medaille

Militaire to Sergeant Leonard Albert Allen, RAF, was extremely well researched, including the fact that Allen was shot in the chest on August 21, 1918 (bullet included in the lot!). The lot achieved £9,430.

One of the lots sold at **DNW, December 1, 2010**, was a magnificent group to Richard Carr: Military Cross and Bar (GV), DCM (GV) (16th Lancers), 1914 Star & Bar Trio (MiD), 1939-45/Africa Stars, Defence & War Medals. Carr started the war as a regular Sergeant, 16th Lancers, but was commissioned into the Royal Lancaster Regiment, with whom he won his two MCs in 1918. For this the successful bidder paid £13,200. At the same sale an incredible group to Chief Petty Officer Richard Henry Homer comprised Conspicuous Gallantry Medal (GV) (Howe Battalion, RND), QSA no clasp, AGS clasp *Aro 1901-1902* (both HMS *Thrush*), 1914 Star & Bar Trio (MiD), Long Service Medal (2nd RN Brigade);

Medal with bar, Australian Defence Medal, Australian Anniversary of National Service Medal, Vietnam Cross of Gallantry (two silver stars), South Vietnam Medal 1964 clasp *1960*, Pingat Jasa Malaysia. Research revealed that Petersen was sent to Vietnam to train guerrilla squads. Sold by order of the recipient, this group and its associated research archive sold for £72,000. Another "colonial" lot was awarded to (Lieutenant-General) George Peter Walls (1926–2010), whose career was phenomenal: Zimbabwe Independence Medal 1980, Rhodesian Grand Order of the Legion of Merit, Rhodesian Officer of the Legion of Merit, Rhodesian Defence Cross for Distinguished Service, Rhodesian General Service Medal, Rhodesian Exemplary Service Medal and bar, MBE, War Medal, GSM 1918 clasp *Malaya*, Coronation 1953. He fought a punishing campaign in the Rhodesian Bush War, and the successful bidder was happy to pay £76,800.

Bosleys sold the important and highly unusual Royal Marine's DFM group for £132,250.

the CGM was awarded for the Third Battle of Krithia, and the lot was bid up to £14,400. The group to (Wing Commander) John Hamilton Norton (1896–1975) comprised Member of the Order of the British Empire, MC and bar (GV), British War & Victory Medals, Territorial Force War Medal (Private, Essex Yeomanry), Defence Medal, Canadian Voluntary Service Medal 1939–45 with clasp, War Medal (MiD). The catalogue recorded Norton's career, from his childhood to his amazing World War I career; accompanied by an archive of documents, the lot achieved £33,600. The group to (Captain) Arthur Barry Petersen was extremely impressive: MC (EII 1965), Australian Active Service Medal clasps *Vietnam, Malaysia, Malaya*, GSM 1918 clasp *Malaya*, GSM 1962 clasps *South Vietnam, Borneo*, Vietnam Medal (MiD), Australian Service Medal clasp *Thai-Malay*, Australian Defence Force Service Medal with clasp, Australian National

Warwick & Warwick, February 9, 2011 offered the group to (Air Marshal Sir) Paul Davie Holder (1911–2001): Knight Commander of the Order of the British Empire, Commander of the Bath, DSO, DFC (1941), 1939–45/Air Crew Europe/Africa Stars, Defence & War Medals, GSM 1918 clasp *Malaya*, 1953 Coronation. This stunning group was well researched with citations for both the DSO and the DFC, and sold for £8,625.

Bosleys, March 2, 2011 included an amazing group. This was awarded to (Sergeant) William Christopher O'Brien, RM, and comprised DFM (EII), GSM 1962 clasps *Northern Ireland, Iraq & S Turkey*, South Atlantic Medal (rosette), Operational Service Medal clasp *Afghanistan*, Golden Jubilee, Long Service Medal. This superb lot was bid up to £132,250.

A splendid Air Force Medal group, at **Lockdales, March 27, 2011**, was awarded to

17

The WWI balloonist's group realised £18,174 at Lockdales.

George Ernest Long, for *"conspicuous devotion to duty in circumstances of exceptional difficulty and danger on board HMA R33"*. The group consisted of the AFM (2nd Coxswain, HMA R33), 1914 Star & Bar Trio (RNAS), British Empire Medal, 1935 Jubilee, Defence Medal. Long had an unrivalled career in the development of ballooning (his BEM award related to this), and the lot achieved £18,174.

The group of Major-General Sir Herbert Aveling Raitt (1858–1935), comprising Knight Commander of the Indian Empire, CB, South Africa Medal 1877 clasp *1878-9* (80th Foot), QSA clasps *Cape Colony, Wittebergen, Transvaal* (South Staffs Regiment), KSA two clasps, 1914–15 Star Trio, Coronation 1911, was offered at **DNW, March 30, 2011**. The catalogue provided a detailed resume of Raitt's long military career, in particular his command of the successful expedition in 1915 against the Kachins in Burma, and the lot sold for £7,800. At the same sale a rare Air Force Cross group to (Commander) Geoffrey Lytleton Lowis, RNAS and RAF, comprised AFC (GV), 1914–15 Star Trio, 1939-45 / Atlantic Stars, Defence & War Medals. Lowis made airships his career in the RNAS, flying over 400 hours in the Sea Scout type; the successful bidder had to pay £7,200. The group awarded to Charles Gordon Ross consisted of Commander of the Order of the British Empire (Military), DFC* (GV), British War & Victory Medals (Captain, RAF), War Medal, Africa Service Medal, Jubilee 1935, Coronation 1953, Belgian Croix de Guerre. Ross moved to South Africa in 1902; transferring to the RFC in 1917, he joined 29 Squadron in March 1918, and between then and November he was credited with at least twelve kills. The lot was knocked down for £30,000.

The DFC group to (Squadron Leader) Brian Hibbs Walker consisted of the DFC (EII), 1939-45 / France & Germany Stars, Defence & War Medals, GSM 1918 clasp *Malaya*. The DFC was awarded for Malaya, where he served with 148 Squadron. The lot made £4,700 at **Bonhams,**

April 20, 2011. Also in this sale a lovely group to (CQMS) W. J. Gibbs, consisting of a MM (GV) (3 / London Regiment), QSA clasps *Cape Colony, Orange Free State, Johannesburg, Diamond Hill* (CIV), British War & Victory Medals, TFWM, Territorial Force Efficiency Medal (3 / London Regiment), was bid up to £2,820, even without research.

At **Spink, April 21, 2011,** the group to George Parker Bevan (1878–1920) showed a superb example of gallantry and disregard for personal safety: Breast Badge of St Michael & St George, DSO, Albert Medal Second Class, 1914–15 Star Trio (MiD), France Legion d'Honneur, Russia Order of St Anne Third Class, Memorial Plaque. The AM was awarded in July 1918, for rescuing the Mate of the *Earl of Forfar* in Archangel Harbour in November 1916. The successful bidder paid £31,360. At the same sale a fine CGM, 1914–15 Star Trio to Leading Seaman James Dewar, RNVR, for picking up a live grenade in a trench and throwing it away, realised £9,600. The group awarded to the naturalist Sir Peter Scott (1909–89) comprised Companion of Honour, CBE, DSC and Bar, 1939–45 / Atlantic Stars, Defence and War Medals (MiD), Netherlands Order of the Golden Ark. The catalogue devoted several pages to the actions for which he was awarded his gallantry decorations. This achieved £31,200.

At **TRM, May 6, 2011**, the DCM, 1939–45 / Africa / Italy Stars, Defence & War Medals, General Service Medal 1918 clasp *Palestine 1945–48* to (WO III) P. Monaghan, RA included an amazing citation mentioning his *"courage, foresight and initiative"*; the lot was knocked down for £3,680.

A very impressive group, offered at **DNW, May 18, 2011**, was that to (General Sir) John Maxwell (1859–1929. This comprised twenty-five items: GCB, KCMG, CVO, DSO (V) (for Ginnis), Egypt Medal clasps *Tel-el-Kebir, The Nile 1884–85, Gemaizah 1888, Toski 1889*, Queen's Sudan Medal, QSA Medal clasps *Cape Colony, Orange Free State, Johannesburg,* KSA Medal two clasps, 1914 Star & Bar Trio, Coronation 1911, and foreign awards. Maxwell started his army career in the Black Watch, and was a generally successful commander; it was his misfortune to be in command in Ireland after the Rising. The lot achieved £31,200. The group awarded to (Lieutenant-Colonel) Ronald Bolton Litteldale, KRRC (1902–44) comprised: DSO (GVI) (1943), GSM 1918 clasp *Palestine*, 1939–45/France & Germany Stars, War Medal. Captured near Calais in May 1940, he escaped from Colditz in October 1942 with three others, eventually reaching the UK via Switzerland, Spain and Gibraltar. Sadly he was killed in September 1944. Extremely well researched, the lot was bid up to £39,600.

At **Bosleys, June 1, 2011**, an amazing group was awarded to (Warrant Officer) Shaun Anthony Wyatt, RA and Army Air Corps. This comprised DFC (EII, 1994), GSM 1962 clasp *Northern Ireland*, South Atlantic Medal with rosette, Gulf Medal with clasp, UN Medals for Cyprus and UNPROFOR, NATO Medal for Former Yugoslavia, Golden Jubilee Medal, Long Service Medal (EII). His DFC was gazetted in April 1994 for *"gallantry and distinguished services in Northern Ireland"*. The details of these "services" (surrounding his skill as a helicopter pilot) were set out in the catalogue. The lot was finally knocked down for a monumental £108,100.

£9,775 secured the delightful Victorian campaign group at Bosleys.

A very unusual, and probably unique, group was offered at **Morton & Eden, June 14, 2011**. This consisted of DSO (GV), 1914-15 Star Trio, GSM 1918 clasp *S Persia*, India General Service Medal 1908 clasp *Waziristan 1919–1921*, Sea Gallantry Medal (GV) to (Lieutenant-Colonel) Willoughby Lugard Hogg, 3/Brahmin Regiment. The DSO was awarded for distinguished service with the Waziristan Field Force; the Sea Gallantry Medal was for directing fire-fighting operations on the SS *Ouro* in Muscat harbour, and for rescuing a Lascar. The group sold for £4,200.

CAMPAIGN MEDALS

Among the campaign medals at **DNW, July 7–8, 2010**, appeared the IGS Medal 1854 clasp *Perak*, South Africa 1877 Medal clasp *1878–9* to T. Westwood, 80th Foot. Westwood was rescued at Fugitive's Drift, after the battle of Isandhlwana, by his comrade in the Mounted Infantry, Samuel Wassall, who received the Victoria Cross for this action. The successful bidder paid £33,600, apparently because the recipient was rescued by a VC winner!

At **Spink, July 22, 2010** a superb lot was the South Africa 1877 Medal clasp *1877-8-9* to Sub-Lieutenant Thomas Llewellyn George Griffith, 2/24th Foot (1857–79), the youngest of the battalion's five officers killed at Isandhlwana. This achieved £28,800. At the same sale the Naval General Service Medal clasp *Sybille 28 Feby 1799* to Commander James Long (1774–1864), who took part in the famous action against the French ship *La Ferte* in the Bay of Bengal, realised £15,000, and the unique four-clasp combination to Commander William Hole, whose clasps demonstrated the war in the Americas (*Martinique, 13 Dec Boat Service 1809, Guadaloupe, 14 Dec Boat Service 1814*), was bid up to £20,400.

At **Bosleys, September 1, 2010**, the delightful group to Edward Cormick comprised the Military General Service Medal clasps *Roleia, Vimiera* (20th Light Dragoons), Cabul 1842, Sutlej Medal reverse Moodkee, clasps *Ferozeshuhur, Sobraon* (3rd Light Dragoons). Cormick, who had an astonishingly long career for his time, died in service at the age of 63, and his medals realised £9,775. In the same sale an amazing long service group was awarded to (Captain) James Frederick Maynard (1875–1968): Queen's Sudan 1898, 1914 Star Trio, Defence and War Medals, Long Service Medal (EVII), Khedive's Sudan (three clasps), and Royal Humane Society Medal. Maynard had a very full career, even receiving a commission in World War II. The successful bidder paid £7,130.

Several campaign medals sold at **DNW, September 16–17, 2010**, were exceptional. A nine-clasp QSA (*Belmont* to *Wittebergen* plus *South Africa 1901*) to Corporal F. W. B. Smith, Damant's Horse, with clasp confirmation, achieved £4,800. The NGSM clasps *Trafalgar, Java*, to Francis

James (Landsman, HMS *Royal Sovereign* for the former, Able Seaman, HMS *Nisus* for the latter) sold at £7,440. Even this price was beaten by that paid for the MGSM clasps *Busaco, Fuentes D'Onor, Ciudad Rodrigo, Salamanca* to (Lieutenant-General) John Fraser (1790–1862), 24th Foot. The catalogue described his bravery at Burgos in October 1812, and this lovely medal realised £9,600. The South Africa 1877 Medal clasp *1877-8-9* to James Dunbar, 2/24th Foot, a confirmed Rorke's Drift defender, made £36,000. Another similar medal was named for Henry Turner, 1/24th Foot. The catalogue discussed why a 1/24th man should be at Rorke's Drift, nevertheless the successful bidder paid £16,800. The superb pair to (Major) Peter Deshon (1776-1852), 43rd & 85th Foot, comprised a Field Officer's gold medal for Nive, and a MGSM clasps *Busaco, St Sebastian, Nivelle;* the catalogue sketched out Deshon's career in some detail, and the lot made £31,200. A group (surely unique?) to (Major) James Anstruther McGowan (1820-1855) comprised Candahar Ghuznee Cabul 1842 Medal (40th Foot), Maharajpoor Star 1843 (40th Foot), Crimea Medal clasps *Alma, Balaklava* (93rd Regiment) (impressed). McGowan, wounded at Sevastopol, died of his wounds as a prisoner of war, and the lot was bid up to £16,800. The group awarded to a confirmed Light Brigade "Charger", John Mortimer, 8th Hussars comprised Crimea Medal four clasps, Indian

Mutiny Medal clasp *Central India*, Long Service Medal (V), Turkish Crimea, and achieved £8,400. A superb group to (WO II) John Vaughan (1928–2010), Glosters, comprised Queen's Korea, UN Korea, AGSM clasp *Kenya*, GSM 1918 clasp *Cyprus*, Long Service Medal (EIIR). He was wounded and taken prisoner in Korea, and the group achieved £5,160.

At **Bonhams, Sept-ember 29, 2010**, a NGSM clasp *Trafalgar* to AB Edward Morgan, HMS *Ajax*, made the high price of £11,515, and a fascinating MGSM with nine clasps to James Hughes, 83rd Foot, with detailed research, was bid up to £6,463. An example of the Order of St Stanislaus (pictured above) originally awarded to a Mr Arnstein, who practised dentistry on the Tsar, made £37,600.

At **Brightwells, October 13, 2010**, a MGSM clasps *Talavera, Busaco, Salamanca,* awarded to Captain Joseph Nicholson, 53rd Foot, achieved £2,820.

A Waterloo Medal to Alexander Frazer, 2/Coldstream Guards, even with an edge bruise and without research, made £3,525 at **The Cotswold Auction Company, October 26, 2010**.

The Queen's Sudan, Long Service Medal (GV), Khedive's Sudan clasp *Khartoum* to Private William Walker, alias Squadron Quarter-Master-Sergeant William Ernest Butchers, 21st Lancers, was sold at **Spink, November 25, 2010**. Walker changed his name to Butchers during his service career, and wrote a very circumstantial account

SQMS Butcher's Omdurman group sold for £6,420 at Spink.

---

of his experiences in the famous charge. £6,240 was needed to buy it. In the same sale, a Field Officer's Small Army Gold Medal for Nive awarded to (Captain) Charles Mosse (1785–1831), Royal Horse Artillery, was bid up to £15,600.

A MGSM clasps *Vittoria, Pyrenees*, to Matthias Asch (or Esch), 60th Rifles, sold for £5,760 at **Morton & Eden, November 30, 2010,** and at the same sale an attractive Victorian pair awarded to (Major-General) Astley Fellowes Terry (1840–1926), 3/60th Rifles, consisting of a South Africa 1877 Medal clasp *1879*, and a rare Cape of Good Hope General Service Medal 1880 clasp *Transkei*, achieved £4,200.

An excellent Victorian pair to (Captain) William English FitzEdward Barnes (1810–81), 3rd Light Dragoons comprising Sutlej Medal for Moodkee clasps *Ferozeshuhur, Sobraon,* Punjab Medal clasps *Chilianwala, Goojerat*, was bid up to £6,960 at **DNW, December 1, 2010.** The NGSM clasp *Camperdown* to John Tracy, Master's Mate, who was wounded on *Ardent* during the battle, attracted £9,360.

A quirky British War & Victory Medal pair to Gunner A. Mitchell, RA, was sold at **Warwick & Warwick, December 8, 2010.** The recipient was apparently Henry Abraham ("Abe") Mitchell, the golf professional who taught Sam Ryder how to play the game. As a reward Ryder had Mitchell memorialised as the figure on the Ryder Cup. The successful bidder paid £978.

£11,750 was paid at **Bonhams, December 15, 2010,** for the Waterloo Medal to Captain Edwin Sandys, 12th Light Dragoons, who died of wounds received in the battle; this, therefore, was one of those scarce Waterloo Medals awarded to fatal casualties. At the same sale the officially impressed Crimea Medal clasps *Alma, Balaklava*, to George Flowers, 17th Lancers, who was killed in the charge, reached £10,810.

A superb Long Service group to Albert Gooderham, 9th Foot/Norfolk Regiment, was sold at **Lockdales, January 16, 2011.** Consisting of Second Afghan War Medal 1878, IGSM 1854 clasps *Jowaki 1877–8, Burma 1887–89*, Long Service Medal (V), MSM (GV), 1902 Coronation, 1911 Coronation, and with research showing that he came from Stowmarket, the lot was bid up to £2,463.

The highlight in the **TRM, January 28, 2011,** sale was the MSM and BWM awarded to CQMS D. Stephenson, 2/Newfoundland Regiment (pictured left). Clearly this was a very rare MSM, and the successful bidder had to pay £1,265 for the lot.

The MGSM clasps *Ciudad Rodrigo, Badajoz, Salamanca, Vittoria, Pyrenees, Orthes, Toulouse,* and Waterloo pair to Francis Gibbs, 2/95th Foot, was sold at **Bosleys, March 2, 2011**; accompanied by an original pension document, indicating that he had lost his right arm at Waterloo, the pair reached £8,280. In the same sale appeared a rare pair: Sutlej Medal reverse Moodkee clasp *Ferozeshuhur*, IGS Medal 1854 clasp *Pegu* to (Lieutenant) Henry Knightly Burne (1825–1901), 2nd Regiment Native Infantry. The medals were with a watercolour portrait, and the ribbons appeared "original". Burne became a General (CB), and the bidding stopped at £2,300. In the same sale appeared a very unusual, even rare, modern pair comprising Operational Service Medal clasp *DROC*, European Security and Defence Policy Service Medal clasp *Artemis* to Sapper G. M. Griffiths, RE. The catalogue claimed that *"only 250 personnel were eligible"* for the former medal, and this particular combination must therefore be extremely rare. This intriguing lot was bid up to £4,025.

At **DNW, March 30, 2011,** the Army of India Medal 1799 awarded to Dennis Driscoll, 29th Light Dragoons had the clasps *Allighur, Laswarree, Capture Of Deig,* and was described by one of its previous owners as *"a rare and remarkable medal"*. It was bid up to £10,800. The NGSM awarded to James Aitken (right) had clasps for *Camperdown, Egypt, Trafalgar*, and Aitken was confirmed as Ordinary Seaman on board HMSS *Venerable, Kent, Defence* respectively. With a resume of Aitken's naval career, the lot made £9,840. A lovely trio comprising Crimea Medal (engraved) four clasps, French Medaille Militaire (citation quoted), Turkish Crimea (Sardinian), to (Sergeant) John Andrews, 4th Light Dragoons, who was a confirmed "Charger", made £8,160. At the same sale a really unusual World War I group was awarded to (Petty Officer) Lloyd Clarence May Milner, RNAS, consisting of British War & Victory Medals (Machine Gun Corps), Russian Medal of St George for Bravery 4th Class, French Croix de Guerre (unverified). The Russian medal was awarded for his action in November 1916 on the Caucasian front in the Dobrudsha operations, when he *"brought shells and petrol for the Armoured Cars"*; the lot was bid up to £6,600.

In a class of its own at **Bonhams, April 20, 2011**, was the Sir Gilbert Blane gold medal, impressed to Dr Thomas R. Dunn, Surgeon, HMS *Fisgard*. The very attractive medal was housed in a contemporary frame with two Portuguese medals, one of which was a Knight's Breast Badge of the Military Order of the Tower and the Sword. A career history was provided, but gave no reason for the award of any of the decorations. The lot realised an astonishing £17,625. A rather unusual pair to (Lieutenant) A. Ormond comprised British South Africa Company's Medal 1890, Rhodesia 1896 reverse (Trooper, Gifford's Horse), QSA clasps *Relief Of Mafeking, Transvaal, South Africa 1901* (Lieutenant, Imperial Light Horse). Ormond was killed in action at Naauwpoort on January 5, 1901, and the lot was bid up to £4,935.

The First Class Gold Medal of Pao Hsing was awarded to William Cartwright (1847–1911), Chinese Imperial Maritime Customs Service; this was China's first official medal realising £67,200 at **Spink, April 21, 2011.** Among the single campaign medals at that sale was the Field Officer's Small Army Gold Medal for Orthes awarded to Major the Honourable Edward Mullins, 28th Foot (pictured above). The successful bidder paid £27,600.

A NGSM clasp *Trafalgar* to Thomas Brooks was sold at **Lockdales, May 15, 2011.** Apparently Brooks served as Boy on HMS *Defence*, and although another man of the same name appears on the roll for *Navarino*, the successful bidder was prepared to pay £3,870.

A very desirable George Cross group, sold at **Bosleys, June 1, 2011**, was awarded to (Corporal) William Jones, RE: GC, 1939–45/ France & Germany Stars, Defence and War Medals. Jones was trained as a bomb disposal expert, and was serving with T-Force attached to 1st Canadian Army in September 1944. His citation praised him for taking charge of a difficult situation and for remaining calm and professional at all times. The lot achieved £6,900.

The Waterloo Medal awarded to (Ensign) John Pasley Dirom, 3/Grenadier Guards, who retired in 1838 with the rank of Lieutenant-Colonel, even with little biographical research, sold for £6,960 at **Morton & Eden, June 14, 2011.**

At **Warwick & Warwick, June 15, 2011**, an extremely unusual lot comprised a Constabulary Medal for Ireland 1921, BWM (disc only), France and Germany Star, Defence & War Medals awarded to Eric William George Gurr. On the BWM he was AB, RN, and on the Constabulary Medal he was a Constable. This medal was awarded for his involvement in the Connors Hill ambush, County Kerry, on February 26, 1921, and attracted a winning bid of £6,900.

At the same sale a superb Army of India Medal clasp *Poona* was awarded to Brigadier Colin James Milnes, 65th Foot. The catalogue indicated that he was entitled to a MGSM clasp *Egypt* (10th Foot). The successful bidder was happy to pay £8,050.

Polar Medals always seem to attract big bidders, and at **DNW, September 16–17, 2010**, the Arctic Medal 1818–55 to Admiral Sir Francis Leopold McClintock (1819–1907), with a family photograph album and much biographical research, reached £7,800.

At another sale by **DNW, December 1, 2010,** the group to Arthur Samuel Bailey attracted attention: 1914–15 Star Trio (MiD) (CPO, RN), Polar Medal 1904 clasp *Antarctic 1910-13* (PO, *Terra Nova*), Long Service Medal (CPO, HMS

Queen), as well as his Royal Geographical Society Scott Memorial Medal 1913 (PO1, Terra Nova B.A.E.). Accompanied by detailed biographical research, this superb historical lot was knocked down for £12,600.

At Spink, April 21, 2011, the Polar Medal 1904 clasp *Antarctic 1910–13* to Petty Officer 2nd Class Frank Vernon Browning, *Terra Nova*, who was a member of the expedition during which the death occurred of Robert Falcon Scott, the father of Peter Scott, achieved £13,200.

Life-saving medals have been selling well in recent years, and this was true, at **Warwick & Warwick, October 13, 2010**, of the group to (Police Constable) Robert Geoffrey McNeill, RMP and Cambridgeshire Constabulary: Royal Humane Society Police Medal (silver gilt), Royal Humane Society small bronze (successful) Medal, GSM 1962 clasp *Northern Ireland*, Iraq Medal with clasp, Iraq Reconstruction Service Medal, Jubilee Medal 2002, Volunteer Reserves Service Medal. McNeill was awarded his gallantry medal for saving the lives of two men trapped by fire in a house in Peterborough. For this unique group the successful bidder paid £5,750.

The Royal National Lifeboat Institution Medal in silver (GV) with two additional clasps awarded to George James Grigson, Coxswain of the Clacton Lifeboat, sold at **Lockdales, November 21, 2010**. The catalogue detailed the dates of the awards, and the lot achieved £4,690. The Edward Medal For Industry in Silver was awarded to Arthur Frankland, who was working at an explosives factory in Ardeer, Glasgow, in July 1915 when he rescued a man, but was badly injured in the process. The lot reached £6,000 at **DNW, March 30, 2011**. At the same sale the Albert Medal (GV) was awarded to acting bosun Albert Charles Mattison, Royal Canadian Navy, who, on the occasion of the explosion of a munitions ship in Halifax Harbour, Nova Scotia, in December 1917 attempted to save lives on the burning steamship *Mont Blanc* (see *Medal News*, October 2010, for an account). Unfortunately the ship blew up as their boat drew alongside and all were killed. The medal realised £22,800. **At Spink, April 21, 2010,** the Medal of the Royal National Institution for the Preservation of Life from Shipwreck, awarded to Richard Eddy, Pilot, in March 1834, sold for £9,000.

GUIDE TO PRICES PAID WHEN BUYING AT AUCTION

Buying at auction can be confusing to those not used to it—it isn't like buying from a dealer's list nor, crucially, like buying from an Internet auction. With a dealer the price you see is the price you pay (unless you can do some haggling that is) and with eBay and the like you bid up to the price you want and the price the auction ends at is how much the item will cost. "Real" auctions are a little different and you have to remember that when the hammer falls the final price might not be what you think.

Auctioneers make their money through buyers' premiums (and sellers' premiums' but that's another matter) i.e. a "fee" on top of the hammer price that goes directly to them not the vendor. On top of that premium is VAT—which as of January 1, 2011 will stand at 20% in the UK. VAT is only really relevant to those in the EU—buyers from outside are exempt although they may be liable for their own import duties and other taxes so it's always worth checking.

These "extras", often referred to by seasoned auction goers as the "bits", can add a significant sum to your purchase. For example, if you bid on an item up to £100 and that's where the hammer falls it isn't £100 you pay—you will have to find that £100 plus the premium (this varies from Auction house to auction house) plus VAT on that premium (not on the £100, just the premium)—that can add up to £24 to the original hammer price—not something to be ignored! It can all get rather confusing and can come as a shock to those new to the game or only used to buying at on-line auctions (it's worth noting that even if you bid on-line at a "real" auction you are still liable for the "bits": there have been those who believe that on-line bidding exempts them from the fees as they treat it like eBay!). Some buyers ignore the "bits" and concentrate on the hammer price, worrying about the extras only when they've secured their purchase. But as premiums rise most of us have to factor them in at the start—so remember, if you have a strict budget you may well have to stop bidding quite a bit before that figure is reached in order to come in on target. Of course, when you just have to have something, what do budgets matter…?

Below is an indication of what you will have to pay on certain hammer prices depending on the Premium (we've given you 10%, 15% 17.5% and 20% options—the actual premium varies so check with the auctioneer before bidding). These figures assume VAT at 20%. Happy bidding!

10 %			15%		
Hammer	Plus premium	Plus premium and VAT	Hammer	Plus premium	Plus premium and VAT
£75	£82.5	£84	£75	£86.25	£88
£175	£192.50	£196	£175	201.25	£206.50
£500	£550	£560	£500	£575	£590
£1500	£1650	£1680	£1500	£1725	£1770
£2500	£2750	£2800	£2500	£2875	£2950

17.5%			20%		
Hammer	Plus premium	Plus premium and VAT	Hammer	Plus premium	Plus premium and VAT
£75	£88.13	£90.75	£75	£90	£93
£175	£205.62	£211.75	£175	£210	£217
£500	£587.50	£605	£500	£600	£620
£1500	£1762.50	£1815	£1500	£1800	£1860
£2500	£2937.50	£3025	£2500	£3000	£3100

RECHERCHÉ

Medals Mounted & Framed   **Photos & Documents Restored**
Bespoke handcrafted designs to suit your individual needs

1. *George Cross group mounted for the late Daphne Pearson now in the Imperial War Museum*
2. *Royal Humane Society of Australasia Medal, & Commendation for Brave Conduct mounted for Shane Harding*
3. *WWI Australian group - from Egypt to the Western front includes originals & replicas*
4. *WW I to WW II including civil OBE on display Returned and Services League of Australia, Warrnambool, Victoria*
5. *MBE & insignia for Pauline Gower - founder women's section of the Air Transport Auxiliary WWII - framed for the family*

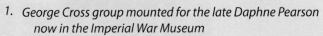

Replicas supplied

Recherché Specialty Picture Framing
17 Albert St. Northcote Vic. Australia
frame@recherche.alphalink.com.au

www.recherchframing.com.au
61 (0)3 9486 1236

OPERATIONAL HONOURS

Included here are the Operational Honours Lists which have appeared in the *London Gazette* since the previous edition of the *Medal Yearbook* was published (September 2010).

The LONDON GAZETTE OF SEPTEMBER 24, 2010

AFGHANISTAN

Order of the British Empire (OBE)

Lieutenant Colonel Henry Robert Downing FULLERTON, The Life Guards, 526294.

Lieutenant Colonel Nicholas John LOCK, The Royal Welsh, 531016.

Member of the British Empire (MBE)

Major Christopher David DAVIES, The Royal Anglian Regiment, 544305.

Major Timothy John HARRIS, The Rifles, 547927.

Major Patrick Simon REEHAL, The Royal Logistic Corps, 545585.

Major Richard Giles STREATFEILD, The Rifles, 545446.

Major Toby Patrick Oughtred TILL, Coldstream Guards, 540069.

Distinguished Service Order (DSO)

Brigadier James Michael COWAN, OBE, late The Royal Regiment of Scotland, 517898.

Lieutenant Colonel Harry Arthur Blair HOLT, OBE, Irish Guards, 526422.

Lieutenant Colonel Nicholas Jan KITSON, The Rifles, 532903.

Lieutenant Colonel Charles Roland Vincent WALKER, Grenadier Guards, 536349.

Conspicuous Gallantry Cross (CGC)

Corporal Lee BROWNSON, The Rifles, 25053532 (killed in action).

Private Graham Stuart HORN, The Parachute Regiment, 25170883.

Rifleman James Lee MCKIE, The Rifles, 30076292.

Captain Robin Edwin Geoffrey BOURNE-TAYLOR, The Life Guards, 565224.

Corporal Robert TURNER, Royal Marines, P053814G.

Military Cross (MC)

Sergeant Paul Edward BAINES, Coldstream Guards, 25050922.

Lance Corporal Sarah Louise BUSHBYE, Royal Army Medical Corps, Q1048823.

Lieutenant Douglas Anthony Keith DALZELL, Coldstream Guards, 25214573 (killed in action).

Lance Corporal Daniel John FLETCHER, Royal Army Medical Corps, 25124538.

Corporal Ricky Paul FURGUSSON, The Rifles, 25136900.

Sergeant Ashley Robert HILL, The Royal Anglian Regiment, 25067216.

Rifleman Harry LANCELEY, The Rifles, 25225947.

Lieutenant Colin William LUNN, The Yorkshire Regiment, 25221734.

Major Angus Donald MACGILLIVRAY, The Royal Regiment of Scotland, 530110.

Lance Corporal Marc Anthony READER, Coldstream Guards, 25214842.

Corporal George Finau SALE, The Royal Welsh, 25168351.

Lieutenant Craig Angus SHEPHARD, Grenadier Guards, 25198907.

Major Nigel John Powell SOMERVILLE, MBE, Royal Marines, N029204N.

Lance Sergeant Adam Charles SWIFT, Coldstream Guards, 25046210.

Acting Corporal Andrew WARDLE, The Yorkshire Regiment, 25195007.

Corporal David Thomas WILLIAMS, The Royal Welsh, 25157469.

Acting Sergeant Richard Edward WISEMAN, Royal Marines, P054464P.

Staff Sergeant Gareth David WOOD, The Royal Logistic Corps, 25087716.

Distinguished Flying Cross (DFC)

Flight Lieutenant Ian Anthony FORTUNE, Royal Air Force, 2670728L.

Flight Lieutenant Andrew Michael NETHAWAY, Royal Air Force, 8700033U.

Flight Lieutenant Timothy Richard POLLARD, Royal Air Force, 2671037B.

George Medal (GM)

Staff Sergeant Karl John Fairfax LEY, The Royal Logistic Corps, 25107461.

Queen's Gallantry Medal (QGM)

Private Callum John BROTHERSTON, The Royal Regiment of Scotland, 30071385.

Corporal John Alexander HARDMAN, The Yorkshire Regiment, 25041192.

Lance Corporal Julie Elizabeth MAY, Royal Army Medical Corps, Q1053799.

Corporal Robert Alan NEALEY, The Royal Logistic Corps, 25200741.

Rifleman Ross David ROBINSON, The Rifles, 30070566 (since deceased).

Sergeant John Arthur SWITHENBANK, The Yorkshire Regiment, 25048253.

Rifleman Reece William Stevenson TERRY, The Rifles, 30022014.

Mentioned in Despatches (MID)

Guardsman Emmanuel ATTUQUAYEFIO, Grenadier Guards, 30044006.

Lance Corporal Lee Colum BLAKE, The Parachute Regiment, 25063724.

The LONDON GAZETTE OF SEPTEMBER 24, 2010 continued...

Private Nikotimo BOLATAGANE, The Yorkshire Regiment, 25141123.

Lance Corporal Daniel Colin James BRAMLEY, Grenadier Guards, 25211671.

Lieutenant Simon Mark BROOMFIELD, The Royal Anglian Regiment, 25147884.

Corporal Daryl Alan BRYANT, The Rifles, 25104180.

Guardsman Lewis Nigel COULBERT, Grenadier Guards, 30020436.

Colour Sergeant Christopher Stephen Mark DUNDON, The Royal Welsh, 25030868.

Acting Major Hugo James Edward FARMER, CGC, The Parachute Regiment, 562140.

Sergeant Paul Maurice FOX, Corps of Royal Engineers, 25035075 (killed in action).

Senior Aircraftman Johnathon Tony FREEMAN, Royal Air Force, 30000801.

Lance Bombardier Craig FROGGETT, Royal Regiment of Artillery, 25139956.

Lance Sergeant David Marc Eric GREENHALGH, Grenadier Guards, 25124116 (killed in action).

Corporal Paul Michael GEORGE, The Royal Welsh, 25145730.

Marine Tobias GUTTERIDGE, Royal Marines, P065066N.

Lieutenant Stephen James HEALEY, The Royal Welsh, 30010991.

Acting Sergeant Paul Andrew HOWARD, The Royal Tank Regiment, 25018216.

Lieutenant Richard David HUTTON, Grenadier Guards, 25197261.

Warrant Officer Class 2 Patrick HYDE, The Rifles, 25020031.

Lance Corporal Alexander David John JONES, The Royal Welsh, 25173106.

Corporal Steven Wayne MARTIN, The Rifles, 24963839.

Sergeant Brian MCINTYRE, The Royal Logistic Corps, 25005729.

Captain Andrew Donald MICHAEL, The Rifles, 565782.

Lance Sergeant Nathan Joseph OWEN, Coldstream Guards, 25134300.

Lance Sergeant William Edwards PATES, Coldstream Guards, 25108097.

Sergeant Quintin Benjamin POLL, The Parachute Regiment, 25058746.

Private David John RADBAND, The Parachute Regiment, 25177381.

Sergeant Gareth Desmond REID, The Royal Logistic Corps, 25017193.

Acting Corporal Liam Matthew RILEY, The Yorkshire Regiment, 25193706 (killed in action).

Major Stuart Roderick SMITH, The Royal Anglian Regiment, 540343.

Corporal Daniel SPRUCE, The Royal Logistic Corps, 25208940.

Lance Corporal Alan Robert TAYLOR, The Royal Anglian Regiment, 25206842.

Corporal Robert James TORDOFF, Corps of Royal Engineers, 25106011.

Rifleman Mark TURNER, The Rifles, 25216154 (killed in action).

Acting Sergeant Ryan James VICKERY, The Royal Anglian Regiment, 24964855.

Lance Sergeant Mathew James WALLIS, Coldstream Guards, 25080795.

Lance Corporal Ryan Joseph WALTON, The Duke of Lancaster's Regiment, 25131321.

Lieutenant Charles Edward Rufus WINSTANLEY, The Rifles, 25199844.

Queen's Commendation for Bravery (QCB)

Lance Corporal George BURGESS, Royal Marines, P060621A.

Warrant Officer Class 2 Andrew David GOODWIN, The Royal Logistic Corps, 25044078.

Lance Corporal Jamie HASTIE, The Yorkshire Regiment, 25222641.

Colour Sergeant Mark Stuart KNOWLES, Royal Marines, P039597Q.

Rifleman Peter Leslie Matthew MATTHEWS, The Rifles, 25233274.

Second Lieutenant Connor Neil Heriot MAXWELL, The Rifles, 30031234.

Rifleman Daniel Vincent NICKSON, The Rifles, 25198076.

Captain Daniel READ, The Royal Logistic Corps, 562251 (killed in action).

Rifleman Gareth Edward SUTHERLAND, The Rifles, 25198456.

Rifleman Aselemo Kokoidabuli VETANIBUA, The Rifles, 30036071.

Lance Sergeant David WALKER, Scots Guards, 25029834 (killed in action).

Staff Sergeant Paul Thomas John WRIGHT, Corps of Royal Engineers, 25051640.

Queen's Commendation for Bravery in the Air

Flight Lieutenant Alexander Nicholas Riddell TOWNSEND, Royal Air Force, 2670054J.

Queen's Commendation for Valuable Service (QCVS)

Reverend James William AITCHISON, Chaplain to the Forces 3rd Class, Royal Army Chaplains' Department, 536260.

Air Commodore Stuart David ATHA, DSO, Royal Air Force, 2627100L.

Lieutenant Colonel Matthew Timothy George BAZELEY, Corps of Royal Engineers, 539402.

Second Lieutenant Daniel James BENSTEAD, The Royal Anglian Regiment, 30023267.

Major James Maurice Hannan BOWDER, MBE, Grenadier Guards, 544881.

Major Oliver Charles Christopher BROWN, The Royal Anglian Regiment, 547284.

Major Ash Giles ALEXANDER-COOPER, The Royal Gurkha Rifles, 544502.

Squadron Leader Daniel Joseph ENDRUWEIT, Royal Air Force, 8196994H.

Acting Group Captain Alan Kenneth GILLESPIE, Royal Air Force, 2637703G.

Sergeant Frederick John GOODING, Corps of Royal Engineers, 25002206.

Corporal Pritabahadur GURUNG, The Queen's Own Gurkha Logistic Regiment, 21169511.

Sergeant Nicholas HARRINGTON, The Parachute Regiment, 24898090.

Major Richard Alexander HEAD, MC, The Rifles, 538701.

Sapper Johnathan Robert HORNER, Corps of Royal Engineers, 25229266.

Second Lieutenant Philip Robert Anthony LENTHALL, The Royal Anglian Regiment, 25147826.

The LONDON GAZETTE OF SEPTEMBER 24, 2010 continued...

Surgeon Lieutenant Colonel Jeremy Hart LEWIN, Royal Army Medical Corps, 539247.

Captain Jonathan Paul NOLAN, Queen Alexandra's Royal Army Nursing Corps Territorial Army, 30018549.

Captain David John POLLOCK, The Royal Tank Regiment, 557536.

Major Andrew Michael ROE, The Yorkshire Regiment, 538105.

Warrant Officer Class 2 Justin Terence Gordon SEARLE, Royal Regiment of Artillery, 25002457.

Captain James Andrew SEDDON, Grenadier Guards, 557669.

Major Graeme Crichton WEARMOUTH, The Royal Regiment of Scotland, 543363.

SERVICES IN THE FIELD

Officer of the Order of the British Empire (OBE)

Captain Nigel Anthony JONES, Royal Fleet Auxiliary, 154356J.

Member of the British Empire (MBE)

Sergeant Philip John CARR, Scots Guards, 25029245.

Queen's Commendation for Bravery (QCB)

Corporal Calvin James COULTER, The Parachute Regiment, 25115021.

Lance Corporal Jamie Martyn TAYLOR, The Royal Logistic Corps, 24920904.

Queen's Commendation for Valuable Service (QCVS)

Acting Corporal Andrew Steven BURROWS, Royal Corps of Signals, 24946834.

Corporal Marc David KEECH, Royal Corps of Signals, 25015788.

Warrant Officer Class 2 Peter Joseph LINDSAY, Army Air Corps, 24651005.

Commodore Timothy Miles LOWE, Royal Navy, C029858A.

Lieutenant Gary MCCALL, Royal Navy, C038693C.

Air Force Cross (AFC)

Flight Sergeant Anthony Richard Davey, Royal Air Force, F8424849.

Queen's Gallantry Medal (QGM)

Petty Officer Aircrewman Dian Jonathan LACY, Royal Navy, D213442P.

Queen's Commendation for Bravery in the Air (QCBA)

Corporal Carl Michael BOOTH, Royal Air Force, F8436427.

FOREIGN AWARDS Her Majesty the Queen has graciously granted permission for the wearing of the following awards:

FOREIGN AWARDS— AFGHANISTAN

Canada

Meritorious Service Medal

Colonel P. M. L. NAPIER, OBE, late Royal Welsh 524781.

USA

Legion of Merit (Degree of Officer)

Major General C. C. WILSON, CB, CBE, late Royal Regiment of Artillery 495598.

Brigadier S. P. WOLSEY, OBE, late Royal Regiment of Artillery 511932.

Bronze Star Medal

Lieutenant Colonel C. B. B. CLEE, CBE, The Blues and Royals (Royal Horse Guards and 1st Dragoons) 518400.

Lieutenant Colonel P. R. CORDEN, The Princess of Wales's Royal Regiment 507424.

Lieutenant Colonel R. C. COLE-MACKINTOSH, The Royal Regiment of Scotland, 520345.

Lieutenant Colonel R. A. WINCHESTER, Royal Regiment of Artillery 507564. Air Medal (with "V" device)

Captain J. A. KAY, Army Air Corps 556729.

Air Medal

Flight Lieutenant M. J. BRUNTON, Royal Air Force 5208471D.

For other Afghanistan awards please see Foreign Awards— General.

FOREIGN AWARDS—IRAQ

USA

Legion of Merit (Degree of Officer) 1st Oak Leaf Cluster

Lieutenant General P. R. NEWTON, CBE, late The Princess of Wales's Royal Regiment 499752.

Legion of Merit (Degree of Officer)

Lieutenant General Sir James DUTTON, KCB, CBE, Royal Marines N022005F.

Major General R. L. BARRONS, CBE, late Royal Regiment of Artillery 504825.

Major General B. BREALEY, late Royal Regiment of Artillery 515939.

Brigadier J. M. CASTLE, OBE, late Kings Own Scottish Borderers 508821.

Lieutenant General J. COOPER, CB, DSO, MBE, late Kings Own Scottish Borderers 499682.

Brigadier S. M. GLEDHILL, late Royal Regiment of Artillery 501006.

Brigadier M. G. LACEY, late Royal Regiment of Artillery 508860.

Major General R. J. M. PORTER, MBE, late The Royal Welsh Fusiliers 510368.

Brigadier D. R. POTTS, MBE, late Royal Regiment of Artillery 501678.

Brigadier E. J. TORRENS-SPENCE, CBE, late The Royal Dragoon Guards 493268.

Lieutenant General B. W. B. WHITE-SPUNNER, CBE, late The Blues and Royals (Royal Horse Guards and 1st Dragoons) 501534.

Brigadier J. E. THOMAS, MBE, late Royal Corps of Signals 499777.

Bronze Star Medal

Captain P. ABRAHAM, Royal Navy C027471H.

Lieutenant Colonel A. S. ATKINSON, Corps of Royal Electrical and Mechanical Engineers 535983.

Wing Commander J. R. BROADBENT, Royal Air Force 2629478K.

Commander R. J. F. BUCKLAND, Royal Navy C026094X.

Major G. W. DAVEY, Royal Logistic Corps 526348.

Major C. H. F. DOBSON, The Mercian Regiment 530070.

Lieutenant Colonel S. D. ETHERINGTON, The Royal Anglian Regiment 515967.

Lieutenant Colonel J. P. EYRE, The Blues and Royals (Royal Horse Guards and 1st Dragoons), 532077.

Colonel T. M. A. FLEETWOOD, late Royal Regiment of Artillery 508837.

Colonel B. J. W. GREEN, late Royal Tank Regiment 509520.

Major J. P. HILL, Royal Marines N029253J.

Captain N. J. HUGHES, Royal Navy C026149L.

Captain R. G. INGRAM, Royal Navy C027460Y.

Colonel P. LONGMORE, late Corps of Royal Electrical and Mechanical Engineers 515335.

Lieutenant Colonel T. D. MCMURTRIE, OBE, The Rifles 519697.

Major E. J. A. MURPHY, The Royal Regiment of Scotland 527339.

Colonel R. J. PULVERTAFT, Royal Marines N028134C.

Captain K. V. PALASTANGA, Royal Regiment of Artillery 564623.

Major G. H. POLLARD, MBE, Adjutant General's Corps (Royal Military Police) 542583.

Captain A. D. RADAKIN, Royal Navy C032545M.

Captain N. SAVAGE, The Royal Logistic Corps 557345.

Major R. A. SCOTT, The Parachute Regiment 536469.

Squadron Leader P. A. SMITH, Royal Air Force 2633376F.

Captain T. M. STOCKINGS, Royal Navy C032934C.

Group Captain P. A. STOREY, Royal Air Force 5205486V.

Lieutenant Colonel J. D. STUART, Scots Guards 512691.

Colonel I. TINSLEY, late Royal Regiment of Artillery 514423.

Colonel W. R. WIELOCH, late The Queen's Royal Lancers 508911.

Captain S. A. W. WILKINSON, The Royal Logistic Corps 24809925.

Lieutenant Colonel T. G. W. WOODMAN, MBE, The Royal Logistic Corps 508258.

Air Medal

Flight Lieutenant A. J. L. BALMER, Royal Air Force 2653645C.

FOREIGN AWARDS—GENERAL

DENMARK

In recognition of personal attention to a Head of State, on the occasion of State or official visits by such personages:

Commander First Class in the Order of the Dannebrog

Lieutenant General P. R. NEWTON, CBE, late The Princess of Wales's Royal Regiment 499752.

REPUBLIC OF ESTONIA

The Order of the Cross of the Eagle (4th Class)

Lieutenant Colonel R. H. C. LUCAS, The Royal Anglian Regiment 500968.

SLOVAK REPUBLIC

In recognition of services to Slovak troops in peace support and mentoring operations in Afghanistan:

Medal for Peace Support and Mentoring Operations

Air Commodore A. D. FRYER, Royal Air Force 8027356J.

REPUBLIC OF BULGARIA

In recognition of services to the Bulgarian contingent participating in the operations of the International Support Assistance Forces (ISAF) in Afghanistan:

St George II Class Honorary Distinction Decoration

Air Commodore R. W. JUDSON, Royal Air Force 8027799C.

The LONDON GAZETTE OF March 25, 2011

AFGHANISTAN

Commander of the British Empire (CBE)

Brigadier Richard Friedrich Patrick FELTON, OBE, late Army Air Corps, 522846.

Group Captain Neil William George LAIRD, Royal Air Force, 5206523C.

Colonel Gerhard Horst WHEELER, OBE, late The Royal Welsh, 523050.

Officer of the Order of the British Empire (OBE)

Lieutenant Colonel John Andrew MATTHEWS, The Royal Regiment of Fusiliers, 529807.

Lieutenant Colonel Andrew Paul MOSS, The Royal Logistic Corps, 529195.

Lieutenant Colonel David William SOUTHALL, MBE, Corps of Royal Engineers, 525893.

Member of the British Empire (MBE)

Lieutenant Commander Ian Graham BERRY, RD, Royal Naval Reserve, C985849Q.

Major Thomas Howard BEWICK, The Rifles, 546093.

Warrant Officer Class 2 Martin James COX, The Parachute Regiment, 24688889.

Major Paul Mark DUPUY, Royal Regiment of Artillery, 543707.

Major Richard Charles Owen GROVER, The Mercian Regiment, 556367.

Lance Corporal Isobel Ann HENDERSON, Royal Army Medical Corps, Q1051705.

Warrant Officer Class 2 Anthony Edward HIGGINBOTTOM, The Mercian Regiment, 24906671.

Staff Sergeant Paul George MCINTOSH, Royal Marines, P052283G.

Major Philip Mark TOTTEN, Royal Marines, N029309N.

Distinguished Service Order (DSO)

Major General Nicholas Patrick CARTER, CBE, late The Royal Green Jackets, 505216.

Lieutenant Colonel Charles Seymour COLLINS, MBE, The Rifles, 542143.

Lieutenant Colonel Paul Melvyn JAMES, Royal Marines, N028434H.

Major Marcus James MUDD, The Queen's Royal Lancers, 549583.

Lieutenant Colonel Gerald Mark STRICKLAND, MBE, The Royal Gurkha Rifles, 533572.

Conspicuous Gallantry Cross (CGC)

Marine Mark Anthony JACKSON, Royal Marines, 30060425.

Acting Sergeant Dipprasad PUN, The Royal Gurkha Rifles, 21170401.

Corporal Seth Vincent Scott STEPHENS, Royal Marines, P999732L (killed in action).

Military Cross (MC)

Lieutenant Jack ANRUDE, Royal Marines, P903592A.

Acting Corporal James Andrew BEDFORD, Corps of Royal Engineers, 25162280.

Colour Sergeant Brian BRIDGER, Royal Marines, P051960H.

Rifleman Sunil LIMBU, The Royal Gurkha Rifles, 30085704.

Marine Lewis LOCKWOOD, Royal Marines, 30004758.

Major James Rowland MARTIN, The Princess of Wales's Royal Regiment, 544003.

Lance Corporal Stephen Daniel MONKHOUSE, Scots Guards, 25183321 (killed in action).

Corporal Billy George MURPHY, Royal Marines, P060325K.

Lance Corporal Alan REDFORD, The Mercian Regiment, 25031185.

The LONDON GAZETTE OF MARCH 25, 2011 continued...

Captain Sean Alan SCOTT, The Royal Logistic Corps, 24839217.

Acting Corporal Matthew James STENTON, The Royal Dragoon Guards, 25154047 (killed in action).

Corporal Mark WARD, The Mercian Regiment, 25176588.

Lance Corporal Kylie Elizabeth WATSON, Royal Army Medical Corps, Q1060658.

Lance Corporal James Gerard WHITE, The Parachute Regiment, 25210810.

Distinguished Flying Cross (DFC)

Flight Lieutenant Matthew David ROBERTS, Royal Air Force, 550799.

Air Force Cross (AFC)

Flight Lieutenant Stephen Douglas BADHAM, Royal Air Force, 8300932P.

Flight Lieutenant James Patrick Michael DONOVAN, Royal Air Force, 8700045L.

Royal Red Cross (ARRC)

Major Ruth TRUSCOTT, Queen Alexandra's Royal Army Nursing Corps, 557268.

George Medal (GM)

Staff Sergeant Brett George LINLEY, The Royal Logistic Corps, 25130109 (killed in action).

Marine Ryan SHELLEY, Royal Marines, P061442J.

Queen's Gallantry Medal (QGM)

Warrant Officer Stephen Charles BOWDEN, Royal Air Force, R8122965.

Private Daniel James HELLINGS, The Mercian Regiment, 30074669.

Staff Sergeant William Ernest MCFARLAND, The Royal Logistic Corps, 24804668.

Captain Benedict Lincoln STEPHENS, The Mercian Regiment, 560346.

Mentioned in Despatches (MID)

Lance Corporal Andrew Christopher ATHERTON, Scots Guards, 25176625.

Squadron Leader Howard Robin BAILEY, Royal Air Force, 5207703V.

Sergeant Sven BAKER, The Duke of Lancaster's Regiment, 25040442.

Lance Corporal Christopher Stephen BOON, The Mercian Regiment, 25222390.

Flight Lieutenant Adam Thomas Owen BOOTH, Royal Air Force, 8701507K.

Private Stephen Edward BROWN, The Parachute Regiment, 25187098.

Lieutenant Commander Stephen Glyn BROWN, Royal Navy, C039085B.

Lance Corporal Christopher Elliot BURNS, The Royal Regiment of Scotland, 25163570.

Major Shaun William Mark CHANDLER, The Royal Gurkha Rifles, 552326.

Corporal Raymond Dino DALLAT, The Parachute Regiment, 25002636.

Corporal John Lee DARE, The Mercian Regiment, 25070113.

Corporal Toni GALACKI, Royal Marines, P059094Q.

Sergeant Anthony Carl GIBSON, Scots Guards, 25086148.

Rifleman Maniraj GURUNG, The Royal Gurkha Rifles, 30048314.

Captain Peter Alexander HOULTON-HART, The Royal Gurkha Rifles, 565289.

Lance Corporal Scott Henry HENDERSON, The Royal Regiment of Scotland, Territorial Army, 25135816.

Kingsman Callum Michael John HOWIE, The Duke of Lancaster's Regiment, 30049122.

Private Robert Oliver JACK, The Mercian Regiment, 25228158.

Corporal Dean JONES, The Parachute Regiment, P056287A.

Staff Sergeant Kevin KEENAN, The Parachute Regiment, 24903119.

Captain Michael John KERRIGAN, The Parachute Regiment, 563971.

Lance Corporal Paul Anthony LANGTON, The Mercian Regiment, 25183192.

Lance Sergeant Christopher LEYDEN, Scots Guards, 25096682.

Warrant Officer Class 2 Stephen Thomas MCDERMOTT, The Duke of Lancaster's Regiment, 24899394.

Sergeant Dean Wayne MCHUGH, The Duke of Lancaster's Regiment, 25065476.

Guardsman Glen MCNALLY, Coldstream Guards, 25149897.

Acting Sergeant George William MOITT, The Mercian Regiment, 25064155.

Sergeant Rory Patrick George O'CONNOR, The Parachute Regiment, P053753R.

Lance Corporal Anthony Joseph OWEN, The Parachute Regiment, 25184448.

Fusilier Jason Palmer, The Royal WELSH, Territorial Army, 30093336.

Captain Jonathan James PHELPS, Royal Marines, 25213288.

Lance Corporal Joeli RADUVA, The Royal Regiment of Scotland, 25133820.

Lance Corporal Nabin RAI, The Royal Gurkha Rifles, 21171210.

Warrant Officer Class 2 Paul William RYAN, Royal Marines, P045870P.

Acting Corporal Craig Colin SAXTON, The Royal Dragoon Guards, 25177699.

Flight Lieutenant Andrew Neil SCRASE, Royal Air Force, 8700207L.

Corporal Darren William George SIMPSON, Royal Marines, P055815M.

Flight Lieutenant Jonathan Arvind SINGH, Royal Air Force, 2659544D.

Captain Shureshkumar THAPA, The Royal Gurkha Rifles, 21168659.

Marine Alexander Charles George TOSTEVIN, Royal Marines, 30063068.

Lieutenant William John Lewis TULLOCH, Scots Guards, 25199842.

Private Mitchell Scott TYLER, The Mercian Regiment, 25142270.

Warrant Officer Class 2 Stephen Paul WATTS, The Rifles, 25010378.

Captain Malcolm James WHEELER, The Mercian Regiment, 25231200.

Queen's Commendation for Bravery (QCB)

Lance Corporal Michael Charles BRACEGIRDLE, Royal Army Medical Corps, 25207519.

Corporal Bryan GILSTON, The Duke of Lancaster's Regiment, 25199784.

The LONDON GAZETTE OF MARCH 25, 2011 continued. . .

Kingsman Scott David GLENDINNING, The Duke of Lancaster's Regiment, 30095569.

Lance Corporal Andrew James HAAG, The Mercian Regiment, 25205203.

Lance Corporal Greg HIND, Corps of Royal Engineers, 25139131.

Staff Sergeant Ian Barry JOHNSTON, The Royal Logistic Corps, 24908460.

Sapper Matthew John MORRIS, Corps of Royal Engineers, 25193170.

Sergeant David Anthony QUINN, The Duke of Lancaster's Regiment, 25031344.

Lance Corporal Richard John RADCLIFFE, Royal Air Force, E8448102.

Lance Corporal Dennis Robert SKINNER, The Royal Regiment of Scotland, 25160112.

Sapper Roy WATSON, Corps of Royal Engineers, 25157579.

Queen's Commendation for Valuable Service (QCVS)

Captain Alasdair James AKERMAN, The Royal Regiment of Scotland, 548730.

Captain Thomas Simon BODKIN, The Parachute Regiment, 564496.

Lieutenant Commander Nicholas John BOWSER, Royal Navy, C038638E.

Captain Matthew Anthony COX, Adjutant General's Corps (Royal Military Police), 562112.

Squadron Leader Gerard John Julian CURRIE, Royal Air Force, 8300829F.

Brigadier Richard Roderick Davis, CBE, late Corps of Royal Engineers, 514841.

Corporal Simon Lauchlan DONE, The Mercian Regiment, 25069439.

Sergeant Duncan GILHOOLY, Royal Marines, P053478C.

Corporal Manoj GURUNG, The Royal Gurkha Rifles, 21168949.

Lieutenant Colonel Andrew Nicholas HADFIELD, The Mercian Regiment, 530085.

Acting Colonel Charles Leonard Gordon HERBERT, OBE, The Royal Regiment of Scotland, 533080.

Staff Sergeant Andrew Derek JOHNSON, Corps of Royal Engineers, 24929217.

Lieutenant Colonel Lincoln Peter Munro JOPP, MC, Scots Guards, 525875.

Major Rupert Edward Charles KITCHING, Scots Guards, 548966.

Lieutenant Colonel Frazer Michael LAWRENCE, OBE, The Duke of Lancaster's Regiment, 533497.

Lance Sergeant Cameron MACDOUGALL, Scots Guards, 25077502.

Lieutenant Colonel Michael Stewart McGINTY, Army Air Corps, 527152.

Sergeant Robert James MOYLAN, Royal Air Force, K8436975.

Lance Corporal Paul Edward RAMSAY, Scots Guards, 25198683.

Squadron Leader Catherine Ann ROGERS, Royal Air Force, 8701427L.

Private Kyle SALISBURY, The Parachute Regiment, 25187431.

Sergeant Duncan STEVENSON, The Parachute Regiment, 24968296.

Warrant Officer Gareth WILLIAMS, Royal Air Force, Q8181581.

Acting Captain Michael George Bovill WHITEHEAD, The Royal Wessex Yeomanry, Territorial Army, 561394.

Flight Lieutenant Richard John WOOLLS, Royal Air Force, C8175034.

SERVICES IN THE FIELD

Officer of the Order of the British Empire (OBE)

Colonel Guy Hugh John DEACON, late 1st The Queen's Dragoon Guards, 519416.

Queen's Commendation for Bravery (QCB)

Craftsman Roy Thomas BOWDEN, Corps of Royal Electrical and Mechanical Engineers, 24929488.

Warrant Officer Class 1 Nicholas Francis HANDY, The Royal Logistic Corps, 25042465.

Sergeant Lewis Donald HORSBURGH, The Parachute Regiment, 25008692.

Queen's Commendation for Valuable Service (QCVS)

Chief Technician David Edward COLLINS, Royal Air Force, C8151662.

Sergeant Rudy McCLENAGHAN, Corps of Royal Electrical and Mechanical Engineers, 25058399.

NON-COMBATANT GALLANTRY

Air Force Cross (AFC)

Lieutenant Peter Martin HIGGINS, Royal Navy, C040089L.

Queen's Commendation for Bravery (QCB)

Petty Officer (Diver) Simon John SPENCEr, Royal Navy, D216996S.

Queen's Commendation for Bravery in the Air (QCBA)

Lieutenant Commander Graham John CHESTERMAN, Royal Navy, C029083X.

WEARING AWARDS

The wearing of Orders, Decorations and Medals is a complex subject too complicated to cover in a publication such as this. However, there are a number of questions that collectors frequently ask, so we have attempted to deal with these as fully as possible.

Full-size Awards Mounted for Wear

Orders, decorations and medals are worn on the left breast in a line suspended from a single brooch mount or a rectangular frame (court mounted), the latter gives a firmer grip which occasions less damage than medals hanging more loosely from a brooch. The brooch/frame is covered by the medal ribbons. The most senior medal (see the following Order of Precedence) is furthest from the left shoulder. The obverse of the medals should show (this will usually be the sovereign's head, coat of arms, cypher, etc.).

If more than five medals are worn (three for the Navy), they should not be suspended side by side, but overlapped, the senior medal and ribbon is the one to be positioned so it can be seen completely. Medals should be lined up straight by the bottom rim/point, the length of ribbon should be one and a quarter inches (33mm) from the top of the mount to the first clasp or the suspension, which ever is appropriate (one and three quarters (45mm) for the Navy). Where the awards differ in size then a ribbon adjustment will be necessary to ensure a straight line.

Emblems for Mentions-in-Despatches or King's and Queen's Commendations for personnel and civilians should be worn on the relevant campaign medal, for example on the Victory Medal for the First World War and the War Medal 1939–45 for the Second World War. Where a recipient has no relevant campaign medal, the MID or commendation emblem is worn directly on the coat after any medal ribbons, or if no ribbons then in the position of a single ribbon.

There are a number of awards for which the sovereign has granted permission that they be worn on the right breast, including:

Royal Humane Society Medals
Stanhope Gold Medal
Royal National Lifeboat Institution Medals
Order of St John of Jerusalem Life Saving Medal.

Foreign Orders, Decorations and Medals

The British sovereign's subjects are not permitted to accept and wear the orders, decorations and medals of a foreign country of which the sovereign is not head of state. Application can be made for wear and permission is of two types: (a) restricted, that is instructions are given as to the exact occasions on which the award(s) may be worn; (b) unrestricted which allows the item(s) to be worn on all occasions according to the Order of Precedence, that is, generally speaking, arranged after British awards by date—first orders, then decorations, followed by medals (there are exceptions for the members of the armed services serving in an overseas force and receive that country's awards).

Awards are worn on a variety of State, evening or other occasions and the rules governing the wearing of orders according to dress are quite detailed. The subject is covered fully in Medals Will Be Worn *by Lieutenant Colonel Ashley R. Tinson (Token Publishing Ltd., 1999) and in* Spink's Guide to the Wearing of Orders, Decorations and Medals *(Spink, 1990). The wearing of awards in civilian clothes is also fully detailed in* Wearing Your Medals in Civilian Clothes *by Lieutenant Colonel Ashley R. Tinson (Token Publishing Ltd., 2003).*

THE ORDER OF WEAR

The order in which decorations and medals should be worn in the United Kingdom and the Commonwealth, is set out below, as announced by the Central Chancery of the Orders of Knighthood.

Victoria Cross
George Cross
Most Noble Order of the Garter
Most Ancient and Most Noble Order of the Thistle
Most Illustrious Order of St Patrick (obsolete since the death of the Duke of Windsor, the last holder)
Knights Grand Cross, The Most Honourable Order of the Bath
Order of Merit
Knight Grand Commander, The Most Exalted Order of the Star of India
Knights Grand Cross, The Most Distinguished Order of St. Michael and St. George
Knight Grand Commander, The Most Eminent Order of the Indian Empire
The Order of the Crown of India
Knights Grand Cross, The Royal Victorian Order
Knights Grand Cross, The Most Excellent Order of the British Empire
Order of the Companions of Honour
Knight Commander, The Most Honourable Order of the Bath
Knight Commander, The Most Exalted Order of the Star of India
Knight Commander, The Most Distinguished Order of St. Michael and St. George
Knight Commander, The Most Eminent Order of the Indian Empire
Knight Commander, The Royal Victorian Order
Knight Commander, The Most Excellent Order of the British Empire
Baronet's Badge
Knight Bachelor's Badge
Companion, The Most Honourable Order of the Bath
Companion, The Most Exalted Order of the Star of India
Companion, The Most Distinguished Order of St. Michael and St. George
Companion, The Most Eminent Order of the Indian Empire
Commander, The Royal Victorian Order
Commander, The Most Excellent Order of the British Empire
Distinguished Service Order
Lieutenant, The Royal Victorian Order
Officer, The Most Excellent Order of the British Empire
Imperial Service Order

Member, The Royal Victorian Order
Member, The Most Excellent Order of the British Empire
Indian Order of Merit—Military

DECORATIONS
Conspicuous Gallantry Cross
Royal Red Cross, Class 1
Distinguished Service Cross
Military Cross
Distinguished Flying Cross
Air Force Cross
Royal Red Cross, Class II
Order of British India
Kaisar-I-Hind Medal
Order of St John

GALLANTRY AND DISTINGUISHED CONDUCT MEDALS
Union of South Africa Queen's Medal for Bravery in gold
Distinguished Conduct Medal
Conspicuous Gallantry Medal
Conspicuous Gallantry Medal (Flying)
George Medal
Queen's Police Medal for Gallantry
Queen's Fire Service Medal for Gallantry
Royal West African Frontier Force Distinguished Conduct Medal
King's African Rifles Distinguished Conduct Medal
Indian Distinguished Service Medal
Union of South Africa Queen's Medal for Bravery in silver
Distinguished Service Medal
Military Medal
Distinguished Flying Medal
Air Force Medal
Constabulary Medal (Ireland)
Medal for Saving Life at Sea
Indian Order of Merit (Civil)
Indian Police Medal for Gallantry
Ceylon Police Medal for Gallantry
Sierra Leone Police Medal for Gallantry
Sierra Leone Fire Brigades Medal for Gallantry
Colonial Police Medal for Gallantry
Queen's Gallantry Medal
Royal Victorian Medal (gold, silver and bronze)
British Empire Medal
Canada Medal
Queen's Police Medal for Distinguished Service

Queen's Fire Service Medal for Distinguished Service
Queen's Volunteer Reserves Medal
Queen's Ambulance Service Medal
Queen's Medal for Chiefs

CAMPAIGN MEDALS

Campaign Medals and Stars, including authorised UN, EU, EC and NATO medals in order of date of participation in the campaign for which awarded, as well as GSMs and OSMs.
Polar Medals—in order of date of award

MEDALS FOR VALUABLE SERVICE

Imperial Service Medal
Indian Police Medal for Meritorious Service
Ceylon Police Medal for Merit
Sierra Leone Police Medal for Meritorious Service
Sierra Leone Fire Brigades Medal for Meritorious Service
Colonial Police Medal for Meritorious Service
Badge of Honour

JUBILEE, CORONATION, DURBAR MEDALS

Queen Victoria's Jubilee Medal 1887 (gold, silver and bronze)
Queen Victoria's Police Jubilee Medal 1887
Queen Victoria's Jubilee Medal 1897 (gold, silver and bronze)
Queen Victoria's Police Jubilee Medal 1897
Queen Victoria's Commemoration Medal 1900 (Ireland)
King Edward VII's Coronation 1902
King Edward VII's Police Coronation 1902
King Edward VII's Durbar 1903 (gold, silver and bronze)
King Edward VII's Police Medal 1903 (Scotland)
King's Visit Commemoration Medal 1903 (Ireland)
King George V's Coronation Medal 1911
King George V's Police Coronation Medal 1911
King George V's Visit Police Commemoration Medal 1911 (Ireland)
King George V's Durbar Medal 1911 (gold, silver and bronze)
King George V's Silver Jubilee Medal 1935
King George VI's Coronation Medal 1937
Queen Elizabeth II's Coronation Medal 1953
Queen Elizabeth II's Silver Jubilee Medal 1977
Queen Elizabeth II's Golden Jubilee Medal 2002
King George V's Long and Faithful Service Medal
King George VI's Long and Faithful Service Medal
Queen Elizabeth II's Long and Faithful Service Medal

EFFICIENCY AND LONG SERVICE DECORATIONS AND MEDALS

Medal for Meritorious Service
Accumulated Campaign Service Medal
Medal for Long Service and Good Conduct, Army
Naval Long Service and Good Conduct Medal
Medal for Meritorious Service (Royal Navy 1918–28)
Indian Long Service and Good Conduct Medal (for Europeans of Indian Army)
Indian Meritorious Service Medal (for Europeans of Indian Army)
Royal Marines Meritorious Service Medal (1849–1947)
Royal Air Force Meritorious Service Medal 1918–28

Royal Air Force Long Service and Good Conduct Medal
Ulster Defence Regiment Long Service and Good Conduct Medal
Indian Long Service and Good Conduct Medal (Indian Army)
Royal West African Frontier Force Long Service and Good Conduct Medal
Royal Sierra Leone Military Forces Long Service and Good Conduct Medal
King's African Rifles Long Service and Good Conduct Medal
Indian Meritorious Service Medal (for Indian Army)
Police Long Service and Good Conduct Medal
Fire Brigade Long Service and Good Conduct Medal
African Police Medal for Meritorious Service
Royal Canadian Mounted Police Long Service Medal
Ceylon Police Long Service Medal
Ceylon Fire Services Long Service Medal
Sierra Leone Police Long Service Medal
Colonial Police Long Service Medal
Sierra Leone Fire Brigade Long Service Medal
Mauritius Police Long Service and Good Conduct Medal
Mauritius Fire Service Long Service and Good Conduct Medal
Mauritius Prisons Service Long Service and Good Conduct Medal
Colonial Fire Brigades Long Service Medal
Colonial Prison Service Medal
Army Emergency Reserve Decoration
Volunteer Officers' Decoration
Volunteer Long Service Medal
Volunteer Officers' Decoration (for India and the Colonies)
Volunteer Long Service Medal (for India and the Colonies)
Colonial Auxiliary Forces Officers' Decoration
Colonial Auxiliary Forces Long Service Medal
Medal for Good Shooting (Naval)
Militia Long Service Medal
Imperial Yeomanry Long Service Medal
Territorial Decoration
Ceylon Armed Service Long Service Medal
Efficiency Decoration
Territorial Efficiency Medal
Efficiency Medal
Special Reserve Long Service and Good Conduct Medal
Decoration for Officers of the Royal Naval Reserve
Decoration for Officers of the Royal Naval Volunteer Reserve
Royal Naval Reserve Long Service and Good Conduct Medal
Royal Naval Volunteer Reserve Long Service and Good Conduct Medal
Royal Naval Auxiliary Sick Berth Reserve Long Service and Good Conduct Medal
Royal Fleet Reserve Long Service and Good Conduct Medal
Royal Naval Wireless Auxiliary Reserve Long Service and Good Conduct Medal
Royal Naval Auxiliary Service Medal
Air Efficiency Award
Volunteer Reserves Service Medal
Ulster Defence Regiment Medal
Queen's Medal (for Champion Shots of the Royal Navy and Royal Marines)

Queen's Medal (for Champion Shots of the New Zealand Naval Forces)
Queen's Medal (for Champion Shots in the Military Forces)
Queen's Medal (for Champion Shots of the Air Force)
Cadet Forces Medal
Coast Guard Auxiliary Service Long Service Medal
Special Constabulary Long Service Medal
Canadian Forces Decoration
Royal Observer Corps Medal
Civil Defence Long Service Medal
Ambulance Service LS & GCM
Royal Fleet Auxiliary Service Medal
Rhodesia Medal
Royal Ulster Constabulary Service Medal
Union of South Africa Commemoration Medal
Indian Independence Medal
Pakistan Medal
Ceylon Armed Services Inauguration Medal
Ceylon Police Independence Medal (1948)
Sierra Leone Independence Medal
Jamaica Independence Medal

Uganda Independence Medal
Malawi Independence Medal
Fiji Independence Medal
Papua New Guinea Independence Medal
Solomon Islands Independence Medal
Service Medal of the Order of St. John
Badge of the Order of the League of Mercy
Voluntary Medical Service Medal
Women's Voluntary Service Medal
South African Medal for War Services
Colonial Special Constabulary Medal
Honorary Membership of Commonwealth Orders (instituted by the Sovereign, in order of date of award)
Other Commonwealth Members, Orders, Decorations and Medals (instituted since 1949 otherwise than by the Sovereign, and awards by States of Malaysia and Brunei in order of date of award)
Foreign Orders in order of date of award
Foreign Decorations in order of date of award
Foreign Medals in order of date of award

THE ORDER IN WHICH CAMPAIGN STARS AND MEDALS AWARDED FOR SERVICE DURING WORLD WAR I AND II ARE WORN

1914 Star with dated "Mons" clasp " 15th AUGUST–22nd NOVEMBER 1914"
1914 Star
1914/15 Star
British War Medal
Mercantile Marine War Medal
Victory Medal
Territorial Force War Medal
1939/45 Star
Atlantic Star
Air Crew Europe Star
Africa Star
Pacific Star

Burma Star
Italy Star
France and Germany Star
Defence Medal
Canadian/Newfoundland Volunteer Service Medal
1939/45 War Medal
1939/45 Africa Service Medal of the Union of South Africa
India Service Medal
New Zealand War Service Medal
Southern Rhodesia Service Medal
Australian Service Medal

POST-NOMINAL LETTERS (as published in the *London Gazette*)
Recipients of some awards are entitled to use post-nominal letters including the following:

AE	Air Efficiency Award (officers)	CVO	Commander, The Royal Victorian Order
AFC	Air Force Cross	DBE	Dame Commander, The Most Excellent Order of the British Empire
AFM	Air Force Medal		
AM	Albert Medal	DCB	Dame Commander, The Most Honourable Order of the Bath
ARRC	Royal Red Cross, Second Class		
BEM	British Empire Medal	DCMG	Dame Commander, The Most Distinguished Order of St Michael and St George
BGM	Burma Gallantry Medal		
Bt or Bart	Baronet		
CBE	Commander, The Most Excellent Order of the British Empire	DCM	Distinguished Conduct Medal (King's African Rifles)
CB	Companion, The Most Honourable Order of the Bath	DCM	Distinguished Conduct Medal (West Africa Frontier Force)
CD	Canadian (Forces) Decoration	DCM	Distinguished Conduct Medal
CGC	Conspicuous Gallantry Cross	DCVO	Dame Commander, The Royal Victorian Order
CGM	Conspicuous Gallantry Medal		
CH	Order of the Companion of Honour	DFC	Distinguished Flying Cross
CIE	Companion, The Most Eminent Order of the Indian Empire	DFM	Distinguished Flying Medal
		DSC	Distinguished Service Cross
CI	The Order of the Crown of India (women only)	DSM	Distinguished Service Medal
		DSO	Distinguished Service Order
CM/M du C	Canada Medal	ED	Efficiency Decoration
CMG	Companion, The Most Distinguished Order of St Michael and St George	EGM	Empire Gallantry Medal
		EM	Edward Medal
CPM	Colonial Police Medal	ERD	Army Emergency Reserve Decoration
CSI	Companion, The Most Exalted Order of the Star of India	GBE	Knight Grand Cross, The Most Excellent Order of the British Empire

GCB	Knight Grand Cross, The Most Honourable Order of the Bath
GCIE	Knight Grand Commander. The Most Eminent Order of the Indian Empire
GCMG	Knight Grand Cross—The Most Distinguished Order of St Michael and St George
GCSI	Knight Grand Commander, The Most Exalted Order of the Star of India
GCVO	Knight Grand Cross, The Royal Victorian Order
GC	George Cross
GM	George Medal
IDSM	Indian Distinguished Service Medal
IOM	Indian Order of Merit (civil)
IOM	Indian Order of Merit (military)
ISO	Imperial Service Order
KBE	Knight Commander, The Most Excellent Order of the British Empire
KCB	Knight Commander, The Most Honourable Order of the Bath
KCIE	Knight Commander, The Most Eminent Order of the Indian Empire
KCMG	Knight Commander, The Most Distinguished Order of St Michael and St George
KCSI	Knight Commander, The Most Exalted Order of the Star of India
KCVO	Knight Commander, The Royal Victorian Order
KG	Knight, Most Noble Order of the Garter
KP	Knight, Most Illustrious Order of St Patrick

KPFSM	King's Police and Fire Service Medal
KPM	King's Police Medal
KT	Knight, Most Ancient and Most Noble Order of the Thistle
LVO	Lieutenant, The Royal Victorian Order
MBE	Member, The Most Excellent Order of the British Empire
MC	Military Cross
MM	Military Medal
MSM	Meritorious Service Medal (Navy, awards up to 20.7.28)
MVO	Member, The Royal Victorian Order
OBE	Officer, The Most Excellent Order of the British Empire
OBI	Order of British India
OB	Order of Burma (distinguished service)
OB	Order of Burma (gallantry)
OM	Order of Merit
QFSM	Queen's Fire Service Medal
QGM	Queen's Gallantry Medal
QPM	Queen's Police Medal
QVRM	Queen's Volunteer Reserves Medal
RD	Royal Naval Reserve Decoration
RRC	Royal Red Cross First Class
RVM	Royal Victorian Medal
SGM	Sea Gallantry Medals
TD	Territorial Decoration
UD	Ulster Defence Regiment Medal (officers)
VC	Victoria Cross
VD	Volunteer Officers' Decoration
VRD	Royal Naval Volunteer Reserve Decoration

COLLECTING MEDAL RIBBONS

There is nothing new or old about collecting medal ribbons, in fact the founders of the present Orders and Medals Research Society originally set out as medal ribbon collectors. The ribbon has, ever since the early 18th century, been an important complement to the medal or badge of an order and its importance has grown over the years. Since those early orders of chivalry when it was deemed necessary to identify the various religious or secular orders one belonged to by the colour of its ribbon, the emphasis has been on the ribbon to identify the order or medal. This practice has continued down through the centuries, even to today when the avid enthusiast can recognise a warriors medals simply by identifying his ribbons.

However, times are changing. The practice of wearing medals is on the decline, reserved only for ceremonial occasions, whilst the wearing of ribbon bars and the awarding of a single campaign or service medal with different ribbons to denote specific operations is on the increase. Our very own Operational Service Medal (OSM), the NATO medal and of course the plethora of United Nations medals are all classic examples of today's expansion of the medal ribbon. There is of course the growing cost of collecting medals and decorations compared to that of medal ribbons. There is also the down side to all of this, as the opportunity to acquire medal ribbons has become a challenge to many, as sources such as tailor's shops, small ribbon manufacturers or numerous regimental or quartermasters stores have all gone into decline, if not altogether vanished.

Before one can collect ribbons properly one must first be able to identify them. It is therefore important to have a reasonable reference library— nothing elaborate or expansive is needed. It is probably wise to start collecting ribbons of the United Kingdom before branching out into those of other countries. There are several good books on the subject and ribbons can be obtained quite easily.

The more one handles ribbons the quicker one starts to get a feel for the subject and gets to know which colours are used by certain countries or organisations, whether they always use silk or fine cottons, prefer moiré (watered) or corded ribbons whether they use wide or narrow ribbons, all are skills one picks up along the way, though sadly this art is slowly dying as the quality of many modern manufactured ribbons is really quite poor compared to the silk watered ribbons of bygone days.

Once over the initial teething problems of deciding how to store ribbons and ultimately mount or display them, the desire to expand and even specialise creeps in. Do you collect ribbons from just one country, state or organisation such as the Red Cross or the United Nations? Campaign medals and their numerous emblems? Famous chests? Regimental battle streamers? Religious or chivalric orders past and present? British or foreign orders and their various rosettes? The choice can be endless. Whatever the path you choose, you will almost certainly have to do a little research to obtain the reason for the award and the colours adopted for the ribbon. In reality, a true ribbon collector will know just as much about the medal or decoration as they will about the ribbon. Depending on the amount of time you have, research can lead you to museums, reading rooms or even portrait galleries, as well as societies such as the Ribbon Branch of the Orders and Medals Research Society. But whatever path is chosen you will be in awe of the sacrifices made by mankind down the centuries.

MINIATURE MEDALS & DECORATIONS

The collecting of miniature medals has gained in popularity over the past few years and as a result groups and single miniatures that were once sold with their full-size counterparts, as an added extra, are now being traded in their own right. The market prices for these attractive and often superbly-produced little pieces are included in the catalogue section. Collectors wishing to learn more about miniature medals are invited to contact the Miniature Medals Branch of the Orders & Medals Research Society whose address can be found opposite.

Miniatures are small versions of orders, decorations and medals designed for formal evening wear. The custom appears to have developed in Continental Europe in the early years of the 18th century, but is now more or less universal, although the actual practice varies from country to country. In the United Kingdom, for example, miniatures are usually confined to mess kit and evening dress, although nowadays there is a tendency to wear them with dinner jacket, as in the United States. In Europe, miniatures are often worn without ribbons, suspended from a tiny chain, but in Britain and elsewhere miniatures are worn with exact replicas of the appropriate ribbons correspondingly reduced in size.

The scale of miniatures likewise varies from country to country. In Britain miniatures are usually half the size of the full-sized medals, but the Scandinavian countries use a 17mm size, while France and the Low Countries prefer a 14mm size, calculated from the diameter of medals or the badges of orders.

In the 18th and early 19th centuries the breast stars of orders were also worn in miniature, but nowadays only the badges of the orders are miniaturised. In Europe the higher classes of orders are designated by placing wings in silver, gold and silver, or gold, according to the class, below the rosette on the riband of the Officer Class. In Britain, however, miniatures are exact replicas of the badges they represent, and no additional rosettes or emblems are added to the ribands to denote a particular class.

Miniatures differ in one major respect from the full-scale; whereas the latter were produced by specific contractors, the former have been manufactured by many jewellers and goldsmiths. Consequently, the quality may vary considerably, from a very faithful replica (doubtless produced by the same firm that made the originals and using scaled-down dies for the purpose), to quite crude imitations that differ in many details from the full sized version. In many instances, miniature medal groups may be found with the original case as supplied by the jeweller, so that identification is not a problem. Many other groups, however, have long since parted company from their presentation cases, and identification is then only possible from other factors, either stylistic or from marks. Some miniatures are hallmarked (i.e. they bear the punches of an assay office and the mark of the manufacturer), and in such cases the miniature can not only be identified, but even the date of manufacture adduced from the year letter. Not all miniatures by any means are hallmarked, especially if they fall below the statutory minimum weight, so that this aid to identification is not always present.

The value placed on miniatures is governed by condition, of course, but other factors that must be taken into consideration are the provenance and authenticity of the medal or group. Miniatures which are contemporary with the original award are rated more highly than replacements procured many years later. And miniature groups which can definitely be assigned to a particular recipient are worth a premium over those whose original owner cannot be determined. Unlike the full-scale originals, miniatures very seldom bear the name of the recipient. Nevertheless, this is a fascinating aspect of medal collecting, much less expensive than the full-size medals but often as rewarding for the human interest which miniatures represent.

Today many miniatures of old medals are being produced and are readily available. The prices quoted in this publication are for contemporary medals unless otherwise stated.

ORDERS OF KNIGHTHOOD

The most colourful and romantic of all awards are those connected with the orders of chivalry. Many of them have their origins in the Middle Ages, when knights in armour formed the elite fighting force in every European country. From the idea of a select band of knights, pledged to the support of a king or an ideal (usually religious), sprang the orders of chivalry.

Many of the orders of chivalry existed in the Middle Ages but most of them died out as feudalism went into decline. In some cases they survived; in others they disappeared for centuries, only to be resurrected at a later date. Still others were devised and instituted in relatively modern times, and indeed, continue to evolve. For example, Canada instituted the Order of Canada in 1967 and both Australia and New Zealand introduced their own orders in 1975.

In their original form membership of the orders of chivalry were just as highly coveted as they are today, but the insignia was usually simple or even non-existent. The complicated system of insignia which now surrounds these orders is fairly modern, dating from the 16th century or later. Nowadays most orders also exist in several classes, with the insignia becoming increasingly elaborate with each higher class.

Britain's senior order is the Garter, and although it consists of one class only it provides a good example of the pomp and ceremony which often surrounds these awards. It was founded by King Edward III and is said to derive its name from the fact that the King was attending a dance one day, when a lady's garter slipped from her leg and fell to the floor. To save her the embarrassment of retrieving her garter—and thus letting everyone know it was hers—the King himself picked it up and tied it round his own leg. Lest anyone should doubt that it was his garter he said, in court French, "Let evil be to him who evil thinks". From this curious incident came the idea of a very exclusive order of knighthood, consisting of the sovereign and 26 knights.

The insignia of this order consists of a Garter, a mantle of blue velvet lined with taffeta with the star of the Order embroidered on the left breast, a hood of crimson velvet, a surcoat of crimson velvet lined with white taffeta, a hat of black velvet lined with white taffeta, with a plume of white ostrich and black heron feathers fastened by a band of diamonds, a collar of gold composed of buckled garters and lovers' knots with red roses, the George (an enamelled figure of St George slaying the dragon) suspended from the collar, the Lesser George or badge, worn from a broad blue sash passing over the left shoulder to the right hip,

and the star, a silver eight-pointed decoration bearing the red cross of St George surrounded by the garter and motto.

The insignia is exceptionally elaborate, the other orders of chivalry varying considerably in their complexity according to the class of the order. The full insignia is only worn on special occasions. In the case of the Garter usually the Lesser George and the breast star are worn on their own.

On the death of a Knight of the Garter the insignia should be returned to the Central Chancery of Orders of Knighthood, and therefore few examples of the Garter ever come on to the market. Those that do are usually examples from the 17th and 18th centuries when regulations regarding the return of insignia were not so strict. In the case of the lesser orders, insignia is returnable on promotion to a higher class. All collar chains are returnable, although that of the Order of St Michael and St George could be retained prior to 1948.

British orders are manufactured by firms holding contracts from the Central Chancery of Orders of Knighthood, and the values quoted in this Yearbook are for the official issues. It should be noted, however, that holders of orders frequently have replicas of breast stars made for use on different uniforms and it is sometimes difficult to tell these replicas from the originals as in many cases the replicas were made by the court jewellers responsible for making the originals. In addition, many jewellers in such European capitals as Vienna, Berlin and Paris have a long tradition of manufacturing the insignia of orders for sale to collectors.

The badges and breast stars of orders of chivalry are very seldom named to the recipient and therefore lack the personal interest of campaign medals and many gallantry awards. For this reason they do not command the same interest or respect of collectors. Nevertheless, in cases where the insignia of orders can be definitely proved to have belonged to some famous person, the interest and value are enhanced. In any case, these orders are invariably very attractive examples of the jeweller's art, and they often possess titles and stories as colourful and romantic as their appearance.

1. THE MOST NOBLE ORDER OF THE GARTER

KG Star
(a Victorian example)

Lesser George
(this early example has the
garter enamelled in blue)

Instituted: 1348.

Ribbon: 100mm plain dark blue. Not worn in undress uniform.

Garter: Dark blue velvet. Two versions may be encountered, with embroidered lettering and other details, or with gold lettering, buckle and tab. Worn on the left leg by gentlemen and on the left forearm by ladies.

Collar Chain: Gold composed of alternate buckled garters, each encircling a red enamelled rose, and lovers' knots in gold although sometimes enamelled white.

Collar badge: An enamelled figure of St George fighting the dragon.

Star: Originally always embroidered in metal thread, a style which continues in the mantle to this day. Prior to 1858 knights often purchased metal stars in addition and since that date metal stars have been officially issued. These consist of a silver eight-pointed radiate star bearing in its centre and red cross of St George on a white ground, surrounded by the garter and motto HONI SOIT QUI MAL Y PENSE (evil be to he who evil thinks).

Sash Badge: The Lesser George, similar to the collar badge but encircled by an oval garter bearing the motto.

Comments: *Membership of the Order of the Garter is confined to the reigning sovereign, the Prince of Wales and 25 other Knights, and is the personal gift of the monarch. In addition to the 25 Knights there have, from time to time, been extra Knights, occasionally non-Christians such as the Sultans of Turkey or the Emperor of Japan. The Emperor Hirohito, incidentally had the dubious distinction of being the only person awarded the Garter twice: in 1922 and again in 1971, having forfeited the original award as a result of the Japanese entry into the Second World War in 1941. Sir Winston Churchill was invested with the insignia originally presented in 1702 to his illustrious ancestor, the Duke of Marlborough. All official insignia is returnable to the Central Chancery of Knighthood on the death of the holder. Ladies (other than royalty) are now eligible for the Order.*

VALUE:

Collar chain	Rare
Collar badge (the George)	£50,000–100,000*
Star (in metal)	£3000–7000
Star (embroidered)	£850–2000
Mantle star	£850–1000
Sash badge (Lesser George)	£5000–40,000
Garter (embroidered)	£800–1000
Garter (gold lettering and buckle)	£3000–5000

Miniature

Star (metal)	£350–400
Collar badge	£650–750
Sash badge	£300–350

Prices are for privately made examples many of which are jewelled and enamelled.

2. THE MOST ANCIENT AND MOST NOBLE ORDER OF THE THISTLE

Instituted: 1687.

Ribbon: 100mm plain dark green. Not worn in undress uniform.

Collar Chain: Gold of alternate thistles and sprigs of rue enamelled in proper colours.

Collar Badge: The jewel is a gold and enamelled figure of St Andrew in a green gown and purple surcoat, bearing before him a white saltire cross, the whole surrounded by rays of gold.

Star: Silver, consisting of a St Andrew's cross, with other rays issuing between the points of the cross and, in the centre, on a gold background, a thistle enamelled in proper colours surrounded by a green circle bearing the Latin motto NEMO ME IMPUNE LACESSIT (no one assails me with impunity).

Sash Badge: The medal of the Order is a gold figure of St Andrew bearing before him a saltire cross, surrounded by an oval collar bearing the motto, surmounted by a gold cord fitted with a ring for suspension. Examples are found in plain gold, or with enamelling and / or set with jewels.

Comments: *This order is said to have been founded in AD 787, alluding to barefoot enemy soldiers who cried out when they trod on thistles and thus alerted the Scots of an imminent attack. The order had long been defunct when it was revived by King James VII and II and re-established in December 1703 by Queen Anne. It now consists of the sovereign and 16 Knights, making it the most exclusive of the orders of chivalry. At death, the official insignia is returned to the Central Chancery. Ladies (other than royalty) are now eligible for the Order.*

KT Star

VALUE:

Collar chain	Rare
Collar badge	Rare
Star (metal)	£1500–4000
Star (embroidered)	£800–1000
Mantle star	£750–1400
Sash badge	£3000–8000

Miniature

Star (metal)	£400–500
Collar badge	£450–550
Sash badge	£350–400

Examples of Sash Badges

3. THE MOST ILLUSTRIOUS ORDER OF ST PATRICK

KP Star

Sash badge

Instituted: February 5, 1783.

Ribbon: 100 mm sky-blue. Not worn in undress uniform.

Collar Chain: Gold, composed of five roses and six harps alternating, each tied together with a gold knot. The roses are enamelled alternately white petals within red and red within white.

Collar Badge: An imperial crown enamelled in proper colours from which is suspended by two rings a gold harp and from this a circular badge with a white enamelled centre embellished with the red saltire cross on which is surmounted a green three-petalled shamrock its leaves decorated with gold crowns, the whole surrounded by a gold collar bearing the Latin motto QUIS SEPARABIT (who shall separate us?) with the date of foundation in roman numerals round the foot MDCCLXXXIII.

Star: A silver eight-pointed star, having in its centre, on a white field, the saltire cross of St Patrick in red enamel charged with a green trefoil bearing a gold crown on each leaf.

Sash Badge: The saltire cross in red enamel surmounted by a green shamrock with gold crowns as above, surrounded by an oval collar of pale blue with the Latin motto round the top and the date of foundation round the foot, the whole enclosed by a gold and white enamel surround charged with 32 shamrocks.

Comments: *Founded by King George III to reward the loyalty of Irish peers during the American War of Independence, it originally comprised the monarch and 15 Knights. In 1833 it was extended to include the Lord-Lieutenant of Ireland and 22 Knights, with certain extra and honorary knights. Appointments of non-royal Knights to the Order ceased with the partition of Ireland in 1922, although three of the sons of King George V were appointed after that date—the Prince of Wales (1927), the Duke of York (1936) and the Duke of Gloucester (1934). It became obsolete in 1974 with the death of the last holder. All items of official insignia were returned at death. Unlike the other two great orders, the sash for this Order is worn in the manner of the lesser orders, over the right shoulder.*

VALUE:

Collar chain	Rare
Collar badge	£8000–12,000
Star (metal)	£2500–4500
Star (embroidered)	£800–1000
Mantle star	£800–1200
Sash badge	£4000–6000
Miniature	
Star (metal)	£350–400
Collar/Sash badge	£550–650

4. THE MOST HONOURABLE ORDER OF THE BATH

GCB Star (Military)

Instituted: 1725.

Ribbon: 38mm deep red.

Collar Chain: Gold composed of nine crowns and eight devices, each consisting of a rose, a thistle and a shamrock issuing from a sceptre all enamelled in their proper colours. The crowns and devices are joined by gold, white-enamelled knots.

Collar Badge: A skeletal gold badge with an oval collar inscribed TRIA JUNCTA IN UNO (three joined in one) in white enamelled letters, enclosing a thistle, rose and shamrock issuing from a sceptre, with a crown above the sceptre and two crowns below, at the sides.

Star: A silver flaming star surmounted by a circular gold band enamelled red bearing the motto round the top and having a laurel spray round the foot, enclosing three gold crowns enamelled in red.

Sash Badge: As the Collar Badge but smaller and without white enamelling.

Comments: *Established by King George I, this was a single-class Order comprising the monarch, a prince of the blood royal, a Great Master and 35 Knights of Companions (KB). It was re-organised at the conclusion of the Napoleonic Wars (see below). Ladies (other than royalty) are now eligible for the Order. Promotion to a different division permits the wearing of both types of insignia.*

VALUE:

Collar chain	£18,000–25,000
Collar badge	£3000–4000
Star (metal)	£2000–3500
Star (embroidered)	£400–800
Sash badge	£2000–3000

KNIGHT GRAND CROSS (GCB)

The Order was re-organised in 1815 in two divisions, Military and Civil. The Military Division had three classes: Knight Grand Cross (GCB), Knight Commander (KCB) and Companion (CB), while the Civil Division continued with the single class of Knight Grand Cross. In 1847 the Civil Division came into line with the Military, and divided into three classes.

Metal: Gold (1815–87), silver-gilt (1887–1901), silver gilt with gold centre (1902 on).

Collar Badge: The Military Badge is a gold Maltese cross of eight points, each point tipped with a small gold ball, and in each angle between the arms of the cross is a gold lion. In the centre of the cross is a device comprising a rose, thistle and shamrock issuing from a sceptre, and three imperial crowns . This device is surrounded by a red enamelled circle on which appears the Latin motto TRIA JUNCTA IN UNO (three joined in one) in gold lettering. The circle is surrounded by two branches of laurel, enamelled green, and below is a blue enamelled scroll with the German motto ICH DIEN (I serve) in gold.

The Civil Badge is of gold filigree work, and oval in shape. It consists of a bandlet bearing the motto, and in the centre is the usual device of the rose, thistle and shamrock issuing from a sceptre, together with the three crowns.

Star: A gold Maltese cross of the same pattern as the Military Badge, mounted on a silver flaming star (Military); or a silver eight-pointed star with a central device of three crowns on a silver ground, encircled by the motto on a red enamelled ribbon (Civil).

Sash Badges: Similar to the Collar Badges, they were originally made in gold but since 1887 silver-gilt has been substituted. They may now be worn at the neck when sashes are not worn.

VALUE:	Military	Civil
Collar chain (gold)	£18,000–25,000	£18,000–25,000
Collar chain (silver gilt)	£8000–10,000	£8000–10,000
Collar badge (gold)	£2000–3500	£1000–1500
Star (metal)	£1000–1500	£450–550
Star (embroidered)	£300–500	£200–300
Mantle star	£700–1000	£600–800
Sash badge (gold)	£1800–3000	£1200–1500
Sash badge (gilt)	£1000–1500	£600–800

4. THE MOST HONOURABLE ORDER OF THE BATH *continued*

KCB Star (Civil)

GCB Sash badge (Civil)

KCB Neck badge (Military)

KNIGHTS COMMANDERS (KCB) AND COMPANIONS (CB)

Holders of the KCB wear a neck badge suspended by a ribbon as well as a breast star. Prior to 1917 Companions wore a breast badge, the same way as a medal: but in that year it was converted into a neck badge.

Star: (KCB): (Military) a star with the gold Maltese cross omitted, and in the shape of a cross pattée, the three crowns and motto in the centre surrounded by a green enamelled laurel wreath. (Civil) similar but omitting the laurel wreath.

Breast Badge (CB): Similar to the Star but smaller.

Neck Badge (KCB): Similar to the Collar badges of the GCB but smaller, in Military and Civil versions as above.

Neck Badge (CB): Similar to the above, but smaller.

VALUE:

	Military	Miniature	Civil	Miniature
Knight Commander				
Star (metal)	£850–1200		£500–700	
Star (embroidered)	£250–400		£200–350	
Neck badge (gold)	£3000–3500		£800–1000	
Neck badge (gilt)	£750–1000		£500–700	
Companion				
Breast badge (gold)	£2000–2500	£100–150	£700–800	£80–100
Breast badge (gilt)	£800–1000	£50–75	£350–4000	£45–75
Neck badge (gilt)	£800–900		£300–350	

5. THE ROYAL GUELPHIC ORDER

Instituted: 1815.
Ribbon: 44mm light blue watered silk.

KNIGHTS GRAND CROSS (GCH)

KCH Star (Military)

Collar Chain: Gold, with lions and crowns alternating, linked by scrolled royal cyphers.
Collar Badge: An eight-pointed Maltese cross with balls on each point and a lion passant gardant in each angle. (Obverse) in the centre, on a ground of red enamel, is a white horse of Hanover surrounded by a circle of light blue enamel with the motto in gold lettering NEC ASPERA TERRENT (difficulties do not terrify). Surrounding this circle is a green enamelled laurel wreath. (Reverse) the monogram GR in gold letters on a red ground, surmounted by the British crown and surrounded by a gold circle with the date of the institution MDCCCXV. In the Military version two crossed swords are mounted above the cross and below a Hanoverian crown. In the Civil version the swords are omited, and the wreath is of oak-leaves instead of laurel.
Star: A radiate star with rays grouped into eight points, the centre being similar to the Collar Badge. Behind the laurel wreathed centre are two crossed swords (Military); in the Civil version the swords are omitted and the wreath is of oak leaves.
Sash Badge: Similar to the Collar Badge but smaller.

Comments: *Founded by HRH the Prince Regent (later King George IV), it took its name from the family surname of the British sovereigns from George I onwards and was awarded by the crown of Hanover to both British and Hanverian subjects for distinguished services to Hanover. Under Salic Law, a woman could not succeed to the Hanoverian throne, so on the death of King William IV in 1837 Hanover passed to Prince Augustus, Duke of Cumberland, and thereafter the Guelphic Order became a purely Hanoverian award.*

VALUE:

	Military	Civil
Collar chain (gold)	£10,000–15,000	£8000–12,000
Collar chain (silver gilt)	£6000–8000	£4000–5000
Collar Chain (copper gilt)	£4000–6000	£3000–4000
Collar badge	£5000–6000	£2500–3500
Star	£2000–2500	£1500–2000
Sash badge	£6000–8000	£3000–4000

KNIGHTS COMMANDERS (KCH) AND KNIGHTS (KH)

Knights Commanders wore a neck badge suspended by a ribbon, and a breast star, while Knights wore a breast badge only.
Star: As above, but smaller.
Neck Badge: Similar to the Collar Badge but smaller.
Breast Badge: Two versions, in gold and enamel or silver and enamel.

VALUE:

	Military	Miniature	Civil	Miniature
Star	£1500–2000		£1000–1200	
Neck badge	£2500–3500		£1500–2000	
Breast badge (gold)	£2500–3000	£350–450	£1200–1500	£400–500
Breast badge (silver)	£600–800			

KH Breast Badge (Military)

6. THE MOST DISTINGUISHED ORDER OF ST MICHAEL AND ST GEORGE

Instituted: 1818.
Ribbon: 101mm, 51mm, 38mm three equal bands of Saxon blue, scarlet and Saxon blue.

KNIGHTS GRAND CROSS (GCMG)

Knights Grand Cross wear a mantle of Saxon blue lined with scarlet silk tied with cords of blue and scarlet silk and gold, and having on the left side the star of the Order. The chapeau or hat is of blue satin, lined with scarlet and surmounted by black and white ostrich feathers. The collar, mantle and chapeau are only worn on special occasions or when commanded by the sovereign, but in ordinary full dress the badge is worn on the left hip from a broad ribbon passing over the right shoulder and the star on the left breast.

Collar Chain: Silver gilt formed alternately on lions of England, Maltese crosses enamelled in white, and the cyphers SM and SG with, in the centre, two winged lions of St Mark each holding a book and seven arrows.

Star: A silver star of seven groups of rays, with a gold ray between each group, surmounted overall by the cross of St George in red enamel. In the centre is a representation of St Michael encountering Satan within a blue circular riband bearing the motto AUSPICIUM MELIORIS AEVI (A token of a better age).

Sash Badge: A gold seven-pointed star with V-shaped extremities, enamelled white and edged with gold, surmounted by an imperial crown. In the centre on one side is a representation in enamel of St Michael encountering Satan and on the other St George on horseback fighting the dragon. This device is surrounded by a circle of blue enamel bearing the Latin motto in gold lettering. Silver-gilt was substituted for gold in 1887.

Comments: *Founded by HRH the Prince Regent and awarded originally to citizens of Malta and the Ionian Islands in the Adriatic Sea, both of which had been ceded to Britain during the Napoleonic Wars. The Ionian Islands were transferred to Greece in 1859. Towards the end of the 19th century, however, the Order was awarded to those who had performed distinguished service in the colonies and protectorates of the British Empire and in more recent times it has been widely used as an award to ambassadors and senior diplomats as well as colonial governors. Ladies are now eligible for this Order. In recent operations a number of awards have been made to military officers, presumably for "diplomatic" work.*

VALUE:

Collar chain	£2000–2600
Star	£1000–1500
Sash badge (gold)	£3500–4500
Sash badge (gilt)	£1400–1600

GCMG Star

6. THE MOST DISTINGUISHED ORDER OF ST MICHAEL AND ST GEORGE *continued*

KCMG Star

KNIGHTS COMMANDERS (KCMG) AND COMPANIONS (CMG)

Knights Commanders wear the badge suspended round the neck from a narrower ribbon of the same colours, and a breast star; Companions wear a neck badge. In undress uniform Knights Grand Cross and Knights Commanders wear the ribbon of Companions of the Order. Prior to 1917 Companions wore a breast badge, worn the same way as a medal, but this was then changed to a neck badge.

Star: A silver eight-pointed star charged with the red St George's cross and having the same central device as the GCMG Star. This was introduced in 1859.

Neck Badge: Similar to the sash badge of the GCMG but smaller. Those worn by Knight Commanders were of gold and enamel until 1887 but silver-gilt and enamel thereafter. The CMG neck badges are invariably of enamel and silver-gilt.

Breast Badge: Similar to the star of the KCMG but smaller and made of gold and enamel till 1887, and silver gilt and enamel from then till 1917.

VALUE:		*Miniature*
Knight Commander		
Star	£800–1000	
Neck badge (gold)	£1500–1800	
Neck badge (gilt)	£600–800	
Companion		
Breast badge (gold)	£1000–1200	£80–100
Breast badge (gilt)	£600–800	£60–75
Neck badge (gilt)	£500–550	

7. THE MOST EXALTED ORDER OF THE STAR OF INDIA

Instituted: 1861.
Ribbon: Broad light blue with white edges (GCSI); 50mm plain white (KCSI); 38mm plain white (CSI).

KNIGHTS GRAND COMMANDERS (GCSI)

KCSI Neck badge

The insignia consisted of a gold collar and badge, a mantle of light blue satin with a representation of the star on the left side and tied with a white silk cord with blue and silver tassels. The collar and mantle were only worn on special occasions and in ordinary full dress uniform a GCSI wore the star on the left breast and the badge on the left hip from a broad sash of light blue edged in white.

Collar Chain: Gold formed of lotus flowers, palm branches and united red and white roses. Later chains are silver-gilt.

Badge: An onyx cameo bearing the left-facing bust of Queen Victoria wearing an imperial crown, set in a gold ornamental oval containing the motto of the Order HEAVEN'S LIGHT OUR GUIDE in diamonds, on a pale blue ground surmounted by a five-pointed star in chased silver.

Star: A five-pointed star in diamonds resting on a circular riband of light blue enamel bearing the motto in diamonds, the whole set on a circular star of golden rays.

Comments: *Founded by Queen Victoria a few years after the British Crown took over the administration of India from the Honourable East India Company, it was intended primarily as an award to loyal Indian princes. The highest class was designated Knight Grand Commander, rather than Cross, because the majority of recipients were not Christians (either Hindus or Muslims). The Order at first consisted of the sovereign, a Grand Master (the Viceroy of India), 36 Knights Grand Commanders (18 British and 18 Indian), 85 Knights Commanders and 170 Companions. The GCSI was the most lavish of all British orders. It lapsed in 1947 when the sub-continent attained independence. Until then all insignia of this Order was returnable on the death of recipients. After 1947, however, recipients or their heirs were allowed in certain cases to purchase the star and badges of any of the three applicable classes, but not the collar chain of the Knight Grand Commander.*

VALUE:
Collar chain	—
Star and badge	£30,000–40,000

KNIGHTS COMMANDERS (KCSI) AND COMPANIONS (CSI)

Knights Commanders wore a badge round the neck and a star on the left breast, while Companions originally had a breast badge which was transmuted into a neck badge from 1917 onwards.

Star: Similar to that of the GCSI but in silver.

Neck Badge: Similar to the collar badge of the GCSI but smaller and less ornate.

Breast Badge: Similar to the above but smaller and less ornate and fitted with a straight bar suspender. Subtle differences in the ornament at the foot of the blue border and the external ornament at the sides and foot of the oval.

Comments: *The second and third classes of the Order were awarded to Indian and British subjects of the armed forces and Indian Civil Service for distinguished service of not less than 30 years' duration.*

VALUE:
		Miniature
Star and Neck badge (KCSI)	£10,000–12,000	
Breast badge (CSI)	£4500–5000	£250–350 (gold), £150–175 (silver gilt),
Neck badge (CSI)	£3500–4000	

8. THE MOST EMINENT ORDER OF THE INDIAN EMPIRE

Instituted: 1878.
Ribbon: Deep indigo blue.

KNIGHTS GRAND COMMANDERS (GCIE)

KCIE Neck badge

The insignia consisted of a collar, badge and mantle of imperial purple or dark blue satin lined with white silk and fastened with a white silk cord with gold tassels, and having on the left side a representation of the Star of the Order. On ordinary full-dress occasions, however, Knights Grand Commanders wore the badge on the left hip from a broad sash, and a star on the left breast.

Collar Chain: Silver-gilt, composed of elephants, lotus flowers, peacocks in their pride and Indian roses with, in the centre, the imperial crown, the whole linked together by chains.

Badge: A gold five-petalled rose, enamelled crimson and with a green barb between each petal. In the centre is an effigy of Queen Victoria on a gold ground, surrounded by a purple riband originally inscribed VICTORIA IMPERATRIX but from 1901 onwards inscribed IMPERATRICIS AUSPICIIS (under the auspices of the Empress). The letters I N D I A are inscribed on the petals in the first version, but omitted in the second.

Star: Composed of fine silver rays with smaller gold rays between them, the whole alternately plain and scaled. In the centre, within a purple circle bearing the motto and surmounted by the imperial crown in gold, is the effigy of Queen Victoria on a gold ground.

Comments: *Founded by Queen Victoria after assuming the title of Empress of India, it was originally confined to Companions only, together with the Sovereign and Grand Master. Members of the Council of the Governor-General were admitted* ex officio *as Companions. It was intended for award in respect of meritorious services in India but from the outset it was regarded as a junior alternative to the Star of India. In 1886 the Order was expanded to two classes by the addition of Knights Commanders up to a maximum of 50 in number. In 1887, however, it was again re-organised into three classes: up to 25 Knights Grand Commanders (GCIE), up to 50 Knights Commanders (KCIE) and an unlimited number of Companions (CIE). The Order has been in abeyance since 1947.*

VALUE:

Collar chain	£12,000–15,000
Star and badge	£4500–5500

KNIGHTS COMMANDERS (KCIE) AND COMPANIONS (CIE)

The insignia of Knights Commanders consisted of a neck badge and a breast star, while that of Companions was originally a breast badge, converted to a neck badge in 1917.

Star: Similar to that of the GCIE but fashioned entirely in silver.

Neck badge: Similar to the collar or sash badge of the GCIE but in correspondingly smaller sizes and differing in minor details.

Breast badge: Similar to the sash badge of the GCIE but differing in minor details, notably the spacing ornament at the foot of the blue circle. Two versions exist, with or without INDIA on the petals of the lotus flower.

VALUE:		*Miniature*
Knights Commanders		
Star and Neck badge	£4000–4500	
Companions		
Breast badge (INDIA)	£1500–2000	£350–400 (gold)
Breast badge (smaller, without INDIA)	£800–1000	£200–250 (gold)
Neck badge	£750–850	£100–200 (gilt)

9. THE ROYAL FAMILY ORDER

Instituted: 1820.

Ribbon: 50mm sky blue moiré (1820); 38mm dark blue bordered by narrow stripes of yellow and broader stripes of crimson with narrow black edges (1902); 50mm pale blue moire (1911); 50mm pink moire (1937); 50mm pale yellow silk moire (1953). These ribbons are tied in a bow and worn on the left shoulder.

Descriptions: An upright oval heavily bordered by diamonds and surmounted by a crown, also embellished in diamonds. The oval contains a miniature portrait of the sovereign in enamels.

Comments: *Awarded to the Queen and female relatives of the reigning monarch. It was instituted by King George IV who conferred such orders on his sister, Princess Charlotte Augusta, wife of Frederick William, King of Wurttemberg, and his niece Princess Augusta Caroline, who married the Grand Duke of Mecklenburg-Strelitz. Queen Victoria instituted a separate Order (see next entry), but this Order was revived by King Edward VII in 1902 and continued by successive sovereigns ever since. Special badges are given to ladies-in-waiting. The insignia of these Family Orders very seldom appear on the market and on account of their immense rarity they are unpriced here.*

Edward VII

George VI

VALUE:

George IV	Rare
Edward VII	Rare
George V	Rare
George VI	Rare
Elizabeth II	Rare
Ladies-in-waiting badges	From £1000

George V

Elizabeth II

10. THE ROYAL ORDER OF VICTORIA AND ALBERT

Instituted: 1862.

Ribbon: 38mm white moiré, in the form of a bow worn on the left shoulder.

Description: An upright oval onyx cameo bearing conjoined profiles of HRH Prince Albert, the Prince Consort and Queen Victoria. The badges of the First and Second Classes are set in diamonds and surmounted by an imperial crown similarly embellished, the badge of the Second Class being rather smaller. The badge of the Third Class is set in pearls, while that of the Fourth Class takes the form of a monogram "V & A" set with pearls and surmounted by an imperial crown.

Comments: *Personally awarded to female members of the Royal Family by Queen Victoria. This order became obsolete in 1981 with the death of Princess Alice, Countess of Athlone, the last surviving grandchild of Queen Victoria.*

VALUE:

First Class	£24,000–26,000
Second Class	£16,000–18,000
Third Class	£10,000–12,000
Fourth Class	£4000–5000

11. THE IMPERIAL ORDER OF THE CROWN OF INDIA

Instituted: January 1, 1878.

Ribbon: 38mm light blue watered silk with narrow white stripes towards the edges, formed in a bow worn on the left shoulder.

Description: A badge consisting of the royal and imperial monogram VRI in diamonds, turquoises and pearls, surrounded by an oval frame and surmounted by a jewelled imperial crown.

Comments: *Awarded by Queen Victoria to the princesses of the royal and imperial house, the wives or other female relatives of Indian princes and other Indian ladies, and of the wives or other female relatives of any of the persons who had held or were holding the offices of Viceroy and Governor-General of India, Governors of Madras or Bombay, or of Principal Secretary of State for India, as the sovereign might think fit to appoint. Her Majesty the Queen is the only surviving member of the Order.*

VALUE:

Breast badge	£8000–12,000	*Miniature*	£400–500

12. THE ROYAL VICTORIAN ORDER

Instituted: April 1896.
Ribbon: Dark blue with borders of narrow red, white and red stripes on either side, 44mm (KCVO and CVO), or 32mm (LVO, MVO and RVM). When insignia not worn only the 32mm width is used by all classes on uniforms.

KNIGHTS GRAND CROSS AND DAMES GRAND CROSS (GCVO)

The insignia consists of a mantle of dark blue silk, edged with red satin, lined with white silk, and fastened by a cordon of dark blue silk and gold; a gold collar and a badge, worn only on special occasions. Knights wear the badge on the left hip from a broad ribbon worn over the right shoulder, with a star on the left breast, while Dames wear a somewhat narrower ribbon over the right shoulder with the badge, and a star similar to that of the Knights. Dames' insignia are smaller than those of the Knights.

Collar: Silver gilt composed of octagonal pieces and oblong perforated and ornamental frames alternately linked together with gold. The pieces are edged and ornamented with gold, and each contains on a blue-enamelled ground a gold rose jewelled with a carbuncle. The frames are gold and each contains a portion of inscription VICTORIA BRITT. DEF. FID. IND. IMP. in letters of white enamel. In the centre of the collar, within a perforated and ornamental frame of gold, is an octagonal piece enamelled blue, edged with red, and charged with a white saltire, superimposed by a gold medallion of Queen Victoria's effigy from which is suspended the badge.

Badge: A white-enamelled Maltese cross of eight points, in the centre of which is an oval of crimson enamel bearing the cypher VRI in gold letters. Encircling this is a blue enamel riband with the name VICTORIA in gold letters, and above this is the imperial crown enamelled in proper colours.

Star: Of chipped silver of eight points on which is mounted a white-enamelled Maltese cross with VRI in an oval at the centre.

Comments: *Awarded for extraordinary, important or personal services to the Sovereign or the Royal Family. Ladies became eligible for the Order in 1936. Most of the badges of the Royal Victorian Order are numbered on the reverse and are returnable on promotion. Honorary awards are unnumbered.*

VALUE:	Knights	Dames	*Miniature*
Collar			
gold	£10,000–12,000	£12,000–15,000	
silver gilt	£5000–6000	£7000–9000	
Star and Badge (GCVO)	£1400–1600	£1200–1500	£200–250

GCVO star

KNIGHTS COMMANDERS (KCVO), DAMES COMMANDERS (DCVO), COMMANDERS (CVO), LIEUTENANTS (LVO) AND MEMBERS (MVO)

The insignia of the Second, Third, Fourth and Fifth Classes follows the usual pattern. Knights wear a neck badge and a breast star, Dames a breast star and a badge on the left shoulder from a ribbon tied in a bow, Commanders the same neck badge (men) or shoulder badge (women), Lieutenants a somewhat smaller breast badge worn in line with other medals and decorations (men) or a shoulder badge (women) and Members breast or shoulder badges in frosted silver instead of white enamel. The two lowest classes of the Order were originally designated member Fourth Class or member Fifth Class (MVO), but in 1984 the Fourth Class was renamed Lieutenant (LVO) and the Fifth Class simply Member (MVO).

VALUE:	Gentlemen	*Miniature*	Ladies
Neck badge and breast star (KCVO)	£1200–1400	£200–250	£1200–1400
Neck badge (CVO)	£480–520	£30–50	£450–500
Breast or shoulder badge (LVO)	£350–400	£30–50	£370–400
Breast or shoulder badge (MVO)	£300–350	£25–30	£300–350

13. ROYAL VICTORIAN MEDAL

Instituted: April 1896.

Ribbon: As for the Royal Victorian Order (above); foreign Associates, however, wear a ribbon with a central white stripe added.

Metal: Silver-gilt, silver or bronze.

Size: 30mm.

Description: (Obverse) the effigy of the reigning sovereign; (reverse) the royal cypher on an ornamental shield within a laurel wreath.

Comments: *Awarded to those below the rank of officers who perform personal services to the sovereign or to members of the Royal Family. Originally awarded in silver or bronze, a higher class, in silver-gilt, was instituted by King George V. Only two medals (both silver) were issued in the brief reign of King Edward VIII (1936) and only four bronze medals were issued in the reign of King George VI. Any person in possession of the bronze medal to whom a silver medal is awarded, can wear both, and the silver-gilt medal in addition if such be conferred upon him or her. Clasps are awarded for further services to each class of the medal, while the medals may be worn in addition to the insignia of the Order if the latter is subsequently conferred. To distinguish between British and foreign recipients, King George VI decreed in 1951 that the ribbon worn by the latter should have an additional stripe, these recipients to be designated Associates. In 1983 the order for wearing this medal was altered and it was no longer to be worn after campaign medals but took precedence over them.*

Ribbon for foreign Associates.

VALUE:

	Silver-gilt	Miniature	Silver	Miniature	Bronze	Miniature
Victoria	—	£65–75	£250–300	£65–75	£180–200	£50–60
Edward VII	—	—	£250–300	£55–65	£175–200	£40–50
George V	£300–350	—	£180–200	£30–35	£250–300	£20–25
Edward VIII	—	—	Rare	—	—	—
George VI	£300–350	—	£180–200	£15–20	Rare	£12–18
Elizabeth II	£300–350	—	£180–200	£15–20	£250–300	£12–18

14. THE ROYAL VICTORIAN CHAIN

Instituted: 1902.

Ribbon: None.

Metal: Silver gilt

Description: A chain consisting of three Tudor roses, two thistles, two shamrocks and two lotus flowers (the heraldic flowers of England, Scotland, Ireland and India respectively), connected by a slender double trace of gold chain. At the bottom of the front loop is a centre piece consisting of the royal cypher in enamel surrounded by a wreath and surmounted by a crown. From this centrepiece hangs a replica of the badge of a Knight Grand Cross of the Royal Victorian Order. Ladies wear the insignia in the form of a shoulder badge suspended from a miniature chain with links leading to a rose, thistle, shamrock and lotus. An even more elaborate collar, with diamonds encrusting the crown and cypher, was adopted in 1921 and there is a ladies' version of this as well.

Comments: *Sometimes regarded as the highest grade of the Royal Victorian Order, it is actually a quite separate Order and was introduced by King Edward VII for conferment as a special mark of the sovereign's favour, and then only very rarely, upon Royalty, or other especially distinguished personages, both foreign and British.*

VALUE

	Gentlemen	Ladies
Chain (1902–21)	Rare	Rare
Chain with diamonds	Rare	Rare

15. ORDER OF MERIT

Order of Merit obverse

Instituted: 1902.
Ribbon: 50mm half blue, half crimson.
Metal: Gold.
Size: Height 50mm; max. width 35mm.
Description: A pattée convexed cross, enamelled red, edged blue. (Obverse) FOR MERIT in the centre surrounded by a white band and a laurel wreath enamelled in proper colours. (Reverse) the royal cypher in gold on a blue ground with a white surround and a laurel wreath as above. The cross is surmounted by a Tudor crown to which is attached a ring for suspension. Naval and military recipients have crossed swords in the angles of the cross.
Comments: *This highly prestigious Order consists of the sovereign and a maximum of 24 members in one class only. There is, however, no limit on the number of foreign honorary members, although only 11 have so far been admitted to the Order. It is intended to honour exceptionally meritorious service in the Crown Services or towards the advancement of the Arts, Learning, Literature and Science or other exceptional service. To date 185 awards have been made, including only nine ladies, from Florence Nightingale (1907) to Baroness Boothroyd (2005). The insignia of those appointed since 1991 have to be returned on the death of the recipient. The insignia of members appointed prior to that date is retained, but understandably few items have come on to the market.*

VALUE:

	Military	Civil
Edward VII	£6000–8000	£5000–7000
George V	£6000–8000	£5000–7000
George VI	Rare	£6000–7000
Elizabeth II	Rare	£5500–6500
Miniature	£150–200	

Order of Merit reverse

16. THE MOST EXCELLENT ORDER OF THE BRITISH EMPIRE

Instituted: June 1917.

Ribbon: 38mm originally purple, with a narrow central scarlet stripe for the Military Division; rose-pink edged with pearl grey, with a narrow central stripe of pearl-grey for the Military Division (since 1936). A silver crossed oakleaf emblem for gallantry was instituted in 1957.

Comments: *Founded by King George V during the First World War for services to the Empire at home, in India and in the overseas dominions and colonies, other than those rendered by the Navy and Army, although it could be conferred upon officers of the armed forces for services of a non-combatant character. A Military Division was created in December 1918 and awards made to commissioned officers and warrant officers in respect of distinguished service in action. The insignia of the Civil and Military Divisions is identical, distinguished only by the respective ribbons. A promotion in a different division permits the wear of both types of insignia and in the case of gallantry awards a third type may be worn. A lapel emblem for wear on ordinary clothing was introduced in December 2006.*

GBE Star (2nd type)

KNIGHTS AND DAMES GRAND CROSS (GBE)

The insignia includes a mantle of rose-pink satin lined with pearl-grey silk, tied by a cord of pearl-grey silk, with two rose-pink and silver tassels attached. On the left side of the mantle is a representation of the star of the First Class of the Order. The mantle, collar and collar badge are only worn on special occasions. In dress uniform, however, the badge is worn over the left hip from a broad (96mm) riband passing over the right shoulder, while Dames wear the badge from a narrower (57mm) ribbon in a bow on the left shoulder; both with the breast star of the Order.

Collar: Silver-gilt with medallions of the royal arms and of the royal and imperial cypher of King George V alternately linked together with cables. In the centre is the imperial crown between two sea lions. The collar for Dames is somewhat narrower than that for Knights.

Badge: A cross patonce in silver-gilt the arms enamelled pearl-grey. In the centre, within a circle enamelled crimson, the figure of Britannia, replaced since 1936 by the conjoined left-facing crowned busts of King George V and Queen Mary, surrounded by a circle inscribed FOR GOD AND THE EMPIRE.

Star: An eight-pointed star of silver chips on which is superimposed the enamelled medallion as for the badge (Britannia or George V and Queen Mary). The star worn by Dames is smaller.

VALUE:	1st type Britannia	2nd type King and
Knights Grand Cross		**Queen**
Collar	£5000–6000	£5000–6000
Badge and star	£1700–1800	£1800–2000
Dames Grand Cross		
Collar	£6000–7000	£6000–7000
Badge and star	£1200–1400	£1400–1800
Miniature stars	£200–250	£200–250

CBE Badge (2nd type)

65

16. THE MOST EXCELLENT ORDER OF THE BRITISH EMPIRE *continued*

KBE Star

KNIGHTS COMMANDERS (KBE), DAMES COMMANDERS (DBE), COMMANDERS (CBE), OFFICERS (OBE) AND MEMBERS (MBE)

The insignia of these five Classes follows the same pattern as other Orders. Both Britannia and King and Queen medallion types have been issued.

Star: A star of four large points and four minor points in chipped silver, with the enamelled medallion superimposed. The star worn by Dames is smaller.

Neck Badge: Similar to the badge of the GBE but smaller and worn from a 44mm ribbon round the neck (men) or from a shoulder bow (ladies). Worn by KBE, DBE and CBE.

Breast Badge: As above, but in silver-gilt (OBE) or frosted silver (MBE), with shoulder versions for ladies, worn with a 38mm ribbon.

Gallantry Award: An emblem of silver crossed oak leaves was added to the ribbon of the CBE, OBE and MBE (1957–74).

Oak leaf emblem for gallantry (smaller when ribbon only worn).

VALUE:	1st type Britannia	Miniature	2nd type King&Queen	Miniature
Badge and Star (KBE)	£850–1000	£200–250	£850–1000	£200–250
Badge and Star (DBE)	£850–1000		£850–1000	
Neck badge (CBE)	£345–380	£25–30	£340–380	£25–30
Shoulder badge (CBE)	£340–380		£340–380	
Breast badge (OBE)	£110–120	£10–15	£110–120	£10–15
Shoulder badge (OBE)	£110–120		£110–120	
Breast badge (MBE)	£110–120	£10–12	£110–120	£10–12
Shoulder badge (MBE)	£110–120		£110–120	

OBE badge (silver-gilt) and reverse of the MBE badge (frosted silver).

Ribbons: (top to bottom) OBE (Military) 1st type, OBE (Military) 2nd type, OBE (Civil) 1st type, OBE (Civil) 2nd type.

17. MEDAL OF THE ORDER OF THE BRITISH EMPIRE

Civil ribbon

Military ribbon

Instituted: June 1917.

Ribbon: 32mm plain purple (Civil), with a narrow scarlet central stripe (Military).

Medal: Silver.

Size: 30mm.

Description: (Obverse) a seated figure of Britannia facing right, her left arm extended and her right holding a trident, with the inscription FOR GOD AND THE EMPIRE round the upper part of the circumference; (reverse) the royal and imperial cypher GRI surmounted by a Tudor crown, the whole enclosed in a cable circle. Fitted with a plain ring for suspension.

Comments: *Instituted as a lower award connected with the Order, it consisted originally of a Civil Division, but a Military Division, distinguishable solely by the ribbon, was added in December 1918. This medal was issued unnamed but many were subsequently engraved or impressed on the rim privately. Fewer than 2000 medals were awarded before they were discontinued in 1922.*

VALUE:

		Miniature
Medal unnamed as issued	£250–300	£60–80
Attributable medal	£350–500	

18. EMPIRE GALLANTRY MEDAL

Instituted: December 29, 1922.

Ribbon: Originally plain purple (Civil), with a thin scarlet central stripe (Military); from July 1937 rose-pink with pearl-grey edges (Civil) and a central pearl-grey stripe (Military). A silver laurel branch was added to the ribbon (1933), with a smaller version for wear on the ribbon alone.

Metal: Silver.

Size: 36mm.

Description: (Obverse) the seated figure of Britannia, her left hand resting on a shield and her right holding a trident, with a blazing sun upper right. The words FOR GOD AND THE EMPIRE inscribed round the upper part of the circumference, with FOR in the wave lower left above the exergue which bears the word GALLANTRY. (Reverse) 1st type has six lions passant gardant, with the Royal cypher in the centre surmounted by an imperial crown. The George VI issue has four lions, two either side and round the foot, in two concentric arcs, the words INSTITUTED BY KING GEORGE V. It is suspended from a straight bar ornamented with laurel leaves. Named in seriffed capitals engraved round the rim.

Comments: *This medal, officially known as the Medal of the Order of the British Empire for Gallantry, replaced the Medal of the Order of the British Empire and was awarded for specific acts of gallantry. It was abolished on the institution of the George Cross in September 1940, while it was announced in the London Gazette of April 22, 1941 that a recipient still living on September 24, 1940 but including posthumous awards after September 3, 1939 should return it to the Central Chancery of the Orders of Knighthood and become a holder of the George Cross instead. Not all EGMs, however, were exchanged or returned. Only 130 medals were issued, 64 being civil, 62 military and four honorary.*

1st type rev.

VALUE:

		Miniature
George V	£3000–3500	£100–150
George VI	£3000–3500	£150–200

Civil 1922

Military 1922

Civil 1937

Military 1937

(emblem smaller when ribbon only worn).

19. BRITISH EMPIRE MEDAL

Civil 1922

Military 1922

Civil 1937

Military 1937

Instituted: December 1922.

Ribbon: As above, but without the silver laurel branch.

Metal: Silver.

Size: 36mm.

Description: As above, but with the words MERITORIOUS SERVICE in the exergue. Suspended from a straight bar ornamented with oak leaves. A silver bar decorated with oak leaves was introduced in March 1941 for further acts, and is denoted by a silver rosette on the ribbon worn on its own. An emblem of crossed silver oak leaves was introduced in December 1957 to denote a gallantry award, a smaller version being worn on the ribbon alone. Named in engraved capitals round the rim.

Comments: *Formally entitled the Medal of the Order of the British Empire for Meritorious Service, it is generally known simply as the British Empire Medal. It is awarded for meritorious service by both civil and military personnel although for some years it was issued as a third grade bravery award, particularly for air raid deeds not considered to be of the level of the GC or GM. The medal may be worn even if the recipient is promoted to a higher grade of the Order. The gallantry awards, instituted in December 1957, ceased in 1974 on the introduction of the Queen's Gallantry Medal. No British awards have been made for the BEM since 1995 but Commonwealth awards are still being made. The Order of the British Empire emblem instituted in December 2006 may also be worn by holders of the BEM.*

VALUE:

	Military	Civil	Miniature
George V	£375–450	£250–300	£15–20
George VI GRI cypher	£275–350	£200–250	£10–15
George VI GVIR cypher	£275–350	£200–250	£10–15
Elizabeth II	£250–300	£200–250	£10–15
Elizabeth II with gallantry emblem	£650–950	£600–800	

19A. QUEEN'S VOLUNTEER RESERVES MEDAL—See 48A

20. THE ORDER OF THE COMPANIONS OF HONOUR

Instituted: June 1917.
Ribbon: 38mm carmine with borders of gold thread.
Metal: Silver gilt.
Size: Height 48mm; max. width 29mm.
Description: An oval badge consisting of a medallion with an oak tree, a shield bearing the royal arms hanging from one branch, and on the left a knight armed and in armour, mounted on a horse. The badge has a blue border with the motto IN ACTION FAITHFUL AND IN HONOUR CLEAR in gold letters. The oval is surmounted by an imperial crown. Gentlemen wear the badge round their necks, while ladies wear it from a bow at the left shoulder.
Comments: *Instituted at the same time as the Order of the British Empire, it carries no title or precedence although the post-nominal letters CH are used. The Order consists of the sovereign and one class of members. Not more than 50 men or women who have rendered conspicuous service of national importance were admitted, but in 1943 this was increased to 65. The Order is awarded in Britain and the Commonwealth on a quota basis: UK (45), Australia (7), New Zealand (2), other countries (11). It is awarded for outstanding achievements in the arts, literature, music, science, politics, industry and religion.*

VALUE
Gentlemen	£2500–3000
Ladies	£2500–3000

Miniature	Uniface	£150–200	Monogrammed reverse £250–300

21. THE BARONET'S BADGE

Instituted: 1629.
Ribbon: 30mm orange watered silk (Nova Scotia); 44mm orange bordered with narrow blue edges (other Baronets).
Metal: Gold or silver-gilt.
Size: Height 55mm; max. width 41mm(Nova Scotia) or 44mm (later badges).
Description: An upright oval badge with a plain ring suspension. The badge of the Baronets of Nova Scotia was originally skeletal, with a shield bearing the lion rampant of Scotland, decorated with pearls and enamels, surmounted by a Scottish crown and surrounded by a blue border inscribed in gold FAX MENTIS HONESTAE GLORIÁ. The remaining badges (authorised in 1929) have a solid ground and a central shield with the red hand of Ulster surmounted by a crown and a border of gold and blue enamel decorated with roses (England), shamrocks (Ireland), roses and thistles combined (Great Britain) or roses, thistles and shamrocks combined (United Kingdom). Often engraved on the reverse with the recipient's title and date of creation.
Comments: *By Letter Patent of 1611 James I created Baronets whose knighthood became hereditary. In 1624, to raise money independently of Parliament, James I sold grants of land in Nova Scotia (New Scotland) to Scotsmen. In 1625 Charles I conferred on the holders of this land the title and dignity of Baronets of Nova Scotia with the title of Sir, and decreed that they should wear round their necks "an orange tawny ribbon whereon shall be pendent an escutcheon". After the Union with England (1707) English and Scottish baronetcies ceased to be created, being replaced by baronetcies of Great Britain. Irish baronetcies continued to be created until 1801 after which all new creations were of the United Kingdom.*

Baronet's badge — United Kingdom

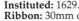

(Nova Scotia)

(other Baronets)

VALUE:	Gold	Silver-gilt
Nova Scotia, 18th–early 19th centuries	£2000–3000	£800–1000
Nova Scotia, late 19th and 20th centuries	£1500–1800	£600–1000
England (rose surround)	£800–1200	£800–1000
Ireland (shamrock surround)	£800–1200	£800–1000
Great Britain (roses and thistles)	£800–1200	£800–1000
United Kingdom (roses, thistles and shamrocks)	£800–1200	£800–1000

22. THE KNIGHT BACHELOR'S BADGE

Instituted: April 21, 1926.

Ribbon: 38mm scarlet with broad yellow borders.

Metal: Silver-gilt and enamels. Some pre-war breast badges in base metal.

Size: Height 76.50mm; max. width 56.50mm. Reduced in 1933 and 1973.

Description: An upright oval medallion enclosed by a scroll, bearing a cross-hilted sword, belted and sheathed, pommel upwards, between two spurs, rowels upwards, the whole set about with the sword-belt.

Comments: *The title Knight Bachelor (KB) was introduced by King Henry III to signify a battelier (one who fought in battle). The badge was authorised by King George V in response to a request from the Imperial Society of Knights Bachelors who wished to have a distinctive badge denoting their rank. The original badge was of the dimensions given above and affixed to the breast by means of a pin on the reverse. This badge was reduced in size in 1933 and again in 1973 when it was fitted with a ring for suspension by a ribbon round the neck. On 4 December 1998 Her Majesty the Queen signed an amending warrant permitting recipients of this honour to wear both a neck badge and breast badge.*

VALUE:

		Miniature
First type (1929)	£350–400	£30–40
Smaller type (1933)	£350–400	(Skeletal type
Neck badge (1974)	£350–400	£20–35)

23. THE ORDER OF ST JOHN

Neck badge

Breast badge

Shoulder badge

Instituted: May 14, 1888 and at various dates in other countries.

Ribbon: Plain black watered silk. Sash ribbons for Bailiffs, 102mm; Dames Grand Cross, 57mm. Ribbons for Knights, 51mm; Ribbons for Dames were formerly in a 32mm bow and ribbons for Commanders, officers and Serving Brothers 38mm and 32mm for ladies, but under new regulations (October 2001) all ribbons below Grand Cross are now standardised at 38mm. In 1947, for all grades of the Order, when the ribbon only is worn, a small Maltese Cross in silver is carried on the ribbon to distinguish it against a dark background.

Metal: Gold, silver-gilt and silver, or base metal.

Sash badge: An eight-pointed gold Maltese cross in white enamel with two lions and two unicorns in the angles (other countries have different animals in the angles). Confined to Bailiffs and Dames Grand Cross.

Neck badge: Hitherto in the grades Knight/Dame, Commander and Officer badges worn by women were smaller than those worn by men, but in 2001 this distinction was abolished. The badges worn by Knights of Justice and Chaplains are in gold, while those worn by Knights of Grace and Commanders are in silver.

Star: The eight-pointed Maltese cross in white enamel without the lions and unicorns (Grand Cross and Justice) or with lions and unicorns (Grace and Sub-Prelate). A sub-Prelate is an Order Chaplain (so his badge is

71

included above) who held high rank in the Church as distinct from the Order. The order ceased appointing Sub-Prelates in 1999, and as a result the Sub-Prelate's star (gilt with animals) is now obsolescent.

Shoulder badge: Worn by Dames of Justice in gold and Dames of Grace, Commanders, Serving Sisters and Officers (Sisters) in silver. It is now mounted on a ribbon with "tails" as in other British orders.

Breast badges: Officers (Brothers) is the Order badge with animals, in silver (1926–36) and in silver and enamel subsequently. Those worn by Serving Brothers have undergone six main phases:

1892–1939: a circular badge with crosses and animals raised above the surface of the medal.

1939–1949: circular skeletal badge with ring suspension and the eight-point cross set in a silver rim.

1949–1974: the first badge resumed.

1974–1984: a badge of the same design but with the cross and animals flush with their background.

1984–1991: the cross and animals in white metal, slightly smaller than the Officer (Brother) cross and the whole convex on the obverse.

Since 1991: Cross and animals thicker, with each arm raised and shaped on both sides of a central channel, the whole in rhodium. Since 1999 a woman Officer or Serving Sister who was in uniform is invested with her breast badge on a straight ribbon.

Donats' badges: Gold, silver or bronze, consisting of the badge of the Order with the upper arm of the cross replaced by an ornamental piece of metal for suspension.

Comments: *The Most Venerable Order of the Hospital of St John of Jerusalem was incorporated by Royal Charter of Queen Victoria and granted the epithet Venerable in 1926 and Most in 1955; despite its title, it has no connection with the Knights Hospitallers of Jerusalem, who were subsequently based at Rhodes and Malta and now have their headquarters in Rome. In 1926 the Order was reorganised into five Classes like certain other Orders. A sixth class was added later. Both men and women are eligible for membership. Her Majesty the Queen is the Sovereign Head of the Order. Next in authority is the Grand Prior, followed by Bailiffs and Dames Grand Cross, Chaplains, Knights and Dames of Justice, Knights and Dames of Grace, Commanders, Officers, Serving Brothers and Sisters and Esquires. Associates were people who were not citizens of the United Kingdom, the British Commonwealth or the Republic of Ireland, or are non-Christians, who have rendered conspicuous service to the Order and may be attached to any grade of the Order. They wear the insignia of that grade, at one time distinguished only by a central narrow white stripe on the ribbon, but now all ribbons are identical. Donats are people who have made generous contributions to the funds of the Order. They are not enrolled as members of the Order but receive badges in gold, silver or bronze. The Statutes and Regulations were revised in 2004. The grade of Chaplain (gold badge) was abolished, but existing Chaplains could retain their insignia or be regarded as Commanders. Before 1999 a Chaplain could be appointed a Sub-Prelate if he held high office in the Church. A sub-Prelate wore the badge of a Chaplain and also a star with gilt lions and unicorns. Those few remaining have now been renamed Honorary Sub-Prelates, a term revived to designate the senior ecclesiastical officer of a Priory. This appointment carries no distinctive insignia.*

VALUE:

	Gold	Silver/Gilt	Bronze	Miniature
Bailiff badge and star	£1500–2500	£800–1000	—	
Dame Grand Cross	£1500–2500	£600–700	—	
Knight of Justice				
neck badge and star	£900–1000	£500–600	£175–275	
Dame of Justice				
shoulder badge and star	£900–1000	£500–600	£200–300	
Knight of Grace				
neck badge and star	—	£350–400	£150–250	
Dame of Grace				
shoulder badge and star	—	£350–400	£150–250	£15–20
Sub-Prelate neck badge		£150–200	£75–100	
Commander (Brother) neck badge	—	£150–200	£60–80	
Commander (Sister) shoulder badge	—	£50–75	£30–50	
Officer breast badge, plain silver	—	£50–70	—	£10–15
Officer breast badge, enamelled	—	£65–75	£30–50	£15–20
Officer (Sister) enamelled badge	—	£65–75	£30–50	
Serving Brother/Sister 1926–39	—	£50–75	£30–50	£10–12
Serving Brother/Sister 1939–49	—	£45–65	£40–60	£10–12
Serving Brother/Sister 1949–	—	—	£30–50	
Donat's badge	£150–200	£45–55	£30–40	£25–30

DECORATIONS

The award of decorations for distinguished military service is an ancient institution. In his Antiquities of the Jews, the historian Josephus relates that, in the second century BC, King Alexander was so pleased with Jonathan the High Priest that he sent him a gold button as a mark of favour for his skill in leading the Jews in battle. Subsequently Jonathan was presented with a second gold button for his gallant conduct in the field, making these incidents among the earliest recorded for which specific military awards were granted. The award of jewels, gold buttons and badges for valour was carried on in most European countries on a sporadic basis but the present system of decorations is essentially a modern one dating back no farther than the middle of the seventeenth century. Earlier medals were quasi-commemorative and include the famous Armada Medal of 1588. A few medals in silver or gold were awarded to officers for distinguished service during the English Civil War, although the first "official" rewards in Britain were probably those issued by Parliament to naval officers following their victories over the Dutch fleet in 1653.

Decorations may be divided into those awarded for individual acts of heroism and those conferred in recognition of distinguished military, political or social service. In general terms collectors prefer a decoration awarded for bravery in the field rather than a political honour given automatically to a civil servant, just because he happens to have been in a particular grade for a certain number of years. The debasement of civil awards, such as the OBE and MBE, is reflected in the relative lack of interest shown by collectors.

It is generally true to say that military decorations are more desirable, but it is important to note that one decoration may be more highly prized than another, while the same decoration may well be more valuable to collectors when issued in one period rather than in another. At one extreme is the greatly coveted Victoria Cross, only 1354 of which (including three bars) have been awarded since its inception. VCs won during the Crimean War (111 awarded) are usually less highly regarded than Crosses awarded during the First World War, where, although numerically greater (633) they were far more dearly won. Second World War Crosses are correspondingly more expensive as only 182 were awarded and even now comparatively few of them have ever come on to the market. Today, while pre-1914 Crosses would rate at least £100,000 and those from the First World War slightly more, Second World War Crosses start around £120,000 but have been known to fetch several times as much, depending on the precise circumstances and the branch of the services.

At the other extreme is the Military Medal, of which no fewer than 115,589 were awarded during the First World War alone. For this reason a MM from this period can still be picked up for under £600, whereas one from the Second World War would usually fetch about four times as much, and awards made during the minor campaigns of the 1930s or the Korean War often rate at least ten times as much.

The value of a decoration, where its provenance can be unquestionably established, depends largely on the decoration itself, whether awarded to an officer or an enlisted man, the individual circumstances of the award, the campaign or action concerned, the regiment, unit or ship involved, and the often very personal details of the act or acts of bravery. These factors are extraordinarily difficult to quantify, hence the frequent large discrepancies in the prices fetched by decorations at auction.

The addition of even relatively common decorations, such as the Military Cross or the Military Medal to the average First World War campaign medal group, invariably enhances its value very considerably while the addition of bars for subsequent awards likewise rates a good premium. Decorations awarded to officers tend to fetch more than those awarded to other ranks, mainly because they are proportionately rarer but also because it is usually easier to trace the career details of an officer.

Sometimes the rank of the recipient may have a bearing on the demand for a particular decoration: e.g. Military Crosses awarded to warrant officers are scarcer than those awarded to subalterns and captains. The branch of the armed services may also have some bearing. Thus a Military Medal awarded to a member of the RAF rates far higher than one awarded to a soldier, while a medal awarded to a seaman in one of the naval battalions which fought on the Western Front is also equally desirable.

Initially the Distinguished Service Order could be won by commissioned officers of any rank but after 1914, when the Military Cross was instituted, it was usually restricted to officers of field rank. DSOs awarded to lieutenants and captains in the Army in both World Wars are therefore comparatively rare and invariably expensive, usually as they were awarded for acts of heroism which in earlier campaigns might have merited the VC. As part of the 1993 review of awards, the Conspicuous Gallantry Coss (CGC) replaced the DSO, CGM and DSM to remove the distiction between officers and other ranks.

The opportunity for individual acts of bravery varied from service to service, and in different conflicts. Thus sailors in the Second World War generally had less scope than air crew. Consequently specifically naval awards, such as the Conspicuous Gallantry Medal and the Distinguished Service Cross, are much more scarce than the corresponding RAF awards for Conspicuous Gallantry and the Distinguished Flying Cross.

The addition of bars to gallantry decorations greatly enhances the scarcity and value of such medals. The VC, for example, has been won by only three men on two occasions; none of these VC and bar combinations has ever come on the market, but should one come up for sale, it is certain that the price would be spectacular. The average First World War MM is today worth around £500, but with a bar for second award its value immediately jumps to about three times as much, while MMs with two or more bars are very much more expensive.

It is important to note that in some cases (the DSO for example) decorations were issued unnamed; for this reason the citation or any other supporting documents relevant to the award should be kept with the decoration wherever possible to confirm its attribution.

Engraving of Gallantry Decorations

After the special investiture for the South Atlantic campaign held on February 8, 1983, the question as to why certain awards were engraved with the date only was raised within the Ministry of Defence. A joint service working party considered the matter and recommended that procedures for all decorations and medals for gallantry in the face of the enemy and for the Air Force Cross when awarded for a specific act of gallantry should be brought into line. A submission was accordingly made to the Queen by the Committee on the Grant of Honours, Decorations and Medals and in April 1984 Her Majesty approved the following:

(i)   That the Distinguished Service Cross, Military Cross, Distinguished Flying Cross and Air Force Cross when awarded for gallantry should be engraved with the personal details of the recipient with effect from January 1, 1984.

(ii) That there should be no retrospection;

(iii) That the badge of a Companion of the Distinguished Service Order should not be engraved (in common with the badges of other orders); and

(iv) That the Royal Red Cross (RRC and ARRC) and the Air Force Cross when awarded for meritorious service should not be engraved.

Condition

The same terms are applied to describe the condition of medals and decorations as apply to coins, although the wear to which they are put is caused by other factors. In modern times, when the number of occasions on which medals are worn are relatively few and far between, the condition of most items will be found to be Very Fine (VF) to Extremely Fine (EF). Indeed, in many cases, the medals may never have been worn at all. A good proportion of Second World War medals and decorations are found in almost mint condition as they were not issued till long after the war, by which time their recipients had been demobilised. In some cases they even turn up still in the original cardboard box in which they were posted to the recipients or their next-of-kin.

Before the First World War, however, the wearing of medals was customary on all but the most informal occasions and when actually serving on active duty. Thus medals could be, and often were, subject to a great deal of wear. Medals worn by cavalrymen are often found in poor condition, with scratches and edge knocks occasioned by the constant jangling of one medal against another while on horseback. Often the medals in a group have an abrasive effect on each other. For this reason the Queen's Medal for Egypt (1882) is comparatively rare in excellent condition, as it was usually worn in juxtaposition to the bronze Khedive's Star whose points were capable of doing considerable damage to its silver companion. Apart from these factors it should also be remembered that part of the ritual of "spit and polish" involved cleaning one's medals and they were therefore submitted to vigorous cleaning with metal polish over long periods of service.

For these reasons medals are often sold by dealers "as worn"—a euphemism which conceals a lifetime of hardy service on the chest of some grizzled veteran. Because of the strong personal element involved in medal-collecting, however, genuine wear does not affect the value of a medal to the same degree that it would in other branches of numismatics. There is a school of thought which considers that such signs enhance the interest and value of a medal or group.

This line of thinking also explains the controversy over medal ribbons. Some military outfitters still carry extensive stocks of medal ribbons covering every campaign from Waterloo onwards, so that it is a very easy matter to obtain a fresh length of ribbon for any medal requiring it, and there is no doubt that the appearance of a piece is greatly improved by a clean, bright new ribbon. On the other hand, that ribbon was not the one actually worn by Corporal Bloggs on parade and, to the purist, it would spoil the total effect of the medal. Some collectors therefore retain the original ribbon, even though it may be faded and frayed. As ribbons are things which one cannot authenticate, however, there seems to be little material benefit to be gained from clinging rigidly to a tattered strip of silk when an identical piece can be obtained relatively cheaply. In reality, most collectors compromise by obtaining new ribbons while preserving the old lengths out of sentiment.

The prices quoted in this publication are average figures for medals and decorations as individual items. Combinations with other decorations and campaign medals will produce a value usually well in excess of the aggregate of the individual items. Value will depend to a large extent on the personal factors and circumstances of the award, but where general factors are involved (e.g. the design of the medal, the period of issue or the campaign concerned, or in some cases the branch of the services) these are itemised separately. "—" indicates that either no examples have come onto the market or no examples have been issued. The figure in brackets (where available) is the approximate number awarded. In the lists which follow, it should be assumed that decorations were instituted by Royal Warrant, unless otherwise stated.

Warwick & Warwick

AUCTIONEERS AND VALUERS
www.warwickandwarwick.com

SELLING YOUR MEDALS?

Warwick and Warwick have an expanding requirement for medal collections, medal groups and related documentation and individual medals of value. Our customer base is increasing dramatically and we need an ever larger supply of quality material to keep pace with demand. The market has never been stronger and if you are considering the sale of your medals, now is the time to act.

FREE VALUATIONS
We will provide a free, professional and without obligation valuation of your collection. Either we will make you a fair, binding private treaty offer, or we will recommend inclusion of your property in our next public auction.

FREE TRANSPORTATION
We can arrange insured transportation of your collection to our Warwick offices completely free of charge. If you decline our offer, we ask you to cover the return carriage costs only.

FREE VISITS
Visits by our valuers are possible anywhere in the country or abroad, usually within 48 hours, in order to value larger collections. Please telephone for details.

VALUATION DAYS
We are staging a series of valuation days, covering the entire country. Please visit our website or telephone for further details.

EXCELLENT PRICES
Because of the strength of our customer base we are in a position to offer prices that we feel sure will exceed your expectations.

ACT NOW
Telephone or email Richard Beale today with details of your property.

Warwick & Warwick Ltd.
Chalon House, Scar Bank, Millers Road, Warwick CV34 5DB England
Tel: (01926) 499031 • Fax: (01926) 491906
Email: richard.beale@warwickandwarwick.com
www.warwickandwarwick.com

24. THE VICTORIA CROSS

Instituted: January 1856.

Ribbon: Crimson. Originally naval crosses used a blue ribbon, but since 1918 the crimson (Army) ribbon has been used for all awards. A miniature cross emblem is worn on the ribbon alone in undress uniform.

Metal: Bronze, originally from Russian guns captured in the Crimea. Modern research, however, reveals that guns captured in other conflicts, e.g. China, have also been used at various periods.

Size: Height 41mm; max. width 36mm.

Description: A cross pattée. (Obverse) a lion statant gardant on the royal crown, with the words FOR VALOUR on a semi-circular scroll. (Reverse) a circular panel on which is engraved the date of the act for which the decoration was awarded. The Cross is suspended by a ring from a seriffed "V" attached to a suspension bar decorated with laurel leaves. The reverse of the suspension bar is engraved with the name, rank and ship, regiment or squadron of the recipient.

Comments: *Introduced as the premier award for gallantry, available for all ranks, to cover all actions since the outbreak of the Crimean War in 1854, it was allegedly created on the suggestion of Prince Albert, the Prince Consort. Of the 1357 awards since 1856, 835 have gone to the Army, 107 to the Navy, 31 to the RAF, ten to the Royal Marines and four to civilians. Second award bars have been awarded three times. The facility for posthumous awards, made retrospective to 1856, began in 1902 and was confirmed in 1907, while the early practice of forfeitures (eight between 1863 and 1908) was discontinued after the First World War. Two posthumous awards were made in the Falklands War. In 2005 Pte. Johnson Beharry was awarded the VC for valour in Iraq, while Corporal Bryan Budd was posthumously awarded for Afghanistan in 2006. In 2002 the Government increased the annuity paid to £1,500, tax free.*

VALUE:

	Royal Navy/Army	RFC/RAF	Miniature
1856–1914 (522)	£80,000–100,000	—	£50–80
1914–18 (633)	£80,000–120,000	£100,000–150,000	£20–30
1920–45 (187)	£100,000–150,000	£150,000–200,000	£20–30
post-1945 (14)	From £150,000	—	£10–20

NB These prices can only be construed as a general guide. Quite a few awards would exceed these price ranges, particularly Commonwealth examples or those appertaining to well known actions.

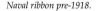

Naval ribbon pre-1918.   *Naval, Army and RAF ribbon since 1918.*

25. NEW ZEALAND CROSS

Instituted: 10 March 1869 (by an Order in Council, Wellington).

Ribbon: 38mm crimson. A silver miniature cross emblem is worn on the ribbon alone.

Metal. Silver with gold appliqué.

Size: Height 52mm; max. width 38mm.

Description: A silver cross pattée with a six-pointed gold star on each limb. In the centre are the words NEW ZEALAND within a gold laurel wreath. The cross is surmounted by a gold Tudor crown which is attached by a ring and a seriffed "V" to a silver bar ornamented with gold laurel leaves, through which the ribbon passes. The recipient's name and details are engraved on the reverse.

Comments: *The rarest of all gallantry awards, it was conferred for bravery during the second series of Maori Wars (1860-72). Only 23 Crosses were awarded, the last being authorised in 1910. This medal was called into being solely because local volunteer forces were not eligible for the VC. Today the Cross, with slight amendments to the design, is New Zealand's premier civilian award for bravery (see NZ2).*

VALUE: £30,000–40,000
Modern copy £650–750

Miniature	
Contemporary	£750–1000
Modern copy	£15–20

26. GEORGE CROSS

Instituted: 24 September 1940.

Ribbon: 38mm dark blue (originally 32mm). A silver miniature cross emblem is worn on the ribbon alone.

Metal: Silver.

Size: Height 48mm; max. width 45mm.

Description: A plain bordered cross with a circular medallion in the centre depicting the effigy of St George and the Dragon after Benedetto Pistrucci, surrounded by the words FOR GALLANTRY. In the angle of each limb is the Royal cypher GVI. The plain reverse bears in the centre the name of the recipient and date of the award. In the case of exchange awards, the date of the deed is given. The Cross hangs by a ring from a bar adorned with laurel leaves.

Comments: *The highest gallantry award for civilians, as well as for members of the armed forces in actions for which purely military honours would not normally be granted. It superseded the Empire Gallantry Medal whose holders were then required to return it and receive the GC in exchange. By Warrant of December 1971 surviving recipients of the Albert and Edward Medals were also invited to exchange their awards for the GC—a move which created a controversy which is still continuing, particularly among those who received the Albert Medal. Perhaps the most famous Cross was that conferred on the island of Malta in recognition of its gallantry during the Second World War. To date no second award bars have been awarded. Since its inception in 1940 the George Cross has been awarded 161 times, including four women (85 of these have been posthumous). In addition, 112 Empire Gallantry medallists, 65 Albert medallists and 68 Edward medallists who were eligible to exchange their awards for the GC have increased the total to 406. Most awards were made during World War II but it should be noted that since 1947 the GC has been awarded only 58 times (including one woman and the collective award to the Royal Ulster Constabulary, presented by Her Majesty the Queen at Hillsborough Castle on 12 April 2000). Arthur Bywater (who died in April 2005) was the only civilian to win both the GC and the GM but seven servicemen have won both. In 2002 the Government increased the annuity paid to £1,500, tax free.*

VALUE:

Service awards 1940 to date	£20,000–25,000
Civilian awards 1940 to date	£8,000–20,000
Service exchange pre-1940	£9000–11,000
Civilian exchange pre-1940	£8000–10,000
Miniature	**£15–20** *(in silver add £10)*

27. DISTINGUISHED SERVICE ORDER

Instituted: 1886.
Ribbon: 29mm crimson with dark blue edges.
Metal: Originally gold; silver-gilt (since 1889).
Size: Height 44mm; max. width 41.5mm.
Description: A cross with curved ends, overlaid with white enamel. (Obverse) a green enamel laurel wreath enclosing an imperial crown; (reverse) the royal monogram within a similar wreath. It is suspended from its ribbon by a swivel ring and a straight laureated bar. Additional awards are denoted by bars ornamented by a crown. Silver rosettes on the ribbon alone are worn in undress uniform. Since its inception, the DSO has been issued unnamed, but since 1938 the year of award has been engraved on the reverse of the lower suspension bar as well as the reverse of the bars for second or subsequent awards.
Comments: *Intended to reward commissioned officers below field rank for distinguished service in time of war, and for which the VC would not be appropriate. Previously the CB had sometimes been awarded to junior officers, although intended mainly for those of field rank. It was also available to officers in both the other armed services. In September 1942 the regulations were amended to permit award of the DSO to officers of the Merchant Navy who performed acts of gallantry in the presence of the enemy. As a result of the 1993 Review of gallantry awards and resultant changes to the operational gallantry award system, the DSO is now awarded for "Leadership" only—theoretically to all ranks (it is not awarded posthumously). It has been replaced by the Conspicuous Gallantry Cross as the reward for gallantry.*

VALUE:	Unnamed single	Attributable group	*Miniature*
Victoria, gold (153)	£4000–5500	£6000–10,000	£100–120
Victoria, silver-gilt (1170)	£1200–1500	£3000–7500	£60–80
Edward VII (78)	£1500–1800	£4500–5500	£85–120 (gold)
George V (9900)	£1000–1200	£1500–2500	£45 (gilt), £100 (gold)
George VI 1st type 1938–48 (4880)	£1500–2000	£3000–5000	£45 (gilt)
George VI 2nd type 1948–52 (63)	£1800–2200	£4500–6000	£45 (gilt)
Elizabeth II	£3000–3500	£6000–8000	£35

28. IMPERIAL SERVICE ORDER

Instituted: August 1902.
Ribbon: 38mm three equal sections of crimson, blue and crimson.
Metal: Silver with gold overlay.
Size: Height 61mm; max. width 55mm.
Description: The badge consists of a circular gold plaque bearing the royal cypher and surrounded by the words FOR FAITHFUL SERVICE. This plaque is then superimposed on a seven-pointed silver star surmounted by a crown and ring for suspension. The badge of the ISO awarded to women is similar but has a laurel wreath instead of the star-shaped base.
Comments: *Instituted by King Edward VII as a means of rewarding long and faithful service in the Administrative and Clerical grades of the Civil Service at home and overseas. Women were admitted to the order in 1908. The order was awarded after at least 25 years service at home, 20 years and 6 months (India) and 16 years in the tropics, but in exceptional cases awards were made for "eminently meritorious service" irrespective of qualifying period. No UK awards have been made since 1995 but some Commonwealth awards continue to this day.*

VALUE:			*Miniature*
Edward VII	Gentleman (489)	£250–300	£25–30
	Lady (4)	£2000–2500	£200–300
George V	Gentleman (909)	£275–300	£20–25
	Lady (2)	£2200–2700	£200–300
George VI	Gentleman (608)	£250–300	£15–20
	Lady (8)	£1200–1500	£200–300
Elizabeth II	Gentleman (2,153)*	£200–250	£10–15
	Lady (114)*	£600–800	£150–200

*1953–94

29. IMPERIAL SERVICE MEDAL

Instituted: August 1902.
Ribbon: Same as above.
Metal: Silver and bronze.
Size: 32mm
Description: Originally similar to the ISO but with a silver plaque and bronze star or wreath. In 1920 the ISM was transformed into a circular medal of silver with the sovereign's effigy on the obverse and a reverse depicting a naked man resting from his labours, with FOR FAITHFUL SERVICE in the exergue.
Comments: *Instituted at the same time as the ISO but intended for junior grades of the Civil Service.*

VALUE:

			Miniature
Edward VII, 1903–10 (c. 4,500) Star (Gentleman)	£75–100	£15–20
Wreath (Lady)	£275–400	£200–300
George V, 1911-20 (c. 6,000) Star (Gentleman)	£65–75	£12–15
Wreath (Lady)	£300–400	£200–300
George V Circular type		
Coinage profile, 1920–31 (c. 20,000)	£20–25	£10–15
Crowned bust, 1931–37 (c. 16,000)	£20–25	£10–15
George VI		
Crowned bust INDIAE:IMP, 1938–48 (c. 36,000)	£20–25	£10–15
Crowned bust FID:DEF, 1949–52 (c. 16,000)	£20–25	£10–15
Elizabeth II		
Tudor crown BRITT:OMN, 1953–54 (c. 9,000)	£20–25	£10–15
Tudor crown DEI:GRATIA, 1955– (c. 150,000)	£20–25	£10–15

30. INDIAN ORDER OF MERIT

Instituted: 1837 (by the Honourable East India Company).
Ribbon: Dark blue with crimson edges (military) or crimson with dark blue edges (civil).
Metal: Silver and gold.
Size: Height 41mm; max. width 40mm.
Description: An eight-pointed star with a circular centre surrounded by a laurel wreath and containing crossed sabres and the relevant inscription. The star is suspended by a curvilinear suspension bar. The different classes were denoted by the composition of the star, noted below.
Comments: *The oldest gallantry award of the British Empire, it was founded in 1837 by the Honourable East India Company. Twenty years later it became an official British award when the administration of India passed to the Crown after the Sepoy Mutiny. Originally known simply as the Order of Merit, it was renamed in 1902 following the introduction of the prestigious British order of that name. There were three classes of the order, promotion from one class to the next being the reward for further acts of bravery. A civil division (also in three classes) was introduced in 1902. Ten years later the military division was reduced to two classes, when troops of the Indian Army became eligible for the VC. The civil division became a single class in 1939 and the military in 1945. Both divisions came to an end with the British Raj in 1947.*

Military

Civil

VALUE:
Military Division
1837-1912 Reward of Valour

1st class in gold (42)	£4500–6000
2nd class in silver and gold (130)	£2500–3500
3rd class in silver (2740)	£1000–1500

1912-39 Reward of Valour

1st class in silver and gold (26)	£4500–6000
2nd class in silver (1215)	£450–550

continued

30. INDIAN ORDER OF MERIT continued

1939-44 Reward of Gallantry	
1st class in silver and gold (2)	Rare
2nd class in silver (332)	£750–100
1945-47 Reward of Gallantry (44mm diameter)	£1800–2500
Civil Division	
1902-39 For Bravery (35mm diameter)	
1st class in gold (0)	—
2nd class in silver and gold (0)	—
3rd class in silver (39)	£1500–1800
1939-47 For Bravery (26mm diameter)	
Single class (10)	£2500–3500
Miniature	£150–250

NB These prices represent unattributable pieces. Values can climb rapidly when in company with related campaign medals, particularly for the Victorian era.

30A. CONSPICUOUS GALLANTRY CROSS

Instituted: October 1993.
Ribbon: White with blue edges and a red central stripe.
Metal: Silver.
Size: Max. width 36mm
Description: A cross pattée imposed on a wreath of laurel, with the royal crown in a circular panel in the centre. Suspended by a ring from a plain suspension bar.
Comments: *As part of the decision to remove distinctions of rank in awards for bravery, this decoration replaced the DSO for gallantry as well as the Conspicuous Gallantry Medal and the Distinguished Conduct Medal. It was first awarded in 1995 to Corporal Wayne Mills of the Duke of Wellington's Regiment and in 1996 to Colour Sergeant Peter Humphreys of the Royal Welch Fusiliers, both for gallantry in action during service with the UN Peacekeeping Forces in Bosnia. Two awards were made in respect of gallantry by members of the SAS and SBS in Sierra Leone in May–June 2000. A further two awards were made to members of the SAS and two awards to members of the SBS in Afghanistan in October 2001–March 2002, while awards to Justin Thomas, RM, and Lance Corporal Michael Flynn, Blues and Royals, both for gallantry in Iraq, were gazetted in October 2003, and that to Sqdn Ldr I. J. McKechnie, Royal Air Force, was gazetted on 9 September 2005, making a total of 11 in the first decade. Since then other awards have ben made taking the total number of awards to date to 50, including a collective award to the Royal Irish Regiment which appeared in the LG Supplement, December 18, 2006 and one posthumous award.*

VALUE: £50,000–100,000   *Miniature*   £20–25

31. ROYAL RED CROSS

First Class obverse

Instituted: 27 April 1883.

Ribbon: 25mm dark blue edged with crimson, in a bow.

Metal: Gold (later silver-gilt) and silver.

Size: Height 41mm; max. width 35mm.

Description: (Obverse) The *1st class* badge was originally a gold cross pattée, enamelled red with gold edges, but from 1889 silver-gilt was substituted for gold. At the centre was a crowned and veiled portrait, with the words FAITH, HOPE and CHARITY inscribed on three arms, and the date 1883 on the lower arm. Subsequently the effigy of the reigning monarch was substituted for the allegorical profile; (reverse) crowned royal cypher. *2nd Class:* in silver, design as the 1st class but the inscriptions on the arms appear on the reverse. Awards from 1938 have the year of issue engraved on the reverse of the lower arm.

Comments: *This decoration had the distinction of being confined to females until 1976. It is conferred on members of the nursing services regardless of rank. A second class award was introduced in November 1915. Bars for the first class were introduced in 1917. Holders of the second class are promoted to the first class on second awards. Holders of the first class decoration are known as Members (RRC) while recipients of the second class are Associates (ARRC). The second type GVI award is surprisingly scarce as only 50 first class and 100 second class were awarded.*

VALUE:	First class (RRC)	Miniature	Second class (ARRC)	Miniature
Victoria, gold	£1000–1200	£90–100	—	
Victoria, silver-gilt	£400–500	£60–70	—	
Edward VII, gold	£800–1000	£90–100	—	
George V	£300–350	£20–30	£120–150	£10–25
George V, with bar	£450–550	£50–60	—	
George VI GRI	£300–350	£20–30	£180–220	£10–25
George VI GVIR	£350–450	£20–30	£250–300	£10–25
Elizabeth II	£300–350	£20–30	£200–250	£10–25

32. DISTINGUISHED SERVICE CROSS

Instituted: June 1901.

Ribbon: 36mm three equal parts of dark blue, white and dark blue.

Metal: Silver.

Size: Height 43mm; max. width 43mm.

Description: A plain cross with rounded ends. (Obverse) crowned royal cypher in the centre, suspended by a ring; (reverse) plain apart from the hallmark. From 1940 onwards the year of issue was engraved on the reverse of the lower limb.

Comments: *Known as the Conspicuous Service Cross when instituted, it was awarded to warrant and subordinate officers of the Royal Navy who were ineligible for the DSO. In October 1914 it was renamed the Distinguished Service Cross and thrown open to all naval officers below the rank of lieutenant-commander. Bars for second awards were authorised in 1916 and in 1931 eligibility for the award was enlarged to include officers of the Merchant Navy. In 1940 Army and RAF officers serving aboard naval vessels also became eligible for the award. Since 1945 fewer than 100 DSCs have been awarded. As a result of the 1993 Review of gallantry awards and resultant changes to the operational gallantry award system, this award is now available to both officers and other ranks, the DSM having been discontinued.*

VALUE:	Unnamed single	Attributable group	Miniature
Edward VII	—	£5500–7000	£200–250
George V	£700–800	£1500–2500	£20–30
George VI GRI	£750–850	£1500–2500	£15–20
George VI GVIR	—	£2500–3500	£25–30
Elizabeth II	—	£3500–5000	£12–15

33. MILITARY CROSS

Instituted: 31 December 1914.

Ribbon: 38mm three equal stripes of white, deep purple and white.

Metal: Silver.

Size: Height 46mm; max. width 44mm.

Description: An ornamental cross with straight arms terminating in broad finials decorated with imperial crowns. The royal cypher appears at the centre and the cross is suspended from a plain silver suspension bar.

Comments: *There was no gallantry award, lesser than the VC and DSO, for junior Army officers and warrant officers until shortly after the outbreak of the First World War when the MC was instituted. Originally awarded to captains, lieutenants and warrant officers of the Army (including RFC), it was subsequently extended to include equivalent ranks of the RAF when performing acts of bravery on the ground and there was even provision for the Royal Naval Division and the Royal Marines during the First World War. Awards were extended to majors by an amending warrant of 1931. Bars for second and subsequent awards have a crown at the centre. The MC is always issued unnamed, although since 1937 the reverse of the cross or bar is officially dated with the year of issue. As a result of the 1993 Review of gallantry awards and resultant changes to the operational gallantry award system, this award is now available to both officers and other ranks, the Military Medal having been discontinued.*

VALUE:	Unnamed single	Attributable group	Miniature
George V 1914-20 (37,000)	£550–625	£1000–1750	£20–25
George V 1914-20 one bar (3000)	£800–950	£1400–2000	
George V 1914-20 two bars (170)	£850–1200	£3500–4500	
George V 1914-20 three bars (4)	—	£8000–10,000	
George V 1921-36 (350)	—	£1800–2500	
George V 1921-36 one bar (31)	—	£3000–5000	
George VI GRI 1937-46 (11,000)	£575–675	£1400–2200	£20–25
George VI GRI one bar (500)	£550–700	£3000–4000	
George VI GVIR (158)	—	£3500–5500	£30–35
Elizabeth II	£650–750	£3500–5500	£20–25
Elizabeth II one bar	—	—	

34. DISTINGUISHED FLYING CROSS

Post-1919 ribbon.

Original ribbon.

Instituted: June 1918.

Ribbon: 30mm originally horizontal but since June 1919 diagonal alternate stripes of white and deep purple.

Metal: Silver.

Size: Height 60mm; max. width 54mm.

Description: (Obverse) a cross flory terminating with a rose, surmounted by another cross made of propeller blades charged in the centre with a roundel within a laurel wreath. The horizontal arms bear wings and the crowned RAF monogram at the centre; (reverse) the royal cypher above the date 1918. The cross is suspended from a bar decorated with a sprig of laurel.

Comments: *Established for officers and warrant officers of the RAF in respect of acts of valour while flying in active operations against the enemy. The DFC is issued unnamed, but Second World War crosses usually have the year of issue engraved on the reverse of the lower limb. As a result of the 1993 Review of gallantry awards and resultant changes to the operational gallantry award system, this award is now available to both officers and other ranks, the Distinguished Flying Medal having been discontinued.*

VALUE:	Unnamed single	Attributable group	Miniature
George V 1918-20 (1100)	£1600–1800	£2500–3500	£20–25
George V 1918-20 one bar (70)	£1800–2000	£5500–6500	
George V 1918-20 two bars (3)	—	—	
George V 1920-36 (130)	—	—	
George V 1920-36 one bar (20)	—	—	
George V 1920-36 two bars (4)	—	—	
George VI GRI 1939-45 (20,000)	£1700–2000	£2500–3500	£20–25
George VI 1939-45 one bar (1550)	£2000–2500	£4000–6000	
George VI 1939-45 two bars (42)	—	—	
George VI GVIR 1948-52 (65)	—	—	£30–35
Elizabeth II	£1600–2000	£6000–8000	£20–25 (in silver add £5)

35. AIR FORCE CROSS

Instituted: June 1918.

Ribbon: 30mm originally horizontal but since June 1919 diagonal alternate stripes of white and crimson.

Metal: Silver.

Size: Height 60mm; max. width 54mm.

Description: (Obverse) the cross consists of a thunderbolt, the arms conjoined by wings, base bar terminating in a bomb, surmounted by another cross of aeroplane propellers, the finials inscribed with the royal cypher. A central roundel depicts Hermes mounted on a hawk bestowing a wreath; (reverse) the royal cypher and the date 1918.

Comments: *This decoration, awarded to officers and warrant officers of the RAF, was instituted in June 1918 for gallantry on non-operational missions and for meritorious service on flying duties. Since the 1993 Review of gallantry awards it is now available to all ranks (the Air Force Medal having been discontinued) for non-operational gallantry in the air only (no longer for meritorious service also).*

Post-1919 ribbon.

Original ribbon.

VALUE:

	Unnamed single	Attributable group	Miniature
George V 1918-20 (678)	£900–1000	£1500–2500	£20–25
George V 1918-20 one bar (12)	—	—	
George V 1918-20 two bars (3)	—	—	
George V 1920-36 (111)	£1200–1500	£1800–3000	
George VI GRI (2605)	£850–950	£1800–3000	£20–25
George VI one bar (36)	£950–1200	£2750–3500	
George VI two bars (1)	—	—	
George VI GVIR (411)	£950–1200	£1500–2000	£30–35
Elizabeth II	£950–1250	£1800–2500	£20–25

(in silver add £5)

36. ORDER OF BRITISH INDIA

Instituted: 1837 by the Honourable East India Company.

Ribbon: Worn around the neck, the base colour of the ribbon was originally sky blue but this was altered to crimson in 1838, allegedly because the hair oil favoured by Indians of all classes would soon have soiled a light ribbon. From 1939 onwards the first class ribbon had two thin vertical lines of light blue at the centre, while the second class ribbon had a single vertical line. Originally these distinctive ribbons were only worn in undress uniform (without the insignia itself), but from 1945 they replaced the plain crimson ribbons when worn with the decoration.

Metal: Gold.

Size: Height 42mm; max. width 38mm.

Description: The first class badge consists of a gold star with a crown between the upper two points and a blue enamelled centre bearing a lion surrounded by the words ORDER OF BRITISH INDIA enclosed in a laurel wreath. The second class badge is smaller, with dark blue enamel in the centre and with no crown.

Comments: *Intended for long and faithful service by native officers of the Indian Army, it was thrown open in 1939 to officers of the armed forces, frontier guards, military police and officers of the Indian native states. There were two classes, promotion to the first being made from the second. Recipients of both classes were entitled to the letters OBI after their names, but holders of the first class had the rank of Sardar Bahadur, while those of the second were merely Bahadur. A few awards were made by Pakistan to British officers seconded to the Pakistani forces at the time of independence.*

Original ribbon.

1838 ribbon.

1st class, post-1939 ribbon.

2nd class, post-1939 ribbon.

VALUE:

		Miniature
1st class, light blue centre and dark blue surround	£1200–1500	£200–250
1st class, sky blue centre and surround (1939)	£1000–1200	£200–250
2nd class	£1000–1200	£200–250

NB The prices quoted are for unattributable awards.

37. ORDER OF BURMA

Instituted 1940.
Ribbon: 38mm dark green with light blue edges.
Metal: Gold.
Size: Height 52mm; max. width 38mm.
Description: The badge consists of a gold-rayed circle with a central roundel charged with a peacock in his pride azure, surmounted by an imperial crown.
Comments: *Instituted by King George VI, three years after Burma became independent of British India. Only 24 awards were made, to Governor's Commissioned Officers for long, faithful and honourable service in the army, frontier force and military police of Burma. By an amendment of 1945 the order could also be awarded for individual acts of heroism or particularly meritorious service. It was abolished in 1947.*

VALUE: £4000–5000   *Not known in miniature*

38. KAISAR-I-HIND MEDAL

Victoria obv.   *Victoria rev.*

Instituted: May 1900.
Ribbon: 37mm bluish green.
Metal: Gold, silver or bronze.
Size: Height 61mm; max. width 34mm.
Description: An oval badge surmounted by the imperial crown. (Obverse) the royal cypher set within a wreath; (reverse) FOR PUBLIC SERVICE IN INDIA round the edge and KAISAR-I-HIND (Emperor of India) on a scroll across the centre against a floral background.
Comments: *Queen Victoria founded this medal for award to those, regardless of colour, creed or sex, who had performed public service in India. Originally in two classes George V introduced a 3rd Class in bronze. The medals were originally large and hollow but were changed to smaller in diameter and solid during the reign of George V.*

VALUE:	1st class (gold)	*Miniature*	2nd class (silver)	*Miniature*	3rd class (bronze)	*Miniature*
Victoria	£1500–1800	£150–200	£350–450	£85–100	—	
Edward VII	£1500–1800	£150–200	£350–450	£85–100	—	
George V 1st	£1200–1400	£85–150	£350–450	£35–50	—	
George V 2nd	£1200–1400	£85–150	£300–400	£35–50	£125–150	£25–30
George VI	£1200–1400	£150–200	£350–400	£50–80	£125–150	£25–30

39. ALBERT MEDAL

Instituted: 7 March 1866.
Ribbons:

Gold (1st Class) Sea
16mm blue with two white stripes (1866)
35mm blue with four white stripes (1867–1949)
Bronze (2nd Class) Sea
16mm blue with two white stripes (1867–1904)
35mm blue with two white stripes (1904–71)

Gold (1st Class) Land
35mm red with four white stripes (1877–1949)

Bronze (2nd Class) Land
16mm red with two white stripes (1877–1904)
35mm red with two white stripes (1904–71)

Metal: Gold (early issues gold and bronze); bronze.
Size: Height 57mm; max. width 30mm.
Description: The badge consists of an oval enclosing the entwined initials V and A. The sea medals have, in addition, an anchor. The oval is enclosed by a bronze garter with the words FOR GALLANTRY IN SAVING LIFE, with AT SEA or ON LAND as appropriate, and enamelled in blue or crimson respectively. The whole is surmounted by a crown pierced by a ring for suspension. The first class medal was originally worked in gold and bronze and later in gold alone, the second class in bronze alone.

2nd class land service medal.

2nd class land and sea service ribbons (until 1904).

1st class land service ribbon.

2nd class land service ribbon.
See also ribbon chart

Comments: *Named in memory of the Prince Consort who died in 1861, this series of medals was instituted for gallantry in saving life at sea. An amendment of 1867 created two classes of medal and ten years later awards were extended to gallantry in saving life on land. In 1917 the title of the awards was altered, the first class becoming the Albert Medal in Gold and the second class merely the Albert Medal. It was last awarded in gold to a living recipient in April 1943, the last posthumous award being in May 1945. The last bronze medal awarded to a living recipient was in January 1949, and posthumous in August 1970. In 1949 the Medal in Gold was abolished and replaced by the George Cross and henceforward the Albert Medal (second class) was only awarded posthumously. In 1971 the award of the medal ceased and holders were invited to exchange their medals for the George Cross. Of the 65 eligible to exchange, 49 did so.*

VALUE:

	Civilian	Service	Miniature
Gold Sea (25)	£8000–14,000	£10,000–15,000	£70–90*
Bronze Sea (211)	£6000–8000	£6000–9000	£50–70
Gold Land (45)	£8000–14,000	£8000–15,000	£70–90*
Bronze Land (290)	£5000–7000	£6000–8000	£50–70
		*assumed gilt	

40. UNION OF SOUTH AFRICA KING'S/ QUEEN'S MEDAL FOR BRAVERY (WOLTEMADE MEDAL)

Instituted: 1939 by the Government of the Union of South Africa.
Ribbon: Royal blue with narrow orange edges.
Metal: Gold or silver.
Size: 37mm.
Description: (Obverse) an effigy of the reigning sovereign; (reverse) a celebrated act of heroism by Wolraad Woltemade who rescued sailors from the wreck of the East Indiaman *De Jong Thomas* which ran aground in Table Bay on 17 June 1773. Seven times Woltemade rode into the raging surf to save fourteen seamen from drowning, but on the eighth attempt both rider and horse perished.
Comments: *This medal was awarded to citizens of the Union of South Africa and dependent territories who endangered their lives in saving the lives of others. It was awarded very sparingly, in gold or silver.*

VALUE:

		Miniature
George VI Gold (1)	£2000–2500	£250–300
George VI Silver (34)	£1500–2000	£150–200
Elizabeth II Silver (1)	£1800–2200	£150–200

41. DISTINGUISHED CONDUCT MEDAL

Instituted: 1854.

Ribbon: 32mm crimson with a dark blue central stripe.

Metal: Silver.

Size: 36mm.

Description: (Obverse) originally a trophy of arms but, since 1902, the effigy of the reigning sovereign; (reverse) a four-line inscription across the field FOR DISTINGUISHED CONDUCT IN THE FIELD.

Comments: *The need for a gallantry medal for other ranks was first recognised during the Crimean War, although previously the Meritorious Service Medal (qv) had very occasionally been awarded for gallantry in the field. The medals have always been issued named, and carry the number, rank and name of the recipient on the rim, together with the date of the act of gallantry from 1881 until about 1901. Bars are given for subsequent awards and these too were dated from the first issued in 1881 until 1916 when the more usual laurelled bars were adopted. Since 1916 it has ranked as a superior decoration to the Military Medal. As a result of the 1993 Review of gallantry awards and resultant changes to the operational gallantry award system, the decoration has been replaced by the Conspicuous Gallantry Cross.*

1st type obv.

VALUE:

Crimea (800)	£2500–5000
Indian Mutiny (17)	£7000–10,000
India general service 1854–95	£4000–6000
Abyssinia 1867–68 (7)	£4500–5500
Ashantee 1873–64 (33)	£3500–5000
Zulu War 1877–79 (16)	£6000–10,000
Afghanistan 1878–80 (61)	£4000–6000
First Boer War 1880–81 (20)	£6500–10,000
Egypt & Sudan 1882–89 (134)	£5000–8000
India 1895–1901	£5000–6500
Sudan 1896–97	£4500–6500
Second Boer War 1899–1902 (2090)	£2000–3500
Boxer Rebellion 1900	£4500–8000
Edward VII	Many rarities
George V 1st type (25,000)	£1000–2500
ditto, unnamed (as issued to foreign recipients)	£350–400
George V 2nd type 1930–7 (14)	£6000–8000
George VI, IND IMP 1937–47	£4000–6000
ditto, unnamed (as issued to foreign recipients)	£500–600
George VI, 2nd type 1948–52 (25)	£12,000–15,000
Elizabeth II, BR: OMN:	£10,000–15,000
Elizabeth II, DEI GRATIA	£10,000–16,000
Miniature (in silver add £5)	
Victoria	£75–85
Edward VII	£45–55
George V	Type I £35–45, II £70–100
George VI	Type I £15–20, II £25–40
Elizabeth II	£15–20

42. DISTINGUISHED CONDUCT MEDAL (DOMINION & COLONIAL)

Instituted: 31 May 1895.

Ribbon: 32mm crimson with a dark blue central stripe.

Metal: Silver.

Size: 36mm.

Description: As above, but the reverse bears the name of the issuing country or colony round the top.

Comments: *A separate DCM for warrant officers, NCOs and men of the colonial forces. Medals were struck for the Cape of Good Hope, Natal, New Zealand, New South Wales, Queensland, Tasmania, Natal and Canada, but only the last two actually issued them and the others are known only as specimens.*

VALUE:

Victoria Canada (1)	Rare
Victoria Natal (1)	Rare
Edward VII Natal (9)	Rare

43. DISTINGUISHED CONDUCT MEDAL (KAR & WAFF)

Instituted: early 1900s.

Ribbon: Dark blue with a central green stripe flanked by crimson stripes.

Metal: Silver.

Size: 36mm

Description: As no. 42, with either King's African Rifles or West Africa Frontier Force around the top of the reverse.

Comments: *Separate awards for gallantry were instituted in respect of the King's African Rifles (East Africa) and the West Africa Frontier Force (Nigeria, Sierra Leone, Gambia and the Gold Coast). These were issued until 1942 when they were superseded by the British DCM.*

VALUE:	Attributable groups
Edward VII KAR (2)	Rare
Edward VII WAFF (55)	£2500–3500
George V KAR (190)	£1500–2000
George V WAFF (165)	£1500–2000

44. CONSPICUOUS GALLANTRY MEDAL

Instituted: 1855.

Ribbon: 31mm white (RN) or sky blue (RAF) with dark blue edges. The Royal Navy ribbon was originally dark blue with white central stripe.

Metal: Silver.

Size: 36mm.

Description: (Obverse) the effigy of the reigning monarch; (reverse) the words FOR CONSPICUOUS GALLANTRY in three lines within a crowned laurel wreath.

Comments: *Conceived as the naval counterpart to the DCM, it was instituted for award to petty officers and seamen of the Royal Navy and to NCOs and other ranks of the Royal Marines. Originally awarded only for gallantry during the Crimean War, it was revived in 1874 to recognise heroism during the Ashantee War and has since been awarded, albeit sparingly, for other wars and campaigns. The Crimean issue utilised the dies of the Meritorious Service Medal which had the date 1848 below the truncation of the Queen's neck on the obverse. The raised relief inscription MERITORIOUS SERVICE on the reverse was erased and the words CONSPICUOUS GALLANTRY engraved in their place. When the decoration was revived in 1874 a new obverse was designed without a date while a new die, with the entire inscription in raised relief, was employed for the reverse. In 1943 the CGM was extended to NCOs and other ranks of the RAF. Both naval and RAF medals are identical, but the naval medal has a white ribbon with dark blue edges, whereas the RAF award has a pale blue ribbon with dark blue edges. It ranks as one of the rarest decorations: the only three medals issued in the present reign were awarded to Cpl. J. D. Coughan, RAAF, for gallantry in Vietnam (1968), to Staff-Sergeant James Prescott, RE, during the South Atlantic War (1982) (posthumous) and to CPO Diver Philip Hammond, RN, during the Gulf War (1991). As a result of the 1993 Review and resultant changes to the operational gallantry award system, the decoration has been replaced by the Conspicuous Gallantry Cross.*

RN first type ribbon

RN

RAF

VALUE:	Attributable groups
Victoria 1st type (11)	£6000–10,000
Victoria 2nd type (50)	£6500–8500
Edward VII (2)	£10,000–15,000
George V (110)	£7000–9000
George VI Navy/RM (72)	£7500–10,000
George VI RAF (103)	£8000–10,000
Elizabeth II (3)	—
Miniature	
Victoria	£50–80
Edward VII	£50–80
George V	£20–30
George VI	£15–20
Elizabeth II	£15–20

45. GEORGE MEDAL

Instituted: 1940.
Ribbon: 32mm crimson with five narrow blue stripes.
Metal: Silver.
Size: 36mm.
Description: (Obverse) the effigy of the reigning monarch; (reverse) St George and the Dragon, modelled by George Kruger Gray, after the bookplate by Stephen Gooden for the Royal Library, Windsor.
Comments: *Awarded for acts of bravery where the services were not so outstanding as to merit the George Cross. Though primarily a civilian award, it has also been given to service personnel for heroism not in the face of the enemy. Of the approximately 2,000 medals awarded, 1,030 have been to civilians. 27 second award bars have been issued, the latest posthumously to WOII Gary O'Donnell, Royal Logistic Corps, who was killed in Afghanistan in September 2008.*

VALUE:

	Civilian	Service
George VI 1st type 1940-47	£2500–3500	£2500–3500
George VI 2nd type 1948-52	£2500–3500	£2500–3500
Elizabeth II 1st type 1953	£2000–2800	£2500–3500
Elizabeth II 2nd type	£2000–2800	£2500–3500

Miniature	
George VI, Type I	£15–20 (Silver £20–25)
Type II	£20–25 (Silver £30–40)
Elizabeth II	£10–15 (Silver £20–25)

46. KING'S POLICE MEDAL

Instituted: 7 July 1909.
Ribbons: 36mm Originally deep blue with silver edges, but in 1916 a central silver stripe was added. Gallantry awards have thin crimson stripes superimposed on the silver stripes.
Metal: Silver.
Size: 36mm.
Description: (Obverse) the monarch's effigy; (reverse) a standing figure with sword and shield inscribed TO GUARD MY PEOPLE. The first issue had a laurel spray in the exergue, but in 1933 two separate reverses were introduced and the words FOR GALLANTRY or FOR DISTINGUISHED SERVICE were placed in the exergue.
Comments: *Instituted to reward "courage and devotion to duty" in the police and fire services of the UK and overseas dominions. Recognising the bravery of the firemen during the Blitz, the medal was retitled the King's Police and Fire Services Medal in 1940, but no change was made in the design of the medal itself. From 1950, the gallantry medals were only awarded posthumously and all medals were discontinued in 1954 when separate awards were established for the two services (see numbers MYB47 and 48).*

VALUE:

		Miniature
Edward VII (100)	£800–1000	£25–30
George V 1st type coinage head (1900)	£500–700	£20–25
George V 2nd type crowned head	£500–700	£40–50
George V for Gallantry (350)	£850–1400	£15–20
George V for Distinguished Service	£400–500	£15–20
George VI 1st type for Gallantry (440)	£800–1000	£10–15
George VI 2nd type for Gallantry (50)	£1500–2000	£10–15
George VI 1st type for Distinguished Service	£400–500	£10–15
George VI 2nd type for Distinguished Service	£400–500	£10–15

KPM

KPM (Gallantry)

47. QUEEN'S POLICE MEDAL

Instituted: 19 May 1954.
Ribbon: Three silver stripes and two broad dark blue stripes. Gallantry awards have thin crimson stripes superimposed on the silver stripes.
Metal: Silver.
Size: 36mm.
Description: (Obverse) effigy of the reigning sovereign; (reverse) a standing figure (as on the KPM) but the laurel spray has been restored to the exergue and the words FOR GALLANTRY or FOR DISTINGUISHED POLICE SERVICE are inscribed round the circumference.
Comments: *The QPM for Gallantry has been effectively redundant since November 1977 when it was made possible to award the George Medal posthumously. Prior to this the QPM was the posthumous equivalent of the GM for police officers. Issued in New Zealand under Regulations dated November 18, 1959 by the Minister in Charge of Police.*

VALUE:		Miniature
Elizabeth II for Gallantry (23)	£1500–2000	£30–40
Elizabeth II for Distinguished Service (1100)	£500–700	£20–30

Gallantry

48. QUEEN'S FIRE SERVICE MEDAL

Instituted: 19 May 1954.
Ribbon: Red with three yellow stripes (distinguished service) or similar, with thin dark blue stripes bisecting the yellow stripes (gallantry).
Metal: Silver.
Size: 36mm
Description: (Obverse) effigy of the reigning monarch; (reverse) standing figure with sword and shield (as on KPM), laurel spray in the exergue, and inscription round the circumference FOR GALLANTRY or FOR DISTINGUISHED FIRE SERVICE.
Comments: *To date no award of this medal, which can be awarded posthumously, has been made for gallantry.*

VALUE:		Miniature
Elizabeth II for Gallantry	—	£30–40
Elizabeth II for Distinguished Service	£550–650	£20–30

Gallantry

48A. QUEEN'S VOLUNTEER RESERVES MEDAL

Instituted: 1999.
Ribbon: Dark green with three narrow gold stripes.
Metal: Silver.
Size: 36mm.
Description: (Obverse) effigy of Queen Elizabeth II; (reverse) five ribbons containing the words THE QUEEN'S VOLUNTEER RESERVES MEDAL. The medal is fitted with a large ring for suspension.
Comments: *Awarded to men and women of any rank in the volunteer reserves of all three services in recognition of outstanding service which formerly would have merited an award within the Order of the British Empire. Holders are entitled to the post-nominal letters QVRM.*

VALUE: £300–500   *Miniature* £10–15

49. KING'S POLICE MEDAL (SOUTH AFRICA)

Instituted: 24 September 1937.
Ribbon: Silver with two broad dark blue stripes. Red stripes are added for gallantry awards.
Metal: Silver.
Size: 36mm.
Description: (Obverse) effigy of George VI and title including the words ET IMPERATOR (1937-49), George VI minus IMPERATOR (1950-52) and Queen Elizabeth II (1953-60). (Reverse) as UK (no. 47 above) but inscribed in English and Afrikaans. Inscribed FOR BRAVERY VIR DAPPERHEID or FOR DISTINGUISHED SERVICE VIR VOORTREFLIKE DIENS.
Comments: *Awarded to members of the South Africa Police for courage and devotion to duty. In 1938 it was extended to cover the constabulary of South West Africa.*

VALUE:
    George VI 1st type 1937-49
        for Gallantry (10)   —
        for Distinguished Service (13)   —
    George VI 2nd type 1950-52
        for Distinguished Service (13)   —
    Elizabeth II 1953-60
        for Gallantry (20)   —
    Elizabeth II 1953-69
        for Distinguished Service (3)   —

Not seen in Miniature

50. EDWARD MEDAL (MINES)

Instituted: July 1907.
Ribbon: Dark blue edged with yellow.
Metal: Silver or bronze.
Size: 33mm.
Description: (Obverse) the monarch's effigy; (reverse) a miner rescuing a stricken comrade, with the caption FOR COURAGE across the top (designed by W. Reynolds-Stephens).
Comments: *Awarded for life-saving in mines and quarries, in two grades: first class (silver) and second class (bronze). Interestingly, the cost of these medals was borne not by the State but from a fund created by a group of philanthropic individuals led by A. Hewlett, a leading mine-owner. Medals were engraved with the names of the recipient from the outset, but since the 1930s the date and sometimes the place of the action have also been inscribed. Since 1949 the medal was only granted posthumously and in 1971 living recipients were invited to exchange their medals for the GC, under Royal Warrant of 1971. Two silver and seven bronze medallists elected not to do so. This is one of the rarest gallantry awards, only 77 silver and 318 bronze medals having been granted since its inception. Only two second award bars have been awarded—both for mine rescues.*

VALUE:	Silver	Bronze
Edward VII	£1000–1500	£850–1000
George V 1st type	£1000–1500	£850–1000
George V 2nd type	£1500–2000	£1000–1500
George VI 1st type	£1800–2500	£1500–1750
George VI 2nd type	—	£1800–2000
Elizabeth II	Not issued	From £2000
Miniature		
Edward VII	£80–90	£70–80
George V	£70–80	£60–70
George VI	£70–80	£60–70

51. EDWARD MEDAL (INDUSTRY)

1st type rev.

2nd type rev.

Instituted: December 1909.
Ribbon: As above.
Metal: Silver or bronze.
Size: 33mm.
Description: (Obverse) effigy of the reigning monarch; (reverse) originally a worker helping an injured workmate with a factory in the background and the words FOR COURAGE inscribed diagonally across the top. A second reverse, depicting a standing female figure with a laurel branch and a factory skyline in the background, was introduced in 1912.
Comments: *Awarded for acts of bravery in factory accidents and disasters. Like the Mines medal it was also available in two classes, but no first class medals were awarded since 1948. Since 1949 the medal was only granted posthumously and in 1971 living recipients were invited to exchange their medals for the GC, under Royal Warrant of 1971. A total of 25 silver and 163 bronze awards have been issued. Two awards were made to women, the rarest gallantry award to a lady.*

VALUE:	Silver	Bronze
Edward VII	£1500–2000	£1000–1500
George V 1st Obv, 1st Rev	—	£1500–1800
George V 1st Obv, 2nd Rev	£1400–1500	£1000–1200
George V 2nd Obv, 2nd Rev	—	£1200–1400
George VI 1st type	Unique	£1000–1200
George VI 2nd type	Not issued	£1500–2000
Elizabeth II 1st type	Not issued	£1500–2000
Elizabeth II 2nd type	Not issued	£1500–2000
Miniature		
George V	£150–200	£100–150
George VI	£70–80	
George VI Modern example	£15–20	

52. INDIAN DISTINGUISHED SERVICE MEDAL

Instituted: 25 June 1907.
Ribbon: Crimson with broad dark blue edges.
Metal: Silver.
Size: 36mm.
Description: (Obverse) the sovereign's effigy; (reverse) the words FOR DISTINGUISHED SERVICE in a laurel wreath.
Comments: *Awarded for distinguished service in the field by Indian commissioned and non-commissioned officers and men of the Indian Army, the reserve forces, border militia and levies, military police and troops employed by the Indian Government. An amendment of 1917 extended the award to Indian non-combatants engaged on field service, bars for subsequent awards being authorised at the same time. It was formally extended to the Royal Indian Marine in 1929 and members of the Indian Air Force in 1940. Finally it was extended in 1944 to include non-European personnel of the Hong Kong and Singapore Royal Artillery although it became obsolete in 1947.*

VALUE:

		Miniature
Edward VII (140)	£1000–1200	£80–90
George V KAISAR-I-HIND (3800)	£800–1200	£50–60
George V 2nd type (140)	£1250–1650	£50–60
George VI (1190)	£950–1350	£40–50

53. BURMA GALLANTRY MEDAL

Instituted: 10 May 1940.
Ribbon: Jungle green with a broad crimson stripe in the centre.
Metal: Silver.
Size: 36mm.
Description: (Obverse) the effigy of King George VI; (reverse) the words BURMA at the top and FOR GALLANTRY in a laurel wreath.
Comments: *As Burma ceased to be part of the Indian Empire in April 1937 a separate gallantry award was required for its armed services. The Burma Gallantry Medal was awarded by the Governor to officers and men of the Burma Army, frontier forces, military police, Burma RNVR and Burma AAF, although by an amendment of 1945 subsequent awards were restricted to NCOs and men. The medal became obsolete in 1947 when Burma became an independent republic and left the Commonwealth. Just over 200 medals and three bars were awarded, mainly for heroism in operations behind the Japanese lines.*

VALUE:
£3500–4500

Miniature
£15–20 for late example, contemporary example unknown

54. DISTINGUISHED SERVICE MEDAL

Instituted: 14 October 1914.
Ribbon: Dark blue with two white stripes towards the centre.
Metal: Silver.
Size: 36mm.
Description: (Obverse) the sovereign's effigy; (reverse) a crowned wreath inscribed FOR DISTINGUISHED SERVICE.
Comments: *Awarded to petty officers and ratings of the Royal Navy, NCOs and other ranks of the Royal Marines and all other persons holding corresponding ranks or positions in the naval forces, for acts of bravery in face of the enemy not sufficiently meritorious to make them eligible for the CGM. It was later extended to cover the Merchant Navy and Army, the WRNS and RAF personnel serving aboard ships in the Second World War. Of particular interest and desirability are medals awarded for outstanding actions, e.g. Jutland, Q-Ships, the Murmansk convoys, the Yangtze incident and the Falklands War. First World War bars for subsequent awards are dated on the reverse, but Second World War bars are undated. As a result of the 1993 Review of gallantry awards and resultant changes to the operational gallantry award system, this award has been replaced by the DSC which is now available both to officers and other ranks.*

VALUE:

		Miniature
George V uncrowned head 1914-30 (4100)	£800–1200	£20–25
George VI IND IMP 1938-49 (7100)	£800–1200	£15–20
George VI 2nd type 1949-53	£3000–4000	£30–40
Elizabeth II BR OMN 1953-7	£4000–5000	£8–10
Elizabeth II 2nd type	£3500–4500	£8–10

(in silver add £5)

55. MILITARY MEDAL

Instituted: 25 March 1916.
Ribbon: Broad dark blue edges flanking a central section of three narrow white and two narrow crimson stripes.
Metal: Silver.
Size: 36mm.
Description: (Obverse) the sovereign's effigy—six types; (reverse) the crowned royal cypher above the inscription FOR BRAVERY IN THE FIELD, enclosed in a wreath.
Comments: *Awarded to NCOs and men of the Army (including RFC and RND) for individual or associated acts of bravery not of sufficient heroism as to merit the DCM. In June 1916 it was extended to women, two of the earliest awards being to civilian ladies for their conduct during the Easter Rising in Dublin that year. Some 115,600 medals were awarded during the First World War alone, together with 5796 first bars, 180 second bars and 1 third bar. Over 15,000 medals were conferred during the Second World War, with 177 first bars and 1 second bar. About 300 medals and 4 first bars were awarded for bravery in minor campaigns between the two world wars, whilst some 932 medals and 8 first bars have been conferred since 1947. As a result of the 1993 Review of gallantry awards and resultant changes to the operational gallantry award system, this award has been replaced by the MC which is now available both to officers and other ranks.*

*Groups to RFC, RAF and RND will be considerably higher and obviously, medals with second (or more) award bars are also worth much more.

VALUE:

		Miniature
George V uncrowned head 1916-30		
Corps/RA—single	£300–400	£15–20
in group	£450–550*	
Regiment—single	£350–450	
in group	£750–1000	
named to a woman	£3000–3500	
unnamed as awarded to foreign recipients	£270–300	
George V crowned head 1930-38	£3000–5000	£70–100
George VI IND IMP 1938-48		
Corps	£1000–1250	£10–15
Regiment	£1500–2500	
unnamed as awarded to foreign recipients	£400–500	
George VI 2nd type 1948-53	£2500–3500	£25–40
Elizabeth II BR: OMN 1953-8	£3500–5000	£10–15
Elizabeth II 2nd type	£5000–7500	£10–15

(in silver add £5)

56. DISTINGUISHED FLYING MEDAL

Instituted: 1918.

Ribbon: Originally purple and white horizontal stripes but since July 1919 thirteen narrow diagonal stripes alternating white and purple.

Metal: Silver.

Size: 42mm tall; 34mm wide.

Description: An oval medal, (obverse) the sovereign's effigy; (reverse) Athena Nike seated on an aeroplane, with a hawk rising from her hand. Originally undated, but the date 1918 was added to the reverse with the advent of the George VI obverse. The medal is suspended by a pair of wings from a straight bar.

Comments: *Introduced at the same time as the DFC, it was awarded to NCOs and men of the RAF for courage or devotion to duty while flying on active operations against the enemy. During the Second World War it was extended to the equivalent ranks of the Army and Fleet Air Arm personnel engaged in similar operations. First World War medals have the names of recipients impressed in large seriffed lettering, whereas Second World War medals are rather coarsely engraved. Approximately 150 medals have been awarded since 1945. As a result of the 1993 Review of gallantry awards and resultant changes to the operational gallantry award system, this award has been replaced by the DFC which is now available both to officers and other ranks.*

Pre-1919

Post-1919

VALUE:		Miniature
George V uncrowned head 1918–30 (105)	£4500–6500	£18–20
George V crowned head 1930–38	£8000–12,000	£70–100
George VI IND IMP 1938–49 (6500)	£1750–2500	£10–12
George VI 2nd type 1949–53	£4000–5000	£25–40
Elizabeth II	£4000–6000	£10–12

(in silver add £5)

Example of WWI impressed naming

WWII engraved naming.

57. AIR FORCE MEDAL

Instituted: 1918.

Ribbon: Originally horizontal narrow stripes of white and crimson but since July 1919 diagonal narrow stripes of the same colours.

Metal: Silver.

Size: 42mm tall; 32mm wide.

Description: An oval medal with a laurel border. (Obverse) the sovereign's effigy; (reverse) Hermes mounted on a hawk bestowing a laurel wreath. The medal is suspended by a pair of wings from a straight bar, like the DFM.

Comments: *Instituted at the same time as the AFC, it was awarded to NCOs and men of the RAF for courage or devotion to duty while flying, but not on active operations against the enemy. About 100 medals and 2 first bars were awarded during the First World War, 106 medals and 3 bars between the wars and 259 medals during the Second World War. After the 1993 Review of gallantry awards the AFM was discontinued; the AFC is now available both to officers and other ranks.*

VALUE:

		Miniature
George V uncrowned head 1918–30	£1550–1850	£25–30
George V crowned head 1930–38	£3000–4000	£80–100
George VI IND IMP 1939–49	£2000–2750	£10–15
George VI 2nd type 1949–53	£2000–2750	£30–40
Elizabeth II	£2000–2500	£10–15

(in silver add £5)

Pre-1919

Post-1919

58. CONSTABULARY MEDAL (IRELAND)

1st type obv.

2nd type obv.

Instituted: 1842.
Ribbon: Originally light blue, but changed to green in 1872.
Metal: Silver.
Size: 36mm.
Description: (Obverse) a crowned harp within a wreath of oak leaves and shamrocks, with REWARD OF MERIT round the top and IRISH CONSTABULARY round the foot. In the first version the front of the harp took the form of a female figure but later variants had a plain harp and the shape of the crown and details of the wreath were also altered. These changes theoretically came in 1867 when the Constabulary acquired the epithet Royal, which was then added to the inscription round the top, although some medals issued as late as 1921 had the pre-1867 title. (Reverse) a wreath of laurel and shamrock, within which are engraved the recipient's name, rank, number, date and sometimes the location of the action.
Comments: *Originally awarded for gallantry and meritorious service by members of the Irish Constabulary. From 1872, however, it was awarded only for gallantry. It was first conferred in 1848 and became obsolete in 1922 when the Irish Free State was established. Bars for second awards were authorised in 1920. About 315 medals and 7 bars were awarded (or, in some cases, second medals—the records are inconclusive), mostly for actions in connection with the Easter Rising of 1916 (23) or the subsequent Anglo-Irish War of 1920 (180) and 1921 (55).*

VALUE:		Miniature
First type	£10000–15000	—
Second type	£10000–15000	£200–250

Original ribbon

Post-1872 ribbon

59. INDIAN POLICE MEDAL

1st type

2nd type (after 1944)

Instituted: 23 February 1932.
Ribbon: Crimson flanked by stripes of dark blue and silver grey. From 1942 onwards additional narrow silver stripes appeared in the centre of the blue stripe intended for the gallantry medal.
Metal: Bronze.
Size: 36mm.
Description: (Obverse) the King Emperor; (reverse) a crowned wreath inscribed INDIAN POLICE, with the words FOR DISTINGUISHED CONDUCT across the centre. In December 1944 the reverse was re-designed in two types, with the words FOR GALLANTRY or FOR MERITORIOUS SERVICE in place of the previous legend.
Comments: *Intended for members of the Indian police forces and fire brigades as a reward for gallantry or meritorious service. The medal became obsolete in 1948 when India became a republic.*

VALUE:

		Miniature
George V	£475–550	£35–45
George VI Distinguished Conduct	£475–575	£35–45
George VI for Gallantry	£575–775	£45–55
George VI for Meritorious Service	£425–525	£35–45

From 1942 for gallantry

60. BURMA POLICE MEDAL

Instituted: 14 December 1937.
Ribbon: A wide central blue stripe flanked by broad black stripes and white edges.
Metal: Bronze.
Size: 36mm.
Description: (Obverse) the effigy of George VI; (reverse) similar to the Indian medal (first type)and inscribed FOR DISTINGUISHED CONDUCT, irrespective of whether awarded for gallantry or distinguished service.
Comments: *Introduced following the separation of Burma from India, it was abolished in 1948. All ranks of the police, frontier force and fire brigades, both European and Burmese, were eligible.*

VALUE:		Miniature
For Gallantry (53)	£1500–2000	£40–50
For Meritorious Service (80)	£900–1200	£40–45

61. COLONIAL POLICE MEDAL

Instituted: 10 May 1938.
Ribbon: Blue with green edges and a thin silver stripe separating the colours, but the gallantry award had an additional thin red line through the centre of each green edge stripe.
Metal: Silver.
Size: 36mm.
Description: (Obverse) the sovereign's effigy; (reverse) a policeman's truncheon superimposed on a laurel wreath. The left side of the circumference is inscribed COLONIAL POLICE FORCES and the right either FOR GALLANTRY or FOR MERITORIOUS SERVICE.
Comments: *Intended to reward all ranks of the police throughout the Empire for acts of conspicuous bravery or for meritorious service. The number to be issued was limited to 150 in any one year. Only 450 were awarded for gallantry (with nine second award bars), whilst almost 3000 were issued for meritorious service.*

Ribbon for gallantry award

VALUE:		Miniature
George VI GRI for Gallantry	£800–1200	£40–50
George VI GRI for Meritorious Service	£350–450	£30–40
George VI GVIR for Gallantry	£800–1200	£40–50
George VI GVIR for Meritorious Service	£350–450	£30–40
Elizabeth II 1st type for Gallantry	£800–1200	£40–50
Elizabeth II 1st type for Meritorious Service	£350–450	£30–40
Elizabeth II 2nd type for Gallantry	£800–1200	£40–50
Elizabeth II 2nd type for Meritorious Service	£350–450	£30–40

62. COLONIAL FIRE BRIGADE MEDAL

Instituted: 10 May 1938.
Ribbon: As above.
Metal: Silver.
Size: 36mm.
Description: (Obverse) the effigy of the reigning sovereign; (reverse) a fireman's helmet and axe, with the inscription COLONIAL FIRE BRIGADES FOR GALLANTRY or FOR MERITORIOUS SERVICE.
Comments: *This medal was intended to reward all ranks of the Colonial fire brigades for gallantry or meritorious service but very few were awarded for gallantry.*

VALUE:		Miniature
George VI GRI for Gallantry	Rare	£40–50
George VI GRI for Meritorious Service	Rare	£30–40
George VI GVIR for Gallantry	Rare	£40–50
George VI GVIR for Meritorious Service	£300–500	£30–40
Elizabeth II 1st type for Gallantry	From £750	£40–50
Elizabeth II 1st type for Meritorious Service	£300–500	£30–40
Elizabeth II 2nd type for Gallantry	£600–800	£40–50
Elizabeth II 2nd type for Meritorious Service	£300–450	£30–40

63. QUEEN'S GALLANTRY MEDAL

Instituted: 20 June 1974.

Ribbon: Blue with a central pearl-grey stripe bisected by a narrow rose-pink stripe.

Metal: Silver.

Size: 36mm.

Description: (Obverse) the Queen's effigy; (reverse) an imperial crown above THE QUEEN'S GALLANTRY MEDAL flanked by laurel sprigs.

Comments: *Awarded for exemplary acts of bravery. Although intended primarily for civilians, it is also awarded to members of the armed forces for actions which would not be deemed suitable for a military decoration. With the introduction of the QGM the gallantry awards in the Order of the British Empire came to an end. To date, about 1,000 QGMs have been awarded, including 18 bars. A bar is added for a second award. A post-1990 SAS QGM and bar group sold at a recent auction for £26,000.*

VALUE:		Miniature
Service award	From £2500	£10–12
Civilian award	From £1500	

64. ALLIED SUBJECTS' MEDAL

Instituted: November 1920.

Ribbon: Bright red with a light blue centre, flanked by narrow stripes of yellow, black and white (thus incorporating the Belgian and French national colours).

Metal: Silver or bronze.

Size: 36mm.

Description: (Obverse) the effigy of King George V; (reverse) designed by C. L. J. Doman, the female allegory of Humanity offering a cup to a British soldier resting on the ground, with ruined buildings in the background.

Comment: *Shortly after the cessation of the First World War it was proposed that services rendered to the Allied cause, specifically by those who had helped British prisoners of war to escape, should be rewarded by a medal. The decision to go ahead was delayed on account of disagreement between the War Office and the Foreign Office, but eventually the first awards were announced in November 1920, with supplementary lists in 1921 and 1922. Medals were issued unnamed and almost half of the total issue, namely 56 silver and 247 bronze medals, were issued to women.*

VALUE:		Miniature
Silver (134)	£1000–1250	£40–50
Bronze (574)	£500–600	£45–55

NB These prices are for unattributable awards.

65. KING'S MEDAL FOR COURAGE IN THE CAUSE OF FREEDOM

Instituted: 23 August 1945

Ribbon: White with two narrow dark blue stripes in the centre and broad red stripes at the edges.

Metal: Silver.

Size: 36mm.

Description: (Obverse) the crowned profile of King George VI; (reverse) inscribed, within a chain link, THE KING'S MEDAL FOR COURAGE IN THE CAUSE OF FREEDOM.

Comments: *Introduced to acknowledge acts of courage by foreign civilians or members of the armed services "in the furtherance of the British Commonwealth in the Allied cause" during the Second World War. Like its First World War counterpart, it was intended mainly to reward those who had assisted British escapees in enemy-occupied territories. About 3200 medals were issued, commencing in 1947.*

VALUE: £250–300 (unattributable)   *Miniature* £30–40

101

66. KING'S MEDAL FOR SERVICE IN THE CAUSE OF FREEDOM

Instituted: 23 August 1945.
Ribbon: White with a central red stripe flanked by dark blue stripes.
Metal: Silver.
Size: 36mm.
Description: (Obverse) effigy of King George VI; (reverse) a medieval warrior in armour carrying a broken lance, receiving nourishment from a female.
Comments: *Introduced at the same time as the foregoing, it was intended for foreign civilians who had helped the Allied cause in other less dangerous ways, such as fund-raising and organising ambulance services. 2490 medals were issued.*

VALUE: £200–250 (unattributable)   *Miniature*   £15–20

67. SEA GALLANTRY MEDAL

Instituted: 1855, under the Merchant Shipping Acts of 1854 and 1894.
Ribbon: Bright red with narrow white stripes towards the edges.
Metal: Silver or bronze.
Size: 58mm or 33mm.
Description: (Obverse) Profile of Queen Victoria; (reverse) a family on a storm-tossed shore reviving a drowning sailor. Both obverse and reverse were sculpted by Bernard Wyon.
Comments: *Exceptionally, this group of medals was authorised not by Royal Warrant but by Parliamentary legislation, under the terms of the Merchant Shipping Acts of 1854 and 1894. The 1854 Act made provision for monetary rewards for life saving at sea, but in 1855 this was transmuted into medals, in gold, silver or bronze, in two categories, for gallantry (where the rescuer placed his own life at risk) and for humanity (where the risks were minimal). The gold medal, if ever awarded, must have been of the greatest rarity. These medals, issued by the Board of Trade, were 58mm in diameter and not intended for wearing. The only difference between the medals lay in the wording of the inscription round the circumference of the obverse. In 1903 Edward VII ordered that the medal be reduced to 1.27 inches (33mm) in diameter and fitted with a suspension bar and ribbon for wearing. Both large and small medals were always issued with a minimum of the recipient's name and date of rescue round the rim. The last medal was awarded in 1989 when it was superseded by the Queen's Gallantry Medal. Only one second award clasp has ever been issued—that to Ch.Off James Whiteley in 1921.*

VALUE:

	Silver	Bronze	*Miniature*
Victoria Gallantry	£550–650	£400–500	£100–150
Victoria Humanity (to 1893)	£850–1250	£1000–1500	
Edward VII Gallantry (large)	£1600–2000	£1450–1600	
Edward VII Gallantry (small)	£600–750	£550–650	£100–150
Edward VII (2nd small type)	£500–650	£450–550	
George V	£450–600	£350–450	£50–75
George VI 1st type	£1200–1500	—	
George VI 2nd type	—	—	
Elizabeth II	—	—	

68. SEA GALLANTRY MEDAL (FOREIGN SERVICES)

Type 4 rev.

Original ribbon

Post-1922 ribbon

Instituted: 1841.

Ribbon: Plain crimson till 1922; thereafter the same ribbon as the SGM above.

Metal: Gold, silver or bronze.

Size: 36mm or 33mm.

Description: The large medal had Victoria's effigy (young head) on the obverse, but there were five reverse types showing a crowned wreath with PRESENTED BY (or FROM) THE BRITISH GOVERNMENT inside the wreath. Outside the wreath were the following variants:

1. Individually struck inscriptions (1841-49 but sometimes later).
2. FOR SAVING THE LIFE OF A BRITISH SUBJECT (1849-54)
3. FOR ASSISTING A BRITISH VESSEL IN DISTRESS (1849-54)
4. FOR SAVING THE LIVES OF BRITISH SUBJECTS (1850-54)

There are also unissued specimens or patterns with a Latin inscription within the wreath VICTORIA REGINA CUDI JUSSIT MDCCCXLI.

The small medal, intended for wear, has five obverse types combined with four reverse types: as 2 above (1854-1906), as 3 above (1854-1918), as 4 above (1854-1926), or FOR GALLANTRY AND HUMANITY (1858 to the present day).

Comments: *Although intended to reward foreigners who rendered assistance to British subjects in distress some early awards were actually made for rescues on dry land. Originally a special reverse was struck for each incident, but this was found to be unnecessarily expensive, so a standard reverse was devised in 1849. Medals before 1854 had a diameter of 45mm and were not fitted with suspension. After 1854 the diameter was reduced to 33mm and scrolled suspension bars were fitted. Of the large medals about 100 gold, 120 silver and 14 bronze were issued, while some 10 gold and 24 bronze specimens have been recorded. The small bronze medal is actually the rarest of all, only six medals being issued.*

VALUE:	Gold	Silver	Bronze
Victoria large	—	£550–750	£450–550
Victoria small	£1500–1800	£300–450	—
Edward VII	£1500–2000	£450–550	—
George V	£1500–1800	£350–450	—
George VI	—	—	—
Elizabeth II	—	—	—
Miniature			£175–225

69. BRITISH NORTH BORNEO COMPANY'S BRAVERY CROSS

Instituted: 1890.

Ribbon: Gold (later yellow) watered silk 34mm.

Metal: Silver or bronze.

Size: 36mm.

Description: The cross pattée has a central medallion bearing a lion passant with the Company motto PERGO ET PERAGO (I carry on and accomplish) within a garter. The arms of the cross are inscribed BRITISH NORTH BORNEO with FOR BRAVERY in the lower limb. Three crosses have been recorded with the lower inscription for bravery omitted.

Comments: *Manufactured by Joseph Moore of Birmingham. The silver version bears the Birmingham hallmark for 1890. The reverse of the bronze medal is smooth. The cross was awarded for bravery in some 17 actions between 1883 and 1915, to the Company's Armed Constabulary Several of these actions involved fewer than 40 combatants, but at the other extreme 144 men took*

69. BRITISH NORTH BORNEO COMPANY'S BRAVERY CROSS *continued*

part in the major battle at Tambunan in 1900. Only five silver and four bronze crosses are known to have been awarded. Jemadar Natha Singh was the only officer to win both bronze (1892) and silver (1897). Examples with the word STERLING on the reverse are modern copies.

VALUE:

Silver	£750–1000	*Not known in miniature.*
Bronze	£400–500 (but much more in either case if attributable)	
Specimens/Copies	£100	

70. KING'S MEDAL FOR NATIVE CHIEFS

Instituted: 1920.
Ribbon: Yellow with two white central stripes (silver-gilt) or a single white stripe (silver).
Metal: Silver or silver-gilt.
Size: Oval 40mm x 34mm or circular 36mm x 32mm.
Description: Originally an oval badge with collar. (Obverse) the crowned effigy of the monarch; (reverse) a warship, symbolic of imperial power. The medals of Elizabeth II come in two versions: the original larger size with collar and the smaller size (1955) fitted with a plain ring for suspension from a yellow watered silk ribbon with or without a narrow central white stripe.

Comments: *Various large silver medals were struck for award to native chiefs in various parts of the world, from the eighteenth century onwards, and of these the awards to American Indian chiefs are probably the best known. In 1920, however, a standard King's Medal for Chiefs was instituted. It was awarded exceptionally in silver-gilt (first class), and usually in silver (second class). The oval medal was worn round the neck from a silver collar. The more modern issues, however, are smaller and intended for wear with a ribbon from the breast. The medal is normally returned on the death of the recipient.*

VALUE:	Silver-gilt	Silver
George V		
First (couped) type	£1000–1200	£700–800
Second (larger bust) type	£1000–1200	£650–750
George VI	£1000–1200	£600–700
Elizabeth II		
First type	£1000–1200	£600–700
Second (small) type	£350–400	£300–400

MENTIONS AND COMMENDATIONS

A description of the various emblems denoting Mentions in Despatches and King's (or later Queen's) Commendations was published as a Supplement to the London Gazette, July 27, 1951. A special emblem to signify a Mention in Despatches was instituted during the First World War and continued to be awarded for active service up to August 10, 1920. It was worn on the ribbon of the Victory Medal (no. 170) and consisted of a bronze spray of oak leaves.

For Mentions in Despatches after August 10, 1920, or a King's Commendation for Brave Conduct or Valuable Service in the Air, a bronze emblem consisting of a single oak leaf was worn on the appropriate medal ribbon, either a General Service Medal or the War Medal, 1939–45. King's or Queen's Commendations for Brave Conduct or Valuable Service in the Air, in cases where no campaign or war medal was awarded, were worn on the breast in the position where an appropriate medal ribbon would have been worn, generally on the uniform tunic after any medal ribbons.

King's or Queen's Commendations in respect of bravery, granted to civilians for acts during or since the Second World War, are denoted by a silver emblem in the form of a spray of laurel leaves (this was originally a plastic oval badge). The emblem was worn on the ribbon of the Defence Medal (no. 185) for bravery in situations earning the medal. Where no medal was awarded, it was sewn directly on to the coat. For civilians the King's or Queen's Commendation for Valuable Service in the Air, during the Second World War and subsequently, consisted of an oval silver badge, worn on the coat below any medals or medal ribbons, or in civil airline uniform, on the panel of the left breast pocket.

Since 2003 all MiD, QCB, QCBA and QCVS emblems may be worn on UK, UN, NATO or EC/EU medal ribbons.

Mention in Despatches emblem 1914–20

Mention in Despatches emblem 1920–94

King's Commendation for Brave Conduct plastic badge for civilians (1942–45).

King's Commendation for Valuable Service in the Air silver badge for civilians (1942–93).

The emblems for Mentions and Commendations were revised in 1994, as shown in the table below.

FOR GALLANTRY			FOR VALUABLE SERVICE
IN ACTION WITH THE ENEMY (ALL ENVIRONMENTS)	NOT IN ACTION WITH THE ENEMY or OUT OF THEATRE (EXCEPT FLYING)	NOT IN ACTION WITH THE ENEMY or OUT OF THEATRE (FLYING)	IN-THEATRE BUT NOT IN ACTION WITH THE ENEMY
MENTION IN DESPATCHES	QUEEN'S COMMENDATION FOR BRAVERY	QUEEN'S COMMENDATION FOR BRAVERY IN THE AIR	QUEEN'S COMMENDATION FOR VALUABLE SERVICE
A single oak leaf in SILVER	A spray of laurel leaves in SILVER	A new emblem in SILVER	A spray of oak leaves in SILVER

CAMPAIGN MEDALS

The evolution of medals struck to commemorate, and later to reward participants in, a battle or campaign was a very gradual process. The forerunner of the modern campaign medal was the Armada Medal, cast in gold or silver, which appears to have been awarded to naval officers and distinguished persons after the abortive Spanish invasion of 1588. The obverse bears a flattering portrait of Queen Elizabeth (thought to have been designed by Nicholas Hilliard, the celebrated miniaturist) with a Latin inscription signifying "enclosing the most precious treasure in the world" (i.e. the Queen herself). On the reverse, the safety of the kingdom is represented by a bay tree growing on a little island, immune from the flashes of lightning which seem to strike it. This medal, and a similar type depicting the Ark floating calmly on a stormy sea, bore loops at the top so that a chain or cord could be passed through it for suspension from the neck of the recipient.

The Civil War produced a number of gallantry medals, mentioned in the previous section; but in 1650 Parliament authorised a medal which was struck in silver, bronze or lead to celebrate Cromwell's miraculous victory over the Scots at Dunbar. This was the first medal granted to all the participants on the Parliamentary side, and not restricted to high-ranking officers, or given for individual acts of heroism.

The Dunbar Medal thus established several useful precedents, which were eventually to form the criteria of the campaign medal as we know it today. After this promising start, however, the pattern of medals and their issue were much more restrictive. Naval medals were struck in gold for award to admirals and captains during the First Dutch War (1650–53), while the battle of Culloden (1746) was marked by a medal portraying the "Butcher" Duke of Cumberland, and granted to officers who took part in the defeat of the Jacobites.

In the second half of the eighteenth century there were a number of medals, but these were of a private or semi-official nature. The Honourable East India Company took the lead in awarding medals to its troops. These medals were often struck in two sizes and in gold as well as silver, for award to different ranks. The siege of Gibraltar (1779–83) was marked by an issue of medals to the defenders, but this was made on the initiative (and at the expense) of the garrison commanders, Generals Eliott and Picton, themselves.

During the French Revolutionary and Napoleonic Wars several medals were produced by private individuals for issue to combatants. Alexander Davison and Matthew Boulton were responsible for the medals granted to the officers and men who fought the battles of the Nile (1798) and Trafalgar (1805). Davison also produced a Trafalgar medal in pewter surrounded by a copper rim; it is recorded that the seamen who received it were so disgusted at the base metal that they threw it into the sea! At the same time, however, Government recognition was given to senior officers who had distinguished themselves in certain battles and engagements and a number of gold medals were

awarded. The events thus marked included the capture of Ceylon (1795–96) and the battles of Maida, Bagur and Palamos.

Towards the end of the Napoleonic Wars an Army Gold Medal was instituted in two sizes—large (generals) and small (field officers). Clasps for second and third battles and campaigns were added to the medal, but when an officer became eligible for a third clasp the medal was exchanged for a Gold Cross with the names of the four battles engraved on its arms. Clasps for subsequent campaigns were then added to the cross (the Duke of Wellington receiving the Gold Cross with nine clasps). A total of 163 crosses, 85 large and 599 small medals was awarded, so that, apart from their intrinsic value, these decorations command very high prices when they appear in the saleroom.

The first medal awarded to all ranks of the Army was the Waterloo Medal, issued in 1816 shortly after the battle which brought the Napoleonic Wars to an end. No action was taken to grant medals for the other campaigns in the Napoleonic Wars until 1847 when Military and Naval General Service Medals were awarded retrospectively to veterans who were then still alive. As applications were made, in some cases, in respect of campaigns more than fifty years earlier, it is hardly surprising that the number of medals awarded was comparatively small, while the number of clasps awarded for certain engagements was quite minute. The Military General Service Medal was restricted to land campaigns during the Peninsular War (1808–13), the American War (1812–14) and isolated actions in the West Indies, Egypt and Java, whereas the Naval GSM covered a far longer period, ranging from the capture of the French frigate La Cleopatra by HMS Nymphe in June 1793, to the naval blockade of the Syrian coast in 1840, during the British operations against Mehemet Ali. Thus Naval Medals with the clasp for Syria are relatively plentiful (7057 awarded) while in several cases clasps were awarded to one man alone, and in seven cases there were no claimants for clasps at all. It is worth bearing in mind that applications for the medals and clasps resulted mainly from the publicity given by printed advertisements and notices posted up all over the country. With the poor general standard of literacy prevalent at the time, many people who were entitled to the medals would have been quite unaware of their existence.

The Naming of Medals

The Military and Naval GSMs, with their multitudinous combinations of clasps, have long been popular with collectors, but the other campaign medals of the past century and a half have a strong following as well. With the exception of the stars and medals awarded during the Second World War, all British campaign medals have usually borne the name of the recipient and usually his (or her) number, rank and regiment, unit or ship as well. This brings a personal element into the study of medals which is lacking in most other branches of numismatics. The name on a medal is very important for two reasons. It is a means of testing the genuineness, not only of the medal itself, but its bar combination, and secondly it enables the collector to link the medal not only with the man who earned it, but with his unit or formation, and thus plays a vital part in the development of naval or military history, if only a small part in most cases.

Much of the potential value of a medal depends on the man who won it, or the unit to which he belonged. To form a coherent collection as opposed to a random accumulation of medals, the collector would be well advised to specialise in some aspect of the subject, restricting his interests perhaps to one medal (the Naval GSM) or a single group (British campaigns in India), or to medals awarded to the men of a particular regiment. The information given on the rim or back of a medal is therefore important in helping to identify it and assign it to its correct place. Even this has to be qualified to some extent. Some regiments are more popular than others with collectors and much depends on the part, active or passive, played by a unit in a particular battle or campaign for which the medal was awarded. Then again, the combination of event with the corps or regiment of the recipient must also be considered.

At one extreme we find the Royal Regiment of Artillery living up to its motto Ubique (everywhere) by being represented in virtually every land action (and not a few naval actions, as witness the Atlantic Star worn by former Maritime Gunners), so that a comprehensive collection of medals awarded to the RA would be a formidable feat.

At the other extreme one finds odd detachments, sometimes consisting of one or two men only, seconded from a regiment for service with another unit. The Indian GSM, with clasp for Hazara (1891), is usually found named to personnel of the 11th Bengal Lancers and various battalions of the Bengal Infantry, but according to the medal rolls it was also given to six men of the 2nd Manchester Regiment, two men of the Queen's Regiment and one each to troopers of the 2nd and 7th Dragoon Guards. Whereas a specimen of the IGS medal with this bar is not hard to find named to a soldier in one of the Bengal units, it constitutes a major rarity when awarded to one of the "odd men" and its value is correspondingly high.

As the personal details given on a medal regarding the recipient are so important, it is necessary for the collector to verify two facts—that the person whose name is on the medal was actually present at the action for which either the medal or its bars were awarded, and secondly, that the naming of the bar and the attachment of the bars is correct and not tampered with in any way. As regards the first, the Public Record Office at Kew, London is a goldmine of information for all naval and military campaigns. Apart from despatches, reports and muster rolls covering the actions, there are the medal rolls compiled from the applications for medals and bars. Transcriptions of the medal rolls are held by regimental museums and also by such bodies as the Military Historical Association and the Orders and Medals Research Society. Details of these and other clubs and societies devoted to medal collecting can be found in the later chapters.

The presence of a name on the roll does not mean that a medal or clasp was inevitably awarded; conversely authenticated medals are known to exist named to persons not listed on the medal roll. There are often divergences between the muster and medal rolls. Moreover, discrepancies in the spelling of recipients' names are not uncommon and bars are sometimes found listed for regiments which were not even in existence when the battle was fought! This is explained, however, by the fact that a man may have been serving with one unit which took part in the campaign and subsequently transferred to another regiment. When claiming his medal he probably gave his present unit, rather than the one in which he was serving at the time of the action.

Unfortunately cases of medals having been tampered with are by no means rare, so it is necessary to be able to recognise evidence of fakery. A favourite device of the faker is to alter the name and personal details of the recipient and to substitute another name in order to enhance the medal's value. This is done simply by filing the inscription off the rim and adding a new one. In order to check for such alterations a similar medal of proven genuineness should be compared with a pair of fine callipers. Take the measurements at several points round the rim so that any unevenness should soon be apparent.

We cannot stress too much the importance of being closely familiar with the various styles of naming medals. Over the past 150 years an incredible variety of lettering—roman, italic, script, sans-serif, seriffed in all shapes and sizes—has been used at one time or another. In some cases the inscription was applied by impressing in raised relief; in others the inscription was punched in or engraved by hand. If a medal is normally impressed and you come across an engraved example you should immediately be on your guard. This is not an infallible test, however, as medals have been known with more than one style of naming, particularly if duplicates were issued at a much later date to replace medals lost or destroyed.

A rather more subtle approach was adopted by some fakers in respect of the Naval GSM. The three commonest clasps—Algiers (1362), Navarino (1137) and Syria (7057)—were awarded to many recipients possessing common names such as Jones or Smith which can be matched with recipients of some very rare clasps. In the case of the Naval GSM the ship on which the recipient served is not given, thus aiding the fraudulent substitution of clasps. It is necessary, therefore, to check the condition of clasps, even if the naming appears to be correct. Points to watch for are file or solder marks on the rivets which secure the clasps to each other and to the suspender of the medal. This test is not infallible as clasps do occasionally work loose if subject to constant wear (particularly if the recipient was a cavalryman, for obvious reasons). But clasps whose rivets appear to have been hammered should automatically be suspect, until a check of the medal rolls pass them as authentic. Examples of the earlier medals, particularly those awarded to officers may be found with unorthodox coupling. Major L. L. Gordon in his definitive British Battles and Medals, mentions a Naval GSM awarded to one of his ancestors with clasps for Guadaloupe and Anse la Barque in a large rectangular style which must have been unofficial. The medal is quite authentic, so it must be presumed that officers were allowed a certain degree of latitude in the manner in which they altered their medals.

Medals with clasps awarded for participation in subsequent engagements are invariably worth much more than the basic medal. In general, the greater number of clasps, the more valuable the medal, although, conversely, there are a few instances in which single-clasp medals are scarcer than twin-clasp medals. There is no short answer to this and individual rare clasps can enhance the value of an otherwise common medal out of all proportion. Thus the Naval GSM with clasp for Syria currently rates £350–400, but one of the two medals known to have been issued with the Acheron clasp of 1805 would easily rate twelve times as much. Again, relative value can only be determined by reference to all the circumstances of the award.

The person to whom a medal was issued has considerable bearing on its value. If the recipient belonged to a regiment which played a spectacular part in a battle, this generally rates a premium. The rank of the recipient also has some bearing; in general the higher the rank, the more valuable the medal. Medals to commissioned officers rate more than those awarded to NCOs and other ranks, and the medals of British servicemen rate more as a rule than those awarded to native troops. Medals granted to women usually command a relatively good premium. Another grim aspect is that medals issued to personnel who were wounded or killed in the campaign also rate more highly than those issued to servicemen who came through unscathed.

With the collector of British campaign medals the person to whom the medal was awarded tends to become almost as important as the medal itself. It is often not sufficient to collect the medal and leave it at that. The collector feels that he must investigate it and delve into the archives to find out all that he can about the recipient. The National Archives (Public Record Office) and regimental museums have already been mentioned, but do not overlook the usefulness of such reference tools as the monumental Mormon International Genealogical Index (now on microfiche

and available in good public libraries and county record offices). All of these should help you to flesh out the bare bones of the details given in the muster and medal rolls.

Medal Groups

Apart from the combination of clasps on a medal and the significance of the recipient, there is a third factor to be considered in assessing the value of medals, namely the relationship of one medal to another in a group awarded to one person. Just as the number of clasps on a medal is not in itself a significant factor, so also the number of medals in a group is not necessarily important per se. Groups of five or more medals, whose recipient can be identified, are by no means uncommon. For example, a fairly common five medal group would consist of 1914–15 Medal, War Medal and Victory Medal (for the First World War) and the Defence Medal and War Medal (for the Second World War). Thousands of men served throughout the first war to do duty, in a less active role, during a part at least of the second, long enough to qualify for the latter pair of medals.

It should be noted that none of the medals awarded for service in the Second World War was named to the recipient, so that groups comprising such medals alone cannot be readily identified and are thus lacking in the interest possessed by those containing named medals. Six-medal groups for service in the Second World War are not uncommon, particularly the combination of 1939–45 Star, Africa Star, Italy Star, France and Germany Star, Defence Medal and War Medal awarded to Army personnel who served from any time up to late 1942 and took part in the campaigns of North Africa and Europe.

Conversely it would be possible for troops to have served over a longer period and seen more action, and only been awarded the 1939–45 Star, Burma Star (with Pacific bar) and the War Medal. Naval groups consisting of the 1939–45 Star, Atlantic Star (with bar for France and Germany), Italy Star and War Medal are less common and therefore more desirable (with, of course, the rider that it must be possible to identify the recipient), while the most desirable of all is the three-medal group of 1939–45 Star (with Battle of Britain bar), Air Crew Europe Star (with bar for France and Germany) and the War Medal. Such a group, together with a Distinguished Flying Cross awarded to one of The Few, is a highly coveted set indeed, providing, as always, that one can prove its authenticity. In any event, the addition of a named medal to a Second World War group (e.g. a long service award, a gallantry medal, or some other category of medal named to the recipient), together with supporting collateral material (citations, log-books, pay-books, service records, newspaper cuttings, etc), should help to establish the provenance of the group.

The prices quoted in this publication are average figures for medals and decorations as individual items. Combinations with other decorations and campaign medals will produce a value usually well in excess of the aggregate of the individual items. Value will depend to a large extent on the personal factors and circumstances of the award, but where general factors are involved (e.g. the design of the medal, the period of issue or the campaign concerned, or in some cases the branch of the services) these are itemised separately. "—" indicates that either no examples have come onto the market or no examples have been issued. The figure in brackets (where available) is the approximate number awarded. Where the term RARE is used for a value this does not necessarily refer to the scarcity of the award in terms of numbers issued but rather their scarcity to market. It is possible that we have been able to ascertain prices for medals that were only issued in their tens as they regularly come up for sale whereas others, with higher issue numbers, haven't appeared on lists or at auction for some while and thus a true value has been difficult to obtain. Of course often the term will apply to those medals that rarely come up for sale simply because so few of them were issued!

71. LOUISBURG MEDAL

Date: 1758.
Campaign: Canada (Seven Years War).
Branch of Service: British Army and Navy.
Ribbon: 32mm half yellow, half blue, although not originally intended for wear and therefore not fitted with suspension or ribbon.
Metals: Gold, silver or bronze.
Size: 42mm.
Description: (Obverse) the globe surrounded by allegorical figures of victory and flanked by servicemen; (reverse) burning ships in the harbour.
Comments: *More in the nature of a decoration, this medal was only given to certain recipients for acts of bravery or distinguished service in the capture in July 1758 of Louisburg in Canada during the Seven Years War. James Wolfe and Jeffrey Amherst commanded the land forces and Edward Boscawen the fleet.*

VALUE:
Gold	Rare
Silver	£3000–4000
Bronze	£1500–2000

72. CARIB WAR MEDAL

Date: 1773.
Campaign: Carib rebellion, St Vincent.
Branch of Service: Local militia or volunteers.
Ribbon: None.
Metal: Silver.
Size: 52mm.
Description: (Obverse) bust of George III in armour; (reverse) Britannia offering an olive branch to a defeated Carib, the date MDCCLXXIII in the exergue.
Comments: *The Legislative Assembly of St Vincent in the West Indies instituted this award to members of the militia and volunteers who served in the campaign of 1773 which put down a native rebellion that had been fomented by the French.*

VALUE:
Silver	£1700–2000

73. DECCAN MEDAL

Date: 1784.
Campaign: Western India and Gujerat 1778-84.
Branch of Service: HEIC forces.
Ribbon: Yellow cord.
Metals: Gold or silver.
Size: 40.5mm or 32mm.
Description: (Obverse) a rather languid Britannia with a trophy of arms, thrusting a laurel wreath towards a distant fort. (Reverse) an inscription in Farsi signifying "As coins are current in the world, so shall be the bravery and exploits of these heroes by whom the name of the victorious English nation was carried from Bengal to the Deccan. Presented in AH 1199 [1784] by the East India Company's Calcutta Government".
Comments: *The first medals struck by order of the Honourable East India Company were conferred on Indian troops for service in western India and Gujerat under the command of Warren Hastings. They were struck at Calcutta in two sizes; both gold and silver exist in the larger size but only silver medals in the smaller diameter.*

VALUE:
40.5mm gold	£4000–6000
40.5mm silver	£1800–2000
32mm silver	£1400–1800

74. DEFENCE OF GIBRALTAR

Eliott's medal   Picton's medal

Date: 1783.

Campaign: Siege of Gibraltar 1779-83.

Branch of Service: British and Hanoverian forces.

Ribbon: None.

Metal: Silver.

Size: 59mm (Picton) and 49mm (Eliott).

Description: Eliott's medal was confined to the Hanoverian troops, hence the reverse inscribed
BRÜDERSCHAFT (German for "brotherhood") above a wreath containing the names of the three
Hanoverian commanders and General Eliott. The obverse, by Lewis Pingo, shows a view of the Rock and
the naval attack of 13 September 1782 which was the climax of the siege. Picton's medal, awarded to the
British forces, has a larger than usual diameter, with a map of the Rock on the obverse and a 22-line text—the
most verbose British medal—above a recumbent lion clutching a shield bearing the castle and key emblem of
Gibraltar on the reverse.

Comments: *Several medals of a private nature were struck to commemorate the defence of Gibraltar during the Franco-
Spanish siege of 1779–83, but those most commonly encountered are the silver medals which were provided by George
Augustus Eliott and Sir Thomas Picton, the military commanders.*

VALUE:

Picton medal	£1000–1200
Eliott medal	£700–1000

75. MYSORE MEDAL

Date: 1792.
Campaign: Mysore 1790-92.
Branch of Service: HEIC forces.
Ribbon: Yellow cord.
Metal: Gold or silver.
Size: 43mm or 38mm.
Description: (Obverse) a sepoy of the HEIC Army holding British and Company flags over a trophy of arms with the fortress of Seringapatam in the background; (reverse) a bilingual inscription (in English and Farsi). The medal has a ring for suspension round the neck by a cord.
Comments: *Indian officers and men who served under Marquis Cornwallis and Generals Abercromby and Meadows received this medal for service in the campaign which brought about the downfall of Tippoo Sultan of Mysore.*

VALUE:
43mm gold (subadars)	£6000–10000
43mm silver (jemadars)	£2500–2800
38mm silver (other ranks)	£1500–1800

76. ST VINCENTS BLACK CORPS MEDAL

Date: 1795.
Campaign: Carib rebellion 1795.
Branch of Service: Local militia volunteers.
Ribbon: None.
Metal: Bronze.
Size: 48.5mm.
Description: (Obverse) the winged figure of Victory brandishing a sword over a fallen foe who has abandoned his musket; (reverse) native holding musket and bayonet, BOLD LOYAL OBEDIENT around and H.G.FEC. in exergue.
Comments: *Awarded to the officers and NCOs of the Corps of Natives raised by Major Seton from among the island's slaves for service against the rebellious Caribs and French forces.*

VALUE:
Bronze	£1000–1200

77. CAPTURE OF CEYLON MEDAL

Date: 1796.
Campaign: Ceylon 1795.
Branch of Service: HEIC forces.
Ribbon: Yellow cord.
Metal: Gold or silver.
Size: 50mm.
Description: The plain design has an English inscription on the obverse, and the Farsi equivalent on the reverse.
Comments: *Awarded for service in the capture of Ceylon (Sri Lanka) from the Dutch during the French Revolutionary Wars. It is generally believed that the gold medals were awarded to Captains Barton and Clarke while the silver medals went to the native gunners of the Bengal Artillery.*

VALUE:
Gold (2)	—	
Silver (121)	£1500–2000 (original striking)	£400–500 (later striking)

78. DAVISON'S NILE MEDAL

Date: 1798.
Campaign: Battle of the Nile 1798.
Branch of Service: Royal Navy.
Ribbon: None, but unofficially 32mm, deep navy blue.
Metal: Gold, silver, gilt-bronze and bronze.
Size: 47mm.
Description: (Obverse) Peace caressing a shield decorated with the portrait of Horatio Nelson; (reverse) the
British fleet at Aboukir Bay. The edge bears the lettering "A TRIBUTE OF REGARD FROM ALEX^r DAVISON,
ESQ^r ST JAMES'S SQUARE=".
Comments: *Nelson's victory at the mouth of the Nile on 1 August 1798 was celebrated in a novel manner by his prize
agent, Alexander Davison, whose name and London address appear in the edge inscription of the medal designed by
Kuchler. Originally issued without a suspender, many recipients added a ring to enable the medal to be worn. Admiral
Nelson's medal was stolen in 1900 and is believed to have been melted down. Prices quoted below are for unnamed
specimens, contemporary engraved medals are usually worth about twice as much.*

VALUE:	Gold (Nelson and his captains)	£6000–8000		Gilt-bronze (petty officers)	£750–900
	Silver (junior officers)	£1500–2000		Bronze (ratings)	£300–400

79. SERINGAPATAM MEDAL

Date: 1808.
Campaign: Seringapatam, India, 1799.
Branch of Service: HEIC forces.
Ribbon: 38mm gold.
Metal: Gold, silver-gilt, silver, bronze and pewter.
Size: 48mm or 45mm.
Description: (Obverse) the British lion defeating Tiger of Mysore
(Tippoo Sultan) with the date of the capture of the fortress IV
MAY MDCCXCIX (1799) in the exergue; (reverse) the assault on
Seringapatam.
Comments: *The British and native troops who took part in the renewed
campaign against Tippoo Sultan were awarded this medal in 1808 in various
metals without suspension (a number of different types of suspenders and
rings were subsequently fitted by individual recipients). The medal was
designed by Kuchler and struck in England (48mm) and Calcutta, the latter
version being slightly smaller (45mm). There are several different strikings of
these medals.*

VALUE:

Gold 48mm (113)	£6000–8000
Silver-gilt 48mm (185)	£1200–1500
Silver 48mm (3636)	£950–1150
Bronze 48mm (5000)	£250–300
Pewter 48mm (45,000)	£250–300
Gold 45mm	£3000–4000
Silver 45mm	£750–850
Miniature	Silver £200–250

80. EARL ST. VINCENT'S MEDAL

Date: 1800.   **Campaign:** Mediterranean.
Branch of Service: Royal Navy.
Ribbon: None.
Metal: Gold or silver.   **Size:** 48mm
Description: (Obverse) left-facing bust of the Earl in Admiral's uniform; (reverse) a sailor and marine.
Comments: *A private medal presented by Earl St Vincent, when he struck his flag and came ashore in 1800, to the petty officers and men of his flagship* Ville de Paris *as a token of appreciation to his old shipmates. Contemporary engraved and named pieces with researched provenance are worth at least twice as much as unnamed specimens.*

VALUE:
Gold	£4500–6000
Silver	£450–650

81. EGYPT MEDAL 1801

Date: 1801.   **Campaign:** Egypt 1801.
Branch of Service: HEIC forces.
Ribbon: Yellow cord.
Metal: Gold or silver.   **Size:** 48mm.
Description: (Obverse) a sepoy holding a Union Jack, with an encampment in the background. A four-line Farsi text occupies the exergue; (reverse) a warship and the Pyramids.
Comments: *Issued by the Honourable East India Company to British and Indian troops in the Company's service who took part in the conquest of Egypt under Generals Baird and Abercromby.*

VALUE:
Gold (16)	—	
Silver (2200)	£1200–1400 (original striking)	£400–500 (later striking)

82. SULTAN'S MEDAL FOR EGYPT

Date: 1801.
Campaign: Egypt 1801.
Branch of Service: British forces.
Ribbon: The gold medals were originally suspended by gold hook and chain as shown. The silver medals were hung from a sand-coloured ribbon.
Metals: Gold or silver.
Size: Various (see below).
Description: The very thin discs have an elaborate arabesque border enclosing the *toughra* or sign manual of the Sultan.
Comments: *This medal was conferred by Sultan Selim III of Turkey on the British officers and NCOs who took part in the campaign against the French. It was produced in five gold versions for award to different ranks of commissioned officers, as well as one in silver for award to sergeants and corporals.*

VALUE:

Gold 54mm studded with jewels	—
Gold 54mm plain (less than 100 issued)	£5000–7000
Gold 48mm	£3500–4500
Gold 43mm	£4000–4500
Gold 36mm	£3500–4000
Silver 36mm	£2500–3500

Miniature

Gold	£150–200
Silver	£100–150

83. HIGHLAND SOCIETY'S MEDAL FOR EGYPT 1801

Date: 1801.
Campaign: Egypt 1801.
Branch of Service: British forces.
Ribbon: None.
Metals: Gold, silver and bronze.
Size: 49mm.
Description: The medal was designed by Pidgeon. (Obverse) the right-facing bust of General Sir Ralph Abercromby, with a Latin inscription alluding to his death in Egypt; (reverse) a Highlander in combat with the Gaelic inscription NA FIR A CHOISIN BUAIDH SAN EPHAIT(These are the heroes who achieved victory in Egypt) and the date 21 MAR 1801. On the edge is the inscription "On choumun Chaeleach D'on Fhreiceadan Dubh Na XLII RT" (From the London Highland Society to the Black Watch or 42nd Regt.).
Comments: *The Highland and Agricultural Society (now Royal) was founded in 1784 to promote the development of agriculture in Scotland generally and the Highlands in particular. General Abercromby (born at Tullibody, 1734) commanded the British expedition to Egypt, and the landing at Aboukir Bay on 2 March 1801 in the face of strenuous French opposition, is justly regarded as one of the most brilliant and daring exploits of all time. The French made a surprise attack on the British camp on the night of 21 March and Abercromby was struck by a ricochet; he died aboard the flagship seven days later. Medals in gold were presented to the Prince Regent and Abercromby's sons, but silver and bronze medals were later struck and awarded to senior officers of the expedition as well as soldiers who had distinguished themselves in the campaign.*

VALUE:

Gold	—
Silver	£600–800
Bronze	£250–300

84. BOULTON'S TRAFALGAR MEDAL

Date: 1805.
Campaign: Battle of Trafalgar 1805.
Branch of Service: Royal Navy.
Ribbon: None, but unofficially 32mm navy blue (originally issued without suspension).
Metals: Gold, silver, white metal, gilt-bronze or bronze.
Size: 48mm.
Description: (Obverse) bust of Nelson; (reverse) a battle scene.
Comments: *Matthew Boulton of the Soho Mint, Birmingham, struck this medal on his own initiative for presentation to the survivors of the battle of Trafalgar. It was awarded in white metal, but bronze and gilt-bronze specimens also exist. It was subsequently restruck on at least two occasions, the first and second strikings have the inscription impressed in large capitals around the rim TO THE HEROES OF TRAFALGAR FROM M:BOULTON, the last having the inscription omitted. As the original dies were used for each striking, they had to be polished before reuse, so the fine detail on Nelson's uniform and in the battle scene is less pronounced in the second and subsequent strikings. Examples of the original striking can sometimes be found engraved in various styles, but great care should be taken over checking the authenticity of such pieces. All gold specimens are restrikes. Silver medals were not awarded but were later ordered from Boulton or his descendants by officers who wished to have a medal to form a group with the 1848 NGS.*

VALUE:

Gold (c. 1905)	£2500–3500	Gilt-bronze	£500–700
Silver (1820–50)	£1500–1800	Bronze	£200–300
White metal	£400–600		

NB These prices are based on medals ssued from the original striking and are dependent on attribution and generally in EF to Mint condition.

85. DAVISON'S TRAFALGAR MEDAL

Date: 1805.
Campaign: Battle of Trafalgar 1805.
Branch of Service: Royal Navy.
Ribbon: None, but unofficially 32mm navy blue.
Metal: Pewter with a copper rim.
Size: 52mm.
Description: (Obverse) bust of Nelson; (reverse) a man-of-war with an appropriate biblical quotation from Exodus "The Lord is a Man-of-War".
Comments: *Alexander Davison, Nelson's prize agent, had this medal struck for award to the ratings of HMS* Victory *who took part in the battle.*

VALUE: £1200–1500

86. CAPTURE OF RODRIGUEZ, ISLE OF BOURBON AND ISLE OF FRANCE

Date: 1810.
Campaign: Indian Ocean 1809-10.
Branch of Service: HEIC forces.
Ribbon: Yellow cord.
Metal: Gold or silver.
Size: 49mm.
Description: (Obverse) a sepoy in front of a cannon with the Union Jack; (reverse) a wreath with inscriptions in English and Farsi.
Comments: *The East India Company awarded this medal to native troops of the Bengal and Bombay Armies for the capture of three French islands in the Indian Ocean (the latter two being better known today as Mauritius and Reunion) between July 1809 and December 1810.*

VALUE:	Original striking	Later striking
Gold (50)	£6000–8000	—
Silver (2200)	£2000–2500	£450–550

87. BAGUR AND PALAMOS MEDAL

Date: 1811.
Campaign: Peninsular War 1810.
Branch of Service: Royal Navy.
Ribbon: Red with yellow edges (illustration at right has faded ribbon).
Metal: Gold or silver.   **Size:** 45mm.
Description: (Obverse) the conjoined crowned shields of Britain and Spain in a wreath with ALIANZA ETERNA (eternal alliance) round the foot; (reverse) inscription in Spanish GRATITUDE OF SPAIN TO THE BRAVE BRITISH AT BAGUR 10 SEPT. 1810, PALAMOS 14 SEPT. 1810.
Comments: *Awarded by the Captain General of Catalonia to General Sir Charles Doyle and the Royal Marines and a limited number of officers and seamen from the British frigate* Cambrian, *for two actions on the coast of Catalonia in September 1810. Only awarded to those who actually went ashore: General Doyle, the Royal Marines, Captain Francis Fane and three of his officers received the medal for their participation in the attack on Bagur, while Lieutenant Benjamin Baynton and the launch crew received the medal for their participation at Palamós. Awarded in gold to officers and silver to other ranks.*

VALUE: **Gold (8)**   £6000–10,000   **Silver (72+)**   £800–1000

88. JAVA MEDAL

Date: 1811.
Campaign: Java 1811.
Branch of Service: HEIC forces.
Ribbon: Yellow cord.
Metals: Gold or silver.
Size: 49mm.
Description: (Obverse) the assault on Fort Cornelis; (reverse) inscriptions in English and Farsi.
Comments: *Awarded by the HEIC for the seizure of Java from the Dutch. The 750 British officers and men who took part in the operation were not only awarded this medal but were eligible for the Military GSM with Java clasp, issued 38 years later. Senior officers of the Company were given the gold medal, while junior officers, NCOs and sepoys received the silver version.*

VALUE:	Original striking	Later striking
Gold (133)	£8000–10,000	£3000–3500
Silver (6519)	£1200–1600	£400–500

89. NEPAUL MEDAL

Date: 1816.
Campaign: Nepal 1814-16.
Branch of Service: HEIC native troops.
Ribbon: Yellow cord.
Metal: Silver.
Size: 51mm.
Description: (Obverse) a fortified mountain-top with a cannon in the foreground; (reverse) Farsi inscription.
Comments: *This medal marked the campaign to pacify Nepal led by Generals Marley, Ochterlony and Gillespie (the last named being killed in action). At the conclusion of the war Ochterlony began recruiting Gurkha mercenaries, a policy which has continued in the British Army to this day. The clasp "Nepaul" was granted with the Army of India Medal to British forces in 1851.*

VALUE: Original striking £1800–2000   Later striking £450–500
(as illustrated)

90. CEYLON MEDAL

Date: 1818.
Campaign: Ceylon (Sri Lanka) 1818.
Branch of Service: British and HEIC forces.
Ribbon: 38mm deep navy blue.
Metal: Gold or silver.
Size: 35mm.
Description: The very plain design has "Ceylon 1818" within a wreath (obverse) and REWARD OF MERIT at top and bottom of the reverse, the personal details being engraved in the centre.
Comments: *Awarded by the Ceylon government for gallant conduct during the Kandian rebellion. Only selected officers and men of the 19th, 73rd and 83rd Foot, the 1st and 2nd Ceylon Regiments and 7th, 15th and 18th Madras Native Infantry received this medal.*

VALUE:

Gold (2)	—
Silver (45)	£2000–3000

91. BURMA MEDAL

Date: 1826.
Campaign: Burma 1824-26.
Branch of Service: HEIC native forces.
Ribbon: 38mm crimson edged with navy blue.
Metals: Gold or silver.
Size: 39mm.
Description: (Obverse) the Burmese elephant kneeling in submission before the British lion; (reverse) the epic assault on Rangoon by the Irrawaddy Flotilla.
Comments: *Granted to native officers and men who participated in the campaign for the subjugation of Burma. This was the first of the HEIC campaign medals in what was to become a standard 1.5 inch (38mm) diameter. The medal was fitted with a large steel ring for suspension and issued unnamed. British troops in this campaign were belatedly (1851) given the clasp "Ava" to the Army of India Medal.*

VALUE:

		Miniature
Gold (750)	£3500–4500	—
Silver-gilt	£1500–1800	—
Silver (24,000)	£1000–1200	£250–300

92. COORG MEDAL

Date: 1837.
Campaign: Coorg rebellion 1837.
Branch of Service: HEIC loyal Coorg forces.
Ribbon: Yellow cord.
Metals: Gold, silver or bronze.
Size: 50mm.
Description: (Obverse) a Coorg holding a musket, with kukri upraised; (reverse) weapons in a wreath with the inscription FOR DISTINGUISHED CONDUCT AND LOYALTY TO THE BRITISH GOVERNMENT COORG APRIL 1837, the equivalent in Canarese appearing on the obverse.
Comments: *Native troops who remained loyal during the Canara rebellion of April-May 1837 were awarded this medal by the HEIC the following August. Bronze specimens were also struck but not officially issued and may have been restrikes or later copies. Bronzed and silvered electrotype copies are also known.*

VALUE:	Original striking	Later striking
Gold (44)	£5000–8000	—
Silver (300)	£1500–1800	£400–500
Bronze	£300–400	—

93. NAVAL GOLD MEDAL

Date: 1795.
Campaign: Naval actions 1795-1815.
Branch of Service: Royal Navy.
Ribbon: 44mm white with broad dark blue edges.
Metal: Gold.
Size: 51mm and 38mm.
Description: The medals were glazed on both sides and individually engraved on the reverse with the name of the recipient and details of the engagement in a wreath of laurel and oak leaves. (Obverse) the winged figure of Victory bestowing a laurel wreath on the head of Britannia standing in the prow of a galley with a Union Jack shield behind her, her right foot on a helmet, her left hand holding a spear.
Comments: *Instituted in 1795, a year after Lord Howe's naval victory on "the glorious First of June", this medal was awarded continually till 1815 when the Order of the Bath was expanded into three classes. Large medals were awarded to admirals and small medals went to captains. As medals were awarded for separate actions it was possible for officers to wear more than one; Lord Nelson himself had three. Two miniatures are recorded and would probably fetch at least £1000 if they came onto the market.*

VALUE:

Large medal (22)	**From £80,000**	
Small medal (117)	**From £50,000**	*Miniature* £300–350

94. NAVAL GENERAL SERVICE MEDAL

Date: 1847.

Campaign: Naval battles and boat actions 1793-1840.

Branch of Service: Royal Navy.

Ribbon: 32mm white with dark blue edges.

Metal: Silver.

Size: 36mm.

Description: (Obverse) the Young Head profile of Queen Victoria by William Wyon; (reverse) Britannia with her trident seated on a sea horse.

Clasps: No fewer than 230 different clasps for major battles, minor engagements, cutting-out operations and boat service were authorised. These either have the name or date of the action, the name of a ship capturing or defeating an enemy vessel, or the words BOAT SERVICE followed by a date. No fewer than 20,933 medals were awarded but most of them had a single clasp. Multi-clasp medals are worth very considerably more. The greatest number of clasps to a single medal was seven (three awards made); four medals had six clasps and 26 medals had five clasps. For reasons of space only those clasps which are met with fairly often in the salerooms are listed below. At the other end of the scale it should be noted that only one recipient claimed the clasps for *Hussar* (17 May 1795), *Dido* (24 June 1795), *Spider* (25 August 1795), *Espoir* (7 August 1798), *Viper* (26 December 1799), *Loire* (5 February 1800), *Louisa* (28 October 1807), *Carrier* (4 November 1807), *Superieure* (10 February 1809), *Growler* (22 May 1812) and the boat actions of 15 March 1793, 4 November 1803, 4 November 1810 and 3-6 September 1814. In several cases no claimants came forward at all. The numbers of clasps awarded are not an accurate guide to value, as some actions are rated more highly than others, and clasps associated with actions in the War of 1812 have a very strong following in the USA as well as Britain. Clasps for famous battles, such as Trafalgar, likewise command a high premium out of all proportion to the number of clasps awarded. A medal to HMS *Victory* would be worth in excess of £15,000.

Comments: *Instituted in 1847 and issued to* **surviving** *claimants in 1848, this medal was originally intended to cover naval engagements of the French Revolutionary and Napoleonic Wars (1793-1815) but was almost immediately extended to cover all naval actions of a more recent date, down to the expedition to Syria in 1840. It was fitted with a straight suspender.*

VALUE (for the most commonly encountered clasps):

v.	1 June 1794 (583)	£3000–3500	cxxviii.	Guadaloupe (484)	£1200–1500
ix.	14 March 1795 (114)	£3000–3500	cxli.	Lissa (124)	£2500–3000
xv.	23 June 1795 (200)	£3000–3500	cxlvi.	Java (695)	£1500–1800
xxxi.	St Vincent (364)	£3000–3500	clxi.	Shannon wh Chesapeake (42)	£5000–6000
xxxiv.	Camperdown (336)	£3000–3500	clxiii.	St Sebastian (288)	£3000–3500
xxxvi.	Mars 21 April 1798 (26)	£5000–7000	clxv.	Gluckstadt 5 Jany 1814 (45)	£4000–5000
xxxviii.	Lion 15 July 1798 (23)	£5000–7000	clxxvi.	Gaieta 24 July 1815 (89)	£3000–3500
xxxix.	Nile (351)	£3500–4000	clxxvii.	Algiers (1,362)	£1300–1500
xli.	12 Octr 1798 (79)	£3500–4000	clxxviii.	Navarino (1,137)	£1200–1600
xlv.	Acre 30 May 1799 (50)	£4000–5000	clxxix.	Syria (7,057)	£700–800
lxii.	Egypt (618)	£1800–2000			
lxiii.	Copenhagen (545)	£3000–3500	**Boat Service**		
lxv.	Gut of Gibraltar (144)	£3000–4000	cxcii.	16 July 1806 (52)	£2500–3500
lxxv.	Trafalgar (1,710)	£6000–7500	ccvi.	1 Novr 1809 (110)	£2000–3000
lxxvi.	4 Novr 1805 (297)	£2500–3000	ccx.	28 June 1810 (27)	£3000–4000
lxxvii.	St Domingo (406)	£3000–3500	ccxxiii.	29 Sepr 1812 (25)	£3000–4000
lxxix.	London 13 March 1806 (27)	£4000–6000	ccxxvii.	8 Ap and May 1813 (57)	£3000–4000
lxxxv.	Curacao 1 Jany 1807 (67)	£3500–4500	ccxxviii.	2 May 1813 (48)	£3000–4000
xcvii.	Stately 22 March 1808 (31)	£4000–5000	ccxxix.	April 1814 (24)	£4000–5000
cxiii.	Martinique (506)	£1200–1600	ccxxx.	24 May 1814 (14)	£5000–6000
cxvii.	Basque Roads (551)	£2500–3000	ccxxxiii.	14 Decr 1814 (205)	£2000–2500

Miniature
  Without clasp   £100–150, for each clasp add £75+ depending on the action.

Below are listed all of the clasps authorised for wear on the Naval General Service Medal. As they were not issued until some years after the events, in some cases very few were ever claimed and in some instances there were no claimants at all. The numbers issued are indicated in brackets.

i.	Nymphe 18 June 1793 (4)		lxiv.	Speedy 6 May 1801 (7)
ii.	Crescent 20 Octr 1793 (12)		lxv.	Gut of Gibraltar 12 July 1801 (144)
iii.	Zebra 17 March1794 (2)		lxvi.	Sylph 28 Septr 1801 (2)
iv.	Carysfort 29 May 1794 (0)		lxvii.	Pasley 28 Octr 1801 (4)
v.	1 June 1794 (583)		lxviii.	Scorpion 31 March 1804 (4)
vi.	Romney 17 June 1794 (2)		lxix.	Beaver 31 March 1804 (0)
vii.	Blanche 4 Jany 1795 (5)		lxx.	Centurion 18 Septr 1804 (12)
viii.	Lively 13 March 1795 (6)		lxxi.	Arrow 3 Feby 1805 (8)
ix.	14 March 1795 (114)		lxxii.	Acheron 3 Feby 1805 (2)
x.	Astraea 10 April 1795 (2)		lxxiii.	San Fiorenzo 14 Feby 1805 (13)
xi.	Thetis 17 May 1795 (2)		lxxiv.	Phoenix 10 Aug 1805 (29)
xii.	Hussar 17 May 1795 (1)		lxxv.	Trafalgar (1,710)
xiii.	Mosquito 9 June 1795 (0)		lxxvi.	4 Novr 1805 (297)
xiv.	17 June 1795 (42)		lxxvii.	St. Domingo (406)
xv.	23 June 1795 (200)		lxxviii.	Amazon 13 March 1806 (30)
xvi.	Dido 24 June 1795 (1)		lxxix.	London 13 March 1806 (27)
xvii.	Lowestoffe 24 June 1795 (6)		lxxx.	Pique 26 March 1806 (8)
xviii.	Spider 25 August 1795 (1)		lxxxi.	Sirius 17 April 1806 (20)
xix.	Port Spergui (4)		lxxxii.	Blanche 19 July 1806 (22)
xx.	Indefatigable 20 April 1796 (8)		lxxxiii.	Arethusa 23 Aug 1806 (17)
xxi.	Unicorn 8 June 1796 (4)		lxxxiv.	Anson 23 Aug 1806 (11)
xxii.	Santa Margarita 8 June 1796 (3)		lxxxv.	Curacoa 1 Jany 1807 (67)
xxiii.	Southampton 9 June 1796 (8)		lxxxvi.	Pickle 3 Jany 1807 (2)
xxiv.	Dryad 13 June 1796 (6)		lxxxvii.	Hydra 6 Aug 1807 (12)
xxv.	Terpsichore 13 Oct 1796 (3)		lxxxviii.	Comus 15 Aug 1807 (9)
xxvi.	Lapwing 3 Decr 1796 (2)		lxxxix.	Louisa 28 Octr 1807 (1)
xxvii.	Minerve 19 Decr 1796 (4)		xc.	Carrier 4 Novr 1807 (1)
xxviii.	Blanche 19 Decr 1796 (4)		xci.	Ann 24 Novr 1807 (0)
xxix.	Indefatigable 13 Jany 1797 (8)		xcii.	Sappho 2 March 1808 (4)
xxx.	Amazon 13 Jany 1797 (6)		xciii.	San Fiorenzo 8 March 1808 (17)
xxxi.	St Vincent (364)		xciv.	Emerald 13 March 1808 (10)
xxxii.	San Fiorenzo 8 March 1797 (8)		xcv.	Childers 14 March 1808 (4)
xxxiii.	Nymphe 8 March 1797 (5)		xcvi.	Nassau 22 March 1808 (31)
xxxiv.	Camperdown (336)		xcvii.	Stately 22 March 1808 (31)
xxxv.	Phoebe 21 Decr 1797 (5)		xcviii.	Off Rota 4 April 1808 (19)
xxxvi.	Mars 21 April 1798 (26)		xcix.	Grasshopper 24 April 1808 (7)
xxxvii.	Isle St. Marcou (3)		c.	Rapid 24 April 1808 (1)
xxxviii.	Lion 15 July 1798 (23)		ci.	Redwing 7 May 1808 (7)
xxxix.	Nile (351)		cii.	Virginie 19 May 1808 (21)
xl.	Espoir 7 Aug 1798 (1)		ciii.	Redwing 31 May 1808 (7)
xli.	12 Octr 1798 (79)		civ.	Seahorse wh Badere Zaffer (32)
xlii.	Fisgard 20 Octr 1798 (9)		cv.	Comet 11 Aug 1808 (4)
xliii.	Sybille 28 Feby 1799 (12)		cvi.	Centaur 26 Aug 1808 (42)
xliv.	Telegraph 18 March 1799 (0)		cvii.	Implacable 26 Aug 1808 (44)
xlv.	Acre 30 May 1799 (50)		cviii.	Cruizer 1 Novr 1808 (4)
xlvi.	Schiermonnikoog 12 Aug 1799 (9)		cix.	Amethyst wh Thetis (31)
xlvii.	Arrow 13 Sept 1799 (2)		cx.	Off the Pearl Rock 13 Decr 1808 (16)
xlviii.	Wolverine 13 Sept 1799 (0)		cxi.	Onyx 1 Jany 1809 (5)
xlix.	Surprise wh Hermione (7)		cxii.	Confiance 14 Jany 1809 (8)
l.	Speedy 6 Novr 1799 (3)		cxiii.	Martinique (506)
li.	Courier 22 Novr 1799 (3)		cxiv.	Horatio 10 Feby 1809 (13)
lii.	Viper 26 Decr 1799 (2)		cxv.	Supérieure 10 Feby 1809 (1)
liii.	Harpy 5 Feby 1800 (4)		cxvi.	Amethyst 5 April 1809 (27)
liv.	Fairy 5 Feby 1800 (4)		cxvii.	Basque Roads 1809 (551)
lv.	Peterel 21 March 1800 (2)		cxviii.	Recruit 17 June 1809 (7)
lvi.	Penelope 30 March 1800 (11)		cxix.	Pompee 17 June 1809 (47)
lvii.	Vinciego 30 March 1800 (2)		cxx.	Castor 17 June 1809 (13)
lviii.	Capture of the Désirée (24)		cxxi.	Cyane 25 and 27 June 1809 (5)
lix.	Seine 20 August 1800 (7)		cxxii.	L'Espoir 25 and 27 June 1809 (5)
lx.	Phoebe 19 Feby 1801 (6)		cxxiii.	Bonne Citoyenne wh Furieuse (12)
lxi.	Egypt (618)		cxxiv.	Diana 11 Septr 1809 (8)
lxii.	Copenhagen 1801 (545)		cxxv.	Anse la Barque 18 Decr 1809 (51)

cxxvi.	Cherokee 10 Jany 1810 (4)
cxxvii.	Scorpion 12 Jany 1810 (8)
cxxviii.	Guadaloupe (484)
cxxix.	Thistle 10 Feby 1810 (0)
cxxx.	Surly 24 April 1810 (1)
cxxxi.	Firm 24 April 1810 (1)
cxxxii.	Sylvia 26 April 1810 (1)
cxxxiii.	Spartan 3 May 1810 (30)
cxxxiv.	Royalist May and June 1810 (3)
cxxxv.	Amanthea 25 July 1810 (23)
cxxxvi.	Banda Neira (68)
cxxxvii.	Staunch 18 Septr 1810 (2)
cxxxviii.	Otter 18 Septr 1810 (8)
cxxxix.	Boadicea 18 Septr 1810 (15)
cxl.	Briseis 14 Octr 1810 (2)
cxli.	Lissa (124)
cxlii.	Anholt 27 March 1811 (40)
cxliii.	Arrow 6 April 1811 (0)
cxliv.	Off Tamatave 20 May 1811 (87)
cxlv.	Hawke 18 Aug 1811 (6)
cxlvi.	Java (695)
cxlvii.	Skylark 11 Novr 1811 (4)
cxlviii.	Locust 11 Novr 1811 (2)
cxlix.	Pelagosa 29 Novr 1811 (74)
cl.	Victorious wh Rivoli (67)
cli.	Weasel 22 Feby 1812 (6)
clii.	Rosario 27 March 1812 (7)

cliii.	Griffon 27 March 1812 (3)
cliv.	Northumberland 22 May 1812 (63)
clv.	Growler 22 May 1812 (1)
clvi.	Malaga 29 May 1812 (18) (the date should have been 29 April 1812)
clvii.	Off Mardoe 6 July 1812 (47)
clviii.	Sealark 21 July 1812 (4)
clix.	Royalist 29 Decr 1812 (4)
clx.	Weasel 22 April 1813 (8)
clxi.	Shannon wh Chesapeake (42)
clxii.	Pelican 14 Aug 1813 (4)
clxiii.	St. Sebastian (288)
clxiv.	Thunder 9 Octr 1813 (9)
clxv.	Gluckstadt 5 Jany 1814 (45)
clxvi.	Venerable 16 Jany 1814 (42)
clxix.	Cyane 16 Jany 1814 (7)
clxx.	Eurotas 25 Feby 1814 (32)
clxxi.	Hebrus wh L'Etoile (40)
clxxii.	Phoebe 28 March 1814 (36)
clxxiii.	Cherub 28 March 1814 (7)
clxxiv.	The Potomac 17 Aug 1814 (108)
clxxv.	Endymion wh President (58)
clxxvi.	Gaieta 24 July 1815 (89)
clxxvii.	Algiers (1,362)
clxxviii.	Navarino (1,137)
clxxix.	Syria (7,057)

BOAT SERVICE

These clasps have the words BOAT SERVICE separating the month and the years of the dates. They were only awarded for actions which culminated in an officer or the senior member present being promoted.

clxxx.	15 March 1793 (1)
clxxxi.	17 March 1794 (29)
clxxxii.	29 May 1797 (3)
clxxxiii.	9 June 1799 (4)
clxxxiv.	20 Decr 1799 (3)
clxxxv.	29 July 1800 (4)
clxxxvi.	29 Aug 1800 (25)
clxxxvii.	27 Octr 1800 (5)
clxxxvii.	21 July 1801 (7)
clxxxviii.	27 June 1803 (5)
clxxxix.	4 Novr 1803 (2)
cxc.	4 Feby 1804 (11)
cxci.	4 June 1805 (10)
cxcii.	16 July 1806 (52)
cxciii.	2 Jan 1807 (3)
cxciv.	21 Jan 1807 (8)
cxcv.	19 April 1807 (0)
cxcvi.	13 Feby 1808 (2)
cxcvii.	10 July 1808 (8)
cxcviii.	11 Aug 1808 (17)
cxcix.	28 Novr 1808 (2)
cc.	7 July 1809 (35)
cci.	14 July 1809 (7)
ccii.	25 July 1809 (36)
cciii.	27 July 1809 (10)
cciv.	29 July 1809 (11)
ccv.	28 Aug 1809 (15)
ccvi.	1 Novr 1809 (100)

ccvii.	13 Decr 1809 (9)
ccviii.	13 Feby 1810 (20)
ccix.	1 May 1810 (15)
ccx.	28 June 1810 (27)
ccxi.	27 Sept 1810 (36)
ccxii.	4 Novr 1810 (1)
ccxiii.	23 Novr 1810 (42)
ccxiv.	24 Decr 1810 (6)
ccxv.	4 May 1811 (10)
ccxvi.	30 July 1811 (4)
ccxvii.	2 Aug 1811 (9)
ccxviii.	20 Sept 1811 (6)
ccxix.	4 Decr 1811 (19)
ccxx.	4 April 1812 (4)
ccxxi.	1st Sept 1812 (21)
ccxxii.	17 Sept 1812 (11) (Bars are known dated 17 Decr 1812 in error)
ccxxiii.	29 Sept 1812 (25)
ccxxiv.	6 Jany 1813 (25)
ccxxv.	21 March 1813 (3)
ccxxvi.	29 April 1813 (2)
ccxxvii.	Ap and May 1813 (51)
ccxxviii.	2 May 1813 (48)
ccxxix.	8 April 1814 (24)
ccxxx.	24 May 1814 (14)
ccxxxi.	Aug and Septr 1814 (1)
ccxxxii.	3 and 6 Septr 1814 (1)
ccxxxiii.	14 Decr 1814 (205)

95. ARMY GOLD CROSS

Date: 1813.
Campaigns: Peninsular War and War of 1812.
Branch of Service: British Army.
Ribbon: 38mm crimson edged with dark blue.
Metal: Gold. **Size:** 38mm.
Description: A cross pattée with a laurel border having a rose at
the centre on each of the four flat ends. At the centre of the cross
appears a British lion statant. The scrolled top of the cross is fitted
with an elaborate ring decorated with laurel leaves looped through
a plain swivel ring fitted to the suspender. The arms of the cross on
both obverse and reverse bear the names of four battles in relief.
Clasps: Large borders of laurel leaves enclosing the name of a battle
in raised relief within an elliptical frame, awarded for fifth and
subsequent battles.
Comments: *Arguably the most prestigious award in the campaign series,
the Army Gold Cross was approved by the Prince Regent in 1813. It was
granted to generals and officers of field rank for service in four or more
battles of the Peninsular War. Three crosses had six clasps, two had seven,
while the Duke of Wellington himself had the unique cross with nine
clasps, representing participation in thirteen battles.*

VALUE:

Gold cross without clasp (61)	From £25,000
Miniature	£450–550

96. MAIDA GOLD MEDAL

Date: 1806.
Campaign: Peninsular War, Battle of Maida 1806.
Branch of Service: British Army.
Ribbon: 38mm crimson edged with navy blue.
Metal: Gold.
Size: 39mm.
Description: (Obverse) laureated profile of George III; (reverse) winged figure of Victory hovering with a laurel wreath over the head of Britannia, shield upraised, in the act of throwing a spear. The name and date of the battle appears on Britannia's left, with the *trinacria* or three-legged emblem on the right.
Clasps: None.
Comments: *This small gold medal was authorised in 1806 and awarded to the thirteen senior officers involved in the battle of Maida in Calabria when a small British force under General Sir John Stuart defeated a much larger French army with heavy loss. A small unknown number of gold and silver specimens are known to exist.*

VALUE: from £45,000

97. ARMY GOLD MEDAL

Date: 1810.
Campaigns: Peninsular War 1806-14 and War of 1812.
Branch of Service: British Army.
Ribbon: 38mm crimson edged with navy blue.
Metal: Gold.
Size: 54mm and 33mm.
Description: (Obverse) Britannia seated on a globe, holding a laurel wreath over the British lion and holding a palm branch in her left hand while resting on a shield embellished with the Union Jack. The name of the first action is generally engraved on the reverse.
Clasps: For second and third actions.
Comments: *The Maida medal (no. 96) established a precedent for the series of medals instituted in 1810. The name of the battle was inscribed on the reverse, usually engraved, though that for Barossa was die-struck. These medals were struck in two sizes, the larger being conferred on generals and the smaller on officers of field rank. Second or third battles were denoted by a clasp appropriately inscribed, while those who qualified for a fourth award exchanged their medal and bars for a gold cross. The award of these gold medals and crosses ceased in 1814 when the Companion of the Bath was instituted.*

VALUE*:
Large medal	£25,000–35,000
Small medal	£12,000–18,000

***Medals to British officers in the Portuguese Service generally sell for 20% less. Only one miniature is known to exist.**

98. MILITARY GENERAL SERVICE MEDAL

Date: 1847.

Campaigns: French Revolutionary and Napoleonic Wars 1793-1814.

Branch of Service: British Army.

Ribbon: 31mm crimson edged with dark blue.

Metal: Silver.

Size: 36mm.

Description: (Obverse) the Wyon profile of Queen Victoria; (reverse) a standing figure of the Queen bestowing victor's laurels on a kneeling Duke of Wellington. The simple inscription TO THE BRITISH ARMY appears round the circumference, while the dates 1793-1814 are placed in the exergue. Despite this, the earliest action for which a clasp was issued took place in 1801 (Abercromby's Egyptian campaign).

Clasps: Only 29 battle or campaign clasps were issued but multiple awards are much more common than in the naval medal, the maximum being fifteen. While it is generally true to say that multi-clasp medals are worth more than single-clasp medals, there are many in the latter category (noted below) which command higher prices. The figures quoted below are based on the commonest regiments. Clasps awarded to specialists and small detached forces rate more highly than medals to the principal regiment in a battle or campaign. In particular, it should be noted that one naval officer, Lieut. Carroll, received the Military GSM and clasp for Maida, while a few other officers of the Royal Navy and Royal Marines received the medal with the clasps for Guadaloupe, Martinique or Java, and these, naturally, are now very much sought after. Paradoxically, the clasps for Sahagun and Benevente alone are very much scarcer than the clasp inscribed Sahagun and Benevente, awarded to surviving veterans who had participated in both battles. The clasps are listed below in chronological order. Medals to officers rate a premium.

Comments: *Like the Naval GSM, this medal was not sanctioned till 1847 and awarded the following year. Unlike the Naval medal, however, the Military GSM was confined to land actions up to the defeat of Napoleon in 1814 and the conclusion of the war with the United States. The regiment is now having a bearing on price, with medals to the 52nd, 88th or 95th Foot worth a good premium.*

VALUE:

i.	Egypt	£900–1250	xxi.	Chateauguay	£3250–4000
ii.	Maida	£1300–1550	xxii.	Chrystler's Farm	£3250–4000
iii.	Roleia	£955–1150	xxiii.	Vittoria	£800–900
iv.	Vimiera	£900–1000	xxiv.	Pyrenees	£900–1000
v.	Sahagun	£1750–2000	xxv.	St Sebastian	£900–1000
vi.	Benevente	£4500–6000	xxvi.	Nivelle	£900–1000
vii.	Sahagun and Benevente	£1750–2000	xxvii.	Nive	£750–850
viii.	Corunna	£800–900	xxviii.	Orthes	£750–850
ix.	Martinique	£800–900	xxix.	Toulouse	£850–1000
x.	Talavera	£800–900	2 clasps		£1000–1250
xi.	Guadaloupe	£900–1100	3 clasps		£1100–1250
xii.	Busaco	£900–1100	4 clasps		£1500–1750
xiii.	Barrosa	£900–1100	5 clasps		£1700–2000
xiv.	Fuentes D'Onor	£900–1100	6 clasps		£2000–2400
xv.	Albuhera	£950–1250	7 clasps		£2200–2600
xvi.	Java	£900–1000	8 clasps		£2600–3000
xvii.	Ciudad Rodrigo	£1000–1250	9 clasps		£3000–3600
xviii.	Badajoz	£1000–1300	10 clasps		£3400–4000
xix.	Salamanca	£900–1000	11 clasps		£3800–4600
xx.	Fort Detroit	£3000–3500	12 or more clasps		From £5000

Miniature **without clasp** £100–150, for each clasp add £75+ depending on the action.

99. WATERLOO MEDAL

Date: 1815.

Campaign: Waterloo 1815.

Branch of Service: British Army.

Ribbon: 38mm, crimson edged in dark blue.

Metal: Silver.

Size: 37mm.

Description: (Obverse) the profile of the Prince Regent; (reverse) the seated figure of Victory above a tablet simply inscribed WATERLOO with the date of the battle in the exergue.

Comments: *This was the first medal awarded and officially named to all ranks who took part in a particular campaign. It was also issued, however, to those who had taken part in one or more of the other battles of the campaign, at Ligny and Quatre Bras two days earlier. The ribbon was intended to be worn with an iron clip and split suspension ring but many recipients subsequently replaced these with a more practical silver mount which would not rust and spoil the uniform. Some 39,000 medals were issued. The value of a Waterloo medal depends to a large extent on the regiment of the recipient. Medals awarded to those formations which saw the heaviest action and bore the brunt of the losses are in the greatest demand, whereas medals named to soldiers in General Colville's reserve division which did not take part in the fighting, are the least highly rated.*

VALUE:

Heavy Cavalry	£2500–3000
Scots Greys	£3500–4000
Light Cavalry	£2500–3500
Royal Artillery	£1000–1500
Royal Horse Artillery	£1300–2000
Foot Guards	£1500–2500
1st, 27th, 28th, 30th, 42nd, 44th, 52nd, 73rd, 79th, 92nd, 95th Foot	£2500–3500
Other Foot regiments	£1500–2000
Colville's division (35th, 54th, 59th, 91st Foot)	£1200–1500
King's German Legion	£1200–1500

Miniature

Original	£50–200
Modern copy	£5–10

100. BRUNSWICK MEDAL FOR WATERLOO

Date: 1817.

Campaign: Battle of Waterloo 1815.

Branch of Service: Brunswick troops.

Ribbon: Cream with light blue stripes towards the edges.

Metal: Bronze.

Size: 35mm.

Description: (Obverse) Duke Friedrich Wilhelm of Brunswick who was killed in the battle; (reverse) a wreath of laurel and oak leaves enclosing the German text "Braunschweig Seinen Kriegern" (Brunswick to its warriors) and the names of Quatre Bras and Waterloo.

Comments: *The Prince Regent authorised this medal for issue to the contingent from the Duchy of Brunswick.*

VALUE:	£350–400
	Casualty £2000–2500
Miniature	Modern copy £5–10

101. HANOVERIAN MEDAL FOR WATERLOO

Date: 1818.
Campaign: Battle of Waterloo 1815.
Branch of Service: Hanoverian troops.
Ribbon: Crimson edged with light blue.
Metal: Silver.
Size: 35mm.
Description: (Obverse) the Prince Regent, his name and title being rendered in German. (Reverse) a trophy of arms below the legend HANNOVERISCHER TAPFERKEIT (Hanoverian bravery), with the name and date of the battle wreathed in the centre.
Comments: *The Prince Regent authorised this medal on behalf of his father George III in his capacity as Elector of Hanover and this was conferred on survivors of the battle. Suspension was by iron clip and ring similar to the British Waterloo Medal.*

VALUE:	£500–600
Miniature	£100–150
Modern copy	£5–10

102. NASSAU MEDAL FOR WATERLOO

Date: 1815.
Campaign: Battle of Waterloo 1815.
Branch of Service: Nassau forces.
Ribbon: Dark blue edged in yellow.
Metal: Silver.
Size: 28mm.
Description: (Obverse) Duke Friedrich of Nassau; (reverse) the winged figure of Victory crowning a soldier with laurels, the date of the action being in the exergue.
Comments: *Friedrich Duke of Nassau distributed this medal on 23 December 1815 to all of his own troops who had been present at the battle.*

VALUE: £300–400

103. SAXE-GOTHA-ALTENBURG MEDAL

Date: 1816.
Campaign: Germany and Waterloo 1814-15.
Branch of Service: Saxe-Gotha-Altenburg Foreign Legion.
Ribbon: Green with black edges and gold stripes.
Metal: Gilt bronze or bronze.
Size: 42mm.
Description: (Obverse) a crown with the legend IM KAMPFE FUER DAS RECHT (in the struggle for the right); (reverse) an ornate rose motif with the name of the duchy and the dates of the campaign in roman numerals.
Comments: *Gilded medals were issued to officers, NCOs received bronze medals with gilt raised points and other ranks a bronze version.*

VALUE:
Gilt-bronze	£400–450
Bronze	£300–350

104. ARMY OF INDIA MEDAL

Date: 1851.
Campaigns: India 1803–26.
Branch of Service: British and HEIC troops.
Ribbon: 32mm pale blue.
Metal: Silver.
Size: 35mm.
Description: (Obverse) the Wyon profile of Queen Victoria; (reverse) the seated figure of Victory beside a palm tree, with a wreath in one hand and a laurel crown in the other. The medal is fitted with an ornamental scroll suspender.
Clasps: The medal was not awarded without a campaign clasp and, unusually, in multi-clasp medals, the last clasp awarded was mounted closest to the medal itself, so that the battle roll has to be read downwards. There were two dies of the reverse, leading to the long- or short-hyphen varieties, both of comparable value. In all, some 4500 medals were awarded, but there is a very wide divergence between the commonest and rarest bars. Multi-clasp medals are rare, and medals awarded to Europeans are much scarcer than those to Indian troops.
Comments: *The last of the medals authorised in connection with the Napoleonic Wars, it was instituted and paid for by the Honourable East India Company in March 1851 for award to surviving veterans of the battles and campaigns in India and Burma between 1803 and 1826. Despite the dates 1799–1826 in the exergue, the medal was in fact awarded for service in one or other of four wars: the Second Mahratta War (1803–4), the Nepal War (1814–16), the Pindaree or Third Mahratta War (1817–18) and the Burmese War (1824–26), together with the siege of Bhurtpoor (1825–26). The medal is scarce, and examples with the clasps for the Second Mahratta War are much sought after, partly because few veterans were still alive 48 years after the event to claim their medals, and partly because of the war's association with Arthur Wellesley, the Duke of Wellington, who died in the very year in which the medal was awarded. Medals to the Royal Navy with the Ava clasp are very rare.*

Rev. die a, short hyphen

Rev. die b, long hyphen

VALUE:
Prices for medals bearing the following clasps are for European recipients. Medals to Indians are generally less expensive.

i.	Allighur (66)	£3000–3500
ii.	Battle of Delhi (40)	£3500–4500
iii.	Assye (87)	£3000–3500
iv.	Asseerghur (48)	£3500–4500
v.	Laswarree (100)	£3000–3500
vi.	Argaum (126)	£2500–3000
vii.	Gawilghur (110)	£3000–3500
viii.	Defence of Delhi (5)	—
ix.	Battle of Deig (47)	£3500–4500
x.	Capture of Deig (103)	£3000–3500
xi.	Nepaul (505)	£1500–1800
xii.	Kirkee (5)	—
xiii.	Poona (75)	£3000–3500
xiv.	Kirkee and Poona (88)	£3000–3500
xv.	Seetabuldee (2)	—
xvi.	Nagpore (155)	£2500–3000
xvii.	Seetabuldee and Nagpore (21)	£6000–8000
xviii.	Maheidpoor (75)	£3000–3500
xix.	Corygaum (4)	£6000–10,000
xx.	Ava (2325)	£1000–1200
xxi.	Bhurtpoor (1059)	£1200–1500
	2 clasps (300)	£2500–3500
	3 clasps (150)	£6000–8000
	4 clasps (23)	£9500–12,000
	5 or more clasps (10 x 5, 2 x 6, 1 x 7)	—
	Glazed gilt specimen	£400

*Miniature**
One clasp Ava	£200–250
Further clasps	£100–150 each

*Note there are many silver reproductions and clasps on the market, value £10–20.

105. GHUZNEE MEDAL

Date: 1839.

Campaign: Ghuznee 1839.

Branch of Service: British and HEIC forces.

Ribbon: 35mm half crimson, half dark green (originally green and yellow)

Metal: Silver.

Size: 37mm.

Description: (Obverse) the impressive gateway of the fortress of Ghuznee; (reverse) a mural crown enclosed in a laurel wreath with the date of capture.

Comments: *This was the second medal awarded for a particular campaign (after Waterloo) and was granted to both British and Indian troops who took part in the assault on Ghuznee in July 1839 which brought the first Afghan War to a close, overthrew the pro-Russian Dost Mohamed and restored Shah Soojah who instituted the Order of the Dooranie Empire (awarded to British generals and field officers) in appreciation. The Ghuznee medal was issued unnamed by the Honourable East India Company, but many recipients subsequently had their names impressed or engraved in various styles. No clasps were issued officially, but unauthorised clasps are occasionally encountered.*

VALUE:

British recipient	£600–800
Indian recipient	£450–650
Unnamed as issued	£475–575
Miniature	£150–300

Original type ribbon.

105A. BRITISH LEGION MEDAL

Date: 1836.
Campaign: First Carlist War.
Branch of Service: British Auxiliary Legion, plus a battalion of Royal Artillery seconded to the forces loyal to Queen Isabella.
Ribbon: Broad blue with narrow yellow stripes towards the edges.
Metal: Silver.
Size: 36mm.
Description: (Obverse) A cross pattee with the word TUJO in a laurel wreath at the centre; (reverse) ESPANA / AGRADECIDA (Grateful Spain) with a British lion enclosed by the cordon of the Golden Fleece. The medal is fitted with a ring for suspension from a double-looped bar and has a brooch fitment at the top of the ribbon. The medal was struck in Birmingham.
Comments: *The British Auxiliary Legion, commanded by General Sir George De Lacey Evans (1787-1870), volunteered for service in Spain in support of Isabella II who, at the age of three (1833) succeeded her father as monarch. Her uncle, Don Carlos, opposed this and triggered off a war which lasted till 1840 and was largely fought in the northern provinces. The inscription on the obverse alludes to the battle at Laguna del Tujo near Castilla la Mancha.*

VALUE: £400–450
(one Continental size miniature example with engraved details to reverse is known)

106. ST. JEAN D'ACRE MEDAL

Date: 1840.
Campaign: Syria 1840.
Branch of Service: Royal Navy, Royal Marines and British Army.
Ribbon: Red with white edges.
Metal: Gold, silver or copper (bronzed).
Size: 30mm.
Description: (Obverse) a fortress flying the Ottoman flag, with six five-pointed stars round the top. A commemorative inscription and date in Arabic appear at the foot; (reverse) the Toughra of the Sultan in a laurel wreath.
Comments: *Awarded by the Sultan of Turkey to British, Austrian and Turkish forces under Sir Charles Napier, taking part in the liberation of this important city on the Syrian coast after eight years of Egyptian occupation. The medal has a plain ring suspension. The clasp "Syria" to the Naval GSM was awarded in 1848 in respect of this operation, and this medal generally accompanies the St Jean d'Acre medal.*

VALUE:		Miniature
Gold (captains and field officers)	£4500–5000	—
Silver (junior officers)	£350–400	£150–200
Copper (petty officers, NCOs and other ranks)	£150–200	—

107. CANDAHAR, GHUZNEE, CABUL MEDAL

Date: 1842.
Campaign: Afghanistan 1841–42.
Branch of Service: British and HEIC troops.
Ribbon: 40mm watered silk of pink, white, yellow, white and blue representing an eastern sky at sunrise.
Metal: Silver.
Size: 36mm.
Description: Although the medals have a uniform obverse, a profile of the Queen captioned VICTORIA VINDEX, reverses are inscribed with the names of individual battles, or combinations thereof, within wreaths surmounted by a crown.
Comments: *The Honourable East India Company instituted this series of medals in 1842 for award to both HEIC and British troops who took part in the First Afghan War. The issue of this medal to units of the British Army, to Europeans serving in the Company's forces, and to Indian troops is further complicated by the fact that unnamed medals are generally common. In addition, the medal for Cabul is known in two versions, with the inscription CABUL or CABVL, the latter being a major rarity as only fifteen were issued. Only 160 medals with Candahar reverse were issued to Europeans. Beware of modern copies of the Candahar and Cabul medals.*

VALUE:	Imperial Regiments	Indian Units	Unnamed
i. Candahar	£850–1000	£425–550	£400–550
ii. Cabul	£600–750	£375–450	£400–550
iii. Cabvl (15)	—	—	—
iv. Ghuznee/Cabul	£750–850	£425–500	£400–550
v. Candahar/Ghuznee/ Cabul	£800–1000	£425–500	£400–550
Miniature	from £250 (depending on reverse)		

108. JELLALABAD MEDALS

Type 1

Date: 1842.
Campaign: Afghanistan 1841-42.
Branch of Service: British and HEIC forces.
Ribbon: 44mm watered silk red, white, yellow, white and blue representing an eastern sky at sunrise.
Metal: Silver.
Size: 39mm and 35mm.
Description: There are two different types of this medal, awarded by the HEIC to surviving defenders of the fortress of Jellalabad between 12 November 1841 and 7 April 1842. The first, struck in Calcutta, has a mural crown and JELLALABAD on the obverse, with the date of the relief of the garrison on the reverse; the second type shows the Wyon profile of Victoria (obverse) and the winged Victory with mountain scenery in the background and JELLALABAD VII APRIL round the top and the year in roman numerals in the exergue (reverse).
Comments: *The first type, struck in Calcutta, was considered to be unsuitable and holders were invited to exchange their medals for the second, more attractive, issue which was produced in London, although very few recipients took up the offer. The latter type was also awarded to the next of kin of soldiers killed in action.*

VALUE:	Imperial Regiments	Indian Units	Unnamed	*Miniature*
i. First type (Crown)	£850–950	£550–650	£500–600	£350–400
ii. Second type (Victory)	£1200–1500	—	£550–650	£250–350

109. MEDAL FOR THE DEFENCE OF KELAT-I-GHILZIE

Date: 1842.
Campaign: Afghanistan 1842.
Branch of Service: European and native troops, HEIC.
Ribbon: 40mm watered silk red, white, yellow, white and blue representing an eastern sky at sunrise.
Metal: Silver.
Size: 36mm.
Description: (Obverse) a shield bearing the name of the fort, surmounted by a mural crown and encircled by laurels; (reverse) a trophy of arms above a tablet inscribed INVICTA (unbeaten) and the date in roman numerals.
Comments: *Awarded to those who took part in the defence of the fort at Kelat-i-Ghilzie in May 1842, it is the rarest medal of the First Afghan War. No British imperial regiments took part, but 55 Europeans in the Company's service received the medal. It was also awarded to 877 native troops (including a contingent supplied by Shah Soojah) but few of their medals appear to have survived.*

VALUE:

European recipients	£5500–6500
Indian recipients	£3000–3500
Unnamed	£1500–1800
Miniature	£300–400

110. CHINA WAR MEDAL

Issued reverse

Date: 1842.
Campaign: China 1841-42.
Branch of Service: British and HEIC forces.
Ribbon: 39mm crimson with deep yellow edges the heraldic colours of Britain and China respectively.
Metal: Silver.
Size: 36mm.
Description: The medal has the usual Wyon obverse, but the reverse was to have shown a British lion with its forepaws on a dragon. This was deemed to be offensive to the Chinese and was replaced by an oval shield bearing the royal arms and a palm tree flanked by a capstan, anchor and naval cannon representing the Royal Navy (left) and a field gun, drum and regimental flag representing the Army (right), with the Latin motto ARMIS EXPOSCERE PACEM (to pray for peace by force of arms) round the top and CHINA 1842 in the exergue.
Comments: *Originally intended for issue to all ranks of the Honourable East India Company, it was subsequently awarded by the British government in 1843 to all who had taken part in the campaign in China popularly known as the First Opium War which ended with the seizure of Nanking.*

VALUE:

Royal Navy	£650–750
Indian and Bengal marine units	£550–650
British imperial regiments	£550–650
Indian Army	£500–600
Specimens of the original reverse	£800–1000
Miniature	£150–250

111. SCINDE MEDAL

Date: 1843.
Campaign: Scinde 1843.
Branch of Service: HEIC forces and 22nd Foot.
Ribbon: 44mm watered silk red, white, yellow, white and blue representing an eastern sky at sunrise.
Metal: Silver.
Size: 36mm.
Description: The usual Wyon profile obverse was married to three different reverse types showing a crowned laurel wreath inscribed with the name of one or two campaigns and the date.
Comments: *Authorised in September 1843, this silver medal marked Sir Charles Napier's conquest of Scinde. The two major battles in the campaign, at Meeanee and Hyderabad, accomplished the complete rout of the forces of the Amirs of Scinde. The medals were originally issued with steel suspenders but the commanding officer of the 22nd Foot had the medals awarded to his men fitted with silver suspenders, at his own expense. Medals to the Indus Flotilla are particularly sought after by collectors.*

VALUE:

	22nd Foot	Indian units	HEIC ships
i. Meeanee	£1000–1200	£500–575	£1500–2000 (38)
ii. Hyderabad	£1000–1200	£500–575	£1500–2000 (52)
iii. Meeanee/Hyderabad	£750–850	£500–575	

Miniature	£150–250

112. GWALIOR STAR

Date: 1843.
Campaign: Gwalior 1843.
Branch of Service: British and HEIC forces.
Ribbon: 44mm watered silk red, white, yellow, white and blue representing an eastern sky at sunrise.
Metals: Bronze, with a silver centre.
Size: Max. width 45mm; max. height 52mm.
Description: Six-pointed bronze star with a silver centre star. The silver stars in the centre bear the name of one or other of the battles and the date 29 December 1843 on which both battles were fought. The plain reverse bears the name and regiment of the recipient.
Comments: *Bronze from guns captured at the battles of Maharajpoor and Punniar during the Gwalior campaign was used in the manufacture of these stars, thus anticipating the production of the Victoria Cross in the same manner. They were presented by the Indian government to all ranks who took part in these actions. When first issued, these stars were fitted with hooks to be worn like a breast decoration, but later ornate bar or ring suspensions were fitted to individual fancy and worn with the standard Indian ribbon of the period.*

VALUE:

			Miniature
i.	Maharajpoor	£550–650	£200–250
ii.	Punniar	£550–650	£250–350

*Awards to Indian recipients are usually somewhat less.

113. SUTLEJ MEDAL

Date: 1846.
Campaign: Sutlej 1845-46.
Branch of Service: British and HEIC forces.
Ribbon: Dark blue with crimson edges.
Metal: Silver.
Size: 36mm.
Description: (Obverse) Wyon profile of Queen Victoria; (reverse) standing figure of Victory holding aloft a laurel crown, with a pile of captured weapons at her feet. The legend ARMY OF THE SUTLEJ appears round the top. The medal was fitted with an ornamental scroll suspender.
Clasps: Mounted above the suspender with roses between: Ferozeshuhur, Aliwal or Sobraon.
Comments: *The practice of issuing medals inscribed with different battles now gave way to the style of medals with specific battle or campaign clasps which set the precedent for the Naval and Military GSMs and later awards. As a compromise, however, the exergue of the reverse bears the name and date of the action for which the medal was first granted, and thus several different types are known.*

VALUE:	British regiments	Europeans in HEIC units	Indian units
i. Moodkee	£400–475	£300–500	£325–375
Moodkee 1 clasp	£500–575	£400–550	£375–425
Moodkee 2 clasps	£700–825	£600–750	£475–575
Moodkee 3 clasps	£875–1000	£800–950	£725–925
ii. Ferozeshuhur	£400–475	£300–400	£325–375
Ferozeshuhur 1 clasp	£500–575	£400–500	£375–425
Ferozeshuhur 2 clasps	£700–825	£600–750	£475–575
iii. Aliwal	£350–425	£300–400	£325–375
Aliwal 1 clasp	£500–575	£400–550	£375–475
iv. Sobraon	£400–525	£350–450	£375–475
Glazed gilt specimen	£375–475		
Miniature	£100–150, for each clasp add £50		

114. PUNJAB MEDAL

Date: 1849.
Campaign: Punjab 1848-49.
Branch of Service: British and HEIC forces.
Ribbon: Dark blue with yellow stripes towards the edges.
Metal: Silver.
Size: 36mm.
Description: (Obverse) Wyon profile of Queen Victoria; (reverse) Sir Walter Gilbert receiving the Sikh surrender. TO THE ARMY OF THE PUNJAB appears round the top and the year in roman numerals in the exergue. The medal has a scroll suspender.
Clasps: Mooltan, Chilianwala, Goojerat. Unusually the clasps read downwards from top to bottom
Comments: *This medal was granted to troops taking part in the campaigns which ended in the annexation of the Punjab. Unlike the Sutlej medal, however, this silver medal had a standard design. Large numbers of this medal were awarded to native troops, however many were melted down and therefore surprisingly few remain on the market in comparison with medals to European recipients.*

VALUE:	British units	Europeans in HEIC units	Indian units
No clasp	£325–375	£350–400	£225–275
i. Mooltan	£425–475	£400–450	£325–375.
Chilianwala	£425–475	£400–450	£325–375
iii. Goojerat	£425–475	£400–450	£325–375
iv. Mooltan/Goojerat	£600–750	£650–700	£425–525
Chilianwala/Goojerat	£550–750	£650–700	£425–525
24th Foot casualty at Chilianwala	£1000–1500	—	—
Glazed gilt specimen	£250–350		
Miniature	£75–100, for each clasp add £25		

115. SOUTH AFRICA MEDAL

Date: 1854.

Campaigns: Southern Africa 1834–53.

Branch of Service: Royal Navy and Army.

Ribbon: Gold with broad and narrow deep blue stripes towards each end.

Metal: Silver.   **Size:** 36mm.

Description: (Obverse) Wyon profile of Queen Victoria; (reverse) an African lion crouching in submission beside a protea shrub, the date 1853 being in the exergue.

Clasps: None.

Comments: *Authorised in November 1854, this medal was awarded in respect of three campaigns in southern Africa: 1834–35, 1846–47 and 1850–53, but as the medal was issued with a standard reverse and no campaign clasps it is impossible to tell when and where the recipient served without reference to the medal rolls. The majority of recipients were British troops but several hundred sailors of the Royal Navy also received the medal and a much smaller number of local forces. Medals to proven recipients who took part in well-known sieges or battles such as the siege of Port Natal (1842), Fort Cox (1850) or the battles of Zwartkopje (1845) or Boomplaats (1848) for example, are worth a considerable premium. Also of particular interest are medals awarded to men who survived the sinking of the troopship* Birkenhead *on its way to the Eastern Cape from Simons Town and medals awarded to those in clashes with Boer forces.*

VALUE:

British Army	£450–575
Royal Navy	£400–500
HMS *Birkenhead*	From £2000
Local forces (levies, burghers and colonial units	£1000
Miniature	£75–100

116. SIR HARRY SMITH'S MEDAL FOR GALLANTRY

Date: 1851.

Campaign: Eighth Kaffir War 1850-51.

Branch of Service: Army and Colonial Forces.

Ribbon: Dark blue with crimson edges.

Metal: Silver.

Size: 34mm.

Description: (Obverse) British lion passant gardant with a laurel wreath over its head; date 1851 in the exergue. (Reverse) PRESENTED BY round top and FOR GALLANTRY IN THE FIELD round the foot. HIS EXCELLENCY SIR H. G. SMITH and the name of the recipient appear across the centre.

Comments: *Sir Harry Smith (1787–1860) served with distinction in the Kaffir War of 1834–35, gained his KCB in the Gwalior campaign and a baronetcy for his decisive victory at Aliwal in the Sikh War. In 1847 he returned to South Africa as governor of Cape Colony. Although short of troops he conducted the eighth Kaffir War (1850–53) with great resourcefulness but was recalled to England in 1852 before the Xhosas had been subdued. Harrismith in the Orange Free State was named in his honour, while Ladysmith in Natal was named after his beautiful and spirited Spanish wife Juanita, the forces' sweetheart of her day. Sir Harry had this medal struck at his own expense and, according to unconfirmed accounts, awarded to troopers of the Cape Mounted Rifles who took part in the epic ride through the enemy lines from Fort Cox to Kingwilliamstown in 1851. Only 31 medals were presented, of which 22 are believed to be still extant.*

VALUE:

Unnamed	£3000–4000
Named and appearing on 1853 medal roll or muster rolls	£7000–10,000

One contemporary miniature example is known

117. INDIA GENERAL SERVICE MEDAL

Date: 1854.
Campaigns: Indian 1854-95.
Branch of Service: British and Indian forces.
Ribbon: Three crimson and two dark blue stripes of equal width.
Metal: Silver or bronze.
Size: 36mm.
Description: (Obverse) Wyon profile of Queen Victoria; (reverse) Victory crowning a semi-nude seated warrior.
Clasps: 24 (see below).
Comments: *This medal was the first of four general service medals issued to cover minor campaigns in India. It was instituted in 1854 and continued for forty-one years, retaining the original Wyon profile of Queen Victoria throughout the entire period. Although the medal itself is quite common, some of its clasps are very rare, notably* Kachin Hills 1892–93 *awarded to the Yorkshire Regiment and* Chin Hills 1892–93 *awarded to the Norfolk Regiment. The maximum number of clasps to one medal recorded is seven. At first the medal was awarded in silver to all ranks regardless of race or branch of the services, but from 1885 onwards it was issued in bronze to native support personnel such as bearers, sweepers and drivers.*

VALUE:		RN/RM	British Army	Indian Army	Bronze
i.	Pegu	£275–325	£285–350	£220–260*	—
ii.	Persia	—	£425–550	£250–335	—
iii.	Northwest Frontier	—	£285–350	£185–235	—
iv.	Umbeyla	—	£285–350	£185–235	—
v.	Bhootan	—	£350–375	£185–235	—
vi.	Looshai	—	—	£385–485	—
vii.	Perak	£275–300	£325–350	£235–275	—
viii.	Jowaki 1877-8	—	£250–300	£185–235	—
ix.	Naga 1879–80	—	—	£375–450	—
x.	Burma 1885–7	£150–200	£175–225	£135–150	£130–185
xi.	Sikkim 1888	—	£350–375	£160–185	£160–200
xii.	Hazara 1888	—	£250–285	£160–185	£160–200
xiii.	Burma 1887–89	—	£235–275	£135–175	£160–200
xiv.	Burma 1887–9	—	£185–250	—	—
xv.	Chin Lushai 1889–90	—	£285–375	£185–220	£220–275
xvi.	Lushai 1889–92	—	£450–525	£220–265	£420–500
xvii.	Samana 1891	—	£275–325	£160–185	£160–200
xviii.	Hazara 1891	—	£235–285	£160–185	£160–200
xix.	NE Frontier 1891	—	£325–375	£160–185	£160–200
xx.	Hunza 1891	—	—	£500–550	£850–1000
xxi.	Burma 1889–92	—	£200–250	£160–185	£135–185
xxii.	Chin Hills 1892–93	—	£650–800	£385–475	£860–1000
xxiii.	Kachin Hills 1892–93	—	£850–1000	£360–435	£860–1000
xxiv.	Waziristan 1894–95	—	£225–275	£160–185	£160–200

Miniature   £20–30, for each clasp add £10–15
(*Hunza, Chin Hills* and *Kachin Hills* clasps are rare)

* In addition a number of Indian ships were present—medals to Indian naval or marine recipients are rare.

118. BALTIC MEDAL

Date: 1856.
Campaign: Baltic Sea 1854–55.
Branch of Service: Royal Navy, Royal Marines and Royal Sappers and Miners.
Ribbon: Yellow with light blue edges.
Metal: Silver.
Size: 36mm.
Description: (Obverse) Wyon profile of Queen Victoria; (reverse) Britannia seated on a plinth decorated by a cannon, with a coastal scene in the background and BALTIC round the top.
Comments: *Authorised in 1856, this medal was granted to officers and men of the Royal Navy and Royal Marines for operations against Russia in the Baltic at the same time as the war in the Crimea. It was also awarded to about 100 members of the Royal Sappers and Miners engaged in the demolition of Russian fortifications of Bomarsund and Sveaborg. Medals were generally issued unnamed but often privately named afterwards, the exception being medals to the Sappers and Miners which were officially impressed.*

VALUE:
Unnamed	£180–200
Privately named	£180–200
Officially impressed to Sappers and Miners	£800–1000
Miniature	£40–50

119. CRIMEA MEDAL

Date: 1854.
Campaign: Crimea 1854–56.
Branch of Service: British Army, Navy and Marines.
Ribbon: Pale blue with yellow edges.
Metal: Silver.
Size: 36mm.
Description: (Obverse) Wyon profile of Queen Victoria; (reverse) a Roman soldier, armed with circular shield and short sword, being crowned by a flying Victory.
Clasps: Unusually ornate, being shaped like oak leaves with acorn finials: Alma, Balaklava, Inkerman, Sebastopol, Azoff, but the maximum found on any medal is four. Recipients of the Balaklava clasp were invariably entitled to other clasps. Unofficial clasps for Traktir, Mamelon Vert, Malakoff, Mer d'Azoff and Kinburn are sometimes found on medals awarded to French troops.
Comments: *Medals may be found unnamed, unofficially or regimentally named, or officially impressed. Medals awarded to participants in the most famous actions of the war — the Thin Red Line (93rd Foot) and the Charge of the Light and Heavy Brigades — rate a very high premium. The prices quoted are for medals named to the Army. Clasps awarded to the Royal Navy and Royal Marines (Azoff, Balaklava, Inkerman, Sebastopol) rate a good premium, especially those named to personnel on board HM Ships* London, Niger, Rodney *and* Wasp.* *No fewer than 19 VCs were awarded for gallantry at Inkerman alone, the largest number for a single action.*

VALUE :	Unnamed	Engraved	Regimentally impressed	Officially impressed Army
No clasp	£125–165	£140–165	£150–175	£150–195
i. Alma	£150–195	£165–220	£175–200	£200–275
ii. Balaklava	£175–225	£165–220	£200–250	£300–375
93rd Foot*	—	£465–565	£800–1000	£1000–1200
Heavy Brigade*	—	£675–865	£950–1250	£1500–2000
Light Brigade (Charger)*	—	£1650–2000	£3500–4500	£10,000–12,000
iii. Inkerman	£150–190	£165–220	£150–175	£200–275
iv. Sebastopol	£150–175	£165–220	£185–250	£250–325
v. Azoff	£275–365	£275–320	—	£500–650
2 clasps	£200–275	£275–320	£225–275	£350–485
3 clasps	£300–375	£365–425	£375–450	£550–675
4 clasps	£375–450	£465–650	£450–600	£1000–1200
Miniature	£20–30, for each clasp add £15			

It is always difficult to price scarce or rare medals such as those marked as we have seen many engraved or Depot-style impressing that were probably named in the past 30 to 40 years. Also an engraved Crimea, together with a Mutiny and/or LS&GC would be worth considerably more than the prices indicated. Buyer beware!

120. TURKISH CRIMEA MEDAL

Date: 1855.
Campaign: Crimea 1855-56.
Branch of Service: British, French and Sardinian forces.
Ribbon: Crimson with green edges.
Metal: Silver.
Size: 36mm (originally 18mm wide).
Description: (Obverse) a cannon, weapons and the four Allied flags with the name and date in the exergue; (reverse) the Toughra and Arabic date according to the Moslem calendar.
Clasps: None.
Comments: *Instituted by the Sultan of Turkey, this silver medal was conferred on troops of the three Allies who fought in the Crimea. The obverse types differed in the arrangement of the flags, corrsponding with the inscription in English, French or Italian in the exergue. Although the medals were intended to be issued to British, French and Sardinian troops respectively, they were issued haphazardly due to most of the British version being lost at sea. They were unnamed, but many were privately engraved or impressed later. Dangerous copies, emanating from the West Country of the UK, are known to be circulating.*

VALUE:			Miniature
i.	CRIMEA (British Issue)	£120–140	£35–40
ii.	LA CRIMEE (French Issue)	£220–230	Not seen
iii.	LA CRIMEA (Sardinia Issue)	£120–140	£25–30

121. INDIAN MUTINY MEDAL

Date: 1858.
Campaign: Sepoy Mutiny, India 1857-58.
Branch of Service: British Army, Navy and Indian forces. It was also awarded to many civilians who took part in suppressing the Mutiny.
Ribbon: White with two red stripes, representing blood and white bandages.
Metal: Silver.
Size: 36mm.
Description: (Obverse) Wyon profile of Queen Victoria; (reverse) the standing figure of Britannia bestowing victor's laurels, with the British lion alongside. INDIA appears round the top with the dates 1857-1858 in the exergue.
Clasps: Delhi, Defence of Lucknow, Relief of Lucknow, Lucknow, Central India. The maximum recorded for a single medal is four (Bengal Artillery) or three (imperial troops, 9th Lancers).
Comments: *This medal was awarded to troops who took part in operations to quell the Sepoy mutiny which had been the immediate cause of the uprising, although it also served to focus attention on the Honourable East India Company's conduct of affairs and led directly to the transfer of the administration of India to the Crown. Medals with the clasp for the defence of Lucknow awarded to the original defenders rate a considerable premium, as do medals awarded to members of the Naval Brigade which witnessed most of the fighting in the mopping-up operations. Medals to Indian recipients although scarcer on the market, generally bring a little less than their British counterparts. Four-clasp medals to the Bengal Artillery bring from £3000 if verified.*

VALUE:

		Royal Navy	British Army	Miniature
	No clasp	£800–1000*	£235–295	£25–35
i.	Delhi	—	£450–500	£40–45
ii.	Defence of Lucknow			
	original defender	—	£1300–1500	£45–50
	first relief force	—	£750–850	
iii.	Relief of Lucknow	£700–800	£400–450	£30–40
iv.	Lucknow	£700–800	£400–450	£40–45
v.	Central India	—	£400–450	£40–45, add
	2 clasps	£700–800	£550–650	£15 for each
	3 clasps (9th Lancers)	—	£900–1200	additional clasp
	4 clasps (Bengal Arty.)	—	£3000–4500	

66 medals to HMS Shannon and 253 to HMS Pearl.

122. SECOND CHINA WAR MEDAL

Date: 1861.

Campaign: Second China War 1857-60.

Branch of Service: British Army and Navy.

Ribbon: 33mm crimson with yellow edges (originally five equal stripes of green, white, red, yellow and blue, edged with red).

Metal: Silver.

Size: 36mm.

Description: As the First China War Medal (no. 110), but without the year 1842 at the foot.

Clasps: Fatshan 1857, Canton 1857, Taku Forts 1858, Taku Forts 1860, Pekin 1860.

Comments: *This medal was awarded to British sevicemen who took part, alongside the French, in the campaign against China which had been provoked by hostile acts against European nationals. The Royal Navy, under Admiral Sir Michael Seymour, destroyed a Chinese flotilla at Fatshan Creek, preparing the way for the attack on Canton whose capture brought the first phase to an end in June 1858. Reinforcements were meanwhile diverted to help put down the Indian mutiny. Fighting broke out again and this time large numbers of troops were involved in the assault on the Taku forts and the sack of Pekin (Beijing). Examples of the China medal of 1842, with or without clasps for 1857-60, have been recorded to recipients who fought in the Second China War. Medals may be found unnamed or with names officially engraved (Indian Army) or impressed (British Army, Indian Navy). Although those to the Navy were all issued unnamed, they are occasionally encountered unofficially named. Awards to Army and Navy personnel are other factors governing values.*

Original ribbon.

Second type ribbon.

VALUE:	Unnamed	Army/Navy officially impressed	Miniature
No clasp	£100–150	£145–180	£40–45
i. China 1842	—	—	£120–150
ii. Fatshan 1857	£160–185	£275–300	£55–65
iii. Canton 1857	£160–185	£275–300	£55–65
iv. Taku Forts 1858	£160–185	£275–300	£45–55
v. Taku Forts 1860	£160–185	£275–300	£45–55
vi. Pekin 1860	£160–185	£275–300	£45–55
2 clasps	£225–250	£325–400	For each
3 clasps	£265–300	£450–550	clasp add
4 clasps	£325–400		£15
5 clasps	£400–450		

123. NEW ZEALAND MEDALS

Date: 1869.
Campaigns: First and Second Maori Wars 1845–47 and 1860–66.
Branch of Service: Army, Navy and local volunteers.
Ribbon: Blue with a central orange stripe.
Metal: Silver.
Size: 36mm.
Description: (Obverse) Veiled head of Queen Victoria. (Reverse) Date
 of service in a wreath, with NEW ZEALAND round the top and
 VIRTUTIS HONOR (honour of valour) round the foot. Suspender
 ornamented with New Zealand fern fronds.
Comments: *These medals were unusual in having the recipient's dates
 of service die-struck on the centre of the reverse, though medals were
 also issued without dates. As the medal was only awarded to surviving
 veterans, the numbers issued in respect of the earlier conflict are
 understandably small. Many of the dates are very scarce, especially those
 issued to naval personnel in the first war when only naval personnel
 received dated medals. A hitherto unknown 1845-dated medal appeared at
 Stride & Son's auction in January 2010 where it sold for a hammer price of
 £12,800. This medal wa named to Captain David Robertson, HMS Hazard.*

VALUE:		Army	RN/RM
First war			
i.	Undated	£450–500	—
ii.	1845–46 (155)	—	£1300–1600
iii.	1845–47 (36)	—	£1400–1700
iv.	1846–47 (69)	—	£1300–1600
v.	1846 (10)	—	£1500–2000
vi.	1847 (20)	£800–1000	£1500–2000
Second war			
vii.	Undated	£375–475	—
viii.	1860	£700–800	—
ix.	1860-61	£475–525	£650–750
	(*to Australians*)	£2000–2300	—
x.	1860-63	From £1550	—
xi.	1860-64	£425–475	—
xii.	1860-65	£425–475	—
xiii.	1860-66	£425–475	—
xiv.	1861	—	—
xv.	1861-63	—	—
xvi.	1861-64	£425–475	—
xvii.	1861-65	—	—
xviii.	1861-66	£425–475	—
xix.	1861-66		
	(*Waikato Regt issues*)	From £700	—
xx.	1862-66	—	—
xxi.	1863	£425–500	—
xxii.	1863-64	£425–500	£650–750
xxiii.	1863-65	£425–500	—
xxiv.	1863-66	£425–500	—
xxv.	1864	£425–500	—
xxvi.	1864-65	£425–500	—
xxvii.	1864-66	£425–500	—
xxviii.	1865	£425–500	£650–750
xxvix.	1865-66	£425–500	—
xxx.	1866	£425–500	—
Miniature			
Undated		£85–100	
Dated		£70–£80	

124. ABYSSINIAN WAR MEDAL

Date: 1869.
Campaign: Abyssinia (Ethiopia) 1867–68.
Branch of Service: Royal Navy, British and Indian Armies.
Ribbon: Red with broad white edges.
Metal: Silver.
Size: 33mm diameter.
Description: (Obverse) the veiled portrait of Victoria framed by a zigzag pattern with floral ornament alternating with the letters of the name ABYSSINIA. The recipient's name and unit were embossed in the centre of the reverse except most to Indian troops which were impressed. Suspension is by a ring via a large crown standing proud from the top of the medal.
Clasps: None.
Comments: *The imprisonment of British subjects by King Theodore of Abyssinia precipitated a punitive expedition under General Sir Robert Napier involving ships of the Royal Navy, a naval brigade and troops of the British and Indian armies. Because casualties were unusually light (only two killed and 27 wounded), medals from this campaign are not so highly rated as those from other nineteenth century wars.*

VALUE:

British troops	£350–400
Royal Navy	£350–400
RN Rocket Brigade	£550–650
Indian troops	£280–320
Miniature	£100–150

125. CANADA GENERAL SERVICE MEDAL

Date: 1899.
Campaign: Canada 1866–70.
Branch of Service: Royal Navy, British Army and Canadian units.
Ribbon: Three equal stripes of orange-red, white and orange-red.
Metal: Silver.
Size: 36mm.
Description: (Obverse) crowned and veiled Old Head bust of Queen Victoria by Sir Thomas Brock (reflecting the very late issue of the medal). (Reverse) Canadian flag surrounded by maple leaves.
Clasps: Fenian Raid 1866, Fenian Raid 1870, Red River 1870.
Comments: *This medal was not authorised until January 1899, thirty years after the event, and was issued by the Canadian government to British and Canadian local forces who took part in operations to put down the Fenian raids of 1866 and 1870 and the Red River rebellion of the latter year. Of the 16,100 medals awarded, 15,000 went to local forces. Naval medals command a premium.*

VALUE:

	Canadian forces	British Army	Royal Navy	*Miniature*
i. Fenian Raid 1866	£295–325	£400–450	£500–550	£60
ii. Fenian Raid 1870	£295–325	£400–450	—	£65
iii. Red River 1870	£1500–1800	£1500–2000	£1000–1500	£85
2 clasps*	£365–465	£850–950	—	£80
3 clasps	Rare	—	—	—

*Two 2-clasp medals were awarded to men of the 1st Bn 60th Foot (KRRC) and ten to the 4th Bn.

126. ASHANTEE MEDAL

Date: 1874.
Campaign: Gold Coast 1873–74.
Branch of Service: Royal Navy, Army and native troops.
Ribbon: Orange with black stripes at the sides and two narrow black stripes towards the centre.
Metal: Silver.　　**Size:** 36mm.
Description: The obverse and reverse are similar to the East and West Africa Medal of 1887–1900, differing solely in thickness and the method of naming. The veiled profile of Victoria graces the obverse while the reverse, designed by Sir Edwin Poynter, shows a skirmish in the jungle between British soldiers and Ashantee warriors.
Clasps: Coomassie.
Comments: *All ranks who took part in operations against King Kalkali of Ashantee, Gold Coast, were awarded this medal, approved in June 1874. The campaign was fought in difficult and hostile terrain, requiring the building of a road through dense rain forest, the construction of many staging posts, camps, bridges and a telegraph. The movement of troops and supplies was met with skirmishes and ferocious battles developed as the column approached Kumasi in the final four weeks and resulted in the award of four VCs. There was also a very high incidence of sickness and disease among the troops, notably the naval contingent. Unusually the medals are named in engraved capitals filled in with black.*

VALUE	Navy	Army	Natives	Miniature
No clasp	£300–350	£300–350	£200–250	£45–50
i. Coomassie	£450–500	£450–500	£280–350	£65–70

127. SOUTH AFRICA MEDAL

Date: 1879.
Campaign: South Africa 1877–79.
Branch of Service: Royal Navy, Army and colonial units.
Ribbon: Gold with broad and narrow deep blue stripes towards each end.
Metal: Silver.
Size: 36mm.
Description: The same design as no. 115, except that the date 1853 in the exergue is replaced by a Zulu shield and four crossed assegais.
Clasps: 1877, 1877–8, 1877–9, 1877–8–9, 1878, 1878–9, 1879.
Comments: *The campaign began in 1877 with an attack on the Fingoes by the Galeka and Gaika tribes and culminated in the showdown between the Zulus and the British when Lord Chelmsford's column was annihilated at Isandhlwana. When the 3,000 Zulus advanced on Rorke's Drift, however, they were checked with heavy losses by a tiny garrison of 139 men. During the defence no fewer than eleven VCs were won—a very large number for a single action. The campaign concluded with the defeat of Cetshwayo's warriors at Ulundi. A number of recipients of the medal stayed on in the country and took part in the first Anglo-Boer War of 1880–81. Medals confirmed to these men, particularly those who took part in the sieges of Wakkerstroom, Rustenburg, Standerton, Marabastadt or Lydenburg or well-known battles such as Swartkoppies, are worth a considerable premium.*

VALUE:	RN	Army	Colonial	Miniature
No clasp	£285–350	£300–350	£300–350	£25–30
i. 1877	—	Unique	£1750–2500	£100–150
ii. 1877–8	£780–850	£475–550	£350–450	£50–60
iii. 1877–9	—	Unique	£4500–6000	—
iv. 1877–8–9	£700–850	£475–575	£375–450	£35–40
v. 1878	—	£425–525	£375–450	£50–60
vi. 1878–9	—	£475–575	£375–450	£50–60
vii.1879	£625–700	£475–575	£375–450	£50–60

Isandhlwana casualty	£6000–10,000
Rorke's Drift participant	£30,000–35,000
Isandhlwana escapee	£10,000–12,000

128. AFGHANISTAN MEDAL

Date: 1881.
Campaign: Afghanistan 1878–80.
Branch of Service: British and Indian Armies.
Ribbon: Dark green, the sacred colour of the prophet with broad crimson edges, the heraldic colour of Britain.
Metal: Silver.
Size: 36mm.
Description: (Obverse) veiled profile of Queen Victoria. (Reverse) a column on the march, with an elephant carrying cannon. The dates 1878–79–80 appear in the exergue.
Clasps: Ali Musjid, Peiwar Kotal, Charasia, Kabul, Ahmed Kel, Kandahar. Maximum number of clasps per medal is four.
Comments: *This medal was awarded to all who took part in the campaigns against Afghanistan known as the Second Afghan War. In 1877 the Amir refused to accept a British resident and the following year raised an army which began harrassing the Indian frontier. A treaty with Russia, however, granting it protective rights in Afghanistan, precipitated an armed response from Britain. In 1880 General Roberts led a column from Kabul to Kandahar to relieve General Burrows and the resulting battle led to the defeat of the Afghans and the conclusion of the war. Medals awarded to the 66th Foot (Berkshire regiment) and E Battery of B Brigade, Royal Artillery rate a high premium as these units sustained the heaviest casualties at the battle of Maiwand in July 1880.*

VALUE:	British units	Indian units	Miniature
No clasp silver	£200–250	£150–175	£20–30
i. Ali Musjid	£275–300	£200–250	£30–40
ii. Peiwar Kotal	£275–300	£200–250	£30–40
iii. Charasia	£275–300	£200–250	£30–40
iv. Kabul	£275–300	£200–250	£25–30
v. Ahmed Khel	£275–300	£200–250	£30–40
vi. Kandahar	£275–300	£200–250	£25–30
2 clasps	£400–450	£275–350	£55–65
3 clasps	£475–550	£375–475	£75–85
4 clasps	£750–1000	£475–585	£85–95
Maiwand casualties:			
66th Foot	£2250–2750	—	
E Bty, B Bde RHA	£2250–2750	—	

129. KABUL TO KANDAHAR STAR

Date: 1881.
Campaign: Afghanistan 1878–80.
Branch of Service: British and Indian Armies.
Ribbon: 40mm watered silk of pink, white, yellow, white and blue representing an eastern sky at sunrise.
Metal: Bronze from captured guns.
Size: Height 60mm, width 45mm.
Description: (Obverse) a rayed five-pointed star surmounted by a crown with a ring for suspension. The centre is inscribed KABUL TO KANDAHAR with 1880 at the foot and the VRI monogram of the Queen Empress in the centre. Stars were either issued unnamed, or had the recipient's name impressed (to British) or engraved (to Indian troops) on the reverse.
Clasps: None.
Comments: *This star, struck by Jenkins of Birmingham, was awarded to those who took part in the epic 300-mile march from the Afghan capital to Kandahar, led by General Roberts to relieve the beleaguered forces of General Burrows.*

VALUE:

Unnamed	£120–150
Impressed (British troops)	£300–350
Engraved (Indian troops)	£200–250
Miniature	Early pierced crown £50–65
	Later solid crown £40–50

130. CAPE OF GOOD HOPE GENERAL SERVICE MEDAL

Date: 1900.
Campaign: Uprisings in Transkei, Basutoland and Bechuanaland 1880-97.
Branch of Service: Local forces and volunteers.
Ribbon: Dark blue with a central yellow stripe.
Metal: Silver.
Size: 36mm.
Description: (Obverse) Jubilee bust of Queen Victoria by Sir Joseph Boehm; (reverse) arms of Cape Colony.
Clasps: Transkei, Basutoland, Bechuanaland.
Comments: *Instituted by the Cape government, this medal acknowledged service in putting down the Transkei (September 1880–May 1881), Basutoland (September 1880–April 1881) and Bechuanaland (December 1896–July 1897) rebellions in those areas. The medal was awarded, with one or more campaign clasps, to local forces and volunteer regiments. Recent research has shown that the medal could not be awarded without a clasp. The previously held notion that ten medals were awarded without clasps, was brought about by an error in transcribing the medal rolls.*

VALUE:

			Miniature
i.	Transkei (562)	£300–365	£50–60
ii.	Basutoland (1589)	£200–235	£50–60
iii.	Bechuanaland (2483)	£180–220	£50–60
	2 clasps (585)	£350–475	£65–80
	3 clasps (23)	£3000–4000	—

131. EGYPT MEDAL 1882–89

Dated rev.

Undated rev.

Date: 1882.

Campaign: Egypt 1882–89.

Branch of Service: Royal Navy and Army.

Ribbon: Three blue and two white stripes, (the Blue and White Niles).

Metal: Silver.

Size: 36mm.

Description: (Obverse) the veiled profile of Queen Victoria; (reverse) the Sphinx.

Clasps: 14, listed below. Maximum number for one medal is 7, but only one such award was made. Common two-clasp combinations are denoted below by / .

Comments: *British involvement in Egypt deepened after the opening of the Suez Canal in 1869, many British officers being seconded to the Khedive's Army. When the Army mutinied in 1882 and triggered off a general anti-European uprising, an Anglo-French expedition was mounted. Subsequently the French withdrew before a landing was effected. Trouble erupted in the Sudan (under Anglo-Egyptian administration) in 1884 where General Gordon was besieged at Khartoum. Further campaigns aimed at the overthrow of the Mahdi and the reconquest of the Sudan. These prolonged operations created immense logistical problems. Nile transportation in particular was a matter resolved only when Canadian voyageurs were recruited to handle the river-boats. In addition, a contingent of troops from New South Wales "answered the Empire's call" and medals awarded to them for the Suakin campaign of 1885 are much sought after. Except where noted, the prices quoted below are for medals awarded to British Army personnel. Medals awarded to Indian or Egyptian troops are generally worth about 25 per cent less than comparable awards to British Army units.*

VALUE:

			Miniature
i.	No clasp (dated)	£100–175	£25–30
ii.	No clasp (undated)	£100–175	£25–30
iii.	Alexandria 11th July	£250–280	£40–45
iv.	Tel-el-Kebir	£200–250	£40–45
v.	El-Teb	£275–325	£40–45
vi.	Tamaai	£275–325	£40–45
vii.	El-Teb–Tamaai	£240–300	£40–45
viii.	Suakin 1884	£200–245	£40–45
ix.	The Nile 1884-85	£240–280	£40–45
x.	The Nile 1884-85/Abu Klea	£650–950	£40–45
xi.	The Nile 1884-85/Kirbekan	£280–350	£40–45
xii.	Suakin 1885	£200–245	£40–45
xiii.	Suakin 1885/Tofrek	£280–350	£40–45
xiv.	Gemaizah 1888	£280–325	£40–50
xv.	Toski 1889	£450–650	£50–60
xvi.	Gemaizah 1888-Toski 1889		
	Egyptian troops	£260–300	
	20th Hussars	£350–450	
2 clasps		£250–300	Add £15
3 clasps		£300–350	for each
4 clasps		£400–500	clasp
5 clasps		£1100–1500	—
Canadian boatmen		£1500–2000	
NSW units (Suakin 1885)		£3500–4000	

132. KHEDIVE'S STAR

Date: 1882.
Campaign: Egypt 1882–91.
Branch of Service: Royal Navy and Army.
Ribbon: 37mm deep blue.
Metal: Bronze.
Size: Height 60mm; width 45mm.
Description: A five-pointed star with a circular centre showing the Sphinx and Pyramids surrounded by a band inscribed EGYPT followed by a year round the top, with 'Khedive of Egypt' and the year in the Moslem calendar in Arabic at the foot. (Reverse) the Khedive's monogram surmounted by a crown. The star is suspended by a ring from an ornamental clasp in the centre of which is a star and crescent.
Clasps: Tokar.
Comments: *This star, struck by Jenkins of Birmingham, was conferred by Khedive Tewfik of Egypt on those who qualified for the Egypt medal and it was invariably worn alongside, to the detriment of the silver medal which suffered abrasion from the points of the star. There was also an undated version found with or without a campaign clasp for Tokar, awarded in 1891. These stars were issued unnamed.*

VALUE:			Miniature
i.	1882	£80–100	£10–15
ii.	1884	£80–100	£12–16
iii.	1884-86	£80–100	£15–20
iv.	Undated	£80–100	£15–20
v.	Undated with Tokar bar	£200–250	£60-100

133. GENERAL GORDON'S STAR FOR THE SIEGE OF KHARTOUM

Date: 1884.
Campaign: Mahdist uprising, Sudan 1884.
Branch of Service: British and Sudanese forces.
Ribbon: Deep blue (?) or red (?).
Metal: Silver or pewter.
Size: Height 80mm; maximum width 54mm.
Description: Star with three concentric circles and seven groups of rays on which are superimposed seven crescents and stars. Suspension by a ring from a Crescent and Star ornament.
Clasps: None.
Comments: *To boost the morale of the defenders Charles Gordon, commanding the garrison at Khartoum, had this star cast locally in a sand mould, using his own breast star of the Order of Mejidieh as the model. Exceptionally, recipients had to purchase their medals, the proceeds going to a fund to feed the poor.*

VALUE:
Silver gilt	£1000–1200
Silver	£700–900
Pewter	£600–800

134. NORTH WEST CANADA MEDAL

Date: 1885.
Campaign: Riel's rebellion 1885.
Branch of Service: Mainly local forces.
Ribbon: Blue-grey with red stripes towards the edges.
Metal: Silver.
Size: 36mm.
Description: (Obverse) bust of Queen Victoria; (reverse) the inscription NORTH WEST CANADA 1885 within a frame of maple leaves.
Clasps: Saskatchewan,
Comments: *Paradoxically, while the medal for the Fenian Raids of 1866–70 was not sanctioned till 1899, this medal for service in the North West was authorised immediately after the conclusion of operations against the Metis led by Louis Riel. It was issued unnamed, with or without the clasp for Saskatchewan where the bulk of the action took place. Of particular interest are medals to officers and men aboard the steamship* Northcote *involved in a boat action; exceptionally, their medals were impressed. Other medals may be encountered with unofficial naming. The medal was awarded to sixteen British staff officers but the majority of medals (5600 in all) went to local forces.*

VALUE:		*Miniature*
i. No clasp	£300–350	£50–60
ii. Saskatchewan	£550–650	£65–75
Northcote recipient	£1600–2000	

135. ROYAL NIGER COMPANY'S MEDAL

Date: 1899.
Campaign: Nigeria 1886–97.
Branch of Service: Officers and men of the Company's forces.
Ribbon: Three equal stripes of yellow, black and white.
Metal: Silver or bronze.
Size: 39.5mm.
Description: (Obverse) the Boehm bust of Queen Victoria; (reverse) the Company's arms in a laurel wreath.
Clasps: Nigeria 1886-97 (silver), Nigeria (bronze).
Comments: *This medal was issued in silver to Europeans and bronze to natives for service in the vast territories administered by the Royal Niger chartered company. Silver medals were impressed in capitals, but those in bronze were more usually stamped with the recipient's service (constabulary) number. Specimens of both versions were later struck from the original dies but these lack name or number.*

VALUE:

		Miniature
Silver named (85)	£3000–4000	no clasp £150–200
Silver specimen	£80–100	—
Bronze oficially numbered (250)	£650–850	Nigeria clasp £200–250
Bronze specimen	£60–80	—

136. IMPERIAL BRITISH EAST AFRICA COMPANY'S MEDAL

Date: 1890.
Campaign: East Africa (Kenya and Uganda) 1888–95.
Branch of Service: Company forces.
Ribbon: Plain dark blue.
Metal: Silver.
Size: 40mm.
Description: (Obverse) the Company badge, a crowned and radiant sun, with a Suaheli inscription in Arabic round the foot signifying "the reward of bravery"; (reverse) plain except for a wreath. Suspension is by a plain ring or an ornamental scroll.
Comments: *The rarest of the medals awarded by the chartered companies, this medal was originally intended solely as a gallantry award; but after the BEA Company was wound up in 1895 further issues were authorised by the Foreign Office for service in Witu (1890) and the Ugandan civil war (1890-91). Less than thirty medals are known.*

VALUE: £4000–5000   *Miniature* £300–400

137. EAST AND WEST AFRICA MEDAL

Date: 1892.
Campaigns: East and West Africa 1887–1900.
Branch of Service: Royal Navy, Army and native forces.
Ribbon: As 126.
Metal: Silver or bronze.
Size: 36mm.
Description: As the Ashantee Medal (no. 126), distinguished only by its clasps.
Clasps: 22 (see below). A 22nd operation (Mwele, 1895–96) was denoted by engraving on the rim of the medal.
Comments: *This medal was awarded for general service in a number of small campaigns and punitive expeditions. Though usually awarded in silver, it was sometimes struck in bronze for issue to native servants, bearers and drivers. British regiments as such were not involved in any of the actions, but individual officers and NCOs were seconded as staff officers and instructors and their medals bear the names of their regiments. Units of the Royal Navy were also involved in many of the coastal or river actions. Especially sought after are naval medals with the bar for Lake Nyassa 1893 in which the ships* Pioneer *and* Adventure *were hauled in sections overland through 200 miles of jungle.*

			Royal Navy	Europeans		
VALUE:						
Natives	*Miniature*					
i.	1887–8		£850–1250	£425–625	£400–450	£40–45
ii.	Witu 1890		£200–250	£200–250	£150–180	£45–50
iii.	1891–2		£225–275	£200–250	£150–180	£45–50
iv.	1892		£1250–1500	£200–250	£150–180	£45–50
v.	Witu August 1893		£225–250	—	£150–180	£60–70
vi.	Liwondi 1893		£2250–2500	—	—	—
vii.	Juba River 1893		£2250–2500	—	—	—
viii.	Lake Nyassa 1893		£2500–3500	—	—	—
ix.	1893–94		£750–900	£200–250	£150–180	£50–60
x.	Gambia 1894		£325–375	—	£150–180	£50–60
xi.	Benin River 1894		£350–400	£200–250	£150–180	£40–50
xii.	Brass River 1895		£325–375	—	—	£45–50
xiii.	M'wele 1895–6		£175–200	£200–250	£140–160	£100
	(Bronze)				£800–1000	
xiv.	1896–98		—	£375–475	£220–300	£30–45
xv.	Niger 1897		—	£375–425	£220–300	£45–55
xvi.	Benin 1897		£200–250	£200–250	£220–300	£35–45
xvii.	Dawkita 1897		—	—	—	£100
xviii.	1897–98		—	£325–425	£220–250	£45–50
xix.	1898		£725–950	£325–425	£220–250	£45–50
xx.	Sierra Leone 1898–9		£225–275	£325–425	£220–250	£45–50
xxi.	1899		£925–1250	£325–375	£220–250	£45–50
xxii.	1900		—	£325–375	£220–250	£45–50
	2 clasps		£475–525	£325–375	£250–300	
	3 clasps		£575–675	—	£350–400	—

138. BRITISH SOUTH AFRICA COMPANY'S MEDAL

1st type rev.

Mashonaland (2nd) rev.

Date: 1896.
Campaign: South Africa 1890-97.
Branch of Service: British Army and colonial units.
Ribbon: Seven equal stripes, four yellow and three dark blue.
Metal: Silver.
Size: 36mm.
Description: (Obverse) the Old Head bust of Queen Victoria; (reverse) a charging lion impaled by a spear, with a mimosa bush in the background and a litter of assegais and a shield on the ground.
Clasps: Mashonaland 1890, Matabeleland 1893, Rhodesia 1896, Mashonaland 1897.
Comments: *Originally instituted in 1896 for award to troops taking part in the suppression of the Matabele rebellion of 1893, it was later extended to cover operations in Rhodesia (1896) and Mashonaland (1897). The medal, as originally issued, had the inscription MATABELELAND 1893 at the top of the reverse. The medal was re-issued with RHODESIA 1896 or MASHONALAND 1897 inscribed on the reverse, but holders of medals for their first campaign only added clasps for subsequent campaigns. Rather belatedly, it was decided in 1927 to issue medals retrospectively for the Mashonaland campaign of 1890; in this instance the name and date of the campaign were not inscribed on the reverse though the details appeared on the clasp. Although 705 men were entitled, only 200 claimed the medal and clasp. An unusually ornate suspender has roses, thistles, shamrocks and leeks entwined. Only two medals are known with all four clasps, while only fifteen medals had three clasps.*

VALUE:		*Miniature*
a. Undated reverse with		
Mashonaland 1890 clasp	£800–1000	£45–60
i. Matabeleland 1893	Rare	—
ii. Rhodesia 1896	Rare	—
iii. Mashonaland 1897	Rare	—
b. Matabeleland 1893 rev.	£300–350	£40–45
ii. Rhodesia 1896	£400–450	£50–60
iii. Mashonaland 1897	£400–450	£50–60
with 2 clasps	£600–800	£65–75
c. Rhodesia 1896 rev.	£300–350	£50–60
iii. Mashonaland 1897	£450–500	£60–70
d. Mashonaland 1897	£280–350	£50–60
Shangani Patrol confirmed member £1800–2200		

139. HUNZA NAGAR BADGE

Date: 1891.
Campaign: Hunza and Nagar 1891.
Branch of Service: Jammu and Kashmir forces.
Ribbon: Large (46mm x 32mm) with a broad red diagonal band and white centre stripe and green upper left and lower right corners.
Metal: Bronze.
Size: 55mm x 27mm.
Description: A uniface rectangular plaque featuring three soldiers advancing on the crenellated hill fort of Nilt, with mountains in the background. The inscription HUNZA NAGAR 1891 appears lower right. It was intended to be worn as a brooch at the neck but subsequently many were fitted with a suspender for wear with a red and green ribbon.
Clasps: None.
Comments: *Gurney of London manufactured this badge which was awarded by the Maharajah of Jammu and Kashmir to his own troops who served in the operation against the border states of Hunza and Nagar and qualified for the Indian general service medal with clasp for Hunza 1891. The punitive expedition was led by Colonel A. Durand in response to the defiant attitude of the Hunza and Nagar chiefs towards the British agency at Gilgit.*
VALUE: £450–600

151

140. CENTRAL AFRICA MEDAL

Date: 1895.
Campaigns: Central Africa 1891–98.
Branch of Service: Mainly local forces.
Ribbon: Three equal stripes of black, white and terracotta representing the Africans, Europeans and Indians.
Metal: Silver or bronze.
Size: 36mm.
Description: Obverse and reverse as the East and West Africa (Ashantee) medal, distinguished only by its ribbon.
Clasps: Originally issued without a clasp but one for Central Africa 1894–98 was subsequently authorised.
Comment: *Though generally issued in silver, a bronze version was awarded to native servants. The first issue of this medal had a simple ring suspension and no clasp. For the second issue a clasp, Central Africa 1894–98 was authorised and the medal was issued with a straight bar suspender, which is very rare.*

VALUE:		Miniature
Without clasp (ring suspension)		
To natives	£600–800	£80–100
To Europeans	£2000–3000	
With clasp (ring suspension)	£700–900	—
To natives	£900–1200	
To Europeans	£2000–3000	
With clasp (bar suspension)	£1300–1600	£80–100
Bronze, unnamed	From £500	—

141. HONG KONG PLAGUE MEDAL

Date: 1894.
Campaign: Hong Kong, May-September 1894.
Branch of Service: Royal Navy, Royal Engineers, KSLI and local personnel.
Ribbon: Red with yellow edges and two narrow yellow stripes in the centre.
Metal: Silver.
Size: 36mm.
Description: (Obverse) a Chinese lying on a trestle table being supported by a man warding off the winged figure of Death while a woman tends the sick man. The year 1894 appears on a scroll in the exergue, while the name of the colony in Chinese pictograms is inscribed on the left of the field. (Reverse) inscribed PRESENTED BY THE HONG KONG COMMUNITY round the circumference, and FOR SERVICES RENDERED DURING THE PLAGUE OF 1894 in seven lines across the centre. It was fitted with a plain ring for suspension.
Clasps: None.
Comments: *The colonial authorities in Hong Kong awarded this medal to nurses, civil servants, police, British Army and Royal Navy personnel who rendered assistance when the crown colony was stricken by a severe epidemic of bubonic plague in May 1894. Despite stringent measures, over 2500 people died in the ensuing three months. About 400 medals were issued in silver and awarded to 300 men of the King's Shropshire Light Infantry, 50 petty officers and ratings of the Royal Navy and NCOs and other ranks of the Royal Engineers, as well as about the same number of police and junior officials, while 45 were struck in gold for award to officers, nursing sisters and senior officials. However, the medal was not authorised for wear on uniform by British troops.*

VALUE:

		Miniature
Gold (45)	From £6000	£200–300
Silver (400)	£2000–2500	£150–200

142. INDIA MEDAL

Date: 1896.
Campaign: India 1895–1902.
Branch of Service: British and Indian forces.
Ribbon: Crimson with two dark green stripes—the heraldic colour of Britain and the sacred colour of the prophet.
Metal: Silver or bronze.
Size: 36mm.
Description: Issued with two different obverses, portraying Queen Victoria (1895–1901) and King Edward VII in field marshal's uniform (1901–02). (Reverse) British and Indian soldiers supporting a standard. The Edward VII reverse is undated.
Clasps: Seven, mainly for actions on the North West Frontier (see below).
Comments: *This medal replaced the India GSM which had been awarded for various minor campaigns over a period of four decades from 1854. Combatant troops were given the medal in silver but native bearers and servants received a bronze version. Although the clasp Waziristan 1901–2 is rare to British recipients it was awarded to a number of regiments.*

VALUE:

	British regiments	Indian Army	Bronze	Miniature
i. Defence of Chitral 1895	—	£1500–2000	£3000–4000	£80–100
ii. Relief of Chitral 1895	£200–225	£150–175	£125–175	£25–30
iii. Punjab Frontier 1897-98	£200–225	£150–175	£100–150	£20–25
iv. Malakand 1897*	£500–700	£150–200	£150–200	£50–60
v. Samana 1897*	£200–225	£150–185	£100–150	£35–40
vi. Tirah 1897-98*	£200–250	£150–185	£100–150	£45–50
vii. Waziristan 1901-2	£350–450	£150–175	£100–150	£55–65
3 clasps	£275–350	£200–250	£175–250	£50–60
4 clasps	—	£200–250	—	£60–80

These clasps are always paired with clasp iii.

143. JUMMOO AND KASHMIR MEDAL

Date: 1895.
Campaign: Defence of Chitral 1895.
Branch of Service: Native levies.
Ribbon: White with red stripes at the edges and a central green stripe.
Metal: Bronze, silver.
Size: 35mm high; 38mm wide.
Description: This medal, by Gurney of London, has a unique kidney shape showing the arms of Jummoo (Jammu) and Kashmir on the obverse. (Reverse) a view of Chitral fort with troops in the foreground.
Clasps: Chitral 1895.
Comments: *Awarded by the Maharajah of Jummoo (Jammu) and Kashmir to the Indian troops who participated in the defence of Chitral (a dependency of Kashmir) during the siege of 4 March to 20 April by Chitralis and Afghans led by Umra Khan and Sher Afzul.*

VALUE:

Named	£500–700
Unnamed	£400–600
Silver	—

144. ASHANTI STAR

Date: 1896.
Campaign: Gold Coast 1896.
Branch of Service: British forces.
Ribbon: Yellow with two black stripes.
Metal: Bronze.
Size: 44mm.
Description: A saltire cross with a four-pointed star in the angles, surmounted by a circular belt inscribed ASHANTI 1896 around a British crown. The plain reverse is simply inscribed FROM THE QUEEN.
Clasps: None.
Comments: *Issued unnamed, but the colonel of the West Yorkshire Regiment had the medals of the second battalion engraved at his own expense. Some 2000 stars were awarded to officers and men serving in the expedition led by Major-General F.C. Scott against the tyrannical King Prempeh. It is believed that the star was designed by Princess Henry of Battenberg whose husband died of fever during the campaign.*

VALUE:

Unnamed	£200–220
Named to West Yorkshire Regiment	£400–450
In attributable group	£400–450
Miniature	£40–50

145. QUEEN'S SUDAN MEDAL

Date: 1899.
Campaign: Reconquest of the Sudan 1896–97.
Branch of Service: Royal Navy, Army and local forces.
Ribbon: Half-yellow and half-black representing the desert and the Sudanese nation, divided by a thin crimson stripe representing the British forces.
Metal: Silver or bronze.
Size: 36mm.
Description: (Obverse) the Jubilee bust of Queen Victoria. (Reverse) a seated figure of Victory holding palms and laurels with flags in the background, the word SUDAN appearing on a tablet at her feet.
Clasps: None.
Comments: *Unusually, no clasps were granted for individual actions which included the celebrated battle of Omdurman in which young Winston Churchill charged with the cavalry. Medals named to the 21st Lancers are especially desirable on that account.*

VALUE:

Bronze	
unnamed	£150–200
named	£250–300
Silver	
unnamed	£180–200
named to British Regt	£300–350
Indian Regt	£200–250
21st Lancers (confirmed charger)*	£2000–2500
RN/RM (46)	£1500–2000
War correspondent	£1000–1500

* Dependent on which Company the recipient served in.

Miniature	£35–45

146. KHEDIVE'S SUDAN MEDAL 1896–1908

(reverse)

Date: 1897.
Campaign: Sudan 1896-1908.
Branch of Service: Royal Navy and British and Egyptian Armies.
Ribbon: 38mm yellow with a broad central deep blue stripe, symbolising the desert and the River Nile.
Metal: Silver or bronze.
Size: 39mm.
Description: (Obverse) an elaborate Arabic inscription translating as 'Abbas Hilmi the Second' and the date 1314 (AD 1897); (reverse) an oval shield surrounded by flags and a trophy of arms. Bar suspender.
Clasps: Fifteen (see below) but medals with more than the two clasps 'The Atbara' and 'Khartoum' are unusual. Inscribed in English and Arabic to British recipients.
Comments: *Instituted by the Khedive of Egypt in February 1897 and granted to those who served in the reconquest of Dongola province in the Sudan (1896-8) as well as in subsequent operations for the pacification of the southern provinces. It was awarded to officers and men of the British and Egyptian Armies and Royal Navy personnel who served on the Nile steamboats. In addition, the crews of the Royal Naval ships HMS Melita (139) and HMS Scout (149) were awarded silver medals with no clasps for Dongola 1896 (but were not awarded the Queen's Sudan Medal 1896–98). Medals to Royal Naval personnel with clasps are rare and command a high premium: Hafir (16), The Atbara (6), Sudan 1897 (12), Khartoum (33), Gedaref (9), Gedid (5) and Sudan 1899 (6).*

VALUE:

No clasp silver		
named to British regt	£150–175	
named to Indian regt	£150–175	
No clasp silver (RN)	£350–450	
No clasp bronze	£125–150	
i. Firket	£125–155	
ii. Hafir	£125–155	
iii. Abu Hamed	£125–155	
iv. Sudan 1897	£125–155	
v. The Atbara	£135–155	
vi. Khartoum	£200–250	
vii. Gedaref	£125–155	
viii. Gedid	£125–155	
ix. Sudan 1899	£125–155	
x. Bahr-el-Ghazal 1900–2	£180–220	
xi. Jerok	£125–150	
xii. Nyam-Nyam	£150–180	
xiii. Talodi	£150–180	
xiv. Katfia	£150–180	
xv. Nyima	£150–180	
2 clasps	£150–200	
3 clasps	£180–220	
4 clasps	£240–280	
5 clasps	£300–350	
6 clasps	£350–380	
7 clasps	£400–450	
8 clasps	£450–500	

Miniature
No clasp silver £35–50
With any single clasp £50–80
Add £15 for each additional clasp

147. EAST AND CENTRAL AFRICA MEDAL

Date: 1899.
Campaigns: East and Central Africa 1897–99.
Branch of Service: British, Indian and local forces.
Ribbon: Half yellow, half red.
Metal: Silver or bronze.
Size: 36mm.
Description: (Obverse) the Jubilee bust of Queen Victoria; (reverse) a standing figure of Britannia with the British lion alongside.
Clasps: Four (see below).
Comments: *Instituted for service in operations in Uganda and the southern Sudan, it was awarded in silver to combatants and in bronze to camp followers. Most of the medals were awarded to troops of the Uganda Rifles and various Indian regiments. The few British officers and NCOs were troop commanders and instructors seconded from their regiments and their medals are worth very much more than the prices quoted, which are for native awards.*

VALUE:

	Europeans	Natives	Miniature
No clasp			
silver	—	£250–275	£45–55
bronze	—	£325–425	—
i. Lubwa's (with clasp			
Uganda 1897-98)	—	£375–475	£75–85
ii. Uganda 1897-98	£600–800	£325–425	£65–75
iii. 1898 (silver)	—	£325–425	£65–75
iv. 1898 (bronze)	—	£525–625	—
v. Uganda 1899	—	£325–425	£65–75

147A. UGANDA STAR

Instituted: 1897–98.
Campaign: Mutiny of Sudanese troops in Uganda.
Branch of Service: African civilians and soldiers.
Ribbon: None.
Metal: Silver.
Description: An eight-pointed uniface star surmounted by a crown, with the dates 1897 and 1898 on a circular rim enclosing the Old Head or Veiled Bust of Queen Victoria. Brooch-mounted. Manufactured by Carrington of London and issued in a blue plush-lined case.
Comments: *This award, approved by the Foreign Office and sanctioned by Queen Victoria, acknowledged the loyalty of African tribal leaders but, in a few cases, was also awarded to Sudanese troops (one, in fact, a Tunisian) who fought gallantly in quelling the serious mutiny of Sudanese troops of the Uganda Rifles. It was for this action that British, Indian and Local forces were awarded the East and Central Africa Medal with the bar for Lubwa's (see above). Only 39 stars were awarded.*

VALUE: From £2500

148. BRITISH NORTH BORNEO COMPANY'S MEDAL 1888–1916

Instituted: 1897.

Campaign: North Borneo (now Sabah, Malaysia), 1897-1916.

Ribbon: Initially gold (later yellow) watered silk 32mm, replaced in 1917 by a 32mm ribbon with maroon edges, two yellow stripes and a dark blue central stripe. The central stripe was originally 6mm wide but modern ribbons have a 10mm stripe.

Metal: Silver or bronze.

Size: 38mm, with a thickness of 5mm.

Description: (Obverse) the shield of the Company, supported by a warrior on either side. The Company motto at the foot is PERGO ET PERAGO (I carry on and accomplish); (reverse) the British lion facing left, standing in front of a bush adorned with the Company flag, with a small wreath in the exergue.

Clasps: Punitive Expedition (1897), Punitive Expeditions (1898-1915), Rundum (1915). The Punitive Expeditions clasp was awarded to those who took part in two or more actions, but it also replaced the earlier single Expedition clasp in due course.

Comments: *These medals were awarded for service in the 15 minor expeditions between 1883 and 1915, excluding the major action at Tambunan. The manufacturers, Spink, supplied 12 silver medals in 1898–9 for award to officers (only three being named). In 1906 a further 74 silver medals were issued, to be exchanged for the bronze medals initially awarded to other ranks. A further 11 silver medals were supplied later on, all unnamed. A total of 75 bronze medals were supplied, 25 of them stamped with a name and sometimes rank and number as well, and issued, both stamped and engraved, to other ranks.*

First type ribbon.   *Second type ribbon.*

VALUE:

		Type	Officially Named	Unnamed original	Spink copy	Stamped "Specimen"	Miniature
i.	Punitive Expedition	Silver	£1500–1800	£350–500	£50–60	£60–80	£150–180
		Bronze	£1500–1800	£350–500	£50–60	£60–80	
ii.	Punitive Expeditions	Silver	£1500–1800	£350–500	£50–60	£60–80	£150–180
		Bronze	£1500–1800	£350–500	£50–60	£60–80	
iii.	Rundum	Silver	£1500–1800	£350–500	£50–60	£60–80	£150–180

148A. BRITISH NORTH BORNEO COMPANY'S MEDAL 1899–1900

Instituted: 1900.

Campaign: The final expedition in the Tambunan Valley against Mat Salleh.

Ribbon: 32mm yellow with a 10mm green stripe down the centre.

Metal: Silver or bronze.

Size: 38mm. Officially named medals are 5mm thick.

Description: (Obverse) the shield of the British North Borneo Company with BRITISH NORTH BORNEO round the top and the date 1900 below; (reverse) a wreath enclosing a device of one clothed and one naked arm supporting the Company's flag. The motto PERGO ET PERAGO is inscribed outside the wreath. The inscription SPINK & SON, LONDON appears in very tiny lettering at the foot.

Clasps: Tambunan.

Comments: *Instituted for award to those officers and men who took part in the expedition of January-February 1900 against Mat Salleh who had roused the Tegas against the Tiawan Dusuns in the Tambunan Valley. Salleh was killed on February 1, 1900 when Company forces stormed his stronghold and his followers were dispersed or killed. Eight silver medals were originally awarded to officers, but in 1906 some 106 were issued to be exchanged for the bronze medals initially issued to other ranks. A further 22 silver medals were later supplied, unnamed. A total of 125 bronze medals were supplied, 118 of them stamped with a name and sometimes also a rank and number, and issued, both stamped and engraved, to other ranks. Only 36 are recorded as replaced by silver medals, but it is known that some of these bronze medals were not returned to the authorities.*

VALUE:

Type	Officially Named	Unnamed original	Spink copy	Stamped "Specimen"
Silver	£1800–2000	£300–500	£50–60	£60–80
Bronze	£1000–1500	£300–500	£50–60	£60–80

Miniature £150–180

149. SULTAN OF ZANZIBAR'S MEDAL

Date: 1896.

Campaign: East Africa 1896.

Branch of Service: Sultan's forces.

Ribbon: Plain bright scarlet.

Metal: Silver.

Size: 36mm.

Description: (Obverse) a facing bust of Sultan Hamid bin Thwain surrounded by a Suaheli inscription in Arabic; (reverse) same inscription set in four lines.

Clasps: Pumwani, Jongeni, Takaungu, Mwele (inscribed only in Arabic).

Comments: *Awarded to the Zanzibari contingent who served under Lieut. Lloyd-Matthews RN in East Africa alongside British and Imperial forces.*

VALUE: £400–500 *Miniature* £500–600

150. QUEEN'S SOUTH AFRICA MEDAL

Date: 1899.

Campaign: Anglo-Boer War 1899-1902.

Branch of Service: British and Imperial forces.

Ribbon: Red with two narrow blue stripes and a broad central orange stripe.

Metal: Silver or bronze.

Size: 36mm.

Description: (Obverse) the Jubilee bust of Queen Victoria; (reverse) Britannia holding the flag and a laurel crown towards a large group of soldiers, with warships offshore. The words SOUTH AFRICA are inscribed round the top.

Clasps: 26 authorised but the maximum recorded for a single medal is nine to the Army and eight to the Navy.

Comments: *Because of the large number of British and imperial forces which took part and the numerous campaign and battle clasps awarded, this is one of the most popular and closely studied of all medals, offering immense scope to the collector. A total of 178,000 medals were awarded. Numerous specialist units were involved for the first time, as well as locally raised units and contingents from India, Canada, Australia and New Zealand. Of particular interest are the medals awarded to war correspondents and nurses which set precedents for later wars. Although nurses received the medal they were not issued with clasps to which they were entitled. A small number of bronze medals without a clasp were issued to bearers and servants in Indian units. The original issue of the QSA depicts Britannia's outstretched hand pointing towards the R of AFRICA and bears the dates 1899–1900 on the reverse field. Less than 70 of these were issued to Lord Strathcona's Horse who had returned to Canada before the war ended, but as the war dragged on the date was removed before any other medals were issued, although some medals can be found with a "ghost" of this date still to be seen. On the third type reverse there is again no date but Britannia's hand points towards the F. The prices for clasps given overleaf are for* clasps issued in combination with others. Some clasps are much scarcer when issued singly than combined with other clasps and conversely some clasps are not recorded on their own. Verified ten-clasp medals to South African units are known. It is important to note that the following list is very basic and represents the value of straightforward medals and clasps. Confusion can sometimes occur as single clasps and combinations of two or three clasps can command higher premiums than medals with a greater number of clasps. It is beyond the remit of this book to give the value of every possible combination of clasps. A very rough guide would be to take the most valuable clasp as a starting point and add 25% of this value for each Battle clasp and 10% for each State clasp, however, this is by no means infallible. An example would be to take a three-clasp medal which has Elandslaagte (£350–400), Belfast (£80–90) and Relief of Kimberley (£80–100) which as a simple 3-clasp medal would be valued at £100–130 — however, on the rough guide system it would be valued at c. £550. Certain clasp combinations will always command a higher premium, for example Relief of Ladysmith/ Relief of Mafeking, Defence of Ladysmith/Relief of Mafeking, Elandslaagte/Defence of Ladysmith, Defence of Kimberley/Paardeberg, etc.*

1st type rev.

2nd type rev. (occasionally ghost dates can be seen)

3rd type rev.

150. QUEEN'S SOUTH AFRICA MEDAL *continued*

VALUE:

		RN	British Army	SA/Indian	Aus/NZ	Canadian
	No clasp bronze	—	—	£150–250	—	—
	No clasp silver	£150–160	£65–85	£75–85	£125–175	£125–175
i.	Cape Colony	£180–200	£65–85	£80–100	£125–175	£125–175
ii.	Rhodesia	£1000–1250	£325–375	£160–200	£225–350	£350–400
iii.	Relief of Mafeking	—	—	£300–350	£350–450	£400–450
iv.	Defence of Kimberley	—	£300–325	£220–250	—	—
v.	Talana	—	£350–400	£250–350	—	—
vi.	Elandslaagte	—	£350–450	£300–350	—	—
vii.	Defence of Ladysmith	£750–850	£250–300	£140–180	—	—
viii.	Belmont	£300–350	£100–125	—	£250–300	—
ix.	Modder River	£300–350	£100–125	—	£250–300	—
x.	Tugela Heights	£300–350	£95–120	—	—	—
xi.	Natal	£300–350	£100–160	£120–150	—	£220–250
xii.	Relief of Kimberley	£750–900	£100–125	£80–100	£125–175	—
xiii.	Paardeberg	£250–300	£85–100	£80–100	£125–175	£175–200
xiv.	Orange Free State	£180–220	£75–95	£65–85	£125–175	£175–200
xv.	Relief of Ladysmith	£250–300	£95–135	£80–100	—	—
xvi.	Driefontein	£240–260	£80–100	—	£125–175	£225–275
xvii.	Wepener	—	£600–800	£400–450	—	—
xviii.	Defence of Mafeking	—	—	£1000–1750	—	—
xix.	Transvaal	£450–600	£75–90	£65–85	£100–150	£225–275
xx.	Johannesburg	£250–300	£85–100	£80–90	£125–175	£125–175
xxi.	Laing's Nek	£500–650	£85–100	—	—	—
xxii.	Diamond Hill	£250–300	£85–100	£80–90	£125–175	£200–225
xxiii.	Wittebergen	£1000–1200	£85–100	£80–90	£125–175	—
xxiv.	Belfast	£250–300	£85–100	£80–90	£125–175	£125–175
xxv.	South Africa 1901	£125–150	£65–90	£55–65	£85–125	£100–150
xxvi.	South Africa 1902	£750–850	£65–90	£50–60	£85–125	£100–150
	2 clasps (see Comment)	£180–220	£90–125	£85–95	£175–200	£175–200
	3 clasps ＂	£250–280	£100–135	£120–145	£185–225	£185–225
	4 clasps	£300–350	£125–155	£120–150	£225–275	£225–275
	5 clasps*	£380–450	£135–175	£120–155	£275–300	£225–275
	6 clasps*	£550–650	£155–185	£180–200	£325–375	£325–375
	7 clasps*	£800–900	£450–500	£400–450	£850–1000	—
	To Royal Marines	£1200–1300				
	8 clasps*	£1200–1500	£600–800	£850–1000	—	—
	9 clasps	—	—	£2000–2400	—	—
	Relief dates on reverse					
	(Lord Strathcona's Horse)	—	—	—	—	£3000–3500
	Nurses	—	£250–350	—	—	—
	War Correspondents	—	£1100–1200	—	—	—

* excluding date clasps

Miniature
From £15 with no clasp to £50 with 6 fixed clasps—"slip-on" style clasps approx. 20% less.
With dated reverse £100–150

Battle of Modder River

151. QUEEN'S MEDITERRANEAN MEDAL

Date: 1899.
Campaign: Mediterranean garrisons 1899-1902.
Branch of Service: British militia forces.
Ribbon: Red with two narrow dark blue stripes and a central broad orange stripe (as for Queen's South Africa Medal).
Metal: Silver.
Size: 36mm.
Description: Similar to the Queen's South Africa Medal but inscribed MEDITERRANEAN at the top of the reverse.
Clasps: None.
Comments: *Awarded to officers and men of the militia battalions which were sent to Malta and Gibraltar to take over garrison duty from the regular forces who were drafted to the Cape.*

VALUE:

Silver (5000)	£300–350	*Miniature* £65–75

152. KING'S SOUTH AFRICA MEDAL

Date: 1902.
Campaign: South Africa 1901–02.
Branch of Service: British and imperial forces.
Ribbon: Three equal stripes of green, white and orange.
Metal: Silver.
Size: 36mm.
Description: (Obverse) bust of King Edward VII in field marshal's uniform; (reverse) as for Queen's medal.
Clasps: Two: South Africa 1901, South Africa 1902.
Comments: *This medal was never issued without the Queen's medal and was awarded to all personnel engaged in operations in South Africa in 1901–02 when fighting was actually confined to numerous skirmishes with isolated guerrilla bands. Very few medals were awarded to RN personnel as the naval brigades had been disbanded in 1901. Apart from about 600 nurses and a few odd men who received the medal without a clasp, this medal was awarded with two clasps—most men were entitled to both clasps, single clasp medals being very rare. Only 137 were awarded to New Zealand troops.*

VALUE:

No clasp (Conductors and associated ranks in the ASC (106) and nurses)	£300–400
i. South Africa 1901	
ii. South Africa 1902	
Single clasp 1902 (ii) (502 to Imperial troops, none known for Colonial troops)	From £200
Two clasps (i and ii)	
RN (33)	£1200–1800
Army	£80–100
Canada (160)	£80–100
Australia (*not issued on its own, in a pair with any QSA to an Australian*)	£2500–2600
New Zealand	£300–350
South African units	£60–80
St John Ambulance Brigade (12)	£250–300
Miniature	
No clasp	£12–15
2-clasps	£15–20

The Orders & Medals Research Society

Founded in 1942, the Orders and Medals Research Society (OMRS) aims to promote a general interest in orders, decorations and medals as well as to assist members in pursuing their research. The Society also aims to publish any information that may be of benefit to members.

Subscribers of the Society enjoy the advantage of a quarterly journal offering informative articles, advise on medals and military history and an active website at **www.omrs.org.uk**

Numerous branches are located world-wide holding regular meetings and discussion groups. Once a year an annual convention is held in London marking the highlight of the researchers' and medal collectors' year.

For further details please contact The Membership Secretary at:
PO Box 248,
Snettisham,
King's Lynn
PE31 7TA

153. ST JOHN AMBULANCE BRIGADE MEDAL FOR SOUTH AFRICA

Date: 1902.
Campaign: South Africa 1899–1902.
Branch of Service: St John Ambulance Brigade.
Ribbon: Black with narrow white edges.
Metal: Bronze.
Size: 37mm.
Description: (Obverse) King Edward VII; (reverse) the arms of the Order with a legend in Latin, SOUTH AFRICA and the dates 1899 and 1902.
Clasps: None.
Comments: *Issued by the Order of St John of Jerusalem to the members of its ambulance brigade who served during the Boer War or who played an active part in the organisation, mobilisation and supply roles. Medals were engraved on the edge with the recipient's name and unit. It is most often associated with the two South Africa medals, but fourteen members who went on from South Africa to serve during the Boxer Rebellion were also awarded the China Medal.*

VALUE: Bronze (1,871)   £350–450   *Miniature* £150–175 *(in silver slightly less)*

153A. NATIONAL FIRE BRIGADE'S UNION MEDAL FOR SOUTH AFRICA

Date: 1902.
Campaign: South Africa 1899–1902.
Branch of Service: National Fire Brigade's Union.
Ribbon: Red with narrow orange edges and two orange stripes near the centre.
Metal: Silver.
Size: 36mm.
Description: (Obverse) King Edward VII; (reverse) A bust of a helmeted fireman with a Geneva cross in the sky above. Around the circumference a spray of laurel leaves between the dates 1899 and 1902 and SOUTH AFRICA at top.
Comments: *Awarded to a small detachment of volunteers of the National Fire Brigades Union (Ambulance Department) who served in South Africa as stretcher bearers and ambulance personnel. Each volunteeer also received the St John's Ambulance Medal for South Africa and the Queen's South Africa Medal with the clasp Cape Colony. Only 42 were awarded.*

VALUE: £1200–1500   *Miniature* (silver)   £200–300

154. KIMBERLEY STAR

Date: 1900.
Campaign: Defence of Kimberley 1899–1902.
Branch of Service: British and local forces.
Ribbon: Half yellow, half black, separated by narrow stripes of red, white and blue.
Metal: Silver.
Size: Height 43mm; max. width 41mm.
Description: A six-pointed star with ball finials and a circular centre inscribed KIMBERLEY 1899–1900 with the civic arms in the middle. (Reverse) plain, apart from the inscription MAYOR'S SIEGE MEDAL 1900. Suspended by a plain ring from a scrolled bar.
Clasps: None
Comments: *The Mayor and council of Kimberley awarded this and the following medal to the defenders of the mining town against the Boer forces. Two medals were struck in gold but about 5000 were produced in silver. Those with the "a" Birmingham hallmark for 1900 rate a premium over stars with later date letters.*

VALUE:
Hallmark "a"   £250–280   *Miniature*   £125–150
Later date letters   £220–250

155. KIMBERLEY MEDAL

Date: 1900.
Campaign: Defence of Kimberley 1899–1900.
Branch of Service: Local forces.
Ribbon: As above.
Metal: Silver
Size: 38mm.
Description: (Obverse) the figure of Victory above the Kimberley Town Hall, with the dates 1899–1900 in the exergue. (Reverse) two shields inscribed INVESTED 15 OCT. 1899 and RELIEVED 15 FEB. 1900. The imperial crown appears above and the royal cypher underneath, with the legend TO THE GALLANT DEFENDERS OF KIMBERLEY round the circumference.
Comments: *Although awarded for the same purpose as MY154, this silver medal is a much scarcer award.*

VALUE: £800–1000

156. YORKSHIRE IMPERIAL YEOMANRY MEDAL

Date: 1900.
Campaign: South Africa 1900–02.
Branch of Service: Yorkshire Imperial Yeomanry.
Ribbon: Dark blue with a central yellow stripe.
Metal: Silver.
Size: 38mm.
Description: Three versions were produced. The first two had the numeral 3 below the Prince of Wales's feathers and may be found with the dates 1900–1901 or 1901–1902, while the third type has the figures 66, denoting the two battalions involved. The uniform reverse has the white rose of Yorkshire surmounted by an imperial crown and enclosed in a laurel wreath with the legend A TRIBUTE FROM YORKSHIRE.
Comments: *Many medals were produced locally and awarded to officers and men of county regiments. The medals struck by Spink and Son for the Yorkshire Imperial Yeomanry, however, are generally more highly regarded as they were much more extensively issued, and therefore more commonly met with.*

VALUE:		Miniature
3rd Battalion 1900–1901	£185–225	£120–140
3rd Battalion 1901–1902	£185–225	£100–120
66th Company 1900–1901	£220–250	Not seen

157. MEDAL FOR THE DEFENCE OF OOKIEP

Date: 1902.
Campaign: Defence of Ookiep 1902.
Branch of Service: British and colonial forces.
Ribbon: Dark brown with a central green stripe.
Metal: Silver or bronze.
Size: 36mm.
Description: (Obverse) a miner and copper-waggon, with the Company name and date of foundation (1888) round the circumference; (reverse) a thirteen-line text. Fitted with a scroll suspender.
Clasps: None.
Comments: *Commonly known as the Cape Copper Co. Medal, this medal was awarded by the Cape Copper Company to those who defended the mining town of Ookiep in Namaqualand when it was besieged from 4 April to 4 May 1902 by a Boer commando led by Jan Christian Smuts, later Field Marshal, Prime Minister of South Africa and a member of the Imperial War Cabinet. The defence was conducted by Lt-Col W. A. D. Shelton, DSO, and Maj J. L. Dean of the Namaqualand Town Guard, the Company's manager. The garrison consisted of 206 European miners, 660 Cape Coloureds, 44 men of the 5th Warwickshire militia and twelve men of the Cape Garrison Artillery.*

VALUE:

Silver (officers)	£6000–8000
Bronze (other ranks)	£1000–1200

158. CHINA WAR MEDAL 1900

Date: 1901.
Campaign: Boxer Rebellion 1900.
Branch of Service: British and imperial forces.
Ribbon: Crimson with yellow edges.
Metal: Silver or bronze.
Size: 36mm.
Description: (Obverse) bust of Queen Victoria; (reverse) trophy of arms, similar to the 1857-60 China Medal but inscribed CHINA 1900 at the foot.
Clasps: Taku Forts, Defence of Legations, Relief of Pekin.
Comments: *Instituted for service during the Boxer Rebellion and the subsequent punitive expeditions, this medal was similar to that of 1857-60 with the date in the exergue altered to 1900. There are three types of naming: in small, impressed capitals for European troops, in large impressed capitals for naval recipients, and in engraved cursive script for Indian forces. The medal was issued in silver to combatants and in bronze to native bearers, drivers and servants. The international community was besieged by the Boxers, members of a secret society, aided and abetted by the Dowager Empress. The relieving force, consisting of contingents from Britain, France, Italy, Russia, Germany and Japan, was under the command of the German field marshal, Count von Waldersee. The British Legation Guard, comprising 80 Royal Marines and a number of 'odd men', won the clasp for Defence of Legations, the most desirable of the campaign bars in this conflict.*

VALUE:	Royal Navy	Army	Indian units	Miniature
Silver no clasp	£190–250	£190–220	£130–175	£20–25
Australian naval forces	£2500–3000 (approx. 550 issued)			
Bronze no clasp	—	—	£175–235	—
i. Taku Forts	£500–600	—	—	£30–40
ii. Defence of Legations	£5000–6000	—	—	£50–60
iii. Relief of Pekin:				
Silver	£400–475	£400–450	£275–350	£25–30
Bronze	—	—	£300–350	—
2 clasps	£600–700	—	—	£40–50
No-clasp medal to a nurse	£1500–2000			
To a war correspondent (9)	£1500–2000			
ditto Relief of Pekin (1)	Rare			

159. TRANSPORT MEDAL

Date: 1903.
Campaigns: Boer War 1899-1902 and Boxer Rebellion 1900.
Branch of Service: Mercantile Marine.
Ribbon: Red with two blue stripes.
Metal: Silver.
Size: 36mm.
Description: (Obverse) bust of King Edward VII in the uniform of an Admiral of the Fleet; (reverse) HMST *Ophir* below a map of the world.
Clasps: S. Africa 1899-1902, China 1900.
Comments: *The last of the medals associated with the major conflicts at the turn of the century, it was instituted for award to the officers of the merchant vessels used to carry troops and supplies to the wars in South Africa and China.*

VALUE:

		Miniature
i. South Africa 1899–1902 (1219)	£650–750	£75–100
ii. China 1900 (322)	£900–1000	£75–100
Both clasps (178)	£1200–1400	£100–150

160. ASHANTI MEDAL

Date: 1901.
Campaign: Gold Coast 1900.
Branch of Service: British and local forces.
Ribbon: Black with two broad green stripes.
Metal: Silver or bronze.
Size: 36mm.
Description: (Obverse) bust of King Edward VII in field marshal's uniform. (Reverse) a lion on the edge of an escarpment looking towards the sunrise, with a native shield and spears in the foreground. The name ASHANTI appeared on a scroll at the foot.
Clasps: Kumassi.
Comments: *A high-handed action by the colonial governor provoked a native uprising and the siege of the garrison at Kumassi. The medal was awarded to the defenders as well as personnel of the two relieving columns. Very few Europeans were involved as most were in South Africa fighting the Boers. The medal was awarded in silver to combatants and bronze to native transport personnel and servants.*

VALUE:

	Silver	Bronze	*Miniature*
No clasp	£300–350	£400–500	£40–60
i. Kumassi	£500–550	Rare	£60–75

161. AFRICA GENERAL SERVICE MEDAL

Date: 1902.
Campaigns: Minor campaigns in Africa 1902 to 1956.
Branch of Service: British and colonial forces.
Ribbon: Yellow with black edges and two thin central green stripes.
Metal: Silver or bronze.
Size: 36mm.
Description: (Obverse) effigies of Edward VII, George V and Elizabeth II; (reverse) similar to that of the East and Central Africa medal of 1897–99, with AFRICA in the exergue.
Clasps: 34 awarded in the reign of Edward VII, ten George V and only one Elizabeth II (see below).
Comments: *This medal replaced the East and West Africa Medal 1887–1900, to which 21 clasps had already been issued. In turn, it remained in use for 54 years, the longest-running British service medal. Medals to combatants were in silver, but a few bronze medals were issued during the 1903–04 operations in Northern Nigeria and the Somaliland campaigns of 1902 and 1908 to transport personnel and these are now much sought after, as are any medals with the effigy of George V on the obverse. With the exception of the 1902–04 Somali campaign and the campaign against the Mau Mau of Kenya (1952–56) European troops were not involved in any numbers, such personnel consisting mostly of detached officers and specialists.*

VALUE:

		RN	British units	African/Indian regiments
i.	N. Nigeria	—	—	£180–210
ii.	N. Nigeria 1902	—	—	£170–190
iii.	N. Nigeria 1903	—	—	£160–180
iv.	N. Nigeria 1903-04	—	—	£200–230
v.	N. Nigeria 1903-04 (bronze)	—	—	£220–240
vi.	N. Nigeria 1904	—	—	£180–210
vii.	N. Nigeria 1906	—	—	£190–210
viii.	S. Nigeria	—	—	£240–270
ix.	S. Nigeria 1902	—	—	£190–210
x.	S. Nigeria 1902-03	—	—	£190–210

continued overleaf

161. AFRICA GENERAL SERVICE MEDAL *continued*

		RN	British units	African/Indian regiments
xi.	S. Nigeria 1903	—	—	£180–200
xii.	S. Nigeria 1903-04	—	—	£210–230
xiii.	S. Nigeria 1904	—	—	£180–200
xiv.	S. Nigeria 1904-05	—	—	£210–230
xv.	S. Nigeria 1905	—	—	£290–340
xvi.	S. Nigeria 1905-06	—	—	£200–220
xvii.	Nigeria 1918	—	—	£170–190
xviii.	East Africa 1902	—	—	£370-410
xix.	East Africa 1904	—	—	£220–260
xx.	East Africa 1905	—	—	£220–260
xxi.	East Africa 1906	—	—	£240–260
xxii.	East Africa 1913	—	—	£240–260
xxiii.	East Africa 1913-14	—	—	£240–260
xxiv.	East Africa 1914	—	—	£240–260
xxv.	East Africa 1915	—	—	£240–260
xxvi.	East Africa 1918	—	—	£240–260
xxvii.	West Africa 1906	—	—	£300–340
xxviii.	West Africa 1908	—	—	£240–280
xxix.	West Africa 1909-10	—	—	£240–260
xxx.	Somaliland 1901	—	—	£310–360
xxxi.	Somaliland 1901 (bronze)	—	—	£290–340
xxxii.	Somaliland 1902-04	£150–175	£150–175	£150–180
xxxiii.	Somaliland 1902-04 (bronze)	—	—	£290–340
xxxiv.	Somaliland 1908-10	£150–170	—	£140–160
xxxv.	Somaliland 1908-10 (bronze)	—	—	£240–290
xxxvi.	Somaliland 1920	£200–300	—	£160–190
	as above but RAF (225 awarded)	—	£650–850	—
xxxvii.	Jidballi (with Somaliland 1902–04)	—	£300–400	£200–260
xxxviii.	Uganda 1900	—	—	£240–290
xxxix.	B.C.A. 1899-1900	—	—	£190–240
xl.	Jubaland	£250–300	—	£200–240
xli.	Jubaland (bronze)	—	—	£540–640
xlii.	Jubaland 1917-18	—	—	£220–240
xliii.	Jubaland 1917-18 (bronze)	—	—	£240–290
xliv.	Gambia	£600–800	—	£260–310
xlv.	Aro 1901-1902	£800–900	—	£240–290
xlvi.	Lango 1901	—	—	£290–340
xlvii.	Kissi 1905	—	—	£390–440
xlviii.	Nandi 1905-06	—	—	£160–190
xlix.	Shimber Berris 1914-15	—	—	£260–290
l.	Nyasaland 1915	—	—	£190–230
li.	Kenya	£350–500	£100–150	£65–100
lii.	Kenya (to RAF)	—	£120–160	—
2 clasps		£150–180	£200–250	£150–250
3 clasps		—	—	£200–400
4 clasps		—	—	£300–450
5 clasps		—	—	£400–600
6 clasps		—	—	£800–1000
Medal to war correspondent		£1200–1500		

Miniature
   Range from £30 to £75 depending upon clasp. "Slip-on" clasps are approx. 20% cheaper. Add £15 for each additional clasp.

162. TIBET MEDAL

Date: 1905.
Campaign: Tibet 1903–04.
Branch of Service: British and Indian regiments.
Ribbon: Green with two white stripes and a broad maroon central stripe.
Metal: Silver or bronze.
Size: 36mm.
Description: (Obverse) bust of King Edward VII; (reverse) the fortified hill city of Lhasa with TIBET 1903–04 at the foot.
Clasps: Gyantse.
Comments: *The trade mission led by Colonel Sir Francis Younghusband to Tibet was held up by hostile forces, against whom a punitive expedition was mounted in 1903. This medal was awarded mainly to Indian troops who took part in the expedition, camp followers being awarded the medal in bronze. A clasp was awarded to those who took part in the operations near Gyantse between 3 May and 6 July 1904.*

VALUE:

	British	Indian	Bronze	Miniature
Without clasp	£500–700	£300–350	£110–125	£40–50
i. Gyantse	£850–1000	£450–500	£350–400	£60–70

163. NATAL REBELLION MEDAL

Date: 1907.
Campaign: Natal 1906.
Branch of Service: Local forces.
Ribbon: Crimson with black edges.
Metal: Silver.
Size: 36mm.
Description: (Obverse) right-facing profile of King Edward VII. (Reverse) an erect female figure representing Natal with the sword of justice in her right hand and a palm branch in the left. She treads on a heap of Zulu weapons and is supported by Britannia who holds the orb of empire in her hand. In the background, the sun emerges from behind storm clouds.
Clasp: 1906.
Comments: *The Natal government instituted this medal for services in the operations following the Zulu rebellion. Local volunteer units bore the brunt of the action and it is interesting to note that one of the recipients was Sergeant-Major M. K. Gandhi who later led India to independence. Medals to officers are engraved in running cursive script.*

VALUE:

		Miniature
No clasp (2000)	£130–165	£40–50
i. 1906 (8000)	£175–200	£50–65
Natal Naval Corps		
without clasp (67)	£150–200	
clasp 1906 (136)	£250–300	

163A. MESSINA EARTHQUAKE COMMEMORATIVE MEDAL

Date: 1908.
Campaign: Messina earthquake relief.
Branch of Service: Royal Navy.
Ribbon: Green with white edges and central white stripe.
Metal: Silver.
Size: 31.5mm.
Description: (Obverse) left-facing profile of King Victor Emanuel III; (reverse) A wreath of oak leaves within which are the words MEDAGLIA COMMEMORATIVA / TERREMOTO CALABRO SICULO 28 DICEMBRE 1908.
Comments: *The King of Italy rewarded Royal Naval and other personnel who went to the aid of victims of the tragic earthquake that hit Messina in December 1908 with this silver medal. Officers and men serving on certain ships were eligible for the award as well as members of the Mercantile Marine and others who were engaged in relief operations. The Admiralty's published list of RN ships is as follows: HMS Duncan, HMS Euralyus, HMS Exmouth, HMS Lancaster, HMS Minerva and HMS Sutlej. However 52 medals were also awarded to personnel from HMS Boxer, which was omitted from the original list and a further 35 medals were awarded to the officers and men of HMS Philomel who had actually "been engaged in work which was directly attributable to the rescue operations". The medal was issued unnamed. In addition to the commemorative medal a special Messina Earthquake Merit Medal was awarded in two sizes (40mm and 30mm) bronze, silver and gold to organisations, vessels and various key individuals who played a part in the rescue operations and examples are known in miniature, in silver.*

VALUE:		Miniature
Unattributed single medal	£100–150	£60–80
Royal Navy (c. 3,500)	£120–160	
Royal Marines (481)	£140–180	
Mercantile Marine (c. 400)	£140–180	
Other	—	
Merit Medal	—	£100–£150

164. INDIA GENERAL SERVICE MEDAL

Date: 1909.
Campaigns: India 1908 to 1935.
Branch of Service: British and Indian forces.
Ribbon: Green with a broad blue central stripe.
Metal: Silver.
Size: 36mm.
Description: Three obverse types were used: Edward VII (1908–10), George V Kaisar-i-Hind (1910–30) and George V Indiae Imp (1930–35). (Reverse) the fortress at Jamrud in the Khyber Pass, with the name INDIA in a wreath at the foot.
Clasps: Twelve, plus two in bronze (see below).
Comments: *This medal was awarded for a number of minor campaigns and operations in India before and after the First World War. The medals were struck at the Royal Mint in London and by the Indian government in Calcutta, the only difference being in the claw suspenders, the former being ornate and the latter plain. Medals with the bars North West Frontier 1908 and Abor 1911–12 were also issued in bronze to native bearers.*

VALUE:

		British Army	RAF	Indian regiments	Miniature
i.	North West Frontier 1908	£125–150	—	£70–95	£20–25
	bronze	—	—	£80–125	
ii.	Abor 1911–12	—	—	£180–225	£20–25
	bronze	—	—	£250–300	—
iii.	Afghanistan NWF 1919	£80–100	£150–180	£35–55	£15–20
iv.	Waziristan 1919–21	£120–150	£180–200	£45–65	£15–20
iv*.	Mahsud 1919–20 (175)	£120–150	£550–650	£60–85	£15–20
v.	Malabar 1921–22	£150–175	—	£110–155	£30–35
vi.	Waziristan 1921–24	£60–90	£150–180	£35–55	£15–20
vii.	Waziristan 1925 (254)	—	£1000–1100	—	£20–25
viii.	NW Frontier 1930–31	£80–100	£150–160	£35–55	£15–20
ix.	Burma 1930–32	£100–150	Rare	£55–85	£15–20
x.	Mohmand 1933	£200–250	£500–600	£40–60	£15–20
xi.	NW Frontier 1935	£80–100	£120–150	£35–55	£20–25

*Usually found in combination with Waziristan 1919-21, but 10 medals were awarded either with this clasp alone or with the Afghanistan NWF clasp.

Royal Mint striking.

Calcutta striking.

165. KHEDIVE'S SUDAN MEDAL 1910

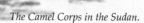

Date: 1911.

Campaign: Sudan 1910 to 1922

Branch of Service: British and Egyptian forces.

Ribbon: Black with thin red and green stripes on either side.

Metal: Silver or bronze.

Size: 36mm.

Description: (Obverse) an Arabic inscription signifying the name of Khedive Abbas Hilmi and the date 1328 in the Moslem calendar (1910 AD) (type I). He was deposed in December 1914 when Egypt was declared a British protectorate, and succeeded by his nephew who was proclaimed Sultan. Sultan Hussein Kamil changed the Arabic inscription and date to AH 1335 (1916–17) on later issues of the medal (type II). (Reverse) a lion poised on a plinth with the sunrise in the background.

Clasps: 16, inscribed in English and Arabic.

Comments: *Introduced in June 1911 as a replacement for the previous Khedive's Sudan medal of 1896–1908, it was awarded for minor operations in the southern Sudan between 1910 and 1922. The silver medal was issued with clasps to combatants, and without a clasp to non-combatants, while the bronze version was granted to camp followers. The medal is usually found unnamed although a few British recipient's medals are found named in small impressed capitals or arabic script. The prices below are for unnamed examples.*

VALUE:

Silver without clasp type I		£200–250
Silver without clasp type II		£180–200
Bronze without clasp type I		£400–450
Bronze without clasp type II		£250–300
i.	Atwot	£260–300
ii.	S. Kordofan 1910	£260–300
iii.	Sudan 1912	£280–310
iv.	Zeraf 1913-14	£300–325
v.	Mandal	£300–325
vi.	Miri	£300–325
vii.	Mongalla 1915-16	£300–325
viii.	Darfur 1916	£290–320
ix.	Fasher	£260–300
x.	Lau Nuer	£265–325
xi.	Nyima 1917-18	£250–300
xii.	Atwot 1918	£250–300
xiii.	Garjak Nuer	£250–300
xiv.	Aliab Dinka	£300–350
xv.	Nyala	£300–350
xvi.	Darfur 1921	£350–400
2 clasps		£350–450

Miniature

Silver type I	£35–50
Silver type II	£35–50
With any single clasp	£50–80

For each additional clasp add £15–30 (slip-on clasps approx. 20% less)

The Camel Corps in the Sudan.

FIRST WORLD WAR MEDALS

World War I medals have enjoyed something of a boom in recent years as more collectors come into the hobby and as more families endeavour to locate the medals of their forebears. The massive popularity in family history research, as shown with the huge attendance at the inaugural "Who do you think you are? Live" event, has gone a long way to encouraging more and more people to find out about their ancestors' military service. The National Archives project to put World War I soldiers' records on-line, in addition to the Medal Index Cards already there, is the most popular starting point for the family historian, thus ensuring the popularity of World War I as a "collecting theme". However, as is inevitable with any boom, there has to be a point at which things cannot go on as they were. The popularity of World War I medals, and in turn the money they were fetching, has led to there being something of a glut in the market recently and whilst prices haven't fallen dramatically they certainly aren't going up as rapidly as they have been in recent years. The prices we have quoted in this year's edition of the Yearbook are broadly similar to last year's and whilst it is true that on some occasions the standard trios, pairs and singles can be found for less than is listed here, these bargains are few and far between and there is not a downward trend—prices just aren't going up as quickly as they were. That, however, is no bad thing as there was a danger for a while that the hobby would price itself beyond the scope of most new collectors, and the fact that the "basic" medals have slowed a little can only be good for us all. World War I still remains a very popular theme and with the hundredth anniversary of the start of the war fast approaching and more records coming to the fore all the time, it is unlikely that its popularity will wane in the foreseeable future. Indeed every month in MEDAL NEWS the Medal Tracker service continues to get more requests for World War I medals than any other and the same is true of Medaltracker.com. As with any area of the hobby, medals with a connection to the more famous actions, in this case particularly the Somme, Gallipoli, the Retreat from Mons, and the battles of Loos and Jutland all command a strong premium (the prices paid for First day of the Somme casualties continue to amaze) and gallantry and complete "sets" to casualties all continue to sell exceptionally well. It should also be noted that medals to Imperial forces, particularly Australian, Canadian and New Zealanders will fetch a considerable premium.

166. 1914 STAR

Date: 1917.

Campaign: France and Belgium 1914.

Branch of Service: British forces.

Ribbon: Watered silk red, white and blue.

Metal: Bronze.

Size: Height 50mm; max. width 45mm.

Description: A crowned four-pointed star with crossed swords and a wreath of oak leaves, having the royal cypher at the foot and a central scroll inscribed AUG NOV 1914. Uniface, the naming being inscribed incuse on the plain reverse.

Clasps: 5th Aug.–22nd Nov. 1914. The clasp was sewn on to the ribbon of the medal, the first of this type. A silver rosette is worn on the ribbon strip if the bar was awarded.

Comments: *Awarded to all those who had served in France and Belgium between 5 August and 22 November 1914. In 1919 King George V authorised a clasp bearing these dates for those who had actually been under fire during that period. The majority of the 400,000 recipients of the star were officers and men of the prewar British Army, the "Old Contemptibles" who landed in France soon after the outbreak of the First World War and who took part in the retreat from Mons, hence the popular nickname of Mons Star by which this medal is often known. Approximately 1000 were awarded to members of the Royal Flying Corps of which about 300 received the bar, hence they command a premium.*

VALUE:		*Miniature*
1914 Star	£65–85	£3–5
To RN	£200–300	
RM	£100–120	
RND	£150–200	
1914 Star/BWM/Victory trio		
Corps	from £95	
British Regiments	from £175	
Canadian Regiments	from £850	
Australian Regiments	from £1200	
Trio with plaque (no. 172)		
Corps	£200–250	
Regiments	£350–450	
RFC	£1500–2000	
i. 5th Aug.–22nd Nov. 1914		
("Mons") clasp	£100–150	£5–7

167. 1914–15 STAR

Date: 1918.
Campaign: First World War 1914–15.
Branch of Service: British and imperial forces.
Ribbon: Watered silk red, white and blue (as above).
Metal: Bronze.
Size: Height 50mm; max. width 45mm.
Description: As above, but AUG and NOV omitted and scroll across the centre inscribed 1914–15.
Clasps: None.
Comments: *Awarded to those who saw service in any theatre of war between 5 August 1914 and 31 December 1915, other than those who had already qualified for the 1914 Star. No fewer than 2,350,000 were awarded, making it the commonest British campaign medal up to that time.*

VALUE:

1914–15 Star	£25–55	*Miniature*	*£3–4*
1914–15 Star/BWM/Victory trio			
Corps	from £55		
RN	from £75		
Regiments	from £80		
Trio with plaque (no. 172)			
Corps	£200–250		
Regiments/RN	£300–350		

168. BRITISH WAR MEDAL 1914–20

Date: 1919.
Campaign: First World War, 1914–20.
Branch of Service: British and imperial forces.
Ribbon: Orange watered centre with stripes of white and black at each side and borders of royal blue.
Metal: Silver or bronze.
Size: 36mm.
Description: (Obverse) the uncrowned left-facing profile of King George V by Sir Bertram Mackennal. (Reverse) St George on horseback trampling underfoot the eagle shield of the Central Powers and a skull and cross-bones, the emblems of death. Above, the sun has risen in victory. The figure is mounted on horseback to symbolise man's mind controlling a force of greater strength than his own, and thus alludes to the scientific and mechanical appliances which helped to win the war.
Clasps: None.
Comments: *This medal was instituted to record the successful conclusion of the First World War, but it was later extended to cover the period 1919–20 and service in mine-clearing at sea as well as participation in operations in North and South Russia, the eastern Baltic, Siberia, the Black Sea and Caspian. Some 6,500,000 medals were awarded in silver, but about 110,000 in bronze were issued mainly to Chinese, Indian and Maltese personnel in labour battalions. It was originally intended to award campaign clasps, but 79 were recommended by the Army and 68 by the Navy, so the scheme was abandoned as impractical. The naval clasps were actually authorised (7 July 1920) and miniatures are known with them, though the actual clasps were never issued.*

VALUE:

		Miniature
Silver (6,500,000)	£20–30*	£4–5
Bronze (110,000)	£90–125	£15–20
BWM/Victory pair		
Corps	from £30	
Regiments/RN	from £40	
Pair with plaque (no. 172)		
Corps	from £180	
Regiment/RN	from £200	

* Current prices are being dictated by world silver markets. The BWM being 1oz of silver, as the price of silver fluctuates so will the price of the BWM.

169. MERCANTILE MARINE WAR MEDAL

Date: 1919.
Campaign: First World War 1914–18.
Branch of Service: Mercantile Marine.
Ribbon: Green and red with a central white stripe, symbolising port and starboard steaming lights.
Metal: Bronze.
Size: 36mm.
Description: (Obverse) Mackennal profile of King George V; (reverse) a steamship ploughing through an angry sea, with a sinking submarine and a sailing vessel in the background, the whole enclosed in a laurel wreath.
Clasps: None.
Comments: *Awarded by the Board of Trade to members of the Merchant Navy who had undertaken one or more voyages through a war or danger zone.*
VALUE:

Bronze (133,000)	£35–40
To women	£175–250
BWM/Mercantile Marine pair	from £60
To Australians	from £100
To South Africans	from £120
With plaque (no. 172)	from £400
Miniature	£20–25

170. VICTORY MEDAL

Date: 1919.
Campaign: First World War 1914–19.
Branch of Service: British and imperial forces.
Ribbon: 38mm double rainbow (indigo at edges and red in centre).
Metal: Yellow bronze.
Size: 36mm.
Description: (Obverse) the standing figure of Victory holding a palm branch in her right hand and stretching out her left hand. (Reverse) a laurel wreath containing a four-line inscription THE GREAT WAR FOR CIVILISATION 1914–1919.
Clasps: None.
Comments: *Issued to all who had already got the 1914 or 1914–15 Stars and most of those who had the British War Medal, some six million are believed to have been produced. It is often known as the Allied War Medal because the same basic design and double rainbow ribbon were adopted by thirteen other Allied nations (though the USA alone issued it with campaign clasps). The Union of South Africa produced a version with a reverse text in English and Dutch (not Afrikaans as is often stated).*

VALUE:

British pattern	£10–14
South African pattern	£25–35
Dark "Chocolate" colour issue	£15–25
Miniature	
Normal	£3–4
"CIVILIZATION" variety	£20–25
South African pattern	£70–80

171. TERRITORIAL FORCE WAR MEDAL

Date: 1919.
Campaign: First World War 1914–19.
Branch of Service: Territorial forces.
Ribbon: Watered gold silk with two dark green stripes towards the edges.
Metal: Bronze.
Size: 36mm.
Description: (Obverse) effigy of King George V; (reverse) a wreath enclosing the text FOR VOLUNTARY SERVICE OVERSEAS 1914–19.
Clasps: None.
Comments: *Awarded to all those serving with the Territorial Forces on 4 August 1914, or those who had completed four years service before this date and rejoined on or before 30 September 1914, who served overseas during the course of World War I. Those who had already qualified for the 1914 or 1914–15 Stars, however, were excluded. Only 34,000 medals were awarded, making it by far the scarcest of the First World War medals. The value of individual medals depends on the regiment or formation of the recipient.*

VALUE:

Infantry/Corps (23,762)	£175–250
Artillery (6460)	£150–200
Yeomanry (393)	£400–500
Cavalry (95)	£800–1000
RFC, RAF, RNAS (499)	£700–900
Nurses (277)	£550–650
Miniature	£20–25

171A. BRITISH RED CROSS SOCIETY MEDAL FOR WAR SERVICE

Date: 1920.
Campaign: First World War.
Branch of Service: Members of the British Red Cross Society.
Ribbon: Plain white.
Metal: Bronze-gilt.
Size: 31mm.
Description: (Obverse) the Geneva Cross surrounded by a laurel wreath, with the legend BRITISH RED CROSS SOCIETY: FOR WAR SERVICE: 1914–1918 around; (reverse) a wreath enclosing the text INTER/ARMA/CARITAS ("Amidst the arms, love").
Clasps: None.
Comments: *Granted to all members of the BRCS including Voluntary Aid Detachments who had performed one year or 1,000 hours voluntary service during the war and who did not receive any British War Medal for services rendered in respect of Red Cross war work. The medal was unnamed for wear only on Red Cross or similar uniform.*

VALUE: £15–20   *Miniature*   £20–25

172. MEMORIAL PLAQUE

Date: 1919.
Campaign: First World War.
Branch of Service: British forces.
Ribbon: None.
Metal: Bronze.
Size: 120mm.
Description: The plaque shows Britannia bestowing a laurel crown on a rectangular tablet bearing the full name of the dead in raised lettering. In front stands the British lion, with dolphins in the upper field, an oak branch lower right, and a lion cub clutching a fallen eagle in the exergue. The inscription round the circumference reads HE (or SHE) DIED FOR FREEDOM AND HONOVR. A parchment scroll was issued with each plaque giving the deceased's name and unit.
Comments: *Given, with a parchment scroll, to the next of kin of those who lost their lives on active service during the War. Originally it was thought that Naval and Army plaques differed because of the width of the "H" in "HE" however examples of narrow "H" plaques found to Army units and wide "H" plaques to the Navy indicates this to be incorrect. The most likely reason for the narrower "H" is the later decision to add an "S" to allow for female casualty plaques.*

VALUE:		
	"He died" (1,355,000)	From £50
	"She died" (600)	From £2500
	Parchment scroll (male)	From £25
	ditto (female)	From £800
Miniature:	Uniface/unnamed (Contemporary casting)	£30–40

172A. SILVER WAR BADGE

Date: 12 September 1916.
Campaign: First World War.
Ribbon: None.
Metal: Silver.
Size: 33mm.
Description: A brooch-mounted circular badge with the crowned royal monogram in the centre and edge inscription FOR KING AND EMPIRE + SERVICES RENDERED +.
Comments: *Awarded to service personnel who sustained a wound or contracted sickness or disability in the course of the war as a result of which they were invalided out. It was worn on the lapel in civilian clothes. Each badge was numbered on the reverse. The purpose of the badge was to prevent men of military age but not in uniform from being harassed by women pursuing them with white feathers. Later in the War medical restrictions altered and some men re-enlisted and could wear the badge in uniform.*

VALUE:	From £20	*Miniature*:	£15–20

172B. CEYLON VOLUNTEER SERVICE MEDAL

Date: 1919.
Campaign: First World War.
Branch of Service: Ceylon volunteer forces.
Ribbon: None.
Metal: Bronze.
Size: 48mm x 44mm.
Description: An upright oval medal. (Obverse) a seated female figure bestowing a laurel crown on a kneeling soldier, with a radiant sun on the horizon; above, a six-line inscription: PRESENTED BY THE GOVERNMENT OF CEYLON TO THOSE WHO VOLUNTARILY GAVE THEIR SERVICES OVERSEAS IN THE GREAT WAR OF with the dates 1914 1919 in two lines on the right of the field; (reverse) the winged figure of Victory seated on a throne above a tablet inscribed with the name of the recipient.
Comments: *Awarded to volunteers from the Ceylon forces who served abroad during the war. Ceylon (now Sri Lanka) was the only British colony to issue such a medal for war service.*

VALUE: £100–150

173. NAVAL GENERAL SERVICE MEDAL 1915–62

Date: 1915.
Campaigns: Naval actions 1915 to 1962.
Branch of Service: Royal Navy.
Ribbon: White with broad crimson edges and two narrow crimson stripes towards the centre.
Metal: Silver.
Size: 36mm.
Description: (Obverse) effigy of the reigning monarch (see below). (Reverse) Britannia and two seahorses travelling through the sea.
Clasps: 17 (see below).
Comments: *Instituted for service in minor operations for which no separate medal might be issued. Five different obverses were employed: George V (1915-36), George VI Ind Imp (1936-49), George VI Fid Def (1949-52), Elizabeth II Br Omn (1952-53) and Elizabeth II Dei Gratia (1953-62). Medals issued with the first clasp include the name of the recipient's ship but this lapsed in later awards. The MALAYA clasp was issued with three types of medal: the George VI Fid Def and Elizabeth II Dei Gratia being the most common. The clasp BOMB & MINE CLEARANCE 1945–46 is very rare as it was apparently only awarded to the Royal Australian Navy. The clasp CANAL ZONE was instituted in October 2003 for service between October 1951 and October 1954.*

VALUE:			Miniature
i.	Persian Gulf 1909-1914		*(in silver add £5)*
	RN (7,127)	£150–180	
	Army (37)	£800–1000	£15–25
ii.	Iraq 1919-20 (116)	£1800–2000	£15–25
iii.	NW Persia 1919–20 (4)*	Rare	£25–50
iv.	Palestine 1936–39 (13,600)	£125–150	£15–25
v.	SE Asia 1945–46 (2,000)	£200–250	£15–25
vi.	Minesweeping 1945–51 (4,750)	£175–200	£15–25
vii.	Palestine 1945–48 (7,900)	£150–180	£15–25
viii.	Malaya (George VI, Elizabeth II		
	2nd type) (7,800)	£100–140	£15–25
	(Elizabeth II 1st type)	£125–155	£15–25
ix.	Yangtze 1949 (1,450)	£800–1000	£15–25
	to HMS *Amethyst*	£1500–2000	
x.	Bomb & Mine Clearance 1945–53 (145)	£800–1000	£40–60
xi.	Bomb & Mine Clearance 1945–46	Very rare	£40–60
xii.	Bomb & Mine Clearance		
	Mediterranean (60)	£2000–2500	£40–60
xiii.	Cyprus (4,300)	£150–200	£15–25
xiv.	Near East (17,800)	£95–125	£15–25
xv.	Arabian Peninsula (1,200)	£200–250	£15–25
xvi.	Brunei (900)	£250–300	£15–25
xvii.	Canal Zone	£250–350	—

The clasp NW Persia 1920 was withdrawn in favour of the clasp NW Persia 1919–20. Recipients were supposed to return their first clasp in exchange for the latter.

174. GENERAL SERVICE MEDAL 1918–62

Date: 1923.

Campaigns: Minor campaigns 1918 to 1962.

Branch of Service: Army and RAF.

Ribbon: Purple with a central green stripe.

Metal: Silver.

Size: 36mm

Description: (Obverse) six different effigies of the reigning monarch [George V coinage head (1918–30), George V crowned and robed bust (1931–36), George VI Ind Imp (1937–49), George VI Fid Def (1949–52), Elizabeth II Br Omn (1952–54) and Elizabeth II Dei Gratia (1955–62)]. (Reverse) a standing figure of Victory in a Greek helmet and carrying a trident, bestowing palms on a winged sword.

Clasps: 18 (see below).

Comments: *Awarded to military and RAF personnel for numerous campaigns and operations that fell short of full-scale war. It did not cover areas already catered for in the Africa and India general service medals. The George V crowned and robed bust was used only on the medal for Northern Kurdistan in 1931. The clasp CANAL ZONE was instituted in October 2003 for service between October 1951 and October 1954.*

VALUE:

		British units	RAF	Indian and local units	Miniature (in silver add £5)
i.	S. Persia (Brit. officers)	£150–200	£3000–3500	£60–90	£15–25
ii.	Kurdistan	£80–110	£250–300	£60–90	£15–25
iii.	Iraq	£75–125	£200–250	£60–90	£15–25
iv.	N.W. Persia	£90–120	£300–350	£60–90	£15–25
v.	Southern Desert Iraq	—	£500–600	—	£20–30
vi.	Northern Kurdistan	£350–450	£1000–1200	—	£90–100
vii.	Palestine	£80–120	£100–150	£75–100	£15–25
viii.	S.E. Asia 1945-46	£80–110	£80–100	£45–65	£15–25
ix.	Bomb and Mine Clearance 1945-49	£400–450	£400–450	—	£40–60
x.	Bomb and Mine Clearance 1945-56	—	—	£475–550*	£40–60
xi.	Palestine 1945-48	£60–85	£50–60	£85–100	£15–25
xii.	Malaya (George VI)	£60–85	£50–60	£55–65	£15–25
xiii.	Malaya (Elizabeth II)	£60–85	£50–60	£55–65	£15–25
xiv.	Cyprus	£60–85	£50–60	£55–65	£15–25
xv.	Near East	£80–125	£80–120	—	£15–25
xvi.	Arabian Peninsula	£80–125	£60–80	£65–70	£15–25
xvii.	Brunei	£200–250	£180–220	£125–155	£15–25
xviii.	Canal Zone	£250–350	£250–350	—	

*Australian units

174A. IRAQ ACTIVE SERVICE MEDAL

Date: May 1926.
Campaign: Iraq, 1924–38.
Branch of Service: Army and RAF.
Ribbon: 31mm in equal stripes of green, white and green.
Metal: Bronze.
Size: 38mm.
Description: (Obverse) a crescent forming the lower part; with an Arabic inscription above signifying "General Service" in two laurel branches. The medal is superimposed on crossed rifles, with rays in the arc between the muzzles, to which is joined a flattened loop suspender. (Reverse) The name of King Faisal I in Arabic and the date (AH) 1344 (i.e. 1926).
Clasps: Dates 1930–31, 1932, 1935 or 1936 in Arabic numerals with an Arabic inscription on the left.
Comments: *Also known as King Faisal's War Medal, it was awarded to British Army and RAF personnel stationed in Iraq or serving with the Iraq Levies. It was originally issued without a clasp, but clasps denoted subsequent actions or periods of service. By 1931, however, medals were issued with appropriate clasps from the outset.*

VALUE:

Without clasp	£80–100
With clasps	£100–150

175. INDIA GENERAL SERVICE MEDAL 1936–39

Date: 1938.
Campaign: India 1936–39.
Branch of Service: British and Indian Armies and RAF.
Ribbon: Stone flanked by narrow red stripes, with broad green stripes at the edges.
Metal: Silver.
Size: 36mm
Description: (Obverse) crowned effigy of King George VI; (reverse) a tiger with the word INDIA across the top.
Clasps: North-West Frontier 1936–37, North-West Frontier 1937–39.
Comments: *The fourth and last of the IGS series, it was introduced when the change of effigy from George V to George VI became necessary, anticipating a similarly long life. It was not awarded after the outbreak of the Second World War, while the partition and independence of the Indian sub-continent afterwards rendered it obsolete. The medal was struck at the Royal Mint, London for award to British Army troops and RAF personnel, but the Calcutta Mint struck the medals awarded to the Indian Army.*

VALUE:

	British Army	RAF	Indian Army	Miniature
North West Frontier				
i. 1936-37	£100–150	£100–150	£45–50	£15–20
ii. 1937-39	£100–150	£100–150	£45–50	£15–25
2 clasps	£150–200	£150–200	£50–65	£15–30

(slip-on clasps deduct 20%)

176. BRITISH NORTH BORNEO COMPANY'S GENERAL SERVICE MEDAL 1937–1941

Instituted: 1937.

Campaign: British North Borneo (now Sabah), 1937–41.

Branch of Service: British North Borneo Company staff, Constabulary and various civilians.

Ribbon: 35mm, half dark green, half yellow. Gallantry awards were denoted by a thin red central stripe.

Metal: Silver. Copies were made in bronze.

Size: 38mm diameter, with a thickness of 3mm.

Description: (Obverse) the shield of the Company flanked by warriors as supporters. Above the shield are two arms, one clothed and the other naked, supporting the Company's flag. Below the shield is the motto PERGO ET PERAGO (I carry on and accomplish); (reverse) the seated figure of Britannia facing right, holding a trident in her left hand, with her right hand resting on a shield which bears the Union flag. NORTH BORNEO GENERAL SERVICE MEDAL is inscribed round the top and in the exergue is a branch with 11 leaves.

Clasps: None.

Comments: *Only one gallantry award was ever made, to Leong Yew Pong, aged 15, gazetted August 3, 1939. For specially valuable or long and meritorious services 44 were issued, gazetted in 1937, 1938, 1939 and 1941, with one replacement in 1947. Recipients were government officials, armed constabulary, rubber planters, the Archdeacon of North Borneo, the Chairman of the Chamber of Commerce, railway managers, businessmen and local dignitaries.*

VALUE

Medal	Type	Officially named	Unnamed original	Spink copy	Specimen
For Gallantry	Silver	Unique	Rare	£250–300	£300–350
For Service	Silver	£1500–1750	Rare	£150–200	£150–200
Miniature	£180–200				

176A. SUDAN DEFENCE FORCE GENERAL SERVICE MEDAL

Instituted: November 1933.

Campaign: Minor campaigns in the Sudan after 1933.

Branch of Service: Sudan Defence Force (SDF) and Police.

Ribbon: Central stripe of royal blue, edged by two yellow stripes and two black stripes at the edges.

Metal: Silver.

Size: 36mm.

Description: (Obverse) the seal of the Governor-General of the Sudan; (reverse) a stationary group of Sudanese soldiers, with "The Sudan" in Arabic below.

Clasps: None.

Comments: *The medal was awarded on the recommendation of the Kaid el'Amm (SDF Commander) to native personnel of the SDF, Police and other approved Sudanese who served in the field on such operations as might be considered by the Governor-General as being of sufficient importance to warrant the grant of the medal. It was also awarded for action against Italian forces in the southern Sudan from June 1940 to November 1941. About 9,000 were issued.*

VALUE: £150–£200

SECOND WORLD WAR STARS

Eight different campaign stars were issued for the Second World War. Apart from some Commonwealth issues notably Australia, Pakistan and South Africa, these were issued unnamed. It was decided that the maximum number of stars that could be earned by any one person was five, while those who qualified for more received a clasp to be sewn on the ribbon of the appropriate star. Only one clasp per ribbon was permitted which was the first to be earned after qualifying for that star. Thus the stars could bear the following clasps:

1	1939–45 Star	i. Battle of Britain
2	Atlantic Star	ii. Air Crew Europe *or* iii. France and Germany
3	Air Crew Europe Star	iv. Atlantic *or* iii. France and Germany
4	Africa Star	v. North Africa 1942-43, vi. 8th Army *or* vii. 1st Army
5	Pacific Star	viii. Burma
6	Burma Star	ix. Pacific
7	Italy Star	None
8	France and Germany Star	x. Atlantic

The ribbons are believed to have been designed by King George VI personally and have symbolic significance in each case. When ribbons alone are worn, the clasp is usually denoted by a silver rosette. However, the Battle of Britain clasp is represented by a gilt rosette and the 8th Army and 1st Army clasps by small silver numerals. As the clasps were sewn on to the ribbon and the stars issued unnamed, it is difficult to put valuations on examples with campaign clasps, however, the prices quoted are for medals with the *original* clasps. When purchasing expensive groups it is advisable that the medals be supported by documentary provenance or form part of a group in which at least one of the medals is named to the recipient.

Many of the medals and stars of the Second World War are still being officially produced, therefore there are a number of different die varieties available. There are also a number of dangerous forgeries in existence so care should be taken when purchasing expensive items. In the past few years a number of lapel badges or emblems have been produced for award to veterans—see MYB nos. 242C et seq.

177. 1939–45 STAR

Date: 1945.

Campaign: Second World War 1939–45.

Branch of Service: British and Commonwealth forces.

Ribbon: Equal stripes of dark blue, red and light blue symbolising the Royal Navy, Army and RAF respectively. The 1939–43 ribbon was authorised in November 1943 and worn by those awarded this proposed Star which became the 1939–45 Star when finally issued.

Metal: Bronze.

Size: Height 44mm; max. width 38mm.

Description: The six-pointed star has a circular centre with the GRI/VI monogram, surmounted by a crown and inscribed THE 1939-1945 STAR round the foot.

Clasps: Battle of Britain, sewn directly on to the ribbon.

Comments: *The first in a series of eight bronze stars issued for service in the Second World War, it was awarded to personnel who had completed six months' service in specified operational commands overseas, between 3 September 1939 and 2 September 1945, though in certain cases the minimum period was shortened. Any service curtailed by death, injury or capture also qualified, as did the award of a decoration or a mention in despatches. The clasp awarded to RAF aircrew for action during the Battle of Britain was denoted by a gilt rosette when the ribbon was worn alone. It is ironic that RAF ground crews who kept the Battle of Britain fighters in the air did not qualify for the 1939–45 Star and only received the Defence and War Medals, although those who assisted with the evacuation of troops from the beaches of Dunkirk did qualify.*

VALUE:		Miniature
1939-45 Star	£10–12	£3–5
Battle of Britain clasp	£1500–1800	£6

178. ATLANTIC STAR

Campaign: Atlantic 1939-45.
Branch of Service: Mainly Royal and Commonwealth Navies.
Ribbon: Watered silk blue, white and green representing the ocean.
Metal: Bronze.
Size: Height 44mm; max. width 38mm.
Description: As above, but inscribed THE ATLANTIC STAR.
Clasps: Air Crew Europe, France and Germany.
Comments: *This star was awarded in the Royal Navy for six months' service afloat between 3 September 1939 and 8 May 1945 in the Atlantic or home waters, and to personnel employed in the convoys to North Russia and the South Atlantic. Personnel must have already qualified for the 1939–45 Star with the qualifying period for this not counting towards the Atlantic Star. Merchant Navy personnel also qualified, as did RAF and Army (maritime gunners and air crews—the latter only requiring 2 months service) who served afloat. In the last six months of operational service up to 8 May 1945, the Atlantic Star was awarded but not the 1939–45 Star. Entitlement to the France and Germany or Air Crew Europe stars was denoted by clasps to that effect, if the Atlantic Star was previously awarded. Only one clasp could be worn. Only two awards were made to WRNS: to an officer and a rating.*

VALUE:		Miniature
Atlantic Star	£30–35	£3
Air Crew Europe clasp	Add £35	£6
France and Germany clasp	Add £20	£6

179. AIR CREW EUROPE STAR

Campaign: Air operations over Europe 1939-44.
Branch of Service: RAF and Commonwealth aircrew.
Ribbon: Pale blue (the sky) with black edges (night flying) and a narrow yellow stripe on either side (enemy searchlights).
Metal: Bronze.
Size: Height 44mm; max. width 38mm.
Description: As above, but inscribed THE AIR CREW EUROPE STAR.
Clasps: Atlantic or France and Germany.
Comments: *Awarded for operational flying from UK bases over Europe, for a period of two months between 3 September 1939 and 4 June 1944. Entitlement to either the Atlantic Star or France and Germany Star was denoted by the appropriate bar. This star is by far the most coveted of all the Second World War stars. Officially named stars to South Africans are the rarest of all the Second World War medals.*

VALUE:		Miniature
Air Crew Europe Star	£225–250	£3
Atlantic Clasp	Add £60	£6
France and Germany Clasp	Add £15	£6

180. AFRICA STAR

Campaign: Africa 1940-43.
Branch of Service: British and Commonwealth forces.
Ribbon: Pale buff symbolising the sand of the desert, with a broad red central stripe, a dark blue stripe on the left and a light blue stripe on the right symbolising the three services.
Metal: Bronze.
Size: Height 44mm; max. width 38mm.
Description: As above, but inscribed THE AFRICA STAR.
Clasps: North Africa 1942-43, 8th Army, 1st Army.
Comments: *Awarded for entry into an operational area in North Africa between 10 June 1940 (the date of Italy's declaration of war) and 12 May 1943 (the end of operations in North Africa), but service in Abyssinia (Ethiopia), Somaliland, Eritrea and Malta also qualified for the award. A silver numeral 1 or 8 worn on the ribbon denoted service with the First or Eighth Army between 23 October 1942 and 23 May 1943. A clasp inscribed North Africa 1942-43 was awarded to personnel of the Royal Navy Inshore Squadrons and Merchant Navy vessels which worked inshore between these dates. RAF personnel also qualified for this clasp, denoted by a silver rosette on the ribbon alone.*

VALUE:		Miniature
Africa Star	£12–15	£3
8th Army clasp	Add £20	£8
1st Army clasp	Add £20	£8
North Africa 1942–43 clasp	Add £20	£10

181. PACIFIC STAR

Campaign: Pacific area 1941-45.
Branch of Service: British and Commonwealth forces.
Ribbon: Dark green (the jungle) with a central yellow stripe (the beaches), narrow stripes of dark and light blue (Royal Navy and RAF) and wider stripes of red (Army) at the edges.
Metal: Bronze.
Size: Height 44mm; max. width 38mm.
Description: As above, but inscribed THE PACIFIC STAR.
Clasps: Burma.
Comments: *Awarded for operational service in the Pacific theatre of war from 8 December 1941 to 15 August 1945. Service with the Royal and Merchant navies in the Pacific Ocean, Indian Ocean and South China Sea and land service in these areas also qualified. Personnel qualifying for both Pacific and Burma Stars got the first star and a clasp in respect of the second.*

VALUE:		Miniature
Pacific Star	£35–40	£3
Burma clasp	Add £40	£6

182. BURMA STAR

Campaign: Burma 1941-45.
Branch of Service: British and Commonwealth forces.
Ribbon: Three equal bands of dark blue (British forces), red (Commonwealth forces) and dark blue. The dark blue bands each have at their centres a stripe of bright orange (the sun).
Metal: Bronze.
Size: Height 44mm; max. width 38mm.
Description: As above, but inscribed THE BURMA STAR.
Clasps: Pacific.
Comments: *Qualifying service in the Burma campaign counted from 11 December 1941 and included service in Bengal or Assam from 1 May 1942 to 31 December 1943, and from 1 January 1944 onwards in these parts of Bengal or Assam east of the Brahmaputra. Naval service in the eastern Bay of Bengal, off the coasts of Sumatra, Sunda and Malacca also counted.*

VALUE:		Miniature
Burma Star	£15–20	£3
Pacific Clasp	Add £40	£6

183. ITALY STAR

Campaign: Italy 1943-45.
Branch of Service: British and Commonwealth forces.
Ribbon: Five equal stripes of red, white, green, white and red (the Italian national colours).
Metal: Bronze.
Size: Height 44mm; max. width 38mm.
Description: As above, but inscribed THE ITALY STAR.
Clasps: None.
Comments: *Awarded for operational service on land in Italy, Sicily, Greece, Yugoslavia, the Aegean area and Dodecanese islands, Corsica, Sardinia and Elba at any time between 11 June 1943 and 8 May 1945.*

VALUE:		Miniature
Italy Star	£12–15	£3

184. FRANCE AND GERMANY STAR

Date: 1945.
Campaign: France and Germany 1944-45.
Branch of Service: British and Commonwealth forces.
Ribbon: Five equal stripes of blue, white, red, white and blue (the national colours of the United Kingdom, France and the Netherlands).
Metal: Bronze.
Size: Height 44mm; max. width 38mm.
Description: As above, but inscribed THE FRANCE AND GERMANY STAR.
Clasps: Atlantic.
Comments: *Awarded for operational service in France, Belgium, the Netherlands or Germany from 6 June 1944 to 8 May 1945. Service in the North Sea, English Channel and Bay of Biscay in connection with the campaign in northern Europe also qualified. Prior eligibility for the Atlantic or Air Crew Europe Stars entitled personnel only to a bar for France and Germany. Conversely a first award of the France and Germany Star could earn an Atlantic bar.*

VALUE:		Miniature
France and Germany Star	£18–20	£3
Atlantic Clasp	Add £60	£6

185. DEFENCE MEDAL

Date: 1945.
Campaign: Second World War 1939-45.
Branch of Service: British and Commonwealth forces.
Ribbon: Two broad stripes of green (this green and pleasant land) superimposed by narrow stripes of black (the black-out), with a wide stripe of orange (fire-bombing) in the centre.
Metal: Cupro-nickel or silver.
Size: 36mm.
Description: (Obverse) the uncrowned effigy of King George VI; (reverse) two lions flanking an oak sapling crowned with the dates at the sides and wavy lines representing the sea below. The words THE DEFENCE MEDAL appear in the exergue.
Clasps: King's Commendation for Brave Conduct.
Comments: *Awarded to service personnel for three years' service at home, one year's service in a non-operational area (e.g. India) or six months' service overseas in territories subjected to air attack or otherwise closely threatened. Personnel of Anti-Aircraft Command, RAF ground crews, Dominion forces stationed in the UK, the Home Guard, Civil Defence, National Fire Service and many other civilian units* qualified for the medal. The medal was generally issued unnamed in cupro-nickel, but the Canadian version was struck in silver.*

VALUE:		Miniature
Cupro-nickel	£16–18	£8
Silver (Canadian)	£25–30	£12

*The definitive list of eligible recipients was published by the Ministry of Defence in 1992 — Form DM1/DM2 and Annexe. This lists 50 different organisations and 90 sub-divisions of eligible personnel.

186. WAR MEDAL 1939–45

Date: 1945.
Campaign: Second World War 1939-45.
Branch of Service: British and Commonwealth forces.
Ribbon: Narrow red stripe in the centre, with a narrow white stripe on either side, broad red stripes at either edge and two intervening stripes of blue.
Metal: Cupro-nickel or silver.
Size: 36mm.
Description: (Obverse) effigy of King George VI; (reverse) a triumphant lion trampling on a dragon symbolising the Axis powers.
Clasps: None.
Comments: *All fulltime personnel of the armed forces wherever they were serving, so long as they had served for at least 28 days between 3 September 1939 and 2 September 1945 were eligible for this medal. It was granted in addition to the campaign stars and the Defence Medal. A few categories of civilians, such as war correspondents and ferry pilots who had flown in operational theatres, also qualified. No clasps were issued with this medal but a bronze oak leaf denoted a mention in despatches. The medal was struck in cupro-nickel and issued unnamed, but those issued to Australian and South African personnel were officially named with SA prefixes (see MYB189). The Canadian version of the medal was struck in silver.*

VALUE:

		Miniature
Cupro-nickel (32g)	£10–12	£8
Officially named	£20–25	
Silver (36g) (Canadian)	£25–35	£12

186A. KING'S BADGE

Date: 1941.
Campaign: Second World War.
Ribbon: None.
Metal: Silver.
Size: 26mm.
Description: A circular buttonhole badge with the crowned monogram GRI in script capitals in the centre, inscribed FOR LOYAL SERVICE.
Comments: *Awarded to personnel who had been invalided out of the services and were in receipt of a war disablement pension. The badges are not numbered or named. For further information see MEDAL NEWS, September 2008.*

VALUE: £15–20   *Miniature* £15–20

187. INDIA SERVICE MEDAL

Date: 1945.
Campaign: India 1939-45.
Branch of Service: Indian forces.
Ribbon: Dark blue with two wide and one central thin pale blue stripes. The colours of the Order of the Indian Empire and the Order of the Star of India
Metal: Cupro-nickel.
Size: 36mm.
Description: (Obverse) the effigy of the King Emperor; (reverse) a map of the Indian sub-continent with INDIA at the top and 1939-45 at foot.
Clasps: None.
Comments: *Awarded to officers and men of the Indian forces for three years' non-operational service in India. In effect, it took the place of the Defence Medal in respect of Indian forces.*

VALUE: £12–15   *Miniature* £10–12

188. CANADIAN VOLUNTEER SERVICE MEDAL

Date: 22 October 1943.
Campaign: Second World War 1939-45.
Branch of Service: Canadian forces.
Ribbon: Narrow stripes of green and red flanking a broad central stripe of dark blue.
Metal: Silver.
Size: 36mm.
Description: (Obverse) seven men and women in the uniforms of the various services, marching in step; (reverse) the Canadian national arms.
Clasps: Maple leaf clasp to denote overseas service. A clasp inscribed DIEPPE and surmounted by the Combined Operations emblem, was instituted on 28 April 1994 for award to all servicemen who took part in the Dieppe raid of 19 August 1942. A clasp inscribed Hong Kong, the 2 words being separated by the letters HK entwined within a circle, was instituted on 28 April 1994 for award to those involved in the Battle of Hong Kong from 8–25 December 1941.
Comments: *Awarded for eighteen months' voluntary service in the Canadian forces from 3 September 1939 to 1 March 1947. The seven marching personnel are based on real people taken from National Defence photographs, representing the land, sea and air forces plus a nurse. The individuals are: first row: centre, 3780 Leading Seaman P. G. Colbeck, RCN; left, C52819 Pte D. E. Dolan, 1 Can. Para Bn; right, R95505 F/ Sgt K. M. Morgan, RCAF. Second row: centre, W4901 Wren P. Mathie, WRCNS; left, 12885 L/Cpl J. M. Dann, CWAC; right, W315563 LAW O. M. Salmon, RCAF; back row: Lt N/S E. M. Lowe, RCAMC. 650,000 have been awarded including 525,500 with the overseas bar.*

VALUE:		Miniature
Silver medal	£30–£45	£8
i. Maple Leaf clasp	£30–£35	£12
ii. Dieppe clasp	£35–45	£15
iii. Hong Kong clasp	£35–45	

188A. CANADIAN MEMORIAL CROSS

Instituted: 1 December 1919.
Branch of Service: Relatives of deceased Canadian forces.
Ribbon: Violet 11mm with ring suspension only.
Metal: Dull silver.
Size: 32mm.
Description: A Greek cross with the royal cypher at the centre, superimposed on another with arms slightly flared at the ends. Maple leaves adorn three of the arms while the top arm has a crown surmounted by a suspension ring. (Reverse) The service number, rank, initials and name of the person being commemorated are engraved. There is also a sterling mark on the lower arm. Four versions of the cross exist: the original, with GRI cypher (1914–19), with GVIR cypher and ring suspension (1940–45), GVIR cypher with suspension bar (1945–52) and an EIIR version for Korea and later conflicts.
Comments: *Issued to wives and mothers of servicemen who had died during World War I. A second version was introduced in August 1940 for award to widows and mothers of World War II servicemen, but this was extended to include those of merchant seamen and civilian firefighters. Newfoundland service personnel became eligible after April 1, 1949.*

VALUE:	Named	Unnamed
GVR, ring suspension (58,500)	From £120	£50–60
GVIR, ring suspension ⎫ (32,500)	From £120	£50–60
GVIR, bar suspension ⎭	From £120	£50–60
EIIR, bar suspension (500)	From £150	£60–70
Miniature £70–90		

189. AFRICA SERVICE MEDAL

Date: 1943.
Campaign: Second World War 1939-45.
Branch of Service: South African forces.
Ribbon: A central orange stripe, with green and gold stripes on either side.
Metal: Silver.
Size: 36mm.
Description: (Obverse) depicts a map of the African Continent; (reverse) bears a leaping Springbok. Inscribed AFRICA SERVICE MEDAL on the left and AFRIKADIENS-MEDALJE on the right.
Clasps: None, but a Protea emblem is worn on the ribbon by recipients of the King's Commendation.
Comments: *Awarded to Union service personnel who served at home and abroad during the War for at least thirty days. Medals were fully named and gave the service serial number of the recipient, prefixed by various letters, for example N (Native Military Corps), C (Cape Corps), M (Indian and Malay Corps), etc., no prefix indicated a white volunteer.*

VALUE:
Silver medal (190,000)	£25–40	*Miniature* £10–12

190. AUSTRALIA SERVICE MEDAL 1939–45

Date: 1949.
Campaign: Second World War 1939-45.
Branch of Service: Australian forces.
Ribbon: Dark blue representing the Royal Australian Navy, Khaki representing the Army, light blue representing the R.A.A.F and red representing the Mercantile Marine.
Metal: Cupro-nickel.
Size: 36mm.
Description: (Obverse) the effigy of King George VI; (reverse) the Arms of the Commonwealth of Australia surrounded by the inscription "THE AUSTRALIA SERVICE MEDAL 1939–45".
Clasps: None.
Comments: *Awarded to all Australian personnel who had seen eighteen months' overseas or three years' home service. The medals were named to the recipients. In the case of Army personnel, their service numbers were prefixed by the initial of their state: N (New South Wales), Q (Queensland), S (South Australia), T (Tasmania), V (Victoria) and W (Western Australia). X prefix is for AIF (Australian Imperial Forces or Volunteer Overseas Service). In 1999 the time served for eligibility was reduced.*

VALUE:
Cupro-nickel medal (600,000)	£40–50	*Miniature* £12–15

191. NEW ZEALAND WAR SERVICE MEDAL

Date: 1946.
Campaign: Second World War 1939-45.
Branch of Service: New Zealand forces.
Ribbon: Black with white edges.
Metal: Cupro-nickel.
Size: 36mm.
Description: (Obverse) effigy of King George VI; (reverse) the text FOR SERVICE TO NEW ZEALAND 1939-45 with a fern leaf below. Suspension was by a pair of fern leaves attached to a straight bar.
Clasps: None.
Comments: *Issued unnamed, to all members of the New Zealand forces who completed one month full-time or six months part-time service between September 1939 and September 1945, provided the applicant carried out the prescribed training or duties. This included Home Guard service and Naval Auxiliary Patrol service.*
VALUE:
Cupro-nickel medal (240,000)	£25–30	*Miniature* £7–10

191A. NEW ZEALAND MEMORIAL CROSS

Instituted: 1960.
Campaign: Second World War, 1939–45.
Branch of Service: Relatives of deceased New Zealand forces personnel.
Ribbon: 12mm royal purple
Metal: Dull Silver.
Size: 32 mm.
Description: A cross surmounted by a St Edward Crown, with fern leaves on each arm, in the centre, within a wreath, the Royal Cypher; (reverse) details of the person in respect of whose death the cross is granted.
Comments: *First announced in the New Zealand Gazette dated at Wellington, September 12, 1947 and approved by the King but not instituted until August 16, 1960. Originally granted to the next-of-kin of persons who had lost their lives on active service with the New Zealand forces during the Second World War, or who had subsequently died of wounds or illness contracted during that conflict. Provision was made for the grant of crosses to the parent(s) as well as the wife or eldest surviving daughter or son. It was subsequently awarded in respect of postwar campaigns: Korea (47), Malaya, South Vietnam (37), and East Timor (3).*

VALUE:	Named	Unnamed
GVIR	From £90	£50–60
EIIR	Rare	£50–60
Miniature £180–200		

192. SOUTH AFRICAN MEDAL FOR WAR SERVICE

Date: 1946.
Campaign: Second World War 1939–46.
Branch of Service: South African forces.
Ribbon: Three equal stripes of red, white and blue, the South African national colours.
Metal: Silver.
Size: 36mm.
Description: (Obverse) South African arms; (reverse) a wreath of protea flowers enclosing the dates 1939 and 1945. Inscribed in English and Afrikaans: SOUTH AFRICA FOR WAR SERVICES on the left and SUID AFRIKA VIR OORLOGDIENSTE on the right.
Clasps: None.
Comments: *Men and women who served for at least two years in any official voluntary organisation in South Africa or overseas qualified for this medal so long as the service was both voluntary and unpaid. Those who already had the Africa Service Medal were ineligible, but exceptions exist. The medals are named as per MYB 189.*

VALUE: Silver (17,500) £35–40 *Miniature* £15–18

192A. SOUTH AFRICAN MEMORIAL PLAQUE

Date: 1946.
Campaign: Second World War 1939–46.
Branch of Service: South African forces.
Metal: Bronze.
Size: Wood backing 135x106.4mm.
Description: The South African arms in a wreath superimposed on a a Maltese cross with torches in the angles. Below is a separate panel containing the details of the deceased. Mounted on a wooden panel.
Comments: *The plaque was given to the next of kin to personnel who lost their lives whilst on active service. The name and the cause of death are inscribed thereon. A numbered brooch of a similar design was also issued. Plaques to personnel killed in famous actions or in well-known theatres of war are worth a considerable premium, as are those named to SAAF aircrew, SANF personnel or plaques named to women. Plaques bearing the Star of David signifying that the person was of the Jewish faith are extremely rare.*

VALUE: Plaque from £50, brooch from £25

193. SOUTHERN RHODESIA WAR SERVICE MEDAL

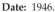

Date: 1946.
Campaign: Second World War 1939-45.
Branch of Service: Southern Rhodesian forces.
Ribbon: Dark green with black and red stripes at each edge.
Metal: Cupro-nickel.
Size: 36mm.
Description: (Obverse) King George VI; (reverse) the Southern Rhodesian national arms. FOR SERVICE IN SOUTHERN RHODESIA round the top and the dates 1939-1945 at the foot.
Clasps: None.
Comments: *This very scarce medal was awarded only to those who served in Southern Rhodesia during the period of the War but who were ineligible for one of the campaign stars or war medals.*

VALUE:
    Cupro-nickel (1700)   £260–280   *Miniature* £20–25

194. NEWFOUNDLAND VOLUNTEER WAR SERVICE MEDAL

Date: 1981.
Campaign: Second World War 1939-45.
Branch of Service: Newfoundland forces.
Ribbon: Deep claret with edges of red, white and blue.
Metal: Bronze.
Size: 37mm.
Description: (Obverse) the royal cypher of George VI surmounted by a crown topped by a caribou, the Newfoundland national emblem; (reverse) Britannia on a scallop shell background guarded by two lions.
Comments: *While the Second World War was being fought, Newfoundland was still a separate British colony which did not enter the Canadian Confederation till 1949. Consequently Newfoundland servicemen did not qualify for the Canadian Volunteer Service medal, and this deficiency was not remedied until July 1981 when the Newfoundland provincial government instituted this medal. Those who had served with the Canadian forces, on the other hand, and already held the Canadian medal, were not eligible for this award. The medal could be claimed by next-of-kin of those who died in or since the war.*

VALUE: Bronze (7500)   £450–550   *Miniature* £60–70

194A. THE ELIZABETH CROSS

Instituted: 2009.
Campaign: Post World War II.
Branch of Service: Relatives of deceased UK forces personnel.
Ribbon: None.
Metal: Oxidised silver.
Size: 31 mm.
Description: A Greek cross superimposed on another cross, with a crowned Royal cypher at its centre, within a wreath. The arms of the outer cross bear the national emblems of the British Isles: the Rose (England), Thistle (Scotland), Shamrock (Ireland) and the Daffodil (Wales).
Comments: *The Cross was first announced in July 2009 and complements the existing Canadian Memorial Cross (MYB 188A) and the New Zealand Memorial Cross (MYB 191A). Only one Cross will be available to the next of kin of any service personnel who died whilst on operational duty or as a consequence of an act of terrorism. Awards of the Cross have been back-dated to 1 January 1948 to cover deaths that occurred after World War II or as a result of service in Palestine since 27 September 1945. It is accompanied by a memorial scroll, except in the case of Korean War casualties, as a scroll has already been issued for that conflict—in this instance the Cross alone will be issued. Crosses are named to the individual commemorated.*

VALUE: —

195. KOREA MEDAL

Date: July 1951.
Campaign: Korean War 1950-53.
Branch of Service: British and Commonwealth forces.
Ribbon: Yellow, with two blue stripes .
Metal: Cupro-nickel or silver.
Size: 36mm.
Description: (Obverse) Right-facing bust of Queen Elizabeth II by Mary Gillick; there are two obverse types, with or without BR: OMN; (reverse) Hercules wrestling with the Hydra, KOREA in the exergue.
Clasps: None.
Comments: *Awarded to all British and Commonwealth forces who took part in the Korean War between July 1950 and July 27, 1953. British and New Zealand medals were issued in cupro-nickel impressed in small capitals, medals to Australian forces were impressed in large capitals and the Canadian version was struck in silver and has CANADA below the Queen's bust. Particularly prized are medals issued to the "Glorious Gloucesters" who played a gallant part in the battle of the Imjin River.*

VALUE:

		Miniature
British, first obverse		
Regiments	£240–300	£12–15
Corps/RN	£130–180	
RAF	£600–850	
British, second obverse	£120–150	£12–15
To Gloucester Regiment	£650–750	
Australian or New Zealand naming	£250–300	
Canadian, silver (over 20,000)	£100–150	£15–20

196. SOUTH AFRICAN MEDAL FOR KOREA

Date: 1953.
Campaign: Korea 1950-53.
Branch of Service: South African forces.
Ribbon: Sky blue central stripe flanked by dark blue stripes and edges of orange.
Metal: Silver.
Size: 38mm.
Description: (Obverse) maps of South Africa and Korea with an arrow linking them and the words VRYWILLIGERS and VOLUNTEERS in the field. (Reverse) the then South African arms surmounted by the crowned EIIR.
Clasps: None.
Comments: *Awarded to the 800 personnel in the contingent sent to Korea by the Union of South Africa. Suspension is by a ring and claw.*

VALUE:

Silver (800)	£400–500	*Miniature*	£35–45
Pilot's issue	£1200–1500		

191

197. UNITED NATIONS KOREA MEDAL

Date: December 1950.
Campaign: Korea 1950-53.
Branch of Service: All UN forces.
Ribbon: Seventeen narrow stripes alternating pale blue and white.
Metal: Bronze.
Size: 35mm.
Description: (Obverse) the wreathed globe emblem of the UN; (reverse) inscribed FOR SERVICE IN DEFENCE OF THE PRINCIPLES OF THE CHARTER OF THE UNITED NATIONS.
Clasps: Korea.
Comments: *National variants were produced, but the British type was granted to all personnel of the British and Commonwealth forces who had served at least one full day in Korea or in support units in Japan. Moreover, as those who served in Korea after the armistice in July 1953 were also entitled to the UN medal it is sometimes found in groups without the corresponding British medal. The award was extended to cover the period up to July 27, 1954, the first anniversary of the Panmunjom Truce. Issues to Australian, South African and Canadian personnel were named on the rim.*

VALUE: £20–25   *Miniature* £8–10

198. GENERAL SERVICE MEDAL 1962–2007

Date: 1964.
Campaign: Minor campaigns and operations since 1962.
Branch of Service: British forces.
Ribbon: Deep purple edged with green.
Metal: Silver.
Size: 36mm.
Description: (Obverse) a crowned bust of Queen Elizabeth II; (reverse) an oak wreath enclosing a crown and the words FOR CAMPAIGN SERVICE. It has a beaded and curved suspension above which are mounted campaign clasps.
Clasps: 13 to date (see below); the maximum clasps awarded so far seems to be six.
Comments: *This medal was instituted for award to personnel of all services, and thus did away with the need for separate Army and Navy general service medals. Awards range from a mere 70 for South Vietnam to over 130,000 for service in Northern Ireland. The eligibility for the Northern Ireland clasp ceased at midnight on 31 July 2007—the eligibility period having been from 14 August 1969, almost 38 years, the longest period for any individual clasp. This medal is also commonly known as the Campaign Service Medal 1962.*

VALUE:

			Miniature
i.	Borneo	£70–90	£10–12
ii.	Radfan	£90–120	£10–12
iii.	South Arabia	£60–100	£10–12
iv.	Malay Peninsula	£65–90	£10–12
v.	South Vietnam	Rare	£15–20
vi.	Northern Ireland	£60–85	£10–12
vii.	Dhofar	£170–225	£10–12
viii.	Lebanon	£800–900	£10–12
ix.	Mine Clearance, Gulf of Suez	£1600–1800	£10–12
x.	Gulf	£240–280	£10–12
xi.	Kuwait	£400–450	£10–12
xii.	N. Iraq & S. Turkey	£350–450	£10–12
xiii.	Air Operations Iraq	£350–450	£12–16
	2 clasps	£80–120	£12–16
	3 clasps	£150–180	£15–20
	4 clasps	£220–280	£20–25

198A. OPERATIONAL SERVICE MEDAL 2000

Date: 1999.

Campaign: Operations after May 5, 2000.

Branch of Service: All branches of the armed forces.

Ribbon: Broad central red stripe, flanked by royal blue and light blue with green edge stripes (Sierra Leone), buff edge stripes (Afghanistan) or ochre edge stripes (Congo). The colours represent the three services.

Metal: Silver.

Size: 36mm.

Description: (Obverse) crowned profile of Queen Elizabeth; (reverse) a four-pointed star with different crowns impaled on each point, the centre having the Union Jack in a circle surrounded by the inscription FOR OPERATIONAL SERVICE. The medal has a scrolled suspender with ornamental finials.

Clasp: Afghanistan, D.R.O.C. (Congo), silver rosette.

Comments: *Intended for minor campaigns for which a separate medal is not awarded. It replaces the General Service Medal 1962–2007, except for Northern Ireland and Air Operations Iraq. It has so far been awarded for operations in Afghanistan (from 11 September 2001), Sierra Leone (5 May 2000–31 July 2002) and the Democratic Republic of the Congo (14 June–10 September 2003). The award of a clasp is denoted by a silver rosette on the ribbon when only the ribbon is worn. For operations Maidenly and Barras (Sierra Leone) a "South Atlantic" type rosette is worn with the medal, and a smaller version on the ribbon alone. The D.R.O.C. clasp is especially sought after.*

Sierra Leone—see ribbon chart for others.

VALUE:				
	Cavalry	£600–800	*Miniature*	£12–15
	Line regiment	£400–500		
	Corps	£300–400		
	Royal Marines	£400–500		
	RAF	£400–500		

198B. ACCUMULATED CAMPAIGN SERVICE MEDAL

Instituted: January 1994.

Branch of Service: All branches of the armed services.

Ribbon: Purple and green with a gold stripe.

Metal: Silver.

Size: 36mm.

Description: (Obverse) crowned effigy of Queen Elizabeth; (reverse) the inscription FOR ACCUMULATED CAMPAIGN SERVICE set within a four-part ribbon surrounded by a branch of oak leaves with laurel and olive leaves woven through the motto ribbon.

Comments: *The ACSM is awarded for aggregated service since August 14, 1969 in those theatres of operations where the General Service Medal (GSM) 1962 with clasp is awarded. The GSM (MYB198) has subsequently been replaced by the Operational Service Medal. The following medals count towards the award: South Atlantic, Gulf, Iraq Medal, GSM 1962–2007 with the clasps for Northern Ireland, Dhofar, Lebanon, Mine Clearance–Gulf of Suez, Gulf, Kuwait, Northern Iraq and Southern Turkey, Air Operations Iraq; the Operational Service Medal awarded since 2000 for Sierra Leone, Afghanistan and the Democratic Republic of Congo. Further periods of 36 months accumulated campaign service will be denoted by a clasp, indicated as a silver rosette when the ribbon alone is worn. A gilt rosette is worn on the ribbon alone to denote the award of four silver clasps. A further gilt rosette is awarded for a further three silver clasps and a third gilt rosette for another two silver clasps. Service on UN, NATO EC or EU missions is not allowed to count towards the qualifying service. This was the first British medal put out to competitive tendering, a contract won by the Royal Mint. As such, the medal is not only silver but hallmarked (believed to be the first medal, although hallmarking is a feature of certain decorations and orders).*

VALUE:	£350–450	*Miniature*	£8–12

199. UNITED NATIONS EMERGENCY FORCE MEDAL

Date: 1957.
Campaign: Israel and Egypt 1956–57.
Branch of Service: All UN forces.
Ribbon: Sand-coloured with a central light blue stripe and narrow dark blue and green stripes towards each edge.
Metal: Bronze.
Size: 35mm.
Description: (Obverse) the UN wreathed globe emblem with UNEF at the top; (reverse) inscribed IN THE SERVICE OF PEACE. Ring suspension.
Clasps: None.
Comments: *Awarded to all personnel who served with the UN peace-keeping forces on the border between Israel and Egypt following the Sinai Campaign of 1956. These medals were awarded to troops from Brazil, Canada, Colombia, Denmark, Finland, Indonesia, Norway, Sweden and Yugoslavia.*

VALUE:

Bronze original issue	£35–45	*Miniature* £6–8

200. VIETNAM MEDAL (no. A25)

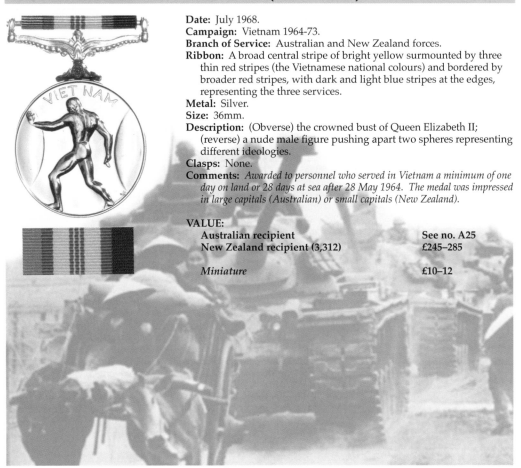

Date: July 1968.
Campaign: Vietnam 1964-73.
Branch of Service: Australian and New Zealand forces.
Ribbon: A broad central stripe of bright yellow surmounted by three thin red stripes (the Vietnamese national colours) and bordered by broader red stripes, with dark and light blue stripes at the edges, representing the three services.
Metal: Silver.
Size: 36mm.
Description: (Obverse) the crowned bust of Queen Elizabeth II; (reverse) a nude male figure pushing apart two spheres representing different ideologies.
Clasps: None.
Comments: *Awarded to personnel who served in Vietnam a minimum of one day on land or 28 days at sea after 28 May 1964. The medal was impressed in large capitals (Australian) or small capitals (New Zealand).*

VALUE:

Australian recipient	See no. A25
New Zealand recipient (3,312)	£245–285
Miniature	£10–12

200A. VIETNAM LOGISTIC AND SUPPORT MEDAL (no. A26)

Instituted: 1993.
Campaign: Vietnam 1964–68.
Branch of Service: Australian forces.
Ribbon: A broad central stripe of yellow with three narrow red stripes superimposed. On the left are stripes of red and dark blue and on the right stripes of dark brown and light blue.
Metal: Nickel-silver.
Size: 36mm.
Description: (Obverse) crowned effigy of Queen Elizabeth and titles; (reverse) as MYB200 above but with a cartouche containing a ram's head (Royal Australian Mint's mark) near the man's right foot. With a straight bar suspension.
Clasps: None.
Comments: *Awarded to personnel who served in the Vietnam War but who did not qualify for the Vietnam Medal. It is estimated that about 20,000 individuals are eligible for this award. Recipients include Qantas air crew who took troop flights to Saigon, and civilian entertainers.*

VALUE:
Australian recipient (5,121)   See no. A26

201. SOUTH VIETNAM CAMPAIGN MEDAL

Date: May 12, 1964.
Campaign: Vietnam 1964–72.
Branch of Service: Allied forces in Vietnam.
Ribbon: White with two broad green stripes towards the centre and narrow green edges.
Metal: Bronze.
Size: Height 42mm; max. width 36mm.
Description: A six-pointed star, with gold rays in the angles. The gilt enamelled centre shows a map of Vietnam engulfed in flames; (reverse) a Vietnamese inscription in the centre.
Clasps: 1960- (bronze, cupro-nickel or silver gilt).
Comments: *Awarded by the government of South Vietnam to Australian and New Zealand forces who served at least six months in Vietnam from March 1, 1961. The original issue, of Vietnamese manufacture, was relatively crude and issued unnamed. Subsequently medals were produced in Australia and these are not only of a better quality but bear the name of the recipient. A third version, made in the USA, has the suspension ring a fixed part of the medal. The medal was always issued with a clasp.*

VALUE:
Unnamed	£15–20
Named	£20–30
Miniature	enamels £6–10, painted £5–8

202. RHODESIA MEDAL

Date: 1980.
Campaign: Rhodesia 1979–80.
Branch of Service: British and Rhodesian forces.
Ribbon: Sky blue, with a narrow stripe of red, white and dark blue in the centre.
Metal: Rhodium-plated cupro-nickel.
Size: 36mm.
Description: (Obverse) the crowned bust of Queen Elizabeth II; (reverse) a sable antelope with the name of the medal and the year of issue.
Clasps: None.
Comments: *This medal was awarded to personnel serving in Rhodesia for fourteen days between 1 December 1979 and 20 March 1980, pending the elections and the emergence of the independent republic of Zimbabwe. Medals were issued unnamed or named in impressed capitals. It was officially named to the armed forces and RAF personnel but unnamed to participating British Police. Examples with the word COPY in raised capitals immediately below the suspension fitment are believed to have been issued as replacements for lost medals, although examples with "R" for replacement are also known to exist.*

VALUE:
Cupro-nickel (2500)   £350–450   *Miniature*   £30–50

203. SOUTH ATLANTIC MEDAL

Date: 1982.
Campaign: Falkland Islands and South Georgia 1982.
Branch of Service: British forces.
Ribbon: Watered silk blue, white, green, white and blue.
Metal: Cupro-nickel.
Size: 36mm.
Description: (Obverse) crowned profile of Queen Elizabeth II; (reverse) laurel wreath below the arms of the Falkland Islands with SOUTH ATLANTIC MEDAL inscribed round the top.
Clasps: None, but a rosette denoting service in the combat zone.
Comments: *Awarded to all personnel who took part in operations in the South Atlantic for the liberation of South Georgia and the Falkland Islands following the Argentinian invasion. To qualify, the recipient had to have at least one full day's service in the Falklands or South Georgia, or 30 days in the operational zone including Ascension Island. Those who qualified under the first condition were additionally awarded a large rosette for wear on the ribbon.*

VALUE:	With rosette	Without
Army (7000)	£700–850	£500–700
Scots & Welsh Guards	£1000–1350	
Parachute Regiment	£1750–2500	
Royal Navy (13,000)	£650–750	£500–650
Royal Marines (3700)	£1100–1400	£750–1000
Royal Fleet Auxiliary (2000)	£450–550	£300–400
RAF (2000)	£500–650	£350–450
Merchant Navy and civilians (2000)	£500–650	£350–450
Gurkhas	£650–800	£500–650
Miniature	£10–12	

203A. SOVIET 40th ANNIVERSARY MEDAL

40th anniversary

Date: 1985.
Campaign: Second World War.
Branch of Service: British and Canadian forces who served mainly in RN or MN ships on Arctic convoys.
Ribbon: One half red, the other orange with three black stripes, edged with pale blue. Later issues have no blue edges. Worn in the Russian style.
Metal: Bronze.
Size: 32mm.
Description: (Obverse) Group of servicemen and women in front of a five-pointed star flanked by oak leaves and the dates 1945–1985 above; (reverse) 40th anniversary of the Victory in the Great Patriotic War 1941–1945, in Russian.
Clasps: None.
Comments: *In 1994 Her Majesty the Queen approved the wearing of this medal awarded by the Soviet Government to selected ex-Servicemen, bearing in mind the changed circumstances in Russia since the award was first issued. Similar medals have also been issued for the 50th, 55th and 60th and 65th anniversaries.*

VALUE:	British striking	£15–20
	Russian striking	£15–20
	Miniature	£9–10

203B. PINGAT JASA MALAYSIA MEDAL

Instituted: 2005.
Ribbon: Central red stripe, flanked by dark blue and yellow.
Metal: Base metal (brass)-coated nickel silver.
Size: 38mm
Description: (Obverse) arms of the Republic of Malaysia with JASA MALAYSIA below; (reverse) map of Malaysia with P.J.M. below, attached to a scrolled suspension bar by two crossed fern fronds.
Comments: *Awarded by the Malaysian Government to members of the British and Commonwealth Armed Forces who were posted on strength of unit or formation and served in the prescribed operational area of Malaysia and Singapore during the "Confrontation" and "Emergency" periods in direct support of operations for: 90 days or more, in Malaysia between August 31, 1957 and December 31 1966 or Singapore between August 31, 1957 and August 9, 1965; or for 180 days for ADF outside the area but in support of operations for the first two dates. At the time of going to press no permission to wear has been granted. Two types are known, the later striking being of poorer quality than the original.*

VALUE: £30–50   *Miniature*   £10–12

203C. KING HUSSEIN MEDAL

Date: 1970.
Campaign: Jordan Civil War.
Branch of Service: British military medical teams.
Ribbon: Plain crimson.
Metal: Silver with red enamel emblem.
Description: (Obverse) Emblem of the Red Cross and Red Crescent. THE HASHEMITE KINGDOM OF JORDAN and its Arabic equivalent, with the date 1970 and Arabic equivalent at the sides; (rev) seven-line inscription across the centre.
Comments: *Awarded to British and American personnel involved in relief operations codenamed Operation Shoveller during and after the Civil War of September 1970. At the end of the deployment all personnel were presented with the medal by King Hussein. Permission to wear it has never been granted.*

VALUE: —

204. GULF MEDAL

Date: 1992.
Campaign: Kuwait and Saudi Arabia 1990-91.
Branch of Service: British forces.
Ribbon: Sand-coloured broad central stripe flanked by narrow stripes of dark blue, red and light blue (left) or light blue, red and dark blue (right) representing the sands of the desert and the three armed services.
Metal: Cupro-nickel.
Size: 36mm.
Description: (Obverse) crowned profile of Queen Elizabeth II; (reverse) an eagle and automatic rifle superimposed on an anchor, symbolising the three armed services. The dates of the Gulf War appear at the foot.
Clasps: 2 Aug 1990, 16 Jan–28 Feb 1991.
Comments: *Awarded to personnel who had thirty days continuous service in the Middle East (including Cyprus) between 2 August 1990 and 7 March 1991, or seven days between 16 January 1991 and 28 February 1991, or service with the Kuwait Liaison Team on 2 August 1990, the date of the Iraqi invasion. Two clasps were sanctioned and awarded to personnel who qualified for active service with the Liaison Team or in the operations to liberate Kuwait. A rosette is worn on the ribbon alone to denote the campaign clasps. Naming is in impressed capitals. More than 45,000 medals were awarded. See also the Kuwait and Iraq-Turkey clasps awarded to the General Service Medal 1962. About 1,500 civilians, including members of British Aerospace working at Dahran, also received the medal with the clasp 16 Jan to 28 Feb 1991.*

VALUE:

No clasp	£175–250
i. 2 Aug 1990	£2000–3000
ii. 16 Jan to 28 Feb 1991	
Regiments/RN/RAF	£250–350
Corps and Artillery	£200–250
Civilians	£200–250
Miniature	£10–12

204A. BRUNEI GENERAL SERVICE MEDAL

Date: 1968.
Campaign: Service in Brunei.
Branch of Service: British personnel on loan service.
Ribbon: Blue with red edges and a central red stripe.
Description: A radiate star with a central medallion inscribed GENERAL SERVICE MEDAL and its equivalent Pingkat Laila Tugas in Arabic script, the royal insignia of the sultanate appearing in the centre. This insignia has changed several times over the years so varieties are seen. The original versions have a white enamel cross on the star (as illustrated) but the later version has the insignia surrounded by a laurel wreath. Suspended by a plain bar.
Comments: *Awarded to British personnel who completed a minimum of 12 months service. The Queen has granted unrestricted permission to entitled members of the British forces.*

VALUE: £50–75 *Miniature* £15–20

204AA. SIERRA LEONE GENERAL SERVICE MEDAL

Date: 1965.

Campaign: Service in Sierra Leone and neighbouring countries.

Branch of Service: British forces on secondment to the Royal Sierra Leone Military Forces.

Ribbon: Broad central red stripe bordered with narrow green, white and dark blue stripes.

Metal: Bronze.

Size: 36mm.

Description: (Obverse) crowned effigy of Queen Elizabeth; (reverse) arms of Sierra Leone with inscription FOR GENERAL SERVICE / SIERRA LEONE. Fitted with a ring for suspension and a brooch bar at the top of the ribbon.

Clasps: Congo.

Comments: *Worn after medals previously earned and before the United Nations' Congo Medal and Sierra Leone Long Service and Independence medals, with restricted permission. UK personnel qualified for this medal if not eligible for any other general service medal for the same service. British personnel who served in the Congo between January 26, 1962 and February 28, 1963 qualified for the clasp.*

VALUE:	£20–30	Miniature	£10–20

204B. IRAQ MEDAL

Date: 2004.

Campaign: Operation TELIC (the Iraq War).

Branch of Service: All military and civilian personnel, including embedded media, involved in the operations for the liberation of Iraq and the overthrow of Saddam Hussein.

Ribbon: Central narrow stripes of black, white and red (symbolising the Iraq national flag) flanked by broad sand-coloured edges.

Metal: Cupro-nickel.

Size: 36mm.

Description: (Obverse) crowned effigy of Queen Elizabeth; (reverse) image of a Lamassu (ancient Assyrian statue) over the word IRAQ.

Clasps: 19 Mar to 28 Apr 2003.

Comments: *This medal was awarded to all military and civilian personnel involved in Operation TELIC in Kuwait and Iraq from January 20, 2003. Those who took part in the actual combat from March 19, 2003 were awarded the clasp, denoted by a silver rosette on the ribbon alone. The medal is currently awarded to those who have served for 30 days continuously or an aggregate 45 days.*

VALUE:		Miniature
i. With clasp		£10–20
Corps	£300–350	
Regiments	£325–400	
Cavalry	£400–450	
ii. No clasp		£10–15
Corps	£125–175	
Regiments	£155–225	
Cavalry	£300–350	

204C. IRAQ RECONSTRUCTION SERVICE MEDAL

Instituted: January 2007.

Branch of Service: Civilians and members of the Armed Forces who have seen service in Iraq but do not qualify for the Iraq Medal.

Ribbon: Sand-coloured with a broad green central stripe and narrow blue stripes towards the edges.

Metal: Rhodium-plated cupro-nickel.

Size: 36mm.

Description: (Obverse) Rank-Broadley effigy of the Queen; (reverse) cuneiform tablet translated as 'land bringing forth life' with stylised depiction of two rivers based on a relief carving from Mesopotamia in the British Museum.

Comments: *The qualifying period for the medal is set at 40 days continuous service since March 19, 2003, or 40 days of service on working visits within Iraq aggregated over a period of one calendar year, for a minimum of 48 hours each.*

VALUE: £350—£450   *Miniature*   £15–25

204D. THE CIVILIAN SERVICE MEDAL (AFGHANISTAN)

Instituted: April 2011.

Branch of Service: Civilian.

Ribbon: Unknown at this stage

Metal: Rhodium-plated cupro-nickel.

Size: 36mm.

Description: (Obverse) Rank-Broadley effigy of the Queen; (reverse) a stylised depiction of the mountains of Afghanistan with the name of the country, both in English and Afghan surrounding it.

Comments: *Awarded to recognise the role of civilians and others involved in the transition of democracy to Afghanistan. The qualifying period is thirty days continuous or 45 days aggregate service provided that takes place within a single calendar year and the visits are of at least 48 hours each. Those whose service is curtailed by death or injury also eligible. Eligible persons include any Crown Servant (including Members of Her Majesty's UK Armed Forces), under Operational Control of the Foreign and Commonwealth Office (but NOT those under the command of the UK joint task force), Police and Contractors. Locally employed civilians are not eligible.*

VALUE: —

205. SAUDI ARABIAN MEDAL FOR THE LIBERATION OF KUWAIT

Date: 1991.
Campaign: Gulf War 1991.
Branch of Service: British and Allied forces.
Ribbon: Green with edges of red, black and white (the Saudi national colours). The ribbon bar has a gold state emblem (palm tree over crossed scimitars).
Metal: White metal.
Size: approx. 45mm across
Description: The white metal medal has a star of fifteen long and fifteen short round-tipped rays, surmounted by a bronze circle bearing a crowned and enwreathed globe on which appears a map of Arabia. Above the circle is a palm tree with crossed scimitars, the state emblem of Saudi Arabia. A scroll inscribed in Arabic and English LIBERATION OF KUWAIT appears round the foot of the circle.
Clasps: None.
Comments: *Awarded by the government of Saudi Arabia to all Allied personnel who took part in the campaign for the liberation of Kuwait, although only a few of the 45,000 British servicemen were subsequently given permission by the Foreign and Commonwealth Office to wear it. The contract for production was shared between Spink and a Swiss company, but subsequently a flatter version, more practicable for wear with other medals, was manufactured in the United States.*

VALUE: £20   *Miniature*   £12–14

205A. MULTINATIONAL FORCE AND OBSERVERS MEDAL

Date: March 1982.
Campaign: Sinai Peninsula.
Ribbon: 36mm orange with central white stripe flanked by 3mm dark green stripes. The civilian award ribbon is orange with two green 8mm stripes and central 8mm white stripe
Metal: Bronze.
Size: 30mm.
Description: (Obverse) a dove clutching an olive branch surrounded by the inscription MULTINATIONAL FORCE & OBSERVERS; (reverse) UNITED IN SERVICE FOR PEACE in five lines.
Comments: *Awarded to personnel of the Multinational Force and Observers (MFO) created in 1979 to monitor the peace agreement between Egypt and Israel. Eligibility for the medal was originally 90 days continuous service in the force, but this was raised to 170 days in March 1985. Subsequent awards for each completed six-month tour is indicated by a silver numeral affixed to the ribbon. It was originally awarded personally by the MFO's first commander, the Norwegian General Fredrik Bull-Hansen. The Force has 3,000 personnel drawn from the armed services of Australia, Canada, Colombia, Fiji, France, Italy, the Netherlands, New Zealand, UK, USA and Uruguay.*

VALUE: £25–30   *Miniature* £7–10

Civilian

206. KUWAITI LIBERATION MEDALS

Date: 1991.

Campaign: Liberation of Kuwait 1991.

Branch of Service: Allied forces.

Ribbon: Equal stripes of green, white and red with a black quadrilateral at the upper edge, representing the Kuwait national flag.

Metal: Various.

Size: Various.

Description: The circular medals have different decorative treatments of the Kuwaiti state emblem on the obverse, enshrined in a five-petalled flower (Second Grade), a five-pointed star with radiate background (Third Grade) and a plain medallic treatment (Fourth Grade). All grades, however, have a straight bar suspender of different designs.

Clasps: None.

Comments: *This medal was issued in five grades and awarded according to the rank of the recipient. The Excellent Grade was only conferred on the most senior Allied commanders, the First Grade went to brigadiers and major-generals, the Second Grade to officers of field rank (colonels and majors), the Third Grade to junior officers (captains, lieutenants and equivalent ranks in the other services), and the Fourth Grade to all other ranks. HM Government has decreed that British personnel may accept their medals as a keepsake but permission to wear them in uniform has so far been refused. The Canadian Government has followed the same policy, but the personnel of other Allied nations are permitted to wear their medals.*

4th grade

VALUE:		*Miniature*
First Grade	—	—
Second Grade	£40–50	£15–18
Third Grade	£20–30	£15–18
Fourth Grade	£20–30	£15–20 *(silver)*

206A. NATO SERVICE MEDALS

Instituted: December 1994.

Campaigns: Any theatre or area of operations in the service of the North Atlantic Treaty Organization.

Branch of Service: NATO military and service personnel.

Ribbon: NATO blue with narrow white stripes having central metal threads: For engagements in NATO-led Article 5 operations (gold thread): Eagle Assist (central stripe), Active Endeavour (two stripes towards the edges), Non-Article 5 (central stripe with silver thread, from January 2011 two stripes towards the edges with silver thread denote operations) with clasps.

Metal: Bronze.

Size: 36mm.

Description: (Obverse) the NATO star emblem set in a wreath of olive leaves; (reverse) the title NORTH ATLANTIC TREATY ORGANIZATION and the words IN SERVICE OF PEACE AND FREEDOM in English and French. Two versions of this medal have been recorded: (a) light bronze, broad leaves in wreath, (b) dark bronze, narrow leaves.

Clasps: Former Yugoslavia, Kosovo, Article 5 (Eagle Assist), Active Endeavour, Non-Article 5 (superseding the first two clasps), Balkans, ISAF (Afghanistan), NTM (Iraq, Pakistan), Africa (NATO support for the African Union incl. Op. Allied Provider, Allied Protector and Ocean Shield), AMIS (Sudan).

Former Yugoslavia.

Comments: *The NATO medal was first instituted to reward personnel who took part in the Alliance operations in the former Yugoslavia. Any person serving under NATO command or operational control is eligible for the award. UK Service personnel cannot qualify for the NATO Medal and the UNPROFOR Medal (no. 207) in respect of the same period of service. The qualifying period for the medal is to be designated by the Secretary-General, however, for the operations in the former Yugoslavia the period has been set as 30 days continuous or accumulated service within the theatre of operations inside the former Yugoslavia*

Kosovo.

Macedonia.

Non-Article 5.

Eagle Assist.

Active Endeavour.

Afghanistan (ISAF), Africa, Sudan (AMIS), Pakistan, Balkans, Iraq (NATO Training Mission)—denoted by clasp on ribbon (see chart).

and the Adriatic, or 90 days within the area of operations but outside the territory of the former Yugoslavia. The medal takes precedence equal to the General Service Medal in order of date of award. Bronze arabic numerals are worn on the ribbon to denote multiple tours. The Non-Article 5 medal (ribbon) replaces the three other NATO medals (ribbons) for services anywhere in the Balkans, commencing December 3, 2002. Article 5 of the NATO Charter states that an attack on one member state is an attack on the whole Alliance. Non-Article 5 operations are therefore those outside NATO territory. No clasp was issued for the service in Macedonia (Former Yugoslavia) due to objections from Greece which does not recognise the independent sovereignty of that country. The clasps for Kosovo and Former Yugoslavia have now been superseded by the Non Article 5 clasp. The clasp for Afghanistan bears the initials of the International Security Assistance Force. Those serving more than one tour of duty are authorised to wear a bronze arabic numeral on their ribbon to indicate this. Eagle Assist, Active Endeavour, Afghanistan and Iraq medals are not approved or authorised for wear by UK personnel, either in full size or in miniature. If presented they may be retained as keepsake(s). NATO ISAF has now been approved for wear by Australian Forces (military and police). Service on awards for these medal(s) does not count as qualifying service towards the Accumulated Campaign Service Medal. Additionally a NATO Meritorious Service Medal has been instituted—see MYB291AA.

VALUE: £20–£25   *Miniature*   £8–10

206B. EUROPEAN COMMUNITY MONITORING MISSION MEDAL

Date: 1995.
Campaigns: Former Yugoslavia.
Branch of Service: EC Community Peacekeeping.
Ribbon: Navy with stripes of white and red and thin yellow.
Metal: Silver.
Size: 36mm.
Description: (Obverse) Outline map of Yugoslavia surmounted by the words EC MONITOR MISSION surrounded by a ring of stars; (reverse) a dove of peace.
Comments: *Awarded or 21 days service between July 27, 1991 and June 30, 1993, in and around the former Yugoslavia. Service on awards for these medal(s) does not count as qualifying service towards the Accumulated Campaign Service Medal.*

VALUE: £20–£25   *Miniature*   £10–15

206C. WESTERN EUROPEAN UNION MISSION SERVICE MEDAL

Date: 1997.
Campaigns: Operations in the Former Yugoslavia.
Branch of Service: Personnel serving with the Western European Union forces.
Ribbon: Bright blue with central broad bright yellow stripe.
Metal: Silver.
Size: 36mm.
Description: (Obverse) capital letters WEU arranged horizontally with U and O above and below the E to signify "Western European Union" and its French equivalent "Union de l'Europe Occidentale". Ten five-pointed stars are ranged around the lower half of the circumference; (reverse) PRO PACE UNUM ("United for peace") in three lines. A clasp signifying the area of service is worn on the ribbon.
Comments: *This medal was instituted to award service with missions under the auspices of the Western European Union. It was awarded to personnel who had served at least 30 days in the former Yugoslavia or 90 days in the Adriatic, Hungary or Rumania. The first British recipients (March 6, 1997) were 27 police officers who had served with the WEU Police Force in Bosnia-Herzegovina. A total of 15,982 medals had been awarded by September 2000. This medal is also known as the European Union Police Mission Medal. Service for these medal(s) does not count as qualifying service towards the Accumulated Campaign Service Medal.*

VALUE: £50–£70 *Miniature* £10–15

206D. EUROPEAN SECURITY AND DEFENCE POLICY SERVICE MEDAL

Date: 2004.
Campaigns: Any military operations involving the European Union.
Branch of Service: Police.
Ribbon: Bright blue with central yellow stripe with an emblem denoting area of service.
Metal: Silver.
Size: 36mm.
Description: (Obverse) Twelve five pointed stars in a circle; (reverse) PRO PACE UNUM in three lines (roughly translated as "United for peace"). The medal is fitted with a large ring for suspension. A clasp signifying the area of service is worn on the ribbon.
Clasps: Artemis, EUPM, Concordia, Proxima, Althea.
Comments: *This medal has been awarded to police and security personnel serving in any military operation under the auspices of the European Union. It has also been awarded to civilian police missions, as well as Canadian personnel (2005). The clasps denote service in the Democratic Republic of Congo from June to September 2003 (Artemis), with the EU Police mission in Bosnia since January 2003, for service in the former Yugoslav republic of Macedonia from March to December 2003 (Concordia) or December 2003 to December 2004 (Proxima) and service in Bosnia since December 2004 (Althea). Those serving more than one tour of duty are authorised to wear an arabic numeral on their ribbon to indicate this. Service for these medal(s) does not count as qualifying service towards the Accumulated Campaign Service Medal. The ESDP Medal with clasp Althea has been approved for unrestricted acceptance and wearing by UK personnel—headquarters and units serving in Bosnia and Herzegovina, on this operation. The ESDP medal for planning and support for Operation Althea is not approved for acceptance or wear. Those presented may be retained as a keepsake.*

VALUE: — *Miniature* £10–15

207. UNITED NATIONS MEDAL

Style of lettering for clasps.

For the various ribbons for the medal see ribbon charts.

Date: 1951.
Campaigns: Various supervisory or observation roles since 1948.
Branch of Service: UN forces.
Ribbons: Various (see below).
Metal: Bronze.
Size: 35mm.
Description: (Obverse) the wreathed globe emblem surmounted by the letters UN; (reverse) inscribed "IN THE SERVICE OF PEACE".
Clasps: CONGO, UNGOMAP, OSGAP, UNSMIH, MINUGUA, UNCRO, ONUMOZ, UNSCOM, UNAMIC, UNMIH, UNTMIH, UNOSGI, UNMONUA.
Comments: *Apart from the UN Korea and UNEF medals, there have been numerous awards to personnel who served in one or other of the UN peace-keeping actions around the world since the end of the Second World War. The all-purpose medal has been awarded with various distinctive ribbons for service in many of the world's trouble spots. Two versions of the medal exist: globe flat (European) and globe raised (US version). Issues to South African Personnel are named. Eligibility is generally 90 days, but some missions were 180 days. Subsequent awards for each six month tour completed with the same mission are indicated by a silver numeral affixed to the ribbon. Those serving more than one tour of duty are authorised to wear an arabic numeral on their ribbon to indicate this. Service for these medal(s) does not count as qualifying service towards the Accumulated Campaign Service Medal. The missions are listed below in chronological order.*

UNTSO United Nations Truce Supervision Organization (Israel, Egypt, Syria since 1948).
Blue ribbon with two narrow white stripes towards the edges.
UNOGIL United Nations Observation Group in Lebanon (1958).
Same ribbon as UNTSO.
ONUC Organisation des Nations Unies au Congo (1960–64).
Originally the same ribbon as UNTSO with clasp CONGO, but a green ribbon, with white and blue edges was substituted in 1963.
UNTEA United Nations Temporary Exacutive Authority (Netherlands New Guinea, 1962).
Blue ribbon with a white central stripe bordered green.
UNMOGIP United Nations Military Observer Group in India and Pakistan since 1949.
Dark green ribbon shading to light green with white and blue edges.
UNIPOM United Nations India Pakistan Observation Mission (1965–66).
Ribbon as UNMOGIP.
UNYOM United Nations Yemen Observation Mission (1963–64).
Ribbon with brown centre, yellow stripes and light blue edges.
UNFICYP United Nations Force in Cyprus (1964–).
Pale blue ribbon with central white stripe bordered in dark blue. Initially 30, then increased to 90 days.
UNEF 2 United Nations Emergency Force 2 patrolling Israeli-Egyptian cease-fire (1973– 79).
Pale blue ribbon with sand centre and two dark blue stripes.
UNDOF United Nations Disengagement Observer Force, Golan Heights (1974–).
Ribbon of red, white, black and pale blue.
UNIFIL United Nations Interim Force in Lebanon (1978–).
Pale blue ribbon with green centre bordered white and red.
UNGOMAP United Nations Good Offices in Afghanistan and Pakistan.
A bronze bar inscribed UNGOMAP was issued but as the mission was made up from observers from three other missions it can only be found on these ribbons: UNTSO, UNIFIL, UNDOF.
UNIIMOG United Nations Iran-Iraq Monitoring Observation Group.
Pale blue with red, white and green edges.
UNAVEM United Nations Angola Verification Missions: I (1989–91), II (1991–95), III (1995–97).
Pale blue ribbon with yellow edges separated by narrow stripes of red, white and black (same for all three).
ONUCA Observadores de las Naciones Unidas en Centro América (Nicaragua and Guatemala).
Pale blue ribbon with dark blue edges and nine thin central green or white stripes.
UNTAG United Nations Transitional Assistance Group (Namibia, 1989–90).
Sand ribbon with pale blue edges and thin central stripes of blue, green, red, sand and deep blue.
ONUSAL Observadores de las Naciones Unidas en El Salvador.
Pale blue ribbon with a white central stripe bordered dark blue.
UNIKOM United Nations Iraq Kuwait Observation Mission (1991–2003).
Sand ribbon with a narrow central stripe of pale blue.

MINURSO   Mission des Nations Unies pour la Referendum dans le Sahara Occidental (UN Mission for the Referendum in Western Sahara) (1991–).
Ribbon has a broad sandy centre flanked by stripes of UN blue.

UNAMIC   United Nations Advanced Mission in Cambodia (Oct. 1991–March 1992).
Pale blue ribbon with central white stripe bordered with dark blue, yellow and red stripes.

UNTAC   United Nations Transitional Authority in Cambodia (March 1992–Sept. 1993).
Green ribbon with central white stripe edged with red, pale blue and dark blue.

UNOSOM   United Nations Operations in Somalia (I: 1992–93 and II: 1993–95).
Pale yellow ribbon with central blue stripe edged with green.

UNMIH   United Nations Mission in Haiti
Pale blue ribbon with dark blue and red central stripes edged with white.

UNPROFOR   United Nations Protection Force (1992–95) operating in the former Yugoslavia, especially Bosnia. *Blue ribbon with central red stripe edged in white and green or brown edges. See also UNCRO below.*

UNOMIL   United Nations Observer Mission in Liberia (1993–97).
Pale blue ribbon flanked with white stripes with dark blue or red edges.

UNOMUR   United Nations Observer Mission in Uganda/Rwanda (1993–94).
Pale blue central stripe edged by white and flanked by equal stripes of black, orange and red.

UNOMIG   United Nations Observer Mission in Georgia (1993–). For 180 days service.
Pale blue central stripe flanked by equal stripes of white, green and dark blue.

UNAMIR   United Nations Assistance Mission in Rwanda (1993–96).
Pale blue central stripe edged with white and flanked by equal stripes of black, green and red.

UNHQ   General service at UN headquarters, New York.
Plain ribbon of pale blue, the UN colour.

UNPREDEP   United Nations Preventative Deployment in Yugoslavia.
Blue ribbon with central red stripe bearing four yellow lines and flanked by white edging.

UNMOP   United Nations Mission of Observers in Pravlaka.
Dark blue ribbon with central yellow stripe edged with white, and two pale blue stripes.

UNTAES   United Nations Transitional Authority in Eastern Slavonia. (1995-96)
Pale blue ribbon with yellow, red edged with white, and green stripes.

UNMOT   United Nations Peacekeeping Force in Tadjikistan.
Blue ribbon with central green stripe flanked by white stripes.

UNMIBH   United Nations Mission in Bosnia Herzegovina (1995).
Blue ribbon with white central stripe, edged with one green and one red stripe.

UNMOGUA   United Nations Military Observers in Guatemala.
Blue ribbon with central pale blue stripe and two white stripes each with central green line.

UNSMIH   United Nations Support Mission in Haiti (July 1996–2000).
Same ribbon as UNMIH above, but with clasp UNSMIH.

UNCRO   United Nations Confidence Restoration Operation in Croatia (1995–96).
Same ribbon as UNPROFOR above, but with clasp UNCRO.

MINUGUA   Mision de las Naciones Unidas en Guatemala.
Same ribbon as UNMOGUA but clasp with initials in Spanish.

ONUMOZ   Operation des Nations Unies pour le referendum dans Mozambique (1992–95).
Pale blue ribbon edged with white and green stripes.

UNSSM   United Nations Special Service Medal.
Awarded to personnel serving at least 90 consecutive days under UN control in operations for which no other UN award is authorised. Blue ribbon with white edges. Clasps: UNOCHA, UNSCOM. The medal with no clasp was awarded to Operation Cheshire aircrew who had completed 100 landings at Sarajevo or ground crew who had spent 90 days at Anacona, Split or Zagreb between July 3, 1992 and January 12, 1996.

OSGAP   Office of the Secretary General for Afghanistan and Pakistan.
Silver clasp worn by Canadian personnel on the ribbons of UNTSO, UNDOF or UNIFIL.

UNOMSIL   United Nations Observer Mission in Sierra Leone. (1998–)
Awarded for 90 days service. White ribbon with blue edges and the Sierra Leone colours (light blue flanked by green stripes) in the centre. This mission was redesignated UNAMSIL on October 1, 1999.

UNPSG   United Nations Police Support Group Medal.
A support group of 180 police monitors created in January 1998 initially to supervise the Croatian police in the return of displaced persons. 90 days qualifying service. White ribbon with a broad blue central stripe and narrow dark grey (left) and bright yellow (right) stripes towards the edges.

MINURCA   United Nations Verification Mission in the Central African Republic (1998–2000).
Mission instituted April 15, 1998 to monitor the restoration of peace following the Bangui agreement. 90 days qualifying service. Ribbon has a broad blue central stripe flanked by yellow, green, red, white and dark blue stripes on either side.

UNSCOM   United Nations Special Service Medal.
The UN Special Service Medal with UNSCOM clasp is awarded to personnel with a minimum of 90 days consecutive service or 180 days in all, with UNSCOM in Iraq. Ribbon is UN blue with a white stripe at each edge.

UNMIK   United Nations Mission in Kosovo (1999–).
Pale blue ribbon with wide central dark blue stripe edged with white. For 180 days service.

UNAMET   United Nations Mission in East Timor (1999–).
Pale blue ribbon with wide central white stripe edged with yellow and claret.

MONUC   United Nations Mission in the Congo (2000–).
Pale blue ribbon with wide central dark blue stripe edged with yellow.

UNMEE   United Nations Mission in Ethiopia/Eritrea.
Pale blue with central band of sand bisected by narrow dark green stripe.

MIPONUH   United Nations Civil Police Mission in Haiti (1997–2000).
Central bands of dark blue and red, flanked by narrow silver stripes and broad blue bands

UNTMIH   United Nations Transitional Mission in Haiti (July–November 1997).
Same ribbon as MIPONUH but with a bar inscribed UNTMIH.
MICAH   International Civilian Support Mission in Haiti (March 2000–).
Same ribbon as MIPONUH.
UNOSGI   The UN Office of the Secretary General in Iraq.
A clasp issued to a small police group assigned to Baghdad from February 1991 to December 1992.
UNHCR   United Nations High Commission for Refugees.
A clasp issued worldwide and still on-going.
UNAMSIL   United Nations Medal for Service in Sierra Leone (1999–).
Same ribbon as UNOMSIL.
UNMEE   United Nations Medal for Service in Ethiopia and Eritrea.
Pale blue ribbon with a central tan section divided by a narrow green stripe.
MINUCI   United Nations Mission in Cote d'Ivoire (Ivory Coast) (May 2003–April 2004).
Orange, white and green stripes with blue edges.
UNMIL   United Nations Mission in Liberia (September 2003–).
Pale blue with a broad central dark blue stripe edged in red and white.
UNIOCI   United Nations Operations in Cote d'Ivoire (April 2004–).
Similar to MINUCI but central stripes very narrow and blue edges correspondingly wider.
UNOB   United Nations Operations in Burundi (June 2004–).
Central stripes of white, red, dark green and white, flanked by broad pale blue stripes.
MINUSTAH   Mission des Nations Unies Stabilisation dans Haiti (June 2004–).
Narrow central pale blue stripe, flanked by broader equal stripes of white, dark green and dark blue.
UNMIS   United Nations Mission in Sudan (March 2005–).
UN blue with dark blue centre divided by two narrow white stripes.
UNMIT   United Nations Integrated Mission in Timor-Leste (August 2006–)
UN blue with red centre stripe bordered each side with narrow stripes of white, dark blue and yellow.
UNAMID   African Union/United Nations Hybrid operation in Darfur (July 2007–)
Yellow with a central stripe of half blue, half white and with dark blue narrow stripes either side or Blue with central white stripe bordered each side by stripes of green and yellow.
MINURCA   United Nations Mission in the Central African Republic and Chad (September 2007–)
UN blue with five equal narrow stripes of dark blue, white, yellow, green and red.

VALUE:

Any current issue medal regardless of ribbon	£15–25
Original striking for Cyprus	£25–30
Miniature	£6–8

207A. INTERNATIONAL CONFERENCE ON THE FORMER YUGOSLAVIA MEDAL

Date: 1995.
Campaigns: Former Yugoslavia.
Branch of Service: UN Observers.
Ribbon: Central broad orange stripe, flanked by narrow blue and white stripes and broad red edges, mounted in the Danish style.
Metal: Silver.
Size: 38mm.
Description: (Obverse) the wreathed globe emblem of the United Nations surrounded by 15 five-pointed stars representing the member nations of the conference, with the inscription round the edge: INTERNATIONAL CONFERENCE ONTHE FORMER YUGOSLAVIA; (reverse) the Drina River and the mountains of Serbia and Montenegro surmounted by a peace dove in flight, with the words OBSERVER MISSION round the foot.
Comments: *This medal was awarded to about 100 observers who monitored the 17 land and two rail crossings between Serbia and Montenegro and Bosnia-Herzegovina during September 1994.*

VALUE: —   *Miniature*   £10–15

207B. INTERFET MEDAL—International Force East Timor

Instituted: March 7, 2000.
Ribbon: 32mm central thin red stripe, flanked by deep green, white and UN light blue.
Metal: Pewter coloured silver.
Size: 38mm.
Description: (Obverse) central raised stylised dove of peace over the island of Timor, surrounded by raised inscription INTERNATIONAL FORCE EAST TIMOR surmounted by Federation Star and plain suspension bar struck as one unit; (reverse) TOGETHER AS ONE FOR PEACE IN EAST TIMOR around outer circle, inner circle blank for naming.
Method of naming: Pantographed on reverse in capitals with regimental number, initials and surname.
Comments: *The Australian Prime Minister established a specific campaign medal for members of the Australian Defence Forces in East Timor. Australia led the coalition of 17 nations and this is the first Australian medal issued to other countries. Awarded for 30 days service during the INTERFET stage of the conflict. 15,046 medals have been issued, including 8,690 to members of the ADF and 6,356 to members of other countries' military establishments.*

VALUE:		
	To Australian personnel	£500–800
	Others	£700–1000

207C. UNITAS MEDAL

Instituted: 1994.
Ribbon: 32mm, pale blue with central green stripe of 8mm edged each side by a white stripe of 4mm.
Metal: Lacquered brass.
Description: (Obverse) a seven pointed star with central circle enclosing the Greek letter Alpha; (reverse) A small embellished coat of arms of South Africa with date 1994 below. The whole is enclosed by a circle made up of the word "Unity" in all eleven official languages of the new South Africa. Suspender is uniface and struck as one piece with the medal.
Comments: *Awarded to all those who rendered service through being members of a serving force (SA Permanent Force, Citizen Force, Commandos, members of the armed forces of the former self-governing territories, the armed wing of the ANC (the MK) and APLA) during the period of South Africa's first non-racial elections and inauguration of Mr Mandela as the first black State President in South Africa between 27 April and 10 May 1994. Those medals awarded to members of the British Military Advisory Team in South Africa at the time, for which Her Majesty Queen Elizabeth II granted permission for wear must be considered a rarity.*

VALUE:
Miniature

	SA recipient	£15–25	£10–15
	BMA recipient	From £250	

LONG AND MERITORIOUS SERVICE

A large, varied but until recently relatively neglected category comprises the medals awarded for long service and good conduct or meritorious service. Their common denominator is that the grant of such awards is made in respect of a minimum number of years of unblemished service—"undetected crime" is how it is often described in the armed forces. As their title implies, long service and good conduct medals combine the elements of lengthy service with no transgressions of the rules and regulations. Meritorious service, on the other hand, implies rather more. Apart from a brief period (1916-28) when awards were made for single acts of gallantry, MSMs have generally been granted to warrant officers and senior NCOs as a rather superior form of long service medal.

Long service and good conduct medals do not appear to excite the same interest among collectors as campaign medals. Perhaps this may be accounted for by their image of stolid devotion to duty rather than the romantic connotations of a medal with an unusual clasp awarded for service in some remote and all but forgotten outpost of the Empire. Nevertheless their importance should not be overlooked. Especially in regard to groups consisting primarily of the Second World War medals, they serve a useful purpose in establishing the provenance of the group, on account of the fact that they are invariably named to the recipient.

Service medals include not only such well known types as the Army LSGC (known affectionately as "the mark of the beast" on account of its high incidence on the chests of sergeant-majors), but also awards to the Territorial and Reserve forces, the auxiliary forces, the nursing services, and organisations such as the Royal Observer Corps and the Cadet Force, the Police, the Red Cross and St John's Ambulance Brigade. The Special Constabulary and Fire Brigades also have their own medals bestowed according to length of service and distinguished conduct. These medals may lack the glamour of naval and military awards but in recent years they have become increasingly fashionable with collectors and will certainly repay further study in their own right.

As many of these medals have been in use for eighty years or more with a standard reverse, variation usually lies in the obverse, changed for each successive sovereign. In addition, considerable variety has been imparted by the use of crowned or uncrowned profiles and busts, and changes in titles. The following is a summary of the principal obverse types which may be encountered, referred to in the text by their type letters in brackets:

Queen Victoria (A) Young head by William Wyon
Queen Victoria (B) Veiled head by Leonard C. Wyon
Queen Victoria (C) Jubilee head by Sir Joseph E. Boehm
Queen Victoria (D) Old head by Sir Thomas Brock

Edward VII (A) Bareheaded bust in Field Marshal's uniform
Edward VII (B) Bareheaded bust in Admiral's uniform
Edward VII (C) Coinage profile by George W. de Saulles
Edward VII (D) Crowned profile in Coronation robes

George V (A) Bareheaded bust in Field Marshal's uniform
George V (B) Bareheaded bust in Admiral's uniform
George V (C) Crowned bust in Coronation robes
George V (D) Crowned bust in Delhi Durbar robes
George V (E) Coinage profile by Bertram Mackennal

George VI (A) Crowned profile in Coronation robes
George VI (B) Crowned profile INDIAE: IMP 1937–48
George VI (C) Crowned profile FID: DEF 1949–52
George VI (D) Coinage profile IND: IMP 1937–48
George VI (E) Coinage profile FID: DEF 1949–52

Elizabeth II (A1) Tudor crown BR: OMN 1953–54
Elizabeth II (A) Tudor crown BR: OMN omitted 1954–80
Elizabeth II (B) Coinage bust BRITT: OMN 1953–54
Elizabeth II (C) Coinage bust BRITT OMN omitted 1954–80
Elizabeth II (D) St Edward crown 1955–

PRINCIPAL OBVERSE TYPES:

Queen Victoria (A) Young Head

Queen Victoria (B) Veiled Head

Queen Victoria (C) Jubilee Head

Queen Victoria (D) Old Head

Edward VII (A) Bareheaded bust in Field Marshal's uniform

Edward VII (B) Bareheaded bust in Admiral's uniform

George V (A) Bareheaded bust in Field Marshal's uniform

George V (B) Bareheaded bust in Admiral's uniform

George V (C) Crowned bust in Coronation robes

George V (E) Coinage profile by Bertram Mackennal

George VI (B) Crowned profile with INDIAE: IMP in legend 1937–48

George VI (C) Crowned profile with FID: DEF 1949–52

George VI (D) Coinage profile with IND: IMP 1937–48

George VI (E) Coinage profile with FID: DEF 1949–52

Elizabeth II (A1) Tudor crown with BR.OMN. (1953–54)
Elizabeth II (A) BR.OMN. omitted (as above) 1954–80

Elizabeth II (B) Coinage bust with BRITT: OMN, 1953–54

Elizabeth II (C) Coinage bust without BR: OMN.

Elizabeth II (D) St Edward crown 1980–.

208. ROYAL NAVAL MERITORIOUS SERVICE MEDAL

Instituted: 14 January 1919 until 1928 by Order in Council. Reinstituted 1977.

Branch of Service: Royal Navy.

Ribbon: Crimson with three white stripes.

Metal: Silver

Size: 36mm.

Description: (Obverse) effigy of the reigning monarch; (reverse) imperial crown surmounting a wreath containing the words FOR MERITORIOUS SERVICE. The medal was named in large seriffed capitals round the rim.

Comments: *Awarded without annuity or pension to petty officers and ratings of the Royal Navy. Originally it was awarded either for specific acts of gallantry not in the presence of the enemy or for arduous and specially meritorious service afloat or ashore in action with the enemy. Bars were granted for second awards. It was superseded in 1928 by the British Empire Medal for Gallantry or Meritorious Service, but re-instated on 1 December 1977. In this guise it has been awarded to senior petty officers of the Royal Navy, warrant officers and senior NCOs of the Royal Marines, and equivalent ranks in the WRNS and QARNNS, who have at least 20 years service and are already holders of the LSGC medal and three good conduct badges. The medal is not awarded automatically when these criteria are satisfied, as no more than 49 medals may be awarded annually. The revived medal is identical to the Army MSM and can only be distinguished by the naming giving rank and name of ship.*

VALUE:		Miniature
George V (A)	—	—
George V (B) (1020)	£400–500	£20–30
Elizabeth II (D)	£350–450	£15–18

209. ROYAL MARINES MERITORIOUS SERVICE MEDAL

Original ribbon.

Instituted: 15 January 1849, by Order in Council (although medals dated 1848 are unknown).

Branch of Service: Royal Marines.

Ribbon: Plain dark blue, but later replaced by the RN MSM ribbon.

Metal: Silver.

Size: 36mm.

Description: (Obverse) effigy of the monarch; (reverse) a crowned laurel wreath enclosing the words FOR MERITORIOUS SERVICE.

Comments: *Annuities not exceeding £20 a year might be granted in addition to the medal for distinguished service. Sergeants with a minimum of 24 years service (the last fourteen as a sergeant), "with an irreproachable and meritorious character" were considered eligible for the award which was extended to discharged sergeants in 1872 when the service qualification was reduced to 21 years. The award of the MSM for gallantry was discontinued in 1874 when the Conspicuous Gallantry Medal was reconstituted. Only six MSMs for gallantry were ever awarded. The medal was identical with the Army MSM, distinguished solely by its ribbon and the naming to the recipient. Under the royal warrants of 1916-19 Marine NCOs became eligible for immediate awards of the MSM for arduous or specially meritorious service. The medals in this case were worn with crimson ribbons with three white stripes and had the obverse showing the King in the uniform of an Admiral or a Field Marshal, depending on whether the award was for services afloat, or with the naval brigades on the Western Front. The use of this medal ceased in 1928 when the BEM for Gallantry was instituted. The Royal Marines MSM was revived in 1977 solely as a long service award and is the same as the naval MSM already noted, differing only in the details of the recipient.*

VALUE:			Miniature	
	VR dated 1848	£1200–1500		£45–60
	VR	£700–1000		£70–80
	EVIIR	£600–800		£70–80
	GVR	£400–600		£40–50
	GVIR	£600–800		£25–30

210. ARMY MERITORIOUS SERVICE MEDAL

Instituted: 19 December 1845.

Branch of Service: Army.

Ribbon: Plain crimson (till 1916), white edges added (1916-17), three white stripes (since August 1917).

Metal: Silver.

Size: 36mm.

Description: (Obverse) effigy of the monarch; (reverse) a crowned laurel wreath inscribed FOR MERITORIOUS SERVICE.

Comments: *A sum of £2000 a year was set aside for distribution to recipients in the form of annuities not exceeding £20, paid for life to NCOs of the rank of sergeant and above for distinguished or meritorious service. The number of medals awarded was thus limited by the amount of money available in the annuity fund, so that medals and annuities were only granted on the death of previous recipients or when the fund was increased. Until November 1902 holders were not allowed to wear the LSGC as well as the MSM, but thereafter both medals could be worn, the LSGC taking precedence. In 1979, however, the order of precedence was reversed. Until 1951 the MSM could only be awarded when an annuity became available, but since then it has been awarded without the annuity. From 1956 recipients needed at least 27 years service to become eligible, but this was reduced to 20 years in 2002. What was, in effect, a second type of MSM was introduced in October 1916 when immediate awards for exceptionally valuable and meritorious service were introduced. In January 1917 this was extended to include individual acts of gallantry not in the presence of the enemy. No annuities were paid with the immediate awards which terminated in 1928 with the institution of the Gallantry BEM. Bars for subsequent acts of gallantry or life-saving were introduced in 1916, seven being awarded up to 1928. The standard crown and wreath reverse was used but in addition to the wide range of obverse types swivelling suspension was used until 1926, and immediate and non-immediate awards may be distinguished by the presence or absence respectively of the recipient's regimental number. Recent awards of the Elizabethan second bust medals have reverted to swivelling suspension. By Royal Warrant of February 2002 the annual allocation was a maximum of 201 medals: Royal Navy (49), Royal Marines (3), Army (89) and RAF (60).*

First type ribbon.

Second type ribbon.

Third type ribbon.

VALUE:

		Miniature
Victoria (A) 1847 on edge (110)	£800–1000	—
Victoria (A) 1848 below bust (10)	£1500–2000	—
Victoria (A) (990)	£350–450	£30–50
Edward VII (725)	£230–350	£30–40
George V (A) swivel (1050)	£150–250	£18–25
George V (A) non-swivel (400)	£150–250	£15–20
George V (A) Immediate awards 1916–28 (26,211+7 bars):		
For Gallantry (366+1 bar)	£300–400	—
Meritorious services (25,845+6 bars)	£200–300	—
George V (E) (550)	£300–400	£18–25
George VI (D) (1090)	£250–350	£15–20
George VI (E) (5600)	£200–300	£15–20
George VI (B) (55)	£800–1000	£15–20
Elizabeth II (B) (125)	£400–650	£15–20
Elizabeth II (C) (2750)	£250–450	£15–20

211. ROYAL AIR FORCE MERITORIOUS SERVICE MEDAL

Instituted: June 1918
Branch of Service: Royal Air Force.
Ribbon: Half crimson, half light blue, with white stripes at the centre and edges. Since 1977 the same ribbon as the Army MSM.
Metal: Silver.
Size: 36mm.
Description: (Obverse) effigy of the monarch; (reverse) a crowned laurel wreath enclosing the words FOR MERITORIOUS SERVICE. Originally medals were named in large seriffed capitals and were issued in respect of the First World War and service in Russia (1918-20), but later medals were impressed in thin block capitals. The RAF version had a swivelling suspension, unlike its military counterpart.
Comments: *Awarded for valuable services in the field, as opposed to actual flying service. This medal was replaced by the BEM in 1928, but revived in December 1977 under the same conditions as the military MSM. No more than 60 medals are awarded annually. The current issue is similar to the naval and military MSMs, differing only in the naming which includes RAF after the service number.*

Original ribbon.

VALUE:		Miniature
George V (E) (854)	£400–500	£20–30
Elizabeth II (D)	£350–450	£10–15

212. COLONIAL MERITORIOUS SERVICE MEDALS

For the various original ribbons see the ribbon charts at the end of this publication.

Instituted: 31 May 1895.
Branch of Service: Colonial forces.
Ribbon: According to issuing territory (see below).
Metal: Silver.
Size: 36mm.
Description: (Obverse) originally the trophy of arms as MYB 229 but later issues have the head of the reigning monarch; (reverse) as British type, but with the name of the dominion or colony round the top.
Comments: *Awarded for service in the British dominions, colonies and protectorates.*

Canada: Ribbon as for British Army MSM. CANADA on reverse till 1936; imperial version used from then until 1958. No medals with the Victorian obverse were awarded, but specimens exist.
Cape of Good Hope: Crimson ribbon with central orange stripe. Only one or two Edward VII medals issued.
Natal: Crimson ribbon with a central yellow stripe. Exceptionally, it was awarded to volunteers in the Natal Militia. Fifteen Edward VII medals awarded.
Commonwealth of Australia: Crimson ribbon with two dark green central stripes. Issued between 1903 and 1975.
New South Wales: Crimson ribbon with a dark blue central stripe. Issued till 1903.
Queensland: Crimson ribbon with light blue central stripe. Issued till 1903.
South Australia: Plain crimson ribbon. Issued till 1903.
Tasmania: Crimson ribbon with a pink central stripe. Issued till 1903.
New Zealand: Crimson ribbon with a light green central stripe. Issued since 1898 (see also NZ21).

VALUE   Rare   *Miniature*   £100–200

213. INDIAN ARMY MERITORIOUS SERVICE MEDAL 1848

Instituted: 20 May 1848, by General Order of the Indian government.
Branch of Service: Forces of the Honourable East India Company and later the Indian armed services.
Ribbon: Plain crimson.
Metal: Silver.
Size: 36mm.
Description: (Obverse) the Wyon profile of Queen Victoria; (reverse) the arms and motto of the Honourable East India Company.
Comments: *Awarded with an annuity up to £20 to European sergeants, serving or discharged, for meritorious service. It was discontinued in 1873.*

VALUE: £500–600   *Miniature* £200–250

214. INDIAN ARMY MERITORIOUS SERVICE MEDAL 1888

Instituted: 1888.
Branch of Service: Indian Army.
Ribbon: Plain crimson (till 1917); three white stripes added (1917).
Metal: Silver.
Size: 36mm.
Description: (Obverse) the sovereign's effigy; (reverse) a central wreath enclosing the word INDIA surrounded by the legend FOR MERITORIOUS SERVICE with a continuous border of lotus flowers and leaves round the circumference.
Comments: *For award to Indian warrant officers and senior NCOs (havildars, dafadars and equivalent band ranks). Eighteen years of exceptionally meritorious service was the minimum requirement, subject to the availability of funds in the annuity. At first only one medal was set aside for each regiment and thereafter awards were only made on the death, promotion or reduction of existing recipients. On promotion the medal was retained but the annuity ceased. It became obsolete in 1947.*

Original ribbon.

VALUE:		*Miniature*
Victoria (B)	£200–250	£80–100
Edward VII (A)	£160–225	£80–100
George V (D)	£100–150	£80–100
George V (C)	£100–150	£80–100
George VI (B)	£85–125	£80–100

215. AFRICAN POLICE MEDAL FOR MERITORIOUS SERVICE

Instituted: 14 July 1915.

Branch of Service Non-European NCOs and men of the colonial police forces in East and West Africa.

Ribbon: Sand-coloured with red edges.

Metal: Silver.

Size: 36mm.

Description: (Obverse) effigy of the sovereign; (reverse) a crown surmounted by a lion passant gardant within a palm wreath and having the legend FOR MERITORIOUS SERVICE IN THE POLICE and AFRICA at the foot.

Comments: *Awarded for both individual acts of gallantry and distinguished, meritorious or long service. In respect of the lastnamed, a minimum of 15 years exemplary service was required. It was superseded by the Colonial Police Medal in 1938.*

VALUE:

George V (A) IND: IMP 1915-31	£350–450
George V (A) INDIAE IMP 1931-7	£350–450
George VI (B) 1938	Rare
Miniature	£80–1000

216. UNION OF SOUTH AFRICA MERITORIOUS SERVICE MEDAL

Instituted: 24 October 1914, by Government gazette.

Branch of Service: Service personnel of South Africa, Southern Rhodesia and Swaziland.

Ribbon: Crimson with blue edges and a central white, blue and white band.

Metal: Silver.

Size: 36mm.

Description: As British military MSM.

Comments: *A total of 46 awards were made for 21 years service and 300 meritorious service awards were made up to 1952 when the medal was discontinued. Of these only two were awarded to South Africans in the RNVR.*

VALUE: Rare *Miniature* £200–250

217. ROYAL HOUSEHOLD FAITHFUL SERVICE MEDALS

1st type obv.

1st type rev.

GV ribbon.

GVI ribbon.

EII ribbon.

Instituted: 1872 by Queen Victoria.

Branch of Service: Royal Household.

Ribbon: Originally Royal Stuart tartan; later, a different ribbon for each monarch: dark blue and red diagonal stripes descending from left to right (George V), the same but descending from right to left (George VI) or dark blue with three red stripes (Elizabeth II).

Metal: Silver.

Size: 27mm (Victoria); 29mm (later awards).

Description: (Obverse) the sovereign's effigy; (reverse) the personal details of the recipient engraved on it. The Victorian medal has a very elaborate suspension ornamented with the crowned royal monogram, with a laurel bar brooch fitting at the top. This medal was not originally intended to be worn with a ribbon, although it had a strip of Royal Stuart tartan behind it. The same medal, but struck in 22 carat gold, was presented to John Brown, the Queen's personal servant. The concept was revived by George V, a silver medal of more conventional appearance being struck with the text FOR LONG AND FAITHFUL SERVICE on the reverse. Thirty, forty and fifty year service bars were also awarded.

Comments: *Originally intended as a reward to servants of the Royal Household for long and faithful service of at least 25 years but during the reign of George V this was changed to 20 years cumulative service. A further 10 years merited a bar. Different ribbons are used for each monarch, corresponding to the crowned cypher joining the medal to the suspension bar on either side of which the recipient's years of service are inscribed.*

VALUE:

		Miniature
Victoria	From £350	Not seen
Edward VII	—	Not seen
George V (E)	From £350	£80–100
George VI (D)	From £350	£70–80
Elizabeth II (C)	From £400	£30–40

2nd type obv. (George V).

2nd type rev.

218. ROYAL NAVAL LONG SERVICE AND GOOD CONDUCT MEDAL

1st type obv.

1st type rev.

2nd type rev. wide suspender

Later type ribbon.

Instituted: 24 August 1831, by Order in Council.
Branch of Service: Royal Navy.
Ribbon: Plain dark blue (1831); dark blue with white edges (1848).
Metal: Silver.
Size: 34mm (1831); 36mm (1848).
Description: First type: (Obverse) an anchor surmounted by a crown and enclosed in an oak wreath; (reverse) the recipient's details. Plain ring for suspension.

Second type, adopted in 1848: (Obverse) the sovereign's effigy; (reverse) a three-masted man-of-war surrounded by a rope tied at the foot with a reef knot and having the legend FOR LONG SERVICE AND GOOD CONDUCT round the circumference. This medal originally had a wide suspender bar 38mm, but a narrow suspender was substituted in 1874. Normally the obverse was undated, but about 100 medals were issued in 1849-50 with the obverse of the Naval GSM, with the date 1848 below the Queen's bust. Between 1875 and 1877 a number of medals had the years of service added to the recipient's details, either engraved or impressed on the edge—these medals (about 60 known) are now sought after by collectors. Engraved naming was used from 1875 to 1877, but from then until 1901 impressed naming was adopted. Later medals used the various obverse effigies noted below.

Comments: *Originally awarded for 21 years exemplary conduct, but the period was reduced to 10 years in 1874, then later increased to 15 years. Bars for additional periods of 15 years were instituted by George V. In March 1981 commissioned officers of the naval services became eligible after 15 years service, provided at least 12 years were served in the ranks.*

VALUE:

		Miniature
Anchor type obv., 1831–47 (644)	£650–850	—
Victoria (A):		
1848–75, wide suspender (3572)	£450–550	—
Dated 1848 type (100)	£1100–1250	—
1875–77, narrow suspender,		
engraved naming (4400)	£150–200	£30–40
Year on edge variety (c. 40)	£350–450	—
1877–1901		
impressed naming (18,200)	£150–200	—
Year on edge variety (c. 20)	£300–350	—
Edward VII (B)	£65–85	—
George V (B) 1910–20 swivel	£65–85	£10–15
1920–30 non-swivelling bar	£60–75	£5–10
George V (E) 1931–36	£70–90	£10–12
George VI (D) 1937–48	£70–90	£10–12
George VI (E) 1949–52	£70–90	£10–12
Elizabeth II (B) 1953–54	£70–90	£10–12
Elizabeth II (C) 1954–	£70–90	£10–12

2nd type rev. narrow suspender

2nd type obv. George V

219. ROYAL NAVAL RESERVE DECORATION

Instituted: 1908.

Branch of Service: Royal Naval Reserve.

Ribbon: Plain green ribbon, white edges being added from 1941 onwards.

Metal: Silver and silver-gilt.

Size: Height 54mm; max. width 33mm.

Description: A skeletal badge with the royal cypher in silver surrounded by an oval cable and reef knot in silver-gilt, surmounted by a crown and suspension ring.

Comments: *Granted for 15 years commissioned service (sub-lieutenant and above) in the Royal Naval Reserve, active service in wartime counting double. Bars are awarded for additional periods of 15 years. Recipients are entitled to the letters RD after their name. This decoration was replaced by the VRSM (No. 242A) in 2000.*

VALUE:		Miniature
Edward VII	£150–175	£25–30
George V	£170–195	£25–30
George VI (GRI)	£150–175	£25–30
George VI (GVIR)	£150–175	£25–30
Elizabeth II	£175–190	£25–30

2nd type ribbon.

220. ROYAL NAVAL RESERVE LONG SERVICE AND GOOD CONDUCT MEDAL

Instituted: 1908.

Branch of Service: Royal Naval Reserve.

Ribbon: Plain green, white edges and a central white stripe being added in 1941. On the amalgamation of the RNR and RNVR in 1958 the ribbon was changed to five equal stripes of blue, white, green, white and blue.

Metal: Silver.

Size: 36mm.

Description: (Obverse) effigy of the monarch; (reverse) a battleship with the motto DIUTERNE FIDELIS (faithful for ever) at the foot.

Comments: *Awarded to petty officers and ratings of the RNR for 15 years service, war service counting double, with bars for additional 15 year periods. This medal was replaced by the VRSM (No. 242A) in 2000.*

VALUE:		Miniature
Edward VII (B)	£40–50	£25–30
George V (B)	£30–40	£25–30
George V (E)	£30–40	£25–30
George VI (D)	£55–70	£25–30
George VI (E)	£55–70	£25–30
Elizabeth II (B)	£55–70	£25–30
Elizabeth II (C)	£55–70	£25–30

2nd type ribbon.

3rd type ribbon.

221. ROYAL NAVAL VOLUNTEER RESERVE DECORATION

Instituted: 1908.

Branch of Service: Royal Naval Volunteer Reserve.

Ribbon: 38mm originally plain dark green; dark blue with a central green stripe flanked by narrow red stripes (since 1919). Dark blue represents the sea, red represents the Royal Crimson, green represents the Old Volunteer colour

Metal: Silver and silver-gilt.

Size: Height 54mm; max. width 33mm.

Description: Similar to RNR decoration.

Comments: *Awarded to commissioned officers of the RNVR. The qualifying period was 15 years, service in the ranks counting half and war service counting double. In 1966 the decoration was replaced by the RD following the merger of the RNR and RNVR. Holders were entitled to the post-nominals letters VD, until 1947 when the letters VRD were substituted. Additional bars were awarded for each 10 years service.*

VALUE:		Miniature
Edward VII	£160–185	£25–30
George V	£140–160	£25–30
George VI GRI	£140–160	£25–30
George VI GVIR	£130–160	£25–30
Elizabeth II	£160–190	£25–30

222. ROYAL NAVAL VOLUNTEER RESERVE LONG SERVICE AND GOOD CONDUCT MEDAL

Instituted: 1908.

Branch of Service: Royal Naval Volunteer Reserve.

Ribbon: Originally plain green, but subsequently a broad central green stripe edged in red with blue stripes at the ends was adopted.

Metal: Silver.

Size: 36mm.

Description: Identical to the RNR medal, but distinguished by the ribbon and the naming which includes the letters RNVR, RCNVR (Canada), RSANVR (South Africa), etc.

Comments: *Awarded to petty officers and ratings for 12 years service with the necessary training, character assessed as "very good" or better throughout the period. War service counted double. The award was extended to the Colonial Navies during the Second World War.*

VALUE:		Miniature
Edward VII (B)	£350–400	£25–30
George V (B)	£45–60	£25–30
George V (E)	£50–70	£25–30
George VI (D)	£50–65	£25–30
George VI (E)	£50–65	£25–30
Elizabeth II (C)	£70–100	£25–30

223. ROYAL FLEET RESERVE LONG SERVICE AND GOOD CONDUCT MEDAL

Instituted: 1919.
Branch of Service: Royal Fleet Reserve.
Ribbon: Blue bordered with thin red stripes and white edges.
Metal: Silver.
Size: 36mm.
Description: Similar to the RNR LSGC but with ring suspension instead of a bar suspender.
Comments: *Awarded for 15 years service in the Fleet Reserve. This medal was discontinued in 2000.*

VALUE:		Miniature
George V (B)	£45–55	£25–30
George V (E)	£45–55	£25–30
George VI (D)	£45–55	£25–30
George VI (E)	£45–55	£25–30
Elizabeth II (B)	£55–65	£25–30
Elizabeth II (C)	£55–65	£25–30

224. ROYAL NAVAL AUXILIARY SICK BERTH RESERVE LONG SERVICE AND GOOD CONDUCT MEDAL

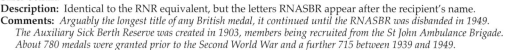

Instituted: 1919.
Branch of Service: Royal Naval Auxiliary Sick Berth Reserve.
Ribbon: Plain green but later green with a white central stripe and white edges.
Metal: Silver.
Size: 36mm.
Description: Identical to the RNR equivalent, but the letters RNASBR appear after the recipient's name.
Comments: *Arguably the longest title of any British medal, it continued until the RNASBR was disbanded in 1949. The Auxiliary Sick Berth Reserve was created in 1903, members being recruited from the St John Ambulance Brigade. About 780 medals were granted prior to the Second World War and a further 715 between 1939 and 1949.*

VALUE:		Miniature
George V (B)	£100–120	£25–30
George V (E)	£100–120	£25–30
George VI (D)	£100–120	£25–30

225. ROYAL NAVAL VOLUNTEER (WIRELESS) RESERVE LONG SERVICE AND GOOD CONDUCT MEDAL

Instituted: 1939.
Branch of Service: Royal Naval Volunteer Wireless Auxiliary Reserve.
Ribbon: A broad central green stripe edged in red with blue stripes at the ends.
Metal: Silver.
Size: 36mm.
Description: Identical to the RNR equivalent, but the letters RNV(W)R after the recipient's name. The last of the service medals with a battleship reverse.
Comments: *Issued till 1957 when the RNWAR was disbanded. It was awarded for 12 years service, only about 200 having been issued.*

VALUE:		Miniature
George VI (D)	£250–350	£25–30
Elizabeth II (C)	£250–350	£25–30

226. ROYAL NAVAL AUXILIARY SERVICE MEDAL

Instituted: July 1965.
Branch of Service: Royal Naval Auxiliary Service (RNXS), formerly the Royal Naval Minewatching Service, disbanded 1994.
Ribbon: Dark blue with a narrow green central stripe and broad white stripes at the edges bisected by thin dark green stripes.
Metal: Cupro-nickel.
Size: 36mm.
Description: (Obverse) the Queen's effigy; (reverse) a fouled anchor in an oak wreath surmounted by a naval crown.
Comments: *Awarded for 12 years service. A bar was awarded for each additional 12 years service. 1,710 were awarded, 131 with one bar and 2 with two bars. Interestingly this medal was the last to be issued with a pure silk ribbon.*

VALUE: Elizabeth II (A)   £180–220   *Miniature*   £25–30

227. ROCKET APPARATUS VOLUNTEER LONG SERVICE MEDAL

First type obverse.

Instituted: 1911 by the Board of Trade.
Branch of Service: Rocket Life Saving Apparatus Volunteers,
Ribbon: Pale blue with broad scarlet edges.
Metal: Silver.
Size: 31mm.
Description: (Obverse) the effigy of the reigning monarch with the date 1911 below the truncation. (Reverse) exists in four types. The first refers to the Board of Trade but when that department handed over responsibility to the Ministry of Transport in 1942 the wording was amended to read ROCKET APPARATUS VOLUNTEER MEDAL round the circumference. In 1953 the inscription was changed to COAST LIFE SAVING CORPS and then in 1968 to COASTGUARD AUXILIARY SERVICE.
Comments: *Awarded for 20 years service with the Rocket Life Saving Apparatus Volunteers. The RLSAV became the Coast Life Saving Corps in 1953 and the Coastguard Auxiliary Service in 1968, these titles being reflected in the wording on the reverse.*

VALUE:		*Miniature*
George V (E)	£95–100	£50–100
George VI (D/E) BoT	£95–100	
George VI (D/E) Rocket Apparatus	£95–100	
Elizabeth II (D) Coast Life Saving	£150–165	
Elizabeth II (D) Coastguard Auxiliary	£150–165	

228. COASTGUARD COMMENDATION

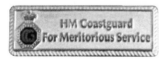

Instituted: 2000.
Branch of Service: HM Coastguard Service.
Ribbon: None.
Metal: Gilt.
Size: 35mm x 12mm.
Description: Pin badge depicting the emblem of HM Coastguard Service (left) with two-line inscription "H.M. Coastguard / For Meritorious Service" (right).
Comments: *Awarded to Coastguard, Auxiliary Coastguard and Coastguard rescue teams for rescuing shipwrecked mariners.*

VALUE: —

229. ARMY LONG SERVICE AND GOOD CONDUCT MEDAL

1st type obv. Trophy of Arms with badge of Hanover.

2nd type obv. with badge of Hanover omitted and swivel suspender.

GV type C obverse with fixed suspender and "Commonwealth" bar.

re-1917 ribbon.

Later ribbon, used from 1917.

Instituted: 1830.

Branch of Service: Army.

Ribbon: Plain crimson was used till 1917 when white stripes were added to the edges. Dominion and colonial medals formerly had crimson ribbons with a narrow central stripe in dark green (Commonwealth of Australia), dark blue (New South Wales), light blue (Queensland), pink (Tasmania), orange (Cape of Good Hope), yellow (Natal), white (Canada), light green (NZ). New Guinea had a scarlet ribbon with a light blue central stripe and South Australia had no central stripe on a plain crimson ribbon.

Metal: Silver.

Size: 36mm.

Description: Over the long period in which this medal has been in use it has undergone a number of changes. Until 1901 the obverse bore a trophy of arms with the royal arms in an oval shield in the centre while the reverse bore the inscription FOR LONG SERVICE AND GOOD CONDUCT. The first issue had the royal arms with the badge of Hanover on the obverse and small suspension ring with a plain crimson ribbon. A large ring was substituted in 1831. On the accession of Queen Victoria in 1837 the Hanoverian emblem was dropped from the arms. In 1855 a swivelling scroll suspension was substituted and in 1859 small lettering replaced the original large lettering on the reverse. From 1901, however, the effigy of the reigning sovereign was placed on the obverse although the reverse remained the same. In 1920 the swivelling scroll suspension gave way to a fixed suspender. In 1930 the title of the medal was changed to the Long Service and Good Conduct (Military) Medal; at the same time the design was modified. A fixed suspension bar was added, bearing the words REGULAR ARMY or the name of a dominion (India, Canada, Australia, New Zealand or South Africa). This replaced the Permanent Forces of the Empire LSGC Medal (see below).

Comments: *Originally awarded to soldiers of exemplary conduct for 21 years service in the infantry or 24 years in the cavalry, but in 1870 the qualifying period was reduced to 18 years and in 1977 to 15 years. During the Second World War commissioned officers were permitted to acquire this medal so long as they had completed at least 12 of their 18 years service in the ranks. Canada discontinued the LSGC medal in 1950 when the Canadian Forces Decoration was instituted, while South Africa replaced it with the John Chard Medal later the same year. From 1930 onwards the lettering of the reverse inscription was in tall, thin letters. In 1940 bars for further periods of service were authorised. The LSGC is invariably named to the recipient. The William IV and early Victorian issues (to 1854) were impressed in the style of the Waterloo Medal and also bore the date of discharge and award. The 1855 issue was not dated, while lettering was impressed in the style of the Military General Service Medal. Later Victorian issues, however, were engraved in various styles, while medals from 1901 onwards are impressed in small capitals of various types. Medals to Europeans in the Indian Army are engraved in cursive script. Recent research by Irvin Mortensen, however, reveals that some medals after 1850 were issued unnamed, and this also accounts for various unofficial styles of naming found on later medals.*

VALUE:		*Miniature*
William IV small ring 1830–31	£850–1000	—
William IV large ring 1831–37	£750–950	—
Victoria without Hanoverian arms 1837–55	£250–350	—
Victoria swivelling scroll suspension 1855–74	£155–225	£30–40
Victoria small reverse lettering 1874–1901	£100–150	£25–30
Edward VII (A) 1902–10	£60–100	£25–30
George V (A) 1911–20	£60–80	£15–20
George V (A) fixed suspender 1920–30	£60–80	£15–20
George V (C) 1930–36, Regular Army bar	£60–80	£15–20
Commonwealth bar	From £75	£15–20
George VI (B) 1937–48, Regular Army bar	£50–80	£15–20
Commonwealth bar	From £75	£15–20
George VI (E) 1949–52, Regular Army bar	£60–85	£15–20
Elizabeth II 1953–54, Regular Army bar	£60–85	£15–20
Elizabeth II 1954–, Regular Army bar	£60–85	£15–20
Commonwealth bar	From £100	£15–20

230. ULSTER DEFENCE REGIMENT MEDAL FOR LONG SERVICE AND GOOD CONDUCT

Instituted: 1982.
Branch of Service: Ulster Defence Regiment.
Ribbon: Similar to the Military LSGC medal but with a central green stripe in addition.
Metal: Silver.
Size: 36mm.
Description: (Obverse) the imperial crowned bust of Queen Elizabeth II; (reverse) similar to the Military LSGC medal. Fitted with a fixed suspension bar inscribed UDR.
Comments: *Granted to personnel for 15 years exemplary service after 1 April 1970, with bars for additional 15-year periods. It is also awarded to officers provided that at least 12 of their 15 years service was in the ranks.*

VALUE:

Elizabeth II (B)	£80–100	*Miniature*	£10–15

231. VOLUNTEER OFFICER'S DECORATION

Instituted: 25 July 1892.
Branch of Service: Volunteer Force.
Ribbon: 38mm plain green, suspended from an oak bar brooch. Members of the Honourable Artillery Company were granted a distinctive ribbon in 1906, half scarlet, half dark blue with yellow edges—King Edward's racing colours.
Metal: Silver and silver-gilt.
Size: Height 42mm; max. width 35mm.
Description: An oval skeletal badge in silver and silver-gilt, with the royal cypher and crown in the centre, within a wreath of oak leaves. It is suspended by a plain ring with a laurel bar brooch fitted to the top of the ribbon. Although issued unnamed, many examples were subsequently engraved or impressed privately. Two versions of the Victorian decoration were produced, differing in the monogram— VR for United Kingdom recipients and VRI for recipients in the dominions and colonies.
Comments: *The basic qualification was 20 years commissioned service in the Volunteer Force, a precursor of the Territorial Army, non-commissioned service counting half. By Royal Warrant of 24 May 1894 the decoration was extended to comparable forces overseas, the qualifying period for service in India being reduced to 18 years. The colonial VD was superseded in 1899 by the Colonial Auxiliary Forces Officers Decoration and the Indian Volunteer Forces Officers Decoration. In the United Kingdom it was superseded by the Territorial Decoration, on the formation of the TF in 1908. A total of 4,710 decorations were awarded. Awards in Bermuda continued until 1930.*

VALUE:		*Miniature*
Victoria VR	£125–150	£35–45
Victoria VRI	£250–300	£85–100
Edward VII	£125–150	£30–40
George V	£125–150	£25–35

HAC ribbon.

232. VOLUNTEER LONG SERVICE AND GOOD CONDUCT MEDAL

HAC ribbon.

Instituted: 1894.

Branch of Service: Volunteer Force.

Ribbon: 32mm plain green, but members of the Honourable Artillery Company were granted a distinctive ribbon in 1906, half scarlet, half dark blue with yellow edges—King Edward's racing colours.

Metal: Silver.

Size: 36mm.

Description: (Obverse) effigy of the reigning monarch; (reverse) a laurel wreath on which is superimposed ribbons inscribed FOR LONG SERVICE IN THE VOLUNTEER FORCE.

Comments: *This medal was awarded for 20 years service in the ranks. Officers could also receive the medal, being eligible on account of their non-commissioned service. Many officers then gained sufficient commissioned service to be awarded either the Volunteer Decoration or (from 1908) the Territorial Decoration. The medal was extended to Colonial Forces in June 1898, the titles of the monarch being appropriately expanded for this version. This medal was superseded by the Territorial Force Efficiency Medal in 1908, although it continued to be awarded until 1930 in Bermuda, India, Isle of Man (Isle of Man Vols.) and the 7th Volunteer Battalion of the King's (Liverpool) Regiment.*

VALUE:

		Miniature
Victoria Regina (C) (UK)	£75–100	
Unnamed	£45–50	£20–25
Victoria Regina et Imperatrix (C) (overseas)	£85–125	£20–25
Edwardus Rex (A)	£85–100	£15–25
Edwardus Rex et Imperator (A) (colonial)	£85–100	£15–25
Edwardus Kaisar-i-Hind (A) (India)	£100–120	£15–25
George V (A)		
India	£85–100	£15–20
Isle of Man	£250–300	£15–20
Bermuda	£150–200	£15–20

233. TERRITORIAL DECORATION

Instituted: 29 September 1908.

Branch of Service: Territorial Force, later Territorial Army.

Ribbon: 38mm plain dark green with a central yellow stripe suspended from an oak bar brooch. Members of the Honourable Artillery Company were granted a distinctive ribbon in 1906, half scarlet, half dark blue with yellow edges—King Edward's racing colours.

Metal: Silver and silver-gilt.

Size: Height 46mm; max. width 35mm.

Description: A skeletal badge with the crowned monogram of the sovereign surrounded by an oval oak wreath, fitted with a ring for suspension.

Comments: *Awarded for 20 years commissioned service, service in the ranks counting half and war service double. It was superseded by the Efficiency Decoration in 1930. A total of 4,783 decorations were awarded.*

VALUE:

		Miniature
Edward VII (585)	£155–185	£15–20
George V (4,198)	£125–175	£10–15

HAC ribbon.

234. TERRITORIAL FORCE EFFICIENCY MEDAL

Original ribbon.

HAC ribbon.

Instituted: 1908.

Branch of Service: Territorial Force.

Ribbon: Originally 32mm plain dark green with a central yellow stripe but members of the Honourable Artillery Company were granted a distinctive ribbon in 1906, half scarlet, half dark blue with yellow edges—King Edward's racing colours. In December 1919 the ribbon was changed to plain dark green with yellow edges.

Metal: Silver.

Size: Height 38mm; max. width 31mm.

Description: An oval medal fitted with claw and ring suspension. (Obverse) the sovereign's effigy; (reverse) inscribed with the name of the medal in four lines.

Comments: *Granted for a minimum of 12 years service in the Territorial Force. It was superseded in 1921 by the Territorial Efficiency Medal when the service was renamed. Bars were awarded for further periods of 12 years service.*

VALUE:

		Miniature
Edward VII (A) (11,800)	£120–140*	£15–20
Of these:		
With bar (537)	£170–200	
with second bars (64)	£220–260	
George V (A) (37,726)	£65–85	£15–20
George V first clasps	£100–150	

*Medals to Yeomanry regiments command a higher premium.

234A. TERRITORIAL FORCE IMPERIAL SERVICE BADGE

Instituted: 1912.

Branch of Service: Members of the Territorial Force.

Ribbon: None.

Metal: Cupro-nickel or brass.

Size: 10mm x 43mm

Description: A horizontal bar surmounted by a royal crown, the bar inscribed in raised lettering IMPERIAL SERVICE.

Comments: *Awarded to members of the Territorial Force who were prepared to serve outside the United Kingdom in defence of the Empire, mainly during the First World War.*

VALUE: £12–15

235. TERRITORIAL EFFICIENCY MEDAL

Instituted: 1921.

Branch of Service: Territorial Army.

Ribbon: 32mm plain dark green with yellow edges.

Metal: Silver.

Size: Height 38mm; max. width 31mm.

Description: As above, but with the name amended and inscribed in three lines.

Comments: *Introduced following the elevation of the Territorial Force to become the Territorial Army. It was superseded by the Efficiency Medal in 1930.*

VALUE:

George V (A)	£70–90	*Miniature*	£10–15

236. EFFICIENCY DECORATION

Original ribbon.

Post-1969 ribbon.

HAC ribbon.

Instituted: 17 October 1930.

Branch of Service: Territorial Army (UK), the Indian Volunteer Forces and the Colonial Auxiliary Forces.

Ribbon: 38mm plain dark green with a central yellow stripe. In 1969, on the introduction of the T&AVR, the ribbon was altered to half blue, half green, with a central yellow stripe. Members of the Honourable Artillery Company wear half blue, half scarlet ribbon, with yellow edges.

Metal: Silver and silver-gilt.

Size: Height 54mm; max. width 37mm.

Description: An oval skeletal badge in silver and silver-gilt with the crowned monogram in an oak wreath, the ring for suspension being fitted to the top of the crown. It differs also from the previous decorations in having a suspender bar denoting the area of service: Territorial (UK), India, Canada, Fiji or other overseas country being inscribed as appropriate, but the previous ribbon was retained.

Comments: *Recipients in Britain were allowed to continue using the letters TD after their names, but in the Commonwealth the letters ED were used instead. The 20-year qualification was reduced to 12 years in 1949, bars for each additional 6 years being added. In 1969 the British bar was changed to T & AVR, on the establishment of the Territorial and Army Volunteer Reserve. In 1982 the title of Territorial Army was resumed, so the inscription on the bar reverted to TERRITORIAL but the blue, yellow and green ribbon was retained. This decoration was superseded in the UK by the VRSM (No. 242A) in 2000. However, it is still current in some Commonwealth countries.*

VALUE:

	Territorial	T&AVR	Commonwealth
George V	£100–125	—	From £175
George VI (GRI)	£85–100	—	From £175
George VI (GVIR)	£85–100	—	—
Elizabeth II	£100–125	£120–150	From £175
Miniature	£10–15	£10–15	£50–75

237. EFFICIENCY MEDAL

Instituted: 17 October 1930.

Branch of Service: Territorial Army (UK), Indian Volunteer Forces and Colonial Auxiliary Forces.

Ribbon: 32mm green with yellow edges. In 1969, on the introduction of the T&AVR, the ribbon was altered to half blue, half green, with yellow edges. Members of the Honourable Artillery Company wear half blue, half scarlet ribbon, with yellow edges.

Metal: Silver.

Original ribbon.

Post-1969 ribbon.

HAC ribbon.

237. EFFICIENCY MEDAL *continued*

Aa

Ab

Size: Height 39mm; max. width 32mm.

Description: An oval silver medal. (Obverse) the monarch's effigy; (reverse) inscribed FOR EFFICIENT SERVICE. In place of the simple ring suspension, however, there was now a fixed suspender bar decorated with a pair of palm leaves surmounted by a scroll inscribed TERRITORIAL or MILITIA (for UK volunteer forces), while overseas forces had the name of the country.

Comments: *This medal consolidated the awards to other ranks throughout the volunteer forces of Britain and the Commonwealth. The basic qualification was 12 years continuous efficient service, but war service and peacetime service in West Africa counted double. Additional bars with a crown were awarded for further periods of six years continuous efficient service. The Militia bar was granted to certain categories of the Supplementary Reserve until the formation of the Army Emergency Reserve in 1951. In 1969 the bar inscribed T & AVR was introduced. The bar TERRITORIAL was resumed in 1982 but the half blue, half green ribbon with yellow edges was retained. For the distinctive medal awarded in the Union of South Africa see number 254. Instead of the second obverse of Queen Elizabeth II, Canada adopted a type showing the Queen wearing the Imperial Crown. This medal was superseded in the UK by the VRSM (No. 242A) in 2000, although it is still current in some Commonwealth countries.*

VALUE:	Territorial	Militia	T&AVR	Commonwealth
George V (C)	£75–100	£85–125**	—	From £85*
George VI (Aa)	£50–85	£75–100	—	From £85*
George VI (Ab)	£50–85	£75–100	—	From £85*
Elizabeth II (A)	£65–90	—	—	From £150*
Elizabeth II (B)	£65–90	—	£85–120	From £150*
Miniature	from £15			£65–85

*These prices are for the commoner Commonwealth types. However, some are extremely rare as can be seen in the table below where the issue numbers are indicated in brackets (where known).
**Only RE (176), R.Signals (94) and RAMC (42).

GEORGE V (C)	GEORGE VI (Aa)	GEORGE VI (Ab)	ELIZABETH II (A)	ELIZABETH II (B)
—	—	—	Antigua (3)	—
Australia	Australia	Australia	Australia	Australia
Barbados	Barbados	Barbados	Barbados	Barbados
Bermuda	Bermuda	Bermuda	Bermuda	Bermuda
British Guiana (15)	British Guiana	British Guiana	British Guiana	—
British Honduras (1)	British Honduras (23)	British Honduras (3)	British Honduras (13)	—
—	Burma (111)	—	—	—
Canada	Canada	Canada	Canada (Rare)	Canada (Rare)
Ceylon	Ceylon	Ceylon	Ceylon (69)	—
—	Dominica (130)	—	—	—
Falkland Islands (29)	Falkland Islands (29)	—	Falkland Islands	Falkland Islands
Fiji (29)	Fiji (35)	Fiji (9)	Fiji (7)	Fiji (33)
—	—	Gibraltar (15)	Gibraltar	Gibraltar
—	Gold Coast (275)	Gold Coast (35)	—	—
—	Grenada (1)	—	—	—
—	Guernsey (3)	Guernsey (4)	Guernsey (3)	Guernsey (35)
Hong Kong (21)	Hong Kong (50)	Hong Kong (224)	Hong Kong (145)	Hong Kong (268)
India	India	—	—	—
Jamaica	Jamaica	Jamaica	Jamaica	—
—	Jersey (40)	Jersey (7)	—	Jersey (1)

237. EFFICIENCY MEDAL *continued*

GEORGE V (C)	GEORGE VI (Aa)	GEORGE VI (Ab)	ELIZABETH II (A)	ELIZABETH II (B)
—	Kenya (1)	Kenya (159)	Kenya (36)	—
—	Leeward Islands (49)	Leeward Islands (14)	Leeward Islands (2)	—
—	Malaya	Malaya	Malaya (54)	—
—	Malta (320)	Malta (31)	—	Malta (36)
—	—	—	Mauritius (71)	—
—	—	—	—	Montserrat (6)
New Zealand (71)	New Zealand (34)	New Zealand	New Zealand	New Zealand
Nigeria (1)	—	Nigeria (7)	Nigeria (3)	—
—	—	—	Rhodesia/Nyasaland (7)	—
—	—	—	St Christopher Nevis (13)	—
—	St Lucia (2)	—	—	—
—	St Vincent (1)	—	—	—
S. Rhodesia (17)	S. Rhodesia (230)	S. Rhodesia (24)	S. Rhodesia (6)	—
—	Trinidad/Tobago (228)	Trinidad/Tobago (46)	Trinidad/Tobago (5)	—

238. ARMY EMERGENCY RESERVE DECORATION

Instituted: 17 November 1952.
Branch of Service Army Emergency Reserve.
Ribbon: 38mm dark blue with a central yellow stripe.
Metal: Silver and silver-gilt.
Size: Height 55mm; max. width 37mm.
Description: An oval skeletal badge, with the monarch's cypher surmounted by a crown in an oak wreath. Suspension is by a ring through the top of the crown and it is worn with a brooch bar inscribed ARMY EMERGENCY RESERVE.
Comments: *Awarded for 12 years commissioned service. Officers commissioned in the Army Supplementary Reserve or Army Emergency Reserve of Offices between 8 August 1942 and 15 May 1948 who transferred to the Regular Army Reserve of Officers after 10 years service were also eligible. War service counts double and previous service in the ranks counts half. The ERD was abolished in 1967 on the formation of the Territorial and Army Volunteer Reserve.*

VALUE:

Elizabeth II	£150–200	*Miniature*	£10–15

239. ARMY EMERGENCY RESERVE EFFICIENCY MEDAL

Instituted: 1 September 1953.
Branch of Service: Army Emergency Reserve.
Ribbon: 32mm dark blue with three central yellow stripes.
Metal: Silver.
Size: Height 39mm; max. width 31mm.
Description: This oval medal is similar to the Efficiency Medal previously noted but has a scroll bar inscribed ARMY EMERGENCY RESERVE.
Comments: *Awarded for 12 years service in the ranks or for service in the Supplementary Reserve between 1924 and 1948 prior to transferring to the Army Emergency Reserve. War service counted double. It was abolished in 1967 following the formation of the Territorial and Army Volunteer Reserve.*

VALUE:

Elizabeth II	£150–180	*Miniature*	£10–12

240. IMPERIAL YEOMANRY LONG SERVICE AND GOOD CONDUCT MEDAL

Instituted: December 1904, by Army Order no. 211.
Branch of Service: Imperial Yeomanry.
Ribbon: 32mm plain yellow.
Metal: Silver.
Size: Height 38mm; max. width 31mm.
Description: Upright oval. (Obverse) the sovereign's effigy; (reverse) inscribed IMPERIAL YEOMANRY round the top and the usual long service and good conduct inscription in four lines across the middle.
Comments: *Awarded to NCOs and troopers of the Imperial Yeomanry for 10 years exemplary service. It became obsolete in 1908 when the Territorial Force was created. Nevertheless 48 medals were awarded in 1909, one in 1910, one in 1914 and one in 1917. All medals were issued with the bust of King Edward VII on the obverse.*

VALUE:

Edward VII (A) (1674)   £375–500   *Miniature*   £60–80

241. MILITIA LONG SERVICE AND GOOD CONDUCT MEDAL

Instituted: December 1904, by Army Order no. 211.
Branch of Service: Militia.
Ribbon: 32mm plain light blue.
Metal: Silver.
Size: Height 38mm; max. width 31mm.
Description: An upright oval medal. (Obverse) the effigy of the monarch; (reverse) similar to the preceding but inscribed MILITIA at the top of the reverse.
Comments: *Qualifying service was 18 years and 15 annual camps. It was superseded by the Efficiency Medal with the Militia bar in 1930. A total of 1,587 medals were awarded between 1905 and 1930 (RGA 341, RE 15, RE Submarine Miners 8, Infantry 988, Channel Islands 89, Malta 131, Bermuda 15).*

VALUE:

		Miniature
Edward VII (A) (1446)	£375–500	£90–120
George V (C) (141)	£600–800	£90–120

242. SPECIAL RESERVE LONG SERVICE AND GOOD CONDUCT MEDAL

Instituted: June 1908, by Army Order no. 126.
Branch of Service: Special Reserve.
Ribbon: Dark blue with a central light blue stripe.
Metal: Silver.
Size: Height 38mm; max. width 31mm.
Description: As the foregoing but inscribed SPECIAL RESERVE round the top of the reverse.
Comments: *Awarded to NCOs and men of the Special Reserve who completed 15 years service and attended 15 camps. A total of 1,078 medals were awarded between 1908 and 1936 with solitary awards in 1947 and 1953. Summary of awards: RA, RFA, RGA 165, RE 9, Royal Anglesey RE 3, Royal Monmouthshire R. 5, RAMC 4, Labour Corps 4, MGC 1. North Irish Horse 16, South Irish Horse 31, King Edward's Horse 14, Infantry 823, Channel Islands 5. Of these, two awards (1 to the RGA, 1 to the South Irish Horse), were subsequently cancelled.*

VALUE:

		Miniature
Edward VII (A) (428)	£400–500	£100–125
George V (C) (650)	£400–500	£100–125

242A. VOLUNTEER RESERVES SERVICE MEDAL

Instituted: 1999.

Branch of Service: Volunteer reserves of all three armed services.

Ribbon: Dark green with three narrow central stripes of dark blue, scarlet and light blue, separated from the green by two narrow stripes of gold. Members of the Honourable Artillery Company wear half blue, half scarlet ribbon, with yellow edges.

Metal: Silver.

Size: Height 38mm; width 32mm.

Description: An oval medal. (Obverse) the sovereign's effigy; (reverse) inscribed FOR SERVICE IN THE VOLUNTEER RESERVES above a spray of oak.

Comments: *Awarded to all ranks of the volunteer reserves who complete ten years of reckonable qualifying service. Bars for additional five-year periods of reckonable qualifying service are also awarded. This medal replaces the Royal Naval Reserve Decoration, the Royal Naval Reserve Long Service and Good Conduct Medal, the Efficiency Decoration, the Efficiency Medal and the Air Efficiency Award. It carries no rights to the use of post-nominal letters.*

VALUE: £250–300   *Miniature*   £10–12

HAC ribbon

242B. ROYAL MILITARY ASYLUM GOOD CONDUCT MEDAL

Instituted: c.1850.

Branch of Service: Students in the Royal Military Asylum.

Ribbon: Plain red or crimson.

Metal: Silver or bronze.

Size: 36mm.

Description: (Obverse) the royal arms, garnished, crested and with supporters; (reverse) ROYAL MILITARY ASYLUM round the circumference enclosing a laurel wreath inscribed across the centre FOR GOOD CONDUCT. Fitted with a scrolled suspender and brooch. Engraved in upright capitals with the name of the recipient.

Comments: *The Royal Military Asylum was established for the education of the sons of soldiers who had been killed in action or who had died while in the service. It was renamed the "Duke of York's Royal Military School" in 1892 and subsequent medals are thus inscribed.*

VALUE: "Asylum"   £125–175
              "School"   £100–150

242C. ARMED FORCES VETERAN LAPEL BADGE

Date: May 2004.

Branch of Service: Former members of HM Armed Forces, Cyprus Regiment, Merchant Navy who took part in a naval action, Home Guard and Polish Forces under UK command.

Ribbon: None.

Description: Badge surmounted by a gold imperial crown with VETERAN on an enamelled scroll at the foot. The badge bears the insignia of the armed services with H.M. ARMED FORCES round the top of the circumference.

Comments: *Originally available to veterans of HM Armed Forces who served up to December 31, 1954, but later extended. It is intended for any service in the Armed Forces.*

VALUE: £10–15

242D. MERCHANT SEAFARERS VETERAN LAPEL BADGE

Instituted: 2006.

Branch of Service: Personnel of the Royal Fleet Auxiliary Service and the Merchant Navy.

Ribbon: None.

Description: Similar to 242C but with the badge superimposed on the Red Ensign.

Comments: *Available to surviving veterans of the Royal Fleet Auxiliary Service and the Merchant Navy who who contributed to HM Armed Forces military operations in World War II.*

VALUE: £15–20

242E. ARCTIC EMBLEM

Instituted: 2006.

Branch of Service: Personnel of the Armed Forces and the Merchant Navy

Ribbon: None.

Description: A white five-pointed star edged in gold, with a red centre, above which is a blue arc bearing the words THE ARCTIC.

Comments: *Available to surviving veterans who served north of the Arctic Circle and west of the Urals for at least one day between 3 September 1939 and 8 May 1945. The emblem is also available to the next of kin of deceased veterans.*

VALUE: £20–25

242F. BEVIN BOYS LAPEL BADGE

Date: 2007.

Branch of Service: Former Bevin Boys.

Ribbon: None.

Description: Oval badge enamelled with the outline of a pit-head winch in white on a black background, surrounded by the words BEVIN BOYS VETERANS and with a silhouette of a miner's head with helmet.

Comments: *Available to surviving veterans of the Bevin Boys of World War II.*

VALUE: £10–15

242G. WOMEN'S LAND ARMY AND TIMBER CORPS LAPEL BADGE

Date: 2007.
Branch of Service: Former members of the Women's Land Army or Women's Timber Corps.
Ribbon: None.
Description: Enamelled replica of the original WLA badge surmounted by a crown.
Comments: *Available to surviving veterans of the Women's Land Army and Women's Timber Corps of World War II.*

VALUE: £10–15

242H. AIR TRANSPORT AUXILIARY LAPEL BADGE

Date: 2008.
Branch of Service: Former members of the Air Transport Auxiliary.
Ribbon: None.
Description: Enamelled badge depicting an eagle in flight on a turquoise background surrounded by the words AIR TRANSPORT AUXILIARY on a dark blue ribbon with laurel wreath surround.
Comments: *Available to veterans of the Air Transport Auxiliary of World War II.*

VALUE: £10–15

242 I. GC & OS LAPEL BADGE

Date: 2012.
Branch of Service: Former employees at Bletchley Park and its outstations.
Ribbon: None.
Description: Enamelled badge depicting the GCHQ emblem surrounded by a laurel wreath and the dates 1939-1945, with the legend GC&OS above, BLETCHLEY PARK AND ITS OUTSTATIONS below.
Comments: *Available to surviving personnel who worked at Bletchley Park during World War II.*

VALUE: £20–25

242 J. MERCHANT NAVY MEDAL

Instituted: 1 June 2005.
Branch of Service: Merchant Navy.
Ribbon: Equal halves of red and green divided by a narrow white stripe. Thin gold edge stripes were added in 2011 to avoid confusion with MYB 169 and to indicate special achievement
Metal: Rhodium plated cupro-nickel. **Size:** 28mm.
Description: (Obverse) The bust of Admiral Nelson surrounded by the legend "THE MERCHANT NAVY MEDAL" above and "1805 - TRAFALGAR - 2005" below; (reverse) the Merchant Navy logo with the inscription "FOR MERITORIOUS SERVICE" below.
Comments: *This medal was instituted to recognise the meritorious service of British registered Merchant Seafarers. The medal is awarded annually to a maximum of 15 men or women who are judged to have made a significant contribution to merchant shipping, its operations, development, personnel, welfare or safety, or who have performed an act of bravery afloat. The names of recipients are listed in the London Gazette and the award carries the post-nominals MNM. A small silver anchor is added to the ribbon to denote an act of bravery at sea.*

VALUE: —

243. INDIAN ARMY LONG SERVICE & GOOD CONDUCT MEDAL FOR EUROPEANS 1848

Instituted: 20 May 1848, by General Order of the Indian Government.
Branch of Service: Indian Army.
Ribbon: Plain crimson.
Metal: Silver.
Size: 36mm.
Description: (Obverse) a trophy of arms, not unlike its British counterpart, but a shield bearing the arms of the Honourable East India Company was placed in the centre. (Reverse) engraved with the recipient's name and service details. In 1859 some 100 medals were sent to India by mistake, these had the Wyon profile of Queen Victoria on the obverse and a reverse inscribed FOR LONG SERVICE AND GOOD CONDUCT within an oak wreath with a crown at the top and a fouled anchor at the foot.
Comments: *Awarded to European NCOs and other ranks of the Indian Army on discharge after 21 years meritorious service. It was discontinued in 1873 after which the standard Army LSGC medal was granted.*

VALUE:

		Miniature
HEIC arms	£500–650	£100–150
Victoria (A) (100)	£650–750	£80–100

Victoria type.

HEIC arms type.

244. INDIAN ARMY LONG SERVICE &GOOD CONDUCT MEDAL (INDIAN)

Instituted: 1888.
Branch of Service: Indian Army.
Ribbon: Originally plain crimson but white edges were added in 1917.
Metal: Silver.
Size: 36mm.
Description: (Obverse) the sovereign's effigy; (reverse) the word INDIA set within a palm wreath surrounded by a border of lotus flowers and leaves. The inscription FOR LONG SERVICE AND GOOD CONDUCT appears between the wreath and the lotus flowers.
Comments: *Awarded to native Indian NCOs and other ranks for 20 years meritorious service. The medal became obsolete in 1947 when India achieved independence.*

VALUE:

		Miniature
Victoria (B) Kaisar-i-Hind	£150–175	£90–100
Edward VII (A) Kaisar-i-Hind	£100–125	£90–100
George V (D) Kaisar-i-Hind	£55–85	£80–90
George V (C) Rex Et Indiae Imp	£55–85	£80–90
George VI (B)	£55–85	£80–90

245. INDIAN VOLUNTEER FORCES OFFICERS' DECORATION

Instituted: May 1899, but not issued until 1903.
Branch of Service: Indian Volunteer Forces.
Ribbon: Plain green (see Comments below).
Metal: Silver and silver-gilt.
Size: Height 65mm; max. width 35mm.
Description: An oval skeletal badge with the royal monogram within an oval band inscribed INDIAN VOLUNTEER FORCES surmounted by a crown fitted with a suspension bar and an elaborate silver brooch.
Comments: *Awarded for 18 years commissioned service, with any service in the ranks counting half. It was superseded by the Efficiency Decoration with* India *bar in 1930, although the first awards were not gazetted until 1933. A total of 1,172 decorations are known to have been awarded, the last in 1934. Although the decoration was issued unnamed, nearly all found so far are named. During the lifetime of the decoration seven different engravers for the naming have been identified. The suspension of the medal is by a flattened loop which is only 32mm wide although it was intended to take a 38mm ribbon—the 32mm ribbon is therefore usually worn on the medal and the 38mm on the tunic.*

VALUE:		Miniature
Edward VII	£275–350	£50–60
George V	£275–350	£30–40

246. COLONIAL AUXILIARY FORCES OFFICERS' DECORATION

Instituted: 18 May 1899.
Branch of Service: Colonial Auxiliary Forces.
Ribbon: Plain green (see Comments below).
Metal: Silver and silver-gilt.
Size: Height 66mm; max. width 35mm.
Description: Similar to the previous decoration, with an oval band inscribed COLONIAL AUXILIARY FORCES.
Comments: *Awarded to officers of auxiliary forces everywhere except in India for 20 years commissioned service. Service in the ranks counting half and service in West Africa counting double. Although issued unnamed, it was usually impressed or engraved privately. Examples to officers in the smaller colonies command a considerable premium. It became obsolete in 1930. The suspension of the medal is by a flattened loop which is only 32mm wide although it was intended to take a 38mm ribbon—the 32mm ribbon is therefore usually worn on the medal and the 38mm on the tunic.*

VALUE:		Miniature
Victoria	£250–300	£80–90
Edward VII	£200–250	£70–80
George V	£150–200	£50–60

247. COLONIAL AUXILIARY FORCES LONG SERVICE MEDAL

Instituted: 18 May 1899.
Branch of Service: Colonial Auxiliary Forces.
Ribbon: Plain green.
Metal: Silver.
Size: 36mm.
Description: (Obverse) the effigy of the reigning monarch; (reverse) an elaborate rococo frame surmounted by a crown and enclosing the five-line text FOR LONG SERVICE IN THE COLONIAL AUXILIARY FORCES.
Comments: *Awarded for 20 years service in the ranks, West African service counting double. It was superseded in 1930 by the Efficiency Medal with the appropriate colonial or dominion bar.*

VALUE:

		Miniature
Victoria (D)	£100–125	£25–35
Edward VII (A)	£80–110	£20–25
George V (A)	£80–110	£15–20

248. COLONIAL LONG SERVICE AND GOOD CONDUCT MEDALS

Instituted: May 31, 1895.
Branch of Service: Indian and Colonial forces.
Ribbon: Crimson with a central stripe denoting the country of service (see no. 212).
Metal: Silver.
Size: 36mm.
Description: Similar to its British counterpart except that the name of the appropriate colony appeared on the reverse. The obverse of the Victorian award for the Colony of Natal depicts the Royal coat of arms.
Comments: *Awarded to warrant officers, NCOs and other ranks for meritorious service and long service and good conduct. Medals of the individual Australian colonies were superseded in 1902 by those inscribed COMMONWEALTH OF AUSTRALIA. The Colonial LSGC medal was replaced in 1909 by the Permanent Forces of the Empire Beyond the Seas LSGC award.*

VALUE: Rare   *Miniature*   £75–100

249. PERMANENT FORCES OF THE EMPIRE BEYOND THE SEAS LONG SERVICE AND GOOD CONDUCT MEDAL

Instituted: 1909.
Branch of Service: Colonial and Dominion forces.
Ribbon: Maroon bearing a broad white central stripe with a narrow black stripe at its centre.
Metal: Silver.
Size: 36mm.
Description: (Obverse) the effigy of the reigning sovereign; (reverse) the legend PERMANENT FORCES OF THE EMPIRE BEYOND THE SEAS round the circumference, with FOR LONG SERVICE AND GOOD CONDUCT in four lines across the centre.
Comments: *This award replaced the various colonial LSGC medals, being itself superseded in 1930 by the LSGC (Military) Medal with appropriate dominion or colonial bar. It was awarded for 18 years exemplary service.*

VALUE:

		Miniature
Edward VII (A)	£300–400	£60–80
George V (A)	£100–150	£50–60

250. ROYAL WEST AFRICA FRONTIER FORCE LONG SERVICE & GOOD CONDUCT MEDAL

Instituted: September 1903.
Branch of Service: Royal West Africa Frontier Force.
Ribbon: Crimson with a relatively broad green central stripe.
Metal: Silver.
Size: 36mm.
Description: (Obverse) the effigy of the reigning monarch. Two reverse types were used, the word ROYAL being added to the regimental title in June 1928.
Comments: *Awarded to native NCOs and other ranks for 18 years exemplary service.*

VALUE: £300–350   *Miniature*   £25–30

251. KING'S AFRICAN RIFLES LONG SERVICE AND GOOD CONDUCT MEDAL

Instituted: March 1907.
Branch of Service: King's African Rifles.
Ribbon: Crimson with a broad green central stripe.
Metal: Silver.
Size: 36mm.
Description: Very similar to the foregoing, apart from the regimental name round the top of the reverse.
Comments: *Awarded to native NCOs and other ranks for 18 years exemplary service.*

VALUE:		*Miniature*
Edward VII	£500–700	—
George V	£250–300	£50–60
George VI (B)	£250–300	£40–50
Elizabeth II	£300–350	£25–35

252. TRANS-JORDAN FRONTIER FORCE LONG SERVICE AND GOOD CONDUCT MEDAL

Instituted: 20 May 1938.
Branch of Service: Trans-Jordan Frontier Force.
Ribbon: Crimson with a green central stripe.
Metal: Silver.
Size: 36mm.
Description: Similar to the previous medals, with the name of the Force round the circumference.
Comments: *This rare silver medal was awarded for 16 years service in the ranks of the Trans-Jordan Frontier Force. Service in the Palestine Gendarmerie or Arab Legion counted, so long as the recipient transferred to the Frontier Force without a break in service. Only 112 medals were awarded before it was abolished in 1948.*

VALUE: £600–800

253. SOUTH AFRICA PERMANENT FORCE LONG SERVICE AND GOOD CONDUCT MEDAL

Instituted: 29 December 1939.
Branch of Service: South African forces.
Ribbon: Crimson with white stripes.
Metal: Silver.
Size: 36mm.
Description: (Obverse) Crowned effigy of King George VI; (reverse) FOR LONG SERVICE AND GOOD CONDUCT in four lines across the upper half and VIR LANGDURIGE DIENS EN GOEIE GEDRAG in four lines across the lower half. It also differs from its British counterpart in having a bilingual suspension bar.
Comments: *Awarded to NCOs and other ranks with a minimum of 18 years service.*

VALUE:		Miniature
George VI (B)	£120–140	£30–40
George VI (C)	£150–170	£30–40

254. EFFICIENCY MEDAL (SOUTH AFRICA)

Instituted: December 1939.
Branch of Service: Coast Garrison and Active Citizen Forces of South Africa.
Ribbon: 32mm plain dark green with yellow edges.
Metal: Silver.
Size: Height 38mm; max. width 30mm.
Description: An oval silver medal rather similar to the Efficiency Medal (number 237) but having a scroll bar inscribed UNION OF SOUTH AFRICA with its Afrikaans equivalent below. The reverse likewise bears a bilingual inscription.
Comments: *Awarded for 12 years non-commissioned service in the Coast Garrison and Active Citizen Forces. A bar, bearing in the centre a crown, was awarded for every six years of additional service. It was replaced in 1952 by the John Chard Medal.*

VALUE:	£65–75	Miniature	£30–40

254A. ROYAL HONG KONG REGIMENT DISBANDMENT MEDAL

Instituted: 1995.
Branch of Service: Royal Hong Kong Regiment (Volunteers).
Ribbon: Half red and half blue with a central yellow stripe.
Metal: Cupro-nickel.
Size: 38mm.
Description: (Obverse) Regimental badge with dates 1854 and 1995 either side and ROYAL HONG KONG REGIMENT THE VOLUNTEERS around. (Reverse) Coat of Arms of Hong Kong with DISBANDMENT MEDAL 3rd SEPTEMBER 1995 (date of disbandment) around.
Comment: *Available to those serving with the Regiment as the end of the Crown Colony became imminent. Recipients, however, had to purchase a full size and a miniature medal in a plush case.*

VALUE:	£75–100	Miniature	£50–60

255 (C32). CANADIAN FORCES DECORATION

Instituted: 15 December 1949.
Branch of Service: Canadian Forces.
Ribbon: 38mm orange-red divided into four equal parts by three thin white stripes.
Metal: Silver-gilt (George VI) or gilded tombac brass or bronze (Elizabeth II).
Size: Height 35mm; max. width 37mm.
Description: A decagonal (ten-sided) medal. The George VI issue has a suspension bar inscribed CANADA and the recipient's details engraved on the reverse, whereas the Elizabethan issue has no suspension bar, the recipient's details being impressed or engraved on the rim and the word "CANADA" appears at the base of the effigy. The reverse has a naval crown at the top, three maple leaves across the middle and an eagle in flight across the foot. The George VI version has the royal cypher superimposed on the maple leaves.
Comments: *Awarded to both officers and men of the Canadian regular and reserve forces for 12 years exemplary service. A bar, gold in colour, bearing the shield from the arms of Canada surmounted by the crown is awarded for each additional 10 years of qualifying service. Approximately 2,400 medals and 3,000 clasps are awarded annually.*

VALUE:		Miniature
George VI (E)	£75–100	£10–20
Elizabeth II (D)	£30–45	£10–20

256. VICTORIA VOLUNTEER LONG AND EFFICIENT SERVICE MEDAL

1st type obv.

Instituted: 26 January 1881 but not given royal sanction until 21 April 1882.
Branch of Service: Volunteer Forces, Victoria.
Ribbon: White, with broad crimson stripes at the sides.
Metal: Silver.
Size: 39mm.
Description: (Obverse) the crowned badge of Victoria with LOCAL FORCES VICTORIA round the circumference; (reverse) inscribed FOR LONG AND EFFICIENT SERVICE. Two types of obverse exist, differing in the motto surrounding the colonial emblem. The first version has AUT PACE AUT BELLO (both in peace and war) while the second version is inscribed PRO DEO ET PATRIA (for God and country).
Comments: *Awarded to officers and men of the Volunteers in the colony of Victoria for 15 years efficient service. Awards to officers ended in 1894 with the introduction of the Volunteer Officers Decoration. This medal was replaced by the Commonwealth of Australia LSGC medal in 1902.*

VALUE: Rare *Miniature* **£200–300**

257. NEW ZEALAND LONG AND EFFICIENT SERVICE MEDAL

Instituted: 1 January 1887.
Branch of Service: Volunteer and Permanent Militia Forces of New Zealand.
Ribbon: Originally plain crimson, but two white central stripes were added in 1917.
Metal: Silver.
Size: 36mm.
Description: (Obverse) an imperial crown on a cushion with crossed sword and sceptre and NZ below, within a wreath of oak-leaves (left) and wattle (right) and having four five-pointed stars, representing the constellation Southern Cross, spaced in the field; (reverse) inscribed FOR LONG AND EFFICIENT SERVICE. Plain ring suspension.
Comments: *Awarded for 16 years continuous or 20 years non-continuous service in the Volunteer and Permanent Militia Forces of New Zealand. It became obsolete in 1931 following the introduction of the LSGC (Military) medal with bar for New Zealand.*

VALUE: 1887-1931 £100–150 *Miniature* £40–50

258. NEW ZEALAND VOLUNTEER SERVICE MEDAL

Instituted: 1902.
Branch of Service: Volunteer Forces, New Zealand.
Ribbon: Plain drab khaki.
Metal: Silver.
Size: 36mm
Description: (Obverse) a right-facing profile of King Edward VII with NEW ZEALAND VOLUNTEER round the top and 12 YEARS SERVICE MEDAL round the foot; (reverse) a kiwi surrounded by a wreath. Plain ring suspension.
Comments: *This rare silver medal (obsolete by 1912) was awarded for 12 years service. Two reverse dies were used. In type I (1902–04) the kiwi's beak almost touches the ground, whereas in Type II (1905–12) there is a space between the tip of the beak and the ground. Only about 100 of Type I were produced, but 636 of Type II.*

VALUE: Type I £250–350 *Miniature* £100–120
Type II £180–220

259. NEW ZEALAND TERRITORIAL SERVICE MEDAL

Instituted: 1912.
Branch of Service: Territorial Force, New Zealand.
Ribbon: Originally as above, but replaced in 1917 by a ribbon of dark khaki edged with crimson.
Metal: Silver.
Size: 36mm.
Description: (Obverse) left-facing bust of King George V in field marshal's uniform; (reverse) similar to the above.
Comments: *It replaced the foregoing on the formation of the Territorial Force on March 17, 1911, from which date the old Volunteer Force ceased to exist but became obsolete itself in 1931 when the Efficiency Medal with New Zealand bar was adopted.*

VALUE:
George V £80–100 *Miniature* £30–50

261. ULSTER DEFENCE REGIMENT MEDAL

Instituted: 1982.
Branch of Service: Ulster Defence Regiment.
Ribbon: Dark green with a yellow central stripe edged in red.
Metal: Silver.
Size: 36mm.
Description: (Obverse) crowned head of Elizabeth II (B); (reverse) crowned harp and inscription ULSTER DEFENCE REGIMENT with a suspender of laurel leaves surmounted by a scroll bar bearing the regiment's initials.
Comments: *Awarded to part-time officers and men of the Ulster Defence Regiment with 12 years continuous service since 1 April 1970. A bar for each additional six-year period is awarded. Officers are permitted to add the letters UD after their names. This medal is superseded by the Northern Ireland Home Service Medal (MYB 261B).*

VALUE:
Elizabeth II (B)   £250–300   *Miniature*   £15–20

261A. ULSTER DEFENCE REGIMENT MEDALLION

Instituted: 1987.
Branch of Service: Relatives of personnel of the Ulster Defence Regiment killed whilst on duty.
Ribbon: Dark green with a yellow central stripe edged in red, as MYB261.
Metal: Silver.
Size: 36mm.
Description: Uniface medal showing a crowned Irish harp flanked by sprays of shamrocks. Ring suspension. Ribbons of awards to widows and other female relatives mounted as a bow with a brooch fitment.
Comments: *Designed by Colour Sergeant Win Clark and struck by Spink & Son, it was commissioned by the Regiment for presentation to the families of UDR personnel killed during the conflict in Northern Ireland as a token of appreciation.*

VALUE: —

261B. NORTHERN IRELAND HOME SERVICE MEDAL

Instituted: 1992.
Branch of Service: Part time members of the Ulster Defence Regiment and the Royal Irish Regiment.
Ribbon: Dark green with a light blue central stripe.
Metal: Silver.
Size: 36mm.
Description: (Obverse) crowned head of Elizabeth II (B); (reverse) a scroll bearing the inscription FOR HOME SERVICE IN NORTHERN IRELAND surmounted by a crown, superimposed on a design of flax with harps below.
Comments: *Awarded to part-time officers and men of the Ulster Defence Regiment or Royal Irish Regiment with 12 years continuous efficient service after 1 July 1980. A bar for each additional six-year period is awarded. Next of kin of eligible deceased members can apply for the medal.*

VALUE: £200–250   *Miniature*   £15–12

262. CADET FORCES MEDAL

Instituted: February 1, 1950.

Branch of Service: Cadet Forces.

Ribbon: A broad green central band bordered by thin red stripes flanked by a dark blue stripe (left) and light blue stripe (right, with yellow edges.

Metal: Cupro-nickel.

Size: 36mm.

Description: (Obverse) the effigy of the reigning monarch; (reverse) a hand holding aloft the torch of learning. Medals are named to recipients on the rim, in impressed capitals.

Comments: *Awarded to uniformed volunteers of the Cadet Forces in recognition of long and exemplary service in the Cadet Forces. Service may reckon from September 3, 1926, with service between September 3, 1939 and September 2, 1945 counting two-fold. Until June 30, 1971, officers and non-commissioned officers only were awarded the medal, the qualification for which was 12 years continuous service, with clasps for successive periods of 12 years service. From July 1, 1971, cadet service over the age of 18 years of age could reckon for the medal and the qualifying period for the clasp was reduced to eight years, which need not be continuous. With effect from April 1, 1999, the qualifying period for the clasp was reduced to six years. Awards are now governed by the Royal Warrant dated November 19, 2001 which consolidates amendments to earlier Royal Warrants and extends the qualification and recognition provisions. Service for either medal or clasp does not need to be continuous.*

The maximum cadet service is four years; other reckonable services includes the UK Volunteer Services, OTC, University Royal Naval Units and University Air Squadrons (maximum three years and not counted towards the Volunteer Services Medal or its predecessors), and Regular forces (maximum three years and not counted towards a long service award). When the ribbon alone is worn, the award of each clasp is denoted by a silver rose. To denote service beyond the award of three clasps, the following are to be worn: Four clasps—one gold rose, Five clasps—one gold rose and one silver rose, Six clasps—one gold rose and two silver roses, Seven clasps—two gold roses. Award of the medal and clasp is promulgated in the London Gazette. Issued to those qualifying in New Zealand under the terms of a Royal Warrant dated February 1, 1950 and the New Zealand Cadet Forces Medal Regulations dated January 13, 1954.

VALUE:		*Miniature*
George VI (C)	£85–120	£8–12
Elizabeth II (A1, BRITT: OMN)	£85–120	£8–12
Elizabeth II (A, DEI GRATIA)	£75–100	£8–12

263. ROYAL OBSERVER CORPS MEDAL

Instituted: 31 January 1950 but not awarded until 1953.

Branch of Service: Royal Observer Corps.

Ribbon: Pale blue with a broad central silver-grey stripe edged in dark blue.

Metal: Cupro-nickel.

Size: 36mm.

Description: (Obverse) effigy of the reigning monarch; (reverse) an artist's impression of a coast-watcher of Elizabethan times, holding a torch aloft alongside a signal fire, with other signal fires on hilltops in the background. The medal hangs from a suspender of an eagle with outstretched wings. An obverse die with the effigy of George VI was engraved, but no medals were struck from it.

Comments: *Awarded to part-time officers and observers who have completed 12 years satisfactory service and full-time members for 24 years service. A bar is awarded for each additional 12-year period. Home Office scientific officers and other non Royal Observer Corps members of the United Kingdom Warning and Monitoring Organisation were eligible for the Civil Defence Medal (no. 264) until being stood down on September 30, 1991. This entailed serving for 15 years alongside ROC members who received their own medal for 12 years' service.*

VALUE:		*Miniature*
Elizabeth II (B)	£250–300	—
Elizabeth II (C)	£120–150	£8–12

264. CIVIL DEFENCE LONG SERVICE MEDAL

Instituted: March 1961.
Branch of Service: Civil Defence and other auxiliary forces.
Ribbon: Blue bearing three narrow stripes of yellow, red and green.
Metal: Cupro-nickel.
Size: Height 38mm; max. width 32mm.
Description: (Obverse) the effigy of the reigning monarch; (reverse) two types. Both featured three shields flanked by sprigs of acorns and oak leaves. The upper shield in both cases is inscribed CD but the initials on the lower shields differ, according to the organisations in Britain and Northern Ireland respectively—AFS and NHSR (British) or AFRS and HSR (Northern Ireland). After 1968 a new reverse was used incorporating the words CIVIL DEFENCE and LONG SERVICE.
Comments: *Issued unnamed to those who had completed 15 years service in a wide range of Civil Defence organisations. It was extended to Civil Defence personnel in Gibraltar, Hong Kong and Malta in 1965. The medal became obsolescent in the UK after the Civil Defence Corps and Auxiliary Fire Service were disbanded in 1968, but members of the CD Corps in the Isle of Man and Channel Islands are still eligible.*

VALUE:		*Miniature*
British version	£35–50	£30–40
Northern Ireland version	£85–120	£100–150
Gibraltar	£100–125	
Hong Kong	£100–125	
Malta	£100–125	
Post 1968 reverse	£75–100	

British reverse.

Northern Ireland reverse.

Post-1968 reverse

264A. AMBULANCE SERVICE (EMERGENCY DUTIES) LONG SERVICE AND GOOD CONDUCT MEDAL

Instituted: 5 July 1996.

Branch of Service: Ambulance services in England and Wales, Scotland, Northern Ireland, the Isle of Man and the Channel Islands.

Ribbon: Green with, on either side, a white stripe on which is superimposed a narrow green stripe.

Metal: Cupro-nickel.

Size: 36mm.

Description: (Obverse) crowned effigy of the reigning monarch, ELIZABETH II DEI GRATIA REGINA F.D.; (reverse) FOR EXEMPLARY SERVICE round the top, with either the emblem of the Ambulance Services of Scotland or the remainder of the United Kingdom in the centre below. Fitted with a ring for suspension.

Comments: *Both full- and part-time members of Ambulance Services are eligible provided they are employed on emergency duties. Service prior to 1974 in ambulance services maintained by local authorities counts. For paramedics and technicians the qualifying service is 20 years. For ambulance officers and other management grades, at least seven of their 20 years' service must have been spent on emergency duties.*

VALUE: £150–160   *Miniature* £35–40

264B. ASSOCIATION OF CHIEF AMBULANCE OFFICERS SERVICE MEDAL

Instituted: —.

Branch of Service: Members of the Ambulance Service.

Ribbon: Dark green with twin central red stripe edged with yellow.

Metal: Bronze.

Size: 36mm.

Description: (Obverse) symbol of the Association (caduceus on a wheel) surrounded by ASSOCIATION OF CHIEF AMBULANCE OFFICERS; (reverse) FOR SERVICE surrounded by a laurel wreath.

Comments: *Issued by members of the Association to ambulance personnel who have performed exemplary service.*

VALUE: £50–75   *Miniature* £50–60

264BB. QUEEN'S AMBULANCE SERVICE MEDAL FOR DISTINGUISHED SERVICE

Instituted: July 2012.

Branch of Service: Members of the NHS Ambulance Service.

Ribbon: Pale green with central silver stripe and silver edges.

Metal: Silver.

Size: 36mm.

Description: (Obverse) the monarch's effigy; (reverse) the inscription FOR DISTINGUISHED AMBULANCE SERVICE around the ambulance service emblem.

Comments: *Issued to recognise exceptional duty and outstanding service of NHS ambulance personnel. The medals are named around the edge and recipients cabn use the post-nominals QAM.*

VALUE: —   *Miniature* —

264C. ROYAL FLEET AUXILIARY SERVICE MEDAL

Instituted: July 24, 2001 by Royal Warrant.
Branch of Service: Royal Fleet Auxiliary Service.
Ribbon: Central band of watered royal blue flanked by narrow stripes of cypress green, yellow-gold and purple.
Metal: Cupro-nickel.
Size: 38mm.
Description: (Obverse) the crowned effigy of the Queen; (reverse) the badge of the Royal Fleet Auxiliary Service with the inscription ROYAL FLEET AUXILIARY — FOR LONG SERVICE.
Comments: *The medal is awarded to all officers, petty officers and ratings of the RFA after 20 years' service. Clasps will be granted for a further 10 years service. The recipient's name and rank, together with date of qualification, are impressed on the rim. The first awards of this medal were made to three petty officers in 2003, a further 400 personnel being eligible.*

VALUE: £200–250   *Miniature*   £40–50

265. WOMEN'S ROYAL VOLUNTARY SERVICE LONG SERVICE MEDAL

Instituted: 1961.
Branch of Service: Women's Royal Voluntary Service.
Ribbon: Dark green with twin white stripes towards the end and broad red edges.
Metal: Cupro-nickel.
Size: 36mm.
Description: (Obverse) the interlocking initials WVS in an ivy wreath; (reverse) three flowers, inscribed SERVICE BEYOND SELF round the circumference.
Comments: *Issued unnamed and awarded for 15 years service. Bars for additional 15 year periods are awarded. Although the majority of the 35,000 (approx.) medals have been awarded to women there has also been a substantial number of male recipients.*

VALUE: £15–20   *Miniature*   £30–40

266. VOLUNTARY MEDICAL SERVICE MEDAL

Instituted: 1932.
Branch of Service: British Red Cross Society and the St Andrew's Ambulance Corps (Scotland).
Ribbon: Red with yellow and white stripes.
Metal: Originally struck in silver but since the 1960s it has been produced in cupro-nickel.
Size: 36mm.
Description: (Obverse) the veiled bust of a female holding an oil lamp, symbolic of Florence Nightingale; (reverse) the crosses of Geneva and St Andrew, with the inscription FOR LONG AND EFFICIENT SERVICE.
Comments: *Awarded for 15 years service, with a bar for each additional period of five years. The service bars are embellished with a Geneva cross or saltire (St Andrew) cross, whichever is the more appropriate.*

VALUE:		*Miniature*
Silver	£25–25	
Cupro-nickel	£15–20	£20–30

267. SERVICE MEDAL OF THE ORDER OF ST JOHN

Ribbon embellishments:

5-year cross

Palm leaf for conspicuous service

Voluntary Aid Detachment

Military Hospital Reserve

Ribbon bars:

5-year bar (second type)

VAD (or MHR) now obsolete

Illustrations by M. Thomas, courtesy of Roy Gould

Instituted: 1898.

Branch of Service: The Most Venerable Order of the Hospital of St John of Jerusalem.

Ribbon: Three black and two white stripes of equal width.

Metal: Silver (1898-1947), silvered base metal (1947-60), silvered cupro-nickel (1960-66) and rhodium-plated cupro-nickel (since 1966).

Size: 38mm.

Description: (Obverse) an unusual veiled bust of Queen Victoria with her name and abbreviated Latin titles round the circumference. A new obverse was adopted in 1960 with a slightly reduced effigy of Queen Victoria and less ornate lettering. (Reverse) the royal arms within a garter surrounded by four circles containing the imperial crown, the Prince of Wales's feathers and the armorial bearings of the Order and of HRH the Prince of Wales, the first Sub-Prior of the Order. Between the circles are sprigs of St John's Wort. Round the circumference is the Latin inscription MAGNUS PRIORATUS ORDINIS HOSPITALIS SANCTI JOHANNIS JERUSALEM IN ANGLIA in Old English lettering.

Comments: *Originally awarded for 15 years service to the Order in the United Kingdom (12 in the Dominions and 10 in the Colonies) but the qualifying period has now been reduced to 12 years service, except that overseas service outside South Africa, New Zealand, Canada and Australia remains 10 years. The medal was designed in 1898 and first presented in 1900. A silver bar was introduced in 1911 for additional periods of five years. From then until 1924 the bar was inscribed 5 YEARS SERVICE but then a design showing a Maltese cross flanked by sprays of St John's Wort was substituted. Bars for 27 years service were subsequently instituted in silver-gilt. Suspension by a ring was changed in 1913 to a straight bar suspender. The medal is worn on the left breast. Although awarded for long service this medal should not be solely referred to as a long service award as it can also be awarded for conspicuous service—when so awarded it was distinguished by the addition of a silver palm leaf on the ribbon. The silver palm was discontinued in 1949, after only three years. It is believed to be the only medal still issued bearing the bust of Queen Victoria (the effigy was first sculpted by HRH Princess Louise, daughter of Queen Victoria).*

VALUE:

		Miniature
Silver, ring suspension	£25–30	£15–20
Silver, straight bar suspension	£20–25	£12–15
Base metal, first obverse	£15–20	£6–10
Base metal, second obverse	£15–20	£6–10

268. ROYAL AIR FORCE LONG SERVICE AND GOOD CONDUCT MEDAL

Instituted: 1 July 1919.

Branch of Service: Royal Air Force.

Ribbon: Dark blue and maroon with white edges.

Metal: Silver.

Size: 36mm.

Description: (Obverse) the effigy of the reigning monarch; (reverse) the RAF eagle and crown insignia.

Comments: *Awarded to NCOs and other ranks of the RAF for 18 years exemplary service, reduced in 1977 to 15 years. Provision for bars for further periods of service was made from 1944 onwards. Before 1945 conduct below the required standard was permitted to count if the airman had displayed higher exemplary conduct against the enemy, gallantry or some special service in times of emergency. From 1944 any prior service in the Navy and Army could be counted. Prior to this date only up to four years service could be counted. In 1947 officers became eligible for the medal provided they had had at least 12 years service in the ranks. Recipients' details are inscribed on the rim. The later issues are of silver-plated base metal.*

VALUE:

		Miniature			Miniature	
George V (E)	£120–150	£20–30	Elizabeth II (B)	£50–60	£20–30
George VI (D)	£75–85	£20–30	Elizabeth II (C)	£50–60	£20–30
George VI (E)	£75–85	£20–30	RCAF recipient	£300–400	

269. ROYAL AIR FORCE LEVIES LONG SERVICE AND GOOD CONDUCT MEDAL

Instituted: 1948.
Branch of Service: RAF Levies, Iraq.
Ribbon: As the preceding.
Metal: Silver.
Size: 36mm.
Description: Similar to the previous type but was fitted with a clasp inscribed ROYAL AIR FORCE LEVIES IRAQ.
Comments: *Awarded to the locally commissioned officers and men of the RAF Levies in Iraq, for 18 years service (the last 12 to be of an exemplary nature). The Iraq Levies were raised in 1919 and became the responsibility of the RAF in 1922, maintaining law and order by means of light aircraft and armoured cars. The force was disbanded in 1955 when the RAF withdrew from Iraq. 309 medals were issued, 115 to officers and 194 to airmen.*

VALUE:

George VI (E)	£800–1000
Elizabeth II (C)	£900–1100
Elizabeth II (D)	£900–1100

270. AIR EFFICIENCY AWARD

Instituted: September 1942
Branch of Service: AAF, RAAF and RAFVR.
Ribbon: Green with two light blue stripes towards the centre.
Metal: Silver.
Size: Height 38mm; max. width 32mm.
Description: An oval medal with a suspender in the form of an eagle with wings outspread. (Obverse) the effigy of the reigning monarch; (reverse) inscribed AIR EFFICIENCY AWARD in three lines.
Comments: *Granted for 10 years efficient service in the Auxiliary and Volunteer Air Forces of the United Kingdom and Commonwealth. A bar was awarded for a further ten-year period. Officers are permitted to add the letters AE after their name. This award was replaced in 2000 by the VRSM (No. 242A).*

VALUE:

George VI (D)	£100–125
George VI (E)	£150–175
Elizabeth II (C)	£100–125
Miniature (all)	£20–30
Named to officers add £40	

271. POLICE LONG SERVICE AND GOOD CONDUCT MEDAL

Instituted: 14 June 1951.
Branch of Service: Police Forces.
Ribbon: Dark blue with twin white stripes towards each end.
Metal: Original issue cupro-nickel, now rhodium plated
Size: 36mm.
Description: The obverse of this medal bears the effigy of the reigning monarch while the reverse has the figure of Justice with scales in her left hand and a wreath in her right surrounded by the inscription 'FOR EXEMPLARY POLICE SERVICE'. The suspender is straight and found in both swivelling and non-swivelling formats
Comments: *Originally awarded to full-time regular police officers within any UK Constabulary for 22 years service. However, following a national campaign by Warwickshire Police Officer Kenneth Fowler, supported by Chief Officers, the Police Federations and Members of Parliament, the award point of the medal was reduced to 20 years service on 19 January 2010, bringing it in line with the Fire, Ambulance and Prison Long Service and Good Conduct Medals which are all awarded after 20 years service. In 1956 this medal was extended to police officers serving in Australia, Papua New Guinea and Nauru. Australia however replaced this medal in 1976 with the National Medal.*

VALUE:

		Miniature
George VI (C)	£40–50	£20–30
Elizabeth II (A)	£40–50	£20–30
Elizabeth II (D)	£40–50	£20–30

272. SPECIAL CONSTABULARY LONG SERVICE MEDAL

Special Constabulary medal.

Ulster Special Constabulary medal.

Instituted: 30 August 1919.
Branch of Service: Special Constabulary.
Ribbon: A broad red stripe in the centre flanked by black and white stripes.
Metal: Bronze.
Size: 36mm.
Description: (Obverse) the effigy of the reigning monarch; (reverse) a partial laurel wreath with a six-line text inscribed FOR FAITHFUL SERVICE IN THE SPECIAL CONSTABULARY. A second reverse was introduced in 1956 for 15 years service in the Ulster Special Constabulary, the text being modified to permit the inclusion of the word ULSTER. A third type was introduced in 1982 for 15 years service in the RUC Reserve and is thus inscribed but with the name change in 2001 a fourth type inscribed Police Service of Northern Ireland was issued.
Comments: *Awarded to all ranks in the Special Constabulary for 9 years unpaid service, with more than 50 duties per annum. War service with at least 50 duties counted triple. A clasp inscribed THE GREAT WAR 1914-18 was awarded to those who qualified for the medal during that conflict. Clasps inscribed LONG SERVICE, with the date, are awarded for additional ten-year periods. To qualify during the two world wars a special constable must have served without any pay for not less than three years, and during that period have performed at least 50 duties a year, and be recommended by a chief officer of police as willing and competent to discharge the duties of special constable as required, i.e. in both world wars service counts treble.*

VALUE:

		Miniature
George V (C)	£15–20	£8–10
With Great War 1914-18 clasp	£20–25	£10–15
George V (E)	£15–20	£8–10
George VI (D)	£15–20	£8–10
George VI (E)	£55–85	£10–15
Elizabeth II (A1)	Very rare	—
Elizabeth II (B)	£55–85	£10–15
Elizabeth II (C)	£45–55	£8–10
Elizabeth II (G/D)		
Northern Ireland types (3)	£175–200	£10–15

273. ROYAL ULSTER CONSTABULARY SERVICE MEDAL

Instituted: 1982.

Branch of Service: RUC and its Reserve.

Ribbon: Green, with narrow central stripes of red, black and dark blue. Following the award of the George Cross to the RUC the ribbon of this medal was modified to reflect the award. The colour of the GC ribbon is now indicated by two vertical blue stripes at the outer edges.

Metal: Cupro-nickel.

Size: 36mm.

Description: (Obverse) the effigy of Queen Elizabeth II; (reverse) the crowned harp insignia of the RUC with the words FOR SERVICE round the foot.

Comments: *Awarded for 18 months continuous service since 1 January 1971, but the award was made immediate on the recipient also being awarded a gallantry decoration or a Queen's commendation.*

VALUE:

Elizabeth II (D)	£200–250	*Miniature*	£15–20

Original ribbon.

Post-2001 ribbon.

274. COLONIAL POLICE LONG SERVICE MEDAL

Instituted: 1934.

Branch of Service: Colonial police forces.

Ribbon: Green centre bordered with white and broad blue stripes towards the edges.

Metal: Silver.

Size: 36mm.

Description: (Obverse) the effigy of the reigning monarch; (reverse) a police truncheon superimposed on a laurel wreath.

Comments: *Originally awarded to junior officers who had completed 18 years exemplary service but latterly awarded to officers of all ranks who have the required service qualification. A bar is awarded on completing 25 years service and a second bar after 30 years. These are represented on the ribbon bar in working dress by silver rosettes. The number (where applicable), rank and name as well as (for George VI and later issues) the relevant force in which the recipient is serving at the time of the award is engraved on the rim, often locally and therefore in a variety of styles.*

VALUE:

		Miniature
George V (C)	£100–120	£20–30
George VI (B)	£75–85	£20–30
George VI (C)	£75–85	£20–30
Elizabeth II (A)	£75–85	£20–30
Elizabeth II (B)	£75–85	£20–30

275. COLONIAL SPECIAL CONSTABULARY LONG SERVICE MEDAL

Instituted: 1957.
Branch of Service: Colonial Special Constabulary.
Ribbon: Two thin white stripes on a broad green centre, with broad blue edges.
Metal: Silver.
Size: 36mm.
Description: (Obverse) the effigy of the reigning monarch; (reverse) the crowned royal cypher above the words FOR FAITHFUL SERVICE in a laurel wreath.
Comments: *Awarded for nine years unpaid or 15 years paid service in a colonial special constabulary. A bar is awarded for further ten-year periods.*

VALUE:

Elizabeth II (A)	£250–300	*Miniature*	£20–30

276. CEYLON POLICE LONG SERVICE AND GOOD CONDUCT MEDAL (I)

Instituted: 1925.
Branch of Service: Ceylon Police.
Ribbon: Very similar to that of the Special Constabulary Long Service Medal—a broad red stripe in the centre flanked by black and white stripes.
Metal: Silver.
Size: 36mm.
Description: (Obverse) coinage profile of King George V by Sir Bertram Mackennal; (reverse) an elephant surmounted by a crown. Ring suspension.
Comments: *Awarded for 15 years active service. It was superseded in 1934 by the Colonial Police Long Service Medal.*

VALUE:

George V (E)	£350–400	*Miniature*	£80–90

277. CEYLON POLICE LONG SERVICE AND GOOD CONDUCT MEDAL (II)

Instituted: 1950.
Branch of Service: Ceylon Police.
Ribbon: Dark blue edged with khaki, white and pale blue.
Metal: Cupro-nickel.
Size: 36mm.
Description: (Obverse) the effigy of the reigning monarch; (reverse) similar to the foregoing, but without the crown above the elephant, to permit the longer inscription CEYLON POLICE SERVICE. Straight bar suspender.
Comments: *Awarded for 18 years exemplary service. Bars for 25 and 30 years service were also awarded. It became obsolete when Ceylon (now Sri Lanka) became a republic in 1972.*

VALUE:

		Miniature
George VI (C)	£450–500	£30–40
Elizabeth II (A)	£400–450	£30–40

278. CEYLON POLICE MEDAL FOR MERIT

Instituted: 1950.
Branch of Service: Ceylon Police.
Ribbon: Broad central khaki stripe, flanked by narrow stripes of white, light blue and dark blue.
Metal: Silver.
Size: 36mm.
Description: (Obverse) the effigy of the reigning monarch; (reverse) an Indian elephant with the legend CEYLON POLICE SERVICE at the top and FOR MERIT at the foot.
Comments: *The medal became obsolete when Ceylon (now Sri Lanka) became a republic in 1972.*

VALUE		*Miniature*
George VI	—	—
Elizabeth II	£400–500	£30–40

278A. CEYLON POLICE MEDAL FOR GALLANTRY

Instituted: 1950.
Branch of Service: Ceylon Police.
Ribbon: As for the Medal for Merit (above) but with the addition of a very narrow red stripe superimposed on the white stripes.
Metal: Silver.
Size: 36mm.
Description: Similar to the Medal of Merit (above) but reverse inscribed FOR GALLANTRY at the foot.
Comments: *It became obsolete when Ceylon (now Sri Lanka) became a republic in 1972.*

VALUE:		*Miniature*
George VI	—	£50–60
Elizabeth II	—	£50–60

279. CYPRUS MILITARY POLICE LONG SERVICE & GOOD CONDUCT MEDAL

Instituted: October 1929.
Branch of Service: Cyprus Military Police.
Ribbon: Yellow, dark green and yellow in equal bands.
Metal: Silver.
Size: 36mm.
Description: (Obverse) King George V; (reverse) the title of the police round the circumference and the words LONG AND GOOD SERVICE in four lines across the middle.
Comments: *Awarded to those who had three good conduct badges, plus six years exemplary service since the award of the third badge, no more than four entries in the defaulters' book and a minimum of 15 years service. Officers who had been promoted from the ranks were also eligible. No more than 7 officers and 54 other ranks were awarded this medal during its brief life before it was superseded in 1934 by the Colonial Police Long Service Medal.*

VALUE:	£800–1000

279A. ROYAL FALKLAND ISLANDS POLICE JUBILEE MEDAL

Date: 1996
Branch of Service: Royal Falkland Islands Police
Ribbon: Blue with a central white stripe edged in black and a thin red central stripe.
Metal: Silver.
Size: 36mm.
Description: (Obverse) Elizabeth II (A); (reverse) arms of the colony; ROYAL FALKLAND ISLANDS POLICE round top and double dated 1846-1996 round foot. Fitted with ring suspension and a brooch clasp at the top of the ribbon.
Comments: *Awarded to all officers serving in the Royal Falkland Islands Police on 15 October 1996. Only 27 medals were awarded.*

VALUE: £1000–1500

280. HONG KONG POLICE MEDAL FOR MERIT

Instituted: May 3, 1862.
Branch of Service: Hong Kong Police.
Ribbon: Various, according to class (see below).
Metal: Gold, silver or bronze.
Size: 36mm.
Description: (Obverse) the effigy of the reigning monarch; (reverse) inscribed HONG KONG POLICE FORCE FOR MERIT within a laurel wreath and beaded circle. Examples have been recorded with the effigy of Queen Victoria as on the Abyssinian and New Zealand Medals (MY123–124), and King George V types C and E.
Comment: *Exceptionally awarded in five different classes according to the length and type of service. The 1st Class medal was struck in gold and worn with a maroon (VC) ribbon, the 2nd Class in silver with a plain yellow ribbon, the 3rd Class in bronze with a central black stripe on the yellow ribbon, the 4th Class in bronze with two central black stripes in the yellow ribbon, and the 5th Class (confined to the Police Reserve) in bronze had a green ribbon with two black central stripes. The 4th Class was engraved on the reverse above the wreath. These medals were superseded in April 1937 by the Hong Kong Police Silver Medal, only four of which were awarded before it was replaced by the Colonial Police Medal for Meritorious Service 1938.*

VALUE:	1st class	2nd class	3rd class	4th class
Victoria	—	£600–700	£500–550	£500–550
Edward VII	Rare	Rare	Rare	Rare
George V (B)	Rare	£500–550	£450–550	£450–500
George V (C)	Rare	£500–550	£450–550	£450–500

Miniature (all, silver or bronze)   Rare

1st Class.   *2nd Class.*   *3rd Class.*   *4th Class.*

280A. HONG KONG DISTRICT WATCH FORCE MERIT MEDAL

Instituted: 1868.
Branch of Service: District Watch Force.
Ribbon: Very dark green with a central deep red stripe.
Metal: Silver or bronze.
Size: 31mm with a prominent rim.
Description: (Obverse) four Chinese characters "Great Britain Hong Kong" above a watchman's lamp, superimposed on a cutlass and police baton, with the Chinese characters for "District Watch Force" and "Medal" at the sides; (reverse) DISTRICT WATCHMEN'S FORCE FOR MERIT within a laurel wreath.
Comment: *While the Hong Kong Police was principally a mixed force of Europeans and Indians, operated in the business and higher class residential areas, and was paid for out of the colony's revenues, the District Watch Force was a purely Chinese organisation, raised by prominent citizens of the colony to patrol and police the Chinese parts of the city. Its members had statutory powers, were uniformed and were trained and functioned in the style of the old parish constables, rather than in the gendarmerie style of the Hong Kong Police which was colonial in nature and imposed on society rather than integrated with it. The District Watch Force ceased to function at the time of the Japanese invasion in 1941 and was not revived on liberation.*

VALUE: £650–700

280B. ROYAL HONG KONG POLICE COMMEMORATIVE MEDAL

Instituted: 1996.
Branch of Service: Royal Hong Kong Police.
Ribbon: Black, magenta and old gold.
Metal: Silver.
Size: 38mm.
Description: (Obverse) the RHKP crest; (reverse) crossed tipstaves inside a laurel wreath with the dates 1844 and 1997.
Comment: *The medal, approved by Commissioner Eddie Hui Ki On, is available on purchase (originally HK$1,000, about £80) to those who served in the Hong Kong Police (1844–1969) and the Royal Hong Kong Police (1969–97). Purchasers' details are often found privately engraved in bold upright capitals in a variety of formats. The medal, worn on the left breast, has the same status as the Royal Hong Kong Regiment Disbandment Medal (254A).*

VALUE: £150–200   *Miniature*   £50–75

280C. ROYAL HONG KONG AUXILIARY POLICE COMMEMORATIVE MEDAL

Instituted: 1996.
Branch of Service: Royal Hong Kong Auxiliary Police.
Ribbon: Black, magenta and old gold.
Metal: Silver.
Size: 38mm.
Description: Similar to the above, but inscribed ROYAL HONG KONG AUXILIARY POLICE FORCE.
Comment: *Similar to the above this medal is available for purchase. Some 5,000 auxiliary policemen and women being eligible for the award.*

VALUE: £150–200   *Miniature*   £50–75

280D. HONG KONG MILITARY SERVICE CORPS MEDAL

Instituted: 1997.
Branch of Service: Hong Kong Military Service Corps.
Ribbon: Red, with a central yellow stripe.
Metal: Cupro-nickel.
Size: 36mm.
Description: (Obverse) a Chinese dragon on a scroll bearing the initials of the Corps. HONG KONG MILITARY SERVICE CORPS inscribed round the top and 1962-1997 at the foot; (reverse) the British royal arms with inscription round the top TO COMMEMORATE DISBANDMENT and the date 31 March 1997 at the foot.
Comments: *The Military Service Corps was a paramilitary unit formed in 1962 for defence of the Crown Colony and recruited locally. Members of the Corps were allowed to purchase this medal following its disbandment prior to the return of Hong Kong to China.*

VALUE: £100–120

281. HONG KONG ROYAL NAVAL DOCKYARD POLICE LONG SERVICE MEDAL

Instituted: 1920.
Branch of Service: Hong Kong Royal Naval Dockyard Police.
Ribbon: Yellow with two royal blue stripes towards the centre.
Metal: Gilt bronze or silver.
Size: 31mm.
Description: (Obverse) the effigy of the reigning monarch; (reverse) the title of the Police within a laurel wreath. Ring suspension (two sizes).
Comments: *Awarded for 15 years service. Although the Dockyard closed in 1961 men who transferred to other police divisions continued to be awarded the medal up to 1973. About 280 medals in all were issued.*

VALUE:		Miniature
George V (E)	£400–500	£100–150
George VI (C)	£400–500	£100–150
George VI (D)	£400–500	£100–150
Elizabeth II (C)	£400–500	£100–150

281A. HONG KONG DISCIPLINED SERVICES MEDAL

Instituted: 1986.
Branch of Service: Hong Kong Customs & Excise and Immigration Service.
Ribbon: Green bordered by vertical stripes of dark blue with a strip of sky blue at each edge.
Metal: Silver.
Size: 36mm.
Description: (Obverse) crowned effigy of Queen Elizabeth II (B); (reverse) armorial bearings of Hong Kong, with the inscription "For Long Service and Good Conduct".
Clasps: Awarded after 25 and 30 years, denoted by silver rosettes on ribband in working dress.
Comments: *Awarded after 18 years continuous service. Engraved with name and rank on rim. Some 1,739 medals were awarded between 1987 and the return of Hong Kong to China on June 30, 1997. No other long service medal to Customs officers has been awarded in the British system.*

VALUE:	Customs	Immigration
Medal	£450–£50	£500–£550
1st clasp	£500–£550	£600–£650
2nd clasp	£600–£650	Unique

281B. TIENTSIN BRITISH EMERGENCY CORPS MEDAL

Instituted: —
Branch of Service: British Municipal Emergency Corps.
Ribbon: Buff with a broad central white stripe.
Metal: Silver.
Size: 36mm.
Description: (Obverse) the arms of the colony supported by a sailor and a Chinese worker surrounded by the words TIENTSIN BRITISH MUNICIPAL EMERGENCY CORPS; (reverse) a wreath surrounding a plain panel engraved FOR LONG SERVICE in three lines, with maker's name in small lettering below: STERLING/ARNOLD.
Comments: *The British Emergency Corps was presumably a paramilitary unit recruited locally. Little is known about these medals or the unit but obviously they were awarded for long service.*

VALUE: £150–200

282. MALTA POLICE LONG SERVICE AND GOOD CONDUCT MEDAL

Instituted: 1921.
Branch of Service: Malta Police.
Ribbon: Dark blue with a narrow central silver stripe.
Metal: Silver.
Size: 36mm.
Description: (Obverse) the effigy of King George V; (reverse) an eight-pointed Maltese cross in a laurel wreath with the title of the service and FOR LONG SERVICE AND GOOD CONDUCT round the circumference.
Comments: *Awarded to sergeants and constables with 18 years exemplary service. Officers who had had 18 years in the ranks were also eligible for the award. It was superseded by the Colonial Police Long Service Medal in 1934. No more than 99 medals were awarded.*

VALUE:		*Miniature*
George V (E)	£350–450	£100–120
George V (C)	£350–450	£100–120

282A. MAURITIUS POLICE LONG SERVICE AND GOOD CONDUCT MEDAL: I

Instituted: —.

Branch of Service: Mauritius Police.

Ribbon: Three types: (a) 36mm half black, half white; (b) 33mm white with a broad royal blue central stripe; (c) blue with two narrow white stripes towards the edges.

Metal: Bronze.

Size: Oval, 40x33mm or 39x31mm.

Description: (Obverse) crown surmounting crossed tipstaves with the motto PAX NOBISCUM (Peace be with us) and the legend POLICE DEPARTMENT round the top and MAURITIUS at the foot; (reverse) palm fronds enclosing a theee-line inscription FOR GOOD CONDUCT. Fitted with a ring for suspension. Medals with 33mm ribbon fitted at top with a pin brooch by Hunt & Roskill.

Comment: *It is believed that the different ribbons indicated different periods of service, but confirmation is sought. It is presumed that this medal was superseded by no. 282B.*

First type ribbon.

VALUE: £200–250 **Miniature** £75–100

282B. MAURITIUS POLICE LONG SERVICE AND GOOD CONDUCT MEDAL: II

Instituted: —.

Branch of Service: Mauritius Police

Ribbon: Green centre flanked by white stripes and broad blue stripes towards the edges.

Metal: Silver.

Size: 36mm.

Description: (Obverse) the effigy of Queen Elizabeth II; (reverse) police truncheon on a laurel wreath.

Comments: *This medal is identical to the Colonial Police Long Service Medal (no. 274) except that the inscription substituted the name MAURITIUS for COLONIAL. It has been recorded in a medal group of 1976 and may have been introduced in or about 1968 when Mauritius attained independence.*

VALUE: £100–150

283. NEW ZEALAND POLICE MEDAL

Instituted: 1886.

Branch of Service: New Zealand Police.

Ribbon: Originally plain crimson but in 1919 it was changed to a pattern very similar to that of the Permanent Forces of the Empire Beyond the Seas LSGC medal (no. 249),

Metal: Silver.

Size: 36mm.

Description: The obverse is identical to that of the NZ Long & Efficient Service Medal (MY257). Issued with a ring suspender until 1919 when a bar suspender was adopted. Clasps for each additional eight years service were introduced at the same time.

Comments: *Granted to sworn police staff for 14 years service. The clasp qualifying period was reduced to seven years in 1963. This medal was rendered obsolete with the introduction, in 1976, of the New Zealand Police Long Service and Good Conduct Medal (NZ26).*

First type obverse.

Second type ribbon.

VALUE: | | *Miniature*
Regalia obverse, bar suspension | £120–140 | £20–30

283A. SEYCHELLES POLICE LONG SERVICE AND GOOD CONDUCT MEDAL

Instituted: —.
Branch of Service: Seychelles Police.
Ribbon: Crimson.
Metal: Bronze.
Size: Oval, 40x33mm.
Description: (Obverse) crown surmounting crossed tipstaves with legend POLICE DEPARTMENT round the top and SEYCHELLES at the foot; (reverse) palm fronds enclosing a three-line inscription FOR GOOD CONDUCT. Fitted with a ring for suspension.
Comments: *This medal is similar to the Mauritius Police Medal (282A) and it is presumed that this medal also became obsolete on the introduction of the Colonial Police Long Service Medal in 1934. Details of qualifying terms of service and other regulations are sought.*

VALUE: £100–150

284. SOUTH AFRICA POLICE GOOD SERVICE MEDAL

Instituted: 1923.
Branch of Service: South Africa Police.
Ribbon: Broad black centre, flanked by white stripes and green borders.
Metal: Silver.
Size: 36mm.
Description: (Obverse) South African coat of arms; (reverse) bilingual inscriptions separated by a horizontal line. Three versions of the medal have been recorded. In the first version inscriptions were in English and Dutch, the latter reading POLITIE DIENST with VOOR TROUWE DIENST (for faithful service) on the reverse. In the second, introduced in 1932, Afrikaans replaced Dutch and read POLIESIE DIENS and VIR GETROUE DIENS respectively. In the third version, current from 1951 to 1963, the Afrikaans was modified to read POLISIEDIENS and VIR TROUE DIENS.
Comments: *Awarded to other ranks for 18 years exemplary service or for service of a gallant or particularly distinguished character. In the latter instance a bar inscribed MERIT-VERDIENSTE was awarded. The medal was replaced by the South African Medal for Faithful Service.*

VALUE:		
	1st type	£30–35
	2nd type	£25–30
	3rd type	£20–25
	Miniature	£10–15

285. SOUTH AFRICAN RAILWAYS AND HARBOUR POLICE LONG SERVICE AND GOOD CONDUCT MEDAL

Instituted: 1934.
Branch of Service: South African Railways and Harbour Police.
Ribbon: Similar to the Police Good Service Medal but with the colours reversed—a green central stripe flanked by white stripes and blue edges.
Metal: Silver.
Size: 36mm.
Description: (Obverse) the Union arms with S.A.R. & H. POLICE at the top and S.A.S.- EN HAWE POLISIE round the foot, but this was changed in 1953 to S.A.S. POLISIE at the top and S.A.R. POLICE at the foot. (Reverse) six line bilingual inscription.
Comments: *Awarded for 18 years unblemished service. Immediate awards for gallant or especially meritorious service earned a bar inscribed MERIT - VERDIENSTE (later with the words transposed). The medal was superseded in 1960 by the Railways Police Good Service Medal.*

VALUE: 1st type   £80–100   2nd type £75–100   *Miniature*   £30–40

286. FIRE BRIGADE LONG SERVICE MEDAL

Instituted: 1 June 1954.
Branch of Service: Fire Services.
Ribbon: Red with narrow yellow stripes towards the end and yellow borders.
Metal: Cupro-nickel.
Size: 36mm.
Description: (Obverse) the Queen's effigy; (reverse) two firemen manning a hose. Ring suspension.
Comments: *Awarded to all ranks of local authority fire brigades, whether full- or part-time for 20 years exemplary service. Prior to the institution of this award most local authorities issued their own medals of individual design.*

VALUE:
  Elizabeth II   £35–50   *Miniature*   £10–12

286A. ASSOCIATION OF PROFESSIONAL FIRE BRIGADE OFFICERS LONG SERVICE MEDAL

Instituted: —
Branch of Service: Association of Professional Fire Brigade Officers.
Ribbon: A red central stripe flanked by narrow white stripes and broad black edges (silver medal) or grey edges (bronze medal).
Metal: Silver or bronze.
Size: 38mm.
Description: (Obverse) allegorical female figure carrying a palm frond and bestowing a laurel crown on a kneeling fireman; an early fire appliance in the background; blank exergue; (reverse) an oak wreath enclosing a four-line inscription ASSOCIATION OF PROFESSIONAL FIRE BRIGADE OFFICERS FOR LONG SERVICE. Fitted with a swivelling bar suspension.
Comments: *The medal in silver was awarded to professional fire brigade officers for a minimum of 20 years full time service and in bronze for lesser periods. Engraved on the rim with the rank and name of the officer, together with the year of the award.*

VALUE: £40–50   *Miniature*   £40–60
Ribbon for silver medal.

286AA. NATIONAL FIRE BRIGADES ASSOCIATION LONG SERVICE MEDAL

Instituted: —
Branch of Service: Fire Services.
Ribbon: Red with a central dark blue stripe flanked by very thin yellow stripes.
Metal: Silver or bronze.
Size: 38mm.
Description: (Obverse) badge of the Association: a wreathed flag within a circle surmounted by a fireman's helmet and surrounded by ladders and hoses inscribed NATIONAL FIRE BRIGADES ASSOCIATION round the central motif; (reverse) LONG SERVICE in minuscule lettering inside an oak wreath with space in the centre for the recipient's name. Fitted with a plain ring for suspension from a broad bar suspender with a clasp bearing the years of service.
Comments: *The medal in silver was awarded to professional fire brigade officers for a minimum of 20 years full time service and in bronze for lesser periods. Engraved on the rim with the rank and number and often the name of the officer, together with the year of the award.*

VALUE: Bronze   £35–55   Silver   £45–65

286AB. NATIONAL FIRE BRIGADES UNION MEDAL

Instituted: —
Branch of Service: Fire Services.
Ribbon: Dark red.
Metal: Silver or bronze.
Size: 38mm.
Description: (Obverse) similar to 286AA but with NATIONAL FIRE
    BRIGADES UNION round the central motif; (reverse) LONG SERVICE
    in minuscule lettering inside an oak wreath with space in the centre for
    the recipient's name. Service number impressed on the rim. Fitted with
    a suspension bar and a brooch bar denoting length of service.
Comments: *The medal in silver was awarded to professional fire brigade officers
    for a minimum of 20 years full time service and in bronze for lesser periods.
    Engraved on the rim with the rank and number and often the name of the
    officer.*

VALUE: Bronze   £35–55   Silver   £45–65

286B. BRITISH FIRE SERVICES ASSOCIATION MEDAL

Instituted: 1949.
Branch of Service: British Fire Services Association.
Ribbon: 33mm with a central silver-grey stripe flanked by black and white
    stripes and a broad red edge. However, the *current* 10 year medal has a
    similar ribbon but with the white stripes to the edges to distinguish it
    from the 20 year ribbon.
Metal: Silver (20 years) or bronze (10 years).
Size: Originally 38mm, now 36mm.
Description: (Obverse) identical to the *obverse* of 286A, i.e allegorical
    female figure and fireman; (reverse) identical to the *obverse* of 286AA
    but with FOR LONG SERVICE & EFFICIENCY, round the central
    motif and THE BRITISH FIRE SERVICES ASSOCIATION round the
    circumference. The medal originally had an ornamental scrolled
    suspender with a bar inscribed BFSA, however it now has a simple
    straight suspender. The recipient's name and service number are
    engraved on the rim. A bar is added for each additional 5 years of
    service
Comments: *The British Fire Services Association was formed in 1949 by the
    amalgamation of the National Fire Brigades Association and the Professional
    Fire Brigades Association. This medal thus superseded 286A and 286AA.*

*Original ribbon and
current 20 year ribbon.*

Current 10 year ribbon.

VALUE:	**Silver**	**£35–50**	*Miniature* **£30–40**
	Bronze	**£20–30**	

286C. BRITISH FIRE SERVICE ASSOCIATION MERITORIOUS SERVICE MEDAL

Instituted: —
Branch of Service: Fire service personnel.
Ribbon: Khaki with a broad central stripe edged with thin black stripes.
Metal: Silver.
Size: 45mm x 36mm.
Description: A circular medallion contained within an upright oval laurel wreath suspended from an ornamental suspender with the initials B.F.S.A. on a scroll superimposed on a laurel spray. The central medallion depicts the Union Jack in a wreath with the inscription FOR MERITORIOUS SERVICE round the circumference. Reverse is plain apart from the maker's mark (foot) and the recipient's rank and name engraved on the medallion.
Comments: *Awarded for outstanding service and gallantry in fire-fighting operations.*

VALUE: —

287. COLONIAL FIRE BRIGADE LONG SERVICE MEDAL

Instituted: 1934.
Branch of Service: Colonial Fire Services.
Ribbon: Blue with twin green central stripes separated and bordered by thin white stripes.
Metal: Silver.
Size: 36mm.
Description: (Obverse) the effigy of the reigning monarch; (reverse) a fireman's helmet and axe. Ring suspension.
Comments: *Awarded to junior officers for 18 years full-time exemplary service. Bars are awarded for further periods of service.*

VALUE:		Miniature
George V (E)	£300–350	£30–40
George VI (D)	£300–350	£30–40
George VI (E)	£300–350	£30–40
Elizabeth II (C)	£300–350	£30–40
Elizabeth II (D)	£300–350	£30–40

288. CEYLON FIRE BRIGADE LONG SERVICE AND GOOD CONDUCT MEDAL

Instituted: 1950.
Branch of Service: Ceylon Fire Service.
Ribbon: Similar to the Police Medal (MYB277), but with a thin central white stripe through the dark blue band.
Metal: Silver.
Size: 36mm.
Description: As the Police Medal, but with a reverse inscribed CEYLON FIRE SERVICES.

VALUE:	
George VI	£300–400
Elizabeth II	£300–400

288A. NORTHERN IRELAND PRISON SERVICE MEDAL

Instituted: 25 February 2002.

Branch of Service: Northern Ireland Prison Service.

Ribbon: Green with a broad navy blue band having at its centre a sky-blue stripe. Prison grade recipients have a ribbon with an additional thin red stripe bisecting the sky-blue stripe.

Metal: Cupro-nickel.

Size: 36mm.

Description: (Obverse) the crowned profile of the Queen with her name and titles; (reverse) a ring of flax flowers with three keys at the top, enclosing a four line inscription NORTHERN IRELAND PRISON SERVICE. The medal is fitted with a plain bar for suspension. The name of the recipient is stamped on the rim.

Comments: *The medal recognises "those who have rendered professional, committed and brave service as members of and by others in support of the Northern Ireland Prison Service".*

VALUE: £150–180

288B. PRISON SERVICE MEDAL

Instituted: 29 April 2008

Branch of Service: Operational grades in HM Prison Services of England and Wales, Northern Ireland, Jersey, Guernsey, Isle of Man and Scotland.

Ribbon: Black with twin stripes towards each end.

Metal: Cupro-nickel.

Size: 36mm.

Description: (Obverse) The effigy of the reigning monarch by Ian Rank Broadley; (reverse) a period archway with the wording "For Exemplary Service", within the archway is Her Majesty's cypher surmounted by a crown.

Comments: *Awarded to operational ranks of the Prison Service of the UK, after completing 20 years service. Naming will include rank, initails, surname and epaulette number, for uniformed ranks.*

VALUE:

288C. BELFAST HARBOUR POLICE MEDAL

Instituted: 1946.

Branch of Service: Belfast Harbour Police Service.

Ribbon: Deep blue with yellow edges. .

Metal: Silver.

Size: 36mm.

Description: (Obverse) A mythical maritime scene—the seal of the Harbour Commissioners—with the words BELFAST HARBOUR COMMISSIONERS around; (reverse) the words WON BY across the centre above the recipient's details with BELFAST HARBOUR POLICE around the edge.

Comments: *The medal is primarily awarded for outstanding meritorious service or when awarded for gallantry a bronze anchor is worn on the ribbon. Since its inception only 16 medals have been awarded, three with the bronze anchor for gallantry, in addition four Harbour Chief Constables have received the medal for long service*

VALUE: £300–500

289. COLONIAL PRISON SERVICE LONG SERVICE MEDAL

Instituted: October 1955.
Branch of Service: Colonial Prison Services.
Ribbon: Green with dark blue edges and a thin silver stripe in the centre.
Metal: Silver.
Size: 36mm.
Description: (Obverse) Queen Elizabeth II; (reverse) a phoenix rising from the flames and striving towards the sun.
Comments: *Awarded to ranks of Assistant Superintendent and below for 18 years exemplary service. Bars are awarded for further periods of 25 or 30 years service.*

VALUE:

Elizabeth II	£250–300	*Miniature*	£30–40

290. SOUTH AFRICAN PRISON SERVICE FAITHFUL SERVICE MEDAL

Instituted: September 1922.
Branch of Service: South African Prison Service.
Ribbon: Broad green centre flanked by white stripes and dark blue edges.
Metal: Silver.
Size: 36mm.
Description: (Obverse) arms of the Union of South Africa, of identical design to no. 284 except with GEVANGENIS DIENST round the top and PRISONS SERVICE round the foot. (Reverse) inscribed FOR FAITHFUL SERVICE across the upper half and in Dutch VOOR TROUWE DIENST across the lower half.
Comments: *Awarded to prison officers with 18 years exemplary service. Immediate awards for gallantry or exceptionally meritorious service received the Merit bar. In 1959 this medal was superseded by a version inscribed in Afrikaans.*

VALUE: £40–50 *Miniature* £30–40

291. SOUTH AFRICA PRISONS DEPARTMENT FAITHFUL SERVICE MEDAL

Instituted: 1959.
Branch of Service: South African Prisons Department.
Ribbon: Broad dark blue centre flanked by white stripes and green edges.
Metal: Silver.
Size: 36mm.
Description: (Obverse) arms of the Union of South Africa, of identical design to no. 284 except with DEPARTEMENT VAN GEVANGENISSE round the top and PRISONS DEPARTMENT round the foot. (Reverse) VIR TROUE DIENS across the upper half and FOR FAITHFUL SERVICE across the lower half.
Comments: *The conditions of the award were similar to the previous medal, the main difference being the change of title and the substitution of Afrikaans inscriptions for Dutch. This medal was superseded by the Prisons Department Faithful Service Medal of the Republic of South Africa, instituted in 1965.*

VALUE: £35–50 *Miniature* £30–40

291AA. NATO MERITORIOUS SERVICE MEDAL

Date: 1994.
Branch of Service: Personnel serving with NATO forces.
Ribbon: NATO blue with white stripes at the edges each having a vertical gold and silver thread.
Metal: Silver.
Size: 36mm.
Description: Obverse and reverse as for the other NATO medals.
Clasps: Silver bar inscribed MERITORIOUS.
Comments: *Awarded for exceptional service to NATO. Not approved for wear by UK personnel either in full size or miniature. If presented it may be retained as a keepsake.*

VALUE: £45–55

CORONATION, JUBILEE AND OTHER ROYAL MEDALS

The first official royal medal was that cast by Henry Basse in 1547 for the accession of the young King Edward VI. It is known cast in gold or silver and is a curious example of bad design and poor workmanship for such an august occasion. No coronation medals were produced in honour of either Mary or Elizabeth I, but under James VI and I there was a small silver medal struck at the Royal Mint to mark the king's accession in 1603. These early medals celebrated the accession of the new sovereign, rather than the act of crowning itself.

To mark the coronation of James I, however, a small silver medalet was struck for distribution among the people who attended the ceremony, and this may be regarded as the forerunner of the modern series. This bore a Latin title signifying that James was Caesar Augustus of Britain and Heir to the Caesars. Thereafter medals in gold, silver or base metals were regularly struck in connection with the coronations of British monarchs. These were purely commemorative and not intended for wear, so they lack rings or bars for suspension.

By the early 19th century medals were being struck by many medallists for sale as souvenirs to the general public. At least fifteen different medals greeted the coronation of William IV in 1830 and more than twice that number appeared seven years later for the coronation of Queen Victoria. That paled into insignificance compared with the number produced for the coronation of Edward VII in 1902. On that occasion numerous civic authorities, organizations, industrial concerns and business firms issued medals in celebration—well over a hundred different medals and medalets were produced.

Sir George Frampton designed two silver medals, and one of these was mounted with a suspender and a blue ribbon with a thin white stripe and scarlet edges. This medal was distributed to notable personages attending the ceremony and established the precedent for subsequent coronation medals which came to be regarded as an award in recognition of services rendered in connection with the coronation,

from the Earl Marshal of England to the private soldiers taking part in the ceremonial parades. In more recent times the coronation medal has even been given to people who were not present at the ceremony but who performed notable public service in the coronation year.

Many other royal events have been commemorated by medals over the centuries. Royal weddings and the birth of the heir to the throne were regularly celebrated in this manner. Important anniversaries in long reigns have been the subject of numerous commemorative medals. The Golden Jubilee of George III in 1809-10, for example, resulted in over 30 different medals. Five times that number greeted the Golden Jubilee of Queen Victoria in 1887, but among them was an official medal intended for wear by those on whom it was conferred.

Even this, however, was not the first of the royal medals intended to be worn. This honour goes to a very large medal celebrating the proclamation of Victoria as Empress of India in 1877. Although fitted with a suspender bar and worn from a ribbon round the neck, it was not permitted for officers and men to wear this medal while in uniform. Later medals, however, were permitted to be worn when in uniform, but after other orders, decorations and campaign medals.

In the following listing (291A–291N) are the official Coronation Medals of James I, 1603, to Victoria, 1838. All were originally non-wearing, i.e. without suspension or ribbon, although some were later pierced or fitted with suspension for wearing. **Values of these are for silver medals only.**

291A. JAMES I CORONATION MEDAL

Date: 1603.
Metal: Silver.
Size: 28mm.
Description: (Obverse) Bust of King James I facing right. Legend: IAC: I: BRIT: CAE: AVG: HAE CAESArum cae D.D. (Reverse) Lion rampant facing left. Legend: ECCE PHA(R)OS POPVLIQ(VE) SALVS (Behold a lighthouse and safety of the people)

VALUE: Silver £350–450

291B. CHARLES I CORONATION MEDAL

Date: 1626.
Metal: Gold, silver.
Size: 28mm.
Designer: Nicholas Briot.
Description: Bust of Charles I facing right. Legend: CAROLVS. I. DG. MAG. BRITAN. FRAN. ET. HIB. REX. (Reverse) An arm issuing from a cloud and holding a sword. Legend: DONEC. PAX. REDDITA. TERRIS. (As long as Peace returns to the lands).

VALUE: Silver £350–450

291C. CHARLES I CORONATION MEDAL

Date: 1633 (Scottish Coronation)
Metal: Gold, silver.
Size: 28mm.
Designer: Nicholas Briot.
Mintage: Gold (3), silver (Unknown)
Description: Bust of Charles I facing left. Legend: CAROLVS DG SCOTIAE. ANGLIAE. FR. ET. HIB. REX. (Reverse) A rose bush surmounted by a thistle. Legend: HINC. NOSTRAE. CREVERE. ROSAE (From this our roses abound). Exergue: CORON. 18 JVNII 1633

VALUE: Silver £350–450

291D. CHARLES II CORONATION MEDAL

Date: 1651 (Scottish Coronation).
Metal: Gold, silver.
Size: 31mm.
Designer: Sir James Balfour.
Description: Bust of Charles II facing right. Legend: CAROLVS.2. D.G. SCO. ANG. FRA. ET. HI. REX. FI. DE. cor. i. ia. scon. 1651. (Reverse) Lion rampant facing left, holding a thistle. Legend: NEMO. ME. IMPVNE. LACESSET (No one provokes me with impunity).

VALUE: Silver £350–450

291E. CHARLES II CORONATION MEDAL

Date: 1661 (English Coronation).
Metal: Gold, silver.
Size: 30mm.
Designer: Thomas Simon.
Description: Bust of Charles II facing right. Legend:
CAROLVS .II.DG ANG. SCO. FR. ET. HI REX. (Reverse)
Charles II, wearing royal robe, seated on throne facing
left, holding sceptre. Angel hovering over him placing
crown on his head. Legend: EVERSO. MISSVS. SVC-
CVRRERE. SECLO. XXIII APR. 1661 (the times having
been turned upside down, he has been sent to succour
us)

VALUE: Silver £250–300

291F. JAMES II CORONATION MEDAL

Date: 1685.
Metal: Gold, silver, copper (?)
Size: 34mm.
Designer: John Roettier.
Mintage: Gold (200), silver (800), copper (Un-
known).
Description: Bust of James II facing right, laure-
ate. Legend: JACOBVS. II. D.G. ANG. SCO. FR.
ET. HI. REX. (Reverse) Hand holding the crown
above a laurel branch resting on a pillow. Legend:
A. MILITARI. AD. REGIAM. (from soldiering to
the palace). Exergue: INAVGVRAT. 23. AP. 1685.

VALUE: Silver £250–350

291G. WILLIAM AND MARY CORONATION MEDAL

Date: 1689.
Metal: Gold, silver, lead.
Size: 34mm.
Designer: John Roettier.
Mintage: Gold (515), silver (1,200), lead (Unknown).
Description: Conjoint busts of William and Mary
facing right. Legend: GVLIELMVS. ET. MARIA.
REX. ET. REGINA. (Reverse) Two-horse vehicle
lower left, Jove in cloud above right. Legend:
NE TOTVS ABSVMATVR. (let not the whole be
consumed). Exergue: INAVGVRAT. II. AP. 1689.

VALUE: Silver £250–350

291H. ANNE CORONATION MEDAL

Date: 1702.
Metal: Gold, silver, base metal.
Size: 34mm.
Designer: John Croker.
Mintage: Gold (858), silver (1,200), base metal (Unknown).
Description: Bust of Queen Anne facing left. Legend: ANNA. D:G: MAG: BR. FR. ET. HIB: REGINA. (Reverse) Pallas Athene, left, with shield and lightning bolts, attacking recumbent monster, right. Legend: VICEM GERIT. ILLA. TONANTIS. Exergue: INAVGVRAT. XXIII. AP. MDCCII. (As, making sounds, she conducts herself).

VALUE: Silver   £250–300

291I. GEORGE I CORONATION MEDAL

Date: 1714.
Metal: Gold, silver, base metal.
Size: 34mm.
Designer: John Croker
Mintage: Gold (330), silver (1,200), base metal (Unknown).
Description: Bust of George I facing right. Legend: GEORGIVS. DG. MAG. BR. FR. ET. HIB. REX. (Reverse) Seated King, left, being crowned by Britannia standing right. Exergue: INAVGVRAT. XX. OCT. MDCCXIIII.

VALUE: Silver   £175–250

291J. GEORGE II CORONATION MEDAL

Date: 1727.
Metal: Gold, silver, base metal.
Size: 34mm.
Designer: John Croker
Mintage: Gold (238), silver (800), base metal (Unknown)
Description: Bust of George II facing left. Legend: GEORGIVS. II. D.G. MAG. BR. FR. ET. HIB. REX. (Reverse) King seated on throne, left being crowned by Britannia, standing right. Legend: VOLENTES. PER. POVLOS (through the will of the people) Exergue: CORON. XI. OCTOB. MDCCXXVII.

VALUE: Silver   £175–250

291K. GEORGE III CORONATION MEDAL

Date: 1761.
Metal: Gold, silver, bronze
Size: 34mm.
Designer: Lorenz Natter.
Mintage: Gold (858), silver (800), bronze (unknown)
Description: Bust of George III facing right. Legend: GEORGIVS. III. D.G. M. BRI. FRA. ET. HIB. REX. F.D. (Reverse) Britannia standing left, crowning King seated right. Legend: PATRIAE. OVANTI. (Crowned as the country rejoices). Exergue: CORONAT. XXII. SEPT. CI ƆI ƆCCLXI

VALUE: Silver £275–350

291L. GEORGE IV CORONATION MEDAL

Date: 1821.
Metal: Gold, silver, bronze
Size: 35mm.
Designer: Benedetto Pistrucci.
Mintage: Gold (1,060), silver (800), bronze (unknown, over 1,525)
Description: Bust of George IV, laureate, facing left. Legend: GEORGIVS IIII D.G. BRITANNIARUM REX F.D. (Reverse) Three standing ladies, left, facing seated King, right. Behind King stands angel holding crown above his head. Legend: PROPRIO JAM JURE ANIMO PATERNO (already by special right, inaugurated in the spirit of his father). Exergue: INAUGURATUS DIE JULII. XIX ANNO. MDCCXXI.
Comments: *A slightly smaller and thinner version of this medal was struck and pierced for suspension from a plain maroon ribbon. These medals are invariably named to members of the Buckinghamshire Yeomanry Cavalry Hussars who took part in lining the route of the procession. This is believed to be the first coronation medal designed to be worn.*

VALUE: Silver £150–175

291M. WILLIAM IV CORONATION MEDAL

Date: 1831.
Metal: Gold, silver, bronze
Size: 34mm.
Designer: William Wyon
Mintage: Gold (1,000), silver (2,000), bronze (1,133)
Description: Head of William IV facing right. Legend: WILLIAM THE FOURTH CROWNED SEP: 8 1831 (Reverse) Head of Queen Adelaide facing right. Legend: ADELAIDE. QUEEN CONSORT. CROWNED SEP: 8 1831.

VALUE: Silver £175–250

291N. VICTORIA CORONATION MEDAL

Date: 1838.
Metal: Gold, silver, bronze.
Size: 36mm.
Designer: Benedetto Pistrucci.
Mintage: Gold (1,369), silver (2,209), bronze (1,871)
Description: Head of Queen Victoria facing left. Legend: VICTORIA D.G. BRITANNIARUM REGINA F.D. (Reverse) Three ladies symbolic of England, Scotland and Ireland, standing left, presenting crown to Queen, seated on a dais, right. A lion lies behind her chair. Legend: ERIMUS TIBI NOBILE REGNUM (We shall be a noble Kingdom to you). Exergue: INAUGURATA DIE JUNII XXVIII MDCCCXXXVIII.

VALUE: Silver   £125–175

292. EMPRESS OF INDIA MEDAL

Date: 1877.
Ribbon: 42mm crimson edged in gold.
Metal: Gold or silver.
Size: 58mm.
Description: (Obverse) a left-facing bust of Queen Victoria wearing a veil and a coronet, her name and the date of her elevation being inscribed round the circumference. (Reverse) a broad zigzag border enclosing the words EMPRESS OF INDIA and its equivalent in Urdu and Hindi across the field.
Comments: *Issued to celebrate the proclamation of Victoria as Empress of India on 1 January 1877. It was awarded in gold to Indian princes and high-ranking British officials. Indian civilians and selected officers and men of the various British and Indian regiments serving in India at the time were awarded the silver medal. It was issued unnamed but many examples were subsequently engraved or impressed privately.*

VALUE:		*Miniature*
Gold	£3500–4500	£250–350
Silver	£400–500	£100–150

292A. VISIT OF THE PRINCE OF WALES TO INDIA MEDAL 1875

(reduced)

Date: 1875–76.
Ribbon: 38mm plain white (gold), pale blue with white edges (silver).
Metal: Gold, silver or white metal with a silver crown.
Size: Oval 48mmx77mm.
Description: (Obverse) left-facing effigy of the Prince of Wales (later King Edward VII) surrounded by a laurel wreath and surmounted by a crown fitted to a suspension ring; (reverse) Prince of Wales's emblem surrounded by the chain of the GCSI.
Comments: *A large oval medal was struck to commemorate the state visit of HRH the Prince of Wales to India. Some 48 medals were struck in gold, 165 in silver and an unknown number in white metal. The gold medals are impressed on the rim with a small numeral, and engraved with the recipient's name in block capitals. The medals were numbered and named in strict order of precedence. The silver medal has a frosted relief on a mirror table. 13 small silver badges were also presented. In addition a small silver medalet was issued to the crews of HMS Renown and Terrible and the Royal Yacht Osborne, with the initials A and E either side of the Prince of Wales' emblem and a reverse inscribed HRH ALBERT EDWARD PRINCE OF WALES INDIA 1875–76 (similar in style to no. 308B).*

VALUE:

Gold (48)	£7000–8000
Silver (165)	£1000–1500
White metal	£200–250
Silver badge (13)	Rare
Silver medalet	£100–150

293. JUBILEE MEDAL 1887

Date: 1887.
Ribbon: Broad central blue band with wide white stripes at the edges.
Metal: Gold, silver or bronze.
Size: 30mm.
Description: (Obverse) the bust of Queen Victoria by Sir Joseph Edgar Boehm; (reverse) an elaborate wreath in which are entwined the heraldic flowers of the United Kingdom. This encloses an eight-line inscription surmounted by a crown: IN COMMEMORATION OF THE 50th YEAR OF THE REIGN OF QUEEN VICTORIA 21 JUNE 1887. The reverse was designed by Clemens Emptmayer
Comments: *Struck to celebrate the 50th anniversary of Victoria's accession to the throne. The medal in gold was given to members of the Royal Family and their personal guests. The silver medal was given to members of the Royal Household, government ministers, senior officials, distinguished foreign visitors, naval and military officers involved in the Jubilee parade on 21 June 1887 and the captains of vessels taking part in the great Naval Review at Spithead. The bronze medal was given to selected NCOs and men who took part in the parade or the Spithead Review. All medals were issued unnamed with a ring for suspension. When the Diamond Jubilee was celebrated ten years later holders of the 1887 medal were given a clasp in the form of a cable entwined around the date 1897 and surmounted by an imperial crown. Twin loops at the ends enabled the clasp to be sewn on to the ribbon.*

VALUE:

	without clasp	with clasp	*Miniature*
Gold	£1350–1500	Rare	£100–150
Silver	£160–180	£200–240	£25–30 (add £30 for clasp)
Bronze	£150–175	£200–240	£25–30 (add £30 for clasp)

294. JUBILEE (POLICE) MEDAL 1887

Date: 1887.
Ribbon: Plain dark blue.
Metal: Bronze.
Size: 36mm.
Description: (Obverse) the veiled profile of Queen Victoria; (reverse) a wreath surmounted by a crown and enclosing the inscription: JUBILEE OF HER MAJESTY QUEEN VICTORIA. The year appears at the foot and the name of the force round the top.
Comments: *Issued to all ranks of the Metropolitan and City of London Police and selected civilian staff to celebrate the Jubilee on 21 June 1887. Clasps for the 1897 Jubilee q.v. were issued to recipients of this medal still serving ten years later.*

VALUE:

	without clasp	with 1897 clasp	*Miniature*
Metropolitan Police (14,000)	£25–35	£35–45	£25–30
City of London Police (900)	£50–60	£70–90	£25–30
			(add £10 for clasp)

295. JUBILEE MEDAL 1897

Date: 1897.
Ribbon: Dark blue with two broad white bands and dark blue edges (as for 293).
Metal: Gold, silver or bronze.
Size: 30mm.
Description: This medal is very similar to the 1887 issue, differing solely in the date and anniversary on the reverse. Around 980 medals were awarded to army officers.

VALUE:

		Miniature
Gold (73)	£1300–1500	£80–100
Silver (3040)	£120–150	£20–30
Bronze (890)	£150–200	£15–20

296. JUBILEE MEDAL (MAYORS AND PROVOSTS) 1897

Date: 1897.
Ribbon: White with two broad dark stripes bands and white edges.
Metal: Gold or silver.
Size: Height 48mm; max. width 40mm.
Description: A diamond-shaped medal with ring suspension, reminiscent of the *Klippe* coinage of central Europe. Both sides had circular centres with trefoil ornaments occupying the angles. (Obverse) the Wyon profile of the young Victoria at the time of her accession; (reverse) Sir Thomas Brock's Old Head veiled bust of the Queen.
Comments: *The gold version was presented to Lord Mayors and Lord Provosts while the silver medal was granted to Mayors and Provosts. Small silver medals of more conventional circular format were produced with these motifs and sold as souvenirs of the occasion.*

VALUE:

		Miniature
Gold (14)	£1000–1400	£800–900
Silver (512)	£350–400	£200–250

297. JUBILEE (POLICE) MEDAL 1897

Date: 1897.
Ribbon: Plain dark blue.
Metal: Bronze.
Size: 36mm.
Description: Very similar to the 1887 issue with the dates suitably amended and the name of the service round the top of the reverse.
Comments: *Separate issues were made in respect of the Police Ambulance service, St John Ambulance Brigade and the Metropolitan Fire Brigade. Holders of the previous medal merely received the 1897 clasp (Metropolitan Police 8708, City of London Police 485).*

VALUE:		Miniature
Metropolitan Police (7481)	£30–35	£50–70
City of London Police (535)	£70–80	£50–70
Police Ambulance (210)	£350–450	£50–70
St John Ambulance Brigade (910)	£60–70	£50–70
Metropolitan Fire Brigade (950)	£60–70	£50–70

298. CEYLON DIAMOND JUBILEE MEDAL 1897

Date: 1897.
Ribbon: Plain red.
Metal: Gold or silver.
Size: 35mm.
Description: (Obverse) the Boehm bust of Queen Victoria with the dates 1837-1897 at the foot. (Reverse) an elephant and a stupa (dome-shaped Buddhist shrine), with two lines of concentric inscriptions: TO COMMEMORATE SIXTY YEARS OF HER MAJESTY'S REIGN and, unusually, THE RT. HON. SIR J. WEST RIDGEWAY K.C.B., K.C.M.G., GOVERNOR. A crown above the rim was fixed to a ring for suspension.
Comments: *Awarded to local dignitaries and leading officials in the Ceylon government.*

VALUE:		Miniature
Gold	£1000–1400	£800–1000
Silver	£200–250	£150–200

299. HONG KONG DIAMOND JUBILEE MEDAL

Date: 1897.
Ribbon: Three equal stripes of dark blue, maroon and dark blue (also known with gold ribbon with two white stripes).
Metal Silver, possibly also bronze.
Size: 36mm.
Description: (Obverse) the Boehm bust of Queen Victoria with the date 1897 at the foot; (reverse) a seascape with a British three-masted sailing ship and a Chinese junk in the background and two figures shaking hands in the foreground. The name of the colony appears at the top, while two concentric inscriptions read SIR WILLIAM ROBINSON G.C.M.G. GOVERNOR and TO COMMEMORATE SIXTY YEARS OF HER MAJESTY'S REIGN 1837-1897.
Comments: *Very little is known for certainty about this medal on account of the fact that the colonial records were destroyed during the Japanese occupation.*

VALUE:	
Silver	£300–400
Bronze	£180–200

299A. LAGOS DIAMOND JUBILEE MEDAL

Date: 1897.
Ribbon: Dark blue with two broad white stripes towards the edges.
Metal Silver.
Size: 36mm.
Description: (Obverse) the veiled crowned profile of Queen Victoria (similar to the Egypt Medal 1882, No. 131) inscribed VICTORIA QUEEN AND EMPRESS with a Tudor rose at the foot; (reverse) QUEEN'S DIAMOND JUBILEE LAGOS round the circumference, with JUNE 22ND 1897 in the centre.
Comments: *Issued to civil and military personnel associated with the Diamond Jubilee celebrations in the crown colony of Lagos (1886–1906 when it was incorporated in the colony and protectorate of Southern Nigeria).*

VALUE: —

299B. INDIA DIAMOND JUBILEE MEDAL

Date: 1897.
Ribbon: White.
Metal Silver.
Size: 36mm.
Description: (Obverse) the veiled crowned profile of Queen Victoria (similar to the Egypt Medal 1882, No. 131) inscribed VICTORIA QUEEN AND EMPRESS with a Star of India at the foot; (reverse) TO COMMEMORATE THE SIXTIETH YEAR OF THE REIGN OF H.M. QUEEN VICTORIA 1897 within a laurel wreath, with royal arms above and the Star of India below.
Comments: *Issued to civil and military personnel associated with the Diamond Jubilee celebrations in India. It was also issued to Native chiefs in the colony of Natal.*

VALUE: £100–150

300. VISIT TO IRELAND MEDAL 1900

Date: 1900.
Ribbon: Plain dark blue.
Metal: Bronze.
Size: 36mm.
Description: (Obverse) a half-length version of the Boehm bust of Queen Victoria; (reverse) the female allegorical figure of Hibernia looking out over Kingstown (Dun Laoghaire) harbour in which the Royal Yacht can be seen (far left). Unusually, the medal was mounted with a suspension bar decorated with shamrocks.
Comments: *The medal designed by G. W. de Saulles commemorated Queen Victoria's visit to Ireland in 1900. It was awarded to officers of the Royal Irish Constabulary and Dublin Metropolitan Police who were involved in security and policing the various events connected with the visit. The medal was worn with the same ribbon as the Jubilee Police medals.*

VALUE:
Bronze (2285)	£120–150	*Miniature*	£100–120

300A. VISIT TO THE COLONIES MEDAL 1901

Date: 1901.
Ribbon: Unknown.
Metal: Silver.
Size: Oval 20 x 24mm.
Description: (Obverse) a crowned anchor with the royal garter and rose emblem inset; (reverse) inscribed T.R.H. DUKE & DUCHESS OF CORNWALL & YORK—BRITISH COLONIES 1901 H.M.S. OPHIR.
Comments: *This small medalet was issued to commemorate the visit of the Duke and Duchess of Cornwall and York to the British Colonies aboard HMS* Ophir *in 1901.*

VALUE: £120–150   *Miniature*   £100–120

301. CORONATION MEDAL 1902

Date: 1902.
Ribbon: Dark blue with a central red stripe and white edges.
Metal: Silver or bronze.
Size: Height 42mm; max. width 30mm.
Description: (Obverse) the left-facing conjoined busts of King Edward VII and Queen Alexandra, both crowned and wearing coronation robes. (Reverse) the crowned royal cypher above the date of the actual ceremony. The medal has an elaborate raised rim decorated with a wreath culminating in a crown through which the ring for suspension was looped.
Comments: *This medal, designed by Emil Fuchs and struck by Messrs. Elkington & Co., celebrated the coronation of King Edward VII on 9 August 1902. It was presented in silver to members of the Royal Family, foreign dignitaries, high officials of the government, senior officials and service officers involved in the celebrations. Selected NCOs and other ranks of the Army and Navy taking part in the parades were awarded the medal in bronze. Both versions were issued unnamed.*

VALUE:		*Miniature*
Silver (3493)	£120–150	£10–15
Bronze (6054)	£70–90	£10–15

302. CORONATION MEDAL (MAYORS AND PROVOSTS) 1902

Date: 1902.
Ribbon: Dark blue with a narrow white central stripe and crimson borders.
Metal: Silver.
Size: 32mm.
Description: (Obverse) conjoined right-facing busts of the King and Queen; (reverse) the crowned cypher and date. It differed from the ordinary medal by having flat, broad borders decorated with the heraldic flowers of the United Kingdom culminating at the top in a simple suspension ring.
Comments: *The medal was designed by Emil Fuchs and struck by Messrs. Elkington & Co.*

VALUE:			
Silver	£140–150	*Miniature*	£100–120

303. CORONATION (POLICE) MEDAL 1902

Date: 1902.
Ribbon: Red, with a narrow dark blue central stripe.
Metal: Silver or bronze.
Size: 36mm.
Description: (Obverse) the left-facing bust of King Edward VII; (reverse) a crown above a nosegay of heraldic flowers with the words CORONATION OF HIS MAJESTY KING EDWARD VII 1902 in the upper field. The name or initials of the service appeared round the top, LCC MFB signifying London County Council Metropolitan Fire Brigade.
Comments: *Issued to all ranks of the police and associated services to celebrate the coronation, and awarded in silver or bronze to officers and other ranks respectively. 97 bronze medals were also issued to police civilian staff. The medal was designed by G. W. de Saulles.*

VALUE:	Silver	Miniature	Bronze	Miniature
Metropolitan Police	£400–500 (51)	£25–35	£25–30 (16,709)	£20–30
City of London Police	£600–800 (5)	£25–35	£60–70 (1060)	£20–30
LCC MFB	—		£50–60 (1000)	£50–60
St John Ambulance Brigade	—		£50–60 (912)	£60–70
Police Ambulance Service	Unique		£300–350 (204)	£90–100

304. CEYLON CORONATION MEDAL 1902

Date: 1902.
Ribbon: Plain blue.
Metal: Gold.
Size: 35mm.
Description: (Obverse) a crowned left-facing bust of King Edward VII; (reverse) the elephant and stupa motif previously used (MYB298). The concentric inscription on the reverse now tactfully omitted any reference to the governor: IN COMMEMORATION OF THE CORONATION OF H.M. KING EDWARD VII 1902. The medal was fitted with a ring for suspension.
Comments: *Like its predecessor, this rare medal was struck for presentation to local dignitaries and government officials.*

VALUE:	—	Miniature	£250–300

305. HONG KONG CORONATION MEDAL 1902

Date: 1902.
Ribbon: None officially designated.
Metal: Bronze.
Size: 36mm.
Description: (Obverse) conjoined right-facing busts of King Edward VII and Queen Alexandra with their names round the circumference; (reverse) the maritime motif of the Diamond Jubilee medal with new inscriptions in two concentric curves: SIR HENRY A. BLAKE G.C.M.G. GOVERNOR (inner) and TO COMMEMORATE THE CORONATION OF THEIR MAJESTIES THE KING & QUEEN (outer). Fitted with a suspension ring.
Comments: *Issued to all British and Indian officers and other ranks serving in the colony as well as local police. Some 6,000 medals were produced by Edmonds & Son, London, and issued in cases.*

VALUE:		
Bronze		£65–85

305A. NATAL CORONATION MEDAL 1902

Date: 1902.
Ribbon: Dark blue with a central claret stripe.
Metal: Silver.
Size: 21mm, 29mm and 51mm.
Description: (Obverse) a right-facing crowned bust of King Edward VII with the inscription TO COMMEMORATE THE CORONATION OF KING EDWARD VII; (reverse) Royal coat of arms above two running wildebeests, inscribed (round top) EDWARDUS DEI GRATIA BRITANNIAR REX F:D and (round bottom) COLONY OF NATAL 26 JUNE 1902. Ring suspension.
Comments: *The small medal was distributed to schoolchildren whereas the large medal was restricted to native chiefs and is relatively scarce. It is believed that the middle-size medal was presented to local dignitaries.*

VALUE:		
	21mm	£20–30
	29mm	£85–100
	51mm	£500–600

306. DELHI DURBAR MEDAL 1903

Date: 1903.
Ribbon: Pale blue with three dark blue stripes—the colours of the Order of the Indian Empire and the Order of the Star of India..
Metal: Gold or silver.
Size: 38.5mm.
Description: (Obverse) a right-facing crowned bust of the King Emperor with DELHI DARBAR 1903 on the right side; (reverse) a three-line inscription in Farsi across the field, which translates as "By grace of the Lord of the Realm, Edward, King, Emperor of India, 1901", with an elaborate border of roses, thistles, shamrocks and Indian flowers. Ring suspension.
Comments: *Struck to celebrate the Durbar of the King Emperor at Delhi on 1 January 1903. It was awarded in gold to the rulers of the Indian princely states and in silver to lesser dignitaries, government officials, and officers and other ranks of the armed services actually involved in the celebrations.*

VALUE:			Miniature
Gold (140)		£1200–1500	—
Silver (2567)		£175–200	£30–40

307. VISIT TO SCOTLAND MEDAL 1903

Date: 1903.
Ribbon: Plain red.
Metal: Bronze.
Size: 36mm.
Description: Very similar to the Police Coronation medal but the year was changed to 1903 and the inscription SCOTTISH POLICE appeared round the top of the reverse. The medal was named to the recipient on the rim. An ornate clasp decorated with a thistle was worn above the suspension bar.
Comments: *This medal was designed by G. W. de Saulles and struck to commemorate Their Majesties' post-coronation tour of Scotland in May 1903. It was awarded to the police and troops involved in parades and escort duties, as well as the ancillary services such as the Fire Brigade and the St Andrew's Ambulance Association.*

VALUE:
Bronze (2957)	£80–100	*Miniature*	£40–50

308. VISIT TO IRELAND MEDAL 1903

Date: 1903.
Ribbon: Pale blue.
Metal: Bronze.
Size: 36mm.
Description: (Obverse) bust of King Edward VII; (reverse) as 1900 medal with the date altered at the foot. The suspension brooch is ornamented with shamrocks.
Comments: *This medal was designed by G. W. de Saulles and struck to mark the King's visit to Ireland in July 1903. It was awarded on the same terms as the Visit to Ireland Medal 1900.*

VALUE:
Bronze (7757)	£80–100	*Miniature*	£60–70

308A. VISIT OF THE PRINCE AND PRINCESS OF WALES TO INDIA

Instituted: 1905–06
Ribbon: Neck ribbon 55mm wide, maroon with wide blue stripes towards each edge.
Metal: Frosted silver.
Size: 46mm.
Description: (Obverse) conjoined busts of the Prince and Princess of Wales (later King George V and Queen Mary), facing right. ELKINGTON (manufacturers) inscribed below busts. (Reverse) badge of the Prince of Wales surrounded by the chain of the GCSI, with legend T.R.H. THE PRINCE & PRINCESS OF WALES VISIT TO INDIA 1905–6.
Comments: *Only 72 medals were struck, 70 of which were bestowed on British and Indian officials.*

VALUE: £400–600 *Miniature* £50–60

308B. GEORGE PRINCE OF WALES MEDAL

Instituted: 1905-06.
Ribbon: 15mm, red, white and blue in equal parts.
Metal: Silver or gold.
Size: Oval 20 x 24mm.
Description: (Obverse) the Prince of Wales's plumes surrounded by the Garter and the chain and badge of the GCSI, flanked in the field by the letters G and M; (reverse) inscription T.R.H. GEORGE PRINCE OF WALES & VICTORIA MARY PRINCESS OF WALES with INDIA 1905-6 in the upper centre.
Comments: *The 26 gold medals were given by Their Royal Highnesses to their personal staff, while a total of 1,625 silver medals were presented to all hands aboard HMS* Renown *and* Terrible *and the Royal Yacht* Osborne.

VALUE:
Gold (26)	£800–1000
Silver (1625)	£80–120

309. CORONATION MEDAL 1911

Date: 1911.
Ribbon: Dark blue with two thin red stripes in the centre.
Metal: Silver.
Size: 32mm.
Description: (Obverse) conjoined left-facing busts of King George V and Queen Mary in their coronation robes within a floral wreath; (reverse) the crowned royal cypher above the date of the coronation itself. Plain ring suspension.
Comments: *Designed by Sir Bertram McKennal, MVO, ARA, these medals were issued unnamed but may sometimes be found with unofficial engraving. Those who were also entitled to the Delhi Darbar Medal received a crowned clasp inscribed DELHI if they had previously been awarded the coronation medal. This was the first occasion that the medal might be awarded to those not actually present at the ceremony itself.*

VALUE:		*Miniature*
Silver (15,901)	£50–65	£5–10
Clasp Delhi (134)	£600–800	£50–60

309A. GUILDHALL CORONATION MEDAL 1911

Date: 1911.
Ribbon: Crimson.
Metal: Silver and enamels.
Size: 37mm.
Description: (Obverse) conjoined left-facing busts of King George V and Queen Mary with their names around, surrounded by a white enamelled ring bearing the words CORONATION RECEPTION . JUNE 1911 with laurel wreath around divided by four shields, surmounted by a crown with three semi-precious stones inset; (reverse) hallmark and pin. Suspended from an ornate clasp (with additional pin) bearing a sword and sceptre.
Comments: *The reception at the Guildhall, London, was a grand affair with members of the Royal family and a number of Heads of State in attendance. The ornate medals were presented in a plush case and were designed to be worn either as a lapel badge or as a conventional medal.*

VALUE: £250–300

310. CORONATION (POLICE) MEDAL 1911

Date: 1911.
Ribbon: Red with three narrow blue stripes.
Metal: Silver.
Size: 36mm.
Description: (Obverse) a crowned left-facing bust of King George V; (reverse) an imperial crown with an ornate surround. The inscription CORONATION 1911 appears at the foot and the name of the service at the top. Ring suspension.
Comments: *By now the number of police and ancillary services had grown considerably, as witness the various reverse types which may be encountered in this medal. The medal was designed by Sir Bertram McKennal, MVO, ARA,*

VALUE:		*Miniature*
Metropolitan Police (19,783)	£25–30	£15–20
City of London Police (1400)	£75–85	£20–25
County and Borough Police (2565)	£70–90	£20–25
Police Ambulance Service*	£400–450	£90–100
London Fire Brigade (1374)	£75–85	£90–100
Royal Irish Constabulary (585)	£100–120	£150–200
Scottish Police (2800)	£80–100	£50–60
St John Ambulance Brigade*	£50–60	£60–70
St Andrew's Ambulance Corps*	£120–150	£100–150
Royal Parks (119)	£300–350	£140–160

* A total of 2623 medals was awarded to these three services, the Police Ambulance medal being the scarcest and St John Ambulance medal the commonest.

311. VISIT TO IRELAND MEDAL 1911

Date: 1911.
Ribbon: Dark green with thin red stripes towards either end.
Metal: Silver.
Size: 36mm.
Description: Very similar to the foregoing, distinguished only by the reverse which is inscribed CORONATION 1911 round the top, with the actual date of the visit round the foot.
Comments: *This medal was designed by Sir Bertram McKennal, MVO, ARA and was granted to prominent civic dignitaries and members of the Irish police forces involved in the royal visit to Ireland which took place on 7-12 July 1911.*

VALUE:
Silver (2477)	£75–90	*Miniature*	£70–80

311A. EAST INDIAN RAILWAY COMPANY ROYAL VISIT TO INDIA MEDAL 1911

Date: 1911.
Ribbon: Dark blue with a central maroon stripe flanked by narrow gold stripes.
Metal: Gilded bronze.
Size: 32mm.
Description: (Obverse) the arms of the East Indian Railway Company surrounded by the inscription EAST INDIAN RAILWAY COMPANY with a winged wheel at the foot; (reverse) a ten-line inscription FOR SERVICES RENDERED DURING THE RAILWAY JOURNEYS OF THEIR MAJESTIES THE KING EMPEROR AND QUEEN EMPRESS IN INDIA 1911.
Comments: *Very little is known about this rare medal, but it is believed to have been awarded to members of the Honour Guard of the East Indian Railway Volunteer Rifle Corps and employees of the company present during the tour of India undertaken in 1911 by King George V and Queen Mary. It is believed that no more than 30 medals were issued.*

VALUE: £100–£120

312. DELHI DURBAR MEDAL 1911

Date: 1911.
Ribbon: Dark blue with two narrow red stripes in the middle.
Metal: Gold or silver.
Size: 38.5mm.
Description: (Obverse) the conjoined crowned busts of King George V and Queen Mary in a floral wreath; (reverse) an elaborate Farsi text which translates as "The Durbar of George V, Emperor of India, Master of the British Lands".
Comments: *This medal marked the Delhi Durbar held in the King Emperor's honour in December 1911. Most of the gold medals went to the Indian princely rulers and top government officials, 10,000 of the 30,000 silver medals were awarded to officers and other ranks of the British and Indian Armies for exemplary service, without their necessarily being present at the Durbar itself.*

VALUE:		Miniature
Gold (200)	£850–1250	£300–400
Silver (30,000)	£60–80	£10–15

312AA. DELHI DURBAR MILITARY TOURNAMENT MEDAL 1911

Date: 1911.
Ribbon: None
Metal: Gold, Silver or Bronze.
Size: 44mm.
Description: (Obverse) the left-facing crowned and robed bust of King George V; (reverse) within a wreath of laurel leaves, three tablets engraved with the words DURBAR, TOURNAMENT and the event for which the medal is awarded, e.g. HOCKEY, with the legend DELHI . CORONATION . DURBAR . 1911 around
Comments: *Minted by the Calcutta Mint, and usually named on the edge with the details of the recipient. These very rare medals were awarded for specific events at the Dehli Durbar, but they are rarely seen.*

VALUE:	Gold (6)	£750–1000
	Silver (15–20)	£250–300
	Bronze (40–50)	£100–150

312A. VISIT OF KING GEORGE V AND QUEEN MARY TO INDIA 1911–12

Date: 1911–12.
Ribbon: None.
Metal: Silver or gold.
Size: Oval 20 x 24mm.
Description: (Obverse): GRI entwined initials as a monogram above the dates 1911–12; (reverse) MRI monogram and dates, suspended from a bar by a simple ring and scroll suspender.
Comments: *Information on the issue of this medalet is sought although it is believed to have been issued to the crew of the royal yacht.*

VALUE:	Gold	£750–1000
	Silver	£60–85

312AB. QUEEN ALEXANDRA'S CHILDREN'S BANQUET MEDAL 1914

Date: 28 December 1914.

Ribbon: White, with red stripes at each edge.

Metal: Bronze.

Size: 38mm.

Description: (Obverse) bust of Queen Alexandra facing right with the inscription A GIFT FROM QUEEN ALEXANDRA; (reverse) central inscription FEAR GOD, HONOUR THE KING surrounded by the legend GUILDHALL BANQUET TO OUR SOLDIERS' & SAILORS' CHILDREN 28th DEC. 1914. The suspension is ornate and has the arms of the City of London superimposed.

Comments: *This medal, designed and manufactured by Elkington, was issued unnamed to 1,300 children and a small number of Chelsea pensioners who attended a banquet at the Guildhall on 28 December 1914. The children, between the ages of eight and thirteen, were the sons and daughters of men in the Fleet or on the Western Front. One child was chosen from each family by Sir James Gildea of the Soldiers' and Sailors' Families' Association. Relatively few medals appear to have survived.*

VALUE: £50–£70

312B. VISIT OF THE PRINCE OF WALES TO INDIA 1921–22

Date: 1921–22.
Ribbon: Neck ribbon 55mm maroon with broad blue stripes towards each edge.
Metal: Frosted silver.
Size: 50mm.
Description: (Obverse) bust of Prince of Wales facing left with inscription EDWARD PRINCE OF WALES INDIA 1921–1922; (reverse) badge of the Prince of Wales surrounded by the chain of the GCSI. Fitted with a plain suspension ring.
Comments: *Only 84 medals were awarded in connection with the visit of HRH the Prince of Wales (later King Edward VIII and Duke of Windsor) to India in the course of his world tour aboard HMS Renown.*

VALUE: £700–900   *Miniature*   £80–100

312C. WELCOME HOME MEDAL FOR THE PRINCE OF WALES

Date: 1922.
Ribbon: Green with red central stripe.
Metal: Silver and bronze.
Size: Oval 43mm x 34mm.
Description: An oval medal with ornate edges. (Obverse) crowned and robed bust of the Prince of Wales with the inscription EDWARD PRINCE OF WALES KG; (reverse) The Prince of Wales's feathers with the inscription WELCOME HOME 1922. With integral ornate loop for suspension.
Comments: *Struck by F. Bowcher to mark the return of the Prince of Wales to England after his world tour.*

VALUE: Gold   £250–350
           Silver   £70–100

312D. VISIT OF THE PRINCE OF WALES TO BOMBAY MEDAL 1921

Date: 1921.
Ribbon: Watered blue/white with central thin white stripe.
Metal: Bronze.
Size: Oval 38mm x 30mm.
Description: An oval medal. (Obverse) bust of the Prince of Wales facing right, with the inscription EDWARD PRINCE OF WALES and surmounted by the Prince of Wales's feathers and motto ICH DIEN; (reverse) VISIT OF HIS ROYAL HIGHNESS BOMBAY NOVEMBER 1921 in six lines.
Comment: *Thought to be presented to the leading military and civil dignitaries present during the visit of the Prince of Wales. New information suggests it was also given to school children although this is unconfirmed. The number issued is not known.*
VALUE: £20–£25

312E. VISIT OF THE PRINCE OF WALES TO PATNA 1921

Date: 1921.
Ribbon: Imperial Purple.
Metal: Bronze.
Size: 40mm.
Description: (Obverse) bust of the Prince of Wales facing with the inscription EDWARD PRINCE OF WALES, in an oval centre-piece, with an ornate floral decoration either side; (Reverse) centre blank, with the inscription VISIT OF HIS ROYAL HIGHNESS around the top half, and PATNA 22ND. DEC 1921 around the lower half of the reverse.
Comment: *Believed to have been presented to the leading military and civil dignitaries present during the visit of the Prince of Wales. The number issued is not known, but is believed to be very small.*

VALUE :   £80–£100

313. JUBILEE MEDAL 1935

Date: 1935.
Ribbon: Red with two dark blue and one white stripes at the edges.
Metal: Silver.
Size: 32mm.
Description: (Obverse) left-facing conjoined half-length busts of King George V and Queen Mary in crowns and robes of state; (reverse) a crowned GRI monogram flanked by the dates of the accession and the jubilee.
Comments: *This medal, designed by Sir William Goscombe John, RA, was issued to celebrate the Silver Jubilee of King George V and widely distributed to the great and good throughout the Empire.*

VALUE:
    Silver (85,234)   £25–30   *Miniature*   £10–15

313A. ISLE OF MAN SILVER JUBILEE MEDAL 1935

Date: 1935.
Ribbon: Three equal stripes of red, white and blue. However some medals had their ribbons substituted with black to mark the death of the King in 1936.
Metal: Silver.
Size: 32mm.
Description: (Obverse) conjoined busts of King George V and Queen Mary in an inner circle surrounded by the legend KING GEORGE V & QUEEN MARY REIGNED 25 YEARS; (reverse) Triskelion emblem with the legend IN COMMEMORATION OF THE SILVER JUBILEE 1935. Suspended from a brooch bar of seven overlapping panels. The centre panel has the royal cypher GvR while the outer panels have two leaves in each.
Comments: *This medal is an unofficial issue struck to celebrate the Silver Jubilee. It is included here as it was apparently presented to civic dignitaries and officials in the island.*

VALUE: £100–120

313B. GUILDHALL JUBILEE MEDAL 1935

Date: 1935.
Ribbon: None.
Metal: Enamelled silver-gilt.
Size: 38mm wide.
Description: (Obverse) Arms of the City of London within a blue enamelled garter with the date 1935 on a white panel, surmounted by the Royal cypher, crown and lion; (reverse) engraved with the date 22nd May 1935. The medal is suspended from a double scroll brooch.
Comments: *This medal was issued to selected dignitaries who attended the banquet at the Guildhall in celebration of the King's Silver Jubilee. It was made by G. Kenning & Son, London.*

VALUE: £250–300

314. CORONATION MEDAL 1937

Date: 1937.
Ribbon: Blue edged with one red and two white stripes.
Metal: Silver.
Size: 32mm.
Description: (Obverse) conjoined busts of King George VI and Queen Elizabeth in their robes of state without any inscription. The stark simplicity of this motif was matched by a reverse showing the crowned GRI over the inscription CROWNED 12 MAY 1937, with the names of the King and Queen in block capitals round the circumference.
Comments: *Issued to celebrate the coronation of King George VI on 12 May 1937.*

VALUE: **Silver (90,000)** £25–35 *Miniature* £10–15

314A. GUILDHALL CORONATION MEDAL 1937

Date: 1937.
Ribbon: None
Metal: Silver-gilt.
Size: 34mm.
Description: A rectangular medal (obverse) conjoined busts of King George VI and Queen Elizabeth in their robes of state on a shield with palm and vine sprigs below and CORONATION in a tablet. The design struck on a rectangular base with two "steps" at each side in art deco style. Reverse blank, inscribed with the name of recipient. The medal is suspended from an ornate crowned coat of arms of the City of London with GUILDHALL above
Comments: Issued by the City of London to selected dignitaries who attended the banquet at the Guildhall to celebrate the coronation of King George VI on 12 May 1937.

VALUE: £150–200

314B. ROYAL VISIT TO SOUTH AFRICA 1947

Reverse i.

Reverse ii.

Date: 1947.
Ribbon: Yellow.
Metal: Silver.
Size: Oval 25mm x 32mm or 65mm x 55mm.
Description: (Obverse) conjoined busts of King George VI and Queen Elizabeth in their robes of state without any inscription. (Reverse) (i) crowned GRE with the inscription ROYAL VISIT 1947; (ii) map of South Africa surmounted by crowned GRE cypher dividing the date 1947 with KONINKLIKE BESOEK above and ROYAL VISIT below.
Comments: *Issued to celebrate the visit of King George VI to South Africa in 1947. Two distinctly different reverses have been seen but little is known about these medals which were issued in two sizes. They appear to have been issued to selected dignitaries and worn from a yellow neck ribbon.*

VALUE: —

315. CORONATION MEDAL 1953

Date: 1953.
Ribbon: Dark red with two narrow blue stripes in the centre and narrow white edges.
Metal: Silver.
Size: 32mm.
Description: (Obverse) a right-facing bust of Queen Elizabeth II in a Tudor crown and robes of state, the field being otherwise plain. (Reverse) a similar crown over the royal monogram EIIR with the legend QUEEN ELIZABETH II CROWNED 2ND JUNE 1953 round the circumference. Ring suspension.
Comments: *This medal celebrated the coronation of Queen Elizabeth II on 2 June 1953. News that Edmund Hillary and Sherpa Tenzing had successfully attained the summit of Everest reached London on the morning of the Coronation. Subsequently the members of the Hunt Expedition were invited to Buckingham Palace on 16 July 1953 where, on Her Majesty's own initiative, they were presented with coronation medals engraved MOUNT EVEREST EXPEDITION on the rim, following the precedent of the Mwele medals of 1895–96.*

VALUE:		*Miniature*
Silver (129,000)	£30–35	£10–12
Mount Everest Expedition (37)	£800–1000	

315A. ROYAL VISIT TO NEW ZEALAND MEDAL 1953–54

Date: 1953.
Ribbon: Dark blue.
Metal: Copper-coloured alloy.
Size: 38mm.
Description: (Obverse) right-facing crowned bust of Queen Elizabeth II wearing Tudor crown; (reverse) the crowned New Zealand coat of arms surrounded by sprays of flowers and the inscription ELIZABETH II ROYAL VISIT 1953–54. The copper-coloured medal is hung by a ring from a scalloped suspender as illustrated.
Comment: *Issued to all New Zealand school-children in 1953, accompanied by a folder telling the story of the Royal Family, with pictures of the Coronation regalia, royal palaces and descriptions. The medals themselves are fairly common, but those with the accompanying folder are quite rare.*

VALUE: £2–3 (with accompanying folder £20–30)

315B. ROYAL VISIT TO MALTA 1954

Date: 1954.
Ribbon: None.
Metal: Gold coloured alloy.
Size: 38mm.
Description: (Obverse) right-facing crowned bust of the Queen; (reverse) shield containing the Maltese flag with the inscription TO COMMEMORATE THE ROYAL VISIT TO MALTA G.C. 1954 round the circumference.
Comments: *Issued to all Maltese schoolchildren, teachers and municipal workers in commemoration of the Royal visit to the island.*

VALUE: £5–10

315C. ROYAL VISIT TO NIGERIA MEDAL 1956

Date: 1956.
Ribbon: None.
Metal: Toned bronze.
Size: 38mm.
Description: (Obverse) Right facing, bare-headed, conjoined busts of HM Queen Elizabeth and Prince Philip, with the inscription "THE ROYAL VISIT" above and "TO NIGERIA 1956" below; (reverse) the crowned Royal coat of arms, with the Royal cypher above and the roman numerals MCMLVI at the foot.
Comments: *This circular medal was struck by the Royal Mint and issued to mark the Royal visit of Queen Elizabeth and Prince Philip to Nigeria, between 28 January and 16 February 1956. The medal was issued to the Royal party and to local dignitaries. A total of 650 medals were issued, each contained in a red leatherette box.*

VALUE: £50-75

316. JUBILEE MEDAL 1977

Date: 1977.
Ribbon: White with thin red stripes at the edges, a broad blue stripe in the centre and a thin red stripe down the middle of it.
Metal: Silver.
Size: 32mm.
Description: (Obverse) Right-facing profile of Queen Elizabeth II wearing the St Edward's crown—the first time this design was employed; (reverse) a crown and wreath enclosing the words THE 25TH YEAR OF THE REIGN OF QUEEN ELIZABETH II 6 FEBRUARY 1977. A distinctive reverse was used in Canada, showing the dates of the reign flanking the royal monogram round the foot, CANADA round the top and a large stylised maple leaf in the centre.
Comments: *The 25th anniversary of the Queen's accession was marked by the release of this unnamed medal.*

VALUE:		Miniature
General issue (30,000)	£160–185	£6–10
Canadian issue (30,000)	£90–120	£6–10

318. GOLDEN JUBILEE MEDAL 2002

Date: February 2002.

Ribbon: Royal blue with thin red stripes at the edges, a broad white stripe in the centre and a thin red stripe down the middle.

Metal: Gold-plated cupro-nickel.

Size: 32mm.

Description: (Obverse) a right facing profile of Queen Elizabeth II wearing a crown; (reverse) the royal coat of arms flanked by the dates 1952 and 2002.

Comments: *Issued to celebrate the 50th anniversary of the Queen's accession. It was granted to all personnel of the armed forces who had completed five or more years service on February 6, 2002. Generals who have been Chief of the General Staff and Chief of the Defence Staff or equivalent RN and RAF ranks were awarded the medal even though retired. It was also issued to members of the police, ambulance, coastguard, fire services, RNLI and mountain rescue services, as well as members of the Royal Household including The Queen's Body Guard of the Yeomen of the Guard, who had completed five years service and holders of the VC or GC. One member of HM Customs & Excise was awarded the medal by the Ministry of Defence to mark his close co-operation in work and liaison between the two departments. Almost 400,000 medals were issued.*

VALUE: £70–80   *Miniature*   £8–10

318A. DIAMOND JUBILEE MEDAL 2012

Date: February 2012.

Ribbon: Dark red with royal blue edges and two narrow white stripes in the centre.

Metal: Nickel-silver.

Size: 32mm.

Description: (Obverse) right facing coinage profile of Queen Elizabeth II by Ian Rank-Broadley; (reverse) the crowned royal cypher surmounted on a faceted diamond dessign, with the dates 1952 – 2002 below.

Comments: *Issued to celebrate the 60th anniversary of the Queen's accession. Awarded to members of the armed forces (Regular and Reserve), certain emergency services and operational prison services personnel and Police Community Support Officers who have completed five years service on February 6, 2012, as well as living holders of the VC or GC and members of the Royal Household.*

VALUE: —   *Miniature*   —

MISCELLANEOUS MEDALS

Under this heading are grouped a very disparate range of medals whose only common denominator is that they do not fit conveniently into one or other of the preceding categories. They are not without considerable interest and many of them have a very keen following and a buoyant market.

319. KING'S AND QUEEN'S MESSENGER BADGE

Date: 1722.
Ribbon: Garter blue.
Metal: Silver gilt.
Size: Earliest issues variable according to monarch and jeweller; since George V—45mm x 34mm.
Description: (Issues since George V) an upright oval fitted with a plain suspension ring and having a greyhound suspended by a ring from the foot of the rim. (Obverse) the Garter inscribed HONI SOIT QUI MAL Y PENSE enclosing the royal cypher; early issues had the Royal coat of arms; (reverse) plain, engraved with an official number of issue and, on occasion, the name of the messenger.
Comments: *Messengers can be traced back to 1199, but prior to George I badges were not issued. Few of the earlier badges can be found due to a hand in and melt down order instituted by George III in 1762. During the reign of Victoria a number of different shapes and sizes were used for the badges due to a misunderstanding whereby individual messengers obtained their insignia from different jewellers instead of the Jewel Office. Since 1870 Garrards have been responsible for the design, submission and production of Messengers badges. From 1876 to 1951 the Foreign Office, as Controllers of the Corps of Messengers, purchased and held all badges for issue to those appointed as messengers. Since 1951 messengers, on satisfactorily completing a period of probation, are given a registered number and letter of permission to purchase their badges through the Crown Jewellers.*

VALUE:		
	George III	£1500–2000
	George IV	£1200–1500
	William IV	£1200–1500
	Victoria	£1000–1500
	Edward VII	£800–1000
	George V	£600–800
	George VI	£600–800
	Elizabeth II	£800–1000

320. ARCTIC MEDAL 1857

Instituted: 30 January 1857.
Ribbon: 38mm watered white.
Metal: Silver.
Size: Height 46mm; max. width 32mm.
Description: An octagonal medal with a beaded rim, surmounted by a nine-pointed star (representing the Pole Star) through which the suspension ring is fitted. (Obverse) an unusual profile of Queen Victoria, her hair in a loose chignon secured with a ribbon. (Reverse) a three-masted sailing vessel amid icebergs with a sledge party in the foreground and the dates 1818-1855 in the exergue. The medal was issued unnamed, but is often found privately engraved.
Comments: *Awarded retrospectively to all officers and men engaged in expeditions to the polar regions from 1818 to 1855, including those involved in the on-going search for the ill-fated Franklin Expedition of 1845-8. Thus the medal was granted to civilians, scientists, personnel of the French and US Navies and employees of the Hudson's Bay Company who took part in a number of abortive search parties for Sir John Franklin and his crew. Some 1106 medals, out of 1486 in all, were awarded to officers and ratings of the Royal Navy.*

VALUE:
(unnamed) £750–850

Miniature £200–300

321. ARCTIC MEDAL 1876

Instituted: 28 November 1876.
Ribbon: 32mm plain white.
Metal: Silver.
Size: 36mm
Description: A circular medal with a raised beaded rim and a straight bar suspender. (Obverse) a veiled bust of Queen Victoria wearing a small crown, dated 1876 at the foot; (reverse) a three-masted ship icebound.

Comments: *Granted to officers and men of HM ships* Alert *and* Discovery *who served in the Arctic Expedition between 17 July 1875 and 2 November 1876. The medal was later extended to include the crew on the second voyage of the private yacht* Pandora *commanded by Allen Young which cruised in Polar waters between 25 June and 19 October 1875 and from 3 June to 2 November 1876. Medals were engraved with the name, rank and ship of the recipient. Only 155 medals were awarded.*

VALUE:
(named) £2000–3000

Miniature £250–300

322. POLAR MEDAL

Instituted: 1904.

Ribbon: 32mm plain white.

Metal: Silver or bronze.

Size: 33mm octagonal.

Description: (Obverse) the effigy of the reigning sovereign; (reverse) a view of the Royal Research Ship *Discovery* with a man-handling sledge party in the foreground.

Comments: *Originally issued in silver, with an appropriate clasp, to the officers and men of Captain Scott's 1902–04 Antarctic Expedition, who went out in the* Discovery *and remained throughout the stay of the ship in the Antarctic Regions, from her arrival until her departure, or to any member compulsorily invalided after 3 January 1902, or to any who joined* Discovery *during her second winter in the Antarctic. It was issued in bronze to officers and men who did not remain, for causes other than sickness, throughout the stay of the ship in Antarctic regions; and also to the officers and men of the relief ships* Morning *and* Terra Nova. *These awards continued for subsequent expeditions: the silver medal being usually awarded to officers and to men who landed or who made more than one voyage, whilst the bronze medal was awarded to those not so exposed to the dangers of the polar environment. The bronze medal ceased being awarded after those awarded for Antarctic Research Work during 1929–39. Apart from the bronze medals awarded for the British Antarctic Expedition 1902–04 and the* Aurora *Relief Expedition 1917 where the year of the expedition was on the rim of the medal, the rest all had a clasp with ANTARCTIC and the year(s) of the expedition; the exception to this being those who took part on Shackleton's expedition and who had previously been awarded the bronze medal, received a clasp to their medal. No bronze medals were awarded for the Arctic. Up to December 2005, 271 bronze awards have been made (to 259 individuals, of whom 10 received one or more additional awards); 1038 silver awards have been made (to 948 individuals, of whom 80 received one or more additional awards), 18 recipients have been awarded both the silver and bronze medals. Only six women have been awarded the medal. Names of recipients are engraved on the earlier and most recent issues, and impressed in small capitals on the earlier Elizabethan issues.*

VALUE:	Silver	Miniature	Bronze (no clasp)	Miniature (no clasp)
Edward VII	from £5000	£100–150	from £3000	£100–150
George V (B)	from £3000	£100–150	from £3000	£100–150
George V (C)	—	£100–150	from £3000	£100–150
George V (E)	from £3000	£100–150	—	£100–150
George VI	from £2500	£100–150	from £3000	£100–150
Elizabeth II	from £2500	£100–150	—	£100–150

Modern examples of miniatures £10–15

323. KING EDWARD VII MEDAL FOR SCIENCE, ART AND MUSIC

Instituted: 1904

Ribbon: 35mm scarlet with a broad central stripe of dark blue and thin white stripes towards the edges.

Metal: Silver.

Size: 32mm.

Description: The raised rim consisted of a laurel wreath and has a ring for suspension. (Obverse) the conjoined busts of King Edward VII and Queen Alexandra; (reverse) the Three Graces engaged in various cultural pursuits.

Comments: *This short-lived medal was discontinued only two years later. It was awarded in recognition of distinguished services in the arts, sciences and music. The medal was struck by Burt & Co.*

VALUE: £1200–1400

324. ORDER OF THE LEAGUE OF MERCY

Modern reverse.

Date: 1898.

Ribbon: 38mm watered white silk with a central broad stripe of black.

Metal: Originally silver, now silver-gilt.

Size: Height 51mm; max. width 39mm.

Description: Originally an enamelled red cross surmounted by the Prince of Wales's plumes enfiladed by a coronet, with a central medallion depicting the emblem of the League, a group of figures representing Charity, set within a laurel wreath. Since 1999: a silver-gilt cross with the emblem in a central medallion. Reverse: a circular plaque inscribed LEAGUE OF MERCY 1999 in four lines.

Comments: *Appointments to the Order were sanctioned and approved by the sovereign on the recommendation of the Grand President of the League of Mercy as a reward for distinguished personal service to the League in assisting the support of hospitals. Ladies and gentlemen who rendered such aid for at least five years were eligible for the award. In 1917 King George V instituted a bar to be awarded to those who gave continuing service over a period of many years after receiving the Order itself. The original Order was last awarded in 1946 and the League itself ceased to exist in 1947. However, in March 1999, 100 years after its institution, the League was re-established and today it awards silver-gilt medals for valuable service. About 150 medals have been awarded since 1999.*

VALUE:

Badge of the Order	Original £50–60	*Miniature* £50–60
	with bar £100–130	

325. QUEEN ALEXANDRA'S IMPERIAL MILITARY NURSING SERVICE CAPE BADGE

Date: 1902–49

Branch of Service: Queen Alexandra's Imperial Military Nursing Service.

Ribbon: Scarlet with two white outer stripes and two black inner stripes.

Metal: Silver.

Size: Oval 55mm by 36mm.

Description: A uniface oval ring surmounted by a Tudor crown fitted to a plain ring for suspension. The ring at the centre has the Cross of the Order of the Dannebrog, with an ornamental cypher of Queen Alexandra. The ring is inscribed in raised lettering QUEEN ALEXANDRA'S IMPERIAL MILITARY NURSING SERVICE.

Comments: *The cape badge was instituted in 1902 and was used until 1949 when the QAIMNS changed its name to the QARANC. It was worn on the right breast on ward dress for commissioned (qualified) nurses. It was issued through stores to each individual.*

VALUE: £20–30 *Miniature* £30–40

325A. QUEEN ALEXANDRA'S IMPERIAL MILITARY NURSING SERVICE RESERVE CAPE BADGE

Date: 1907–50
Branch of Service: Queen Alexandra's Imperial Military Nursing Service Reserve.
Ribbon: Black with two narrow outer white stripes and two inner scarlet stripes.
Metal: Silver.
Size: 38mm.
Description: A uniface ring containing a prominent "R" surmounted by a Tudor crown fitted to a plain ring for suspension. The ring is inscribed in raised lettering QUEEN ALEXANDRA'S IMPERIAL MILITARY NURSING SERVICE RESERVE.
Comments: *The cape badge was instituted in 1907 and was used until 1950 when the QAIMNS(R) was incorporated into the QARTANC. It was worn on the right breast on ward dress for commissioned (qualified) nurses. It was issued through stores to each individual.*

VALUE: £20–30   *Miniature*   £30–40

326. TERRITORIAL FORCE NURSING SERVICE CAPE BADGE

Date: 1907–21.
Branch of Service: Territorial Force Nursing Service.
Ribbon: Scarlet with a narrow central white stripe.
Metal: Silver.
Size: Oval 50mm by 34mm
Description: A uniface oval ring surmounted by a Tudor crown attached to a plain ring for suspension. The ring has at the centre two ornamental letters "A" interlocking and set at an angle. The ring is inscribed in raised lettering: TERRITORIAL FORCE NURSING SERVICE.
Comments: *The cape badge was instituted in 1907 and was used until 1921 when the TFNS was renamed the TANS. It was worn on the right breast on ward dress for commissioned (qualified) nurses. It was issued through stores to each individual.*

VALUE: £25–£35   *Miniature*   £20–30

326A. QUEEN ALEXANDRA'S MILITARY FAMILIES NURSING SERVICE CAPE BADGE

Date: 1921–26.
Branch of Service: Queen Alexandra's Military Families Nursing Service.
Ribbon: Black with a wide central scarlet stripe.
Metal: Silver.
Size: Oval 44mm by 34mm
Description: A uniface oval ring containing an ornamental cypher of Queen Alexandra surmounted by a Tudor crown. Three plain rings are attached to the outer edge of the circle for suspension. The ring is inscribed in raised lettering: QUEEN ALEXANDRA'S MILITARY FAMILIES NURSING SERVICE.
Comments: *The cape badge was instituted in 1921 upon formation of the QAMFNS, and was used until 1926 when the QAMFNS was incorporated into the QARANC. It was worn on the right breast on ward dress for commissioned (qualified) nurses. It was issued through stores to each individual.*

VALUE: £20–£30   *Miniature* £20–30

326B. TERRITORIAL ARMY NURSING SERVICE CAPE BADGE

Date: 1921–50.
Branch of Service: Territorial Army Nursing Service.
Ribbon: Scarlet with a narrow central white stripe.
Metal: Silver.
Size: Oval 38mm by 28mm
Description: A uniface oval ring surmounted by a Tudor crown attached to a plain ring for suspension. The ring has at the centre two ornamental letters "A" interlocking and set at an angle. The ring is inscribed in raised lettering: TERRITORIAL ARMY NURSING SERVICE. Beneath, an ornate scroll bearing the Latin inscription: FORTITUDO MEA DEUS.
Comments: *The cape badge was instituted in 1921 upon the formation of the TANS and was used until 1950 when the TANS was incorporated into the QARANC. It was worn on the right breast on ward dress for commissioned (qualified) nurses. It was issued through stores to each individual.*

VALUE: £20–£30   *Miniature* £20–30

326C. QUEEN ALEXANDRA'S ROYAL ARMY NURSING CORPS CAPE BADGE

Date: 1949.
Branch of Service: Queen Alexandra's Royal Army Nursing Corps.
Ribbon: Scarlet with two white outer stripes and two black inner stripes.
Metal: Silver.
Size: Oval 46mm by 32mm.
Description: A uniface oval ring containing the Cross of the Order of the Dannebrog, with an ornamental cypher of Queen Alexandra, surmounted by a Tudor crown, fitted with a plain ring for suspension. The oval ring is inscribed in raised lettering QUEEN ALEXANDRA'S ROYAL ARMY NURSING COPRS.
Comments: *The cape badge was instituted in 1949 and continues to be issued today to all commissioned (qualified) nurses in the QARANC. It is worn on the right breast on ward dress for both female and, since 1992, male commissioned (qualified) nurses. It is issued through stores to each individual.*

VALUE: £20–30   *Miniature* £30–40

327. INDIAN TITLE BADGE

1st Class

2nd Class

3rd Class

Instituted: 12 December 1911.
Ribbon: Light blue edged with dark blue (1st class); red edged with dark red (2nd class); or dark blue edged with light blue (3rd class).
Metal: Silver or silver-gilt.
Size: Height 58mm; max. width 45mm.
Description: A radiate star topped by an imperial crown with a curved laurel wreath below the crown and cutting across the top of a central medallion surrounded by a collar inscribed with the appropriate title. The medallion bears the crowned profile of King George V or King George VI. From the first issue of King George V's Title Badge on June 1, 1912 until 1933, his bust faced right. As from June 1, 1933 his bust faced left for the remainder of the reign. King George VI's Title Badges had his bust facing left. (Reverse) plain, but engraved with the name of the recipient.
Comments: *Introduced by King George V on the occasion of the Delhi Durbar of 1911 and awarded in three classes to civilians and Viceroy's commissioned officers of the Indian Army for faithful service or acts of public welfare. Recipients proceeded from the lowest grade to higher grades, each accompanied by a distinctive title. Each grade was issued in Hindu and Muslim versions, differing in title: Diwan Bahadur (Muslim) or Sardar Bahadur (Hindu), Khan Bahadur (Muslim) or Rai or Rao Bahadur (Hindu) and Khan Sahib (Muslim) or Rai or Rao Sahib (Hindu), in descending order of grade. These title badges took precedence after all British and Indian orders and decorations, and before campaign medals. In miniatures (at least) the George VI versions, which all have his bust facing right, are rarer than those of King George V which have a left-facing bust.*

VALUE:

Diwan Bahadur	£100–150
Sardar Bahadur	£100–150
Khan Bahadur	£85–120
Rao Bahadur	£85–120
Khan Sahib	£85–120
Rao Sahib	£85–120
Miniatures	
King George V	£50–65
King George VI	£70–85

328. BADGES OF HONOUR (AFRICAN COUNTRIES)

Instituted: 1922.

Ribbon: Plain yellow, 38mm (neck) or 32mm (breast).

Metal: Bronze.

Size: 65mm x 48mm (neck); 45mm x 33mm (breast).

Description: Oval badges with a raised rim of laurel leaves terminating at the top in an imperial crown flanked by two lions. (Obverse) a crowned effigy of the reigning monarch; (reverse) the crowned cypher of the monarch or some emblem symbolic of the particular country with the country name in the exergue.

Comments: *The badge accompanied a certificate of honour awarded to chiefs and other persons of non-European descent who had rendered loyal and valuable service to the government of the territory. The original award was a neck badge suspended by a ribbon, but from 1954 onwards recipients were given the option of taking the award as a neck or breast badge. These awards were quite distinct from the decorations known as the Native Chiefs Medals (see number 70). They were first awarded to Ugandans but later extended to 14 other British territories in East and West Africa as well as the three High Commisson territories in Southern Africa. In particular the Badges issued for Nyasaland under Elizabeth II are rare, as Nyasaland became a Federation with Rhodesia in 1957. They are believed to have fallen into abeyance in the early 1980s.*

VALUE:

George V	£250–350
George VI	£175–250
Elizabeth II (neck)	£150–200
Elizabeth II (breast)	£150–200

329. BADGES OF HONOUR (NON-AFRICAN COUNTRIES)

Instituted: 1926.

Ribbon: 38mm watered silk mustard yellow.

Metal: Silver gilt.

Size: 41mm (George VI) or 32 mm (Elizabeth II).

Description: Circular with a raised rim of laurel leaves bearing a ring for suspension. (Obverse) crowned effigy of the reigning monarch; (reverse) the emblem of the country with the name round the foot.

Comments: *These medals accompanied certificates of honour awarded to indigenous persons who had rendered valuable service to the colony or protectorate. These awards appear to have been in abeyance since the early 1980s. Exceptionally, the New Hebrides badge was awarded to three British officers (Colonel (now General Lord) Guthrie (of Craigiebank), Lieutenant-Colonel C. H. C. Howgill, RM and HRH the Duke of Gloucester) in connection with the "Coconut War" in July 1980 instead of a campaign medal. The reverse types show the badges of 28 colonies or protectorate.*

VALUE:

George V	£300–400
George VI	£300–400
Elizabeth II	£350–450

Miniature £70–90 (only New Hebrides known)

330. NAVAL ENGINEER'S GOOD CONDUCT MEDAL

Instituted: 1842.
Ribbon: Originally plain dark blue but later broad blue with white edges.
Metal: Silver.
Size: 35mm.
Description: (Obverse) a two-masted paddle steamer with a trident in the exergue; (reverse) a circular cable cartouche enclosing a crowned fouled anchor and the legend FOR ABILITY AND GOOD CONDUCT. Between the cable and the rim the details of the recipient were engraved round the circumference. Considering the rarity of the award, it is even more remarkable that the medals have several unique features. Shaw's medal, for example, had oak leaves in the exergue, flanking the trident, but this feature was omitted from later medals. Medals have been recorded with a straight bar suspender, a steel clip and ring suspender or fixed ring suspension with one or two intermediate rings.
Comments: *This medal was abolished five years after it was instituted, only seven medals being awarded in that period: to William Shaw (1842), William Dunkin (1842), William Johnstone (1843), John Langley (1843), J.P. Rundle (1845), George Roberts (1845) and Samuel B. Meredith (1846). Restrikes were produced in 1875 and at a later date. The original medals have a grooved rim, the 1875 restrikes a diagonal grained rim and the later restrikes a plain, flat rim.*
VALUE:

Original	Rare
1875 restrike	£125–150
Later restrike	£80–100

331. INDIAN RECRUITING BADGE (GEORGE V)

Instituted: 1917.
Ribbon: Plain dark green.
Metal: Bronze.
Size: Height 45mm; max. width 48mm.
Description: A five-pointed star with ball finials, surmounted by a wreathed gilt medallion bearing a left-facing crowned bust of King George V, inscribed FOR RECRUITING WORK DURING THE WAR.
Comments: *Awarded to Indian officers and NCOs engaged in recruitment of troops. It could only be worn in uniform when attending durbars or state functions, but at any time in plain clothes.*

VALUE: George V £80–100 *Miniature* £50–60

332. INDIAN RECRUITING BADGE (GEORGE VI)

Instituted: 1940.
Ribbon: Emerald green divided into three sections interspersed by narrow stripes of red (left) and yellow (right).
Metal: Silver and bronze.
Size: Height 42mm; max. width 39mm.
Description: A multi-rayed silver breast badge surmounted by an imperial crown with a suspension ring fitted through the top of the crown. In the centre is superimposed a bronze medallion bearing the left-facing crowned profile of King George VI, within a collar inscribed FOR RECRUITING.
Comments: *Awarded to selected civilian and military pensioners, full-time members of the Indian Recruiting Organisation, fathers and mothers having at least three children in the armed services, and wives having a husband and at least two children serving in the defence forces.*

VALUE: George VI £50–60 *Miniature* £60–70

333. NAVAL GOOD SHOOTING MEDAL

Instituted: August 1902.
Ribbon: Dark blue with a red central stripe edged in white.
Metal: Silver.
Size: 36mm.
Description: (Obverse) the effigy of the reigning monarch; (reverse) a nude figure of Neptune holding five thunderbolts in each hand. In the background can be seen the bows of a trireme and the heads of three horses, with a trident in the field. The Latin motto VICTORIA CURAM AMAT (Victory loves care) appears round the circumference. Fitted with a straight suspension bar. The recipient's name, number, rank, ship and calibre of gun are impressed round the rim.
Comments: *Instituted to promote excellent gunnery performances in the annual Fleet Competitions, it was first awarded in 1903 but was discontinued in 1914. Subsequent success was marked by the issue of a clasp bearing the name of the ship and the date. A total of 974 medals and 62 bars were awarded. 53 men received one bar, three men got two bars and only one achieved three bars.*

VALUE:		Miniature
Edward VII	£300–400	£60–70 (in silver)
George V	£300–400	£60–70 „
With 1 bar	£600–800	

334. ARMY BEST SHOT MEDAL

Instituted: 30 April 1869.
Ribbon: Watered crimson with black, white (or buff*) and black stripes at the edges. *The Regulations state that the stripes should be white but recent medals have been issued with buff stripes.*
Metal: Silver.
Size: 36mm.
Description: (Obverse) the veiled diademmed profile of Queen Victoria; (reverse) Victory bestowing a laurel crown on a naked warrior armed with a quiver of arrows and a bow and holding a target, impaled with arrows, in his other hand. Fitted with a straight suspension bar.
Comments: *This medal, sometimes referred to as the Queen's Medal, was awarded annually to the champion in the Army marksmanship contests held at Bisley. It was originally struck in bronze but was upgraded to silver in 1872. The award ceased in 1882 but was revived in 1923 and thereafter known as the King's Medal. The original reverse was retained, with the appropriate effigy of the reigning sovereign on the obverse. Since 1953 it has been known as the Queen's Medal again. In the post-1923 medals a bar bears the year of the award, with additional year clasps for subsequent awards. Until 1934 a single medal was awarded each year but in 1935 two medals were granted for the champion shots of the Regular and Territorial Armies respectively. Subsequently additional medals have been sanctioned for award to the military forces of India, Canada, Australia, New Zealand, Ceylon, Rhodesia, the British South Africa Police, the Union of South Africa, Pakistan, Jamaica and Ghana.*

VALUE:		Miniature
Victoria bronze	Rare	—
Victoria silver	Rare	—
George V	£1000–1200	£30–40
George VI	£1000–1200	£30–40
Elizabeth II	£1000–1200	£15–20

335. QUEEN'S MEDAL FOR CHAMPION SHOTS OF THE ROYAL NAVY AND ROYAL MARINES

Instituted: 12 June 1953.
Ribbon: Dark blue with a broad red central stripe flanked by white stripes.
Metal: Silver.
Size: 36mm.
Description: (Obverse) the effigy of Queen Elizabeth II; (reverse) Neptune (as on the Naval Good Shooting Medal).
Comments: *Instituted as the naval counterpart of the Army best shot medal with a bar which bears the year of the award.*

VALUE:

Elizabeth II	£1000–1200	*Miniature*	£15–20

336. QUEEN'S MEDAL FOR CHAMPION SHOTS OF THE ROYAL AIR FORCE

Instituted: 12 June 1953.
Ribbon: Broad crimson centre flanked by dark blue stripes bisected by thin light blue stripes.
Metal: Silver.
Size: 36mm.
Description: (Obverse) the effigy of Queen Elizabeth II; (reverse) Hermes kneeling on a flying hawk and holding the caduceus in one hand and a javelin in the other. The medal is fitted with a straight bar suspender. A date clasp is attached to the ribbon.
Comments: *Competed for at the annual RAF Small Arms Meeting at Bisley. The medal was issued to the Champion Shot of the RNZAF under the terms of the same Royal Warrant as the RAF.*

VALUE:

Elizabeth II	£1000–1200	*Miniature*	£15–20

337. QUEEN'S MEDAL FOR CHAMPION SHOTS OF THE NEW ZEALAND NAVAL FORCES

Instituted: 9 July 1958.
Ribbon: Crimson centre bordered with white and broad dark blue stripes at the edges.
Metal: Silver.
Size: 36mm.
Description: (Obverse) the effigy of Queen Elizabeth II; (reverse) similar to that of the Naval Good Shooting Medal of 1903-14. Fitted with a clasp bearing the year of the award and a straight suspension bar.
Comments: *Awards were made retrospective to 1 January 1955. This medal is awarded for marksmanship in an annual contest of the New Zealand Naval Forces. Additional clasps are granted for further success. One contestant, Lt Cdr N. C. G. Peach, RNZN, has won this award ten times*

VALUE:

Elizabeth II	—	*Miniature*	£30–40

338. UNION OF SOUTH AFRICA COMMEMORATION MEDAL

Instituted: 1910.

Ribbon: 38mm orange-yellow with a broad central dark blue stripe.

Metal: Silver.

Size: 36mm.

Description: (Obverse) the uncrowned effigy of King George V; (reverse) Mercury as God of Commerce and Prosperity, bending over an anvil, forging the links of a chain symbolic of the uniting of the four colonies (Cape Colony, Natal, Orange Free State and the Transvaal), with the date 1910 in the exergue and the legend TO COMMEMORATE THE UNION OF SOUTH AFRICA.

Comments: *This was the first medal struck in the reign of George V and resulted from the South Africa Act of 1909. This Act proclaimed the unification on 31 May 1910, of the self-governing four colonies into a legislative Union, becoming provinces of the Union of South Africa. This medal, the obverse of which was designed by Sir Bertram MacKennal, and the reverse by Mr Sydney Marsh, was struck to mark the opening of the first Parliament of the Union by HRH the Duke of Connaught. Awarded to those who took part in the inauguration of the Parliament. Additionally it was also awarded to certain officers and men of HMS Balmoral Castle, a Union Castle liner specially commissioned as a man-of-war to convey HRH the Duke of Connaught as the King's representative to South Africa for the celebrations. A total of 551 medals were struck by the Royal Mint, and were issued unnamed, although privately named medals are in existence.*

VALUE:		
Named	£250–300
Unnamed	£150–200
Miniature	£20–30

339. DEKORATIE VOOR TROUWE DIENST

The other side is similar to no. 340 illustrated opposite

Instituted: 1920.

Ribbon: A broad dark blue central stripe flanked on one side by a gold stripe with a thin red stripe superimposed towards the edge, and on the other side by a yellow stripe with a thin white stripe towards the edge. Transvaal recipients wore the ribbon with the red to the centre of the chest; Orange Free State recipients wore the ribbon with the white stripe to the centre of the chest.

Metal: Silver.

Size: 36mm.

Description: (Obverse) the arms of the Transvaal; (reverse) the arms of the Orange Free State. Fitted with a fixed suspender. Recipients wore the medal with the appropriate state arms showing.

Comments: *This medal which is correctly named the Dekoratie Voor Trouwe Dienst was awarded by the Union of South Africa to officers of the two former Boer republics for distinguished service during the Second Boer War of 1899-1902. Awards to officers and men of the former Boer Republics had to be individually claimed on prescribed forms and were named with rank, initials and surname of the individual. The late Don Forsyth published a roll listing full names and commandos/units of the recipients. This clearly identifies many recipients but cannot differentiate, for example, between any of the 10 issued ABO medals that were named "Burger P. J. Botha". However, the naming style and type of suspender can help to make positive identification possible.*

Medals issued up to October 1937 had a WWI British War Medal (MYB168) suspender and typical SA Mint WWI naming. Between October 1937 and February 1942 the WWI suspender was still used, but the naming was thinner, in a slightly smaller font as on the WWII Africa Service Medal (MYB 189). All subsequent issues have the WWII style naming as well as the "thick-necked" suspender as found on the Africa Service Medal (for details and illustrations see the article by Hent Loots in the OMRS Miscellany of Honours, No. 9, 1992). By comparing the dates on the Medal Application Forms of men with the same initials and surname a particular recipient can sometimes be pinpointed. NB Please note that these medals are often found with the suspender claw flattened to varying degrees: the SA Mint, on occasion, used rather crude methods to "fix" the pin.

VALUE:				
Silver (591)	£750–£900		
Paired with matching MYB340	£1100-1500	*Miniature*	£60–70

340. ANGLO-BOERE OORLOG (WAR) MEDAL

Instituted: 1920.

Ribbon: Broad green and yellow stripes with three narrow stripes of red, white and dark blue in the centre. Transvaal recipients wore the ribbon with the green to the centre of the chest, while Orange Free State recipients wore it with the yellow towards the centre.

Metal: Silver.

Size: 36mm.

Description: Both sides inscribed ANGLO-BOERE OORLOG round the top, with the dates 1899-1902 round the foot. Medallions set in a border of a square and quatrefoil show the arms of the Orange Free State on one side and the Transvaal on the other. The medal was worn with the side showing the arms of the appropriate state uppermost. Fitted with a fixed suspender.

Comments: *Correctly named the Anglo-Boere Oorlog Medal, this was awarded by the Union government to officers and men of the former Boer republics for loyal service in the war against the British. To qualify for the medal proof had to be provided that they had fought against the British without surrendering or taking parole or the oath of allegiance prior to May 31, 1902. See note on no. 339 regarding awards to men of the former Boer Republics.*

VALUE: Silver   £120–150   *Miniature*   £60–70

Lint Voor Wonden (Wound Ribbon) Certificate value: £30; if with corresponding medal: value: £50.

341. COMMONWEALTH INDEPENDENCE MEDALS

Pakistan Independence Medal

For the various ribbons see charts.

Since the partition of the Indian sub-continent in 1947 and the emergence of the Dominions of India and Pakistan, it has been customary for medals to be issued to mark the attainment of independence. As these medals are invariably awarded to British service personnel taking part in the independence ceremonies, they are appended here in chronological order of institution, the date of the actual award, where later, being given in parentheses. These medals usually have symbolic motifs with the date of independence inscribed. The distinctive ribbons are noted alongside. All are 32mm wide unless otherwise stated.

India 1947 (1948) Three equal stripes of orange, white and green

Pakistan 1947 (1950) Dark green with a central thin white stripe

Ghana 1957 Nine alternating stripes of red, yellow and green

Nigeria 1960 (1964) Three equal stripes of green, white and green

Sierra Leone 1961 Three equal stripes of green, white and blue

Jamaica 1962 Black centre flanked by yellow stripes and green edges

Uganda 1962 (1963) Six stripes of black, yellow, red, black, yellow, red

Kenya 1963 Green with two equal red stripes towards the edges

Malawi 1964 Three equal stripes of black, red and green

Guyana 1966 Red centre flanked by yellow stripes and broad green edges. The green and yellow separated (left) by a thin black stripe and (right) by a thin pale blue stripe

Swaziland 1968 Three equal stripes of red, yellow and blue

Fiji 1970 Grey-blue with bars half red, half white, towards each end

Papua New Guinea 1975 Red bordered by thin stripes of yellow and white, with black edges

Solomon Islands 1978 Five equal stripes of blue, yellow, white, yellow and green

Gilbert Islands (Kiribati) 1980 Half red, half black, separated by a thin white stripe, and edged in yellow

Ellice Islands (Tuvalu) 1980 Equal stripes of red, white and red edged yellow. the white stripe bisected by a thin blue stripe

Zimbabwe 1980 Silver or bronze 38mm black centre flanked by red and yellow stripes with edges of green or blue

Vanuatu 1980 (1981) 30mm stripes of red and green with central thinner stripe of yellow edged by black

St Christopher, Nevis and Anguilla 1983 Bars of green (left) and red (right) with a black central bar having two thin white stripes, flanked by yellow stripes

VALUE: From £10   *Miniature*   £10–100

342. MALTA GEORGE CROSS FIFTIETH ANNIVERSARY COMMEMORATIVE MEDAL

Instituted: 1992.

Ribbon: Dark blue with central stripes of white and red (the Maltese national colours).

Metal: Cupro-nickel.

Size: 36mm.

Description: (Obverse) the crowned arms of the island, which include the George Cross in the upper left corner, with the date 1992 at the foot. (Reverse) a replica of the George Cross with the eight-pointed Maltese Cross at the top and the date 1942 at the foot, with a legend BHALA SHIEDA TA'EROIZMU U DEDIKAZZJONI on one side and TO BEAR WITNESS TO HEROISM AND DEVOTION on the other. Suspension is by a fixed bar decorated with laurels, attached to a ring.

Comments: *Sanctioned by the government of Malta to celebrate the fiftieth anniversary of the award of the George Cross by King George VI to the island for its heroic resistance to prolonged Axis attack during the Second World War. The medal has been awarded to surviving veterans who served in Malta in the armed forces and auxiliary services between 10 June 1940 and 8 September 1943. Permission for British citizens to wear this medal was subsequently granted by the Queen. As a number of veterans applied for the medal after the cut-off date of 15 April 1994, the Maltese Government sanctioned a second striking—these medals carry the word COPY below the right arm of the George Cross.*

VALUE:

Cupro-nickel (original striking)	£90–120	*Miniature* £15–20
Official copy	£50–60	

343. SHANGHAI VOLUNTEER CORPS MEDAL

Date: 1854

Ribbon:

Metal: Silver.

Size: 38mm

Description:

Comment: *Awarded to the officers and men of the Shanghai Volunteers who took part in the battle of Soo Chow Creek (also known as the battle of Muddy Flats) which took place in April 28, 1854. Examples are of the greatest rarity and the last one to appear at auction was sold in 1991. Further details are sought.*

VALUE: £800–850

344. SHANGHAI JUBILEE MEDAL

Instituted: 1893.

Ribbon: Watered silk half bright red, half white or red with 4mm central white stripe.

Metal: Silver or bronze.

Size: 36mm.

Description: (Obverse) triple-shield arms of the municipality surrounded by a band with thistles, shamrocks and roses round the foot and NOVEMBER 17 1843 round the top. (Reverse) a scrolled shield with the words SHANGHAI JUBILEE and NOVEMBER 17 1843 and inscribed diagonally across the centre with the recipient's name in block capitals. The shield is flanked by Chinese dragons and above is a steamship and the sun setting on the horizon. The rim is engraved "Presented by the Shanghai Municipality". Issued with a small suspension ring, but often replaced by a straight bar. This medal has also been recorded with an ornamental silver brooch bearing the dates 1843–1893.

Comments: *The British settlement in Shanghai was founded in 1843 and formed the nucleus of the International Settlement established in 1854 under the control of an autonomous Municipal Council. In effect the International Settlement functioned as an autonomous City State administered by a Municipal Committee formed from those nations comprising the Settlement. This was abolished when Shanghai was overrun by Imperial Japanese troops in 1941.*

VALUE:

Silver (625)	£250–300
Bronze (100)	£250–300

345. SHANGHAI FIRE BRIGADE LONG SERVICE MEDAL

Instituted: Before 1904.
Ribbon: Black with broad crimson borders.
Metal: Silver.
Size: 31mm.
Description: (Obverse) an armorial device featuring a Chinese dragon standing on a symbolic high-rise building on which is displayed a flame on a pole crossed by a hook and ladder, with MIH-HO-LOONG SHANGHAI round the top and the motto "Say the word and down comes your house" round the foot; (reverse) engraved with recipient's details. It seems strange that no Chinese characters appear on the medal. Ring and double claw suspension, with a broad silver brooch bar at the top of the ribbon.
Comment: *Awarded for a minimum of twelve years regular service with the Municipal Fire Brigade. The award was presumably in abeyance following the Japanese invasion in 1937 and the wholesale destruction of the international commercial metropolis.*

VALUE: £300–350

346. SHANGHAI VOLUNTEER FIRE BRIGADE LONG SERVICE MEDAL

Instituted: 1904.
Ribbon: Red with white edges.
Metal: Gold, silver or bronze.
Size: 36mm.
Description: (Obverse) the arms and motto of the Municipality surrounded by a collar inscribed SHANGHAI VOLUNTEER FIRE BRIGADE ESTABLISHED 1866. (Reverse) originally simply engraved with name of unit, later a pair of crossed axes surmounted by a fireman's helmet under which is a horizontal tablet on which are engraved the recipient's dates of service. Round the circumference is inscribed FOR LONG SERVICE (top) and WE FIGHT THE FLAMES (foot) with quatrefoil ornaments separating the two inscriptions. Fitted with a swivelling scroll suspender.
Comments: *The medal in silver was awarded to members of the Volunteer Fire Brigade for five years service, for eight years service a clasp was added to the ribbon and for 12 years service the medal was awarded in gold. Bronze medals exist but are believed to have been specimens only.*

VALUE: £475–550

347. SHANGHAI VOLUNTEER CORPS LONG SERVICE MEDAL

Instituted: 1921.
Ribbon: Equal stripes of red, white and blue, the red bisected by a thin green stripe, the white by black and the blue by yellow.
Metal: Silver.
Size: 36mm.
Description: (Obverse) an eight-pointed radiate star bearing a scroll at the top inscribed 4th APRIL 1854. The arms of the Municipality superimposed on the star and surrounded by a collar inscribed SHANGHAI VOLUNTEER CORPS. Round the foot of the medal is a band inscribed FOR LONG SERVICE. (Reverse) plain, engraved with the name of the recipient and his period of service.
Comments: *The Volunteer Corps was raised in 1853 to protect the British and other foreign settlements. The date on the scroll alludes to the Corps' first engagement, the Battle of Muddy Flat. The Corps was cosmopolitan in structure, although the British element predominated. It was disbanded in September 1942, nine months after the Japanese overran the International Settlement. Awarded for 12 years good service. The last medal was awarded in 1941.*

VALUE: £300–350　　　*Miniature* £90–100

303

348. SHANGHAI MUNICIPAL POLICE DISTINGUISHED CONDUCT MEDAL

Instituted: 1924.
Ribbon: Red with a central blue stripe (1st class); red with a blue stripe at each edge (2nd class).
Metal: Silver or bronze.
Size: 36mm.
Description: (Obverse) arms of the Municipality and the inscription SHANGHAI MUNICIPAL POLICE; (reverse) the words FOR DISTINGUISHED CONDUCT. The recipient's name and rank were engraved around the rim.
Comments: *Awarded to officers and men of the Municipal Police in two classes, distinguished solely by their ribbons and the metal used (silver or bronze). A sliding clasp was fitted to the ribbon to denote a second award; this featured the Municipal crest and was engraved on the reverse with the details of the award. It is believed that a total of 223 medals were awarded up to 1942, including 72 to foreign members of the force.*

VALUE: Silver   £850–1000
        Bronze   £650–750

349. SHANGHAI MUNICIPAL POLICE LONG SERVICE MEDAL

Instituted: 1925.
Ribbon: Brown with a central yellow stripe edged in white.
Metal: Silver.
Size: 36mm.
Description: (Obverse) arms of the Municipality within a collar inscribed SHANGHAI MUNICIPAL POLICE; (reverse) plain apart from the inscription FOR LONG SERVICE in two lines across the centre. The recipient's name and rank were engraved round the rim in upper and lower case lettering. Awards to Indians were named in cursive script with the Hindi equivalent alongside. Fitted with a swivelling scroll suspender.
Comments: *Awarded for 12 years good service in the Shanghai Municipal Police, an international force composed largely of Sikhs, Chinese and White Russians as well as British ex-soldiers and policemen. Dated clasps for further five year periods of service were awarded. The medal was abolished in 1942.*

VALUE:		*Miniature*
Without clasp	£300–350	£45–50
With clasp	£400–500	£50–60
2 clasps	£500–600	£60–70

350. SHANGHAI MUNICIPAL POLICE (SPECIALS) LONG SERVICE MEDAL

Instituted: 1929.
Ribbon: Dark brown with three white bars, each bisected by a thin yellow stripe.
Metal: Silver.
Size: 36mm.
Description: (Obverse) the arms of the Municipality with the motto OMNIA JUNCTA IN UNO (all joined in one) round the circumference. (Reverse) inscribed SHANGHAI MUNICIPAL POLICE (SPECIALS) FOR LONG SERVICE in six lines. A unique award to A.L. Anderson (1930) was inscribed on the reverse FOR DISTINGUISHED AND VALUABLE SERVICES.
Comments: *Awarded for 12 years active and efficient service in the Special Constabulary. Some 52 medals and 8 clasps for additional service are recorded in the* Shanghai Gazette, *but the actual number awarded was probably greater. The medal was discontinued in 1942.*

VALUE:
    Without clasp   £450–500   With clasp   Very rare
    Miniature   £200–250

351. SHANGHAI MUNICIPAL COUNCIL EMERGENCY MEDAL

Instituted: 1937.
Ribbon: 38mm bright red, having a broad white central stripe bordered black and yellow edges separated from the red by thin black stripes.
Metal: Bronze.
Size: 40mm.
Description: An eight-pointed star with ring suspension. (Obverse) a central medallion superimposed on the radiate star with the triple-shield arms of the Municipality surrounded by a collar inscribed SHANGHAI MUNICIPAL COUNCIL. (Reverse) a laurel wreath enclosing the words FOR SERVICES RENDERED - AUGUST 12 TO NOVEMBER 12 1937.
Comments: *Awarded to members of the Police, Volunteer Corps, Fire Brigade and civilians for services during the emergency of August-November 1937 when fighting between the Chinese and Japanese in and around Shanghai threatened to encroach on the International Settlement. Issued unnamed, but accompanied by a certificate bearing the name and unit of the recipient. Examples have been seen with the recipient's name engraved on the reverse.*

VALUE:　　　£150–170　　　*Miniature*　　£60–80

351A. CHINESE MARITIME CUSTOMS SERVICE FINANCIAL MEDAL

Obverse

Instituted:
Ribbon: Green, with yellow stripes.
Metal: Gold, silver or bronze according to class.
Size:
Description: An eight-pointed radiate star suspended by a plain ring, having an oval medallion on the obverse inscribed in Chinese and depicting a Chinese junk; (reverse) a horseshoe scroll inscribed THE CHINESE MARITIME CUSTOMS MEDAL with FINANCIAL across the foot. The recipient's name was engraved in the centre.
Comments: *The Chinese Maritime Customs Service was operated and largely staffed at the higher levels by British personnel from 1854 till 1950. Medals were awarded for five years' service or shorter service of exceptional merit and were granted in three classes, each of three grades, making nine variations in all, distinguished by the respective metals, and awarded according to the rank of the recipient.*

VALUE:　　　—　　　*Miniature*　　£90–100

351B. CHINESE MARITIME CUSTOMS SERVICE MERITORIOUS SERVICE MEDAL

Reverse

Instituted:
Ribbon: Green with yellow stripes.
Metal: Gold, silver or bronze according to grade.
Size:
Description: As above, but FOR MERITORIOUS SERVICE in the tablet on the reverse.
Comments: *Awarded for 25 years continuous service, according to the rank of the recipient, but later awards in silver or gold could be made on promotion to a higher rank, or for exceptional service, notably from 1931 onwards, following the outbreak of hostilities with Japan.*

VALUE:　　　—

352. AUTOMOBILE ASSOCIATION SERVICE CROSS

Date: 1956.
Ribbon: Yellow with three narrow black stripes.
Metal: Silver.
Size: 36mm.
Description: A silver cross flory terminating in scrolls, with the AA emblem surmounted in the centre.
Comments: *Established in commemoration of the Association's Golden Jubilee, the Cross is the highest award to AA patrolmen and other uniformed members of staff for conspicuous acts of bravery involving an imminent risk of personal injury whilst on duty in uniform, or whilst engaged in an action related to duty. To date only 15 crosses have been awarded. A monetary reward accompanies the Cross.*

VALUE: —

353. AUTOMOBILE ASSOCIATION SERVICE MEDAL

Date: 1956.
Ribbon: Half yellow, half black.
Metal: Silver.
Size: 36mm.
Description: A circular medal in the form of the AA badge with wings sprouting from the top and flanking a claw and ring suspension. (Obverse) AA superimposed on a wheel, with the inscription AUTOMOBILE ASSOCIATION/SERVICE MEDAL round the circumference; (reverse) details of the award.
Clasp: A silver-gilt and red enamel clasp inscribed 192064 (ie. 20 years good driving, 1964) has been reported.
Comments: *Like the Cross, the Medal of the Association was instituted in commemoration of the Association's Golden Jubilee. The medal is awarded to members of the uniformed staff for courageous or outstanding initiative and devotion to duty. To date, only 60 medals have been awarded, including four in 1997, mainly for life-saving and bravery in accidents. A monetary reward accompanies the Medal. A Service Citation is also awarded for lesser acts, a total of 63 having been bestowed so far.*

VALUE: —

354. SUFFRAGETTE MEDAL

Instituted: 1909.
Campaign: Votes for women.
Ribbon: Three equal stripes of purple, silver and green.
Metal: Silver.
Size: 20mm.
Clasps: A silver dated bar, or an enamelled bar in the WSPU colours with the date on the reverse, or prison bars surmounted by a broad arrow.
Description: A small silver medal suspended by a ring from a bar with scrolled finials, engraved with the date of the award. A similarly scrolled brooch bar at the top of the ribbon is inscribed FOR VALOUR. The plain medal is engraved HUNGER STRIKE in various styles and hallmarked.
Comments: *This medal was awarded by the Women's Social and Political Union (WSPU) to those militant Suffragettes who were imprisoned for various acts of violence and who went on hunger strike while in prison. At first they were forcibly fed under the most barbaric conditions, as a result of which several died. The government then introduced the Cat and Mouse Act, whereby hunger strikers at the point of death were released, but were then re-arrested and returned to prison when they had recovered sufficiently from their ordeal. A silver bar was awarded to those who were imprisoned and went on hunger strike whilst an enamel bar was awarded to those who were force fed in prison. The portcullis badge was given to those imprisoned in Holloway and is occasionally seen separately from the medal.*

VALUE: £3500–£4000 (unboxed)
£6000–£7500 (in personally inscribed case)

355. FLORENCE NIGHTINGALE MEDAL

Date: 1912.
Ribbon: White with narrow yellow and broad red stripes towards the edges.
Metal: Silver with enamels.
Size:
Description: An upright elliptical medal coming to a point at both ends, with a three-quarter length portrait of Florence Nightingale from the Crimean War period, inscribed MEMORIAM FLORENCE NIGHTINGALE 1820–1910 AD. The reverse bears the recipient's name.
Comments: *Instituted by the International Committee of the Red Cross for award to trained nurses, matrons, nursing organisers or voluntary aids for distinguished or exceptional service. Awards are made every other year on the anniversary of Miss Nightingale's birthday. This medal has been awarded very sparingly.*

VALUE: £500–700   *Miniature*   £400–500

356. ANZAC COMMEMORATIVE MEDAL

Date: 1967.
Ribbon: None.
Metal: Bronze.
Size: 76mm x 50mm.
Description: (Obverse) a medallion surmounted by a Royal Crown with a laurel wreath and the word ANZAC in a scroll below. In the field is the date 1915 above a picture of John Simpson and his donkey saving a wounded soldier at Gallipoli (based on a painting by 4/26A Spr Horace Moore-Jones, NZ Engineers. (Reverse) a map of Australia and New Zealand with the Southern Cross constellation. The reverse of the scroll has New Zealand fern leaves.
Comments: *This medal was instituted jointly by the governments of Australia and New Zealand and awarded to surviving veterans of the Australian and New Zealand Army Corps who served in the Gallipoli campaign, all named on the reverse. Designed by Australian artist Raymond Ewers. There is also a half-size lapel badge bearing the obverse design and is numbered on the reverse.*

307

VALUE: Medal   £100–150   Lapel badge   £50–60

357. NEW ZEALAND CADET DISTRICT MEDAL

Date: 1902.
Ribbon: Plain khaki or tan with a central pink flanked by dark green stripes.
Metal: Silver.
Size: 32mm.
Description: (Obverse) profile of Edward VII or George V with inscription FOR KING AND COUNTRY: PUBLIC SCHOOL CADETS, N.Z.; (reverse) DEFENCE NOT DEFIANCE round the top, with DISTRICT PRIZE (or CHALLENGE) MEDAL AWARDED TO in three lines, leaving space for the name of the recipient to be engraved below.
Comments: *These medals were instituted folllowing the establishment of the Public School Cadets in 1902 and were awarded in two classes in Challenge competitions or as prizes in the annual examinations.*

VALUE: District Challenge   £100–150
             District Prize   £90–100

For the sake of continuity, the following medals now appear in the LIFE SAVING section:
358. DICKIN MEDAL—see L44A.
359. NATIONAL CANINE DEFENCE LEAGUE MEDAL—see L31A.
360. THE PEOPLE'S DISPENSARY FOR SICK ANIMALS CROSS—see L31B.
361. OUR DUMB FRIENDS LEAGUE MEDAL—see L31C.

362. CORPS OF COMMISSIONAIRES MEDAL

Date:
Ribbon: Red, white and blue.
Metal: Silver or blackened metal.
Size: 40mm.
Description: A 16-point star bearing a central medallion with the Union Jack in the centre surrounded by the Latin mottoes: VIRTUTE ET INDUSTRIA (top) and LABOR VINCIT OMNIA (foot)—"by valour and industry" and "work conquers all" respectively. Fitted with a plain ring for suspension from the ribbon which bears an elaborate brooch consisting of crossed rifle and sabre on a fouled anchor with a cannon behind, representing the armed forces from which the Corps recruits its members.
Comments: *Awarded by the Corps of Commissionaires for long and exemplary service.*

VALUE: £30–45   *Miniature*   £20–25

363. NATIONAL EMERGENCY MEDAL

Date: 1926.
Ribbon: None.
Metal: Gold or bronze.
Size: 50mm.
Description: (Obverse) Britannia seated holding a laurel branch and resting on a shield. Above the inscription across the field FOR SERVICE IN NATIONAL EMERGENCY MAY 1926 appear the national emblems of England, Wales and Scotland; (reverse) three female figures with arms outstretched holding locomotives dividing the inscription LARGITAS MUNERIS SALUS REIPUBLICAE (the immensity of the task, the well-being of the country).
Comments: *These medals were designed by Edward Gillick and struck by the Royal Mint on behalf of the London, Midland and Scottish Railway for presentation to those volunteers who had served the company throughout the General Strike of May 1926. The medals were struck in bronze and issued in boxes unnamed to the recipients. According to Mint records, a few medals were also struck in gold, but none has so far been recorded.*

VALUE: £45–55

364. ROYAL WARRANT HOLDERS ASSOCIATION MEDAL

Original reverse.

"Jubilee" obverse.

Instituted: 1897.
Ribbon: Dark purple with a central yellow stripe.
Metal: Silver, silver-gilt or gold.
Size: 23mm.
Description: (Obverse) crowned profile of the reigning monarch; (reverse) THE ROYAL WARRANT HOLDERS ASSOCIATION round the edge with the name of the Warrant holder engraved in the centre. The medal was surmounted by an imperial crown fitted to a ring for suspension, with a brooch bar at the top of the ribbon, for issues between those of Queen Victoria and George VI. The medal fell into abeyance in 1946 due to the scarcity of silver. In 1897 the Association issued a medal in silver to commemorate the Diamond Jubilee of Queen Victoria. In 1977, for Her Majesty Queen Elizabeth's Silver Jubilee, a new medal was struck, with the dates 1952–1977 appearing below the bust. This medal is surmounted by a Tudor crown and fitted with a ring for suspension from a bar with a brooch bar at the top of the ribbon. This issue has a special reverse bearing the Royal arms—this special reverse was used again in 2002 on the occasion of the Golden Jubilee.
Comments: *This medal was originally instituted by Queen Victoria for individuals who are granted the Royal Warrant and may be worn at formal occasions of the Association. Until 1911 medals were issues in both silver and silver-gilt to members of the Association. However, from 1911 the silver-gilt and gold medals were only awarded to Council members. Miniature medals were also authorised and are believed to have been issued but they are very rare and were discontinued in 1920. Medals were struck for the reign of Edward VIII but were never issued, however unnamed examples do exist. The 1977 Silver Jubilee medal was designed by Alex Styles of Garrard the Crown jewellers. In 2002 Her Majesty the Queen gave approval for the medal to be issued in silver-gilt or gold to mark the Golden Jubilee, but it reverted to silver in 2003. The medal may be purchased by Warrant holders only.*

VALUE:	Victoria Silver-gilt	£200–250
	Jubilee	£200–250
	Edward VII Silver	£100–150
	Silver-gilt	£200–250
	George V	£150–200
	Edward VIII	£200–250
	George VI	£150–200
	Elizabeth II	£150–200
	1977 Jubilee	£200–250
	2002 Jubilee	£200–250

365. ROYAL NATIONAL LIFEBOAT INSTITUTION DECORATION

Date: 1901, 1913.
Ribbon: Blue watered silk.
Metal: Gold or silver with enamels.
Size: 36mm.
Description: A wavy cross in dark blue enamel, with the initials RNLI in the angles interlaced with a rope, surmounted by a Royal Crown fitted with a ring for suspension. First Class (gold) and Second Class (silver).
Comments: *The original decoration, designed by Charles Dibdin, the RNLI Secretary, was instituted as a reward for Branch Honorary Secretaries and Ladies Auxiliaries for long and devoted service. 36 awards were made initially, followed by 18 other awards in 1902–9. Thereafter a new decoration, awarded to men and women in two classes, was proposed. Designed by Mr Burke of the College of Heralds and manufactured by Garrards in 1912. Objections raised by King George V led to the cross being discontinued on May 14, 1914, by which time only ten gold awards had been made and no silver awards, the latter known only as a sample in the RNLI archives. No record of the design of the 1901–09 award has been preserved.*

VALUE: —

366. MAIDSTONE TYPHOID MEDAL

Date:
Ribbon: Purple with yellow stripes at the edges.
Metal: Silver.
Size: 32mm.
Description: (Obverse) the coat of arms of the town of Maidstone with MAIDSTONE KENT on a ribbon below; (reverse) an ornate panel engraved with the recipient's name in the centre and the words WITH GRATITUDE TO . . . FOR LOVING SERVICES 1897, with an olive branch below.
Comments: *A major epidemic of Typhoid fever broke out in Maidstone, Kent during late August 1897. By 9 September 117 cases had been reported, rising to 774 by the end of the month and by 9 October the number had risen to 1,200, with 42 deaths. By the end of December when the epidemic was considered to be over a total of 132 people had died. Medals were awarded to the nursing staff who served in the town during the epidemic. Many were presented by the Mayor of Maidstone at a special ceremony held at the Museum and Technical School on Wednesday 8 December 1897.*

VALUE:	Unnamed	£150–200
	Named	£300–350

367. BOYS' LIFE BRIGADE MEDAL

Date: 1905.
Ribbon: Red.
Metal: Bronze.
Size: 34mm.
Description: (Obverse) A Geneva cross within a crowned circle and a radiate background, the circle inscribed TO SAVE LIFE; a scroll round the foot inscribed THE BOYS LIFE BRIGADE; (reverse) personal details of the recipient. Fitted with a plain suspension ring. The brooch bar is the form of a scroll with a laurel wreath superimposed on the middle and a clasp bearing the date of the award.
Comments: *This medal was awarded for good attendance. The Boys' Life Brigade amalgamated with the Boys' Brigade in 1926 and the award of this medal was then abolished. The BLB Cross for Courage was also abolished at this time having been awarded only ten times in its history.*

VALUE: £20–30

367A. BOYS' BRIGADE SQUAD MEDAL

Date: 1896.
Ribbon: Originally dark blue, later maroon, suspended from an ornate brooch pin..
Metal: Bronze.
Size: 42mm.
Description: A multi-faceted, eight-pointed star surmounted by the Brigade badge: an anchor with the word SURE on the top cross-member of the anchor and STEDFAST on the lower limbs, the initials BB either side. When the Boys' Brigade amalgamated with the Boys' Life Brigade in 1926 the Geneva cross was added to the design.
Comments: *This medal is believed to have been awarded to the squad who achieved the highest average attendance over one year. The Boys' Brigade issued and continues to issue a large number of badges and medals, most of which are beyond the scope of this publication..*

VALUE: £25–35

368. GIRLS' LIFE BRIGADE MEDAL

Date: 1905.
Ribbon: Red.
Metal: Bronze.
Size: 34mm.
Description: Similar to the above, but inscribed THE GIRLS' LIFE BRIGADE.
Comments: *This medal was awarded to members of the Brigade in similar circumstances to those for the Boys' Life Brigade.*

VALUE: £30–40

368A. RSPCA QUEEN VICTORIA MEDAL

Date: 1875.
Ribbon: White with two blue stripes towards each edge.
Metal: Silver.
Size: 34mm.
Description: (Obverse) a group of animals dominated by a standing horse with the legend ROYAL SOCIETY FOR THE PREVENTION OF CRUELTY OF ANIMALS FOUNDED 1824; (reverse) the throned effigy of Queen Victoria with the word PATRON below, surrounded by a floral wreath.
Comments: *This medal is awarded to people who have made a significant contribution to the Society. It was instituted in 1837 and the young Queen Victoria, an enthusiastic supporter of the Society, actually sketched a cat to be included in the reverse design. The name of the recipient is engraved in the exergue below the animals on the obverse.*

VALUE: £70–100

369. MARINE SOCIETY REWARD OF MERIT

Date: 1875.
Ribbon: Blue.
Metal: Silver.
Size: 47mm.
Description: (Obverse) a depiction of Britannia holding the hand of a young sailor with seascape behind , with MARINE SOCIETY INSTITUTED MDCCLVI around and INCORPORATED MDCCLXXII in exergue ; (reverse) a wreath of rose, thistle and shamrock enclosing inscription REWARD OF MERIT TO and with the name of the recipient engraved. Suspended from a thin straight bar swivel suspension.
Comments: *The Marine Society was instituted in 1756, at the start of the Seven Years War, by Fowler Walker, Sir John Fielding and Jonas Hanway. Its aim was to encourage poor men and boys to join the Royal and Merchant navies. In this it was successful, and by the end of the war in 1764, it had recruited 5,451 men and 5,174 boys for service at sea. Incorporated by Act of Parliament in 1772 to apprentice poor boys to the Royal and Merchant navies; it clothed them and provided them with an education suitable for their future employment. In 1783, Hanway published a paper promulgating the establishment of schools in every seaport for the training of boys for the sea. So large a concept was beyond the means of the Society but it led the way and in 1786 it commissioned the first pre-sea training ship, the* Beatty*, a sloop which housed 30 boys together with a superintendent, mate, schoolmaster, boatswain and cook. In later years, other organisations followed their example. By 1940, when the Society's training ship* Warspite *was broken up, the Society had trained and equipped some 36,000 boys for the Royal Navy and just under 35,000 for the Merchant Navy. Over the years, the Society was influential in the formation of several related organisations, including The Seamen's Hospital Society, Sail Training Association, Nautical Institute and Sea Cadet Corps. In 1976 the Marine Society merged with a number of other related charities: The Sailors' Home and Red Ensign Club (estab. 1830), The London School of Nautical Cookery (estab. 1893), The Incorporated Thames Nautical Training Trust (H.M.S. Worcester) (estab. 1862), The Seafarers Education Service (estab. 1919), College at Sea (estab. 1938), The Merchant Navy Comforts Service Trust (estab. 1940) and the British Ship Adoption Society (estab. 1936). The Society continues to this day as a charity supporting maritime youth organisations.*

VALUE: £70–100

370. ROYAL BRISTOL VOLUNTEERS MEDAL

Date: 1875.
Ribbon: White with two blue stripes towards each edge.
Metal: Silver.
Size: 37mm x 54 max.
Description: (Obverse) Arms of the city of Bristol within a garter bearing the words VIRTUTE ET INDUSTRIA surrounded by ROYAL BRISTOL VOLUNTEERS and IN DANGER READY in scroll below; (reverse) the Volunteers' edict: "IMBODIED FOR THE MAINTENANCE OF PUBLIC ORDER & PROTECTION OF THEIR FELLOW CITIZENS ON THE THREAT OF INVASION BY FRANCE MDCCXCVII. REVIVED AT THE RENEWAL OF HOSTILITIES MDCCCIII. DISBANDED WHEN THE DELIVERANCE OF EUROPE WAS ACCOMPLISHED BY THE PERSEVERENCE & MAGNANIMITY OF GREAT BRITAIN AND HER ALLIES MDCCCXIV" with scroll below bearing the words PRO PATRIA. Suspended from an integral wreath of laurel affixed to an ornamental scroll with the initials GR.
Comments: *This unusual medal was presumably given to all citizens who had volunteered for service when there was the real threat of invasion from France.*

VALUE: £80-£100

371. GRANTON MEDAL FOR ZEAL

Date: 1915–19
Branch of Service: RN, RNR and RNVR.
Ribbon: Unknown.
Metal: Silver.
Size: 31mm.
Description: A thin medal (1mm) with a simple ring suspension. (Obverse) a raised laurel wreath with the words FOR ZEAL in the centre, in two lines; (reverse) A plain, flat disc engraved with the recipient's details.
Comments: *Instituted personally by Commodore (later Admiral and an AM recipient) Sir James Startin, SNO of Granton Naval Base, Edinburgh, and selectively awarded to naval personnel under his command who manned the trawlers, sailing ships and coastal trading boats that were involved in extensive mine clearance and Q-ship activities ranging from the North Sea to the Bay of Biscay during the First World War. This medal was awarded to both officers and men for meritorious service in circumstances that would otherwise have gone unrecognised. Although the recipients were mainly from the RNR and RNVR, these medals were awarded at special parades by visiting dignitaries to the base, including King George V, two Prime Ministers (Asquith and Lloyd George) and the Archbishop of Canterbury. Recipients also included Admiral Lord Beatty and Admiral Lord Jellicoe and a gold medal was presented to and accepted by the King. A miniature version of the medal was also available.*

VALUE: £150–200

372. SECURICOR MEDAL FOR LONG SERVICE

Date: —
Ribbon: Yellow with central dark blue stripe and blue edges.
Metal: Silver.
Size: 31mm.
Description: (Obverse) the cross keys of the company's badge with the name SECURICOR above; (reverse) a laurel wreath with centrre panel engraved with the recipient's details.
Comments: *Awarded to employees of the company who exhibit a high standard of devotion to duty over a sustained period.*

VALUE: £35–40

373. SECURICOR MEDAL FOR BRAVERY

Date: —
Ribbon: Blue with central wide yellow stripe and two thin yellow stripes.
Metal: Silver.
Size: 31mm.
Description: Similar to the above .
Comments: *Awarded to employees of the company who exhibit a particularly high standard of bravery and courage when on duty.*

VALUE: £400–500

374. ST. ANDREW'S ASSOCIATION MEDAL

Date: 1899
Ribbon: Dark red with three narrow yellow stripes.
Metal: Silver.
Size: 36mm.
Description: (Obverse) St Andrew standing before a diagonal cross with the words ST ANDREWS AMBULANCE ASSOCIATION around the circumference; (reverse) a wreath of thistles surrounding the words FOR SERVICE IN THE ST ANDREWS AMBULANCE CORPS.
Comments: *Given for long and faithful service in the Association. Originally the medal, in gold silver or bronze was awarded for bravery in saving life but in 1907 the service medal was introduced for efficient completion of 15 years service. In 1954 the special medal illustrated was issued in celebration of the Association's 50th anniversary and Review by HRH the Duke of Edinburgh in Glasgow, inscribed ST ANDREWS AMBULANCE CORPS 1904–1954, with a yellow ribbon with three narrow red stripes.*

VALUE:	1907 type	£60–75
	1954 issue	£75–100

375. SALVATION ARMY SERVICE MEDAL

Date: —
Ribbon: Maroon with two narrow blue stripes and a central thin orange stripe.
Metal: Silver.
Size: Various.
Description: An ornate cross surmounted in the centre by the Army's badge in enamels and the words LONG AND FAITHFUL SERVICE on four enamel panels around.
Comments: *Little is known about this attractive medal but it is known that the higher the rank, the larger the medal awarded. Further details would be appreciated.*

VALUE: £100–150

376. ROYAL NORFOLK VETERANS ASSOCIATION MEDAL

Date: 1909
Ribbon: Seven stripes consisting of a central 3mm white stripe flanked by two 3mm khaki stripes flanked by two l6mm red stripes edged by two 3mm khaki stripes.
Metal: Bronze.
Size: 31mm.
Description: (Obverse) crowned effigy of Edward VII with a laurel branch extending from the bottom of the medal around the left side and the words EDWARD VII on the right; (reverse) the words TO COMMEMORATE THE INSPECTION OF THE ROYAL NORFOLK VETERANS ASSOCIATION BY HIS MAJESTY KING EDWARD VII 25th OCTOBER 1909 in eight lines.
Comments: *This medal was issued to commemorate the inspection of the Association by King Edward VII at Crown Point, Norwich. In 1902 the King had agreed to become Patron of the Association, granting it the Royal title. The King's continued patronage resulted in the inspection of 25 members of the Association at Sandringham in 1907. In 1909 there was a further inspection by the King which resulted in the medal being struck. It is said that the King designed the ribbon for the medal but there is no documentary proof for this. Since 1902 each successive monarch has been the Patron of the Association.*

VALUE: £40–60

377. THE SHIPPING FEDERATION MEDAL FOR MERITORIOUS SERVICE

Date: 1917
Ribbon: None
Metal: Hallmarked gold or silver
Size: 28mm.
Description: (Obverse) a standing figure of Britannia holding a trident and shield, with a submarine on one side and a merchant ship on the other; (reverse) a fouled anchor above a plaque with the words "Presented by the Shipping Federation", flanked by a fish each side. The whole is surrounded by a laurel wreath with a scroll reading "1914 For services During the War 1918" beneath.
Comments: *Awarded by the Shipping Federation for meritorious service during World War I. Each medal has the recipient's name around the rim and the date of the action for which it was awarded.*

VALUE: —

MEDALS FOR SAVING LIFE

Until the establishment of the government's own gallantry awards for the saving of life (the Sea Gallantry Medal (Foreign Services), instituted in 1841 and the Sea Gallantry Medal of 1854 and the Albert Medal of 1866), it was left entirely to private individuals and organizations to reward those who risked their own lives to save the lives of others. Although the medals granted from the late eighteenth century onwards are unofficial, they are of considerable human interest and are now very much sought after, preferably with the citations, diplomas, printed testimonials and other collateral material. The most commonly found of these medals are listed in broadly chronological order of their institution. However, listed below is the very wide range of Institutions and other bodies who have issued or continue to give awards for life saving, as currently known to the Life Saving Awards Research Society. A few of the medals issued by these institutions are included in the main section of this Yearbook, as they can often be awarded for reasons other than life saving. The Society would be very pleased to hear from readers of this Yearbook of any that are not on the list. Many of the following awards are as yet incompletely researched, and it is our intention to include many of these in this section when the research has been completed by the Life Saving Awards Research Society.

LIFE SAVING SOCIETIES / FUNDS

Royal Humane Society
Bath Humane Society
Bolton & District Humane Society
Bristol Humane Society
Carnegie Hero Fund Trust
Fleetwood Humane Society
Glasgow Humane Society
Grimsby Humane Society
The Hundred of Salford Humane Society
Jersey Humane Society
Lancashire Humane Society
Liverpool Shipwreck & Humane Society
Norfolk Humane Society
Northants Humane Society
Plym, Tamar, Lynher & Tavy Humane Society
Port of Plymouth Humane Society
The Royal National Lifeboat Institution
The (Royal) Society for the Protection of Life from Fire
The Royal Life Saving Society (Mountbatten Medal)
Sheffield Society for the Recognition of Bravery
Shipwrecked Fishermen & Mariners Royal Benevolent Society
Suffolk Humane Society
Tayleur Fund
Tynemouth Trust
Windsor & Eton Humane Society
Wisbech Humane Society

NEWSPAPERS/MAGAZINES

Answers Medal
Associated Newspapers Medal
Daily Herald (Order of Industrial Heroism)
Daily Mirror
Daily Sketch Medal
Fleet (For Merit) Medal
Golden Penny Medal
Pluck Medal
Post Office Magazine (St. Martin's Medal)
The Quiver Medal
Ally Sloper's Medal
To-Day (Gallantry Fund) Medal

MUNICIPAL AND OTHER AUTHORITIES

Binney Memorial Award
Birmingham Fire Medal
Civil Aviation Authority
Dale Award
Dundee Corporation Medal for Bravery
Folkestone Bravery Medal
The Corporation of Glasgow Bravery Medal
Liverpool Corporation Medal for Bravery
Metropolitan/LCC/London Fire Brigade Bravery Medal
Plymouth City Police Bravery Medal
Southend-on-Sea Pier Department Life Saving Medal
The Strathclyde Bravery Medal

YOUTH ORGANISATIONS

Boys' Brigade
Church Lads' and Church Girls' Brigade
Girl Guards (Salvation Army)
Girl Guiding UK
Scout Association
Sea Cadet Corps

ANIMAL SOCIETIES

Belfast Society for the Prevention of Cruelty to
 Animals
Dublin Society for the Prevention of Cruelty to
 Animals
National Canine Defence League
Our Dumb Friends League
Peoples Dispensary for Sick Animals
Royal Society for the Prevention of Cruelty to
 Animals

COMMERCIAL ORGANISATIONS

Automobile Association
Castle Mail Steam Packet Co.
Imperial Chemical Industries
Lloyds
Silk Cut
Surrey Commercial Dock Company

NON-COMMERCIAL ORGANISATIONS

Gallantry Medallists' League Gold Medal for
 Bravery
Imperial Merchant Services Guild
Mercantile Marine Service Association
Royal Society for the Prevention of Accidents
St. Andrews Ambulance Association Bravery
 Medal
Order of St. John of Jerusalem Life Saving Medal
Shipping Federation
Port Sunlight Order of Conspicuous Merit

SPECIFIC RESCUES

Indian Chief Medal (Ramsgate Medal)
Carpathia and *Titanic* Medal
CQD Medal
SS *Drummond Castle*

Folkestone, Hythe & Sandgate Medal
Gorleston *Christean* Medal
Grounding of the TSS *Erinpura*
SS Lusitania (*Wanderer*)
Maharajah of Burdwan's Medal (HMS Goliath)
Osip Medal
HMS *Niger* Medal (Deal)
Henry Vernon Crew Fund Medal
Wreck of the *Chusan*
Wreck of the *Kent*
Wreck of the *Palme*

COLLIERY DISASTERS

Little Hulton 1866
Hamstead Colliery 1908
Hartley Colliery 1862
Hulton Coliery 1910
Sacriston Colliery 1903

OTHER DISASTERS

Glasgow Plague Medal 1900
Hong Kong Plague Medal
Maidstone Typhoid Medal 1897
Moray Floods Medal 1829

RAILWAYS

London, Midland & Scottish Railway
London & North Eastern Railway
London Passenger Transport Board
Midland Railway
Southern Railway

PRIVATE AWARDS

Too numerous to mention—but each a tale of
 heroism in its own right!

*Scottish Society for the
Prevention of Cruelty to
Animals.*

The Golden Penny Award.

*The Liverpool Corporation
Medal for Bravery*

L1. ROYAL HUMANE SOCIETY MEDALS

Date: 1776.

Ribbon: None or blue (1776–1867); plain navy blue (1867); thin central yellow stripe and white edges added (silver medal, 1921). Stanhope medal: plain navy blue until 1921, when changed to blue with yellow and black edges. Police medal: plain navy blue with a central yellow stripe.

Metal: Gold, silver or bronze.

Size: 51mm (1776–1869); 38mm (1867–).

Description: The first Large Medal was engraved by Lewis Pingo and is described: (obverse) a cherub, nude but for a flowing cloak, blowing on a burnt-out torch explained by the Latin legend LATEAT SCINTILLVLA FORSAN (perhaps a tiny spark may be concealed). A three-line Latin text across the exergue reads SOC. LOND. IN RESUSCITAT INTERMORTUORUM INSTIT. with the date in roman numerals. (Reverse) an oak wreath containing the engraved details of the recipient and the date of the life-saving act. Round the circumference is a Latin motto HOC PRETIVM CIVE SERVATO TVLIT (He has obtained this reward for saving the life of a citizen). Around 1826, the dies were worn out and were replaced with dies of a similar design by another engraver, Benedetto Pistrucci, the main difference being a general reworking of the cherub figure on the obverse.

In 1837 a new reverse die was produced which omitted the motto HOC PRETIUM CIVE DONATO TULIT from the circumference. This was to be awarded in the future for "unsuccessful" rescues (note—until this date no distinction had been made between "successful" and "unsuccessful" rescues). Until this time the medal had been awarded in silver (except 13 instances of an honorary gold award), but from now onwards bronze medals were also struck.

In 1867, the "small" version (38mm diameter) of the medal was introduced. This was a wearable version having a scroll suspender fitted with a navy blue ribbon. The reverses of the smaller medals were similar to those of the larger variety except that the area inside the wreath (previously left plain for the engraved details of the rescue) were now replaced for a successful rescue with VIT.OB.SERV.D.D. SOC.REG.HVM (The Royal Humane Society presented this gift for saving life) and for an unsuccessful rescue with VIT.PERIC.EXPOS. D.D. SOC REG.HVM (The Royal Humane Society, his life having been exposed to danger).

Scrolled clasps in silver and bronze were awarded for subsequent acts of bravery deserving of a medal; the silver and bronze clasps corresponded to the previous award (i.e. a silver medal holder would only receive a silver clasp—even if the subsequent rescue was only "bronze standard". However, a bronze medal holder would receive a silver medal if the rescue was "silver standard".

The Stanhope Medal in memory of Captain C. S. S. Stanhope, RN, was struck in gold and first issued in 1873. The medal was similar to the Society's silver medal but has a plaque-shaped bar fixed to the suspender embossed with the year of the award and STANHOPE MEDAL. This plaque was discontinued c. 1937. The medal could be issued with either the "successful" or "unsuccessful" reverses.

Comments: *The Society was formed in 1774 for the specific purpose of diffusing knowledge about the techniques of resuscitation and saving life from drowning. Within two years of its inception, the Society's large medals were struck, chiefly in silver with 13 gold medals being honorary awards for non life saving activities. In addition monetary rewards and testimonials were granted to those who saved life, or attempted to save life from drowning, but later the Society's remit was broadened to include "all cases of exceptional bravery in rescuing or attempting to rescue persons from asphyxia in mines, wells, blasting furnaces or in sewers where foul air may endanger life". In 1837 a new medal specifically for unsuccessful rescues was introduced and at the same time medals were struck in bronze for both types of rescue. In December 1866 the Society was requested by the Duke of Cambridge, the Army's most senior officer that "some alteration might be made in the size of the Medal in question so as to admit of its being worn." The Society rapidly acceded to his request and by late 1867 the first 'wearable' medals were being awarded. Details of the recipient and the act were engraved on the rim. Interestingly it wasn't until 1869 that the Army and Navy formally gave acceptance for the wearing of the Society's medals.*

The Stanhope medal was first awarded in 1873 in memory of Captain C.S.S. Stanhope. This is the highest honour bestowed by the Society and is awarded annually for the most gallant rescue to have been rewarded by the Society. Since 1962, the Liverpool Shipwreck & Humane Society, and the Humane Societies of

Australasia, Canada, New Zealand and New South Wales have also participated by submitting their most gallant rescue. In January 2000, the Society introduced The Police Medal, struck in silver, to honour the police officer who has shown "courage of the highest order" during the preceding year. It is awarded to a policeman or woman who has already been awarded a Society award—usually either a Silver or a Bronze Medal.

VALUE:

	Gold	Silver	Bronze
Large (Type 1, 1774–1837)	—	£600–900	—
Large successful (Type 2, 1837)	—	£550–850	£300–500
Large unsuccessful (Type 2)	—	£400–550	£250–350
Small successful	—	£500–750	£250–450
Small unsuccessful	—	£400–500	£200–300
Stanhope Gold Medal	£4000–5000	—	—
Police Medal	—	—	—
Miniature Undated	£250–350	£55–65	£45–55
Dated	£350–450		

L2. GLASGOW HUMANE SOCIETY MEDALS

Instituted: 1780.
Ribbon: None.
Metal: Gold or silver.
Size: 42mm.
Description: (Obverse) a naturalistic treatment of the elements of the Glasgow civic arms: the tree that never grew, the bird that never flew, the fish that never swam and the bell than never rang, with edge inscription GLASGOW HUMANE SOCIETY INSTITUTED 1780; (reverse) PRESENTED BY THE GLASGOW HUMANE SOCIETY TO above a horizontal tablet engraved with the name of the recipient; below: FOR INTREPIDITY OF COURAGE AND SUCCESS IN SAVING THE LIFE OF A FELLOW CITIZEN.
Comments: *Awarded mainly for saving people from drowning in the Clyde and Kelvin rivers but also for rescues in the Firth of Clyde.*

VALUE:
Gold: —
Silver: £600–850

L3. HUNDRED OF SALFORD HUMANE SOCIETY MEDALS

Date: 1824.
Ribbon: Plain dark blue.
Metal: Gold, silver or bronze.
Size: 32mm (circular type); height 49mm, max. width 41mm (cruciform type).
Description: Circular gold, silver or bronze medals were awarded from 1824 onwards, with the recipient's name and details engraved on the reverse, and featuring a cherub kindling a spark similar to the Royal Humane Society's medal, on the obverse. Around the time of the society's centenary in 1889, however, a more elaborate type of medal was devised, with the circular medal superimposed on a cross of distinctive shape, so that the society's name could be inscribed on the arms. The recipient's details are again found on the reverse.
Comments: *This society was formed in 1789 to serve the needs of the Salford and Manchester area. After a few years it was dissolved, but was revived again in 1824. These awards ceased in 1922. The Society also awarded medals for swimming proficiency in silver and in bronze—see MYBL48.*

VALUE:

	Gold	Silver	Bronze	*Miniature*
Circular medal	—	£250–300	£200–250	—
Cruciform medal	—	£125–175	—	—

L4. ROYAL NATIONAL LIFEBOAT INSTITUTION MEDALS (see also no. 365)

Date: 1825.
Ribbon: Plain blue.
Metal: Gold, silver or bronze.
Size: 36mm.
Description: The first medals bore the effigy of George IV on the obverse and it was not until 1862 that this was replaced by a garlanded profile of Victoria by Leonard C. Wyon. Medals portraying Edward VII and George V were introduced in 1902 and 1911 respectively, but when permission to portray George VI was refused in 1937 the RNLI adopted a profile of its founder, Sir William Hillary, instead. All but the Edwardian medals have a reverse showing a drowning seaman being rescued by three men in a boat with the motto LET NOT THE DEEP SWALLOW ME UP. The Edwardian medals have the seated figure of Hope adjusting the lifejacket on a lifeboatman. The early medals (1825–c. 1831) except some gold examples were pierced below the rim to allow a suspension ring to be fitted. Later a band of the appropriate material was added to the medal having an integral loop which allowed a larger suspension loop to be fitted. The characteristic dolphin suspension made its appearance c. 1852 and is still in use to this day. Rewards for additional rescues were initially recognised by a miniature rowing boat, gold for gold awards and silver for silver awards, suspended from short chains either being attached to the medal riband or from the medal itself. Details of the rescue were engraved on the boat. These were phased out c. 1835 and additional rewards were given by issuing additional medals. This continued until c. 1855 when second, third and subsequent rewards were recognised by the award of "service clasps" fixed to the medal suspension. Details of the rescue are engraved on the reverse of the clasp.

Comments: *The RNLI was founded, as the Royal National Institution for the Preservation of Life from Shipwreck, on 4 March 1824 and began awarding medals the following year to "persons whose humane and intrepid exertions in saving life from shipwreck on our coasts are deemed sufficiently conspicuous to merit honourable distinction". Its title changed to the Royal National Lifeboat Institution in 1854. The medals are engraved on the edge with the recipient's name and date of award.*

VALUE:	Gold (150)	Silver (1,564)	*Miniature*	Bronze (793)	*Miniature*
George IV	£2000–2750	£500–675	—	—	—
Victoria	£2000–2750	£500–800	£150–200	—	—
Edward VII	£2500–3000	£850–1800	£200–250	—	—
George V	£2500–3000	£500–675	£200–250	£350–450	£150–200
Hillary	£2500–3000	£650–850	£200–250	£350–450	£150–200

L4A. PLYM, TAMAR, LYNHER AND TAVY HUMANE SOCIETY MEDALS

Date: 1831
Ribbon: None.
Metal: Silver and bronze.
Size: 48mm.
Description: (Obverse) a winged female figure with a star on her forehead, holding the left wrist of a man who has been raised from the water and lies against a rock. Over the man's head, she is holding an oil lamp in her right hand, with the flame flickering and uncertain. Around the upper perimeter is "LATET SCINTILLULA FORSAN". In the exergue is "MDCCCXXXI"; (reverse) an oak wreath with outside the wreath "THE PLYM TAMAR LYMHER AND TAVY HUMANE SOCIETY". Within the wreath are engraved the recipient's name and details of award. The design of the medal is attributed to Lt. Col. Charles Hamilton Smith, KH, and the medallist was Benjamin Wyon.

Comments: *The Society (initially known as the Plym and Tamar Humane Society) was based on the river systems around Plymouth. The Society owed its origin and establishment to a "medical gentleman of the town" who, during the course of his practice, observed many instances of "suspended animation" where the individuals could have been revived had the necessary apparatus and knowledge been readily available. The objective of the Society was to preserve life, to bestow rewards on all who promptly risked their own lives to rescue those of their fellow creatures; to provide assistance, as far as possible, in all cases of apparent death in the town and neighbourhood; to restore the apparently drowned and dead; and to distinguish by rewards all who may be successful in such restoration. Shortly after the Society's institution in December 1831, they began to issue medals and these were struck in silver and bronze. The medals were issued without means of suspension. There are seven known examples for the period 1832–61 which have an engraved inscription in running script detailing the recipient, place of rescue and date signed by two officials (President, Hon. Secretary or Treasurer). Additionally two examples from the 1870s are recorded with fewer details. A small number of un-named bronze examples and a presentation example to Lt.-Col. H. Smith, the designer of the medal, are known.*

VALUE:	Silver £400–£500	Bronze £350–£400

L4B. PORT OF PLYMOUTH SWIMMING ASSOCIATION AND HUMANE SOCIETY MEDALS

Date: 1831.
Ribbon: Blue.
Metal: Silver and bronze.
Size: ??
Description: The medals were issued in silver and bronze with further acts of gallantry by medal holders being rewarded with bars to their medals. The medal has always had the basic design of a four-armed cross surmounting a wreath, with a round centre and a crown at the top (crown varied according to the reigning monarch). The centres show the swimmer diving from the left or the right to rescue a person in the water, with different scenes in the background. In others, the centres are plain, or in the case of one known award, the initials of the rescuer.
Comments: *Very little is currently known regarding the early history of this Society. It was formed c. 1862 when the Swimming Association and the Humane Society amalgamated although for another century the Society maintained separate sections for Swimming and Humane Society, each with its own Chairman, Secretary and Committee. The Humane Society had responsibility for investigating any acts of bravery in rescuing persons along a section of the Plymouth, Stonehouse and Devonport coastline, with the Devonport Humane Society having responsibility for the remainder of the local coastline. As a result of these investigations the Society awarded medals, certificates, watches and other pecuniary awards in those cases felt worthy of recognition. Many of the Society's records have been lost over the years but extant medals indicate that the medals were awarded from c. 1842 to the Second World War period.*

VALUE: Silver   £350–£450   Bronze   £300–£350

L5. MEDALS OF THE SOCIETY FOR THE PROTECTION OF LIFE FROM FIRE

Date: 1836.
Ribbon: Plain scarlet.
Metal: Silver or bronze.
Size: 52mm (I and II), 45mm (III), 42mm (IV &V) and 40mm (VI).
Description: The first medal (type I) had a radiate eye in garter on the obverse and a reverse giving the recipient's details in an oak-leaf wreath. They were fitted with a ring suspender. The Society was granted the Royal title in 1843 and a new medal (type II) was adopted the following year, with the word ROYAL added and the date at the foot of the obverse changed to 1844. In the early 1850s type III was introduced, with an obverse of a man carrying a woman away from a fire. This and type IV (1892) were struck in silver or bronze. As royal patronage ended with the death of Queen Victoria, a new medal (type V) was required in 1902 without the Royal title. Types IV and V show a man rescuing a woman and two children from a fire. The reverse of this medal has the words DUTY AND HONOR within a wreath, the recipient's details being placed on the rim. Type VI , awarded from 1984, has no suspension, with the recipient's details engraved on the reverse.

VALUE:		Silver	Bronze
I	Eye and garter (1836)	£750–895	—
II	Eye and garter (1844)	£750–895	—
III	Man and woman (1850s)	£450–600	£350–450
IV	Man, woman and children (1892)	£550–650	£400–500
V	As type IV but "Royal" removed (1902)	£350–450	£300–400
VI	As type IV but details on rev.	Unique	£350–450
	Miniature (type IV)	£150–200	—

L6. LLOYD'S MEDALS FOR SAVING LIFE AT SEA

Date: 1836.
Ribbon: Blue, striped white, red and white in the centre.
Metal: Gold, silver or bronze.
Size: 73mm or 36mm.
Description: Both large and small medals had similar motifs. (Obverse) the rescue of Ulysses by Leucothoe; (reverse) an ornate wreath.
Comments: *The first medals, introduced in 1836, had a diameter of 73mm and were not intended for wear, but in 1896 the diameter was reduced to 36mm and a ring fitted for suspension with a ribbon.*

VALUE:		*Miniature*
Large silver	£600–750	—
Large bronze	£350–450	—
Small silver	£350–500	£80–100
Small bronze	£300–400	£60–80

L7. LIVERPOOL SHIPWRECK AND HUMANE SOCIETY'S MARINE MEDALS

1st type

2nd type

Date: 1839.
Ribbon: Plain dark blue.
Metal: Gold, silver or bronze.
Size: 54mm (type I), 45mm x 36mm (oval, type II) or 38mm (type III).
Description: (Obverse) a man on a spar of wreckage, taking an inert child from its drowning mother, with the stark legend LORD SAVE US, WE PERISH. This motif was retained for smaller, oval medals (type II) introduced around 1867 with the name of the Society round the edge, and a simple wreath reverse. The suspender was mounted with the Liver Bird emblem. A smaller circular version (type III) was adopted in 1874/75 and fitted with a scroll suspender. In this type the Liver Bird appeared in a wreath on the reverse. Bars engraved with the details were awarded for subsequent acts of life-saving. In addition to the general Marine medals there were distinctive awards in connection with specific marine rescues and funded separately. These had the type III obverse, but the reverse was inscribed CAMP & VILLAVERDE or BRAMLEY-MOORE. A glazed silver medal inscribed IN MEMORIAM was granted to the next of kin of those who lost their lives while attempting to save the lives of others.
Comments: *The Society was formed in 1839 to administer funds raised to help and reward those who distinguished themselves in saving life as a result of a hurricane which swept the Irish Sea in January of that year. The first medals were struck in 1844 and presented for rescues dating back to November 1839. They were large (54mm) in diameter, without suspension.*

VALUE:

	Gold	Silver	Bronze
Large (54mm) 1844	—	£400–550	—
Oval 1867	—	£500–650	—
Small (38mm) 1874/5	£1500–2000	£175–275	£150–200
Camp & Villaverde	—	£500–650	£450–550
Bramley-Moore	—	£500–650	£450–550
In Memoriam	—	£800–1200	—
Miniature (type II)	£150–200	£100–150	£100–125
(type III)	£150–200	£100–150	£100–125

L8. SHIPWRECKED FISHERMEN AND MARINERS ROYAL BENEVOLENT SOCIETY MEDALS

Date: 1851.
Ribbon: Navy blue.
Metal: Gold or silver.
Size: 36mm.
Description: (Obverse) the Society's arms; (reverse) inscribed PRESENTED FOR HEROIC EXERTIONS IN SAVING LIFE FROM DROWNING with a quotation from Job 29: 13 at the foot. The circumference is inscribed ENGLAND EXPECTS EVERY MAN WILL DO HIS DUTY, a quotation from Lord Nelson's signal to the fleet at Trafalgar, 1805. The first medals had a straight suspender but by 1857 a double dolphin suspender had been adopted (six variations of this suspender can be identified). Details of the recipient's name and the date of the rescue are engraved on the edge.
Comments: *The Society was founded in 1839 to raise funds for shipwrecked fishermen and mariners and the families of those lost at sea. The first medals were awarded in 1851 and the last award was made to Alexander Lamont in 1965.*

VALUE	Gold	Silver
Straight suspender	—	£300–450
Dolphin suspender	—	£300–450
Miniature	£300–400	£150–210

L9. TAYLEUR FUND MEDALS

Date: 1854.
Ribbon: Dark blue.
Metal: Gold or silver.
Size: 45mm.
Description: (Obverse) a sinking ship with the legend TAYLEUR FUND FOR THE SUCCOUR OF SHIPWRECKED STRANGERS; (reverse) details of the award engraved.
Comments: *In January 1854 the emigrant ship* Tayleur *foundered in Bantry Bay, Ireland. A fund was started for the relief of the survivors and the surplus used to issue silver life-saving medals. The first awards were made in 1861. Medals are known to have been awarded for nine separate rescues, the last in 1882. Further awards may be discovered as research on this medal continues. In December 1913 the residue of the Tayleur Fund was transferred to the RNLI and the issue of medals terminated.*

VALUE:
Gold (3)	—
Silver (46)	£400–575

L10. HARTLEY COLLIERY MEDALS

Date: 1862.
Ribbon: None.
Metal: Gold or silver.
Size: 53mm
Description: (Obverse) an angel with mine rescuers and disaster victims. Details of the award were engraved on the reverse.
Comments: *Some 204 miners perished in the disaster which overtook the Hartley Colliery, Northumberland on 10 January 1862. This medal was awarded to those involved in the rescue operations.*

VALUE:
Gold (1)	—
Silver (37)	£850–1200

L10A. JERSEY HUMANE SOCIETY MEDALS

Date: 1865.
Ribbon: Silver medal—purple 32mm wide;
Bronze medal—royal blue 32mm wide.
Metal: Gold, silver or bronze.
Size: 38mm.
Description: The medal has a plain swivel type suspension, curved, 40mm wide. (Obverse) the escutcheon of Jersey—(Three lions passant guardant heraldic "leopards"). Above "HUMANE SOCIETY OF JERSEY" embossed in large capital letters: Below a naked mariner astride a ship's spar in heavy seas waving for assistance. Reverse: With a wreath "PRESENTED TO . . . . . FOR COURAGE AND HUMANITY" embossed in capital letters.
Comments: *The first society meeting to award medals took place in June 1865 when one gold (Philip Ahier Jnr.), and two silver medals (Alex. J. Bellis and Howard Morris) were awarded. Since then, the Society has remained active with only a break during the German Occupation 1940–45, when the Military Authorities ordered the Society to cease its function and hand over all documents and medals to the Germans. These were, however, hidden by the then Secretary until the Liberation.*

VALUE:

Gold (2)	—
Silver (approx. 55)	£900–£1500
Bronze (approx. 110)	£600–£775

L11. MERCANTILE MARINE SERVICE ASSOCIATION MEDALS

Date: 1872.
Ribbon: Blue.
Metal: Gold (2) and silver (74).
Size: 38mm.
Description: The obverse has a border with the legend "MERCANTILE MARINE SERVICE ASSOCIATION". In the centre are two seated figures of Neptune and Britannia. Neptune has a shield decorated with an anchor; Britannia a shield decorated with a sailing ship. Between the two figures are Cornucopias, Mercury's staff and a Liver bird. Beneath the two figures are the words "INCORPORATED BY SPECIAL ACT OF PARLIAMENT", and the maker's name Elkington & Co. Liverpool. The reverse bears a wreath containing the engraved details of the incident and the recipient's name.
Comments: *The medal was instituted by the MMSA in 1875 but the first awards were made retrospectively for rescues in 1872. The award was generally given to the Master and senior officers of ships engaged in life saving actions, but towards the end of its issuance some of the recipients were not officers. The medal was also awarded (in gold and in silver) to the students on the school ship Conway (Boy's training ship on the River Mersey) who had demonstrated "the greatest proficiency in all branches of training and education". The reverse of the medal was engraved with full details of the award. The last known award was made in 1906.*
VALUE:

Gold	Silver
—	£450–575

L12. LIFE SAVING MEDALS OF THE ORDER OF ST JOHN

First type reverse.

Date: 1874.

Ribbon: Black, embroidered with the eight-point cross in white (1874), black watered silk (1888), white inner and red outer stripes added, separated by a black line (1950) which was subsequently removed in 1954.

Metal: Gold, silver or bronze.

Size: 37mm.

Description: The first medals (1874) had a plain eight-pointed cross of the Order on the obverse with the legend AWARDED BY THE ORDER OF ST. JOHN OF JERUSALEM IN ENGLAND; (reverse) a sprig of St John's wort bound by two ribbons, the upper bearing JERUSALEM ACRE and the lower bearing CYPRUS RHODES MALTA, within a circular border the words FOR SERVICE IN THE CAUSE OF HUMANITY. A second type of medal was adopted in 1888 and showed two tiny lions and two tiny unicorns in the interstices of the cross, with the legend FOR SERVICE IN THE CAUSE OF HUMANITY; the reverse shows sprigs of St John's wort bound with a ribbon bearing JERUSALEM ENGLAND, within a circular border AWARDED BY THE GRAND PRIORY OF THE ORDER OF THE HOSPITAL OF ST. JOHN OF JERUSALEM. A third type was adopted in 1980 in the same style as the 1888 type but with the reverse wording changed to read AWARDED BY THE MOST VENERABLE ORDER OF THE HOSPITAL OF ST. JOHN OF JERUSALEM. Bars to the medal were authorised to recognise further acts of gallantry from 1963.

Original ribbon.

Comments: *Instituted on 15 December 1874 and awarded for gallantry in saving life, these medals were originally granted in bronze or silver, but gold medals were also struck from 1907. Of the first type only 34 silver and 18 bronze were awarded. The bar to the medal has only been awarded twice in gold.*

Third type ribbon.

VALUE:

	Gold	Silver	Bronze
1st type 1874	—	£850–1200	£650–850
2nd type 1888	£1250–1950	£850–1200	£450–550
3rd type 1980	—	£750–900	£400–500
Miniature	—	£200–300	£150–200

L12A. MAHARAJAH OF BURDWAN'S MEDAL FOR GALLANT CONDUCT— BURNING OF HMS *GOLIATH* 1875

Date: 1875

Ribbon: Blue.

Metal: Silver. Bronze specimens are known

Size: 36mm.

Description: The medal has a fixed ring suspender. (Obverse) Bust of Queen Victoria wearing a coronet and veil draped behind, she wears the Order of the Star of India. Below "J. S. & A. B. Wyon". Around "VICTORIA REGINA". (Reverse) Surrounding: "THE GIFT OF THE MAHARAJAH OF BURDWAN"; within "PRESENTED BY THE LORD MAYOR OF LONDON FOR GALLANT CONDUCT AT THE BURNING OF H.M.S. GOLIATH 22nd DECr 1875",

Comment: *HMS* Goliath *was a training ship lent by the Royal Navy to Forest Gate School Board in 1870. Moored off Grays, Essex, it held some 450 orphan boys, mostly from the East End of London and was used for training in Naval Service. On December 22, 1875 a fire accidentally broke out in the lamp-room and the ship was completely destroyed. One officer and 19 boys are believed to have died in the disaster. Such was the conduct of the boys that the Maharajah of Burdwan wrote to* The Times *expressing his desire to award a medal, through the Lord Mayor of London, to those boys who had particularly distinguished themselves. The medals were presented at the Mansion House in a private ceremony by the Lord Mayor.*

VALUE: £650–£875

L13. SHROPSHIRE SOCIETY LIFE SAVING MEDAL

Date: —
Ribbon: 30mm with two equal stripes of blue and yellow.
Metal: Silver.
Size: 51mm.
Description: (Obverse) a left-facing profile of Captain Matthew
Webb whose name appears round the top, with the inscription
•BORN IN SHROPSHIRE 1848•SWAM THE CHANNEL 1875•
around; (reverse) two draped females holding wreath above
panel with a swimmer in waves below, with legend •PRESENTED
FOR BRAVERY BY THE SHROPSHIRE SOCIETY IN LONDON.
Panel inscribed with recipient's details. Fitted with a plain ring for
suspension and a brooch bar at the top of the ribbon.
Comment: *Struck by John Pinches and presented by the Shropshire Society in
London (instituted in 1916) for outstanding acts of bravery in Shropshire.
It is not known how many were awarded.*

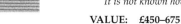

VALUE: £450–675

L14. LIVERPOOL SHIPWRECK AND HUMANE SOCIETY'S FIRE MEDALS

Date: 1883.
Ribbon: Plain scarlet.
Metal: Gold, silver or bronze.
Size: 38mm.
Description: (Obverse) a fireman descending the stairs of a burning house
carrying three children to their kneeling mother, her arms outstretched
to receive them, with FOR BRAVERY IN SAVING LIFE in the exergue;
(reverse) the wreathed Liver Bird previously noted for the third type of
Marine medal (L7 type III). The medal is fitted with a scroll suspender.
Clasps engraved with the details are awarded for subsquent acts.
Comments: *The first recipient was William Oversly in November 1883, for
rescuing a child from a burning house. The first woman recipient was Miss
Julia Keogh (12 February 1895) who saved two children in a house fire.*

VALUE:

	Gold (2)	Silver	Bronze
Fire medal	—	£350–475	£250–300
Miniature	£250–300	£200–275	£150–200

L15. LIVERPOOL SHIPWRECK AND HUMANE SOCIETY'S SWIMMING MEDALS

Date: 1885.
Ribbon: Five equal bars, three blue and two white.
Metal: Silver or bronze.
Size: Height 44mm; max. width 30mm.
Description: This extremely ornate medal has a twin dolphin
suspender and a free form. (Obverse) a wreath surmounted
by crossed oars and a trident, with a lifebelt at the centre
enclosing the Liver Bird emblem on a shield; (reverse) plain,
engraved with the recipient's name and details.
Comments: *Not granted for life-saving as such, but for proficiency in
swimming and life-saving techniques.*

VALUE:	Silver	Bronze
	£100–175	£75–100

L15A. ALLY SLOPER'S MEDAL

Date: c. 1885 (exact date unknown).
Ribbon: Equal stripes of red, white and blue.
Metal: Silver.
Size: 36mm.
Description: (Obverse) Ally Sloper parodying Britannia with an umbrella converted into a trident and a barrel with the words "FOR VALOUR" in place of Britannia's shield. (Reverse) A wreath around the circumference with at the base Ally Sloper's initials intertwined. The centre is plain in which details of the recipient and details of the act which led to the award are engraved. Various suspender types to the medal are known, being either a ring and claw or a bar a claw suspender, with the bar being plain or ornate. One example of the medal with a red/white/blue ribbon is known (John Jones) but this has yet to be confirmed as the ribbon issued with the medal.
Comments: *"Ally Sloper's Half Holiday" was a comic satirical magazine published from 1884 to 1916 and was perhaps the "Private Eye" of its time. The medal was awarded for bravery. It was awarded to the famous (i.e. the explorer H. M. Stanley and Piper Findlater, VC) and to the more humble (David Buchanan, a journeyman painter, William J. Osborn, a coastguard and John Jones, a miner). Details of the full awards can be found in copies of the magazine which are available at the British Museum Newspaper Library.*

VALUE: £350–465

L16. ANSWERS MEDAL FOR HEROISM

Date: 1892.
Ribbon: Equal stripes of blue, white, blue, white and blue.
Metal: Silver.
Size: 38mm.
Description: (Obverse) a wreath enclosing a lion crouching with a sunburst in the background; (reverse) HONORIS CAUSA within a wreath surrounded by the legend PRESENTED BY THE PROPRIETORS OF ANSWERS. Fitted with a scroll suspender.
Comments: *This medal is typical of the many awards made by newspapers and magazines in the late 19th century. The medals were accompanied by a first class diploma. Second class diplomas were projected but never issued. It was also intended to issue a gold medal but no trace of such awards has been found.*

VALUE: £350–495

L17. LLOYD'S MEDALS FOR MERITORIOUS SERVICE

Date: 1893.
Ribbon: Red with blue stripes towards the edges (1893); blue with broad white stripes towards the edges (since 1900).
Metal: Silver or bronze.
Size: 36mm x 38mm (star), 39mm x 29mm (oval), 36mm (circular).
Description: The original medal was a nine-pointed rayed star in bronze with the arms of Lloyd's on the obverse, suspended by a ring from a red ribbon with blue stripes towards the edge. A silver oval medal was introduced in 1900 with Lloyd's arms on the obverse and details of the recipient engraved on the reverse. This medal was fitted with a twin dolphin suspender and a blue ribbon with broad white stripes towards the edge. A third type, introduced in 1913, was a circular medal, struck in silver or bronze, with Lloyd's shield on the obverse. The fourth type, still current, was introduced in 1936 and has the full arms, with crest, motto and supporters, on the obverse. The ribbon is suspended by a ring.
Comments: *These medals have been awarded to officers and men for extraordinary services in the preservation of vessels and cargoes from peril.*

Second type.

VALUE:

	Silver	Bronze
Star 1893	—	£150–200
Oval 1900	£450–550	—
Circular 1913	£350–425	£300–350
Circular 1936	—	—
Miniature (circular)	£200–250	—
(oval)	£250–300	—

L18. LIVERPOOL SHIPWRECK AND HUMANE SOCIETY'S GENERAL MEDALS

Date: 1894.
Ribbon: Five equal stripes, three red and two white.
Metal: Gold, silver or bronze.
Size: 38mm.
Description: (Obverse) a cross pattee with a wreathed crown at the centre and the legend FOR BRAVERY IN SAVING LIFE with the date 1894 at the foot; (reverse) the wreathed Liver Bird of the Marine medal, type III. Fitted with an ornate bar suspender. Bars for subsequent awards are granted.
Comments: *The first award was made on 9 June 1894 to Constables Twizell and Dean who were both injured whilst stopping runaway horses.*

VALUE:

	Gold	Silver	Bronze
General medal	—	£300–400	£250–350
Miniature	£300–350	£150–200	£100–150

L19. TODAY GALLANTRY FUND MEDALS

Date: 1894
Ribbon: Red with a central white stripe.
Metal: Silver and bronze.
Size: 38mm.
Description: (Obverse) standing figure of Britannia, lion and shield within a wreath; (reverse) the heraldic emblems of the United Kingdom with the legend ABSIT TIMOR (let fear depart) and AWARDED BY THE GALLANTRY FUND. The name of the recipient and date of the award are engraved within a wreath. The medal is fitted with an ornamental suspension bar.
Comments: *This medal was awarded by the magazine "To-Day", published between 1893 and 1903. Its first editor was the novelist Jerome K. Jerome who enthusiastically promoted the idea of the Gallantry Fund, but when he gave up the editorship in 1897 the Fund soon fell into disuse. About 30 medals were issued.*

VALUE:
Silver £350–425

Bronze £275–350

L20. IMPERIAL MERCHANT SERVICE GUILD MEDALS

Date: c. 1895.
Ribbon: Blue
Metal: Silver with a silver-gilt rope and enamelled flag on a gold centre.
Size: 40mm and 63mm.
Description: A cross pattée in the centre of which, within a rope ring, is the Guild flag with the initials M.S.G. superimposed. (Reverse) plain but for the details of the recipient engraved with the formula "Presented by the Merchant Service Guild to . . . for heroism at sea (date)". The cross is suspended by a ring and hook, from a rod with a ball and point at each end. There is a brooch of similar design.
Comments: *Only three examples of this medal are known. The medal to C. Wood Robinson is 63mm and those to John H. Collin and W. Nutman are 40mm. No definite dates of issue for this award have been determined, but the rescues for which the known recipients got these awards were in 1895 and 1896.*

VALUE: —

L21. PLUCK MEDAL FOR HEROISM

Date: 1895
Ribbon: Blue
Metal: Silver
Size: 32mm
Description: (Obverse) sprig of laurel and palm on left and right, with a cross pattée in the centre inscribed FOR HEROISM; (reverse) a sprig of laurel on the left of a scroll engraved with the recipient's name alongside the words PRESENTED BY PLUCK.
Comments: *"Pluck" was an adventure magazine for boys published from 1895 to 1916. Medals were issued from the inception of the periodical. In issue 8 it was announced that the award was to be known as the Answers — Pluck Award and until issue 24 the medal was similar to that given by Answers. From number 25 onwards the distinctive Pluck award was used. The last medals appear to have been issued in 1897.*

VALUE: £350–435

L22. TYNEMOUTH MEDALS

Date: 1895.
Ribbon: Dark blue.
Metal: Gold or silver.
Size: Silver 51mm (gold smaller).
Description: Silver: (obverse) a scene viewed from the north of King Edward's Bay at Tynemouth, with Pen Bal Crag surmounted by a lighthouse. In the left foreground is a ship, sinking by the stern and a lifeboat putting off into stormy seas to the rescue. Around the top is the inscription PALAM QUI MERUIT and around the bottom TYNEMOUTH MEDAL; (reverse) recipient's engraved name surrounded by a laurel wreath. The medal is suspended by a scroll suspender with an ornate bar. **Gold:.** The obverse is similar to the silver medal but has no motto and there are numerous changes to the scene. The reverse carries the motto on a large lifebuoy within which are the details of the recipient.
Comments: *The Tynemouth Medal Trust was formed in response to a request from Mr E. B. Convers, a New York lawyer, who had witnessed a rescue in the Tynemouth area. He was so impressed that he had a medal designed and produced and sent 100 silver medals to the Trustees to be awarded for acts of heroism to Tynesiders worldwide, or for acts of heroism in the Tyne and the surrounding area. A variant to the silver medal exists in which the reverse of the medal is inverted in relation to the suspender—this is known as the Tynemouth Extension Medal.*

VALUE:	Silver (approx. 100)	£450–575
	Gold	£850–1400

L23. DRUMMOND CASTLE MEDAL

Date: 1896.
Ribbon: Plain crimson.
Metal: Silver.
Size: 38mm.
Description: (Obverse) the veiled profile of Queen Victoria; (reverse) a wreath enclosing the name of the ship and the date of its sinking with the legend FROM QUEEN VICTORIA A TOKEN OF GRATITUDE. Fitted with a scrolled suspender.
Comments: *Presented on behalf of Queen Victoria by officials from the British Embassy in Paris to inhabitants of Brest, Ushant and Molene for their generosity and humanity in rescuing and succouring the survivors of the SS Drummond Castle which struck a reef off Ushant on 16 June 1896. Of the 143 passengers and 104 crew, all but three perished. 282 medals were struck and 271 of these were awarded to those who helped save the living and assisted in the recovery and burial of the victims.*

VALUE:

Silver (282) £300–365

L24. NEWFOUNDLAND SILVER STAR FOR BRAVERY

Date: 1897.
Ribbon: Two equal stripes of dark blue and crimson.
Metal: Silver.
Size: 36mm max.
Description: A six-pointed radiate star with ball ornaments in the interstices, surmounted by a circular medallion showing a ship in distress and having the inscription FOR BRAVERY AT SEA in a collar. Fitted with a plain ring for suspension.
Comment: *Originally instigated by the Governor of Newfoundland, Sir Terence O'Brien, in 1893, as a bravery award. A total of 27 were made. In 1897 three were awarded to those who assisted in putting out a fire on the SS* Aurora *which, loaded with dynamite, was docked in St John's Harbour, Newfoundland. These three were altered to have the name of SS* Aurora *added to the legend.*

VALUE: £850–1250

L25. QUIVER MEDALS

Date: c.1897.
Ribbon: Dark blue for water rescues, red for land, both with a broad diagonal white stripe from lower left to upper right.
Metal: Silver (29) or bronze (29).
Size: 38mm.
Description: A thick medal weighing two ounces. (Obverse) a naked figure holding a rescued child, with the winged skeletal figure of Death hovering over a stormy sea in the background; (reverse) a laureated tablet bearing the name of the recipient and the date of the act. The circumference is inscribed round the top: FOR HEROIC CONDUCT IN THE SAVING OF LIFE and THE QUIVER MEDAL round the foot. The very elaborate suspension ring is in the form of a laurel wreath and is fitted to the suspender bar by means of a scroll inscribed THE QUIVER MEDAL. Brooch mounting at top of ribbon.
Comments: *The popular Victorian magazine "Quiver" took a keen interest in rewarding heroic deeds and encouraged its readers to submit details of such bravery "to include rescues by land and water, and in any part of the world". "Quiver" also took a particular interest in promoting safety at sea and organised a Lifeboat Fund which provided not only a number of lifeboats named "Quiver" but also this gallantry award. At least 58 silver and bronze medals were awarded of which four were presented to the survivors of the Margate surf boat disaster on December 2, 1897. A specially struck medal (of a different design) was awarded by "Quiver" to Captain Inch of "Volturno" fame.*

VALUE: Silver £450–575   Bronze £350–450

If you know of a British Life Saving medal that is not included in the MEDAL YEARBOOK we would be delighted to hear from you.

Or if you can supply us with a photograph of any of the medals not illustrated in this publication we would be pleased to include it next year.

If you can help, please contact the Managing Editor, John Mussell, telephone 01404 46972 or at the address on page 1. Thank you!

L26. HUMANE SOCIETY OF NEW ZEALAND MEDALS

Date: 1898.

Ribbon: Scarlet edged with broad beige stripes on which was embroidered gold fern leaves (1898–1914) or 32mm plain royal blue (from, 1915).

Metal: Gold, silver and bronze versions.

Size:

Description: Originally an eight-pointed cross with ball points, with a circular medallion at the centre showing two figures surrounded by an inscription ROYAL HUMANE SOCIETY at the top and NEW ZEALAND round the foot, the cross mounted on an oak wreath surmounted by a Royal Crown fitted with a plain ring for suspension. The reverse was engraved with the recipient's name, date and details of the award. The second type consists of a circular medal with (obverse) an allegorical life-saving scene, name of the Society round the top and FOR LIFE SAVING in two lines in the field; (reverse) a laurel wreath with the recipient's name and details engraved in the centre. Early versions of this medal had a scrolled swivel suspension bar but later versions had a plain suspension bar. The top of the ribbon is fitted with a plain brooch.

Comments: *Presented by the Governor General as Patron of the Royal Humane Society of New Zealand. Only one or two awards are made each year. The medal is worn on the right breast. Until 1913 the Society also awarded a special gold medal, known as the Stead Medal, for acts of outstanding bravery. It was similar to the gold medal but had a suspension bar inscribed STEAD MEDAL. It was revived in 1963 for award to unsuccessful nominees for the Stanhope Gold Medal.*

Second type.

VALUE:	Gold	Silver	Bronze
Type I	£2500–3750 (6)	£1250 –1800 (73)	£650–£800 (89)
Type II	£2000–2500 (10)	£650–800 (82)	£450 –550 (449)
Stead Gold Medal —			

L26A. PORT SUNLIGHT ORDER OF CONSPICUOUS MERIT

Date: 1901.

Ribbon: None.

Metal: Gold (15 carat).

Size: 45mm high x 42mm wide.

Description: The medals were only issued in 15 carat gold (Birmingham hallmarks). The medal is in the form of a Maltese cross with a ring suspender (to allow attachment of a chain or similar for suspension). The obverse has a central legend "PORT SUNLIGHT ORDER OF CONSPICUOUS MERIT". The reverse is plain upon which the details of the recipient, the act of bravery and the date and time of the incident are engraved. The hallmark is also impressed on the reverse.

Comments: *In 1887, William Hesketh Lever (later Lord Leverhulme) began looking for a new site on which he could expand his soap-making business, at that time based in Warrington. He purchased 56 acres of unused marshy land at the site which became Port Sunlight (after his best-selling brand of soap), which was relatively flat, allowed space for expansion, and had a prime location between the River Mersey and a railway line. The garden village was founded to house his factory workers. Lever personally helped to plan the village, and employed nearly 30 different architects. He introduced schemes for welfare, education and the entertainment of his workers, and encouraged recreation and organisations which promoted art, literature, science or music. His stated aims were "to socialise and Christianise business relations and he also decided to instigate a form of recognition for the various acts of bravery that they had shown in rescuing those in distress. To this end he founded the Port Sunlight Order of Conspicuous Merit. The first medals were presented at a meeting held in the Hume Hall, Port Sunlight on 26 August 1901, where five awards were made for acts of bravery during that year. The final award was made in 1923—a total of only 19 awards having been made.*

VALUE: —

L27. THE SHEFFIELD SOCIETY FOR THE RECOGNITION OF BRAVERY MEDAL

Date: c. 1903.
Ribbon: Blue.
Metal: Gold, silver and bronze.
Size: 38 mm.
Description: (Obverse) a laurel branch and an oak leaf branch, tied to form a wreath, surmounted by a crown with inside the wreath an array of arrows above three sheaves of corn; (reverse) a laurel wreath upon which is a shield on which are inscribed details of the recipient and the act of bravery, with SHEFFIELD SOCIETY FOR RECOGNISING BRAVERY around.
Comments: *The Society owes its inception to Colonel Sir John E. Bingham, Bt. The rewards were intended to be given to any person residing in the city of Sheffield or within a radius of six miles from the Sheffield Parish Church, including the borough of Rotherham, for a conspicuous act of bravery, but not for rescues or attempted rescues from drowning and rescue or attempted rescues from asphyxia in mines, wells, sewers, and the like, or for any act of bravery that received an award from the Royal Humane Society.*

VALUE:		
	Gold	—
	Silver	£400–525
	Bronze	£300–400

L28. BOYS' BRIGADE CROSS FOR HEROISM

Date: September 1902.
Ribbon: Originally royal blue with two equal white stripes, but changed to plain royal blue in 1941.
Metal: Bronze.
Description: A cross pattée formed of four V-shaped finials linked to a circular disc inscribed the BOYS' BRIGADE CROSS FOR HEROISM and enclosing the emblem of the Boys' Brigade. The cross has a suspension ring and a plain brooch bar at the top of ribbon. There are two types, with or without a Geneva cross behind the anchor in the emblem (added in 1926 when the Boys' Life Brigade amalgamated with the Boys' Brigade).
Comments: *First awarded in 1904, the cross was awarded only 194 times up to the end of 1985, including five posthumous awards. Simon Herriott, aged 8, became the youngest holder in 1980.*

VALUE:		
	First type (without central cross)	£750–1000
	Second type (with central cross)	£500–600

L29 & L29A. BOYS' & GIRLS' LIFE BRIGADE MEDALS see nos. 367 & 368.

L30. CARNEGIE HERO FUND MEDAL

Date: 1908.
Ribbon: None.
Metal: Bronze.
Size: 90mm.
Description: (Obverse) an angel and a nude male figure surrounded by an inscription "HE SERVES GOD BEST WHO MOST NOBLY SERVES HUMANITY"; (reverse) two wreaths surrounding a central tablet inscribed "FOR HEROIC ENDEAVOUR TO SAVE HUMAN LIFE 19…" surrounding a further inscription "PRESENTED BY THE TRUSTEES OF THE CARNEGIE HERO FUND". Details of the recipient are engraved on the rim.
Comments: *The Carnegie Hero Fund Trust was established in Scotland by Andrew Carnegie in 1908. The first medallion was awarded posthumously on 26 November 1909 to Thomas Wright for a life saving act on 23 September 1908. To date 173 medallions have been awarded.*

VALUE:
    Bronze   £850–1300

L31. RSPCA LIFE-SAVING MEDALS

Date: 1909.
Ribbon: Blue with three white stripes in the centre, the central stripe being narrower than the others (silver); blue with a central white stripe flanked by narrow red and white stripes (bronze).
Metal: Silver or bronze.
Size: 36mm.
Description: (Obverse) a seated female figure surrounded by a cow, sheep, cat, dog, goat and horse; (reverse) plain, with an inscription. The recipient's name usually appears on the rim. Both medals have a brooch bar inscribed FOR HUMANITY.
Comments: *Instituted in 1909 by the Royal Society for the Prevention of Cruelty to Animals, this medal is awarded in silver or bronze for acts of gallantry in saving the lives of animals. See also L38.*

VALUE:		*Miniature*
Silver	£300–365	£150–200
Bronze	£175–250	£100–150

L31A. NATIONAL CANINE DEFENCE LEAGUE MEDAL

Date: c. 1900.
Ribbon: Red.
Metal: Silver or bronze.
Size: 30mm.
Description: (Obverse) Victory standing with sword in hand over vanquished dragon, her right hand resting on a dog; NATIONAL CANINE DEFENCE LEAGUE inscribed round the top; (reverse) spray of oak leaves with a placard engraved with the name of the recipient and date of the award. Fitted with a plain ring for suspension
Comments: *Awarded for acts of bravery or exceptional humanity in the rescue of dogs from dangerous situations. Medals in bronze were intended for award to dogs for brave acts.*

VALUE:	Silver (early issue)	£1000–£1600
	Silver (late issue)	£300–375
	Bronze	£250–300

L31B. THE PEOPLE'S DISPENSARY FOR SICK ANIMALS CROSS

Date: —
Ribbon: Broad red band with a narrow blue central stripe and broad white edges.
Metal: Silver.
Size: 32mm.
Description: A plain cross pattée with the initials PDSA on the arms. At the centre is a medallion bearing the figure of St Giles. The reverse is plain except for the name of the recipient and date of the award.
Comments: *Awarded to people who have performed acts of bravery involving animals. The PDSA also award medals to animals, the Dickin Medal (no. 358) being the most important.*

VALUE: £150–265

L31C. OUR DUMB FRIENDS LEAGUE MEDAL

Date: —
Ribbon: Plain red.
Metal: Silver or bronze.
Size: Heart-shaped, 45mm x 50mm.
Description: (Obverse) Figures of a horse, dog, cat and donkey within a heart-shaped ribbon inscribed OUR DUMB FRIENDS LEAGUE A SOCIETY FOR THE ENCOURAGEMENT OF KINDNESS TO ANIMALS; (reverse) engraved with the name of the recipient and date of the award.
Comments: *Awarded by the League for acts of bravery involving the rescue of animals.*

VALUE: Silver £400–475   Bronze £350–400

L32. SCOUT ASSOCIATION GALLANTRY MEDALS

Bronze award ribbon.

Silver award ribbon.

Gilt award ribbon.

Date: 1909.
Ribbon: Red (bronze), blue (silver) or half red, half blue (gilt).
Metal: Bronze, silver and gilt.
Size: 33mm.
Description: The medal is in the form of a cross pattée with the fleur-de-lis emblem at the centre. *Type 1* 1909–19 (obverse) FOR SAVING LIFE and the motto BE PREPARED; (reverse) (i) indent of Scout emblem and motto with ridge underneath; (ii) plain. *Type 2* 1920–66 (obverse) FOR GALLANTRY with motto BE PREPARED, (reverse) plain with maker's name "Collins, London". *Type 3* 1966– date (obverse) FOR GALLANTRY with the new Scout emblem with inverted "V", no emblem; (reverse) plain. The Type 1 medal is suspended from a ring suspender and Types 2 and 3 have a fixed bar suspender.
Comments: *The Scout movement began informally in 1907 and the Boy Scouts Association was founded a year later. The Scout Association's highest award is the Cornwell Scout badge, named after "Boy" Cornwell of Jutland fame. However, gallantry awards were instituted in 1908 and 1909. The bronze cross is the highest award of the Association for gallantry, granted for special heroism or action in the face of extraordinary risk. The silver cross is awarded for gallantry in circumstances of considerable risk. The gilt cross is awarded for gallantry in circumstances of moderate risk. A clasp may be awarded to the holder of any gallantry award for further acts of gallantry in circumstances of similar risk. Collective awards may also be made to Troops, Groups or other Units within the Scout Movement and in 1943 the Boy Scouts of Malta & Gozo received the unique distinction of being awarded the Bronze Cross.*

VALUE: Bronze (148)   £1000–1500
           Silver (1343)   £650–900
           Gilt   £450–650

L32A. CORNWELL SCOUT BADGE

Date: 1916.
Ribbon: None.
Metal: Bronze.
Size: 30 x 25mm.
Description: The fleur de lys of the Scout Association with a stylised capital C in the centre, suspended by a brooch pin with attached safety chain.
Comments: *This award was named after John Travers Cornwell who won a posthumous Victoria Cross at the Battle of Jutland. At the age of 16 Jack Cornwell was one of the youngest winners of the VC and had been a Scout before entering the Navy. It was originally awarded "in respect of pre-eminently high character and devotion to duty, together with great courage and endurance" but is now reserved exclusively to members of a training section of the Scout Association under 25 years of age (until 2002, under 20 years of age) who have an outstanding record of service and efficiency. It is very rarely awarded, the last occasion being in 1998. To date a total of 634 badges have been awarded.*

VALUE: £350–525

L33. C.Q.D. MEDALS

Date: 1909.
Ribbon: Plain dark blue.
Metal: Silver-gilt, silver, bronze.
Size: 45mm.
Description: (Obverse) the SS *Republic* with the initials C.Q.D. at the top; (reverse) the words FOR GALLANTRY across the middle, with a very verbose inscription round the circumference and continued in eight lines across the field. Ring suspension. Issued unnamed, but examples are known with the recipient's name and ship privately engraved.
Comments: *This medal takes its curious name from the CQD signal (All Stations Distress) sent out by the stricken White Star steamship* Republic *after it collided with the Italian steamer* Florida *on January 21, 1909. The liner* Baltic *responded to the call. The* Republic *was the more severely damaged vessel, but all of her passengers and crew were transferred, first to the* Florida *and then to the* Baltic, *before she sank. The saloon passengers of the* Baltic *and* Republic *subscribed to a fund to provide medals to the crews of all three ships in saving more than 1700 lives. Four silver-gilt examples without suspender were presented to the captains of the three ships involved and to Jack Binns, the Marconi operator aboard the* Republic *who sent out the CQD radio signal. Silver medals with ring suspenders were presented to the officers and crews. Binns became a hero when the survivors reached New York and was given a welcome parade. This was the first time that radio was used to effect a rescue at sea and indirectly sealed the fate of the* Titanic *three years later, as the White Star Line wrongly assumed that any larger liner would take several hours to sink and radio would obtain help quickly within well-used shipping lanes and lifeboats would only be required to effect the transfer of passengers and crew. As a result the number of lifeboats on the* Titanic *was severely reduced. Coincidentally, Jack Binns was offered the post of wireless officer on board the new* Titanic *but declined. It is believed that bronze examples exist but the Editor would be pleased to learn of any definite sightings of these.*

VALUE:
Silver-gilt (4)	£850–1300
Silver	£350–450

L33A. BOLTON & DISTRICT HUMANE SOCIETY MEDAL

Date: 1911.
Ribbon: Plain dark blue.
Metal: Bronze.
Size: 34mm.
Description: (Obverse) a vertical flying angel holding out a wreath in the left hand with, around the perimeter, "VIRTUE ET PATIENTIA". At the bottom is a star with the maker's name, "JENKINS B'HAM". (Reverse) around the perimeter "BOLTON AND DISTRICT HUMANE SOCIETY" and in the centre "HULTON COLLIERY DISASTER DECEMBER 21st 1910". The suspender is very similar to that of the Crimea medal. The medal was issued unnamed.
Comments: *At the time this was the largest recorded mine disaster which occurred at the No. 3 Bank (Pretoria) Pit of the Hulton Colliery on 21 December 1910. The pit which was located at Atherton near Bolton, Lancashire and was 400 metres deep, was devastated by an enormous explosion which destroyed part of the upcast shaft with the subsequent fall of earth sealing in the miners below. Whilst a number of miners were killed outright by the explosion, by far the greatest number died of carbon monoxide poisoning. Despite the very real danger to their lives many men volunteered to go below ground to attempt to save the survivors and their bravery was outstanding. Despite their efforts only three men survived the disaster in which the total dead was 370. The bravery of the rescuers was recognised by the Bolton & District Humane Society who presented this specially struck medal to 160 recipients. The Order of St. John awarded one silver and ten bronze medals and the Government recognised the rescuers' bravery with 10 Edward Medals (Mines) 2nd class. In addition, medals awarded by the Lancashire and Cheshire Coal Owners Rescue Station with a clasp "Hulton 1911" are known, of which one extant example is named to a rescuer. Further research is required to establish the relationship of this medal to the disaster.*

VALUE: £300–365

L34. CARPATHIA AND TITANIC MEDALS

Date: 1912.
Ribbon: Maroon.
Metal: Gold, silver or bronze.
Size: Height 40mm; max. width 35mm.
Description: The ornately shaped medal, in the best Art Nouveau style, has the suspension ring threaded through the head of Neptune whose long beard flows into two dolphins terminating in a fouled anchor and ship's spars. (Obverse) the *Carpathia* steaming between icebergs; (reverse) a twelve-line inscription, with the name of the recipient and the name of the manufacturer at the foot. It was worn from a straight bar suspender.
Comments: *This medal recalls one of the greatest tragedies at sea, when the White Star liner* Titanic *struck an iceberg on her maiden voyage and sank with the loss of 1490 lives. The 711 survivors were picked up by the* Carpathia *whose officers and men were subsequently awarded this medal in gold, silver or bronze according to the rank of the recipient.*

VALUE:	Gold (14)	£7500–12,000
	Silver (110)	£3500–6200
	Bronze (180)	£2500–3500

L35. LLOYD'S MEDALS FOR SERVICES TO LLOYD'S

Date: November 1913.
Ribbon: Blue with broad white stripes towards the edge.
Metal: Silver.
Size: 36mm.
Description: (Obverse) Neptune in a chariot drawn by four horses; (reverse) an oak-leaf wreath enclosing a scroll inscribed FOR SERVICES TO LLOYD'S. Fitted with ring suspension.
Comments: *Instituted by Lloyd's Committee, this medal was intended to reward services of a general nature.*

VALUE:		*Miniature*
Gold (14)	£2000–4750	—
Silver (10)	£1000–1250	£200–250

L35A. ERINPURA AND TOPAZE MEDAL

Date: June 1919.
Ribbon: None.
Metal: Silver or bronze.
Size: 32mm.
Description: (Obverse) simple inscription 526 MEN, WOMEN AND CHILDREN . TAKEN OFF . S.S. BRINPURA . AGROUND ON . MUSHEGERA REEF BY H.M.S.TOPAZE . 15.6.19; (reverse) an oak-leaf wreath with A MEMENTO PRESENTED BY THE PASSENGERS within.
Comments: *In a severe dust storm on 15 June 1919 the SS* Erinpura *went aground at full speed on the Mushegera Reef in the Red Sea. HMS* Topaze, *a Gem Class scout cruiser, came to her aid and took off the passengers and most of the crew, leaving a few men on board to maintain the engines. Attempts to refloat her were unsuccessful as the bow section was stuck fast and eventually had to be cut away and completely replaced. The medals were struck on behalf of the grateful passengers and presented to the officers and crew of HMS* Topaze. *The medals are known in bronze although there are unconfirmed reports of examples in silver—perhaps presented to the officers (?). The obverse is incorrectly inscribed* BRINPURA *as the ship has been confirmed as the* Erinpura, *built for the British India Steam Navigation Co. Ltd in 1910 and sunk by German bombers en route to Malta in World War II.*

VALUE:	Bronze	£100–150

L36. ORDER OF INDUSTRIAL HEROISM

Date: 1923.
Ribbon: Bright watered red.
Metal: Bronze.
Size: 28mm.
Description: (Obverse) a modern interpretation of St Christopher carrying Christ (by Eric Gill); (reverse) inscription ORDER OF INDUSTRIAL HEROISM around the perimeter and in the upper half AWARDED BY THE DAILY HERALD above the recipient's name and date of award.
Comments: *Created by the* Daily Herald *and first issued in 1923. It was given as a reward to the "workers" who demonstrated bravery in the workplace and was initially only to be awarded to members of a Trade Union. However, there are numerous examples of the awards being given to non Union members and the definition of "workplace" was wide. The award was intimately associated with the* Daily Herald *throughout the lifetime of the newspaper and when it ceased publication in 1963 the award was discontinued. The medal was always awarded with a certificate and a monetary award. 440 were awarded.*

VALUE:	Bronze	£600–825

L37. CORPORATION OF GLASGOW BRAVERY MEDALS

Type I obverse.

Date: 1924
Ribbon: Green with red edges.
Metal: Gold, silver or bronze.
Size: 38mm (type I), 33mm (type II), 30mm (type III).
Description: Type I: (obverse) Fame blowing a trumpet and holding a laurel wreath in front of a circular scrolled cartouche inscribed FOR BRAVERY; (reverse) plain, engraved with the name and details of the recipient. Type II: (obverse) wreath enclosing the words FOR BRAVERY; (reverse) Arms of the Corporation of Glasgow and details of the recipient. Type III: (obverse) Arms of the Corporation of Glasgow with FOR BRAVERY above and two sprigs of laurel below; (reverse) plain for details of the recipient. Fitted with a ring suspension and an ornate thistle brooch inscribed GALLANTRY in a scroll.
Comments: *Following the reorganisation of local government in Scotland in 1975, the award ceased and was replaced by the Strathclyde Regional Council Medal for Bravery.*

VALUE:	Type I	Type II	Type III
Gold	—	—	£300–430
Silver	£300–400	£300–400	—
Bronze	—	—	—

L37A. IMPERIAL CHEMICAL INDUSTRIES BRAVERY AWARD

Date: 1930.
Ribbon: Blue with gold (9ct) brooch bar "Fortis".
Metal: Gold (9ct) (pre-war), later bronze.
Size: 38mm x 26mm
Description: (Obverse) "Awarded for Bravery" with a lion rampant bearing the letters "I.C.I."; (reverse) inscription in raised letters (name, location and date of incident).
Comments: *A meeting of the ICI Central Council in 1929 proposed an award to be given for outstanding acts of bravery by ICI workers whilst at work. Originally awarded in 9ct gold but after World War II issued in bronze. The first award was made to Harry Smithies in 1929 and the last to James Nicol in 1975. The award is still available for issue. 36 awards have been made to date.*

VALUE:	Gold	£1000–1250
	Bronze	£800–1000

L38. RSPCA MARGARET WHEATLEY CROSS

Date: 1936.
Ribbon: 32mm blue with a white stripe towards each edge.
Metal: Bronze.
Size: 33mm square.
Description: Cross pattée with a central circular cross with rounded ends superimposed. R.S.P.C.A. across the top arm of the outer cross and INSTD. 1936 across the lower arm. THE MARGARET WHEATLEY CROSS inscribed in four lines across the centre. (Reverse) central circle inscribed FOR BRAVING DEATH ON BEHALF OF ANIMALS, above and below a raised horizontal panel engraved with the details of the award. Fixed ring for suspension.
Comments: *The RSPCA's highest award, it was named in memory of 16 year-old Margaret Wheatley who was killed by a train at Grange-over-Sands on June 4, 1936 while saving her dog thsat had got trapped on the railway line. She was posthumously awarded the RSPCA's Silver Medal and was also the first recipient of the cross named in her honour. To date, a total of 70 crosses have been awarded, at least 32 of them posthumously.*

VALUE: —

L39. LLOYD'S MEDAL FOR BRAVERY AT SEA

Date: 1940.
Ribbon: White with broad blue stripes at the sides.
Metal: Silver.
Size: 36mm.
Description: (Obverse) a seated nude male figure holding a laurel wreath, extending his hand towards a ship on the horizon; (reverse) a trident surmounted by a scroll inscribed BRAVERY, enclosed in a wreath of oak leaves. It has a ring suspender.
Comments: *Instituted by Lloyd's Committee, it was awarded to officers and men of the Merchant Navy and fishing fleets for exceptional bravery at sea in time of war. A total of 523 medals was awarded up to December 1947 when it was discontinued.*

VALUE:
| Silver | £550–850 | *Miniature* | £200–250 |

L40. LONDON, MIDLAND AND SCOTTISH RAILWAY MEDAL

Date: 1940.
Ribbon: Dark blue.
Metal: Silver.
Size: 38mm.
Description: (Obverse) Three different steam locomotive chimneys with a radiant sun in the right background with the inscription LONDON, MIDLAND AND SCOTTISH RAILWAY round the circumference; (reverse) a locomotive driving wheel on which is superimposed at the left a sprig of laurel, with the inscription FOR COURAGE or FOR MERIT round the top of the circumference. The date 1940 appears in the exergue. Fitted with a plain ring for suspension.
Comments: *Instituted by the Chairman of the LMS Company for acts of gallantry or meritorious service, hence the two different reverse types. The Chairman, Lord Stamp, was killed in an air raid in 1941 and it is believed that many of the records relating to this medal perished with him. Although the exact number of awards is not known, it is believed that about 20 awards were made.*

VALUE:
For courage —
For merit —

L41. SOUTHERN RAILWAY MERITORIOUS SERVICE MEDAL

Date: 1940.

Ribbon: Green with railway track and sleepers in gold.

Metal: Silver gilt.

Size: 32mm.

Description: (Obverse) a cross formy with SR in a circle at the centre, superimposed on a laurel wreath surrounded by a locomotive driving wheel; (reverse) FOR MERIT in seriffed capitals over a space for the recipient's name and SOUTHERN RAILWAY across the foot. The ornamental suspension bar is in the form of a vehicle spring. This medal was designed by Kruger Gray and struck at the Royal Mint.

Comments: *Instituted by the Directors of the Company for award to those employees who had been honoured by the King. 18 medals were awarded at a ceremony on August 16, 1940, and a further six medals were subsequently awarded.*

VALUE: —

L42. THE DALE AWARD

Instituted: November 1940.

Ribbon: White with broad blue and narrow black stripes towards the edges.

Metal: Silver.

Size: 33mm.

Description: (Obverse) a central medallion enamelled in white bearing the spires of Coventry Cathedral, surrounded by an inscription: THE DALE AWARD / COVENTRY.NOV.14.1940; (reverse) a laurel wreath enclosing a ten-line inscription across the middle: AWARDED BY THE COVENTRY HOSPITAL FUND FOR DEVOTION TO HOSPITAL & AMBULANCE DUTY DURING THE COVENTRY AIR RAID NOVEMBER 14th 1940. The rim bears the Birmingham assay marks and maker's mark of Thomas Fattorini. The medal was not named.

Comments: *This medal is known to have been awarded to a St John's Ambulance driver but nothing further is known and details of the Dale Award and a list of recipients is sought.*

VALUE: —

L43. LONDON PASSENGER TRANSPORT BOARD MEDAL FOR BRAVERY

Instituted: 1940.

Ribbon: Red with green central stripe and four narrow white stripes on either side.

Metal: Cupro-nickel.

Size: 38mm.

Description: (Obverse) a naked man kneeling and turning a large wheel; (reverse) the words LONDON TRANSPORT above a sprig of laurel, with a space for the recipient's name and a three-line inscription across the foot: FOR BRAVERY AND DEVOTION TO DUTY. Plain suspension bar and an ornamental brooch fitment at the top of the ribbon.

Comments: *This medal was instituted by Lord Ashfield, Chairman of the LPTB, to reward "special deeds of bravery" undertaken by LPTB staff during the Blitz. Only nine medals were awarded (all presented on February 21, 1941) before the medal was discontinued, after some government pressure, to encourage nominations for the official civilian bravery awards of the George Cross and George Medal. A few unnamed specimens are known, possibly reaching the market from the stock of John Pinches when they ceased business.*

VALUE:
Named (9)	£750–850
Unnamed	£250–300

L44. LONDON AND NORTH EASTERN RAILWAY GALLANTRY MEDAL

Date: 1941.

Ribbon: Dark blue with a central white stripe flanked by narrow white stripes.

Metal: Silver with a matt finish.

Size: 38mm.

Description: (Obverse) a shield containing the arms of the company, superimposed on a laurel wreath surrounded by the inscription LONDON AND NORTH EASTERN RAILWAY on a raised band; (reverse) a scroll for the recipient's name superimposed on a laurel wreath with the rising sun in the background. The raised band is inscribed FOR COURAGE AND RESOURCE. Fitted with a plain suspension bar and an ornamental brooch bar at the top of the ribbon.

Comments: *Awarded "for outstanding acts of gallantry and resource which are not connected with enemy action, but which are of such a standard as would warrant recommendations for Government recognition had the acts been connected with enemy action". As some of the medals were awarded for actions resulting from enemy air raids the phrase "not connected with enemy action" was very liberally interpreted. A total of 22 medals were awarded, the last in 1947.*

VALUE: —

L44A. DICKIN MEDAL

Date: 1943.
Ribbon: Three equal bands of green, dark brown and pale blue.
Metal: Bronze.
Size: 36mm.
Description: (Obverse) a laurel wreath enclosing the inscription "For Gallantry" in raised cursive script over the motto WE ALSO SERVE in block capitals; the initials PDSA in a tablet at the top of the wreath; (reverse) the date, name of recipient and details of the award. Fitted with a plain ring for suspension.
Comments: *Awarded by the People's Dispensary for Sick Animals to recognise acts of bravery by birds and animals in wartime, and consequently popularly known as the Animals' VC. Originally, Maria Dickin, founder of the PDSA, also instituted a lesser award for acts of bravery by animals, known as the PDSA Silver Medal. The Dickin Medal is very rarely awarded but in recent years three medals were awarded following the terrorist attacks in the USA on September 11, 2001. Two were awarded to guide dogs that assisted their blind handlers to safety and the third was awarded to "Apollo", one of the search and rescue dogs who did such sterling work. "Apollo" was selected by ballot from out of the 300+ dogs involved. More recently in January 2003 another award was made, albeit posthumously, to "Sam" of the Royal Army Veterinary Corps for bravery in war-torn Bosnia in 1998. The latest award is to arms and explosives search dog Treo, a black labrador, for his work in Helmand Province, Afghanistan, over several months during 2008. He is the 27th canine recipient out of a total of 63 awards made to date. Medals to famous animals tend to sell for higher figures.*

VALUE: £10,000–£20,000
   (Spink sold the medal to Rip a mongrel dog for £24,000+, including the buyer's premium, in April 2009)

L45. BINNEY MEMORIAL MEDAL

Date: 1947.
Ribbon: None.
Metal: Bronze.
Size: 48mm.
Description: (Obverse) a bust of Captain R.D. Binney, CBE, RN; (reverse) inscription FOR COURAGE IN SUPPORT OF LAW AND ORDER and AWARDED TO above the recipient's name on a raised tablet.
Comments: *Instituted in memory of Captain Ralph Douglas Binney who was killed on 8 December 1944 in the City of London while attempting to apprehend two armed robbers single-handedly. It is awarded annually to the British citizen who displays the greatest courage in support of law and order within the areas under the jurisdiction of the Metropolitan Police and the City of London Police. The medal is not intended for wear. See MEDAL NEWS, August 1998 for a detailed article on the medal by Victor Knight.*

VALUE: £750–1000

L46. SEA CADET GALLANTRY CROSS

Date:
Ribbon: Red with a central white stripe and blue stripes towards the edges.
Metal: Silver.
Size: 36mm.
Description: (Obverse) a fouled anchor within a wreath superimposed on a cross pattée inscribed FOR GALLANTRY with initials N and L on the left and right arms of the cross to signify the Navy League; (reverse) blank.
Comments: *Awarded by the Sea Cadet Association, originally the Navy League, for gallantry in saving or attempting to save life under circumstances of exceptional danger and personal risk to the saver. It has been very rarely awarded.*

VALUE: £800–1000

L47. SEA CADET GALLANTRY MEDAL

Date:
Ribbon: Red with a central white stripe and blue stripes towards the edges.
Metal: Bronze.
Size: 36mm.
Description: A circular medal with a plain ring suspension. (Obverse) an image of the cross as above but without the initials on the arms; (reverse) blank.
Comments: *Awarded for gallantry in saving or attempting to save life under circumstances of considerable danger and personal risk to the saver. Both the cross and the medal are manufactured by Spink & Son. Gallantry certificates and commendations are also awarded for life saving in lesser circumstances.*

VALUE: —

L47A. GALLANTRY MEDALLISTS' LEAGUE GOLD MEDAL FOR COURAGE

Date: 2006
Ribbon: Red with a dark blue stripe towards the right and light blue towards the left, representing the colours of the Gallantry Medallists League.
Metal: 9ct white gold and gilded.
Size: 36mm.
Description: The medal is made in two pieces. (Obverse) a six-pointed star with a central disc hand painted in enamels surrounded by a red enamel ring bearing the words "FOR COURAGE". The central disc depicts a hand at the top pulling up another hand, symbolising rescue, the upper hand has wings symbolising the innocence of youth. These wings are carried over into the design of the suspension. (Reverse) inscribed with the name of the medal, the recipient and details of the act for which the award is made.
Comments: *The medal is to be presented each year to the most deserving recipient of the* Woman's Own *"Children of Courage" award—a ceremony which was instituted in 1973 to honour ten of the UK's most deserving children who have acted heroically over the previous year. The heroism can take many forms from courage in the face of disability or steadfast devotion to bravery in saving life. The first award was made in December 2006 to nine-year-old Lewis Woodruffe who calmly led his young brothers and sisters to safety during a disastrous fire at the family home.*

VALUE: —

L48. HUNDRED OF SALFORD HUMANE SOCIETY SWIMMING PROFICIENCY MEDALS

Date: c. 1922.

Ribbon: Special Proficiency Medal and Proficiency Medal issued without a ribbon, although often seen with a blue ribbon.

Metal: Both silver.

Size: Special Proficiency Medal—irregular shape with small ring suspender. Proficiency Medal—circular 26mm with a small ring suspender.

Description: Special Proficiency Medal: (obverse) an ornamental pattern of three shields, bearing the arms of Salford backed by crossed tridents. An intertwined blue enamel band around the medal carries the legend HUMANE SOCIETY FOR THE HUNDRED OF SALFORD; (reverse) plain. Proficiency Medal: (obverse) a single shield carrying the arms of Salford surrounded by a blue enamel band that carries the words HUMANE SOCIETY FOR THE HUNDRED OF SALFORD, the whole is encircled by a wreath and is surmounted by a crown; (reverse) plain.

Comments: *Following the discontinuing of awards for life saving in 1921, the Society began to run competitions for children with the object of encouraging swimming proficiency with a view to life saving. Two medals were awarded, the Special Proficiency Medal and the Proficiency Medal. Each year there are a number of winners of the Proficiency Medal and the best boy and girl are selected to receive the Special Proficiency Medal.*

VALUE:

Special Proficiency Medal	£75-£125
Proficiency Medal	£50-£80

L49. ROYAL HUMANE SOCIETY SWIMMING PROFICIENCY MEDAL

Date: 1882.

Ribbon: None.

Metal: Silver.

Size: 51mm.

Description: (Obverse) a life saving scene, circumscribed by the motto NARE EST ALIENAM NOSSE SALUTEM in sans serif capitals and by a heavily beaded border. The exergue is blank to allow the engraved details of the school and the date of award to be entered; (reverse) "Awarded FOR PROFICIENCY IN SWIMMING EXERCISE with reference to saving life from DROWNING". Above this "ROYAL HUMANE SOCIETY", and below "INST: 1774" and again circumscribed by heavy beading.

Comments: *In February 1882, the RHS received a letter from Dr Dukes, the physician at Rugby School, relating to the establishment of a prize "for swimming and for a knowledge of the treatment of the apparently drowned". The Society saw merit in this and by the end of the year the medal was awarded to seven winners of competitions held at seven public schools. The competition grew in popularity and for many years 20 to 30 medals per year were awarded. However, with increasing competition from the Royal Life Saving Society the RHS award declined in popularity and the last awards were made in 1948. The medal was awarded only in silver, although a bronze specimen is known.*

VALUE: £75-£125

L50. THE ROYAL LIFE SAVING SOCIETY— MOUNTBATTEN MEDAL

Date: 1951.
Ribbon: None.
Metal: Silver.
Size: 51mm.
Description: A circular medal without suspender. The medal is cased. The obverse has the family crest of the Mountbatten family and on the reverse is "The Mountbatten Medal of the Royal Life Saving Society for the award holder who makes the best rescue of the year—Presented by the President RLSS The Earl Mountbatten of Burma". The name of the recipient and the year of the award is engraved on the lower rim of the medal.
Comments: *Earl Mountbatten instituted the medal in 1951 and it was to be awarded annually for a rescue adjudged by RLSS Commonwealth Council to be the bravest performed in that year by an award holder of the RLSS who, in the opinion of the Commonwealth president, makes the best rescue of the year. Originally, the conditions of the award required that the potential recipient should, "not been otherwise signally honoured". This effectively disqualified many worthy recipients for consideration of the award, so, in 1965 this condition was removed. Since its inception the medal has generally been awarded annually, but occasionally no award was made, as the rescues in those years were adjudged not to have met the high standard necessary to qualify for the medal. Exceptionally, in 1955, 2004 and 2006 there were two recipients. To date 36 awards have been made.*

Value: £500–600

L51. TYNE & WEAR FIRE AND CIVIL DEFENCE AUTHORITY MEDAL FOR BRAVERY

Date: 1986
Ribbon: Three blue and two white stripes.
Metal: Base metal with colouring according to class.
Size:
Description: (Obverse) The medal took the form of a five winged star representative of the Tyne & Wear Fire Service badge with a central device consisting of an outer collar bearing the words "Tyne and Wear Fire and Civil Defence Authority", the inner circle having stylised flames with "Award for Bravery" incorporated above and below the flames; (reverse) a plain back on which were engraved the recipient's name and the date of act that the medal was awarded for. Details of the act of bravery were not included but were recorded in a Roll of Honour book.
Comments: *The medal was awarded in three classes: Gold, Silver and Bronze to recognise acts of bravery by members of the public in emergency situations in Tyne & Wear. It was also awarded to members of the Fire Service for acts of bravery outside of their normal firefighting duties. In 1992 the award was replaced by a scroll.*

VALUE:

Gold (21)	£100–150
Silver (45)	£90–120
Bronze (84)	£75–100

Once again this year we have included a section on the most common "foreign" medals found in British Groups, i.e. those medals issued by a foreign authority to British or Commonwealth personnel which they in turn have sought permission to wear alongside those medals awarded by their own government. Quite often these medals, when found, were awarded for gallantry where the recipient was directly involved in action with allies from the country who conferred the medal, either fighting alongside them or in an act of heroism involving one of their countrymen.

We are deeply indebted to readers, and especially those members of the British Medal Forum, who have forwarded suggestions for which medals to include within this section to allow it to expand, we do hope that more will be forthcoming in the future. We are particularly interested in any information on numbers of these medals and decorations awarded to British personnel as this will undoubtedly affect value considerably.

It must be stressed that included here are only the most common medals found in British and Commonwealth groups and the list is by no means exhaustive. It has always been common practice amongst high ranking officers of all countries to, in effect, "swap" orders and decorations with allies, some of which would never be received by the ordinary fighting soldier, sailor or airman. Because of the rarity of these awards within British groups it has been decided to exclude them at this stage, although we are grateful for all examples of "one-offs" that have been sent in.

As always it must be stressed that the prices given here are for single examples as found in dealers' lists and websites, when found in an attributable group their value dramatically increases.

BELGIUM

As with most orders, these are awarded in various classes. In this section we have concentrated on those most commonly encountered.

*Order of Leopold II,
Officer's breast badge.*

ORDER OF LEOPOLD II
Commander's neck badge	£180–350
Knight's badge	£55–75
Officer's badge	£45–65
Miniature	£25–35

349

BELGIUM *continued*

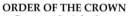

Order of the Crown, Commander's badge,

ORDER OF THE CROWN
Commander's badge	£225–350
Officer's badge	£40–55
Knight's badge	£30–45
Miniature	£25–30

CROIX DE GUERRE
WWI	£30–45
WWII	£35–50
Miniature	£12–15

DECORATION MILITAIRE   £25–35

Miniature   £10–15

FRANCE

LEGION d'HONNEUR 1870–1951
   Commander's neck badge   £350–450
   Officer's badge   £125–175
   Knight's badge   £75–100

   Miniature   £25–30

MÉDAILLE MILITAIRE 1870   £35–45

Miniature   £25–35

CROIX DE GUERRE
   1914–15 reverse   £25–35
   1914–16 reverse   £25–35
   1914–17 reverse   £25–35
   1914–18 reverse   £20–30
   WWII   £34–55
   for each star or palm add £5

   Miniature   £12–15

GREECE

ORDER OF THE REDEEMER
Commander's badge   £400–625
Knight's badge   £250–350
Officer's badge   £150–200

Miniature   £45–55

GREEK WAR CROSS   £50–100

Miniature   £10–15

ITALY

ORDER OF THE CROWN
Commander's badge   £150–225
Officer's badge   £75–100
Knight's badge   £55–75

Miniature   £40–60

AL VALORE (unnamed)
Bronze   £30–45
Silver   £45–55
Silver-gilt   £55–65

Miniature   bronze £15–20
    silver £25–30
    gilt £25–30

Restrikes are also known. They can be distinguished from the originals by the omission of the initials FG at the bottom on the obverse.

In addition to the above medals, the Messina Earthquake Medal, awarded by the King of Italy in 1908 to British personnel who went to the aid of victims of the tragic earthquake at Messina, can be found under Medal No. 163A

ITALY *continued*

WAR MERIT CROSS	£15–30
Miniature	£10–20

JAPAN

ORDER OF THE RISING SUN

3rd Class	£550–650
4th Class	£400–500
5th Class	£250–275
6th Class	£200–225
7th Class	£55–75
8th Class	£35–55
Miniature	£35–55

ORDER OF THE SACRED TREASURE

3rd Class	£460–565
4th Class	£250–300
5th Class	£150–200
6th Class	£100–175
7th Class	£40–50
8th Class	£25–40
Miniature	£40–60

LUXEMBOURG

**CROIX DE GUERRE
WWII**   £60–80

Miniature   £15–20

NORWAY

**KING HAAKON VII
FREEDOM CROSS**   £175–250

Miniature   £15–20

**KING HAAKON VII
FREEDOM MEDAL**   £120–180

Miniature   £15–20

POLAND

**CROSS OF VALOUR
WWII** £55–75

Miniature £10–15

ROMANIA

**ORDER OF THE STAR OF ROMANIA
WITH SWORDS (1864–1931)**
£75–150

Miniature £35–50

ORDER OF THE CROWN (1932–47)
£75–150

Miniature £25–35

355

RUSSIA

ORDER OF ST STANISLAUS
Gold   £4500–£7750+
Silver-gilt   £1200–1700

Miniature   £160–275

ORDER OF ST ANNE

    Gold   £6000–16,000+

    Miniature   £160–265

CROSS OF ST GEORGE
  3rd Class   £350–525
  4th Class   £250–400

  Miniature   £80–100

MEDAL OF ST GEORGE
  3rd Class   £150–265
  4th Class   £100–210

  Miniature   £30–50

MEDAL FOR ZEAL
  Silver   £225–325

  Miniature   £30–50

SOVIET UNION

The Soviet Union awarded some 160 orders and medals to British Servicemen either during or immediately after World War II. The most numerous of these being the Order of the Patriotic War (1st and 2nd class), the Medal for Valour, the Medal for Meritorious Service in Battle and the Order of the Red Star. However the numbers of these awarded to British personnel were still less than 30 in each case and as such documented examples come on the market very rarely making it extremely difficult to give accurate valuations. For more information see MEDAL NEWS June/July 2001.

SERBIA

ORDER OF KARAGEORGE (1904–15)
4th Class £450–565

Miniature £40–60

ORDER OF THE WHITE EAGLE (1882–1915)
Knight's badge £350–475

Miniature £80–100

TURKEY

ORDER OF THE OSMANIEH
1st Class £550–675
2nd Class £450–550
3rd Class £250–350
4th Class £95–150
5th Class £65–85

Miniature £30–50

ORDER OF THE MEDJIDIEH
Commander's badge £550–725
Knight's badge £250–300

Miniature £40–60

UNITED STATES

DISTINGUISHED SERVICE CROSS   from £75
(Army)

US NAVY CROSS   from £75

US AIR FORCE CROSS   from £75

DISTINGUISHED SERVICE MEDAL   from £75
(Army)

Miniatures of US medals are available, prices range from £5–10 for "plain" examples to £10–20 for more sophisticated "fancy" pieces.

UNITED STATES *continued*

US DISTINGUISHED SERVICE MEDAL £20–30
(Navy-Marine Corps)

US DISTINGUISHED FLYING CROSS £20–30

Legionnaire

LEGION OF MERIT

Commander	£150–250
Officer	£120–175
Legionnaire	£75–100

US SILVER STAR £25–30

US BRONZE STAR £20–25

US AIR MEDAL £25–30

359

MEDALS OF THE IRISH REPUBLIC (EIRE)

Since 1921 Ireland has been divided into two distinct countries: the Irish Free State in the south and Ulster in the north, both as separate countries within the British Empire. However, in 1949 the Irish Free State proclaimed itself a republic and became known as Eire. Since that time it has issued its own medals and honours, including a number of retrospective awards for the troubled times prior to independence and for the period before it became a republic. Irish men and women served with the British armed forces at home and overseas and many Irish regiments famously took part in many of the fiercest actions of World War I. Medals and awards for these actions will be found in the main section of this book. During World War II the Irish Defence Forces remained neutral although the Dublin Goverrnment assisted the British war effort in many ways. Today Irish troops regularly serve with the United Nations and have been in action on a number of occasions. Interestingly in the 1950s the Irish Government decided to standardise the Irish language and introduced An Caighdean Ofigiuil, which was a change in the Irish alphabet. The earlier Irish medals carry inscriptions in the old Irish alphabet but to simplify matters we have given the modern Irish equivalent in these listings.

E1. 1916 MEDAL

Instituted: January 1941.
Ribbon: Two equal stripes of green (left) and orange, suspended from an ornate clasp of Celtic design.
Metal: Bronze.
Size: 38mm, max.
Description: (Obverse) based on the cap badge of the Irish Republican Army, viz. an eight-pointed star with "flames" between the points, surmounted by a double circle on which is a depiction of "Cuchulainn", the memorial erected at the General Post Office, Dublin, to commemorate the 1916 uprising; (reverse) central medallion inscribed SEACTMAIN NA CASGA (Easter Week) curved above 1916. With plain ring suspension.
Comments: *The medal, which takes precedence over all other Irish medals, was instituted by the Irish Republican Government to commemorate the Easter Uprising in Dublin, April 1916. Recipients, who were mostly members of the Dublin Brigade of the Irish Republican Army, also received a pension in respect of this medal. Of the 2,000 medals originally struck some 1,906 were issued. Of these 266 were named and presented to the next of kin of those who had died before the date of issue, including the 88 who were killed in the rebellion and 16 executed afterwards; the remainder were issued unnamed. Another 450 medals were struck and issued later.*

VALUE:		
	Original named 1916 casualty (88)	from £55,000
	1941 issue named medal	from £12,000
	Post 1941 named late issue medal	from £6000
	Unnamed	£2000–3000
	Miniature	£150–200

E2. MILITARY MEDAL FOR GALLANTRY

Instituted: 4 December 1944.

Ribbon: Dark green with a central stripe of crimson (1st Class), dark green with crimson edges (2nd Class), dark green with crimson edges and central crimson stripe (3rd Class).

Metal: Silver (1st Class), light bronze (2nd Class), dark bronze (3rd Class).

Size: 36mm.

Description: (Obverse) a Celtic cross with a longer lower limb, surrounded by a laurel wreath with the words DE BARR CALMACTA (For Gallantry) in the centre; (reverse) inscribed AN BONN MILEATA CALMACTA (The Military Gallantry Medal) above a scroll bearing the recipient's name.

Comments: *The medal is intended to be awarded in three different classes to members of the Defence Forces who have performed actions of outstanding gallantry in the course of their military duty whilst not on war service. Only seven medals have so far been awarded in 2nd or 3rd Class. The 1st Class has never been awarded, making this probably one of the rarest gallantry awards.*

VALUE: —

E3. DISTINGUISHED SERVICE MEDAL

Instituted: February 1964.

Ribbon: Dark green with 6mm black centre stripe (1st Class), 5mm black edges (2nd Class) or 3mm black edges and black centre stripe (3rd Class), suspended from a clasp with a stylised Celtic design.

Metal: Silver (1st Class) or bronze (2nd and 3rd Class).

Size: 36mm.

Description: (Obverse) a figure of Cuchulainn driving a two-horse chariot; (reverse) legend AN BONN SEIRBISE DEARSCNA (The Distinguished Service Medal) around. With simple ring suspension.

Comments: *Awarded in three classes for acts of bravery or special devotion to duty which do not merit the award of the Military Medal for Gallantry (MYBE2).*

VALUE:	
1st class	—
2nd class	£500–750
3rd class	£400–600

E4. CIVIL MEDAL FOR BRAVERY

Instituted: —.

Ribbon: Crimson with two narrow white stripes 3mm apart at centre (gold) or dark blue with two narrow white stripes 3mm apart at centre.

Metal: gold (1st Class), silver (2nd Class) and bronze (3rd Class).

Size: 36mm.

Description: (Obverse) a winged figure brandishing a flaming sword standing over another winged figure representing death and the inscription MIR GAILE GNIOM TARRTALA (The Council for Deeds of Bravery) below; (reverse) the words ARNA BRONNAD AG COMAIRLE NA MIR GAILE AR (Awarded by the Council for Deeds of Bravery to) in the top half with the recipient's name engraved to the right of an olive branch below.

Comments: *Awarded by the Department of Justice. The gold and silver medals are awarded for an individual act of bravery in saving life; the bronze is awarded to civilians for brave deeds which do not merit the other awards.*

VALUE:	1st class	2nd class	3rd class
	—	£800–1200	£450–550

E5. GENERAL SERVICE MEDAL 1917–21

Instituted: January 1941.
Ribbon: Two equal stripes of black (left) and orange, suspended from an ornate clasp of Celtic design.
Metal: Bronze.
Size: 38mm.
Clasp: COMRAC (this word has two meanings, combat or action).
Description: (Obverse) a standing figure of a soldier holding a rifle surrounded by the crests of the four provinces of Ireland and bisecting the word "EIRE", at the foot COGAD NA SAOIRSE (War of Independence); (reverse) plain except for a laurel wreath around.
Comments: *Awarded to those who took part in the struggle for independence between the Easter Uprising of 1916 to ratification of the treaty which ensured independence from Britain and the establishment of the Irish Free State in 1921. The COMRAC clasp was awarded to those who took an active part in the military operations. When this clasp is worn the simple ring suspender is exchanged for one of an ornate triangular design. Approximately 15,000 medals were issued with a clasp, and 40,000 without, of these 1,080 Comrac medals and 1,360 no clasp medals were issued named.*

VALUE:	Unnamed	Named	Miniature
With clasp	£350–425	from £1,000	£50–70
Without clasp	£200–275	£300–550	£30–50

E6. THE EMERGENCY SERVICE MEDAL 1939–46

Instituted: 6 October 1944.
Ribbon: Orange-red with two white 4.5mm stripes 1.5mm apart at centre or with one central 10mm stripe, suspended from a bar bearing the words SEIRBHIS NAISIUNTA (National Service).
Metal: Bronze.
Size: 38mm.
Clasp: Laurel spray between the dates 1939 and 1946 for each two years extra service.
Description: (Obverse) a female figure of Ireland holding a sword, with Irish wolf hound on a leash at her side and the legend RE NA PRAINNE (Emergency Period) above and around; (reverse) a branch of laurel and the dates 1939 and 1946, with the recipient's unit above.
Comments: *The medal was instituted to reward Defence Service personnel who served between September 3, 1939 and March 31, 1946. A total of 11 different units were recorded and medals are inscribed on the reverse with the unit in which each recipient served. The most popular unit for collectors is the 26th Battalion which was comprised of veterans from the 1916 Uprising. The qualifying period was one year's service with the Defence Forces, the Chaplaincy Service, the Army Nursing Service or the Local Defence Forces (the ribbons for which have two stripes) or two years with the Air Raid Precautions Service, the Irish Red Cross Society or the Local Security Force (the ribbons for which have one stripe). A clasp was awarded for each extra two years service, with a maximum of two being available.*

VALUE:	
Army, Air Corps, Navy (Na Forsai Cosanta)	£35–50
Naval Reserve (An Sluag Muiri)	£200–265
26th Battalion (An 26u Cathlan)	£300–375
Chaplaincy Service (An Seirbhis Seiplineachta)	£750–1200
Local Defence Force (An Forsa Cosanta Aitiuil)	£35–50
Volunteer Reserve (Forsa na n-Oclac, 2u Line)	£75–100
Army Nursing Service (Seirbis Altranais an Airm)	£500–750
Volunteer Aid (Red Cross) (Ranna Cabair Deontaca Cumann Croise Deirge na h-Eireann)	£75–100
First Aid (Red Cross) (Ranna Cead-Cabair Cumann Croise Deirge na h-Eireann)	£75–100
Air Raid Precautions (Na Seirbisi Reamcuraim In Agaidh Aer-Ruatar)	£40–55
Local Security Force (Na Caomnoiri Aitiula)	£35–55
Miniature	£20–30

E7. MERCHANT SERVICE MEDAL 1939–46

Instituted: 6 October 1944.

Ribbon: Blue with central white stripe, suspended from a clasp bearing the words SEIRBHIS NAISIUNTA (National Service).

Metal: Bronze.

Size: 38mm.

Clasp: Laurel spray between the dates 1939 and 1946 for each two years extra service.

Description: (Obverse) as MYB E6 above,—a female figure holding a sword, with Irish wolf hound at her side and RE NA PRAINNE (Emergency Period) above; (reverse) a steamship sailing left and a sailing ship in the background with the words AN TSEIRBHIS MUIR-TRACTALA (The Merchant Marine Service) above and the dates 1939–1946 over a laurel branch below.

Comments: *Awarded for six months' continuous service on Irish registered merchant ships between September 1939 and March 1946. A total of just over 500 of these medals were issued, including 127 with single extra service bars, 37 with two bars and a further 57 with three bars.*

VALUE:

Without bar	£650–785
One bar	£750–900
Two bars	£800–1000
Three bars	£850–1200

E8. PERMANENT DEFENCE FORCES SERVICE MEDAL

Instituted: 13 September 1944.

Ribbon: There are two types of ribbon for this medal, a plain blue one for 10 years service or blue, with central gold stripe, when long service clasp is added for 15 years service. Both suspended from a bar bearing the word SEIRBIS

Metal: Bronze.

Size: 38mm.

Clasps: Bronze bar with a cross and laurel design for each five years extra service.

Description: (Obverse) Eire, represented as a female figure, placing a wreath on a kneeling soldier and AN BONN SEIRBISE (For good service) to left; (reverse) the words THE SERVICE MEDAL (in English) around with the recipient's details inscribed in the centre.

Comments: *Awarded to non-commissioned members of the Defence Forces for a minimum of ten years service with good conduct.*

VALUE:

	Without bar	£50–£90
	With bar	£100–£125

E10. ST JOHN AMBULANCE BRIGADE OF IRELAND SERVICE MEDAL

Instituted: September 1945.
Ribbon: Watered white with a single black centre stripe with two thinner black stripes each side and green edges.
Metal: Silver or silver-gilt.
Size: 38mm.
Description: (Obverse) the Maltese Cross emblem of the Brigade with sprigs of shamrock in the angles, surrounded by the legend THE ST JOHN AMBULANCE BRIGADE OF IRELAND; (reverse) the words FOR SERVICE inside a wreath of St John's wort leaves and flowers.
Comments: *Awarded in silver to members of the Brigade in Ireland for 15 years service and in silver-gilt for 50 years service.*

VALUE:	Silver	£30–£50
	Silver-gilt	£100–£125

E11. THE UNITED NATIONS PEACEKEEPERS MEDAL

Instituted: 3 October 1989
Ribbon: 32mm wide with central vertical stripe of United Nations blue, 3mm wide, flanked by orange vertical stripes, 4.5mm wide, flanked by white vertical stripes, 5mm wide, with vertical green stripe, 5mm wide each side.
Metal: Nickel-plated brass (silver appearance).
Size: 35mm.
Description: (Obverse) female figure of Eireann standing on a shoreline releasing a dove of peace into the sky with an olive branch in its beak and three wild geese flying into the distance; (reverse) NÁ NÁISIUN AONTAITE DON TSÍOCÁIN—FOR PEACE UNITED NATIONS.
Comments: *The official name of this medal is An Bonn Chosantoiri Síochána na Naisiun Aontaithe (The United Nations Peacekeeper's Medal). Any member of the Irish Defence Forces who is entitled to a United Nations Service medal, is entitled to this medal. Only one United Nations Peacekeeper's Medal is awarded irrespective of how many peacekeeping tours the recipient has taken part in and there are no bars or other indicators to show how many tours the recipient has been on.*

VALUE: £100–175

E12. 1916-1966 "SURVIVORS" MEDAL

Instituted: 1966.
Ribbon: Green with 5mm orange edges and a white 1mm central stripe.
Metal: Hallmarked silver (gilded).
Size: 38mm max.
Description: The same type of ring suspender as the 1916 medal, MYB E1 (qv), with a similar wearing brooch, which has the maker's name stamped on the reverse. (Obverse) as 1916 medal; (reverse) plain circular back with 1916/Ca'isc/1966 (1916 Easter 1966) in three lines.
Comments: *Issued to the recipients of the 1916 medal who were still alive in 1966 on the 50th Anniversary of the Easter Rising. 964 medals were issued. None of these medals were officially named.*

VALUE: £3000–4500

E13. 1921-71 "SURVIVORS" MEDAL

Instituted: 1971.
Ribbon: Orange with green edges and a black central stripe.
Metal: Gilt bronze.
Size: Significantly smaller than the 1917–21 medal.
Description: A circular medal with the same type of ring suspender as the 1917–21 medal (MYB E5) and with a similar wearing brooch. (Obverse) same as 1917–21 medal; (reverse) as the 1917-21 medal except with "1921–71" in the area where the blank space is on the 1917-21 medal.
Comments: *Issued to the recipients of the 1917-21 medal who were still alive in 1971 on the 50th Anniversary of the Truce. There is no difference between the medals issued to combatants and non-combatants. None of these medals were officially named.*

VALUE: £300–350

E14. RESERVE DEFENCE FORCES LONG SERVICE MEDAL

Instituted:
Ribbon: Blue ribbon with yellow edges (7 years), and blue ribbon with yellow edges and a central yellow stripe (12 and 21 years).
Metal: A golden coloured medal.
Size: 38mm.
Description: Circular medal with suspender similar to the Irish UN Service Medal. (Obverse) a Celtic warrior with shield and spear surrounded by the words Cus Na Saoirse/Faire Biodgac; (reverse) plain circle with around the edges An Bonn Seirbise/F.C.A. 7 S.M.
Comments: *Awarded to members of An Forsa Cosanta Aitiuil (Local Defence Force) and An Slua Muiri (Naval Reserve) after 7 years service. A bar is awarded after 12 years service and a further bar is awarded after 21 years service.*

VALUE:	7 years	12 years	21 years
	£100–150	£120–180	£200–275

MEDALS OF AN GARDA SÍOCHÁNA

E15. SCOTT MEDAL FOR VALOR

Instituted: 1923.

Ribbon: 34mm wide. Three equal stripes of green, white and orange.

Metal: Gold (first class), Silver (second class) and Bronze (third class).

Size: 44mm.

Description: The medal is in the form of a Celtic cross. (Obverse) the entwined GS of the Garda crest in the centre with "Walter Scott Medal" on the top arm of the cross and "For Valor" on the bottom arm; the left arm carries the shield and eagle crest of the United States and the right arm the harp and sunburst of Ireland; (reverse) New York City coat of arms surrounded by the coats of arms of each of the four Irish provinces (Leinster, Munster, Connacht, Ulster), one in each of the arms of the cross with the words "Garda Síochána na h-Éireann". The medals are suspended from a pin brooch, on which is engraved the name of the recipient.

Comments: *In 1923, the then Commissioner of the Garda Síochána, General Eoin O'Duffy met Colonel Walter Scott, an Honorary Commissioner of the New York City Police and a well known philanthropist. Colonel Scott expressed the wish to assist in some way with what was, at the time, the world's youngest Police Force, namely the Garda Síochána. He presented to An Garda Síochána a $1,000 gold bond, the interest from which would pay, in perpetuity, for a gold medal. The one condition attached to the award of the Scott Medal was: "No action, however heroic, will merit the award of the Scott medal unless it takes the shape of an act of personal bravery, performed intelligently in the execution of duty at imminent risk to the life of the doer, and armed with full previous knowledge of the risk involved". In 1925, Colonel Scott presented a further $500 bond to provide silver and bronze medals to members who, during the year performed similar acts in the execution of duty but with less risk to their lives and who are next in order of merit. A Scott medal ceremony is held annually when recipients are formally presented with their medals by the Minister for Justice, Equality and Law Reform. The ceremony usually takes place at the Garda College.*

VALUE:　　　　**from £3000**

E16. GARDA SÍOCHÁNA LONG SERVICE MEDAL

Instituted: 1972.

Ribbon: Green ribbon with two white central stripes.

Metal: Silver coloured.

Size: 34mm.

Description: (Obverse) The scales of justice surrounded by the words "Garda Síochána" which are at the centre of a star with 22 points (one for each year of service); (reverse) the words "Seirbhís Fhada" (Long Service) with a Celtic design.

Comments: *Awarded to members of An Garda Síochána after 22 years service. Issued unnamed.*

VALUE:　　　　£100–150

E17. GARDA SÍOCHÁNA GOLDEN JUBILEE MEDAL

Instituted: 1972.

Ribbon: Three equal stripes of yellow, blue, yellow.

Metal: Gold coloured.

Size: 34mm.

Description: (Obverse) The entwined GS of the Garda Síochána crest surrounded by a pentagon with 10 stars; (reverse) a pillar of justice with a scroll going through and around it with the words "Jubaile Orga 1922-1972" (Golden Jubilee 1922-1972).

Comments: *Struck to commemorate the 50th Anniversary of the founding of the force in 1972. The medal was given to anyone serving in the police that year (approx 9,000) and was issued unnamed.*

VALUE: £50–75

E18. GARDA SÍOCHÁNA MILLENNIUM MEDAL

**IMAGE
NOT
AVAILABLE**

Instituted: 2000.

Ribbon: Gold with central thick blue stripe

Metal: Gold coloured.

Size: 34mm.

Description: —

Comments: *Issued unnamed.*

VALUE: £50–75

E19. GARDA UNITED NATIONS SERVICE MEDAL

Instituted:

Ribbon: Dark blue central stripe with equal white stripes each side and narrow light blue edges.

Metal: A gold coloured medal

Size:

Description: (Obverse) The entwined GS of the Garda Síochána crest in a circle below a dove of peace with an olive branch in its beak and the words "Seirbhis Thar Lear" (Overseas Service); (reverse) plain back with the words "Garda Siochana – don tSiochain – Na Naisiuin Aontaithe" (Garda Siochana – for Peace – United Nations).

Comments: *The medal was given to a very few members of the force who served with the United Nations overseas. Issued unnamed*

VALUE: £200–275

E20. CIVIL DEFENCE LONG SERVICE MEDAL

Instituted: 1961.

Ribbon: Pale blue with a single red stripe in the centre for ten years service or two red stripes for twenty years service.

Metal: Gold coloured.

Size: 36mm.

Description: (Obverse) The Celtic Cross with the words "Seirbhis Fada—Long Service" inscribed between the arms of the cross. The centre of the Cross has the International CD badge of a blue triangle on an orange background inset in coloured enamel; (reverse) is concave and blank for recipient's details.

Comments: *The medal is issued by the Minister of Defence and was first awarded in 1997. Suspension is from a straight bar.*

VALUE: —

E21. CIVIL DEFENCE MILLENNIUM MEDAL

Instituted: 2000

Ribbon: Orange with two pale blue stripes separated by a central green stripe with clasp "1950–2000".

Metal: Gold coloured

Size: 36mm

Description: (Obverse) An Irish harp in the centre surrounded by the words "Cosaint Sibhalta—Civil Defence"; (reverse) blank space for recipient's details surrounded by a rope pattern around the edge.

Comments: *The medal was issued by the Civil Defence Officers Association initially in the year 2000 to mark the 50th anniversary of the Civil Defence. Suspension is from a straight bar.*

VALUE: —

The world's only magazine devoted to Medals and Battles

Subscribing is easy!

Call 01404 44166

Complete the order form and send it to—
Token Publishing Ltd,
Orchard House,
Duchy Road, Heathpark,
Honiton, Devon, EX14 1YD

Complete the order form and fax it to 01404 44788

log on to
www.tokenpublishing.com

Subscription Rates
UK £35,
Europe/World Surface £42,
Rest of World Airmail £52

Medal News

Save money when you take out a subscription to *Medal News* for either yourself or a friend. Pay just £35 for 10 issues, or £17.50 for 5 issues, save money on the cover price and enjoy having the world's only magazine devoted to medals and battles delivered to your door before it goes on sale in the newsagents!

Subscriber Benefits

- **FREE** delivery before the magazine goes on sale in the newsagents
- **FREE** classified advertising for all non-trade subscribers
- **FREE** medal tracker for subscribers—find those missing medals
- Never miss an issue!
- **FREE** online version of Medal News to subscribers, with direct links to dealers websites!

(Digital version available separately—see below)

View your monthly magazine on-line at work, on the train, on your phone and never miss out on that bargain again!

MEDAL NEWS SUBSCRIBERS ORDER FORM

Your subscription will start from the next available issue.
(Please tick as appropriate)
❏ UK £35 (10 issues)
❏ UK £17.50 (5 issues)
❏ Europe/World Surface £42
❏ Worldwide Airmail £52
❏ Digital Magazine only £10 Worldwide

YOUR DETAILS

Title _____ Initial _____ Surname _____

Address _____

Postcode _____ Telephone _____

E-mail _____

CREDIT OR DEBIT CARD PAYMENT
❏ Visa ❏ Mastercard ❏ JCB ❏ Switch

Card Number

Issue no. [   ]   Authorisation code* [   ]
Valid from [   ]   Expiry date [   ]

Signature _____

* The last 3 digits from the back of the card

We will not pass your details on to any other organisation, however we may send you information we feel is of interest to you. If you DO NOT want to receive this information please tick this box. ☐   (MYB2012)

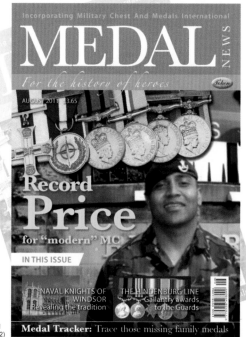

Incorporating Military Chest And Medals International

MEDAL N E W S
For the history of heroes
AUGUST 2011 £3.65

Record **Price** for "modern" MC

IN THIS ISSUE

NAVAL KNIGHTS OF WINDSOR Revealing the tradition

THE HINDENBURG LINE Gallantry awards to the Guards

Medal Tracker: Trace those missing family medals

www.tokenpublishing.com

CJ Medals

- PROFESSIONAL MEDAL MOUNTING & FRAMING
- MEDAL/MILITARIA SALES & AUCTIONS
- VALUATIONS OF MEDALS & COINS

ALL RELATED ENQUIRES WELCOME

SAMUEL ALFRED • MEDAL SPECIALIST

Shop 17 Loganholme Shopping Village
59 Bryants Road, Loganholme, Qld 4129

(07) 3806 5980 • www.cjmedals.com
cjmedals@optusnet.com.au

AWARDS
OF THE BRITISH
COMMONWEALTH

In recent years many countries of the British Commonwealth have created their own individual systems of Honours and Awards. However, some British awards are still recognised within these systems. The medals and awards of these countries instituted prior to their own systems being introduced, are included in the main section of this book. In this section of the YEARBOOK we include the latest honours and awards of AUSTRALIA, CANADA, NEW ZEALAND and SOUTH AFRICA, together with their current Orders of Precedence encompassing their own and former British honours and awards.

There is a website for Australian Honours and Medals, maintained by the Awards and National Symbols branch in Canberra, ACT www.itsanhonour.gov.aus. The site is constantly being updated and, apart from listing the Australian honours and awards, has a search facility to enable researchers to trace medal details of Australians back to 1901, the year of Federation. It is also possible to search for awards by localities, defined by postcodes. This is an essential tool for military historians, medal collectors and family historians.

THE ORDER OF PRECEDENCE IN AUSTRALIA
(including British awards)

Victoria Cross (VC)
George Cross (GC)
Cross of Valour (CV)
Knight/Lady of the Garter
Knight/Lady of the Thistle
Knight/Dame Grand Cross of the Order of the Bath
Order of Merit
Knight/Dame of the Order of Australia (AK/AD)
Knight/Dame Grand Cross of the order of St Michael and St George
Knight/Dame Grand Cross of the Royal Victorian Order
Knight/Dame Commander of the Order of the British Empire
Companion of the Order of Australia (AC)
Companion of Honour
Knight/Dame Commander of the Order of the Bath

Knight/Dame Commander of the Order of St Michael and St George
Knight/Dame Commander of the Royal Victorian Order
Knight/Dame Commander of the Order of the British Empire
Knight Bachelor
Officer of the Order of Australia (AO)
Companion of the Order of the Bath
Companion of the Order of St Michael and St George
Commander of the Royal Victorian Order
Commander of the Order of the British Empire
Star of Gallantry (SG)
Star of Courage (SC)
Companion of the Distinguished Service Order
Distinguished Service Cross (DSC)
Member of the Order of Australia (AM)
Lieutenant of the Royal Victorian Order
Officer of the Order of the British Empire
Companion of the Imperial Service Order

Member of the Royal Victorian Order
Conspicuous Service Cross (CSC)
Nursing Service Cross (NSC)
Royal Red Cross (1st class)
Military Cross
Distinguished Flying Cross
Air Force Cross
Royal Red Cross (2nd class)
Medal for Gallantry (MG)
Bravery Medal (BM)
Distinguished Service Medal (DSM)
Public Service Medal (PSM)
Australian Police Medal (APM)
Australian Fire Service Medal (AFSM)
Ambulance Service Medal (ASM)
Emergency Services Medal (ESM)
Medal of the Order of Australia (OAM)
Order of St John
Conspicuous Service Medal (CSM)
Australian Antarctic Medal (AAM)
Queen's Police Medal for Gallantry
Queen's Fire Service Medal for Gallantry
Military Medal
Distinguished Flying Medal
Air Force Medal
Queen's Gallantry Medal
Royal Victorian Medal
British Empire Medal
Queen's Police Medal for Distinguished Service
Queen's Fire Service Medal for Distinguished
    Service

Commendation for Gallantry
Commendation for Brave Conduct
Queen's Commendation for Brave Conduct
Commendation for Distinguished Service
War Medals
Campaign Medals
Active Service Medals
Service Medals
Police Overseas Medal
Humanitarian Overseas Medal
Civilian Service Medal
Polar Medal
Imperial Service Medal
80th Anniversary Armistice Remembrance
    Medal
Australian Sports Medal
Centenary Medal
Defence Force Service Medal
Reserve Force Decoration
Reserve Force Medal
Defence Long Service Medal
National Medal
Australian Defence Medal
Australian Cadet Forces Service Medal
Champion Shots Medal
Long Service Medals
Anniversary of National Service 1951-72 Medal
Independence and Anniversary Medals (in order
    of date of receipt)
Foreign Awards (in order of date of authorization
    of their acceptance and wearing).

AUSTRALIAN MEDALS

Since 1975 Australia has instituted a number of Australian awards. Medals and decorations pertaining to Australia, instituted prior to 1975 will be found in chronological sequence within the main text of this book. The Australian system was inaugurated on February 14, 1975 when the Order of Australia, four bravery awards and the National Medal were established by Letters Patent. For further information about Australian refer to *Australians Awarded* by Clive Johnson (2008) and *The National Honours & Awards of Australia* by Michael Maton (1995). They are listed below in order of precedence. Most of the illustrations for this section have been generously supplied by the Directorate of Honours and Awards of the Australian Department of Defence.

A1. VICTORIA CROSS FOR AUSTRALIA

Instituted: 1991.
Ribbon: Crimson 38mm wide.
Metal: Bronze.
Size: 35mm at each axis.
Description: As per MYB 24 (UK VC)
Method of naming: To be determined.
Comments: *The Australian VC was established as part of the Australian System of Honours and awards, 15 January 1991. The Victoria Cross for Australia is identical to the original British VC. Recipients are entitled to the post nominal letters VC. Only two have been awarded to date. The first to Trooper Mark Donaldson of the Australian SAS on 16 January 2009 for gallantry in Afghanistan in 2008. The second, awarded on 24 January 2011 to Corporal Benjamin Roberts-Smith M.G., of the Australian SAS for the most conspicuous gallantry and daring in the face of the enemy while in circumstances of extreme peril as a Patrol Second-in-Command, Special Operations Task Group on Operation SLIPPER. On 16 April 2011 The Parliamentary Secretary for Defence, announced that an independent Defence Honours and Awards Appeals Tribunal will inquire into unresolved recognition for past acts of naval and military gallantry and will examine eligibility to receive the Victoria Cross for Australia or other forms of recognition for their service. Thirteen names have been submitted for investigation.*
VALUE: —

A2. CROSS OF VALOUR

Instituted: 1975.
Ribbon: Magenta 38mm wide with a blood-red central band of 16mm.
Metal: 22 carat gold.
Size: 42mm.
Description: A straight-armed Greek cross with diminishing rays between the arms; surmounted by St Edward's crown and an integral suspension bar inscribed FOR VALOUR. The Cross is surmounted by the shield and crest from the Arms of the Commonwealth of Australia.
Method of naming: Recipient's full name pantographed in capital letters on the reverse of the bar. Topped by the Federation Star
Comments: *Intended to replace the British civilian award of the George Cross. Five have been awarded to date: D. J. Tree (saved a child from electrocution); V. A. Boscoe (apprehension of armed robbers); A. Sparkes (rescuing a child from a flooded drain); R. T. Joyes and T. Britten (Bali Bombing). Recipients are entitled to the post nominal letters CV.*

VALUE: **£20,000-35,000.** Obviously value is dependent on the reason for the award and would attain upward of £30,000, especially with other medals).

A3. ORDER OF AUSTRALIA

Instituted: 1975.
Ribbon: Royal blue bearing scattered gold mimosa blossoms of various sizes (General Division); similar, but with gold edges (Military Division)

Neck/shoulder badge

Breast badge

KNIGHTS AND DAMES OF THE ORDER

Instituted: 1975.
Ribbon: Royal blue bearing scattered gold mimosa blossoms of various sizes (General Division); similar, but with gold edges (Military Division).
Metal: 18 carat gold.
Size: Neck badge: 60mm disk; Breast badge: 80mm disk; miniature badge 20mm disk; lapel badge 10mm diameter; ribbon bar 38mm.
Description: The insignia consists of a neck badge and breast badge.
Neck badge: Jewelled and having at its centre the arms of Australia enamelled in full colour on a blue background decorated with two branches of mimosa. The whole is surmounted by the St Edward Crown in full colour with a suspension ring at the top.
In the case of a Dame there was the option of a neck badge or a shoulder badge, the latter being identical in every respect save the mounting. The neck badge is worn with a 16mm ribbon, while the shoulder badge of the Dame is worn with a 28mm ribbon
Breast badge: The emblem of the Order is jewelled, and has the arms of Australia at the centre, surmounted by the St Edward Crown. The breast badge is worn on the left side of a coat or outer garment.
Miniature badge: worn with 16mm ribbon.
Lapel badge: for ordinary civilian wear.
Ladies' badge: mounted on a brooch bar.
Method of naming: Pantographed in the centre of the reverse of the medal.
Comments: *Knights and Dames are entitled to the prefix "Sir" or "Dame" and the use the post nominal letters AK or AD respectively. Between May 24, 1976, when the grade of Knights and Dames was introduced, and March 3, 1986 when these grades were abolished, a total of 12 Knights and two Dames were created, excluding the Queen (Sovereign of the Order) and the Prince of Wales.*

VALUE: £10,000 +

Companion's badge.

COMPANION OF THE ORDER OF AUSTRALIA

Instituted: 1975.

Ribbon: Royal blue bearing scattered gold mimosa blossoms of various sizes (General Division); similar, but with gold edges (Military Division).

Metal: 18ct gold.

Size: 60mm diameter.

Description: The insignia consists of a gold neck badge or shoulder badge, similar to the Knight's badge but having at its centre a circlet of blue enamel edged in gold containing two sprigs of mimosa and inscribed AUSTRALIA at the foot. Miniature, lapel and brooch badges with jewelled centres identical to those of the Knights and Dames are also worn.

Neck badge: Worn with 16mm neck ribbon.

Shoulder badge: Worn with 38mm shoulder bow.

Method of naming: Pantographed in the centre of the reverse of the medal.

Comments: *Companions have the post nominal letters AC after their name. Awarded to civil and military for eminent achievement and merit of the highest degree in service to Australia or to humanity at large. Medals awarded through third party recommendation, which involves in depth information, references and research. Awards published in Australian Honours List on Australia Day 26th January and the Queen's Birthday. 406 (381 Civil and 25 Military) have been awarded to date.*

VALUE:	Civil	£2000–3000
	Military	£3000–5000
	Miniature	£100–120

OFFICER OF THE ORDER

Instituted: 1975.

Ribbon: Royal blue bearing scattered gold mimosa blossoms of various sizes (General Division); similar, but with gold edges (Military Division).

Metal: Gold plated silver.

Size: 55mm diameter.

Description: The insignia of the badge is similar to that of the Companion. The miniature, lapel badge and brooch badges have a blue enamel centre.

Method of naming: Pantographed in the centre of the reverse of the medal.

Comments: *Officers have the postnominal letters AO after their name. Awarded to civil and military for distinguished service at a high degree to Australia or to humanity. Medals awarded through third party recommendation, which involves in depth information, references and research. Awards published in Australian Honours List on Australia Day January 26 and the Queen's Birthday. 2233 (1989 Civil and 244 Military) have been awarded to date.*

VALUE:	Civil	£800–1200
	Military	£1000–2000
	Miniature	£80

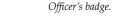

Officer's badge.

MEMBER OF THE ORDER

The insignia is a badge consisting of the emblem of the Order, 45mm in diameter in silver-gilt but without the enamelled centre, although the miniature, lapel badge and brooch badges have a blue enamel centre. Members have the postnominal letters AM.

For further details of Members badge see no. A7

This award, along with all other Australian awards can now be awarded as "honorary" to non-Australians. Medals conferred are termed "Honorary AC, Honorary AO, etc.

For the Medal of the Order of Australia see no. A18.

A4. STAR OF GALLANTRY

Instituted: 1991.

Ribbon: 32mm deep orange with chevrons of light orange, points upwards.

Metal: Silver gilt.

Size: 37mm.

Description: A seven pointed Federation Star surmounted by St Edward's Crown affixed to a suspension bar inscribed FOR GALLANTRY with (obverse) a smaller Federation Star 22mm across, surrounded by stylized flames representing action under fire; (reverse) central horizontal panel on a stepped background.

Method of naming: Full name pantographed on the reverse.

Comments: *Second and subsequent awards are denoted by a silver-gilt 34mm bar with a replica of the Federation Star at the centre. Recipients are entitled to the post nominal letters SG. The Star of Gallantry is awarded for acts of great heroism or conspicuous gallantry in action in circumstances of great peril. An amendment was made to include actions in operations in circumstances similar to armed combat or actual operations. The Star of Gallantry has been awarded four times to date: Sergeant A from 4RAR (Commando)(2006); Lt Col Harry Smith (2008)(retrospective for his leadership and gallantry during the Battle of Long Tan in the Vietnam War in August 1966.); Private S from 2nd Commando (2010). Sergeant P for actions in Afghanistan (2011).*

VALUE: £20000–25000

A5. STAR OF COURAGE

Instituted: 1975.

Ribbon: Blood red 32mm with a magenta central band 16mm wide.

Metal: Sterling silver.

Size: 50mm.

Description: A seven-pointed, ribbed star surmounted by the shield and crest from the Arms of the Commonwealth of Australia and surmounted by a St Edward Crown affixed to a suspension bar inscribed FOR COURAGE.

Method of naming: Full name pantographed on reverse of bar.

Comments: *Subsequent awards are denoted by a silver bar bearing a replica of the star. Recipients are entitled to the post nominal letters SC. Awarded for acts of conspicuous courage in circumstances of great peril. Primarily a civilian award, but can be awarded to military personnel. The award can be made posthumously. 140 have been awarded to date.*

VALUE: £2500-3500 (civil)
         £8200-10000 (military)
         Miniature £50

A6. DISTINGUISHED SERVICE CROSS

Instituted: 1991.
Ribbon: Ochre-red flanked by silver-blue bands.
Metal: Nickel-silver.
Size: 41mm.
Description: (Obverse) a modified Maltese cross with a seven-pointed Federation Star at the centre and flames in the interstices. It is surmounted with a St Edward Crown affixed to a plain suspension bar. (Reverse) plain but for the horizontal panel giving details of the award.
Method of naming: Pantographed service number, initials and surname of recipient.
Clasps: Subsequent awards are denoted by nickel-silver bars with a replica of the Federation Star at the centre.
Comments: *Recipients are entitled to the post nominal letters DSC. 76 have been awarded to date. A bar has been awarded to Colonel 'V' DSC, For distinguished command and leadership in action as a commanding officer on Operation SLIPPER in Afghanistan in June 2009.*

VALUE: £4000–6000

A7. MEMBER OF THE ORDER OF AUSTRALIA (A.M.)

Member's badge.

Instituted: 1975.
Ribbon: Royal blue bearing scattered gold mimosa blossoms of various sizes (General Division); similar, but with gold edges (Military Division).
Metal: Gold plated silver.
Size: 45mm diameter.
Description: The insignia is a badge consisting of the emblem of the Order, 45mm in diameter in silver-gilt but without the enamelled centre, although the miniature, lapel badge and brooch badges have a blue enamel centre. Members have the postnominal letters AM. The badge is worn as a medal or as a shoulder badge by ladies in civilian dress.
Method of naming: Pantographed in the centre of the reverse of the medal.

Comments: *Members have the post nominal letters AM. Awarded to civil and military for service in a particular locality or field of activity to a particular group. Medals awarded through third party recommendation, which involves in depth information, references and research. Awards published in Australian Honours List on Australia Day, 26th January, and the Queen's Birthday. 8099(7039 Civil and 1060 Military) have been awarded to date. This award can also be awarded as "honorary" to non-Australians. Medals conferred are termed "Honorary AM, etc.*

VALUE:
Civil	£400-600
Military	£550-850
Honorary	£350–500
Miniature	£55

A8. CONSPICUOUS SERVICE CROSS

Instituted: 1989.

Ribbon: 32mm wide, with alternate diagonal stripes of bush green and sandy gold 6mm wide.

Metal: Nickel-silver.

Size: 38mm.

Description: A modified Maltese Cross with fluted rays between the arms. (Obverse) the constellation of the Southern Cross within laurel leaves, surmounted with a St Edward's Crown affixed to a plain suspension bar. (Reverse) a horizontal panel for details of the award.

Method of naming: Pantographed service number, initials and surname of recipient on reverse.

Comments: *Recipients are entitled to the post nominal letters CSC. Awarded for outstanding devotion or outstanding achievement in the application of exceptional skills, by members of the Australian Defence Force. Can be awarded posthumously. 792 have been awarded to date, including 5 second award bars.*

VALUE: £1500–2000   *Miniature*   £45

A9. NURSING SERVICE CROSS

Instituted: 1991.

Ribbon: 32mm red flanked by broad white stripes with yellow edges.

Metal: Silver, with enamel.

Size: 43mm.

Description: A stepped cross with straight arms, with a red enamelled plain cross at the centre and surmounted with the St Edward Crown affixed to a plain suspension bar. (Reverse) a horizontal panel superimposed on a pattern of fluted rays.

Method of naming: Pantographed service number, initials and surname of recipient.

Comments: *For members of the Nursing Service of the Army, RAN and RAAF. Recipients are entitled to the post nominal letters NSC. Awarded for outstanding devotion and competency in the performance of nursing duties in support of the armed forces. Presented by the Governor-General on recommendation from the Minister of Defence. Can be awarded posthumously. 29 have been awarded to date, including 1 second award bar. Nominations for the NSC have been discontinued until further notice. Nominations for other operational or non-operational awards, as appropriate, are being made instead.*

VALUE: £4000–6000   *Miniature*   £40

A10. MEDAL FOR GALLANTRY

Instituted: 1991.
Ribbon: 32mm light orange with chevrons of deep orange, points upwards.
Metal: Gold plated silver.
Size: 38mm.
Description: (Obverse) Federation Star surrounded by flames and surmounted by a St Edward Crown affixed to a suspension bar inscribed FOR GALLANTRY; (reverse) horizontal panel on a background of fluted rays.
Method of naming: Pantographed service number, initials and surname of recipient
Comments: *Recipients are entitled to post nominal letters MG. Awarded to all ranks of the armed services for acts of gallantry in action in hazardous circumstances. Can be awarded posthumously. 50 have been awarded to date. Including 21 awarded as part of the Vietnam End of War List review of Australian awards to Service Personnel announced 1998, 1999 and 2010.*

VALUE: **£8000-10000**   *Miniature* **£50-60**
    SAS/Special Forces from £12,000   **End of Vietnam list: £4000–6000**

A11. BRAVERY MEDAL

Instituted: 1975.
Ribbon: 32mm with 15 alternating stripes of blood-red and magenta.
Metal: Bronze.
Size: 38mm.
Description: (Obverse) the shield and crest from the Arms of the Commonwealth of Australia on a circular zigzag border; (reverse) zigzag pattern.
Method of naming:
Comments: *Recipients are entitled to post nominal letters BM. Awarded to civilians and members of the armed services in non-warlike conditions for acts of bravery in hazardous circumstances. Citations are simplified for Gazette details but a full account of the incident is recorded on the certificate which accompanies the award. Types of Gazette entries include "Saved child from burning car", "Saved woman from burning home" and "Saved a swimmer caught in a rip". 1024 have been awarded to date.*

VALUE: **£2000–3000**   *Miniature* **£45–55**

A12. DISTINGUISHED SERVICE MEDAL

Instituted: 1991.
Ribbon: 32mm silver-blue with three stripes of red ochre.
Metal: Nickel-silver.
Size: 38mm.
Description: (Obverse) Federation Star with flames in the angles; (reverse) horizontal panel on a ground of fluted rays.
Method of naming:
Comments: *Recipients are entitled to the post nominal letters DSM. Awarded to all ranks of the armed services for distinguished leadership in action. 110 have been awarded to date, including 2 second award bar. 22 were awarded as part of the Vietnam End of War List review of Australian awards to Service Personnel announced 1998 and 1999 A further retrospective award for Vietnam was gazetted March 2010 to Flight Lieutenant Clifford Doyle for distinguished leadership in action as a captain of an Iroquois helicopter of Number 9 Squadron, Royal Australian Air Force, during the Battle of Long Tan in Vietnam on 18 August 1966. The latest second award bar was awarded on Australia Day 2011to Major 'G' DSC DSM, For distinguished leadership in action while an officer commanding on Operation SLIPPER in Afghanistan in 2009. August 2010, June 2011*

VALUE: £3000–3500   **End of Vietnam list: £15000+**

A13. PUBLIC SERVICE MEDAL

Instituted: 1989.

Ribbon: 32mm with 12 alternating stripes of green and gold of varying widths, the widest green on the left and widest gold on the right.

Metal: Nickel-silver.

Size: 38mm.

Description: (Obverse) an inner circle showing four planetary gears spaced equidistant from a central sun gear, surrounded by the inscription PUBLIC SERVICE. An outer circle shows 36 upright human figures representing a wide range of professions and activities. (Reverse) a wreath of mimosa surrounding the text FOR OUTSTANDING SERVICE.

Comments: *Awarded for outstanding public services at Commonwealth, State or Local Government levels. The number of medals allocated is limited annually to 33 (Commonwealth), 22 (New South Wales), 17 (Victoria), 11 (Queensland), 6 each (Western and Southern Australia), 3 (Tasmania) and 2 (Northern Territory). Awards may be made to Norfolk Island once every three years. Recipients are entitled to the postnominal letters PSM. There have been 1899 issued since its inception.*

VALUE: £200–300   *Miniature*   £40–50

A14. AUSTRALIAN POLICE MEDAL

Instituted: 1986.

Ribbon: 32mm white with a central broad dark blue stripe.

Metal: Nickel-silver.

Size: 38mm.

Description: (Obverse) effigy of Queen Elizabeth within a Federation Star, with an outer pattern of fluted rays; (reverse) wreath of golden wattle enclosing the inscription AUSTRALIAN POLICE MEDAL and FOR DISTINGUISHED SERVICE on a background of flames.

Method of naming: Pantographed name and rank on edge.

Comments: *Recipients are entitled to the post nominal letters APM. Awarded for distinguished service among members of the Australian Federal Police and the forces of the states and territories. Awards are limited annually to no more than one per thousand members in each force, plus one additional medal for the whole of Australia. 1411 awarded to date.*

VALUE: £800–1000   *Miniature*   £40–50

A15. AUSTRALIAN FIRE SERVICE MEDAL

Instituted: 1988.

Ribbon: 32mm central gold band bearing an irregular pattern of red flames and flanked by green stripes.

Metal: Cupro-nickel.

Size: 38mm.

Description: (Obverse) effigy of Queen Elizabeth superimposed on a Federation Star composed of flames; (reverse) inscriptions AUSTRALIA FIRE SERVICE MEDAL and FOR DISTINGUISHED SERVICE on a background of flames.

Method of naming: Pantographed on edge

Comments: *Recipients are entitled to the post nominal letters AFSM. Awarded for distinguished service among members of the fire services on the basis of one annually for every 1,000 full-time and one for every 25,000 part-time or volunteer firemen. 1064 awarded to date.*

VALUE: £500–600

Miniature   £40–50

A16. AMBULANCE SERVICE MEDAL

Instituted: 1999
Ribbon: Chevrons of white, red and silver.
Metal: Silver and bronze bi-metallic.
Size: 38mm.
Description: A circular medal featuring a Maltese Cross, with the seven-pointed Federation Star at the centre, surrounded by 24 dots symbolizing 24 hour service.
Method of naming: Pantographed on edge.
Comments: *Recipients are entitled to the post nominal letters ASM. Awarded for distinguished service by members of the civilian ambulance services. 238 awarded to date.*

VALUE: £500–600   *Miniature £40*

A17. EMERGENCY SERVICES MEDAL

Instituted: 1999.
Ribbon: Orange and white chequered pattern edged in blue
Metal: Silver and bronze, bi-metallic.
Size: 38mm.
Description: (Obverse) a triangular device containing a seven-pointed Federation Star surrounded by 24 dots representing emergency services operating around the clock.
Method of naming: Pantographed.
Comments: *Recipients are entitled to the post nominal letters ESM. Awarded for outstanding duty by members of the emergency services, including state organizations and voluntary emergency services, and to persons who render distinguished service relating to emergency management, training or education. Each Australian emergency service organization may award one ESM for every 1000 full-time members each year and in addition one for every 5000 part time, volunteer or auxiliary members. Recommendations are made by the responsible minister in the Commonwealth and each state and territory, so defined in the medals regulation to the Governor-General for approval. 265 awarded to date.*

VALUE: £350–500   *Miniature £40*

A18. MEDAL OF THE ORDER OF AUSTRALIA

Instituted: 1976.
Ribbon: Royal blue bearing scattered gold mimosa blossoms of various sizes (General Division); similar, but with gold edges (Military Division).
Metal: Gold plated silver.
Size: 40mm.
Description: (Obverse) emblem of the Order of Australia surmounted by St Edward Crown affixed to a plain suspension bar.
Method of naming: Pantographed in the centre of the reverse of the medal.
Comments: *Recipients are entitled to the post nominal letters OAM. Awarded to civil and military division for service worthy of particular recognition. Medals awarded through third party recommendation, which involves in-depth information, references and research. Awards published in Australian Honours List on Australia Day, 26 January, and the Queen's Birthday. 18,569 (17,448 Civil and 1121 Military) have been appointed to date. This total now includes honorary awards—see A7 for explanation.*

VALUE: civil £200–400;   military £500–700   *Miniature £20–25*

A19. CONSPICUOUS SERVICE MEDAL

Instituted: 1989.
Ribbon: 32mm wide with alternating 3mm diagonal stripes of bush
    green and sandy-gold.
Metal: Nickel-silver.
Size: 38mm
Description: (Obverse) the Southern Cross encircled by laurel leaves;
    (reverse) a horizontal panel on a background of fluted rays.
Method of naming:
Clasps: Only one bar to the CSM has been issued, to Major David John
    Rutherford.
Comments: *Comments: Recipients are entitled to the post nominal
    letters CSM. Awarded to all ranks of the Armed forces for meritorious
    achievement or devotion to duty in non-warlike situations. Can be awarded
    posthumously. 910 have been awarded to date, including 1 bar.*

VALUE: £1000–1200   *Miniature £40–50*

A20. AUSTRALIAN ANTARCTIC MEDAL

Instituted: 1987.
Ribbon: 32mm snow-white moiré with 3mm edges in three shades of
    blue merging with the white.
Metal: Nickel-silver.
Size: 38mm.
Description: An octagonal medal surmounted by an ice crystal device
    affixed to a plain suspension bar. (Obverse) a global map of the
    Southern Hemisphere showing Australia and Antarctica, and the
    legend FOR OUTSTANDING SERVICE IN THE ANTARCTIC;
    (reverse) a polar explorer outside Sir Douglas Mawson's hut, leaning
    into a blizzard and wielding an ice-axe.
Method of Clasp: Clasps are inscribed with the years of service.
Comments: *AAwarded to persons who have given outstanding service in
    connection with Australian Antarctic Expeditions, with at least 12 months
    service in Antarctica. The Governor-General makes awards of the medal
    on the recommendation of the Commonwealth Minister responsible for the
    Antarctic Territory. 84 awarded to date. Holders of this award are entitled
    to the post nominal AAM. The most recent awards to Captain Murray
    Patrick Doyle and Dr Stephen Nicol, June 2011*

VALUE: £2000+   *Miniature £45–55*

A21. COMMENDATION FOR GALLANTRY

Instituted: 1991.
Ribbon: Plain orange 32mm wide and 90mm long.
Metal: Silver-gilt.
Size: 22mm.
Description: The insignia consists of a row of flames tapering towards
    the ends, with a seven-pointed Federation Star superimposed.
Method of naming: Pantographed on reverse of insignia with initials,
    surname and date.
Comments: *Awarded for acts of gallantry worthy of recognition considered to be of lesser magnitude than for which the
VC, SG, or MG. 54 have been awarded to date. Including 4 awarded as part of the Vietnam End of War List announced
1998, 1999. 20 retrospective posthumous awards were announced in March 2011 as part of a review of Australian killed
while escaping from Japanese forces during World War II. One award has been made to a member of the British SAS
whilst attached to Australian Forces in Afghanistan (2011).*

VALUE: £3000–5000 Must be with original citation   *Miniature £50–60*
SAS Special forces from £8000
End of Vietnam list: £2000–2500
End of WWII list: £1000-1500

A22. COMMENDATION FOR BRAVE CONDUCT

Instituted: 1975.
Ribbon: Blood-red 32mm wide and 90mm long.
Metal: Silver-gilt.
Size: 30mm.
Description: A sprig of mimosa, mounted diagonally near the foot of the ribbon.
Comments: *Awarded for acts of bravery worthy of recognition considered to be of lesser magnitude than for which the CV, SC, or BM would be awarded. 1462 awarded to date, with 62 in 2008, 35 in 2009. Examples of brief citations include: "assisted in rescue of two children from burning house", "rescue during floods", "rescue of infant from crashed plane". Recipients are not entitled to post nominal letters. 1608 have been awrded to date.*

VALUE: £400–1000
    Civil £500-£600 Must be together with original citation certificate
    Mil £800-£1000 Must be together with original citation certificate

A23. COMMENDATION FOR DISTINGUISHED SERVICE

Instituted: 1991.
Ribbon: Ochre-red 32mm wide by 90mm long.
Metal: Nickel-silver.
Size: 22mm.
Description: A central Federation Star mounted on a row of flames tapering towards the end.
Comments: *Awarded for distinguished performance of duty in war-like operations. 295 gazetted to date, including 36 awarded as part of the Vietnam End of War List review of Australian awards to Service Personnel announced 1998, 1999. Recipients are not entitled to post nominal letters.*

VALUE: £250–300 Must be together with original citation
End of Vietnam list: £100-200 Must be together with original citation

A24. AUSTRALIAN ACTIVE SERVICE MEDAL 1945–1975

Instituted: 1995.
Ribbon: 32mm with central red stripe, flanked by narrow yellow stripes and broad stripes of pale blue, dark green and purple towards edge.
Metal: Nickel silver.
Size: 38mm
Description: (Obverse) a seven-pointed Federation Star surrounded by the legend THE AUSTRALIAN ACTIVE SERVICE MEDAL 1945–1975; (reverse) a wreath of mimosa surrounding a plaque.
Method of naming: Pantographed in capital letters on the reverse in two lines: first line with service number, second line with initials and surname.
Clasps: KOREA, MALAYA, MALAYSIA, THAILAND, THAI-MALAY, VIETNAM. Bars originally slide-on type but later struck as sew-on type.
Comments: *Awarded to all ranks of the Armed Forces for war-like services in theatres of operation between the end of World War II and February 13, 1975. The medal is worn immediately after any World War II awards and before any other campaign medals. Approximately 70,829 issued to date*

VALUE: £100–150   *Miniature £10–12*

A25. VIETNAM MEDAL

Instituted: July 1968.

Ribbon: A broad central stripe of bright yellow surmounted by three thin red stripes and bordered by broader red stripes, with dark and light blue stripes at the edges representing the three services.

Metal: Silver.

Size: 36mm.

Description: (Obverse) the crowned bust of Queen Elizabeth II; (reverse) a naked male figure pushing apart two spheres representing different ideologies.

Method of naming: Impressed on edge with service number, initials and surname. (RAAF medals can be engraved), and all issued since 1996 are pantographed.

Comments: *Awarded for 28 days in ships or craft on inland waters or off the coast of Vietnam; or for one day or more on the posted strengths of a unit or formation on land; or for one operational sortie over Vietnam or Vietnam waters by aircrew posted on strength of unit; or for official visits either continuous or aggregate of 30 days between 1964 and 1972. There are some issues collectors should be aware of if collecting Vietnam medals. Some recipients have received two or more medals due to issuing errors and due to the availability of un-named specimens of this medal, examples have been seen on the market impressed with the details of prominent or desirable veterans (i.e. gallantry, KIA, SAS, etc.). Always ensure that medals*

VALUE:

KIA, SAS or 6 RAR at Battle of Long Tan	£1500–2500
WIA	£500–750
Others	£200–250
Miniature	*£5–10*

A26. VIETNAM LOGISTIC & SUPPORT MEDAL

Instituted: 1993.

Ribbon: A broad central stripe of yellow with three narrow red stripes superimposed. On the left are stripes of red and dark blue and on the right stripes of dark brown and light blue.

Metal: Nickel-silver.

Size: 36mm.

Description: (Obverse) crowned effigy of Queen Elizabeth and titles; (reverse) a naked male figure pushing apart two spheres.

Method of naming: Pantographed on edge in capital stylized letters.

Comments: *Awarded to personnel who served in the Vietnam War but who did not qualify for the Vietnam medal. Recipients include QANTAS air crew who took troop flights to Saigon, civilian entertainers, war correspondents and many RAN personnel.*

VALUE: £200–350   *Miniature £5–10*

A27. AUSTRALIAN ACTIVE SERVICE MEDAL

Instituted: 1991.

Ribbon: 32mm with a central red stripe, flanked by stripes of silver-green, light-green, gold, dark green and brown.

Metal: Nickel-silver.

Size: 38mm.

Description: (Obverse) a seven-pointed Federation Star within a laurel wreath; (reverse) FOR ACTIVE SERVICE within a laurel wreath.

Method of naming: Pantographed on edge with service or PMKeys number, initials and surname.

Clasps: Kuwait, Cambodia, Balkans, Vietnam 1975, East Timor, Somalia, Namibia, Rwanda, ICAT, IRAQ, IRAQ 2003.

Comments: *Awarded for active service in various conflicts, denoted in each case by a campaign clasp. In the past 10 years some campaigns that were determined to be non-active service have now been amended to active service category. Including Rwanda, Cambodia, and Iraq (from 1991-2003). Multiple clasps are now quite common in the Armed Forces. A review of active service categories in 2011 added two new clasps. 'SIERRA LEONE' for OP HUSKY International Military Advisory and Training Team (IMATT) - Sierra Leone for 1 days service from 15 Jan 01to 28 Feb 03. 'MIDDLE EAST' for OP PALADIN. Syria-Lebanon-Israel border for service from 12 July 06 to 14 Aug 06.*

VALUE:

CAMBODIA, KUWAIT, NAMIBIA, SOMALIA, RWANDA	£500-1500
IRAQ 2003, ICAT	£400-600
EAST TIMOR	£200-400
SIERRA LEONE, MIDDLE EAST	£-
VIETNAM 1975, BALKANS	Rare

A28. INTERFET MEDAL—International Force East Timor

Instituted: March 7, 2000.

Ribbon: 32mm central thin red stripe, flanked by deep green, white and light blue.

Metal: Pewter coloured silver.

Size: 38mm.

Description: (Obverse) central raised stylised dove of peace over the island of Timor, surrounded by raised inscription INTERNATIONAL FORCE EAST TIMOR surmounted by Federation Star and plain suspension bar struck as one unit; (reverse) TOGETHER AS ONE FOR PEACE IN EAST TIMOR around outer circle, inner circle blank for naming.

Method of naming: Pantographed on reverse in capitals with service or PMKeyS number, initials and surname.

Comments: *The Prime Minister, John Howard, established a specific campaign medal for members of the Australian Defence Force in East Timor. Australia led the coalition of 17 nations and this is the first Australian medal issued to other countries. Awarded for 30 days service during the INTERFET stage of the conflict. 15,052 medals have been issued, including 8,696 to members of the ADF and 6,356 to members of foreign military establishments.*

VALUE: £500–800

A29. AFGHANISTAN MEDAL

Instituted: Australia Day 2004.

Ribbon: 32mm central red line, flanked by purple, a wider khaki band, white and rimmed with light blue.

Metal: Nickel-silver plated

Size: 37mm.

Description: (Obverse) Australian coat of arms edged by 80 pebbled circles; (reverse) is based on a portion of a snow-capped mountain range with a multi-rayed sun rising behind the mountain. The word AFGHANISTAN appears around the central device on the flan in English and in an Arabic script.

Method of naming: Pantographed around edge, with PMKeyS (identification number superseding service number in Australia), initials and surname in capital letters.

Comments: *Awarded to Australian Defence Force personnel who were assigned to Operation Slipper in Afghanistan, and support operations in surrounding areas, from the beginning of operations on October 11, 2001 to the withdrawal of ADF forces on December 5, 2002. Personnel subsequently deployed to Afghanistan from December 6, 2002 also qualify. Eligibility includes a specified period of (aggregated) service or, in the case of Air Force members, a qualifying number of sorties Personnel are also eligible for clasp ICAT on the AASM.*

VALUE: £700–800

A30. IRAQ MEDAL

Instituted: Australia Day 2004.

Ribbon: 32mm with thin red central stripe, flanked by purple, with two wide bands of gold/yellow.

Metal: Nickel-silver.

Size: 38mm.

Description: (Obverse) a processional lion copied from a relief on the Gateway of the Temple of Ishtar in Babylon, the lion stands on a narrow plinth (for balance) and the inscription IRAQ appears below; (reverse) Australian coat of arms edged by 80 pebbled circles.

Method of naming: Pantographed around edge, with PMKeyS (identification number superseding service number in Australia), initials and surname in capital letters.

Comments: *Awarded to Australian Defence Force personnel who have served at least 30 days in the defined area of operations. The Iraq medal will recognize ADF involvement in and around Iraq from March 18, 2003, in Operations Falconer and Catalyst. Eligibility includes a specified period of (aggregated) service or, in the case of Air Force members, a qualifying number of sorties. Personnel are also eligible for clasp Iraq 2003 on the AASM.*

VALUE: £500–700

A31. AUSTRALIAN SERVICE MEDAL 1945–75

Instituted: 1995.

Ribbon: 32mm central thin yellow stripe flanked by narrow green stripes flanked by khaki with wide navy blue stripe at left and pale blue at right.

Metal: Nickel-silver.

Size: 38mm.

Description: (Obverse) the arms of the Commonwealth of Australia surrounded by the legend THE AUSTRALIAN SERVICE MEDAL 1945-1975; (reverse) seven-pointed Federation Star and a plaque for recipient's details, surrounded by mimosa leaves.

Method of naming: Pantographed service number, initials and surname of recipient in capital letters.

Clasps: Berlin, FESR, Germany, Indonesia, Japan, Kashmir, Korea, Middle East, PNG, SE Asia, Special Ops, SW Pacific, Thailand, W New Guinea (multiple bars are scarce). Originally slide on bars were issued, but proved frail and have been replaced by sew on bars.

Comments: *Awarded to all ranks of the armed forces for 30 days service in a non-warlike theatre outside of Australia between the end of WWII and February 13, 1975. At June 2006, there have been 96,524 medals approved. The medal is worn after campaign awards and before long service and foreign awards. Can be issued as a single award, but is not issued without a bar.*

VALUE:

Berlin, Germany, Indonesia, Kashmir, Middle East, WNG	£600–800
Special Ops, Thailand	£500–700
FESR, Japan, Korea, PNG, SW Pacific, SE Asia	£50–150

A32. AUSTRALIAN SERVICE MEDAL

Instituted: 1991.

Ribbon: 32mm wide with a central brown stripe flanked by stripes of dark green, light green, gold and silver-green.

Metal: Nickel-silver.

Size: 38mm.

Description: (Obverse) a modified heraldic shield on a background of the lines of longitude, surmounted by St Edward Crown affixed to a plain suspension bar; (reverse) clusters of mimosa blossom, surrounding a Federation Star inscribed FOR SERVICE.

Method of naming: Service or PMKeyS number, initials and surname pantographed on rim. Also worthy of note, the early issues were hand engraved—primarily to RAN in crude rim to rim capitals.

Clasps: BALKANS, BOUGAINVILLE, CAMBODIA, CT/SR, EAST TIMOR, ETHIOPIA/ERITREA, GUATEMALA, GULF, HAITI, IRIAN JAYA, IRAN/IRAQ, IRAQ, KASHMIR, KOREA, KUWAIT, MIDDLE EAST, MOZAMBIQUE, PESHAWAR, SE ASIA, SINAI, SIERRA LEONE, SOLOMON ISLANDS I, SOLOMON ISLANDS II, SOMALIA, SPECIAL OPS, S. PACIFIC 2006, SUDAN, UGANDA AND WEST SAHARA.

Comments: *Awarded for 30 days service outside Australia with multinational peace-keeping forces, where time in area qualifies – recipients may also be entitled to an appropriate UN medal. The first strike of this medal produced a 7mm thick medal, crudely named. The ASM may be encountered with no service or PMKeyS number—this indicates award to a civilian. In 2010-2011 three new clasps were created for the Australian Service Medal: 'LEBANON' awarded for service with Operation RAMP and Operation RAMP II. 'CT/SR' for service in a Tactical Assault Group or Recovery Force – 60 days continuous service from 31 August 1979 until present. 'KOREA' for service while assigned for duty to UN Command (MAC) activities in the specified area of the Korean Peninsula. 30 Days from 14 Feb 75 to present.*

VALUE:

Guatemala (2), Gulf (22), Mozambique (40), Uganda (40), Irian Jaya, Ethiopia-Eritrea, West Sahara, Balkans, all considered rare clasps	£2000+
Iran-Iraq (120), Peshawar (190), Kashmir (188)	£1500+
East Timor, Timor-Leste, SE Asia, Solomon Islands and Solomon Islands II	£250-350
All others	£300-350

A32A. GENERAL SERVICE MEDAL

Instituted: 2010.

Ribbon: The ribbon is 32 mm wide with a central yellow stripe flanked by blue stripes and outer white stripes. The ribbon colours are representative of the colours used for the British Korea Medal and the United Nations Service Medal for Korea.

Metal: Antique coloured silver.

Size: 38mm.

Description: The suspender bar features a raised Federation Star. (Obverse) a raised map of South Korea which is superimposed over polar projection lines. The words 'AUSTRALIAN GENERAL SERVICE MEDAL KOREA' are inscribed on the inside of the medal rim with two Federation Stars included in the bottom left and right hand quadrants; (reverse) has the words 'POST ARMISTICE SERVICE 1953 – 1956' surrounded by a wreath of gum leaves and blossoms.

Method of naming: Service number, initials and surname pantographed on rim.

Comments: *The AGSM has been instituted to recognise former Defence Force personnel who completed 30 days participating in operations in South Korea, including any location 161km seaward from the coast of SouthKorea, during the post-armistice period from 28 July 1953 to 19 April 1956. The AGSM is worn in accordance with the Order of Wearing Australian Honours and Awards immediately after the Australian Service Medal (ASM) 1945 -1975.*

VALUE: £200-250

A33. RHODESIA MEDAL (see also no. 202)

Instituted: 1980.

Ribbon: Sky blue, with a narrow stripe of red, white and dark blue in the centre.

Metal: Rhodium-plated cupro-nickel.

Size: 36mm.

Description: (Obverse) the crowned bust of Queen Elizabeth II; (reverse) a sable antelope with the name of the medal and the year of issue.

Method of naming: unnamed (Police) or impressed capitals (RAF and armed forces); replacements show the word COPY or the letter R. Always named to Australians (impressed) as is the Zimbabwe Independence Medal.

Comments: *This medal was awarded to personnel serving in Rhodesia for fourteen days between December 1, 1979 and March 20, 1980, pending the elections and the emergence of the independent Republic of Zimbabwe. Recipients also received the Zimbabwe Independence Medal. At June 2009 there have been 152 medals awarded to Australians.*

VALUE: £2000-3500 to Australians

A34. POLICE OVERSEAS SERVICE MEDAL

Instituted: 1992
Ribbon: 32mm with a chequerboard pattern of black and white squares
Metal: Nickel-silver
Size: 38mm
Description: (Obverse) globe surmounted by a branch of wattle, the whole enclosed in a checkerboard pattern and surmounted by a St Edward's crown affixed to a plain suspension bar.
Method of naming: Pantographed in capital letters on reverse.
Clasps: BOUGAINVILLE, CAMBODIA, CYPRUS, HAITI, MOZAMBIQUE, SOMALIA (SLIP-ON TYPE), EAST TIMOR, SOLOMON ISLANDS, RAMSI, SOLOMON ISLANDS II, SUDAN, TIMOR LESTE.
Comments: *Awarded to members of the Australian Federal Police and small contingents from Australian police forces (about 20 from each state who have mainly served in the Solomon Islands) serving as members of peace-keeping missions under the auspices of the United Nations in areas of conflict and unrest. Consequently recipients also receive the UN medal if their service exceeds 90 days. 4,190 have been issued to date.*

VALUE: £400–600

A35. HUMANITARIAN OVERSEAS SERVICE MEDAL

Instituted: April 16, 1999
Ribbon: Olive green with a central gold stripe
Metal: Nickel-silver in matte pewter finish
Size: 38mm
Description: A circular medal (obverse) a stylized eucalyptus tree surrounded by a ring of gum nuts; (reverse) a ring of gum nuts.
Method of naming: Engraved in centre of reverse with recipient's name in full.
Clasps: AFGHANISTAN, BALKANS, CAMBODIA, EAST TIMOR, GREAT LAKES (AFRICA), INDIAN OCEAN, IRAQ, MOZAMBIQUE, PAKISTAN, NORTHERN IRAQ, PAKISTAN, SOMALIA, SOUTH SUDAN, SOUTH VIETNAM (1975).
Comments: *The medal is awarded to civilians and service personnel who have provided humanitarian service overseas and is believed to be the first medal of its kind. It is awarded to non-government employees or volunteers and may be awarded retrospectively. Following the devastating tsunami on December 26, 2004 the medal was awarded to members of the ADF. 1,993 have been awarded to date.*

VALUE: £800-1200

A36. CIVILIAN SERVICE MEDAL 1939-45

Instituted: 1994.
Ribbon: 32mm ochre-red central stripe flanked by narrow white stripes and broad stripes of opal green towards the edges.
Metal: Bronze.
Size: 38mm.
Description: (Obverse) the Southern Cross superimposed on a globe surrounded by mimosa blossoms; (reverse) horizontal panel for recipient's name, with 1939 above and 1945 below.
Method of naming: Pantographed on reverse.
Comments: *Awarded to civilians who had assisted Australia's war effort in a wide variety of organizations and who served under quasi-military conditions for at least 180 days. Can be awarded posthumously (to next-of-kin). 6,810 have been awarded to date.*

VALUE: £250–300   *Miniature £8–10*

A37. 80th ANNIVERSARY ARMISTICE REMEMBRANCE MEDAL

Instituted: 2000,

Ribbon: Red with a black central stripe and narrow black edges,

Metal: Silver,

Size: 36mm,

Description: (Obverse) a "Digger" in the uniform of World War I with the legend 80TH ANNIVERSARY ARMISTICE REMEMBRANCE MEDAL; (reverse) the words LEST WE FORGET in three lines within a wreath of ferns surmounted by a seven-pointed star. Fitted with a suspension bar with a Tudor crown on both sides.

Method of naming: Pantographed on rim.

Comments: *Awarded to all veterans of World War I who were still alive on November 11, 1998, the 80th anniversary of the Armistice. Only 71 were issued. Alec Campbell was the last surviving Gallipoli veteran for Australia and he passed away May 2002. The "Digger" on the obverse is a representation of the so-called "Bullecourt Digger", a statue that stands in a small memorial park in the French town of Bullecourt.*

VALUE: RARE

A38. AUSTRALIAN SPORTS MEDAL

Instituted: 2000.

Ribbon: Sand-coloured with four narrow dark green stripes, of varying widths, towards the right side.

Metal: Silver plated brass.

Size: 38mm.

Description: (Obverse) a stylized view of the Sydney Olympics Stadium with the Southern Cross constellation above; (reverse) the Olympic Stadium and the inscription "To commemorate Australian sporting achievement" and the date 2000.

Method of naming: Pantographed on the rim.

Comments: *This medal was only awarded during the year of the Sydney Olympic Games and was intended to reward Australian sporting achievement. Both current and former sports men and women have been honoured, as well as coaches, sports scientists, officials, team managers and even those who maintain playing fields and sporting facilities. 18,015 were issued.*

VALUE: £80–150

A39. CENTENARY MEDAL

Instituted: January 2001.

Ribbon: Deep blue with a central yellow stripe bearing three thin red stripes.

Metal: Silver.

Size: 36mm.

Description: (Obverse) a seven-pointed star with a central band inscribed CENTENARY OF FEDERATION 1901-2001.

Method of naming: Pantographed on reverse.

Comments: *The Centenary Medal was awarded to all Australian citizens who were born on or before December 31, 1901, and also acknowledges those who contributed to the success of Australia's first hundred years as a federal nation, recognising the many Australians who laid solid foundations for the nation's future. Each recipient also received a personalised warrant accompanying his or her medal. A total of 15,841 medals were issued. These included close to 1,400 medals awarded to Australian centenarians. The medal is now only open to centenarians*

VALUE: £200–300 (Centenarians)   £100–150 (Contribution to the nation)

A40. DEFENCE FORCE SERVICE MEDAL

Instituted: 1982.

Ribbon: 32mm azure blue with two gold stripes.

Metal: Cupro-nickel.

Size: 38mm.

Description: A circular chamfered medal (affectionately known as the Pizza cutter) bearing a Federation Star on which appears the Australian Defence Force emblem. The medal in surmounted by the St Edward Crown affixed to a plain suspension bar. (Reverse) inscription FOR EFFICIENT SERVICE IN THE PERMANENT FORCES.

Method of naming: Service number, initials and name engraved or pantographed on reverse. May occasionally be encountered with small ram's head engraved below naming, indicating an early issue from Royal Australian Mint.

Clasps: Sew-on bar 4mm high decorated with sprigs of wattle, centered with EIIR cipher, awarded for further periods of five years service.

Comments: *The medal is granted for 15 years in the Defence Force, of which 12 years must have been as a member of the permanent forces. At June 2011 there have been 118,934 medals approved..*

VALUE: £80–150 with no bar
    add £25 for one confirmed bar, £40 (2), £80 (3), £250 (4)

A41. RESERVE FORCE DECORATION

Instituted: 1982.

Ribbon: 32mm azure blue with a broad central band of gold.

Metal: Cupro-nickel.

Size: Oval 44mm high and 36mm wide.

Description: (Obverse) the Australian Defence Force emblem on a radiating background within a wreath of wattle; (reverse) inscribed FOR EFFICIENT SERVICE IN THE RESERVE FORCES.

Clasps: Sew-on gilt bar 4mm high decorated with sprigs of wattle, centered with EIIR cipher. The bar/s awarded for further periods of five years service.

Method of naming: Service number, initials and name engraved or pantographed vertically (to fit medal design) on reverse.

Comments: *Awarded for a minimum of 15 years service as an officer in the Reserve Forces. This is the only long service medal for which recipients are entitled to post nominal letters—RFD. 5,547 decorations have been awarded to date.*

VALUE: £120–180   *Miniature £30–35*
    add £50 for one confirmed bar; £100 (2), £250 (3)

A42. RESERVE FORCE MEDAL

Instituted: 1982.

Ribbon: 32mm azure blue with narrow gold edges.

Metal: Cupro-nickel.

Size: Oval 44mm high and 36mm wide.

Description: (Obverse) insignia of the Australian Defence Force emblem on a rayed background; (reverse) inscription FOR EFFICIENT SERVICE IN THE RESERVE FORCES.

Method of naming: Service number, initials and name engraved or pantographed on reverse.

Clasps: Sew-on bar 4mm high decorated with sprigs of wattle, centered with EIIR cipher, awarded for further periods of five years service.

Comments: *Awarded to non-commissioned officers and other ranks of the reserve forces on completion of 15 years service. 11,204 medals awarded to date.*

VALUE: £175–250   *Miniature £30–35*

A43. DEFENCE LONG SERVICE MEDAL

Instituted: 1998.

Ribbon: 32mm with central 10mm panel of seven narrow alternating stripes of azure blue and gold, flanked by 7mm broad azure stripes and 4mm gold edges.

Metal: Nickel-silver.

Size: 38mm.

Description: A circular medal surmounted with the St Edward Crown attached to the suspension bar. (Obverse) the Australian Defence Force emblem surrounded by two sprays of wattle leaves and blossom; (reverse) a central horizontal panel surrounded by the inscription FOR SERVICE IN THE AUSTRALIAN DEFENCE FORCE.

Method of naming: Pantographed on reverse.

Clasps: Sew-on bar 4mm high decorated with sprigs of wattle, centred with EIIR cipher, awarded for further periods of five years service.

Comments: *This medal is awarded on completion of 15 years service and supersedes the DFSM, the RFD and the RFM. This medal takes in service in both the regular and reserve forces, can accumulate across services and does not discriminate between rank levels. 32,032 medals have been awarded to date.*

VALUE: £100-120
    add £25 for one confirmed bar, £50 (2), £100 (3)

A44. NATIONAL MEDAL

Instituted: 1975.

Ribbon: 32mm with 15 alternating gold and blue stripes.

Metal: Bronze.

Size: 38mm.

Description: (Obverse) arms of the Commonwealth of Australia on a ground of mimosa blossom within a recessed circle. Incuse inscription round the edge THE NATIONAL MEDAL FOR SERVICE. (Reverse) plain

Method of naming: Military (up to and including April 19, 1982) named on reverse in impressed, pantographed or engraved styles with service number, initials and surname.

Clasps: A bronze bar, 5mm high by 32mm wide, designed with 10 orbs framed in a border. The bar is awarded for additional 10 years service, and is sewn to the ribbon 10mm above the metal suspender.

Comments: *Awarded to members of the various uniformed services for long service and good conduct, being a minimum of 15 years in one service or an aggregate on 15 years in two or more services. An amendment by Letters Patent in 1987 extended the award of this medal to the prisons service. There have been 175,257 medals awared to date.*

VALUE: £80–150 with no bars; add £25 for one bar confirmed and £100 for two.

A45. AUSTRALIAN CADET FORCES SERVICE MEDAL

Instituted: December 1999.
Ribbon: 32mm stripes of blue and gold with three outer stripes navy/red/light blue.
Metal: Nickel plated bronze.
Size: 38mm.
Description: (Obverse) the emblem of the Australian Cadet Force surmounted with a St Edward's Crown; (reverse) The Federation Star overlaid by a rectangular panel for recipient details.
Method of naming: Pantographed on reverse.
Clasps: A clasp is awarded for each additional five years service.
Comments: *Awarded to officers and instructors of cadets, for efficient long service of 15 years, replacing the British Cadet Forces medal that ceased to be issued in Australia in 1974. 1,644 medals have been awarded.*

VALUE: £150–200

A46. AUSTRALIAN DEFENCE MEDAL

Instituted: Approved in 2004, instituted April 2006.
Ribbon: 32mm wide, deep red with two inner white stripes and two thin exterior stripes of black on the edge.
Metal: Nickel-silver.
Size: 38mm
Description: (Obverse) central coat of arms of Australia as Australia Service Medal 1939–45 (MYB 190), surrounded by the legend THE AUSTRALIAN DEFENCE MEDAL; (reverse) two sprigs of wattle around an imperial crown and the words FOR SERVICE. Suspended from a ring mount.
Method of naming: Pantographed on the edge with service number or PMKeyS number, initials and surname only.
Comments: *There are no clasps awarded with the medal. Awarded to Regular and Reserve forces for four years service (with a minimum of 21 days in any one year) or completion of initial term of engagement, whichever is the lesser. Also awarded if the member died or was medically discharged prior to completion of time. 242,576 have been awarded to date.*

VALUE: £60–80

A47. CHAMPION SHOTS MEDAL

Instituted: 13 September, 1988.
Ribbon: 32mm central 8mm dark blue stripe flanked by 6mm red and 6mm light blue stripes representing the three forces.
Metal: Antiqued brass.
Size: 38mm.
Description: (Obverse) a eucalyptus wreathed vertical panel (indicating excellence) with the Southern Cross and two crossed 0.303 SMLE rifles; (reverse) plain.
Method of naming: Pantographed on the edge with service number or PMKeyS number, initials and surname only.
Clasps: show year(s) of award.
Comments: *This medal has replaced the Army Best Shot Medal (MYB334) and the Queen's Medal for Champion Shot of the Air Force (MYB335). Only three medals may be awarded annually, to the respective champions of the RAN, RAAF and Army. Notable multiple winners include Stuart Boyd-Law, Peter Kelly and Philip Macpherson (three occasions each), Andrew Bellott (four occasions) and Brett Hartman (five occasions). The medal has been issued on 53 occasions.*

VALUE: £1500+

A48. ANNIVERSARY OF NATIONAL SERVICE 1951–1972 MEDAL

Instituted: April 2001.
Ribbon: White with a central gold stripe flanked by thin royal blue stripes with bottle green, pale blue stripes and sand-coloured edges.
Metal: Bronze.
Size: 36mm.
Description: (Obverse) the emblem of the armed forces surrounded by the text ANNIVERSARY OF NATIONAL SERVICE 1951-1975; (reverse) the sun radiating towards the Southern Cross constellation with a cogwheel surround. The medal is surmounted by a royal crown attached to a bar for suspension.
Method of naming: Pantographed on the edge with service number, initials and surname.
Comments: *All 325,800 National Servicemen, including the next-of-kin of the 187 who were killed on active service, are eligible for this medal. It was struck to publicly recognize all National Servicemen between 1951-72 who played a part in the defence of Australia, with 125,425 issued to date.*

VALUE: £100–200   *Miniature* £10

The Unit Citation for Gallantry, the Meritorious Unit Citation and the Group Citation for Bravery (MYBA49–51) are not positioned in The Order of Wearing Australian Honours and Awards. There is a common misconception that the emblems of the awards are the actual awards. This is incorrect, the award is the signed citation certificate presented to the unit or group. The citation emblems are simply uniform dress or other clothing embellishments issued to signify that the wearer was serving with a unit or group that had been cited. For members of the uniformed services, the emblems are worn in accordance with dress rules of the particular Service concerned. Civilian personnel awarded the Group Citation for Bravery should wear the insignia on the left lapel or breast. Should other honours or awards have been awarded, the Group Citation for Bravery insignia should be worn centrally, approximately 10mm above. Citation valuations are based on official records accompanying a medal group. Unattributed Meritorious Unit Citations are available for around £10.

A49. UNIT CITATION FOR GALLANTRY

Instituted: 1991.
Ribbon: Green encased in a silver-gilt rectangular frame with flame decoration. A seven-pointed Federation Star in silver-gilt is worn in the centre.
Size: 15mm by 32mm.
Comments: *This system was borrowed from the USA, many Australian formations and units receiving American unit citations during the Vietnam War. The citation is worn by all members of the unit receiving the citation for extraordinary gallantry in action, and appears on the right breast (Army and RAAF) or below the medal ribbons on the left breast (RAN). Defence force personnel who join the unit at a later date wear the citation emblem without the Federation Star during the period of their service with the unit only. The Unit Citation for Gallantry has been awarded 3 times. The first Unit Citation for Gallantry was awarded to No. 1 Squadron of the SASR for gallantry in 13 major engagements in Iraq in 2003. The second to 4th Battalion, Royal Australian Regiment (Now 2nd Commando) For gallantry in action in Afghanistan, from 25 August 2005 to 2 September 2006. The latest Unit Citation for gallantry was gazetted 10 March 2010 to Delta Company, 6th Battalion, The Royal Australian Regiment (6RAR) For acts of extraordinary gallantry in action at the Battle of Long Tan in Vietnam on 18 August 1966.*

VALUE: £300–500 with certificate

A50. MERITORIOUS UNIT CITATION

Instituted: 1991.

Ribbon: Gold encased in a rhodium-plated silver frame with flame decoration. A rhodium-plated silver Federation Star is mounted in the centre.

Size: 15mm by 32mm.

Comments: *Awarded to members of a unit for sustained outstanding service in warlike operations. 20 Meritorious Unit Citations have been issued to date. Defence force personnel who join the unit at a later date wear the citation emblem without the Federation Star during the period of their service with the unit only. The latest award was made to the 1st Mentoring Task Force, For sustained outstanding service in warlike operations on Operation SLIPPER in Uruzgan Province, Afghanistan, between 20 January and 30 October 2010.*

VALUE: **£250–300 with certificate**

A51. GROUP CITATION FOR BRAVERY

Instituted:

Description: Rhodium-plated rectangular insignia with bronze waratah blossom mounted in the centre.

Comments: *In addition to individual awards for bravery, a collective act of bravery by a group of persons in extraordinary circumstances may have their actions recognized by a group bravery citation. 64 groups (numbering 448 people) Group Citations for Bravery have been issued to date.*

VALUE: **£100–200 with certificate**

A52. PINGAT JASA MALAYSIA

Instituted: 2005, first awards presented April 2006.

Ribbon: 35mm wide, central red stripe, flanked by dark blue and yellow.

Metal: Nickel-silver.

Size: 35mm, suspender bar 40mm.

Description: (Obverse) arms of the Republic of Malaysia with JASA MALAYSIA below; (reverse) map of Malaysia with P.J.M. below, attached to a scrolled suspension bar by two crossed fern fronds.

Method of naming: Pantographed on edge with service or PM keys number, initials and surname.

Comments: *Awarded by the Government of Malaysia to members of the Australian Defence Force who were posted on the strength of a unit or formation and served in the prescribed operational area of Malaysia and Singapore in direct support of operations for 90 days or more, in Malaysia between August 31, 1957 and December 31, 1966 or Singapore between August 31, 1957 and August 9, 1965; or for 180 days for ADF outside the area but in support of operations for the first two dates. Now being issued in a case with a brass plate inserted into the lid with vote of thanks and gratitude from Malaysia. Worn in Australia as a foreign decoration. There are at least two different strikings of this medal.*

VALUE: **£100–250 dependent on other service medals**

State Awards

Each of the Australian Sates and Territories also have their own system of awards for Police, Ambulance, Fire, Prison and Emergency Services. These awards are covered fully in *Australians Awarded* published by Clive Johnson of CJ Medals in Queensland (see main advert at the beginning of this section). Listed below is *just a cross section* of awards to give some idea of the depth of this exciting, collectable field. Some States authorise the wearing of State Awards on the right hand side of the chest and in the reverse order, i.e. most important medal worn closest to the heart. As so few of these medals are available to the collector, it has been decided not to give valuations at this stage.

A54. NEW SOUTH WALES CORRECTIVE SERVICE BRAVERY MEDAL

Instituted: 1989.
Ribbon: Dark blue with a broad crimson central stripe.
Metal: Silver-gilt.
Description: A cross pattée with radiations in the angles and surmounted by a St Edward's crown fitted to a ring for suspension. (Obverse) the arms of New South Wales within a circular band inscribed CORRECTIVE SERVICE N.S.W., with a scroll at the foot inscribed FOR BRAVERY; (reverse) plain.
Comments: *Awarded to prison officers for bravery*

VALUE: —

A55. NEW SOUTH WALES CORRECTIVE SERVICE EXEMPLARY CONDUCT CROSS

Instituted: 1989.
Ribbon: Navy blue with a broad gold central stripe.
Metal: Silver.
Description: An eight-pointed star with one point obscured by the crown, surmounted by a large St Edward's crown fitted to a suspension ring. (Obverse) the arms of New South Wales within a circular band inscribed CORRECTIVE SERVICE N.S.W., with a scroll at the foot inscribed EXEMPLARY CONDUCT; (reverse) plain.
Comments: *Awarded to prison officers for exemplary conduct.*

VALUE: —

A56. NEW SOUTH WALES CORRECTIVE SERVICE MERITORIOUS SERVICE MEDAL

Instituted: 1989.
Ribbon: Red with a broad central gold stripe.
Metal: Bronze.
Description: An elongated circle fitted with a suspension bar. (Obverse) the arms of New South Wales, with NSW CORRECTIVE SERVICE at the top and LONG SERVICE at the foot; (reverse) FOR TWENTY YEARS SERVICE in four lines within a wreath.
Clasps: A bronze clasp in the form of a five pointed star for 25 years and silver clasps for 30, 35 and 40 years service
Comments: *Awarded for 20 years service in the New South Wales prison service*

VALUE: —

A57. NEW SOUTH WALES CORRECTIVE SERVICE LONG SERVICE MEDAL

Instituted: 1989.
Ribbon: Navy blue with two silver stripes.
Metal: Bronze.
Size: 36mm.
Description: A circular medal fitted with a plain suspension bar. (Obverse) the crowned emblem of the Corrective Service with a wreath at the foot; (reverse) a laurel branch round the left side with the words FOR FIFTEEN YEARS SERVICE in four lines on the right.
Comments: *Awarded for 15 years service in the New South Wales Prison Service.*

VALUE: —

A58. COMMISSIONER'S VALOUR AWARD—NSW

Instituted: 1987.
Ribbon: Light blue with narrow white stripes towards the edges and dark blue edges.
Metal: Silver with enamelled centre.
Description: (Obverse) A cross pattée with a crowned and enamelled centerpiece bearing the insignia of the New South Wales Police Service within a wreath, inscribed NEW SOUTH WALES POLICE FOR BRAVERY.
Comments: *Awarded to police officers where an act of conspicuous merit involving exceptional bravery was in evidence. It is very sparingly awarded, only seven being awarded posthumously since it was instituted.*
VALUE: —

A59. COMMISSIONER'S COMMENDATION (COURAGE)—NSW

Instituted: 1970.
Ribbon: Light blue with a narrow central white stripe and narrow white edges.
Description: A bronze Nemesis device affixed directly to the ribbon.
Comments: *Awarded for outstanding courage in the line of duty. May be awarded posthumously. A bronze bar is awarded for additional acts. There is no restriction to the number of awards and about 90 are made annually.*

VALUE: —

A60. COMMISSIONER'S COMMENDATION(SERVICE)—NSW

Instituted: 1970.
Ribbon: Light blue with narrow white edges.
Description: A bronze Nemesis device affixed directly to the ribbon.
Comments: *Awarded to police officers for outstanding service. About ten commendations are awarded annually.*

VALUE: —

A60A. COMMISSIONER'S OLYMPIC COMMENDATION—NSW

Instituted: 2000.
Ribbon: Five equal stripes of light blue and dark blue.
Description: A bronze device of the Olympic rings affixed directly to the ribbon.
Comments: *Awarded to police officers who performed in an outstanding manner in the planning period leading up to and over the period of the Olympic games in 2000.*

VALUE: —

A60B. COMMISSIONER'S COMMUNITY SERVICE COMMENDATION—NSW

Instituted: 2002.
Ribbon: Narrow blue with narrow white edges
Description: A silver coloured Nemesis device affixed directly to the ribbon
Comments: *Awarded to sworn and unsworn salaried employees of the NSW Police Force who, as representatives of the Force raise significant funds for community causes or raise awareness of indigenous issues or volunteer in an unpaid capacity as a director in a police-related charity.*

VALUE: —

A61. COMMISSIONER'S UNIT CITATION— NSW

Instituted: 1994.

Description: A silver bar in the form of a wreath containing a light blue enamel start. For a subsequent award a star is added upt to a maximum of three.

Comments: *Awarded to units, patrols, groups, squads and commands where outstanding service involving bravery or actions of obvious merit have been evident. The emblem is worn by each member of the unit, while the unit receives a framed citation for display. About five citations are awarded annually.*

VALUE: —

A61A. COMMISSIONER'S COMMUNITY SERVICE CITATION— NSW

Instituted: 1994.

Description: A silver bar in the form of a wreath containing a white insert. For a subsequent award a star is added.

Comments: *Awarded to sworn and unsworn salaried employees who, as representatives of the NSW Police Force, have demonstrated an outstanding level of service as a field officer, camp supervisor or fundraiser for a police-related charity, etc.*

VALUE: —

A61B. COMMISSIONER'S OLYMPIC CITATION— NSW

Instituted: 2000.

Description: A silver bar in the form of a wreath containing a white enamel insert with silver Olympic rings. Only one award can be conferred. .

Comments: *Awarded to officers who had significant involvement during the Olympic Games.*

VALUE: —

A61C. NEW SOUTH WALES POLICE SERVICE MEDAL

Instituted: 2002

Ribbon: Royal blue with two equal stripes of light blue.

Metal: Nickel-plated copper.

Description: (Obverse) St Edward's crown above the badge of the state of New South Wales and the Australian Wedgetail eagle carrying a scroll of Nemesis, with the words NSW POLICE MEDAL—DILIGENT AND ETHICAL SERVICE around.

Comments: *Awarded to police officers for diligent and ethical service of 10 years with the NSW Police. Clasps are awarded for each additional five years service. It can also be awarded for a member who dies in the line of duty with less than 10 years service. Pantographed on the reverse with the recipient's full name.*

VALUE: —

A62. QUEENSLAND PRISON SERVICE SUPERINTENDENT'S LONG SERVICE MEDAL

Instituted: Before 1988.
Ribbon: Dark blue with three narrow silver stripes.
Description: An eight-pointed Maltese Cross superimposed on a wreath surmounted by a St. Edward's crown attached to a ring for suspension from a rectangular bar inscribed MERITORIOUS SERVICE. The centre of the cross has the arms of Queensland.
Method of naming: The top of the ribbon has a brooch bar with the recipient's details engraved on the reverse.

VALUE: —

A63. QUEENSLAND PRISON SERVICE OFFICER'S LONG SERVICE MEDAL

Instituted: Before 1988.
Ribbon: Silver with two narrow dark blue stripes.
Description: A circular medal fitted with a loop for suspension via a ring attached to an ornamental rectangular bar. (Obverse) the crowned and wreathed insignia of the Queensland Prison Service with the inscription LONG AND MERITORIOUS SERVICE round the foot. The top of the ribbon has a brooch bar with the recipient's details engraved on the reverse.

VALUE: —

A64. QUEENSLAND POLICE SERVICE VALOUR AWARD

Instituted: 1993.
Ribbon: Maroon, light blue and dark blue in equal widths.
Metal: Silver.
Description: A Maltese Cross superimposed on a wreath, with an enameled centerpiece featuring the St. Edward's crown within a wreath and surrounded by the inscription QUEENSLAND POLICE VALOUR AWARD.
Method of naming: Pantographed recipient details on reverse.
Clasps: In the event that an officer is awarded the Valour Award on a second occasion, the officer may be granted a silver bar.
Comments: *This award is rightfully seen as the premier award for bravery available to Queensland Police. An officer who performs an act of exceptional bravery in hazardous circumstances may be awarded the Queensland Police Service Valour Award. Including, but not restricted to "arrests of armed offenders", "hostage situation where police show sacrifice by leaving cover and drawing the offender's fire at close range", "rescues in advanced fire situations", "rescues by trained personnel which required extreme sacrifice". This decoration is similar to the Queensland Police Award which was discontinued in the 1930s. May be awarded posthumously or to a person who has left the service.*

VALUE: £1000–1300

A64A. COMMISSIONER'S COMMENDATION FOR BRAVERY (QLD)

Instituted: —

Ribbon: 32mm riband alternating bands of maroon and Queensland Police Flag blue radiating inwards in decreasing widths from opposite sides with a traditional police blue coloured border.

Description: Maltese cross and crown, initially awarded with a clasp FOR BRAVERY, with subsequent awards signified by additional clasps or a rosette for the ribbon bar.

Method of naming: unnamed, but accompanied by attractive illuminated scroll.

Comments: *Awarded to an officer who performs an act of bravery in hazardous circumstances, beyond that which can be adequately recognized by a Commissioner's Certificate. Examples can include, but are not restricted to "arrests or attempted arrests of offenders in possession of firearms", "hostage situations where police intervene with considerable exposure to risk of injury", "intervention of suicidal situations", "rescues from advanced fire, floods, heavy seas, vehicles on fire, cliffs, bridges"*

VALUE: £165+ with scroll

A65. QUEENSLAND POLICE SERVICE MEDAL

Instituted: December 1998.

Ribbon: 32mm blue with broad central stripe of light blue and silver edges.

Metal: Silver.

Size: 36mm.

Description: (Obverse) the Queensland Police emblem with the inscription DILIGENT AND ETHICAL SERVICE round the circumference, surmounted by a St. Edward's crown; (reverse) QUEENSLAND POLICE SERVICE MEDAL round the circumference.

Method of naming: Name of recipient pantographed at centre of reverse.

Clasps: Awarded in five-year increments starting at 15 years service.

Comments: *Awarded to police officers after a minimum of 10 years service, but prospective candidates must demonstrate an unblemished record of diligence and ethical service. A ribbon bar with silver rosette(s) is worn on the day uniform.*

VALUE: £100–150

A65A. VICTORIA POLICE VALOUR AWARD (VA)

Instituted: December 1987.

Ribbon: Watered pale blue.

Metal: Silver and enamels.

Size: 38mm.

Description: A four armed cross with the upper arm surmounted by the Queen's crown and attached to a plain suspension bar by three small rings. (Obverse) cross enamelled in pale blue with a five pointed star on each arm surmounting a square shape made of five silver rays between each pair of arms. A central medallion with the words FOR BRAVERY in the centre and VICTORIA POLICE FORCE around the circumference completes the medal. The word "Force" was removed in 1987. (Reverse) plain

Method of naming: Full name of recipient and date of the act on reverse

Clasps: A silver bar with a central rose design is awarded for any subsequent act of courage deserving the medal.

(Old style, 1956–87)

VALUE: £1000–£1500

A65B. 2010-2011 QUEENSLAND FLOOD AND CYCLONE CITATION

Instituted: 2011.

Size: 34mm.

Description: maroon ribbon with four white vertical stripes representing the four emergency service agencies, surrounded by a bronze metallic frame. The cyclone symbols on both side of the citation represents the time-line of cyclonic events occurring between Cyclone Tasha in December 2010 and Cyclone Yasi in February 2011. The swirls on the top and bottom of the citation represents waves associated with mass flooding which occurred throughout many parts of Queensland.

Comments: *The group citation is issued to employees and volunteers of the Queensland Police Service (QPS) and the Queensland Department of Community Safety who performed duty on at least one shift at any time between 1 December 2010 and 28 February 2011. Duty performed may be in direct response to the flood and cyclone events or maintaining core business during this period. Group citations are not issued for any individual effort, but are issued to acknowledge the performance of a unit or organisation.*

Recipients of the citation receive the citation in a box set which also contains a miniature version of the citation which is worn with Mess Dress or equivalent wear at formal evening dinners or similar events.
First awarded June 4, 2011.

VALUE: —

A66. A.C.T. COMMUNITY POLICING MEDAL

Instituted: 1988.

Ribbon: White with a thin central stripe and broad edges of dark blue, the central stripe flanked by two thin gold stripes.

Metal: Bronze.

Size: Upright oval 52 x 42mm.

Description: (Obverse) the arms of the Australian Capital Territory with the inscription A.C.T. COMMUNITY POLICING MEDAL round the top; (reverse) inscribed FOR DILIGENT SERVICE above a horizontal plaque, fitted with a straight suspension bar.

Method of naming: Name of recipient on reverse.

Clasps: Awarded for 20, 25 and 30 years service, but only one to be worn. A rosette showing the years served is worn on the ribbon.

Comments: *Awarded for service in the AFP ACT Community Policing, recognizing those who have dedicated 10 or more years diligent service by policing in the territory since December 6, 1988, the first day of self-government of the ACT. A ribbon bar with silver rosette(s) is worn on the day uniform.*

VALUE: £100–150

A66A. A.C.T. EMERGENCY MEDAL

Instituted: 2004.

Ribbon: 32mm, flame red with central yellow stripe bisected with a thin blue stripe.

Metal: Bronze with antique finish.

Size: 38mm.

Description: (Obverse) a stylised flower symbolising the Canberra Royal bluebell, surrounded by wind and flame; (reverse) inscribed COURAGE/LEADERSHIP/TEAMWORK/PROFESSIONALISM/INNOVATION/INTEGRITY.

Method of naming:

Clasp: 2003.

Comments: *Commissioned in March 2004 to recognise the efforts of those who worked tirelessly to preserve the community following the devastating bush fires of January 2003. The medal is issued in a black case inscribed ACT EMERGENCY MEDAL.*

VALUE: £100–150

A66B. A.C.T. COMMUNITY PROTECTION MEDAL

Instituted: November 11, 2002

Ribbon: 32mm, scarlet with a central white stripe, two yellow and two blue stripes each of 3mm.

Metal: Bronze.

Size: 36mm.

Description: (Obverse) The Coat of Arms of the Australian Capital Territory. (Reverse) A design of eucalyptus leaves and seed pods. The wording "For Distinguished Service" and a plinth originally for the name of the recipient but now with the date of the award. The name of the recipient is now engraved on the rim of the medal. A maximum of five medals in total will be awarded by the A.C.T. Government each year on Canberra Day (March 15).

Comments: *For sustained distinguished or outstanding service to the A.C.T. Community. One medal to a volunteer or employee of each of A.C.T. Ambulance Service, A.C.T. Emergency Service or A.C.T. Emergency Services Bureau. Also eligible are sworn or unsworn members of the Australian Federal Police working within A.C.T. Community Policing. First presented on Canberra Day 2003.*

VALUE: —

A66C. NORTHERN TERRITORY POLICE SERVICE MEDAL

Instituted: 1999.

Ribbon: Black with a broad central terracotta band flanked by white stripes

Metal: Bronze.

Size: 36mm.

Description: Circular medal attached to a plain suspender by a small circle with two raised crossed batons. (Obverse) the badge of the NT Police service within a raised circle, surrounded by the words NORTHERN TERRITORY POLICE SERVICE MEDAL; (reverse) plain.

Method of naming: Pantographed on reverse.

Comments: *Presented for ten years full or part time continuous service. Bars available for each additional period of ten years service. The first awards in June 1999 were backdated to 1978 (when the NT Police Service was officially recognised) with 60 officers receiving the medal.*

VALUE: £150–200

Unofficial medals

Australia, like many countries has produced a number of unofficial and semi-official medals. Although rejected by many of the ex-servicemen's institutions and RSLs, they are still a popular form of recognition, where recognition is due. Despite not having official status, these awards can still increase the desirability of a group. The Merchant Navy awards listed are an attempt to recognize the merchant seamen whose service often appears to go unrecognized, despite their involvement in both peace time and war. Although not approved within the Australian Honours System, the Merchant Navy Association is following strict protocol with regard to the issue of these medals.

A67. AUSTRALIAN MERCHANT NAVY SERVICE CROSS

Instituted: 1998.
Ribbon: Blue with narrow green, white and red central stripes and white edges.
Metal: Silver gilt.
Size: 36mm wide.
Description: A cross fourchée on which is superimposed a small circular medallion bearing the insignia of the Australian Merchant Navy, fitted with a bar suspender.
Method of naming: Usually hand engraved on reverse, or unnamed.
Clasps: A gold laurel spray is awarded for each 15 years additional service
Comments: *Created to mark United Nations Year of the Ocean, the cross is awarded for 15 years bona fide service on Articles of Agreement.*

VALUE: £50–100

A68. AUSTRALIAN MERCHANT NAVY MERITORIOUS MEDAL

Instituted: 1998
Ribbon: Watered silk, white with broad green and red edges and blue central stripe
Metal: Silver
Size: 38mm
Description: (Obverse) the crowned insignia of the Merchant Navy; (reverse) AUSTRALIAN MERCHANT NAVY MERITORIOUS MEDAL, fitted with ornamental bar suspender.
Method of naming: Hand engraved on rim or unnamed
Comments: *Awarded for exceptional contribution to the Merchant Navy over a long period of time or for an individual act of bravery by a seafarer.*

VALUE: —

A69. AUSTRALIAN MERCHANT NAVY COMMENDATION

Instituted: 1998.
Ribbon: Watered silk with a dark blue centre, white stripes and light green edges with a small laurel spray emblem attached.
Metal: Silver.
Size: 42mm.
Description: A laurel wreath joined at the top by a merchant navy crown attached to a ring for suspension.
Comments: *Awarded unnamed for an ongoing or individual contribution by a person in one of the many fields of maritime endeavour including education, research and development, maritime business, industrial relations and professional achievement. As at December 2007, only 63 had been issued—five to officers of RAN Hydrographic Service.*

VALUE: —

A70. GALLIPOLI STAR

Instituted: April 25, 1990.
Ribbon: Central broad deep blue stripe, flanked by narrow crimson stripes and broad edges of yellow and light blue respectively.
Metal: Bronze.
Size: 36mm.
Description: A small circular medal superimposed on an eight-pointed star with ring suspension. (Obverse) a Tudor crown surrounded by the inscription GALLIPOLI 1914-15.
Method of naming: Unnamed.
Comments: *This medal was originally approved by King George V but was never issued at the time. In April 1990 it was produced and presented unofficially by Mr Ross Smith, a retired army warrant officer and Canberra businessman, to the 200 surviving Gallipoli veterans to mark the 75th anniversary of the ill-fated landings on the Turkish coast. The remaining stars were sold to collectors. However, replicas of this medal have been produced and although not always marked as such, are of much lower quality than the originals, which are stamped with the letters A. J. P. in small 1mm font on the bottom arm.*

VALUE: £100–175

A71. TOBRUK T MEDAL

Ribbon: Khaki, with thin red and dark blue stripes on the left, and thin light blue and red stripes on the right.
Metal: Plated bronze.
Size: 36mm across top of T, 32mm in height.
Description: Large "T" shape, with plain suspension bar. (Obverse) laurel wreath edging and TOBRUK SIEGE 1941 in raised lettering in the centre; (reverse) plain.
Method of naming: Hand engraved usually with regimental number, initials and name on reverse—sometimes with additional information.
Comments: *Issued to Australian, British, Indian, New Zealand and Polish troops who were in action during the siege of Tobruk between April and December 1941. An unofficial award, issued by the "Rats of Tobruk" Association in 1977.*

VALUE: £60–100

A72. FRONT LINE SERVICE MEDAL

Instituted: —

Ribbon: Left half gold, right half dark green, both have a thin red stripe down the middle.

Metal: Bronze.

Size: Long rectangle 40mm by 20mm, with scroll and crossed guns to a total height of 60mm.

Description: (Obverse) A long rectangle edged with a laurel wreath and the raised words FRONT LINE SERVICE, scroll above with INFANTRY, and suspender above in the form of crossed 303 rifles; (reverse) plain.

Method of naming: Usually engraved on reverse.

Comments: *Issued by the 2/12 Battalion Association to identify those that took part in front line actions with the Infantry, thus differentiating them from other units.*

VALUE: £50–60

A73. BRITISH COMMONWEALTH OCCUPATION FORCES—BCOF

Instituted: —

Ribbon: Broad white band flanked by very narrow red bands, with narrow green on left edge and narrow blue on right edge.

Metal: Cupro-nickel.

Size: 38mm.

Description: (Obverse) central King's crown above BCOF scroll and 1946 JAPAN 1952 in raised letters around the top circumference; (reverse) sprigs of laurel, tri-services badges and the words FOR SERVICE WITH THE OCCUPATION FORCES.

Method of naming: Impressed on rim in small capitals.

Comments: *Issued by the Australian BCOF Association to any veteran who had served one day on the strength of the unit with the Commonwealth Forces. Around 8,000 have been issued.*

VALUE: £50–60   *Miniature £10*

A74. RSPCA AUSTRALIA PURPLE CROSS AWARD

Instituted: 1996.
Ribbon: 32mm purple.
Metal: Bright Nickel
Description: a circular medal featuring a resin purple cross at the centre surrounded with the inscription PURPLE CROSS AWARD; the reverse is blank.
Method of naming: Pantographed name on reverse.
Comments: *The award recognises the deeds of animals that have shown outstanding service to humans, particularly exceptional courage in risking their own safety or life to save a person from injury or death. The medal has been awarded only 8 times. 2 awards were made retrospective. The first, to "The Pikeman's Dog Wee Jack" (Eureka Stockade, 1854) and the second, to "Murphy" (on behalf of all donkeys used by John Kilpatrick Simpson at Gallipoli, 1915). The most recent award was to "Sarbi" a nine year old black Labrador. Awarded on 5 April 2011 "for her unquestioning, unwavering service to man". After being separated from her handler during the action which Mark Donaldson was awarded his VC she was missing for 13 months wandering in Afghanistan until found by US Special Forces and returned to Australian Lines.*

VALUE: —

A75. WAR DOG OPERATIONAL MEDAL

Instituted: 2008. The Medal is backdated from 1948 (The Malayan Emergency)
Ribbon: 32mm navy blue, bronze olive green and sky blue, with one blood red stripe down the centre of each colour.
Metal: Bright Nickel
Description: a square medal divided into three sections. The right section features a soldier and his dog with the words "AUSTRALIAN ACTIVE SERVICE MEDAL" underneath; the left section is for naming details; the base section displays the words "AUSTRALIAN DEFENCE FORCE TRACKERS AND WAR DOGS ASSOCIATION"; the reverse is blank.
Method of naming: Pantographed number, name and service on the obverse.
Clasps: MALAYA, MALAYSIA, BORNEO, SOUTH VIETNAM, SOMALIA, EAST TIMOR, TIMOR LESTE, THE SOLOMON ISLANDS, BOUGANVILLE, IRAQ, AFGHANISTAN. Clasps are sew-on type and multiple bars are rare. Only one dog has received three clasps.
Comments: *Although not a federally approved award the Australian Directorate of Honours and Awards of the Department of Defence has outlined that they cannot issue medals to Military Working Dogs. However, they have allowed the Australian Defence Force Trackers and War Dogs Association (ADFTWDA) to design its own medals and medal ribbons for issue to Military Working Dogs and approved them for wear by the recipient dog.*

VALUE: —

A76. CANINE SERVICE MEDAL

Instituted: 2008
Ribbon: 32mm navy blue, red, and sky blue with two white stripes.
Metal: Bright Nickel
Description: a square medal divided into three sections. The right section features a soldier and his dog with the words 'AUSTRALIAN SERVICE MEDAL' underneath; the left section is for naming details; the base section displays the words 'AUSTRALIAN DEFENCE FORCE TRACKERS AND WAR DOGS ASSOCIATION'; the reverse is blank.
Method of naming: Pantographed number, name and service on the obverse.
Clasps: there are no clasps awarded for this medal
Comments: *Much like the War Dog Operational Medal it is not a federally approved award but is approved for issue and wear by Military Working Dogs by the (ADFTWDA). The medal can also be issued to Police/Corrective Services and Customs dogs when they have served 5 years of aggregated service as a working dog on Government security details.*

VALUE: —

CANADIAN MEDALS

Apart from such British campaign awards as the Louisburg Medal of 1758 (71), the Canada General Service Medal (125) awarded to those who helped to put down the Fenian Raids of 1866 and 1870 and the Red River rebellion of the latter year and the North West Canada Medal (134), distinctive medals relating to military service in Canada date from 1902 when Canadian versions of the Meritorious Service Medal (212) and Colonial Long Service and Good Conduct Medal (248) were instituted. Subsequently there were also Canadian versions of the Permanent Forces of the Empire Beyond the Seas Long Service and Good Conduct Medal (249) and the military Long Service and Good Conduct Medal (229). Similarly, both the Efficiency Decoration (236) and the Efficiency Medal (237) were issued with suspension bars denoting service in Canada. Distinctive versions of certain British medals, such as the Defence Medal (185), War Medal (186) and the Korea Medal (195), struck in silver instead of base metal, will also be found in the appropriate sections of this volume.

Several awards which were purely Canadian in character will also be found in earlier sections of this book, as they were authorised or instituted by the imperial government. Thus the Canadian Volunteer Service Medal (188), instituted to recognise volunteer service during World War II, comes under this category, as the various types of Canadian Memorial Cross (188A) awarded to the relatives of service personnel who gave their lives in both world wars and since the Korean War. Also included are awards by Newfoundland which did not enter the Confederation of Canada until 1949. For this reason Newfoundland servicemen were not eligible for the Canadian Volunteer Service Medal, and it was not until 1981 that this deficiency was remedied by the institution of a separate Newfoundland Volunteer War Service Medal (194).

The move towards purely Canadian medals, however, began to develop in the inter-war period, but the earliest awards were confined to the Royal Canadian Mounted Police and include a number of medals which were authorised by the various provinces. In 1967 Canada celebrated the centenary of Confederation and the opportunity was then taken to institute the Order of Canada, with its associated Medal of Service and Medal of Courage, as well as the Centennial Medal. Five years later, Canada inaugurated a full range of honours and awards and over the intervening years this has been extended considerably.

THE ORDER OF PRECEDENCE IN CANADA

Victoria Cross (VC)
Cross of Valour (CV)
Order of Merit (OM)
Companion of the Order of Canada (CC)
Officer of the Order of Canada (OC)
Member of the Order of Canada (CM)
Commander of the Order of Military Merit (CMM)
Commander of the Order of Merit of the Police Forces (COM)
Commander of the Royal Victorian Order (CVO)
Officer of the Order of Military Merit (OMM)
Officer of the Order of Merit of the Police Forces (OOM)
Lieutenant of the Royal Victorian Order (LVO)
Member of the Order of Military Merit (MMM)
Member of the Order of Merit of the Police Forces (MOM)
Member of the Royal Victorian Order (MVO)
The Most Venerable Order of the Hospital of St John of Jerusalem (all grades)
Ordre National du Québec (GOQ, OQ, CQ) (in French only)
Saskatchewan Order of Merit (SOM)
Order of Ontario (OOnt)
Order of British Columbia (OBC)
Alberta Order of Excellence (AOE)
Order of Prince Edward Island (OPEI)
Order of Manitoba (OM)
Order of New Brunswick (ONB)
Order of Nova Scotia (ONS)
Order of Newfoundland and Labrador (ONL)
Star of Military Valour (SMV)
Star of Courage (SC)
Meritorious Service Cross (Military and Civil) (MSC)
Medal of Military Valour (MMV)
Medal of Bravery (MB)
Meritorious Service Medal (Military and Civil) (MSM)
Royal Victorian Medal (Gold, Silver & Bronze) (RVM)
Sacrifice Medal
Korea Medal
Canadian Volunteer Service Medal for Korea
Gulf and Kuwait Medal
Somalia Medal
South-West Asia Service Medal

General Campaign Star with Ribbons
General Service Medal with Ribbons
Operational Service Medal with Ribbons
Special Service Medal with Bars
Canadian Peacekeeping Service Medal
United Nations' Medals
NATO Medals
International Commission and Organisation Medals
Canadian Centennial Medal, 1967
Queen Elizabeth II's Silver Jubilee Medal, 1977
125th Anniversary of the Confederation of Canada Medal, 1992
Queen Elizabeth II's Golden Jubilee Medal, 2002
Queen Elizabeth II's Diamond Jubille Medal, 2012
Royal Canadian Mounted Police Long Service Medal
Canadian Forces Decoration (CD)
Police Exemplary Service Medal
Corrections Exemplary Service medal
Fire Services Exemplary Service Medal
Canadian Coast Guard Exemplary Service Medal
Emergency Medical Services Exemplary Service Medal
Peace Officer Exemplary Service Medal
Queen's Medal for Champion Shot
Ontario Medal for Good Citizenship (OMC)
Ontario Medal for Police Bravery
Ontario Medal for Firefighters Bravery
Saskatchewan Volunteer Medal (SVM)
Ontario Provincial Police Long Service and Good Conduct Medal
Service Medal of the Most Venerable Order of the Hospital of St John of Jerusalem
Commissionaire Long Service Medal
Newfoundland and Labrador Bravery Award
Newfoundland and Labrador Volunteer Service Medal
British Columbia Fire Services Long Service and Bravery Medal
Saskatchewan Centennial Medal
Alberta Centennial Medal
Commonwealth Orders, Decorations and Medals
Foreign Orders, Decorations and Medals

C1. VICTORIA CROSS (CANADA)

Date: 1 January 1993.

Ribbon: Crimson, with a miniature emblem when the ribbon alone is worn.

Metal: An alloy of bronze which includes metal used to make the UK VC (gunmetal from the cascabel of Chinese cannon), a bronze Confederation Metal (1867) and metal found and mined across Canada.

Size: 38mm.

Description: (Obverse) a cross pattée with raised edges having in the centre a lion standing on the royal crown partially circumscribed by a banner bearing the words PRO VALORE; (reverse) a circle containing the date of the action for which it was awarded. A straight suspender bar with a design of laurel leaves is used attached to the upper arm of the cross by a ring and "V" shaped lug.

Comments: *Available with effect from 1 January 1993 to members of the Canadian Forces or a member of an allied force serving with them for an act of supreme courage, self-sacrifice or devotion to duty in the face of an enemy. It is identical to the awards of the UK, Australia and New Zealand with the important exception of the inscription within the banner on the obverse. The two official languages of Canada (English and French) militated against the use of the English inscription FOR VALOUR as on the three other awards and the Latin translation PRO VALORE was chosen for the Canadian award. The decoration is cast by the Government of Canada in a collaboration between the Royal Canadian Mint and Natural Resources Canada. Recipients are entitled to use the post-nominals VC. None have been awarded yet.*

VALUE: —

C2. CROSS OF VALOUR

Date: 1 May 1972.

Ribbon: Light crimson—worn around the neck (men) or on a bow (women), with a miniature emblem when the ribbon alone is worn.

Metal: Gold and red enamel.

Size: 38mm.

Description: (Obverse) a cross with straight arms in red enamel edged in gold with a central medallion of a gold maple leaf on a red enamel ground encircled by a gold wreath of laurel; (reverse) the royal cypher (EIIR) surmounted by a crown on the upper arm with the words VALOUR VAILLANCE across the centre above the engraved name of the recipient and date of the incident.

Comments: *Awarded for acts of conspicuous courage in circumstances of extreme peril to Canadian citizens and foreign nationals for an act in Canada or elsewhere if the act is considered to be in the interest of Canada and merits recognition by the country. A second award is signified by a gold maple leaf worn on the larger of the two suspension rings. The first award was made on 20 May 1972. 20 have been awarded to this date. Recipients are entitled to use the post-nominals CV.*

VALUE: — *Miniature* £50–60

C3. ORDER OF CANADA
COMPANION (CC), OFFICER (OC), MEMBER (CM)

Date: 1 July 1967.
Ribbon: Red with a broad central stripe in white—a neck ribbon for the two higher levels (Companion and Officer) and a breast ribbon for Members. In undress uniform a small maple leaf is worn on the ribbon in red (CC) gold (OC) or silver (CM).
Metal: Silver gilt or silver with enamels.
Size: 57mm (companion), 47.5mm (officer) and 38mm (member).
Description: (Obverse) A white enamelled stylised snowflake of six points (hexagonal in shape) edged in gold or silver with a central medallion comprising a maple leaf in red enamel (CC), gold (OC) or silver (CM) on a white enamel field all surrounded by a red enamel outer band bearing the words DESIDERANTES MELIOREM PATRIAM (they desire a better country) in gold or silver. A St Edward's crown in gold (CC and OC) or silver (CM) with red enamel is placed at the top of the central medallion on the upper point of the snowflake; (reverse) a small box in which is inscribed a serial number with the word CANADA above. The CC and OC are worn with neck ribbons, a ring suspender is used for the CM.
Comments: *Established to reward Canadian citizens who exemplify the highest qualities of citizenship which enrich the lives of their fellow citizens. Honorary membership is available to foreigners. There are three levels—Companion, Officer and Member—with the qualifying criteria differing for each. Appointments are made in July and December each year with a maximum of 15 (CC) Companions, 64 (OC) Officers and 136 (CM) Members appointed each year. The maximum number of living Companions at any one time will not exceed 165 although there is no limit to the number of Officers and Members. The Order initially had a single class—Companion—with the Officer and Member levels being introduced on 1 July 1972. Prior to this a Medal of Service was a part of the Order but it was discontinued in 1972 and all holders made Officers of the Order of Canada. A Medal of Courage was also attached to the Order but was never awarded and discontinued on the introduction of the Bravery Decorations (CV, SC and MB).*

VALUE: Companion (448) £3000–5000
Officer (1871) £2000–4000
Member (3502) £800–1500 *Miniature* £50–60

C4. ORDER OF MILITARY MERIT
COMMANDER (CMM), OFFICER (OMM), MEMBER (MMM)

Date: 1 July 1972.
Ribbon: Blue with gold edges (4.8 mm) worn around the neck (CMM) or on the breast (OMM and MMM).
Metal: Enamelled silver gilt or silver.
Size: 38mm (OMM and MMM).
Description: (Obverse) a cross pattée with the arms in blue enamel edged with gold (CMM and OMM) or silver (MMM). A central medallion has a maple leaf at the centre in red (CMM), gold (OMM) or silver (MMM) on a white background surrounded by an outer band in red enamel inscribed with the words MERIT MÉRITE CANADA in the appropriate metal and surmounted by the crown; (reverse) left plain apart from a serial number. A straight suspender bar with a laurel leaf design is used for Officers (in gold) and Members (in silver).
Comments: *Instituted to recognise conspicuous merit or exceptional service by all members of the Canadian Forces. The total of all levels which can be awarded annually cannot exceed one-tenth of one per cent of the average number of personnel in the preceding year, currently it adds up to about 115 appointments or promotions a year of which 5% are at the CMM level, 20% at the OMM level and 75% at the MMM level. There is no limit to the total number at any level. Commanders are most usually of the rank of Brigadier-General/Commodore and above, Officers are Majors to Colonels and Members all those of lower rank including NCOs and junior officers. Appointments are made in December each year. In undress uniform the level of the award is indicated by a blue cross worn on the ribbon with a maple leaf placed centrally in red, gold or silver. Prior to 1983 a maple leaf of the appropriate colour was worn alone.*

VALUE: Commander (215) £3000–5000
Officer (1084) £1000–2000
Member (2455) £750–1500 *Miniature* £50–60

C5. ORDER OF MERIT OF THE POLICE FORCES

COMMANDER (COM), OFFICER (OOM), MEMBER (MOM)

Date: 2 October 2000.

Ribbon: Bands of blue, gold and blue, all of equal width. A neck ribbon is worn for the rank of Commander and a breast ribbon for Officers and Members.

Metal: Silver gilt or silver and enamels.

Size: 38mm (OOM and MOM).

Description: (Obverse) a cross pattée in dark blue enamel with a central medallion bearing a maple leaf and an outer band inscribed with the word MERIT (left) and MÉRITE (right) in the upper circumference and CANADA at the bottom. A St Edward's crown is on the upper arm of the cross. The maple leaf in the central medallion is red for Commanders, gold for Officers and silver for Members. The outer band is red with gold lettering for Commanders and Officers and red with silver lettering for Members. A silver suspender bar with a laurel leaf pattern and three small rings is used for the MOM, the bar is gold for the OOM.

Comments: *The most recent addition to the awards available to police officers is a continuation of the series of Orders first established in 1967 with the introduction of the Order of Canada and continued in 1972 with the Order of Military Merit. The Order of Merit of the Police Forces ranks immediately after the Order of Military Merit in the order of precedence. It was introduced to recognise the impact of the Police Service on society and honour those officers with careers of particular merit or who otherwise deserve formal recognition and is available in three classes—Commander (COM), Officer (OOM) and Member (MOM). In any one year there will be a maximum number of new appointees equivalent to one-tenth of one per cent of the number of police officers serving in Canada in the preceding year and is expected that they will number no more than 50. Officers from any police force in Canada are eligible although it is a living order and retired officers are not eligible, neither can it be awarded posthumously.*

VALUE:		
	Commander (46)	Rare
	Officer (99)	Rare
	Member (248)	Rare

C6. L'ORDRE NATIONAL DU QUÉBEC

GRAND OFFICIER (GOQ), OFFICIER (OQ), CHEVALIER (CQ)

Date: 20 June 1984.

Ribbon: Blue with a white central stripe, all of equal width. Worn around the neck (Grand Officier and Officier) or on the breast (Chevalier).

Metal: Gold (GOQ) or silver (OQ and CQ).

Size: —

Description: (Obverse) a Greek cross with very broad arms and the space between them so small that it is almost square. The upper left and lower right have an irregular highly polished area resulting in a very reflective quality with the space between the two in a matt finish giving the overall appearance of a river running between two land masses. In the bottom left corner, superimposed on the matt area is a fleur-de-lys. All the elements and ribbon colour are taken from the flag of Québec. The insignia for a Chevalier has the cross mounted on a circular silver disc with a ring suspender.

Comments: *Membership of the Order is open to any citizen of Québec without distinction to recognise outstanding work in the Province for the benefit of all. Any person can nominate any other citizen for the award. Honorary membership is available to those not resident in Québec. An award ceremony takes place once a year although special arrangements can be made if the recipient does not reside in the Province. Recipients are entitled to use the post-nominals GOQ, OQ or CQ.*

VALUE:		
	Grand Officier	£2500–3000
	Officer	£1500–1000
	Chevalier	£500–600

C7. SASKATCHEWAN ORDER OF MERIT

Date: 1985.

Ribbon: Dark green with a gold central stripe, all of equal width. Since 2005 the colours are reversed so that the ribbon is now gold with a green central stripe.

Metal: Enamelled gold.

Size: —

Description: (Obverse) a six-point star in white enamel edged in gold and with gold lines along the centre of each point. There is a central medallion in the shape of the shield from the Saskatchewan coat of arms in enamels (a lion above three sheaves of wheat) surmounted by a crown in gold. Since 2005, the shield is surrounded by the Motto of the Order " MULTIS E GENTIBUS VIRES" on a red circlet.The neck ribbon is attached to the upper point of the star by a small suspender ring.

Comments: *Awarded to recognise individual excellence and outstanding achievement to the social, cultural and economic well-being of the Province and its people. A maximum of ten appointments can be made in any one year. Any resident, past or present of Saskatchewan is eligible for membership although members of parliament, legislative assembly and judges are barred whilst in office. Recipients are entitled to use the post-nominals SOM.*

VALUE: £500–750   *Miniature*   £20–25

C8. ORDER OF ONTARIO

Date: 18 December 1986.

Ribbon: Red with a central stripe in dark green flanked by a white stripe bisected by a thin gold line.

Metal: Enamelled gold.

Size: —

Description: (Obverse) a stylised version of the provincial flower (trillium) with three petals in white enamel superimposed on three dark green enamel sepals, all edged in gold. In the centre is the shield taken from the Ontario coat of arms in enamels surmounted by a crown in gold. A small ring suspender is used.

Comments: *Awarded to residents of Ontario who have shown excellence and achievement of the highest standard and whose contributions have enriched the lives of others and helped make a better society in Ontario. Recipients have the right to use the post-nominals O Ont. Elected officials at federal, provincial or municipal level are barred from membership of the Order whilst in office.*

VALUE: £500–750

C9. ORDER OF BRITISH COLUMBIA

Date: 12 April 1989.

Ribbon: Dark green with two stripes of white either side of a central dark blue stripe each bisected by a thin gold line.

Metal: Gold and enamel.

Size: —

Description: (Obverse) a stylised representation of the six-petal provincial flower of British Columbia (pacific dogwood) in white and green enamels edged by gold. At the centre is the shield of the provincial coat of arms in enamels topped by a crown. A small ring suspender is used.

Comments: *Awarded in recognition of distinction and excellence in any field of endeavour for the benefit of people in British Columbia and elsewhere. Recipients are entitled to use the post-nominals OBC.*

VALUE: £500–750

C10. ALBERTA ORDER OF EXCELLENCE

Date: 16 November 1979.
Ribbon: The same design as the previous order but with the dark green replaced by dark blue.
Metal: Silver gilt and enamel.
Size: —
Description: (Obverse) a cross pattée with the arms in dark blue enamel edged with gold superimposed on a circular disc visible between the arms of the cross and decorated with a design of roses and rose leaves to represent the provincial flower. A central medallion has the full achievement of arms of Alberta on a red background within an outer band of white enamel bearing the words THE ALBERTA ORDER OF EXCELLENCE in gold; (reverse) a maple leaf and sheaf of wheat.
Comments: *Awarded in October each year to Canadian citizens living in Alberta from all walks of life who have performed excellent and distinctive works at provincial, national or international level. It is the highest award that can be bestowed by the Province of Alberta. An important provision is that the work will stand the test of time. Recipients are entitled to use the post-nominals AOE.*

VALUE: £500–750   *Miniature*   £45–50

C11. ORDER OF PRINCE EDWARD ISLAND MEDAL OF MERIT

Date: 1996.
Ribbon: A broad stripe of brown (left) and one of green (right) separated by a narrow white stripe and with a white line at each edge.
Metal: Enamelled gold.
Size: —
Description: (Obverse) circular with the shield from the provincial coat of arms in gold with red and white enamel on a background of gold enamel all within an outer band of blue enamel bearing the words MERIT (upper) and PRINCE EDWARD ISLAND (lower) in gold. A second version with the inscriptions in French is also available— MÉRITE (upper) and ÎLE-DU-PRINCE-EDOUARD. The ribbon, which is worn around the neck attached to the disc by two rings—one small, one large. A miniature is awarded for wear on less formal occasions— the design is the same but the ribbon is green with a central brown band, all of equal width, separated by white lines and with white edges.
Comments: *The Order is the highest that can be bestowed by the Province and given to any resident (present or former long-term) who contributes to the social, economic and cultural life of Prince Edward Island. Not more than three people can be admitted to the Order in any one year. In common with other provincial orders elected officials are not eligible whilst they remain in office. Recipients are entitled to use the post-nominals OPEI.*

VALUE: £500–750

C12. ORDER OF MANITOBA

Date: 14 July 1999.
Ribbon: White with a central stripe in red and a pale blue stripe towards each edge.
Metal: Enamelled gold.
Size: —
Description: (Obverse) a stylised representation of the provincial flower (crocus) with six petals in pale blue enamel edged in gold bearing the shield from the provincial coat of arms at the centre in enamels topped by a crown in gold.
Comments: *Established to recognise current or former long-term residents of Manitoba who have demonstrated excellence and achievement in any field leading to the social, economic or cultural well-being of the Province. A maximum of eight awards can be made in any one year although the initial investiture saw 20 people honoured. Members are entitled to the use of the post-nominals OM. Certain elected officials are not eligible whilst in office.*

VALUE: £500–750

C12A. ORDER OF NEW BRUNSWICK

Instituted: December 2000
Ribbon: Red with a central blue stripe flanked by yellow stripes. Worn as a neck ribbon.
Metal: Gold and enamels.
Description: (Obverse) a stylised purple violet, the provincial floral emblem, in enamels bordered with gold. In the centre is the provincial arms surmounted by a crown, the shield depicting an ancient galley topped by a lion (an allusion to the arms of the Duchy of Brunswick, a possession of King George III in 1784 when New Brunswick was established). The ribbon is attached to the top of the crown between the two uppermost petals of the flower.
Comments: *Awarded to Canadian citizens who are present or long—term residents of New Brunswick and who have distinguished themselves in various fields (as above). A maximum of ten awards will be made each year. Recipients are entitled to the post-nominal letters ONB.*

VALUE: £500–750

C12B. ORDER OF NOVA SCOTIA

Instituted: 2001
Ribbon: Blue with a narrow central stripe of red flanked by white, a black line and a gold line, the colours of the provincial flag. Worn as a neck ribbon.
Metal: Gold and enamels.
Description: (Obverse) in the shape of a stylised mayflower, the provincial floral emblem, in white enamel edged with gold and with green enamel between each petal. In the centre is the provincial coat of arms (a blue Saltire cross surmounted by the Scottish lion in red and gold), all surmounted by a crown on the uppermost petal to which is affixed a thin ring for suspension.
Comments: *Awarded to Canadian citizens who are present or long-term residents of Nova Scotia and who have distinguished themselves by outstanding achievement in a number of fields bringing honour and prestige to the Province. Certain public officials are not eligible while holding office. The award is available posthumously if the person is nominated within a year of death. Five appointments will be made annually after the inaugural year when there were ten recipients. Recipients are entitled to the post-nominal ONS.*

VALUE: £500–750

C12C. ORDER OF NEWFOUNDLAND AND LABRADOR

Date: Instituted: 2001
Ribbon: Edged green with two stripes of white on either side of a dark blue stripe with a thin gold stripe in the center of each white stripe.
Metal: Silver gilt, Labradorite and enamel.
Size: —
Description: (Obverse) a stylized version of the provincial flower (pitcher plant), the main petals are crafted with the provincial mineral, Labradorite, while the smaller petals are enamelled with similar colours. In the center is the shield of the provincial coat of arms enamelled in colour surmounted by the Royal Crown in gold. A ring is affixed to the top petal for suspension.
Comments: *Canadian citizens who are present or former long-term residents of Newfoundland and Labrador are eligible for nomination to the Order which recognizes individuals who have demonstrated excellence and achievement in any field of endeavour benefiting in an outstanding manner Newfoundland and Labrador and its residents. The only exceptions are public officials (members of the Senate, House of Commons, House of Assembly or legislative assembly of a province, or judges), who may not be nominated while they are in office. Other Canadians and foreigners may be appointed as honorary members. A maximum of eight appointments are made annually. Members are entitled to the post-nominal letters ONL.*

VALUE: £500–750

C13. STAR OF MILITARY VALOUR

Date: 1 January 1993.
Ribbon: Crimson with a white stripe towards each edge.
Metal: Silver gilt, silver and enamel.
Size: 44mm
Description: (Obverse) a four-point star with a maple leaf between the points. A central medallion has a maple leaf placed centrally on a red background all surrounded by a circular wreath of laurel in silver; (reverse) the royal cypher (EIIR) surmounted by a crown with the inscription PRO VALORE. The rank and name of the recipient is engraved below the inscription. A suspension ring is attached to the upper point of the star.
Comments: *The second highest military valour decoration in Canada. It is awarded to any member of the Canadian Forces or allies serving with the Canadians for distinguished and valiant service in the presence of an enemy on or after January 1, 1993. Any second or subsequent award is indicated by a gold bar bearing a maple leaf in the centre. It can be awarded posthumously. Recipients are entitled to use the post-nominals SMV or ÉVM in French. 12 have been awarded to date.*

VALUE: —   *Miniature*   £20–25

C14. STAR OF COURAGE

Date: 1 May 1972.
Ribbon: Red with a stripe of blue towards each edge.
Metal: Silver and silver gilt.
Size: 44mm
Description: (Obverse) identical to the Star of Military Valour but in silver with a gold wreath of laurel around the central medallion bearing a gold maple leaf in its center; (reverse) the royal cypher (EIIR) surmounted by a crown on the upper arm of the cross with the inscription COURAGE below. The name of the recipient and date of the act are engraved below.
Comments: *The second highest honour for courage awarded for acts of conspicuous courage in circumstances of great peril. It is available to Canadian citizens and foreign nationals for the performance of an act in Canada or elsewhere if the act is in the interest of Canada. The first award was made on July 20, 1972. Second or subsequent awards are indicated by a gold bar with a maple leaf at its centre. In common with most Canadian national honours the award is named in English and French but the initials of the two are not the same. The post-nominals are therefore different—SC (English) or ÉC (French "Étoile du Courage"). 419 have been awarded to date.*

VALUE: £3000–4500   *Miniature*   £20–25

C15. MERITORIOUS SERVICE CROSS (MILITARY AND CIVIL DIVISIONS)

Date: 11 June 1984 (military) and 6 June 1991 (civil).

Ribbon: Bright blue with a white stripe (6 mm) towards each edge. The civil division is indicated by the addition of a central white stripe (1 mm).

Metal: Originally silver, now rhodium plated red brass.

Size: 38mm.

Description: (Obverse) a Greek cross with splayed ends with a wreath of laurel between the arms. A crown is attached to the upper arm of the cross to which is joined the plain straight suspender bar. A central medallion bears a maple leaf at its centre; (reverse) two concentric circles with the royal cypher (EIIR) in the centre and the words MERITORIOUS SERVICE MÉRITOIRE (separated at the bottom by a maple leaf) around the second of the two circles.

Comments: *The Cross was initially introduced for award to the military only but extended in 1991 to civilians and made retrospective to 1984. The criteria are similar for both divisions—a deed or activity performed in a highly professional manner or of a high standard bringing benefit or great honour to the Canadian Forces (military) or Canada (civil). Second or subsequent awards are indicated by a silver bar with a maple leaf in its centre. Both awards are available to Canadians and foreign nationals. The name of the recipient is engraved at the back of the suspension bar and the date on the reverse of the top arm of the cross. Recipients are entitled to use the post-nominals MSC or CSM in French. 221 MSC's have been awarded to date (189 military, 32 civilian).*

VALUE: £500–1000   *Miniature*   £20–25

C16. MEDAL OF MILITARY VALOUR

Date: 1 January 1993.

Ribbon: Crimson with white stripes in the centre and at each edge.

Metal: Silver gilt.

Size: 36mm.

Description: (Obverse) circular with a maple leaf surrounded by a wreath of laurel tied at its base by a bow; (reverse) the royal cypher (EIIR) surmounted by a crown with the inscription PRO VALORE. The suspender bar is in the shape of a fleur-de-lys attached to the disc by a claw fitting. The rank and name of the recipient are engraved on the rim.

Comments: *Awarded to members of the Canadian Forces and allies serving with or in conjunction with the Canadians for an act of valour or devotion to duty in the presence of an enemy. A gold bar with a maple leaf at its centre is available for any second or subsequent award. It can be awarded posthumously. Recipients are entitled to use the post-nominals MMV or MVM in French. 64 have been awarded to date.*

VALUE: —   *Miniature*   £20–25

C17. MEDAL OF BRAVERY

Date: 1 May 1972.

Ribbon: Crimson with dark blue stripes in the centre and at each edge.

Metal: Silver.

Size: 36mm.

Description: (Obverse) identical to the previous award; (reverse) the royal cypher (EIIR) surmounted by a crown with the words BRAVERY (right) and BRAVOURE (left) at the circumference.

Comments: *Awarded to all Canadian citizens (civilian and military) and foreign nationals as defined for previous awards for acts of bravery in hazardous circumstances. It can be awarded posthumously. The first award was made on 20 July 1972. Bars are of silver with a maple leaf placed centrally. The name of the recipient is engraved on the rim. Recipients are entitled to use the post-nominals MB. 2,571 have been awarded to date.*

VALUE: £650–850   *Miniature*   £20–25

C18. MERITORIOUS SERVICE MEDAL (MILITARY AND CIVIL DIVISIONS)

Date: 6 June,1991.

Ribbon: Bright blue with two white stripes towards each edge. The civil division is indicated by the addition of a central white stripe (1mm).

Metal: Originally silver, now rhodium plated red brass.

Size: 36mm.

Description: (Obverse) a Greek cross with splayed ends with a wreath of laurel between the arms and a maple leaf in the central medallion all superimposed on a disc. A crown is attached to the upper arm of the cross to which is joined the ring suspender; (reverse) two concentric circles with the royal cypher (EIIR) in the centre and the words MERITORIOUS SERVICE MÉRITOIRE (separated at the bottom by a maple leaf) around the second of the two circles.

Comments: The criteria are similar for both divisions—a deed or activity performed in a highly professional manner or of a high standard bringing benefit or honour to the Canadian Forces (military) or Canada (civil). Second or subsequent awards are indicated by a silver bar with a maple leaf in its centre. Both awards are available to Canadians and foreign nationals and can be awarded posthumously. The name of the recipient is engraved on the rim and the date on the top part of the reverse. 986 MSMs have been awarded to date (695 military, 291 civilian). Recipients are entitled to the use of the post-nominals MSM.

VALUE: £350–400   *Miniature* £15–25

C18A. SACRIFICE MEDAL

Date: 29 August 2008.

Ribbon: Two equal red stripes bisected by thin white stripes, divided by a central black stripe.

Metal: Silver.

Size: 36mm

Description: (Obverse) effigy of HM the Queen with the legend ELIZABETH II DEI GRATIA REGINA CANADA around; (reverse) a figure of "Canada" from the National Vimy Memorial and the word SACRIFICE.

Comments: Awarded posthumously to members of the Canadian Forces who die as a result of military service after October 6, 2001. Also awarded to those who, since that date, have been wounded as a direct result of a hostile action on the condition that the wounds that were sustained required treatment by a physician and the treatment has been documented. Accidents and minor wounds are not eligible but 'friendly fire' and operational stress injuries as a direct result of hostile action are eligible under certain circumstances. Additional incidents entitle the holder to a bar. The medal is engraved with the recipient's details on the edge. 689 medals and 17 bars have been awarded to date

VALUE: Rare   *Miniature* £10–15

C19. CANADIAN VOLUNTEER SERVICE MEDAL FOR KOREA

Date: 12 July,1991

Ribbon: Yellow with a broad stripe in UN blue (7mm) at each edge and a central stripe of red, white and red (all 2mm).

Metal: Silver coloured copper and zinc alloy.

Size: 36mm.

Description: (Obverse) the crowned profile of Queen Elizabeth II with the word CANADA below and ELIZABETH II DEI GRATIA REGINA around the circumference; (reverse) a wreath of laurel tied at the base by a bow with a maple leaf above it. In the central field is the inscription KOREA/ VOLUNTEER/1950–1954/VOLONTAIRE/COREE. A plain straight suspender was used.

Comments: *Awarded to former members of the Canadian Forces who were in the qualifying area of Korea and adjacent areas between June 27, 1950 and July 27, 1954 with four further provisos. The recipients were eligible if they were on the strength of a unit in Korea for one day, were on active service aboard a ship for at least 28 days, flew one sortie over Korea or Korean waters or had accumulated at least 28 days service in the qualifying area. The medal could be awarded posthumously and 18,526 awards were made. Issued unnamed.*

VALUE: £60–80   *Miniature*   £10–15

C20. GULF AND KUWAIT MEDAL

Date: 3 June,1991.

Ribbon: A sand coloured central stripe (8mm) flanked by stripes of dark blue (5mm), red (2mm) and light blue (5mm) to represent the three branches of the armed forces.

Metal: Silver coloured copper and zinc alloy.

Size: 36mm.

Description: (Obverse) the crowned profile of Queen Elizabeth II with the word CANADA below and ELIZABETH II DEI GRATIA REGINA around the circumference; (reverse) a wreath of laurel tied at the base by a bow with a maple leaf above it. In the central field is the inscription THE GULF/ AND KUWAIT/1990–1992/LE GOLFE/ET KUWAIT in five lines. A plain straight suspender was used.

Comments: *Awarded to all members of the Canadian Forces who served in the theatre of operations between August 2, 1990 and June 27, 1991 for a minimum of 30 days cumulative service or who served during actual hostilities for at least one day between January 16 and March 30, 1991. The bar was awarded to all those who served during the hostilities for at least one day. The bar has a silver maple leaf at its centre. 4,447 medals were awarded, including 3,195 with bar. Issued unnamed*

VALUE: £80–100   *Miniature*   £10–15

C21. SOMALIA MEDAL

Date: 8 April, 1997

Ribbon: White with United Nations blue stripes (5 mm) at each edge and a central stripe of three colours (dark blue, red and light blue to represent the three armed services) flanked by stripes of a sand colour—all 2.5 mm wide).

Metal: Gold-plated bronze.

Size: 36mm.

Description: (Obverse) three over-lapping Canadian maple leaves above two branches of laurel and with the word CANADA above; (reverse) the royal cypher (EIIR) surmounted by a crown with the words SOMALIA (left) SOMALIE (right) and the dates 1992–93 (lower) around the circumference. A ring suspender was used.

Comments: *Available to any member of the Canadian Forces or anyone attached to or working with them for a minimum of 90 days cumulative service in Somalia between November 16, 1992 and June 30, 1993. Anyone with a minimum of 60 days service who died, was evacuated or redeployed was also eligible. It was awarded posthumously. 1,421 were awarded, it was issued unnamed.*

VALUE: £125–150   *Miniature*   £10–15

C22. SOUTH-WEST ASIA SERVICE MEDAL

Date: 31 July, 2002

Ribbon: 32mm in width with a white stripe in the middle (12mm), on either side of which are stripes of black (4mm), red (2mm) and sand (4mm).

Metal: Originally nickel-plated red brass, now cupro-nickel.

Size: 36mm

Description: (Obverse) the Queen's effigy, wearing the King George IV State Diadem, facing right, circumscribed with the legend: ELIZABETH II • DEI GRATIA REGINA and at the base of the effigy, the word CANADA flanked by two small maple leaves; (reverse) a representation of the mythical figure of Hydra transfixed by a Canadian sword and over the design is the Latin phrase, ADVERSUS MALUM PUGNAMUS - "We are fighting evil". A claw at the top of the medal, in the form of a cluster of olive leaves representing peace is attached to a straight suspension bar.

Comments: *Awarded to Canadian Forces members deployed with, or in direct support of the operations against terrorism in South-West Asia. The medal with the AFGHANISTAN bar is awarded for 30 days cumulative service between 11 September, 2001 and 31 July, 2009 in the theatre of operations of South-West Asia while it is awarded without the bar for a minimum of 90 days cumulative service in direct support of these operations such as service with the Headquarters, Canadian Joint Task Force South-West Asia in Tampa Bay, Florida; the Stragtegic Airlift Detachment in Ramstein, Germany and other similar tasks. Rotation Bars are awarded for each period of 180 days of eligible service following eligibility for the medal with AFGHANISTAN bar (i.e. at 210 days, 390 days, etc.) The medal is issued unnamed. Over 12,631 medals and 12,312 bars have been issued to date.*

VALUE: £100–150   *Miniature*   £10–15

C23. GENERAL CAMPAIGN STAR

Date: 24 March 2004

*Ribbon: 32mm in width with a central stripe of 12mm specific to the theatre or task concerned (light blue for Op ALLIED FORCE, dark green for SOUTH-WEST ASIA and light grey for EXPEDITION) on either side of which are stripes of white (2mm) and dark red (8mm).

Metal: Gold-plated bronze.

Size: 44mm.

Description: A four pointed star bearing (Obverse) a wreath of maple leaves open at the top to include the Royal Crown, two crossed swords, the blades and hilts forming four additional points to the Star, an anchor and a flying eagle; (reverse) within a raised circle, the Royal Cypher ensigned by the Royal Crown, a plain space for engraving and three maple leaves on one stem. A ring is fitted to a small ball at the tip of the top point of the Star. Recipient's details are engraved on the reverse of the Star.

Comments: *Awarded to Canadian Forces members who deploy into a specific theatre of operations to take part in operations in the presence of an armed enemy. The Star is always awarded with a ribbon specific to the theatre or task being recognized, each ribbon having its own criteria. Rotation Bars are awarded for each period of 180 days of eligible service following eligibility for the Star i.e. at 210 days, 390 days, etc.*

*Ribbons: ALLIED FORCE: awarded to fighter pilots and AWACS crew members who took part in at least five missions in the theatre of operations during the air campaign in Kosovo between 24 March and 10 June, 1999. 66 issued.

SOUTH-WEST ASIA: awarded for 30 days of service in Afghanistan as part of the Canadian contribution to the International Security and Assistance Force between 24 April 2003 and 31 July 2009 and for 30 days of service in Afghanistan or the SWA naval theatre since 1 August, 2009. 27,435 issued.

EXPEDITION: awarded for 30 days in approved smaller operations conducted in the presence of an armed enemy. Currently, CF members on exchange with US forces in Iraq are eligible. Seven issued.

VALUE: £200–250   *Miniature*   £10–15

C24. GENERAL SERVICE MEDAL

Date: March 24, 2004

Ribbon: 32mm in width with a dark red central stripe of 18mm on either side of which are stripes of white (2mm) and a colour specific to the threatre or task concerned (light blue. for Op ALLIED FORCE, dark green for SOUTH-WEST AIA and light grey for EXPEDITION) (5mm.)

Metal: Cupro-nickel.

Size: 36mm.

Description: (Obverse) a contemporary crowned effigy of The Queen circumscribed by the inscriptions "ELIZABETH II DEI GRATIA REGINA" and "CANADA" separated by small crosses pattée; (reverse) two crossed swords, an anchor and a flying eagle surmounted by the Royal Crown and surrounded by two branches of maple leaves. The straight suspension bar is ornamented with 3 overlapping maple leaves. Recipient's details are engraved on the rim.

Comments: *Awarded to Canadian Forces members and Canadian civilians who deploy outside Canada but not necessarily into a defined theatre of operations, to provide direct support, on a full-time basis, to operations conducted in the presence of an armed enemy. The Medal is always awarded with a ribbon specific to the theatre or task being recognized, each ribbon having its own criteria. Rotation Bars are awarded for each period of 180 days of eligible service following eligibility for the Medal (i.e. at 210 days, 390 days, etc.).*

Ribbons: ALLIED FORCE: awarded to personnel who served a least 30 days in Aviano and/or Vicenza, Italy in direct support of the air campaign in Kosovo between 24 March and 10 June, 1999. 130 issued.

SOUTH-WEST ASIA: awarded for 30 days of service in locations outside Afghanistan and the SWA naval theatre, such as at Camp Mirage, in direct support of the Canadian operations in SWA since the spring of 2003 (start dates vary depending on location). 4,869 issued.

EXPEDITION: awarded for 30 days in support of approved smaller operations conducted in the presence of an armed enemy. No eligible service as of yet. None issued.

VALUE: £200–250   *Miniature*   £10–15

C24A. OPERATIONAL SERVICE MEDAL

Date: 5 July 2010

Ribbon: 32 mm in width with a central stripe of 22 mm specific to the theatre or task concerned (sand for SOUTH-WEST ASIA, light green for SIERRA LEONE, royal blue for HAITI, dark green for SUDAN, white for HUMANITAS and light grey for EXPEDITION) on either side of which are stripes of white (2.5 mm) and red (2.5 mm).

Metal: Cupro-nickel

Size: 36 mm

Description: (Obverse) a contemporary effigy of The Queen circumscribed by the inscriptions "ELIZABETH II DEI GRATIA REGINA" and "CANADA" separated by small maple leaves; (reverse) from top to bottom appear the Royal Crown on either side of which are three maple leaves conjoined on one stem, a Goode interrupted homolosine equal-area projection of the globe, and a laurel branch crossed with an oak branch. A plain straight suspender is attached by a claw fitting. Recipient's details are engraved on the rim.

Comments: Awarded to Canadian Forces members, Canadian Police Officers and Canadian civilians working for them, who deployed overseas to take part in, or provide direct support to, operations, or who served under dangerous circumstances, provided their service is not eligible for another medal. The Medal is always awarded with a ribbon specific to the theatre or task being recognized, each ribbon having its own criteria. Rotation Bars are awarded for each period of 180 days of eligible service following eligibility for the Medal (i.e. at 210 days, 390 days, etc.).

Ribbons: SOUTH-WEST ASIA: awarded for non military service in that area since 7 October 2001. None issued.

SIERRA LEONE: awarded for 30 days of service in that country since the Armistice of 31 July 2002, mainly with the British-led International Military Advisory Team (IMATT). 37 issued.

HAITI: awarded for 30 days of service in that country since 6 March 2004, mainly with the US-led Multinational Interim Force (6 March to 16 August 2004, as well as support from the Dominican Republic). 622 issued.

SUDAN: awarded for 30 days of service in that country since 15 September 2004, mainly with the African Union-Led mission in Darfur (15 September 2004 to 31 December 2007, as well as support from Ethiopia and Senegal). 19 issued.

HUMANITAS: replaces the HUMANITAS bar to the Special Service Medal (C25) from 1 August 2009 and is awarded for 30 days of service on approved humanitarian missions such as the earthquake relief in Haiti (12 January to 2 May 2010). 364 issued.

EXPEDITION: awarded for 30 days in approved smaller operations not recognized by other medals. This currently includes service in the Middle East with the Office of the US Security Coordinator as well as naval and air antinarcotics operations in the Caribbean Sea, East Pacific and off the West coast of Africa. 20 issued.

VALUE: Rare   *Miniature: £10-15*

C25. SPECIAL SERVICE MEDAL

Date: 16 June 1984.
Ribbon: A dark green central stripe (12mm) flanked by stripes of white (5mm) and red (5mm) at the edges.
Metal: Originally rhodium-plated alloy, now cupro-nickel.
Size: 36mm.
Description: (Obverse) A wreath of laurel tied at the base by a bow with a maple leaf in the central field; (reverse) the Royal cypher (EIIR) surmounted by the Royal Crown with the words SPECIAL SERVICE SPÉCIAL around the circumference. A plain straight suspender bar is used. Issued unnamed.
Bars: PAKISTAN 1989-90: Created 6 June 1991 for 90 days of service with the Mine Awareness and Clearance Training Program in Pakistan from 15 March 1989 to 29 July 1990. 50 were awarded on 27 January 1992. Recipients can now exchange this award for the United Nations Special Service Medal.
PEACE - PAIX: Created 26 November 1992 for 180 days of service in approved peacekeeping operations since November 1947. This bar was superseded by the Canadian Peacekeeping Service Medal (C26) on 21 June 2001. 2,311 Peace Bars have been issued.
ALERT: Created 26 November 1992 for 180 days of service at Canadian Forces Station Alert since 1 September 1958. 7,685 issued.
NATO + OTAN: Created 26 November 1992 for 180 days service with NATO since 1 January 1951 (some restrictions apply). 64,138 issued.
HUMANITAS: Created 9 March 1993 for 30 days of service on approved humanitarian operations between 11 June 1984 and 31 July 2009. 1,089 issued.
JUGOSLAVIJA: Created 9 March 1993 for 90 days of service with the European Community Monitor Mission in Yugoslavia (ECMMY) from 4 September 1991. This bar was cancelled and replaced by the ECMMY Medal (206B).
RANGER: Created 1 October 1999 for 4 years service with the Canadian Rangers including completion of 3 sovereignty patrols in isolated regions of Canada since 1947. To date, more than 3,192 Ranger bars have been issued.
Comments: *Awarded to members of the Canadian Forces for service performed under exceptional circumstances, in a clearly defined locality for a specific duration. The medal is always issued with a bar, each having its own criteria.*
VALUE: £15–25   *Miniature*   £10–15

C26. CANADIAN PEACEKEEPING SERVICE MEDAL

Date: 25 April 1997.
Ribbon: A light blue central stripe flanked by equal stripes of white, red and green.
Metal: Antique Silvered Copper
Size: 36mm.
Description: (Obverse) a depiction of three Canadian peacekeepers taken from the National Peacekeeping Monument in Ottawa. One figure is an unarmed UN military observer holding a pair of binoculars, another a kneeling female figure shouldering a radio and the third a guard with a rifle. The words PEACEKEEPING (upper) and SERVICE DE LA PAIX (lower) lie at the circumference; (reverse) a maple leaf with the royal cypher (EIIR) topped by a crown in the centre with a branch of laurel on either side and the word CANADA below. The plain straight suspender bar is attached by a maple leaf.
Comments: *Inspired by the award in 1988 of the Nobel Peace Prize to all UN peacekeepers. Awarded to Canadian citizens for a minimum of 30 days service on a peacekeeping or observing mission since 14 November 1947. Military personnel, police officers and civilians are eligible. Recipients are also entitled to wear any UN, NATO or other international medal issued. 74,391 have been awarded to date, it is issued unnamed.*

VALUE: £35–40   *Miniature*   £10–15

C27. CANADIAN CENTENNIAL MEDAL

Date: 1 July 1967.
Ribbon: White with four red stripes (1mm) equally spaced and red
  stripes (5mm) at the edges.
Metal: Silver.
Size: 36mm.
Description: (Obverse) the Canadian maple leaf superimposed
  by the royal cypher (EIIR) surmounted by a crown and the
  words CONFEDERATION (left) CANADA (upper) and
  CONFÉDÉRATION (right) around the circumference; (reverse) the
  full achievement of arms of Canada above the dates 1867–1967. A
  plain suspender in a wide, shallow triangular shape was used.
Comments: *Awarded in celebration of the centenary of Canadian
  Confederation to those recommended by national and provincial
  governments and a variety of other bodies and associations. Approximately
  29,500 medals were awarded, including 8,500 to the military.*

VALUE: £60–80   *Miniature*   £25–30

C28. QUEEN ELIZABETH II'S SILVER JUBILEE MEDAL (Canada)

Date: 6 February 1977.
Ribbon: White with thin red stripes at the edges, a broad blue stripe in
  the centre and a thin red stripe down the middle of it.
Metal: Silver
Size: 32mm
Description: (Obverse) Right-facing profile of Queen Elizabeth II
  wearing the St Edward's crown–the first time this design was
  employed; (reverse) a large stylised maple leaf with 'CANADA'
  around the top of the rim and, around the bottom of the rim, the
  Royal Cypher EIIR surmounted by the Crown and the dates 1952
  and 1977 on each side in small lettering.
Comments: *Awarded to Canadians who have made a significant contribution
  to their fellow citizens, their community or to Canada on the occasion of
  the 25th anniversary of Her Majesty's Accession to the Throne as Queen of
  Canada. The recipients were selected by a number of partner organisations
  in every field of Canadian Life. Approximately 30,000 medals were awarded
  including 7,000 to the military.*

VALUE: £90–120   *Miniature*   £10–15

C29. 125th ANNIVERSARY OF THE CONFEDERATION OF CANADA MEDAL

Date: 7 May 1992.

Ribbon: White with five red stripes (1mm) equally spaced and blue stripes (4.5mm) at the edges.

Metal: Rhodium plated copper and zinc alloy.

Size: 36mm.

Description: (Obverse) the Canadian maple leaf superimposed by the royal cypher (EIIR) surmounted by a crown and the words CONFEDERATION (left) and CONFÉDÉRATION (right) and the dates 1867–1992 (lower) around the circumference; (reverse) the shield taken from the Canadian coat of arms within a belt bearing the words DESIDERANTES MELIOREM PATRIAM and surmounted by a lion. The legend A MARI USQUE AD MARE is inscribed around the lower circumference half. A plain straight suspender is used.

Comments: *Awarded to Canadian citizens who had made a significant contribution to Canada, their community or their fellow citizens in celebration of the 125th anniversary of federation. Approximately 44,000 were awarded, including 4,000 to the military.*

VALUE: £45–50   *Miniature* £10–15

C30. QUEEN ELIZABETH II'S GOLDEN JUBILEE MEDAL (Canada)

Date: 23 February 2002.

Ribbon: 32mm in width with two outer stripes of 2mm of red, followed by 10mm stripes of royal blue, 3mm stripes of white and a central 2mm stripe of red.

Metal: Gold-plated bronze.

Size: 32mm.

Description: (Obverse) the 1990-2002 Canadian coinage effigy of HM the Queen with the legend "QUEEN OF CANADA - REINE DU CANADA"; (reverse) the Royal Crown above a stylized maple leaf bearing the Royal Cypher with 1952, 2002 and CANADA around. There is a small ring at the top of the medal, through which passes a larger ring to accommodate the ribbon which is the same as for the British Golden Jubilee Medal.

Comments: *Awarded to Canadians who have made a significant contribution to their fellow citizens, their community or to Canada on the occasion of the 50th anniversary of Her Majesty's Accession to the throne as Queen of Canada. The recipients were selected by a number of partner organisations in every field of Canadian Life. Approximately 46,000 medals were awarded including approximately 9,000 to the military. The Canadian Forces awarded its 9,000 medals proportionally through its ranks according to an automatic formula based on the component, service, rank, trade and length of service of every member of the Canadian Forces.*

VALUE: £45–50   *Miniature* £10–15

C30A. QUEEN ELIZABETH II'S DIAMOND JUBILEE MEDAL (Canada)

Date: 2011

Ribbon: 32 mm in width with a red stripe in the centre (2 mm) on each side of which are white stripes (3 mm) followed by red stripes (10 mm) and blue edge stripes (2 mm).

Metal: Nickel-Silver

Size: 32 mm

Description: (Obverse) a contemporary crowned effigy of The Queen circumscribed by the inscriptions "ELIZABETH II DEI GRATIA REGINA" and "CANADA" separated by small maple leaves; (reverse) a diamond-cut field, on which is superimposed a lozenge inscribed with the Royal Cypher, placed on four maples leaves, incorporating the dates "1952" and "2012" at the sides, and, in base, two scrolls bearing the words "VIVAT" and "REGINA" respectively. Ring suspension.

Comments: To be awarded on the occasion of the 60th anniversary of Her Majesty's Accession to the Throne as Queen of Canada to Canadian citizens or permanent residents of Canada (alive on 6 February 2012) who have made significant contributions to Canada or to a particular province, territory, region or community within Canada, or for an outstanding achievement abroad that has brought great credit to Canada. 60,000 recipients will be selected by a number of partner organizations in every field of Canadian life.

VALUE: *Miniature*   *£10-15*

C31. ROYAL CANADIAN MOUNTED POLICE LONG SERVICE MEDAL

Date: 6 March 1934.

Ribbon: Dark blue with two yellow stripes towards the edges.

Metal: Silver.

Size: 36mm.

Description: (Obverse) the effigy of the reigning monarch; (reverse) the insignia of the RCMP consisting of the head of a buffalo within a buckled belt inscribed with the words MAINTIENS LE DROIT all topped by a crown. On either side of the belt are five maple leaves. The name of the Force is contained in a banner below the belt. The words FOR LONG SERVICE (above) and AND GOOD CONDUCT (below) are inscribed around the circumference. A plain straight suspender is attached by a claw fitting.

Comments: *Awarded for 20 years of service in the RCMP. Different bars exist to denote subsequent periods of service (bronze with one star for 25 years, silver with 2 stars for 30 years, gold with 3 stars for 35 years and gold and silver with 4 stars for 40 years), only the last bar awarded is worn. When Queen Elizabeth came to the throne and the medal was redesigned to display her effigy on the obverse, changes were also made to the reverse to substitute the Queen's crown for the King's that had been used from the medal's introduction. The opportunity was also taken to reduce the size of the insignia of the RCMP and move the inscription to read continuously around the circumference. In 1989 a French language version of this new design was introduced with the inscription on the reverse reading POUR ANCIENNETÉ ET BONNE CONDUITE. The recipients have the right to choose which version they would prefer. The name of the recipient is engraved on the rim. Approximately 75 Medals and close to 1,000 various bars are issued evry year.*

VALUE:

George V (C)	£1250–1000	
George VI (B)	£850–1000	
George VI (C)	£1000–1200	
Elizabeth II (A)	£350–450	
Elizabeth II (French)	£400–500	*Miniature* (all) £45–50

C32. CANADIAN FORCES' DECORATION

Instituted: 15 December 1949.

Branch of Service: Canadian Forces.

Ribbon: 38mm orange-red divided into four equal parts by three thin white stripes.

Metal: Silver-gilt (George VI) or gilded tombac brass or bronze(Elizabeth II).

Size: Height 35mm; max. width 37mm.

Description: A decagonal (ten-sided) medal. The George VI issue has a suspension bar inscribed CANADA and the recipient's details engraved on the reverse, whereas the Elizabethan issue has no suspension bar, the recipient's details being impressed or engraved on the rim and the word "CANADA" appears at the base of the effigy. The reverse has a naval crown at the top, three maple leaves across the middle and an eagle in flight across the foot. In the George VI version the royal cypher is superimposed on the maple leaves.

Comments: *Awarded to both officers and men of the Canadian regular and reserve forces for 12 years exemplary service. A clasp, gold in colour, bearing the shield from the arms of Canada surmounted by the crown is awarded for each additional 10 years of qualifying service. Approximately 2,500 decorations and 3,500 clasps are awarded annually.*

VALUE:			Miniature
	George VI (E)	£75–100	£10–20
	Elizabeth II (D)	£30–40	£10–20

C33. POLICE EXEMPLARY SERVICE MEDAL

Date: 12 August 1982.

Ribbon: Five equal stripes of dark blue (three) and yellow (two).

Metal: Rhodium plated red brass.

Size: 36mm.

Description: (Obverse) a circular medal with a maple leaf in the centre bearing a representation of the scales of justice and an outer band with the words EXEMPLARY SERVICE in the upper half and SERVICES DISTINGUÉS in the lower. It is of a skeletal design with the outer band attached to the leaves and stem of the maple leaf; (reverse) plain apart from the royal cypher (EIIR) topped by the Queen's crown in the centre of the maple leaf.

Comments: *Awarded on completion of 20 years' service to officers of any recognised Canadian police force who showed industry, efficiency and good conduct during their careers. Although members of the RCMP or Canadian Military Police are not eligible, any previous and unrecognized full-time service in either of those bodies can be counted towards the necessary number of years' service. Bars (bearing a stylised maple leaf) are available for additional periods of ten years. The medal is not a purely long service award and will be withheld if an officer with the required number of years' service does not meet the appropriate standards of behaviour necessary. It can be awarded posthumously. The name of the recipient is engraved on the rim. 44,368 have been issued to date.*

VALUE:	£45–60	Miniature	£10–15

C34. CORRECTIONS EXEMPLARY SERVICE MEDAL

Date: 11 June 1984.
Ribbon: Five equal stripes of green (three) and yellow (two).
Metal: Rhodium plated red brass.
Size: 36mm.
Description: (Obverse) a circular medal with a maple leaf in the centre bearing a crossed key and torch and an outer band with the words EXEMPLARY SERVICE in the upper half and SERVICES DISTINGUÉS in the lower. It is of a skeletal design with the outer band attached to the leaves and stem of the maple leaf; (reverse) plain apart from the royal cypher (EIIR) topped by the Queen's crown in the centre of the maple leaf.
Comments: *Awarded on completion of 20 years' full-time paid service to officers of the Canadian Correctional Service (federal, provincial or territorial) who showed industry, efficiency and good conduct during their careers. The service need not have been continuous. Bars (bearing a stylised maple leaf) are available for additional periods of ten years. The medal is not a purely long service award and will be withheld if an officer with the required number of years' service does not meet the appropriate standards of behaviour necessary. It can be awarded posthumously. The name of the recipient is engraved on the rim. 11,952 have been issued to date.*

VALUE: £45–60   *Miniature*   £10–15

C35. FIRE SERVICES EXEMPLARY SERVICE MEDAL

Date: 25 August 1985.
Ribbon: Five equal stripes of red (three) and yellow (two).
Metal: Rhodium plated red brass.
Size: 36mm.
Description: (Obverse) a circular medal with a maple leaf in the centre bearing a pair of crossed axes and fire hydrant within an outer band with the words EXEMPLARY SERVICE in the upper half and SERVICES DISTINGUÉS in the lower. It is of a skeletal design with the outer band attached to the leaves and stem of the maple leaf; (reverse) plain apart from the royal cypher (EIIR) topped by the Queen's crown in the centre of the maple leaf.
Comments: *Awarded on completion of 20 years' service with a recognised Canadian fire service (including fire marshal's offices, fire commissioner's offices and the Canadian Forces Fire Service) to officers who showed industry, efficiency and good conduct during their careers. The service need not have been continuous. Bars (bearing a stylised maple leaf) are available for additional periods of ten years. The medal is not a purely long service award and will be withheld if an officer with the required number of years' service does not meet the appropriate standards of behaviour necessary. It can be awarded posthumously. The name of the recipient is engraved on the rim. 50,248 have been issued to date.*

VALUE: £60–75   *Miniature*   £10–15

C36. CANADIAN COAST GUARD EXEMPLARY SERVICE MEDAL

Date: 14 March 1991.

Ribbon: Dark blue with a narrow white stripe in the centre and a broader yellow stripe towards each edge.

Metal: Rhodium plated red brass.

Size: 36mm.

Description: (Obverse) a solid circular medal with the crest of the Canadian Coast Guard in the centre and an outer band bearing the inscriptions EXEMPLARY SERVICE (left) and SERVICES DISTINGUÉS (right); (reverse) plain apart from the royal cypher (EIIR) topped by the Queen's crown in the centre of the maple leaf.

Comments: *Awarded on completion of 20 years' service with the Department of Transport which must include 10 years with the Canadian Coast Guard in duties with a potential risk. Officers must have shown industry, efficiency and good conduct during their careers. The service need not have been continuous. Bars (bearing a stylised maple leaf) are available for additional periods of ten years, five of which must have involved duties where there was a potential risk of danger. The medal is not a purely long service award and will be withheld if an officer with the required number of years' service does not meet the appropriate standards of behaviour necessary. It can be awarded posthumously. The name of the recipient is engraved on the rim. 532 have been issued to date.*

VALUE: £100–150   *Miniature*   £10–15

C37. EMERGENCY MEDICAL SERVICES EXEMPLARY SERVICE MEDAL

Date: 7 July 1994.

Ribbon: Gold with three stripes of blue all equally spaced and with a stripe of orange bisecting each of the three blue stripes.

Metal: Rhodium plated red brass.

Size: 36mm.

Description: (Obverse) a circular medal with a maple leaf in the centre bearing the star of life, staff and serpent within an outer band with the words EXEMPLARY SERVICE in the upper half and SERVICES DISTINGUÉS in the lower. It is of a skeletal design with the outer band attached to the leaves and stem of the maple leaf; (reverse) plain apart from the royal cypher (EIIR) topped by the Queen's crown in the centre of the maple leaf.

Comments: *Awarded on completion of 20 years' service in the field of pre-hospital emergency medical care. Ten of these years must have involved duties with a potential risk. Recipients must have shown industry, efficiency and good conduct during their careers. The service need not have been continuous. Bars (bearing a stylised maple leaf) are available for additional periods of ten years. The medal is not a purely long service award and will be withheld if an officer with the required number of years' service does not meet the appropriate standards of behaviour necessary. It can be awarded posthumously. The name of the recipient is engraved on the rim. 2,933 have been issued to date.*

VALUE: £100–150   *Miniature*   £10–15

C37A. PEACE OFFICER EXEMPLARY SERVICE MEDAL

Date: June 22, 2004

Ribbon: A central stripe of green flanked by stripes of gold, light blue and dark blue.

Metal: Rhodium plated red brass.

Size: 36mm.

Description: (Obverse) a circular medal with a maple leaf in the center bearing a shield set on a star and an outer band with the words EXEMPLARY SERVICE in the upper half and SERVICES DISTINGUÉS in the lower. It is of a skeletal design with the outer band attached to the leaves and stem of the maple leaf; (reverse) plain apart for the royal cipher (EIIR) surmounted by the Royal Crown in the center.

Comments: *Awarded on completion of 20 years' service as a peace officer with one or more of the following organizations: the Canada Border Service Agency; the Department of Citizenship and Immigration, Environment, Fisheries and Oceans; the Parks Canada Agency or any other organization that employs peace officers and that is deemed eligible by the Advisory Committee. Ten of these years must have involved duties with potential risk. Recipient must have shown industry, efficiency and good conduct during their careers. The service need not have been continuous. Bars (bearing a stylized maple leaf) are available for additional periods of ten years of eligible service. The medal is not a purely long service award and will be withheld if an officer with the required number of years' service does not meet the appropriate standards of behaviour necessary. It can be awarded posthumously. The name of the recipient is engraved on the rim. 3,535 have been awarded to date.*

VALUE:	£100–150	*Miniature*	£10–15

C38. QUEEN'S MEDAL FOR CHAMPION SHOT IN CANADA

Date: 28 August 1991.

Ribbon: Dark crimson with stripes of black, white and black (each 3mm) at the edges.

Metal: Silver.

Size: 38mm.

Description: (Obverse) the crowned head of Queen Elizabeth II with the inscription ELIZABETH II DEI GRATIA REGINA around the circumference and CANADA at the bottom; (reverse) the figure of Fame on the right rising from her throne and crowning a warrior with a laurel wreath. The warrior holds a bow and quiver of arrows in his right hand and has a target with three arrows in the centre resting on his left knee. Until 2002, a plain silver straight suspender was used attached by a claw fitting, since then it is a straight suspender ornamented with a fleur-de-lys. The date of the award is showed on a plain silver clasp. Any subsequent award of the medal is indicated by a clasp only.

Comments: *There are two medals awarded each year, one to the regular member of the Canadian armed forces and another to the officer of the Royal Canadian Mounted Police who obtains the highest aggregate score in the two stages of the Queen's Medal Competition. The name of the recipient is engraved on the rim.*

VALUE:

Victoria bronze	—
Victoria silver	—
George V	£800–1000
George VI	£800–1000
Elizabeth II	£800–1000

C39. ONTARIO MEDAL FOR GOOD CITIZENSHIP

Date: 1973.
Ribbon: White with a central stripe in gold and a broad green stripe at the edges.
Metal: Silver.
Size: 36mm.
Description: (Obverse) circular with the full achievement of arms of Ontario in the lower two-thirds and the inscription FOR GOOD CITIZENSHIP at the upper circumference; (reverse) the provincial flower—a trillium. A scrolled suspender bar is used attached to the top of the disc.
Comments: *Awarded to any citizen of Ontario to recognise good citizenship displayed by their generous, kind or self-effacing manner in improving the quality of life in the Province. It is not awarded posthumously or for acts of courage. A maximum of twelve medals are presented each year. Recipients can use post-nominals OMC.*

VALUE: £100–150

C40. ONTARIO MEDAL FOR POLICE BRAVERY

Date: 1975.
Ribbon: Royal blue with two gold stripes towards the edges.
Metal: Gold plated sterling silver with blue and white enamel.
Size: 57mm wide by 68mm high (with crown).
Description: (Obverse) a cross in blue enamel on gold with the provincial flower (white trillium) in white in a small central medallion and a maple leaf between the arms of the cross. A Queen's crown tops the upper arm; (reverse) left plain.
Comments: *Awarded to officers from any police force in the province to reward any act of superlative courage and bravery performed in the line of duty and is also intended to encourage the virtue of bravery and focus attention and support of the public behind the efforts of the police forces. The medals are presented at a special ceremony held in early November each year.*

VALUE: £125–150

C41. ONTARIO MEDAL FOR FIREFIGHTERS BRAVERY

Date: 1976.

Ribbon: Red with two gold stripes towards the edges.

Metal: Gold plated sterling silver with red and white enamel.

Size: 57mm wide by 68mm high (with crown).

Description: (Obverse) a cross in gold with a pattern on each arm in red enamel to symbolise fire and a maple leaf between the arms. The provincial flower (white trillium) in white enamel lies in a small central medallion. A Queen's crown tops the upper arm; (reverse) left plain.

Comments: *Awarded to firefighters in the Province to reward any act of superlative courage and bravery performed in the line of duty and is also intended to encourage the virtue of bravery and focus attention and support of the public behind the efforts of the firefighters. The medals are presented at a special ceremony held on 9 November each year. The medal can be awarded posthumously.*

VALUE: £125–150

C42. SASKATCHEWAN VOLUNTEER MEDAL

Date: 1995

Ribbon: Green with a gold central stripe, all of equal width.

Metal: Silver and enamel.

Size: 36mm.

Description: (Obverse) a circular silver medal with the shield from the Saskatchewan coat of arms surmounted by a crown placed in the centre. The name of the Province lies along the lower circumference and the inscription NOS IPSOS DEDIMUS (we give of ourselves) at the upper edge. The plain straight suspender bar is attached by a stylised letter "V".

Comments: *Awarded each year to a maximum of ten current or former long-term residents of Saskatchewan who have served in a voluntary capacity above and beyond the call of duty to improve daily life in the Province. Elected officials and members of the judiciary are barred from receiving the award whilst they remain in office. Recipients can use post-nominals SVM.*

VALUE: £25–30

C43. ONTARIO PROVINCIAL POLICE LONG SERVICE AND GOOD CONDUCT MEDAL

Date: 15 December 1949.

Ribbon: Crimson with two green stripes each bordered by white lines on both sides.

Metal: Silver, later in cupro-nickel

Size: 38mm.

Description: (Obverse) the Coat of Arms of the Province of Ontario with the word ONTARIO written below; (reverse) the inscription ONTARIO PROVINCIAL POLICE in three lines in the central field and FOR LONG SERVICE AND GOOD CONDUCT around the circumference and two crossed maple leaves in the exergue. An ornate, non-swivelling, suspender was attached to the top of the medal.

Comments: *Ontario is one of only two provincial police forces that remain in Canada. The medal was awarded to members of the Force who had served for not less than 20 years, the last ten of which must have been with good conduct and satisfactory service. Bars were awarded for each additional period of five years' qualifying service. For 25 and 30 years' service a plain silver bar decorated with one or two white trilliums (the provincial flower) was awarded and for 35 or 40 years qualifying service gold bars were issued also bearing one or two trillium motifs.*

VALUE:	Silver	£200–250
	Cupro-nickel	£30–40

C44. COMMISSIONAIRES LONG SERVICE MEDAL

Date: August 20, 1948.

Ribbon: 32mm in width with a broad centre stripe of crimson on each side of which are stripes of white and navy blue.

Metal: Bronze, nickel-plated copper

Size: 36mm.

Description: (Obverse) within a buckled belt inscribed with the words VIRTUTE ET INDUSTRIA are superimposed on a natural maple leaf a crossed sword and anchor and a flying eagle; (reverse) the inscription THE CANADIAN CORPS OF COMMISSIONAIRES - LE CORPS CANADIEN DES COMMISSIONNARES surrounding a plain field. The medal is attached to a suspension bar bearing the inscription LABOR OMNIA VINCIT by three small rings.

Comments: *Initially awarded in bronze for 10 years but now only awarded in "silver" for 12 years of service in the Canadian Corps of Commissionaires. Bars are awarded for subsequent periods of 5 years of service, a maximum of 3 bars may be awarded to an individual.*

VALUE: £10–15

C45. SASKATCHEWAN CENTENNIAL MEDAL

Date: 2005.

Ribbon: Gold with two green stripes near the edges.

Metal: Bronzed base metal.

Size: 36mm.

Description: (Obverse) The provincial motto on a ribbon under a wreath of western red lilies, surmounted by the St. Edward's Crown, the whole circumscribed with the words "Saskatchewan 1905-2005"; (reverse) the provincial shield of arms.

Comments: *Created to commemorate the 100th anniversary of the creation of the province, the medal recognizes individuals who have made significant contributions to society and honours outstanding achievements. Approximately 4,000 medals were presented during Centennial year and up until the spring of 2006. Many recipients were members of the Canadian Forces or members of the various protective services. Persons not residing in Saskatchewan but have contributed to the province were also eligible.*

VALUE: £50–75

C46. ALBERTA CENTENNIAL MEDAL

Date: 2005

Ribbon: A central red-pink stripe flanked by stripes of white, green, gold and Royal blue.

Metal: Gold-plated bronze

Size: 36mm.

Description: (Obverse) The arms of the province surrounded by a raised circle, the whole circumscribed with the words "Alberta Centennial 1905-2005"; (reverse) the provincial shield of arms charged on a maple leaf, surrounded by a raised circle, the whole circumscribed with the words "Honouring Outstanding Albertans".

Comments: *Created to commemorate the 100th anniversary of the creation of the province, the medal recognizes Albertans whose achievements have benefited their fellow citizens, their community and their province. Approximately 8,000 medals were presented during Centennial year and up until the spring of 2006. Many recipients were members of the Canadian Forces or members of the various protective services. Eligibility was limited to Canadian citizens who reside in, or have resided in, Alberta.*

VALUE: £50–75

In addition to the medals listed in this section there are also a large number of interesting collectable medals issued by the various provinces and by numerous organisations throughout Canada. Many of these are already well known whilst others are seldom seen and are very rare. Here, with the assistance of collector Jack Boddington we include a representative selection. Others will be added in future editions. For ease of identification each has been allotted a Medal Yearbook reference number.

C57. ALBERTA MUNICIPAL ENFORCEMENT LONG SERVICE MEDAL

Date: 2005.
Ribbon: Wide central black stripe, flanked on either side by equal stripes of yellow and green withd narrow white edges. The colours represent the mineral, agricultural and forestry resources of the province and the snow that caps the Rocky Mountains.
Metal: Sterling Silver.
Size: 36mm.
Description: (Obverse) the Shield of Alberta surmounted by a mural crown representing municipal authority and surrounded by 13 maple leaves representing the Canadian provinces and territories with the words MUNICIPAL ENFORCEMENT above. (Reverse) a wild rose, the provincial flower of Alberta, surmounted by a mural crown and surrounded by 13 maple leaves. The words FOR LONG SERVICE and 20 YEARS encircle the whole.
Comments: *The medal was authorised by the Province of Alberta by Ministerial Order on January 16, 2006 to recognise 20 years of service by Municipal enforcement officers. A clasp is awarded for additional five year increments. To date 24 medals have been awarded including 2 for special circumstances, 10 first clasp, and 3 second clasps have been awarded.*

Value   £75–100

C58. ALBERTA EMERGENCY SERVICES MEDAL

Date: 2000
Ribbon: Blue with three central thin white pin stripes. The blue colour represents the province of Alberta and the three white stripes for good service, loyalty and good conduct, bar suspension.
Metal: Silver.
Size: 35mm.
Description: (Obverse) the Alberta shield centred around which are the words: EMERGENCY SERVICES (above) and ALBERTA (below). (Reverse) the Alberta wild rose surrounded by the words: IN THE SERVICE OF ALBERTANS
Comments: *To be eligible for the medal, the recipient must have been serving for a total of at least 12 years of service with one or more municipal emergency services or with the Alberta Emergency Management Agency or Alberta Sustainable Resource Development in the province of Alberta.*

Alberta Emergency Personnel include:
• Members of the emergency services established by an Alberta municipality under the provisions of the Alberta Municipal Government Act (i.e. fire fighters, officers and dispatchers of full-time, part-time or volunteer Fire Services or Search and Rescue volunteers)
• Alberta Emergency Management Agency personnel
• Directors or Deputy Directors of Emergency Management appointed by municipalities under the Emergency Management Act
• Emergency Medical Services (EMS) Paramedicine Practitioners licensed under the Health Professions Act - Paramedic Regulation (i.e licenced Emergency Medical Responders, Emergency Medical Technicians, Emergency Medical Technologists—Paramedic)
•Emergency Medical Dispatchers certified through the National Academy of Emergency Medical Dispatch; or
• Sustainable Resource Development personnel (Fire Protection & Emergency Response).

Value   £75–100

C59. ALBERTA LAW ENFORCEMENT LONG SERVICE MEDAL

Date: 1969 (date of authorisation)

Ribbon: Royal blue with a centre green stripe with on either side, two narrow yellow stripes.

Metal: Silver.

Size: 35mm.

Description: The circular medal is suspended from a straight bar. (Obverse) the Provincial Shield of Alberta with a wheat stalk on either side and the word ALBERTA in styalised form below. (Reverse) the floral emblem of Alberta the prairie rose, with the words TWENTY FIVE YEARS above and LONG SERVICE below

Comments: *The 25 years law enforcement must have been served in Alberta. The medal was introduced by the Solicitor General of the time Roy Farran, renowned for his former SAS service and holder of the DSO, MC with two bars and Legion of Merit (USA), French Croix de Guerre and two Greek medals in addition to his British Campaign Medals. He was the author of the SAS classic "The Winged Dagger".*

Value £75–100

C60. EDMONTON POLICE SERVICE MEDAL OF VALOUR

Date: 2002 (recommendations were dated from 1961)

Ribbon: Blue with broad central white stripe, a red and gold pin line stripes in the centre

Metal: Silver.

Size: 30mm.

Description: (Obverse) round silver medal with the EPS crest centred on top of a solid "V", which symbolises Valour. The suspensory bar has "For Valour", written on it. (Reverse) a wreath surrounding a plain field with space for the engraving of the Register number, name and rank of recipient and date of occurrence.

Comments: *The Medal of Valour is the highest award that may be bestowed upon a member of the service. It is to be conferred upon members of the Edmonton Police Service for outstanding acts of personal heroism or the most conspicuous acts of courage in circumstances of extreme peril and personal hazard to life during the intelligent and appropriate execution of their duty. Nominations for the Medal of Valour would be considered for occurrences dating back to 1961: the year of amalgamation between the Edmonton Police Department and the Beverly Police Department. In the absence of specific criteria the following factors are considered in making determinations in each incident: A member found himself/herself caught in the circumstances as a result of their normal duties and engaged in a brave or heroic initiative taken on their own volition. (Incidents that do not meet these initial criteria will be considered for the officer safety award).*

Value £100–125

C61. EDMONTON POLICE SERVICE MEDAL OF HONOUR

Date: 2002 (recommendations were dated from 1892)
Ribbon: Blue with central broad white stripe and three lines in red, gold and red.
Metal: Silver.
Size: 32mm.
Description: (Obverse) octagonal star shaped silver medal with the EPS Crest centred within a circle. The tip of the top point connects to the suspensory bar. The suspensory bar has "For Honour" written on it. (Reverse) a wreath surrounding a plain field with space for the engraving of the register number, name and rank of the recipient and date of occurrence.
Comments: *The criteria for this medal are as follows: "The Medal of Honour is to be conferred upon members of the Edmonton Police Service, who during the intelligent and appropriate execution of their duty, in an attempt to save or protect life suffered grievous physical injury or permanent disfigurement. The actions were performed in good faith as a peace officer, adhering to proper officer safety protocol and policy. The Medal of Honour will also be awarded posthumously, the surviving family of Edmonton Police Service members who have lost their lives while in the lawful execution of their duties and services to the City of Edmonton".*

Value   £75–100

C62. CANADIAN LIFEBOAT INSTITUTION

Date: 1981
Ribbon: Two version—red with two blue intermediate stripes for patronage; red with two white intermediate stripes for bravery.
Metal: Gold, silver and bronze.
Size: 34mm.
Description: Circular, straight bar suspension. (Obverse) in the centre a fouled anchor surrounded by a roped border with the words CANADIAN LIFEBOAT INSTITUTION and two maple leaves. (Reverse) a cross with a crown and anchor in the centre, around a rope is the motto of the institution THE SEA SHALL NOT HAVE THEM with a maple leaf at the bottom.
Comments: *The ribbon colour identifies whether the medal is issued for patronage or for bravery in saving, or attempting to save human life, the metal distinguishing the level of service.*

	Bronze	Silver	Gold
Value for life saving	£100–120	£150–175	rare
Value for service	£60–80	£80–100	£200

C63. THE CANADIAN RED CROSS SOCIETY ORDER OF THE RED CROSS

Date: 1984
Ribbon: Red with white stripes at outer edge
Metal: Silver or Gold
Size: 38mm across the arms
Description: A cross pattée with a maple leaf in each of the four corners of the arms. Inner green enamelled wreath with a central red cross. The reverse is left plain for naming purposes (the name of the recipient and year of award are always engraved).
Comments: *The Order of the Red Cross has three grades—Companion (neck decoration in gold), Officer (breast cross in gold) and Member (breast cross in silver). The award pays tribute to volunteers and other individuals for their outstanding humanitarian service, dedication and achievements. Appointments to the Order are limited to three Companions, five Officers and twenty-five members.*

Value: —

C64. THE CANADIAN BANKS LAW ENFORCEMENT AWARD

Date: 1972
Ribbon: Off white with wide side stripes in light purple
Metal: Gold
Size: 35mm
Description: Suspended from a straight bar to accommodate the ribbon. (Obverse) an antique bank vault door, the words THE CANADIAN BANKS above and LAW ENFORCEMENT AWARD below. (Reverse) within a narrow wreath the words AWARDED BY THE CANADIAN BANKERS ASSOCIATION FOR DISTINGUISHED LAW ENFORCEMENT. The medal can be worded in French if desired.
Comments: *The Canadian Banks Law Enforcement Award was established after extensive discussion between the Canadian Bankers Association and the Canadian Association of Chief of Police. The purpose of the award is to recognise outstanding police action in combatting crimes against banks.*

Value: £250–300

C65. THE MOOSE JAW MEDAL OF MERIT

Date: 1968
Ribbon: Green with a wide central yellow stripe
Metal: Gold (gilt)
Size: 34mm
Description: A top bar in gilt carrying the words FOR MERIT. (Obverse) the civic coat-of-arms of the city of Moose Jaw, Saskatchewan surmounting the word MOOSOOCHAPISKUN which is the name of the city in the local Indian dialect, wreath of wheat stalks surround with an outer edge inscription CORPORATION OF THE CITY OF MOOSE JAW. (Reverse) plain for appropriate engraving.
Comments: *In addition to life saving "the saving of a life where circumstances involved personal risk or heroism beyond the call of duty" the medal may also be awarded for achievements in athletics, arts and culture and civic actions.*

Value: £50-£150 depending on circumstances.

NEW ZEALAND MEDALS

The New Zealand contribution in this edition has been updated by the New Zealand Defence Force, with the support of the New Zealand Honours Unit, the New Zealand Customs Service, the New Zealand Police and John D. Wills.

Between 1848 and 1996 New Zealanders were eligible for the various British or Imperial honours and awards. The first step towards an independent honours system was taken in 1975 when the Queen's Service Order and Queen's Service Medal were instituted.

Thereafter a range of distinctive New Zealand medals was gradually adopted for the defence forces, the police, fire and prison services, this culminated in the introduction of a totally separate New Zealand Royal Honours System in May 1996. With a few exceptions, all honours and awards are conferred by, or in the name of, the sovereign (Queen Elizabeth) on the advice of Her Majesty's New Zealand ministers. A distinctive feature of many New Zealand orders, decorations and medals is the influence of Maori art forms.

Medals and decorations which were specific to New Zealand but made under Royal Warrants prior to 1975 are listed in the main body of this book. A new range of New Zealand gallantry and bravery awards has recently been developed, and this includes the creation of a Victoria Cross for New Zealand as well as the highest non-combatant bravery award, the New Zealand Cross. The new medals and decorations are given below in order of precedence. To date very few of these awards have come onto the market. and information on their rarity and other details have not been available, so prices in this section, where given, can only be regarded as a rough guide.

In addition to those listed, a number of foreign awards have been approved for acceptance and wear by NZDF personnel and NZ veterans, including the Malaysian PJM, the US Bronze Star and Army Commendation Medals for service in Afghanistan, while NZDF personnel are also in receipt of UN, NATO and ESDP medals as appropriate. These medals can be found in the main section of the book.

Further information on New Zealand medals can be found on the following websites: medals.nzdf.mil.nz; www.archives.govt.nz and www.honours.govt.nz.

THE ORDER OF WEAR IN NEW ZEALAND (including British Awards)

Victoria Cross for New Zealand
New Zealand Cross
George Cross
Knight/Lady of the Order of the Garter
Knight/Lady of the Order of the Thistle
Knight or Dame Grand Cross, The Most Honourable Order of the Bath
Order of Merit
Member of the Order of New Zealand
Baronet's Badge
Knight or Dame Grand Companion of the New Zealand Order of Merit
Knight or Dame Grand Cross of the Order of St Michael and St George
Knight or Dame Grand Cross of the Royal Victorian Order
Knight or Dame Grand Cross of the Order of the British Empire
Member of the Order of Companions of Honour
Knight or Dame Companion of the New Zealand Order of Merit
Knight or Dame Commander of the Most Honourable Order of the Bath
Knight or Dame Commander of the Most Distinguished Order of St Michael and St George
Knight or Dame Commander of the Royal Victorian Order

Knight or Dame Commander of the Order of the British Empire
Knight Bachelor's badge
Companion of the New Zealand Order of Merit
Companion of the Order of the Bath
Companion of the Order of St Michael and St George
Commander of the Royal Victorian Order
Commander of the Order of the British Empire
New Zealand Gallantry Star
New Zealand Bravery Star
Companion of the Distinguished Service Order
Lieutenant of the Royal Victorian Order
Companion of the Queen's Service Order
Officer of the New Zealand Order of Merit
Officer of the Order of the British Empire
Companion of the Imperial Service Order
Member of the Royal Victorian Order
Member of the New Zealand Order of Merit
Member of the Order of the British Empire
New Zealand Gallantry Decoration
New Zealand Bravery Decoration
Royal Red Cross (First Class or Member)
Distinguished Service Cross
Military Cross
Distinguished Flying Cross
Air Force Cross
Royal Red Cross (Second Class or Associate)

Order of St John (All classes)
Distinguished Conduct Medal
Conspicuous Gallantry Medal
George Medal
Distinguished Service Medal
Military Medal
Distinguished Flying Medal
Air Force Medal
Queen's Gallantry Medal
New Zealand Gallantry Medal
New Zealand Bravery Medal
Royal Victorian Medals
Queen's Service Medal
New Zealand Antarctic Medal
New Zealand Distinguished Service Decoration
British Empire Medal
Queen's Police Medal for Distinguished Service
Queen's Fire Service Medal for Distinguished
    Service
War Medals in order of campaign
New Zealand Special Service Medal in order of
    date of award
Polar Medal in order of date of award
Coronation, Jubilee and New Zealand
    Commemoration Medals in date order:
        King George VI Coronation Medal 1937
        Queen Elizabeth II Coronation Medal 1953
        Queen Elizabeth II Silver Jubilee Medal 1977
        Queen Elizabeth II Golden Jubilee Medal
        2002
        New Zealand 1990 Commemoration Medal
        New Zealand Suffrage Centennial Medal
        1993
New Zealand Meritorious Service Medal
New Zealand Armed Forces Award

New Zealand Army Long Service and Good
    Conduct Medal
Royal New Zealand Navy Long Service and Good
    Conduct Medal
Royal New Zealand Air Force Long Service and
    Good Conduct Medal
New Zealand Police Long Service and Good
    Conduct Medal
New Zealand Fire Brigades Long Service and
    Good Conduct Medal
New Zealand Prison Service Medal
New Zealand Traffic Service Medal
Efficiency Decoration
Efficiency Medal
Royal New Zealand Naval Reserve Decoration
Royal New Zealand Naval Volunteer Reserve
    Decoration
Royal New Zealand Naval Volunteer Reserve
    Long Service and Good Conduct Medal
Air Efficiency Award
Queen's Medal for Champion Shots of the New
    Zealand Naval Forces
Queen's Medal for Champion Shots of the Military
    Forces
Queen's Medal for Champion Shots of the Air
    Forces
Cadet Forces Medal
New Zealand Defence Service Medal
Rhodesia Medal 1980
Commonwealth Independence Medals
Service Medal of the Order of St John
Other Commonwealth Members' Orders,
    Decorations and Medals in date of award
Approved Foreign Orders, Decorations and
    Medals in order of date of award

NZ1. VICTORIA CROSS FOR NEW ZEALAND

Instituted: September 20, 1999.
Ribbon: Crimson 38mm wide.
Metal: Bronze.
Size: 35mm at each axis.
Description: A cross pattée with raised edges, identical to the
    British and Australian Victoria Crosses (MYB24 and A1).
Comments: *Although identical to the existing VC, awards will be
    made under a New Zealand, as opposed to a British, Royal Warrant.
    Recipients are entitled to the postnominal letters VC and their name
    will be engraved on each award. It may be awarded posthumously. The
    first VC for NZ was awarded on July 26, 2007 to Corporal Apiata of
    the NZ SAS for gallantry in Afghanistan in 2004.*

VALUE: —

NZ2. NEW ZEALAND CROSS

Instituted: September 20, 1999.
Ribbon: Bright blue. A miniature cross is worn on the ribbon alone.
Metal: Silver with gold appliqué.
Size: Height 52mm, width 38mm.
Description: Similar to the original New Zealand Cross of 1869 (MYB25) but incorporating changes which were first proposed in 1885 and only now implemented, viz. fern fronds have replaced laurel leaves. (Reverse) inscribed FOR BRAVERY—MO TE MAIA.
Comments: *The premier civilian award for bravery, it now supersedes the George Cross so far as New Zealand citizens are concerned. Recipients are entitled to the postnominal letters NZC. To date only two crosses have been awarded, one posthumously.*

VALUE: —

NZ3. ORDER OF NEW ZEALAND

Instituted: 1987.
Ribbon: Red ochre with a narrow white stripe towards either edge.
Metal: 9 carat gold.
Description: An oval medal decorated with coloured enamels bearing in the centre the heraldic shield of New Zealand within a Kowhaiwhai rafter pattern.
Comments: *Instituted as a first-level non-titular order, it is modelled on the British Order of Merit (1917) and the Order of the Companions of Honour (1917). The Order comprises the Queen as Sovereign and no more than 20 ordinary members who are entitled to the postnominal letters ONZ. Additional members may be appointed in commemoration of important royal, state or national occasions. Honorary membership includes citizens of Commonwealth nations of which the Queen is not Head of State, and of foreign countries. The badge must be returned on the death of the holder. No miniature exists, but a lapel badge was instituted in 1990.*

VALUE: —

NZ4. NEW ZEALAND ORDER OF MERIT

Breast star

Instituted: May 30, 1996.

Ribbon: Plain red ochre (kokowai).

Comments: *An order of chivalry designed along British lines and intended to replace the various British orders to which New Zealanders were formerly appointed. It consists of five classes whose insignia are noted separately below. In addition, there is a collar of the order, worn only by the Sovereign of the Order and the Chancellor (the Governor-General of New Zealand). The collar is composed of links of the central badge and gold koru (in the form of the letter S) with a pendant badge featuring the New Zealand arms. Distinctive lapel badges denoting membership of the Order are worn in civilian clothes. On the abolition of Knighthoods an amending warrant dated May 18, 2000, replaced Knights and Dames with Principal and Distinguished Companions. However, in March 2009 Her Majesty approved the reinstatement of the original titles in the New Zealand honours system therefore the titles Knights and Dames are once more current.*

VALUE: —

GRAND COMPANIONS (GNZM)

Badge: A cross in white enamel set in silver-gilt with, in the centre, a medallion comprising the New Zealand arms in coloured enamel surrounded by a circle of green enamel inscribed in gold FOR MERIT / TOHU HIRANGA and surmounted by a royal crown. The badge is worn from a sash over the right shoulder and resting on the left hip.

Star: A gold breast star of eight points, each arm bearing in relief a representation of a fern frond, superimposed in the centre of which is a smaller representation of the badge of the order.

Comments: *Holders of the grades of Knight or Dame Grand Cross (GNZM) are entitled to the titles "Sir" or "Dame".*

KNIGHT AND DAME COMPANION (K/DNZM)

A badge and breast star similar to that above, except that the badge is worn from either a neck ribbon or a bow on the left shoulder. The breast star is in silver, with the badge of the order in the centre. Holders of the grades of Knight or Dame Companion are entitled to the titles "Sir" or "Dame" respectiviely.

COMPANIONS (CNZM)

A badge similar to that above (illustrated left), worn from a 38mm wide neck ribbon or a bow on the left shoulder.

OFFICERS (ONZM)

A smaller representation of the badge in silver-gilt, with the motto in green enamel. Worn from a ribbon on the left lapel or from a 38mm wide ribbon tied in a bow and worn on the left shoulder.

MEMBERS (MNZM)

Badge as for Officers but in silver.

Companions badge

NZ5. NEW ZEALAND GALLANTRY STAR

Instituted: September 20, 1999.
Branch of Service: New Zealand armed forces.
Ribbon: Crimson with a purple central stripe bordered by thin white stripes.
Metal: Silver and gilt.
Size: 45mm.
Description: (Obverse) faceted silver 8-pointed star of equal points surmounted by a gilt crown surrounded by a wreath of New Zealand fern. (Reverse) inscribed FOR GALLANTRY —MO TE TOANGA. With ring suspension.
Comments: *This decoration supersedes the British Distinguished Service Order, Distinguished Conduct Medal and Conspicuous Gallantry Medal. Recipients are entitled to the postnominal letters NZGS and their name will be inscribed on the reverse. The only recipient so far is Colonel N. J. Reilly for gallantry in East Timor, 1999.*

VALUE: —

NZ6. QUEEN'S SERVICE ORDER

Instituted: 1975.
Ribbon: Narrow red ochre edges with a centre of alternating diagonal steps in ochre, white and black descending from left to right. The design is based on the Maori Poutama (stepped) pattern used in Tukutuku wall panels to represent the stairway to heaven, but here denoting the steps of achievement.
Metal: Frosted sterling silver.
Description: A badge based on the stylised representation of a manuka flower, consisting of five large and five small stylised petals. Superimposed in the centre is a silver-gilt medallion bearing the crowned effigy of the Queen within a circle of red enamel bearing the words FOR COMMUNITY SERVICE or FOR PUBLIC SERVICES as appropriate and surmounted by St Edward's Crown. The full name of the recipient is engraved on the reverse. From June 2007 the two divisions of the Order have been amalgamated and the insignia now reads FOR SERVICE—M_NG_MAHI NUI.
Comments: *The single non-titular order is divided into two divisions for Community Service and for Public Services respectively. Ordinary membership is limited to 30 appointments per annum. Members of the Royal Family may be appointed as Extra Companions and include so far the Duke of Edinburgh (1981), Prince Charles (1983) and the Princess Royal (1990). Recipients are entitled to the postnominal letters QSO, and appropriate lapel badges for everyday wear. 91 QSOs were awarded for Community Service and 124 for Public Services.*

VALUE: £500–750   *Miniature*   £150–200

NZ7. NEW ZEALAND GALLANTRY DECORATION

Instituted: September 20, 1999.
Branch of Service: New Zealand armed forces.
Ribbon: 32mm wide. Crimson with central purple stripe and two equal white stripes.
Metal: Silver and gilt.
Size: 46mm.
Description: (Obverse) A simple faceted silver cross surmounted by the royal crown and fern frond wreath emblem; (reverse) inscribed FOR GALLANTRY —MO TE TOANGA. With ring suspension.
Comments: *This decoration supersedes the British DSC, MC, DFC, AFC, DSM, MM, DFM and AFM. Recipients are entitled to the postnominal letters NZGD. So far six awards have been made: two for East Timor, one each for Cambodia and Sierra Leone, and two for Afghanistan.*

VALUE: —

NZ8. NEW ZEALAND BRAVERY STAR

Instituted: September 20, 1999.
Branch of Service: New Zealand police forces, fire brigades and civilians.
Ribbon: 32mm wide. Bright blue with two narrow red ochre stripes.
Metal: Silver and gilt.
Size: 46mm
Description: (Obverse) an 8-pointed faceted star with four long and four short points in the angles surmounted by a gilt royal crown and fern frond wreath emblem; (reverse) inscribed FOR BRAVERY—MO TE MAIA. With ring suspension.
Comments: *This decoration superseded the British George Medal and is the second grade award for civilian acts of bravery. Recipients are entitled to the postnominal letters NZBS. So far 17 awards (two posthumous) have been made.*

VALUE: —

NZ9. NEW ZEALAND BRAVERY DECORATION

Instituted: September 20, 1999.
Branch of Service: Civilians and members of the armed forces in non-combat situations.
Ribbon: 32mm wide. Bright blue with three equal stripes of red ochre.
Metal: Silver and gilt.
Size: 45mm.
Description: (Obverse) a cross pattée surmounted by a small faceted four-pointed star with the royal crown and fern frond wreath emblem; (reverse) inscribed FOR BRAVERY—MO TE MAIA. With ring suspension.
Comments: *This decoration is awarded for acts of bravery in a non-combat situation. It supersedes the British QGM, QPM, QFSM, AFC and AFM. Recipients are entitled to the postnominal letters NZBD. One award has been made to an NZDF employee, T. A. Hood, a civilian employed by the Defence Force, for life-saving in 1989, and 22 other awards have been made to NZ Police personnel and civilians (two posthumous).*

VALUE: —

NZ10. NEW ZEALAND GALLANTRY MEDAL

Instituted: 1998.
Branch of Service: New Zealand armed forces.
Ribbon: 32mm wide. Crimson with two central purple stripes and two outer white stripes.
Metal: Bronze.
Size: 36mm.
Description: (Obverse) the Rank-Broadley effigy of Her Majesty Queen Elizabeth II with the legend ELIZABETH II QUEEN OF NEW ZEALAND; (reverse) FOR GALLANTRY / MO TE TOANGA surrounded by a fern frond wreath with the royal crown above.
Comments: *This decoration replaces the Mention in Despatches. Recipients are entitled to the postnominal letters NZGM. The name of the recipient will be engravd on each award. Two awards have been made so far, to Cpl G. S. Fenton, East Timor, 2005 and another to a member of the NZSAS for gallantry in Afghanistan in 2004.*

VALUE: —

NZ11. NEW ZEALAND BRAVERY MEDAL

Instituted: September 20 ,1999.
Branch of Service: Civilians or members of the New Zealand armed forces in a non-combat situation.
Ribbon: 32mm wide. Bright blue with four red ochre stripes.
Metal: Bronze.
Size: 36mm.
Description: (Obverse) the Rank-Broadley effigy of Her Majesty Queen Elizabeth II with the legend ELIZABETH II QUEEN OF NEW ZEALAND; (reverse) FOR BRAVERY / MO TE MAIA surrounded by a fern frond wreath with the royal crown above.
Comments: *This decoration replaces the Queen's Commendations for Brave Conduct and Valuable Service in the Air. Recipients are entitled to the postnominal letters NZBM. To date 49 awards have been made (four posthumously).*

VALUE: —

NZ12. QUEEN'S SERVICE MEDAL

Instituted: March 13, 1975.
Ribbon: Same as the Queen's Service Order.
Metal: Silver.
Size: 36mm.
Description: (Obverse) effigy of Queen Elizabeth surrounded by the royal styles and titles; (reverse) New Zealand arms with THE QUEEN'S SERVICE MEDAL round the top. Two versions of the reverse exist, inscribed at the foot either FOR COMMUNITY SERVICE or FOR PUBLIC SERVICES. The medal is fitted with a suspension ring. From June 2007 the two divisions have been amalgamated and the insignia now reads FOR SERVICE—M_NG_ MAHI NUI at the foot.
Comments: *Awards are made for valuable voluntary service to the community or meritorious and faithful services to the Crown or similar services within the public sector. Military service is ineligible. The name of the recipient is engraved on the rim. Recipients are entitled to the postnominal letters QSM. 1,987 medals were awarded for Community Service and 1,873 for Public Services. A number of unnamed examples have surfaced following a robbery from a delivery lorry in the UK.*

VALUE: £275–350   *Miniature*   £60–70

NZ12A. NEW ZEALAND ANTARCTIC MEDAL

Instituted: 2006.
Ribbon: White.
Metal: Sterling silver.
Size: 36mm octagonal.
Description: (Obverse) bears the effigy of the Queen by Ian Rank-Broadley, FRBS, FSNAD, of the United Kingdom and the inscription Elizabeth II Queen of New Zealand. This effigy is also used on the New Zealand Gallantry and Bravery Awards; (reverse) shows a group of four Emperor Penguins on an Antarctic landscape with Mt Erebus in the background.
Comments: *Awarded to those New Zealanders and other persons who either individually or as members of a New Zealand programme in the Antarctic region have made an outstanding contribution to exploration, scientific research, conservation, environmental protection, or knowledge of the Antarctic region; or in support of New Zealand's objectives or operations, or both, in the Antarctic region. The Medal will not be awarded for acts of bravery, for short-term acts of extreme endurance, for long service or for service in Antarctica generally. The first three recipients were Prof. John Dudley Bradshaw, Dr. Clive Howard-Williams and Dr. Karl Erb. To date 10 awards have been made. Recipients are entitled to the post nominal letters "NZAM".*

VALUE: —

NZ12B. NEW ZEALAND DISTINGUISHED SERVICE DECORATION

Instituted: 2008.
Ribbon: Red central stripe bounded by thin yellow stripes and dark blue edges..
Metal: Sterling silver.
Size: 36mm octagonal.
Description: (Obverse) A stylised image of eight blades of a *kotiate* (lobed club) surmonted by a royal crown; (reverse) the inscription "For Distinguished Service/mo nga te mahi kahurangi" with the recipient's name engraved between.
Comments: *Awarded to members of the NZ armed forces for distinguished or meritorious service to New Zealand that consists of outstanding performance or individual efforts towards peacetime and humanitarian service. The award can be made for a single accomplishment or for cumulative efforts over a sustained period. A bar to the decoration can be awarded for further qualifying services. Foreign or Commonwealth persons can qualify for an Honorary decoration. Recipients are entitled to the post nominal letters "DSD".*

VALUE: —

NZ13. NEW ZEALAND OPERATIONAL SERVICE MEDAL

Instituted: August 2002.
Branch of Service: All New Zealand personnel previously awarded an operational medal for service since September 3, 1945.
Ribbon: 32mm wide. Black with six white stripes in pairs at the edges and centre.
Metal: Silver.
Size: 38mm.
Description: (Obverse) New Zealand arms; (reverse) a kiwi on six straight lines (land) with NEW ZEALAND between two stars below and three wavy lines (sea) and the inscription FOR OPERATIONAL SERVICE below.
Comments: *Personnel who have been awarded a campaign medal for operational service for New Zealand since September 3, 1945 qualify for the award of the NZOSM, provided that the particular campaign medal has been approved for acceptance and wear by New Zealanders. The medal is worn before all post World War II campaign medals. Issued un-named until July 2009, all are now engraved on issue. Over 20,000 medals have been issued to date. .*

Value:	£50–75	*Miniature*	£25–30

NZ14A. NEW ZEALAND GENERAL SERVICE MEDAL 2002 (SOLOMON ISLANDS)

Instituted: July 2002.
Branch of Service: New Zealand civil and military personnel.
Ribbon: 32mm, dark green with a yellow central stripe flanked by narrow dark blue stripes, the national colours of the Solomon Islands.
Metal: Silver-plated base metal.
Size: 36mm.
Description: (Obverse) the effigy of Queen Elizabeth by Ian Rank-Broadley; (reverse) a wreath of New Zealand flora surmounted by a Royal Crown with the title of the medal in the middle.
Comments: *Awarded to New Zealand personnel (both military and non military) who served in the Solomon Islands and its waters between June 2000 and June 2002 and those who served with the Regional Assistance Mission in the Solomon Islands (RAMSI) since July 24, 2003 and to New Zealand Pol;ice personnel since October 6, 2002. TYhe medal is still being issued. All medals are engraved. Over 1,330 issued to date to NZDF and 528 to NZ Police personnel.*

VALUE: £250–300

NZ14B. NEW ZEALAND GENERAL SERVICE MEDAL 2002 (AFGHANISTAN)

Instituted: July 2002.
Branch of Service: New Zealand civil and military personnel.
Ribbon: 32mm, green with a narrow central black stripe flanked by red stripes (primary operations) or with narrow blue edges (secondary operations).
Metal: Silver-plated alloy.   **Size:** 36mm.
Description: as NZ14A.
Comments: *Awarded to New Zealand personnel (both military and non military) who served in Afghanistan from December 2001 in one of two qualifying geographic areas. The "primary" operational area is within the borders of Afghanistan itself, while the "secondary" operational area includes areas where forces are based to support the operation. Different medal ribbons denote the primary and secondary areas. The NZGSM (Afghanistan) primary has also been awarded to 27 New Zealand Police personnel and to 9 New Zealand Red Cross aid workers. The medal is issued engraved. Over 3,200 issued to date.*

Primary operations

VALUE: £250–300

NZ14C. NEW ZEALAND GENERAL SERVICE MEDAL 2002 (IRAQ 2003)

Instituted: 2004.
Branch of Service: New Zealand civil and military personnel.
Ribbon: 32mm, a central broad red stripe flanked by thin white stripes, then green stripes with thin black edges.
Metal: Silver-plated alloy.
Size: 36mm.
Description: As NZ14A.
Comments: *Awarded to New Zealand personnel (both military and non military) who have served in Iraq from May 27, 2003. The initial NZ Government contribution was personnel who served with the United Nations Mine Action Service's Mine Action Coordination Team based in Basrah. The qualifying period starts from May 27, 2003 for mine clearance operations, and September 17, 2003 for humanitarian and reconstruction service with the British-led Multi-National Division in (Southeast) Iraq. The medal is issued engraved. More than 200 issued to date.*

VALUE: £350–500

NZ14D. NEW ZEALAND GENERAL SERVICE MEDAL 2002 (TIMOR-LESTE)

Instituted: 2007.
Branch of Service: New Zealand civil and military personnel.
Ribbon: 32mm, a central broad red stripe flanked by yellow, black and white stripes.
Metal: Silver-plated alloy.
Size: 36mm.
Description: As NZ14A.
Comments: *Awarded to New Zealand Defence Force and New Zealand Police personnel who have served in Timor-Leste since April 28, 2006, following the outbreak of violence in April 2006. The medal is issued engraved. More than 1,350 NZDF personnel and over 160 New Zealand Police have been issued with the medal to date.*

VALUE: £250–300

NZ14E. NEW ZEALAND GENERAL SERVICE MEDAL 2002 (KOREA)

Instituted: September 11, 2008.
Branch of Service: New Zealand military personnel. To date this has been awarded to any civilians.
Ribbon: 32mm, of dark blue with a red centre flanked by yellow stripes.
Metal: Silver-plated alloy.
Size: 36mm.
Description: As NZ14A.
Comments: *Awarded to New Zealand Defence Force personnel posted to UN Command Military Armistice Commission or the UN Honour Guard Company since January 1, 2001. Qualifying service is 30 days. Medals are issued engraved. More than 50 issued to date.*

VALUE: —

NZ15. NEW ZEALAND SERVICE MEDAL 1946–49

Instituted: November 3, 1995.
Branch of Service: New Zealand armed forces, merchant navy and civil airline crews.
Ribbon: 32mm white with a central red stripe and black stripes at the edges.
Metal: Rhodium plated steel.
Size: 38mm.
Description: (Obverse) New Zealand arms; (reverse) FOR SERVICE TO NEW ZEALAND 1946–1949 with a fern frond below.
Comments: *Awarded to recognise New Zealand military personnel who served in the British Commonwealth Occupation Force in Japan between March 1946 and March 1949 with a minimum of 28 days service required. Sometimes referred to as the "J Force medal". Initially issued un-named, since July 2009 medals are engraved on issue. More than 4,900 issued to date.*

VALUE: £65–75   *Miniature*   £25–30

NZ16. NEW ZEALAND GENERAL SERVICE MEDAL 1992 (WARLIKE)

Instituted: May 7, 1992.
Branch of Service: New Zealand armed forces.
Ribbon: 32mm dark blue with a central black stripe flanked by red stripes.
Metal: Silver.
Size: 38mm.
Description: (Obverse) crowned effigy of Queen Elizabeth; (reverse) THE NEW ZEALAND GENERAL SERVICE MEDAL within a wreath of pohutakawa blossom, fern fronds and kowhai blossom, ensigned by a royal crown affixed to a plain suspension bar.
Clasps: Near East, Malaya 1960–64, Vietnam, Kuwait.
Comments: *Awarded to recognise service in warlike operations for which, initially, no separate New Zealand or British Commonwealth campaign medal was issued. It is worn as a campaign medal, in order of date of qualification. All medals are engraved on issue. Clasp Near East awarded for specified service between October 31, 1956 and December 22, 1956; Malaya 1960-64 between August 1, 1960 and August 16, 1964; Vietnam between December 1, 1962 and 1 May 1, 1975; and Kuwait between December 18, 1990 and March 12, 1991. The most common issue is with the clasp "Vietnam", with more than 2,400 issued to date.*

VALUE: £450–600   *Miniature*   —

NZ17. NEW ZEALAND GENERAL SERVICE MEDAL 1992 (NON-WARLIKE)

Instituted: May 7, 1992.

Branch of Service: New Zealand armed forces.

Ribbon: 32mm dark blue with a white central stripe flanked by narrow red stripes.

Metal: Bronze.

Size: 38mm.

Description: As above.

Clasps: Korea 1954-57, Korea 1958-2000, Thailand, Sinai, Indian Ocean, Peshawar, Iraq, Somalia, Mozambique, Cambodia, Rwanda, Arabian Gulf, Bougainville.

Comments: *Awarded to recognise service in non-warlike operations for which no separate New Zealand, British Commonwealth, United Nations or NATO campaign medal was issued. Thirteen clasps have been issued. The most common clasp issued is 'Sinai' with more than 1,200 issued to date. Clasp Korea 1954–57 awarded for specified service between July 27, 1954 and December 31, 1957; Korea 1958–2000 between January 1, 1958 and December 31, 2000; Thailand, May 25, 1962 and December 15, 1971; Sinai, April 25, 1982 to present; Indian Ocean, June 21, 1982 and September 20, 1983; Peshawar, April 1, 1989 and December 31, 1991; Iraq, August 1, 1991 and January 31, 2003; Somalia, December 26, 1992 and November 30, 1993; Mozambique, February 1, 1994 and June 30, 2005; Cambodia, March 1, 1994 and April 30, 2005; Rwanda, August 1, 1994 and September 17, 1994; Arabian Gulf, October 4, 1995 and December 31, 2001; Bougainville, November 19, 1997 to present. In 2002, the NZGSM 1992 was replaced by the New Zealand General Service Medal 2002.It is worn as a campaign medal, in order of date of qualification. All medals are engraved.*

VALUE: £350–450   *Miniature*   —

NZ18. EAST TIMOR MEDAL

Instituted: April 25, 2000.

Ribbon: 32mm broad green central stripe flanked by narrow red, wider black and white stripes towards the edges.

Metal: Silver-plated alloy.

Size: 36mm.

Description: (Obverse) the effigy of the Queen by Ian Rank-Broadley with ELIZABETH II QUEEN OF NEW ZEALAND round the circumference; (reverse) the head of a kiwi facing right and overshadowing a map of East Timor with the words EAST TIMOR below and a sprig of olive leaves above. Fitted with a plain suspension bar.

Clasp: A silver clasp inscribed EAST TIMOR for additional service of 365 days or more, continuous or aggregate, in the operational area.

Comments: *Awarded to recognise New Zealand personnel (both military and non military) who served in East Timor from the commencement of the New Zealand involvement in June 1999 until April 27, 2006. All medals are engraved. More than 5,000 issued to date.*

VALUE: £300–350   *Miniature*   £30–35

NZ19. NEW ZEALAND SPECIAL SERVICE MEDAL (NUCLEAR TESTING)

Instituted: July 2002.
Branch of Service: New Zealand service personnel and civilians.
Ribbon: 32mm. An orange-yellow central stripe, flanked by narrow crimson stripes, then narrow red and white stripes and thin black edges.
Metal: Gold-plated.
Size: 36mm.
Description: (Obverse) the arms of New Zealand; (reverse) fern fronds and sprigs of pohutakawa, manuka, kowhai blossom and Mount Cook lilies.
Comments: *Awarded to recognise the service of those personnel who were part of an official New Zealand Government presence at an atmospheric nuclear test between 1956 and 1973. Initially issued unnamed, all recent medal issues are engraved. 650 issued as at June 30, 2011.*

VALUE   £150–200   *Miniature*   —

NZ19A. NEW ZEALAND SPECIAL SERVICE MEDAL (ASIAN TSUNAMI)

Instituted: December 2005.
Branch of Service: New Zealand service personnel and civilians.
Ribbon: 32mm, 11 stripes of red, white, blue, orange, green, yellow/green, orange, blue, white, red (colours of the six countries affected).
Metal: Gold-plated.   **Size:** 36mm.
Description: (Obverse) the arms of New Zealand; (reverse) fern fronds and sprigs of pohutakawa, manuka, kowhai blossom and Mount Cook lilies.
Comments: *Awarded to recognise New Zealanders who were involved in rescue, relief and rehabilitation efforts in areas devastated following the earthquake off the coast of Sumatra and the resulting tsunami of December 26, 2004.*
Qualifying service for the medal is 7 days between December 26, 2004 and February 28, 2005, or 14 days between December 26, 2004 and December 26, 2005. All medals are engraved on issue. 447 issued as at June 30, 2011.

VALUE: £150–200   *Miniature*   —

NZ19B. NEW ZEALAND SPECIAL SERVICE MEDAL (EREBUS)

Instituted: November 2006.
Branch of Service: New Zealand police.
Ribbon: 32mm, white with a central black stripe, light blue and dark blue stripes towards the edges.
Metal: Gold-plated.   **Size:** 36mm.
Description: (Obverse) the arms of New Zealand; (reverse) fern fronds and sprigs of pohutakawa, manuka, kowhai blossom and Mount Cook lilies.
Comments: *Awarded to recognise the service of those New Zealanders, and citizens of the United States of America and other countries, who were involved with the extremely difficult and very unpleasant, hazardous, and extreme circumstances associated with the body recovery, crash investigation and victim identification phases of Operation Overdue by the New Zealand Police following the crash of an Air New Zealand DC-10 aircraft on Mt. Erebus, Antarctica on November 28, 1979, with the loss of all 257 passengers and crew on board. Presentations to US citizens (mainly ex US Navy) started in Washington DC in June 2009 and are continuing as retired personnel are located. It is estimated about 70 US citizens will qualify for this award. All medals are engraved. 289 issued as at June 30, 2011.*

VALUE: £400–500   *Miniature*   —   **451**

NZ20. NEW ZEALAND 1990
COMMEMORATION MEDAL

Instituted: February 9, 1990.

Ribbon: 32mm nine narrow stripes, black at the centre flanked by alternate white and red ochre.

Metal: Silver-gilt.

Size: 38mm.

Description: (Obverse) effigy of Queen Elizabeth with inscription ELIZABETH II . QUEEN OF NEW ZEALAND incuse on a raised rim; (reverse) stylised Kotuku or White Heron with inscription NEW ZEALAND 1990 COMMEMORATION.

Comments: *Awarded during the sesquicentennial year of British annexation to recognise achievements of New Zealanders in community service and the public services or their contribution to the country. The medal is accompanied by a certificate. 3,632 were issued unnamed. Good quality copies exist.*

VALUE: £150–200

Miniature —

NZ21. NEW ZEALAND MERITORIOUS
SERVICE MEDAL

Instituted: May 6, 1985.

Branch of Service: NCOs of the rank of sergeant or petty officer or above in the armed forces.

Ribbon: 32mm crimson with a narrow green central stripe.

Metal: Silver.

Size: 38mm.

Description: (Obverse) bare-headed effigy of Queen Elizabeth; (reverse) FOR MERITORIOUS SERVICE within a laurel wreath surmounted by a royal crown and the legend NEW ZEALAND. Reverse similar to 212.

Comments: *Awarded for a minimum of 21 years full-time service in the armed forces, although this may be reduced to 18 years in the case of those invalided out of the services on grounds of disability. The recipient must be in possession of the Long Service & Good Conduct Medal. Service before the age of 17 does not count. At present the medal is limited to 10 serving members of RNZN, 20 Army and 15 RNZAF. The medal is always issued named with number, rank, name and corps.*

VALUE: £350–400

Miniature £45–50

NZ22. NEW ZEALAND ARMED FORCES
AWARD

Instituted: May 6, 1985.

Branch of Service: Officers of the armed forces.

Ribbon: 32mm dark blue, crimson and light blue with a central stripe of black.

Metal: Silver.

Size: 38mm.

Description: (Obverse) crowned effigy of Queen Elizabeth; (reverse) crossed swords, eagle and naval crown with two fronds below and inscription NEW ZEALAND ARMED FORCES AWARD.

Comments: *Awarded to Regular Force commissioned officers of the armed services for 15 years full-time service back-dated to 1977. Clasps for each additional 15 years may be awarded. Where an officer has been commissioned from the ranks at least 8 years must be commissioned service. The medal is always issued named with number, rank, name and regiment.*

VALUE: £300–400

NZ23. ROYAL NEW ZEALAND NAVY LONG SERVICE MEDAL

Instituted: May 6, 1985.
Branch of Service: Royal New Zealand Navy.
Ribbon: 32mm dark blue edged in white.
Metal: Silver.
Size: 38mm.
Description: (Obverse) uncrowned effigy of Queen Elizabeth; (reverse) HMS *Victory* surrounded by the inscription FOR LONG SERVICE AND GOOD CONDUCT.
Comments: *Awarded for naval ratings with 15 years service. Clasps may be awarded for each additional 15 years, denoted in undress uniform by a silver rosette on the ribbon bar. Indistinguishable from the Royal Navy LS&GC Medal, apart from the recipient's details. The medal is always issued named with number, rank, name and regiment.*

VALUE: £70–95

Miniature £15–20

NZ24. NEW ZEALAND ARMY LONG SERVICE & GOOD CONDUCT MEDAL

Instituted: May 6, 1985.
Branch of Service: New Zealand Army, Regular Forces.
Ribbon: 32mm crimson edged in white.
Metal: Silver.
Size: 36mm.
Description: (Obverse) crowned effigy of Queen Elizabeth; (reverse) FOR LONG SERVICE AND GOOD CONDUCT attached to an ornamental title bar bearing the words NEW ZEALAND in raised lettering.
Comments: *Similar to the British Army LS&GC Medal (229) but with a distinctive New Zealand suspension bar. Only soldiers of the Regular Force serving from December 1, 1977 onwards, are eligible for this medal, a minimum of 15 years full-time irreproachable service being required. Clasps for additional periods of 15 years may be granted. The medal is always issued named with number, rank, name and corps.*

VALUE: £60–75   *Miniature* £15–20

NZ25. ROYAL NEW ZEALAND AIR FORCE LONG SERVICE MEDAL

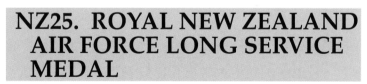

Instituted: May 6, 1985.
Branch of Service: Royal New Zealand Air Force.
Ribbon: 32mm equal stripes of dark blue and crimson edged in white.
Metal: Silver.
Size: 36mm.
Description: (Obverse) uncrowned effigy of Queen Elizabeth; (reverse) an eagle with outstretched wings surmounted by a royal crown encircled by the inscription FOR LONG SERVICE AND GOOD CONDUCT.
Comments: *This medal replaces the award of the British RAF LS&GC Medal (MY 268). It is, in fact, indistinguishable from the British award except for the recipient's details engraved on the rim.*

VALUE: £75–100   *Miniature* £15–20

NZ26. NEW ZEALAND POLICE LONG SERVICE & GOOD CONDUCT MEDAL

Instituted: September 8, 1976.
Ribbon: 32mm crimson with a central dark blue stripe flanked with white stripes.
Metal: Silver.
Size: 38mm.
Description: (Obverse) crowned effigy of Queen Elizabeth; (reverse) St Edward's Crown, sceptre and sword on a cushion within a wreath of oak leaves and fern fronds, surrounded by the inscription NEW ZEALAND POLICE—FOR LONG SERVICE AND GOOD CONDUCT.
Comments: *This medal replaced the New Zealand Police Medal (MY283). It is awarded to sworn police staff on completion of 14 years service. Clasps are awarded for each additional seven years of service. All medals are issued engraved.*

VALUE: £175–250   *Miniature*   £35–40

NZ27. NEW ZEALAND FIRE BRIGADES LONG SERVICE AND GOOD CONDUCT MEDAL

Instituted: September 8, 1976.
Ribbon: 32mm vermilion with a central black stripe flanked by narrow yellow stripes.
Metal: Silver.
Size: 36mm.
Description: (Obverse) crowned effigy of Queen Elizabeth (reverse) NEW ZEALAND FIRE BRIGADES—FOR LONG SERVICE AND GOOD CONDUCT above a fern frond.
Comments: *Originally awarded for 14 years full or part time services as a fireman, but amended by Royal Warrant (October 15, 1981) to include fire brigades maintained or operated by companies as well as the forces under the control of the NZ Fire Service Commission. Clasps are awarded every additional period of seven years service. The recipient's name is engraved on the rim.*

VALUE: £150–175   *Miniature*   £35–40

NZ28. NEW ZEALAND PRISON SERVICE MEDAL

Instituted: October 15, 1981.
Ribbon: 32mm crimson with a central dark blue stripe flanked by narrow green stripes.
Metal: Silver.
Size: 36mm.
Description: (Obverse) crowned effigy of Queen Elizabeth II; (reverse) St Edward's crown and inscription NEW ZEALAND PRISON SERVICE FOR LONG SERVICE AND GOOD CONDUCT.
Comments: *Awarded for 14 years service with bars further 7 year periods. This medal superseded the NZ Prison Service Long Service Medal originally instituted in 1901. The recipient's name is engraved on the rim.*

VALUE: £150–175   *Miniature*   £35–40

NZ29. NEW ZEALAND SUFFRAGE CENTENNIAL MEDAL 1993

Instituted: July 1, 1993.
Ribbon: 32mm purple with narrow central stripes of white, yellow and white.
Metal: Antiqued bronze.
Size: 36mm.
Description: (Obverse) crowned effigy of Queen Elizabeth; (reverse) wreath of fern and camellia enclosing the inscription 1893 THE NEW ZEALAND SUFFRAGE CENTENNIAL 1993.
Comments: *Awarded to 500 men and women who by their virtues, talents and loyalty have made a recognised contribution to the rights of women in New Zealand or to women's issues in New Zealand. It was only awarded during the centennial year of the granting of votes to women—New Zealand being the first country in the world to do so. 546 unnamed medals were issued.*

VALUE: £350–400

NZ30. NEW ZEALAND TRAFFIC ENFORCEMENT LONG SERVICE AND GOOD CONDUCT MEDAL

Instituted: September 28, 1970.
Ribbon: Bright blue with a narrow central white stripe flanked by black stripes.
Metal: Silver
Size: 36mm.
Description: A circular medal bearing (obverse) the coat of arms of the New Zealand Ministry of Transport; (reverse) the inscription FOR LONG SERVICE AND GOOD CONDUCT TRAFFIC ENFORCEMENT, with a suspender of stylised fern leaves.
Comments: *This award, rendered obsolete with the introduction of the New Zealand Traffic Service Medal (NZ31), was awarded to personnel of the traffic enforcement and road safety branches of the Ministry of Transport on completion of 15 years service. Clasps were awarded for each additional 10 years of service. All medals were issued engraved.*

VALUE: £100–150   *Miniature* £50–60

NZ31. NEW ZEALAND TRAFFIC SERVICE MEDAL

Instituted: December 22, 1998.
Ribbon: Bright blue with a narrow central white stripe flanked by black stripes as MYB NZ30 above..
Metal: Silver.
Size: 36mm.
Description: (Obverse) crowned effigy of Queen Elizabeth; (reverse) crowned wreath of fern fronds enclosing the word THE NEW ZEALAND TRAFFIC SERVICE MEDAL.
Comments: *Awarded to both local body and Government traffic enforcement staff who had completed 14 years service on or after January 1, 1987. Clasps were awarded for each seven years additional service. Eligibility for this medal ceased on July 1, 1992, with the merger of the Traffic Safety Service of the Ministry of Transport and the New Zealand Police.*

VALUE: £100–150   *Miniature*   £30–40

NZ32. NEW ZEALAND CUSTOMS SERVICE MEDAL

Instituted: February 20, 2008.

Ribbon: Dark blue with a central stripe of bright blue bordered by yellow stripes.

Metal: Silver

Size: 36mm.

Description: (Obverse) The effigy of Queen Elizabeth by Ian Rank-Broadley and the inscription "Elizabeth II Queen of New Zealand"; (reverse) the badge of the New Zealand Customs Service. The clasp to the medal shall be of silver, oblong in shape, and bear a Royal Crown in the centre. When the ribbon is worn alone, a small silver rosette may be worn for each clasp awarded.

Comments: *Awarded to members of the New Zealand Customs Service employed on or after 1 December 2007 on completion of fourteen years service as a Customs Officer. Clasps are awarded for each additional period of seven years service. The medal is always issued engraved. 369 medals awarded to June 2010: 63 medals alone, 59 medals plus one clasp, 102 medals plus two clasps, 89 medals plus three clasps, 52 medals plus four clasps, 4 medals plus five clasps.*

VALUE: —

NZ34. ROYAL NEW ZEALAND NAVAL RESERVE DECORATION

Instituted: May 6, 1985.

Ribbon: 38mm green edged with white.

Metal: Silver and gold.

Size: 54mm high and 33mm wide.

Description: A skeletal badge consisting of an oval loop of rope in silver surrounding the Royal Cypher in gold.

Comments: *Awarded to commissioned officers of the Royal New Zealand Naval Reserve, with a minimum of 15 years service. Clasps for each additional period of 10 years are also awarded. The names of recipients are engraved on the reverse. Recipients are entitled to the postnominal letters RD. This medal replaced MY219.*

VALUE: £150–200   *Miniature* £20–25

NZ35. ROYAL NEW ZEALAND NAVAL VOLUNTEER RESERVE DECORATION

Instituted: May 6, 1985.
Ribbon: 38mm dark blue with a central broad green stripe flanked by narrow crimson stripes.
Metal: Silver and gold.
Size: 54mm high and 33mm wide.
Description: A skeletal badge, similar in design to the above.
Comments: *Awarded to commissioned officers in the Royal New Zealand Naval Volunteer Reserve, with a minimum of 15 years service. Clasps for each additional period of 10 years are awarded. The names of recipients are engraved on the reverse. Recipients are entitled to the postnominal letters VRD. These decorations replaced the British RD and VRD, the latter being obsolete and the organisation of the Royal New Zealand Navy being such that the British Admiralty Board regulations were no longer applicable.*

VALUE: £150–200   *Miniature*   £20–25

NZ36. ROYAL NEW ZEALAND NAVAL VOLUNTEER RESERVE LONG SERVICE AND GOOD CONDUCT MEDAL

Instituted: 1985.
Ribbon: 32mm dark blue with a central broad stripe of green between narrow crimson stripes.
Metal: Silver.
Size: 36mm.
Description: (Obverse) uncrowned effigy of Queen Elizabeth; (reverse) a battleship with the motto DIUTURNE FIDELIS (faithful of long duration).
Comments: *Awarded to RNZVR ratings serving on or after December 1, 1977, with a minimum of 15 years service. Clasps for each additional period of 10 years are awarded. This medal replaced MY221.*

VALUE: £50–75   *Miniature*   £15–20

NZ37. NEW ZEALAND CHIEF OF DEFENCE FORCE COMMENDATION

Instituted: 2005.
Description: Pale blue ribbon encased in a dark blue frame, on which is superimposed the emblem of the Chief of the Defence Force, in silver, and consisting of a crown over crossed swords and fern leaves with an eagle at the centre.
Comments: *For award to members of the NZDF for performance which would be unlikely to meet the criteria for a New Zealand Honour. Commendations are available to individual military and civilian staff, and to military units. The Commendations are presented with a manuscript narrative outlining the reason for the award. Military personnel wear these commendations on their right breast in uniform. The CDF Commendation takes priority over the lower level single service Chief of Staff Commendations.*

VALUE: —

NZ38. NEW ZEALAND CHIEF OF NAVY COMMENDATION

Instituted: 2005.
Branch of Service: Navy.
Metal: Silver.
Description: A badge surmounted by a naval crown and inscribed CHIEF OF NAVY round the circumference, with twin fern fronds at the foot. The centre depicts the flag of the Chief of the Navy.
Comments: *Awarded to RNZN personnel who deliver excellent performance that is usually of benefit to the RNZN rather than NZDF as a whole.*

VALUE: —

NZ39. NEW ZEALAND CHIEF OF ARMY COMMENDATION

Instituted: 2005.
Branch of Service: Army.
Description: A crimson ribbon (similar to the Victoria Cross) but with the badge of the Army (crossed weapons—a sword and a taiaha—superimposed by a crown surmounted by a lion with NZ and NGATI TUMATAUENGA below) in gold-coloured metal.
Comments: *Awarded to NZ Army personnel who deliver excellent performance that is usually of benefit to the NZ Army rather than NZDF as a whole.*

VALUE: —

NZ40. NEW ZEALAND CHIEF OF AIR FORCE COMMENDATION

Instituted: 2005.
Branch of Service: Air Force.
Description: A blue ribbon with diagonal crimson and pale blue stripes on the left, surmounted by an eagle and two five-pointed stars.
Comments: *Awarded to RNZAF personnel who deliver excellent performance that is usually of benefit to the RNZAF rather than NZDF as a whole.*

VALUE: —

NZ41. NEW ZEALAND DEFENCE SERVICE MEDAL

Instituted: April 2011.
Ribbon: Dark blue, red and light blue stripes. Light green stripes have been added to reflect the volunteer and territorial elements of the Services.
Metal: Antique bronze.
Size: 36mm
Description: (Obverse) The New Zealand coat of arms; (reverse) on the right one large New Zealand fern frond. On the left are the emblems of the Navy, Army and Air Force—the Naval crown, crossed swords and eagle. In the lower section the words "THE NEW ZEALAND DEFENCE SERVICE MEDAL".
Comments: *The New Zealand Defence Service Medal (NZDSM) was instituted to recognise attested military service since September 3, 1945. The Royal Warrant for the NZDSM allows for one or more clasps to be awarded with the medal. The number of clasps awarded to an individual will be determined by the type(s) of military service undertaken. There are four clasps which can be awarded: REGULAR (image shown left), TERRITORIAL, C.M.T. and NATIONAL SERVICE. At least 160,000 NZ ex-Service persons and over 7,000 currently serving NZDF military personnel are expected to be eligible to receive the NZDSM. To issue the medal to all ex-Service persons who apply is expected to take between two and three years, even with extra staff being employed by NZDF for the duration of the project. This will be the largest medal issue project New Zealand has undertaken since 1950–54 when the majority of the World War II medals were issued.*

SOUTH AFRICAN MEDALS

Apart from the various British campaign medals from 1834 onwards, distinctive medals relating to military service in South Africa date from 1896 when a version of the Meritorious Service Medal (MYB210) was provided with the name of the Cape of Good Hope on the reverse. This was accompanied by similar versions of the Distinguished Conduct Medal (MYB42) and the Long Service and Good Conduct Medal (MYB229). The following year similar awards were instituted for Natal. Moreover, there were also a number of military and naval medals issued under Dutch, and later Boer, administrations which are outside the scope of this Yearbook.

Cape and Natal colonists received British awards from the earliest days of the British occupation, and numerous instances have been recorded of awards to South Africans of both the orders of chivalry and gallantry decorations. This situation coninued after the formation of the Union of South Africa in 1910. As a rule, these were identical to the British versions in every respect but there were a few notable exceptions. The Victory Medal (MYB170) was struck with a bilingual (English and Dutch) reverse for award to South African forces. Distinctive medals for the police, railway and harbour police and prison services (MYB284–285 and 290–291) were awarded but as they were instituted by Royal Warrant they are included in the main body of this Yearbook.

Other South African awards which will be found in the main section are the King's Police Medal for gallantry or bravery (MYB49), the Africa Service Medal (MYB189), the South African Medal for War Service (MYB192) and the South African Medal for Korea (MYB196). There were also South African versions of the Efficiency Decoration (MYB236), Efficiency Medal (MYB254), the Permanent Force LS&GC (253) and Air Efficiency Award (MYB270). Finally, there are three miscellaneous medals: the Union of South Africa Commemoration Medal of 1910 (MYB357), the Dekoratie Voor Trouwe Dienst of 1920 (MYB358) and the Anglo-Boere Oorlog Medal instituted at the same time (MYB359).

In 1952 the Union of South Africa instituted its own system of awards for gallantry in action, bravery in a non-combat situation and for distinguished service. Nine of these awards had a standard reverse showing the arms of the Union of South Africa surmounted by the royal cypher. In 1961, when South Africa became a republic and left the Commonwealth, the royal cypher was removed. The tenth award was the Union Medal which was completely redesigned and renamed the Permanent Force Good Service Medal (SA11 below).

For the purposes of this insertion it has been necessary to limit full coverage to military awards because of the absolute plethora of orders, decorations and medals that have made their appearance in the last 50 years while South Africa was ruled by the National Party. Not only were separate and independent award structures set up with their own orders, decorations and medals for all branches of the public service: Military, Police, Railway Police, Prisons, as well as the National Intelligence Service, but the situation was further complicated when the Nationalist Party Government in terms of its apartheid policy set up Homeland Governments that were given independence from the Republic of South Africa, each with their own set of awards for Military, Police and Prison departments—Transkei, Ciskei, KwaZulu, Bophuthatswana, Venda, Lebowa, Gazankulu and Qwa-qwa, etc. After 1994 the situation has been compounded by the issue of medals awarded retrospectively to members of the forces of freedom fighters or terrorists—MK (Mkhonto Wesizwe) and APLA (Azanian People's Liberation Army).

The awards instituted and awarded in South West Africa by the South African Government until this SA administered territory gained its independence and became Namibia in 1990 through world pressure, must not be overlooked either. The South African award system also reveals great instability through the frequent abolition of awards, their supersession and further proliferation by the introduction of new awards! Although this insertion has a primary focus on military awards, some of the awards to the South African Police, Prisons and Railway Police that may occur in medal groups with some regularity, have been included.

For information purposes a full list of orders, decorations and medals instituted since 1952 to the Police, Railway Police and Prisons, appears on the next page. The date in brackets next to each award indicates the year of gazetting of that award. The awards are listed in order of precedence for that particular compartment of the public service. These lists are preceded by a listing of South African civilian orders and decorations that are not confined to any particular public service compartment of awards.

SOUTH AFRICAN CIVILIAN AWARDS

ORDERS
Order of the Southern Cross (1986/87)—Two Classes
Order of the Star of South Africa (Non Military)
(1988)—Five Classes
Order for Meritorious Service (1986)—Two Classes
Order of Good Hope (1973/88)—Five Classes

DECORATIONS FOR BRAVERY
The Queen's Medal for Bravery (Gold and Silver) (1953)
The Woltemade Decoration for Bravery (1970/88)
Gold
The Woltemade Decoration for Bravery (1970/88) Silver
Civil Defence Medal for Bravery (1976)

MERITORIOUS SERVICE
Civil Defence Medal for Meritorious Service (1976)
State President's Sports Merit Award (1971)

SOUTH AFRICAN POLICE

ORDERS
South African Police Star for Distinguished
Leadership (1979)

DECORATIONS FOR BRAVERY
South African Police Cross for Bravery (1963)
South African Police Cross for Bravery (1989)
(Gold/ Silver/ungraded)
South African Police Silver Cross for Gallantry (1985)

**AWARDS FOR DISTINGUISHED, LONG AND
MERITORIOUS SERVICE**
South African Police Star for Distinguished
Service (1963)
South African Police Star for Distinguished
Service (1979)
South African Police Star for Outstanding Service (1979)
South African Police Star for Merit (1963)
South African Police Medal for Faithful Service (1963)
South African Police Star for Faithful Service (1979)

SERVICE
South African Police Medal for Combating
Terrorism (1974)

COMMEMORATIVE
South African Police Seventy-Fifth Anniversary
Commemorative Medal (1988)

SOUTH AFRICAN RAILWAYS POLICE

ORDERS
South African Railways Police Star for
Distinguished Leadership (1980)

DECORATIONS FOR BRAVERY
South African Railways Police Cross for Valour (1966)
South African Railways Police Cross for Valour (1980)

**AWARDS FOR DISTINGUISHED, LONG AND
MERITORIOUS SERVICE**
South African Railways Police Star for
Distinguished Service (1980) *
Decoration for Distinguished Service in the SA
Railways Police Force (1966)
Decoration for Outstanding Service in the South
African Railways Police Force (1980)
Star for Merit in the South African Railways Police
Force (1966)
Star for Merit in the South African Railways Police
Force (1980)
South African Railways Police Star for Faithful
Service (1980)
Medal for Faithful Service in the South African
Railways Police Force (1966)
Medal for Faithful Service in the South African
Railways Police Force (1980)

SERVICE
South African Railways Police Medal for
Combating Terrorism

SOUTH AFRICAN PRISONS
(later Department of
Correctional Services)

DECORATIONS FOR BRAVERY
Decoration for Valour in the South African Prisons
Service (1968)
South African Prisons Service Cross for Valour
(Diamond) (1980)
South African Prisons Service Cross for Valour
(Ruby) (1980)

**AWARDS FOR DISTINGUISHED, LONG AND
MERITORIOUS SERVICE**
South African Prisons Service Star for Excellence
(1980)
South African Prisons Service Star for Distinction
(1980)
South African Prisons Service Star for Merit (1980)
South African Prisons Service Cross for Merit
(1980)
Medal for Merit in the South African Prisons
Service (1968)
South African Prisons Service Medal for Merit
(Commissioned Officers) (1980)
South African Prisons Service Medal for Merit
(Non-Commissioned Officers) (1980)
Faithful Service Medal in the Prisons Department
(1959)
Faithful Service Medal, Prisons Department (1965)
Medal for Faithful Service in the South African
Prisons Service (1968)
South African Prisons Service Medal for Faithful
Service (1980)—Gold Medal (30 years); Silver
Medal (20 years); Bronze Medal (10 years)

* name later changed to Star for Distinguished Devotion

VERIFICATION OF GENUINENESS OF SOUTH AFRICAN MEDALS

The unfortunate incident regarding the naming of South African World War I medals featured in a
recent *OMRS Journal* article has cast unwarranted suspicion on the genuineness of South African-
issued medals. The Military Medal Society of South Africa have a large database and offers to
verify the naming, etc., of medals for a reasonable fee and issue a certificate of authenticity. All
enquiries to be directed to Medal Verification, MMSSA, at hirk@jhb.stormnet.co.za. Hopefully
this will restore confidence in South African medals where this is in doubt.

**SPECIAL NOTE ON THE PRICING OF POST 1952
SOUTH AFRICAN DECORATIONS AND MEDALS AWARDED TO MEMBERS OF
THE ARMY, NAVY AND AIR FORCE**

In 1952 the Union Defence Force made a decision to cease naming its medals. Instead each medal would be impressed with a serial number and the number, rank and name, etc. of the recipient entered against the serial number of the medal recorded down the left-hand margin of the register. The registers have since been misplaced. The register system was replaced by the computer and when a recipient received a medal, the medal number was recorded in many cases on this computerised record of service. However, these records are held by the Department of Defence and their system is not geared up to print out a full list of recipients of a particular medal with medal numbers.

(i)   In certain cases, after the award of the medal, the recipient's number, rank, name and unit, along with the serial number of the medal awarded, was published in Part II Unit orders.

(ii)   Since approximately 1988, the certificates of award have recorded the serial number of the medal awarded. Prior to that time, no medal serial number was printed on the certificate.

In order to establish that the medal in the group or as a singleton was awarded to a particular recipient (i) or (ii) above, are a prerequisite = PRICE A (Medal certificate must be the original in (ii) to qualify).

If a medal is numbered and has an un-numbered original certificate of award as supporting documentation = PRICE B.

If a medal is numbered (or unnumbered) without any supporting documentation = PRICE C.

It must be stressed that even if a recipient was awarded a medal, there is nothing to prove that that particular medal was actually awarded to the recipient, unless the serial number on the medal can be tied to that recipient through supporting documentation. Obviously gallantry awards must be accompanied by a copy of the citation for which the award was made.

An A, B and C price will be given for each SA Military award. For medals awarded to the Police, two prices will be given: named medals and unnamed specimens, as the Police continued to name their medals (they actually impressed the day, month and year of award as well). As Prisons medals were engraved by a variety of jewellers after 1980, three prices are given for medals awarded from 1980. A: with certificate; B: named; C: unnamed.

For verification of the Permanent Force LSGC Medal (18 years) (MYB SA29) and identification of the recipient, an unpublished roll has been compiled from Part II orders. This may be consulted by contacting Mr J. Louw at chevjlouw@hotmail.com. He will provide a copy of the roll entry at a fee. Such verification places verified medals in Category A.

SOUTH AFRICAN DEFENCE FORCE

ORDERS

SA1. STAR OF SOUTH AFRICA

Instituted: 1952.
Ribbon: 44.5mm orange with three 3mm green stripes in centre, 6mm apart.
Metal: Silver.
Description: A multi-facetted five-point star, fitted with a ring and oblong loop through which the ribbon is passed for suspension round the neck.
Comments: *Awarded for recognising exceptionally meritorious service, in time of peace or war, by officers of the SA Defence Force or of other armed forces attached to or serving with, or rendering service to the SA Defence Force. The award could recognize a particular instance or service over a period of time.*
Further awards were denoted by a silver bar embossed in the centre with a miniature replica of the Star. None were awarded but an example of the bar is on display at the SA Museum of Military History. The reverse of the order has the embellished coat of arms of the Union of SA in relief, surmounted by the Royal cypher. After 1961 the Royal cypher was erased from existing medal stock. Those officers who were still serving in 1975 could exchange their Star of South Africa for the Order of the Star of South Africa. Post nominal title: SSA.

VALUE

	A	B	C	Miniature
With Royal cypher	£1000	£600	£300	£80
Royal cypher erased	£750	£250	£150	£20
Coat of arms reverse	£400	£200	£100	£20

SA2. ORDER OF THE STAR OF SOUTH AFRICA (MILITARY)

Instituted: 1975.

Ribbon: Blue, 37mm (neck ribbon), 80mm (sash), 44mm (breast ribbon) or 20mm (miniature). A narrow central white stripe denotes the second class (redesignated silver award in 1977).

Metal: Silver-gilt or silver depending on class.

Description: An eight-pointed Maltese cross with an eight-pointed star superimposed at the centre and having a circular Protea wreath behind. *First Class:* A Protea ornament at the top joins the star to a five-pointed badge in the form of a ground plan of the Castle of Good Hope, enclosing a circular device featuring the insignia of the Defence Force. This is linked by a chain to circular medallions embellished with eight-pointed stars forming the neck collar of the order. In addition to the neck badge and collar there is a gold breast star. An eight pointed multi-rayed star is surmounted by a circular protea wreath superimposed with a blue enamel Maltese Cross edged in gold, in turn surmounted by an eight pointed star with alternate long and short rays in gold. The centre of the neck badge is mounted with a diamond. The neck collar or chain was discontinued in 1978. *Second Class:* award is similar in every respect to the First Class except there is no diamond in the centre and the metal is silver and there is no neck collar.

Comments: *The Order of the Star of SA (Military) is divided into two classes:*

Class I Gold: Post nominal title: SSA. Awarded to generals and higher officers or officers of comparable rank who distinguished themselves by meritorious military service that promoted efficiency and contributed lastingly to the security of the nation.

Class II Silver: Post nominal title: SSAS. Awarded to brigadiers and higher officers or officers of comparable rank who distinguished themselves by exceptionally meritorious service of major military importance.

To all intents and purposes the award of this order was confined to members of the South African Permanent Force. If an officer was promoted to Class I of the order his Class II insignia would be returnable. The 1988 amendments to the warrant eliminated the inclusion of non-South African citizens of the appropriate rank for consideration. The amendments to regulations to cover the division that was not exclusively military but could include civilians, was introduced in 1978 but space does not permit lengthy explanation of the various classes: Grand Cross, Grand Officer, Commander, Officer and Knight.

VALUE:

	A	B	C	Miniature
Class I Neck collar and badge and breast badge in silver-gilt	£2000	£1500	£1000	—
Class I ditto but in base metal gilt plated for presentation purposes or museums	—	—	£500	—
Class I Neck badge and breast badge.	£850	£750	£500	£50
Class I ditto in base metal	—	—	£250	—
Class II Neck and breast badge	£500	£350	£300	£25

DECORATIONS FOR BRAVERY

SA3. CASTLE OF GOOD HOPE DECORATION

Instituted: 1952.
Ribbon: 44.5mm green.
Metal: Gold.
Description: A five-pointed star representing in outline the Castle of Good Hope (the first major fortress in South Africa) the whole surrounded by a moat. The raised centre is in the form of a circle in which is depicted the arrival of Jan Van Riebeek, in his flag ship *Drommedaris* in Table Bay on 6 April 1652 against a background of Table Mountain, surrounded by a garland of Protea (the national flower) and the inscription: CASTEEL DE GOEDE HOOF DEKORASIE round the top and CASTLE OF GOOD HOPE DECORATION round the foot. (Reverse) Serial number and Royal cypher. Recently the loop for neck wear has been replaced by a ring for breast wear.
Comments: *Awarded for a signal act of valour or most conspicuous bravery or some daring or pre-eminent act of self-sacrifice or extreme devotion to duty in the presence of an enemy. The decoration could be awarded posthumously. This is South Africa's highest gallantry award but to date it has not been awarded. As no examples of the full size decoration have been awarded, no price is given—any specimens that come on to the market should be regarded with great suspicion. A gold miniature of the decoration is worn on the ribbon on the tunic.*

VALUE:

		Miniature (hallmarked gold)
Base metal-gilt plated specimen for museums or presentation sets of medals	£150	£170–200

SA4. LOUW WEPENER DECORATION

Instituted: 1952.
Ribbon: 35mm divided into equal stripes, six orange and five white.
Metal: Silver.
Description: Scene at the battle of Thaba Bosigo, Basutoland (now Lesotho) in 1865 in which Louw Wepener, shown in the foreground, was the hero. Inscribed LOUW WEPENER round the top and DECORATION DEKORASIE round the foot. Fitted with a scrolled suspension bar.
Comments: *It was awarded in recognition of acts of most conspicuous courage and self-sacrifice performed in the execution of or beyond the call of military duty in time of peace or war, by members of the SADF or attached troops, in saving or endeavouring to save the lives of others on land, sea or in the air or in the execution of duty for which other purely military honours are not normally granted. Post nominal title: LWD. The award was rendered obsolete by the Honoris Crux Decoration in 1975. Further awards were to have been denoted by a silver bar centred with a silver button inscribed with the initials LWD, but none were ever manufactured.*

VALUE:

	A	B	C	Miniature
Royal cypher reverse	£750	£500	£350	£35
Royal cypher erased	£750	£500	£250	£30
SA coat of arms	£600	£450	£150	£60

SA5. VAN RIEBEECK DECORATION

Instituted: 1952.
Ribbon: 32mm sky blue.
Metal: Silver-gilt.
Description: In shape of a five-pointed star representing the outline of the Castle of Good Hope. The suspension consists of a cluster of eight protea leaves. In the centre of the obverse is the full figure of Jan Van Riebeeck (first Governor of the Cape of Good Hope) in relief against a background of three rings representing his three ships—*Drommedaris, De Rijger* and *De Goede Hoop*.
Comments: *The decoration was awarded to officers of the SA Defence Force or auxiliary services or attached troops who distinguished themselves by outstanding resourcefulness, perseverance or personal courage or by their outstanding leadership or responsibility and personal example against an enemy in the field. Post nominal title: DVR. The award was rendered obsolete by the Honoris Crux Decoration in 1975. A specimen of the bar embossed with a miniature cannon in silver gilt to denote further awards, is on display at the SA Museum of Military History.*

VALUE:

	A	B	C	Miniature
Royal cypher reverse	£650	£450	£150	£30
Royal cypher erased	£650	£450	£150	£60
SA coat of arms reverse	£650	£400	£150	£30

SA6. VAN RIEBEECK MEDAL

Instituted: 1952.
Ribbon: 32mm sky blue with 6mm white central stripe.
Metal: Silver.
Description: Very similar to the Van Riebeeck Decoration (above) but differing in the ribbon. It, too, was discontinued in August 1975.
Comments: *In all respects identical to the Van Riebeeck Decoration except the medal was awarded to Warrant Officers, NCOs and Men. The medal was rendered obsolete by the Honoris Crux Decoration in 1975. Post nominal title: VRM. Additional award bar as for the decoration, except metal is silver. Specimen on display at the SA Museum of Military History.*

VALUE:

	A	B	C	Miniature
Royal cypher reverse	£500	£400	£150	£40
Royal cypher erased	£500	£400	£150	£65
SA coat of arms reverse	£400	£300	£150	£30

SA7. HONORIS CRUX

Instituted: 1952.
Ribbon: 32mm leaf-green with 3mm red outer and 2mm white inner edges.
Metal: Silver gilt and enamels.
Description: An eight-pointed Maltese Cross in silver gilt: in each angle formed by the cross is an eagle in silver gilt, facing to the right. Centre circle of the cross is enamelled in the three colours of the flag of Union of South Africa. The design was significantly influenced by the Order of the Golden Eagle that was proposed in 1894 but was rejected by the Transvaal Volksraad.
Comments: *There have been six recipients of this award. It was awarded to members of the South African Defence Force, auxiliary services, attached troops who regardless of their own safety and through personal courage and determination, perform a gallant act or deed against an enemy in the field. Subsequent deeds may entitle a recipient to a bar in silver-gilt embossed in the centre with a miniature eagle. A specimen bar is on display at the SA Museum of Military History. Post nominal title: HC.*

VALUE:

	A	B	C	Miniature
Royal cypher reverse	£1000	£700	£375	£40
Royal cypher erased	£1000	£700	£375	£40
SA coat of arms	£800	£700	£375	£40

SA8. LOUW WEPENER MEDAL

Instituted: 1967.
Ribbon: 35mm in width, orange divided into five broad stripes of equal width by four white stripes of 1.5mm
Metal: Bronze
Description: Identical to the Louw Wepener Decoration with the words "MEDALJE/MEDAL" substituted for"DECORATION/DEKORASIE".
Comments: *Conditions of award as for Louw Wepener Decoration for deeds of a lesser nature to those for which the Louw Wepener Decoration was awarded. The award could be made posthumously. Subsequent awards were recognized by a bar with a centred circle containing the letters LWM. Post nominal title: LWM. The medal was rendered obsolete by the Honoris Crux Decoration in 1975.*

VALUE:

A	B	C	Miniature
£700	£500	£300	£40

SA9. HONORIS CRUX DECORATION

Instituted: 1975.
Ribbon: 32mm orange with additional white stripes according to class.
Metal: Enamelled gold or silver, according to class.
Description: An eight-pointed enamelled Maltese cross superimposed on a wreath with crossed swords in the angles, with a central roundel divided horizontally into orange, white and blue. Fitted with an ornamental suspension loop.
Comments: *This award replaced SA4, 5, 6, 7 and 8 above and was divided into four classes, distinguished by their ribbons and the embellishment of the obverse.*
Honoris Crux Diamond. Plain orange ribbon, 32mm, with a green circular border to centre roundel mounted with eight diamonds awarded to those who distinguished themselves. Awarded for performing deeds of outstanding valour, at extreme risk to their lives
Honoris Crux Gold. Orange ribbon with a 1mm central white stripe. Made of silver gilt with gold border to centre roundel. Awarded for performing outstanding deeds of bravery in extreme danger.
Honoris Crux Silver. Orange ribbon with a 1mm white stripe 13mm from each edge. Made of silver with silver border to centre roundel. Awarded for performing exceptional deeds of bravery whilst in great danger.
Honoris Crux. Orange with 2mm white edges and 1mm white stripe 5mm from each edge. Made of silver. The centre roundel has a silver border but the arms of the cross are white enamel instead of green as in the other three classes. Awarded for performing deeds of bravery in dangerous circumstances.
The post-nominal titles are: HCD, HCG, HCS and HC respectively. Further awards are denoted by a bar with miniature replica of the decoration—in gold for the first two classes and silver for the second two. Only 4 HCGs were awarded—one with a bar. In 1993 the HCD and HCG were discontinued. The crosses have a SA Mint hallmark. The first striking has voiding round the protea wreath whereas subsequent strikings have no voiding at all.

VALUE:

	A	B	C	Miniature
HC (Diamond)	—	—	300	140
HC (Gold)	£2000	£1700	£275	£120
HC (Silver)	£1700	£1500	£250	£100
HC	£1100	£1000	£200	£100

SA10. PRO VIRTUTE DECORATION

Instituted: 1987.

Ribbon: 32mm in width, 20mm orange central stripe edged with a narrow pale blue stripe of 6mm each.

Metal: 9ct gold.

Description: A five linked white enamelled Maltese Cross edged with gold. The centre is of dark red enamel on which is superimposed the embellished coat of arms of the Republic of South Africa. The cross is connected with the suspender by an inverted V from which extends two proteas. The reverse bears the words "PRO VIRTUTE". Awarded to officers of the SA National Defence Force who have distinguished themselves by distinguished conduct and exceptional combat leadership during military operations.

Comments: *Post Nominal Title PVD. Subsequent awards are denoted by a silver gilt bar with a miniature Protea emblem embossed in the centre of the bar.*

VALUE:

A	B	C	Miniature
£1300	£800	£300	£70

SA11. PRO VIRTUTE MEDAL

Instituted: 1987.

Ribbon: 32mm in width, orange outer stripes of 10mm with two 4mm central light blue stripes divided by an orange 4mm central stripe.

Metal: Silver

Description: The obverse bears the outline of the cross of the Pro Virtute Decoration. The reverse bears the title PRO VIRTUTE Surmounted by the coat of arms of the Republic of South Africa and a wreath of proteas as a surround on three sides.

Comments: *Awarded to warrant officers and other ranks with a similar bar for further awards, except in silver. Conditions of award as for PVD. Post nominal title: PVM.*

VALUE:

A	B	C	Miniature
£700	£500	£175	£50

SA12. AD ASTRA DECORATION

Instituted: 1987.

Ribbon: 30mm diagonal alternating narrow light blue and white stripes of 3mm.

Metal: Gold plated silver with hallmark.

Description: In the centre of a five-pointed star is the outline of the Castle of Good Hope in relief on which is depicted the badge of the SA Air Force in gold on a light blue background edged with white. The reverse shows the embellished coat of arms of the Republic of South Africa above the words "AD ASTRA". The star is suspended from an eagle with outstretched wings attached to a ring at the top of the star.

Comments: *This award is made to air crew members for excellent flying skill or outstanding ingenuity or skill during emergencies or unusual situations on board aircraft. Post nominal title: AAD.*

VALUE:

A	B	C	Miniature
£1300	£700	£300	£50

SA13. THE S.A.D.F. CROSSES

Army Cross

Air Force Cross

Instituted: 1987.

Ribbons: A. Army Cross: 30mm wide. White with central 10mm guardsman red stripe; **B. Air Force Cross:** 30mm wide. White with central broad light blue stripes of 12mm divided by a narrow gold stripe of 2mm; **C. Navy Cross:** 30mm wide. White with central broad navy blue stripe of 10mm; **D. SA Medical Services Cross:** 30mm wide. White with central broad purple stripe of 10mm.

Metal: Silver

Description: A silver cross with fixed straight suspender decorated with laurel leaves. The suspender is attached to the top arm of the cross. The arms of the cross have a double border and rise to a higher point from the edge which is 2mm thick. There is a central roundel for each cross covered in shiny epoxy and bordered with three circles of laurel leaves.

A. Army Cross: orange roundel; with badge of the SA Army in gold; **B. Air Force Cross:** light blue roundel with the badge of the SA Air Force in gold; **C. Navy Cross:** navy blue roundel with the badge of the SA Navy in gold; **D. SA Medical Services Cross:** a purple roundel with the badge of the SA Medical Services in gold.

Comments: *The reverse bears the embellished coat of arms of the Republic of South Africa. A bar in silver denotes a subsequent award and bears a miniature protea. Post-nominal titles are as follows: **A. Army Cross:** CM (Crux Militere); **B. Air Force Cross:** CA (Crux Aeronautica); **C. Navy Cross:** CN (Crux Navalis); **D. SA Medical Services Cross:** CC (Crux Curationis).*

Recent events—the sinking of the Oceana *and the Mozambique floods—have seen a number of these crosses awarded, particularly to Air Force personnel. The crosses are awarded to all ranks of the SA Defence Force and auxiliary service for the SA Defence Force and other armed forces attached to or serving with or rendering service to the SA Defence Force, who have distinguished themselves by their exceptional ingenuity and skill in handling equipment, weapons, vehicles, aircraft and vessels concomitant with exemplary personal leadership, dedication and courage in peril of their lives (non-operational).*

VALUE:

A	B	C	*Miniature*
£1200	£600	£200	£70

Navy Cross

SA Medical Services Cross

MEDALS AWARDED FOR DISTINGUISHED, LONG AND MERITORIOUS SERVICE

SA14. SOUTHERN CROSS MEDAL (1952)

Instituted: 1952.

Ribbon: 32mm dark blue with 3mm orange and white central stripes.

Metal: Hallmarked silver and enamel.

Description: A circular medal with raised 4mm rimmed border decorated with a single wreath of oak leaves with suspender also decorated with oakleaves. Within the wreath the field of dark blue enamel shows the Southern Cross constellation.

Comments: *This decoration was superseded in 1975 when it was split into two classes: the Southern Cross Decoration and the Southern Cross Medal (of different design). Recipients are entitled to the postnominal SM. The medal was awarded in times of peace or war to members of the SA Defence Force, or of an auxiliary service or other attached armed forces, irrespective of rank, who distinguished themselves by displaying outstanding devotion to duty, either in a particular instance or over a period of time.*

VALUE:

	A	B	C	Miniature
Royal cypher reverse	£550	£450	£175	£50
Royal cypher erased	£400	£400	£175	£50
SA coat of arms	£400	£400	£175	£50

SA15. SOUTHERN CROSS DECORATION (1975)

Instituted: 1975.

Ribbon: 32mm blue with 1mm white stripes 13mm from each edge.

Metal: Silver and enamels.

Description: An eight-pointed Maltese cross superimposed on a larger, broader cross in the same form, with a beaded enamelled medallion at the centre bearing the constellation of the Southern Cross. Fitted with a protea emblem for suspension from a straight bar.

Comments: *Awarded to commissoned officers of the South African Defence Force or of related forces who contributed to the security of the nation, in recognition of outstanding service of the highest order and the utmost devotion to duty displayed in time of peace or war. In 1993 a bar (silver gilt) was authorised with a protea emblem embossed in its centre, for subsequent awards. Recipients are entitled to the post-nominal SD.*

VALUE:

A	A with bar	B	C	Miniature
£250	£280	£150	£100	£75

SA16. SOUTHERN CROSS MEDAL (1975)

Instituted: 1975.

Ribbon: (1975)—32mm in width, dark blue with 2mm white edges and 1mm white stripes 13mm from each edge. (1986)—32mm in width, divided as follows: white 4mm, dark blue 9mm, white 1mm, dark blue 4mm and then repeated in reverse.

Metal: Enamelled silver.

Description: A five-pointed radiate star with circular radiate sectors between the arms, having a beaded central medallion depicting the constellation of the Southern Cross. Fitted with a plain ring for suspension from a straight bar.

Comments: *Awarded to commissioned officers of the SA Defence Force or other armed forces attached to or serving with or rendering service to the SADF, in recognition of exceptionally meritorious service and particular devotion to duty displayed in time of peace and war. This medal replaced the Southern Cross 1952 (SA14). Bar for subsequent awards as for Southern Cross Decoration (see SA15). Since 1993, recipients have been entitled to the post-nominal SM.*

VALUE:

A	A with bar	B	C	Miniature
£180	£200	£160	£130	£65

SA17. PRO MERITO MEDAL (1967)

Instituted: 1967.

Ribbon: 32mm sky blue with a dark blue centre flanked by narrow white and orange stripes.

Metal: Oxidised silver.

Description: An enamelled disa flower in relief encircled by a wreath of leafed protea flowers on the obverse. The embellished coat of arms of South Africa is on the reverse. With a foliate suspender.

Comments: *Awarded to Warrant Officers, NCOs and other ranks of the SA Defence Force and related forces for outstanding devotion to duty. 374 medals were awarded in total. Recipients are entitled to the post-nominal PMM. In 1975 this award was discontinued when it was split into two classes: The Pro Merito Decoration and The Pro Merito Medal (of different design).*

VALUE:

A	B	C	Miniature
£300	£200	£150	£25

SA18. PRO MERITO DECORATION (1975)

Instituted: 1975.

Ribbon: 32mm blue with a 4mm white central stripe.

Metal: Enamelled silver gilt.

Description: A white enamelled Maltese Cross bordered in gold with centre roundel charged with a red disa flower. The reverse has the embellished coat of arms of South Africa. At the top is a protea flower emblem for suspension from a straight bar.

Comments: *It is awarded to Warrant Officers and NCOs and other ranks of the SA Defence Force or of related forces contributing to the defence of the Republic of South Africa, who have distinguished themselves by rendering outstanding service of the highest order and displaying the utmost devotion to duty. In 1993 a silver gilt bar with protea emblem on its centre was introduced to denote a subsequent award. Recipients are entitled to the post-nominal PMD.*

VALUE:

A	B	C	Miniature
£200	£250	£120	£35

SA19. PRO MERITO MEDAL (1975)

Instituted: 1975.
Ribbon: (1975)—32mm in width, blue with 2mm white edges and 4mm white central stripe. (1986)—32mm, sky blue edged by 5mm white stripes with one 4mm white central stripe.
Metal: Oxidised silver.
Description: A five pointed radiate star with radiate sectors between the arms, having a beaded central medallion of blue enamel with a red disa flower. The reverse bears the embellished coat of arms of South Africa. In 1993, a silver bar with a protea embossed in its centre was introduced to indicate a susbequent award. In 1993 the post-nominal title of PMM was introduced. Fitted with a plain ring for suspension from a straight bar.
Comments: *This medal replaced the original Pro Merito Medal of 1976 (SA 17) when that decoration was divided into two classes. The medal was awarded for exceptionally meritorious service and particular devotion to duty in peace or war to Warrant Officers, NCOs and other ranks.*
VALUE:

A	B	C	Miniature
£120	£100	£80	£30

SA20. COMMANDANT GENERAL OF THE SOUTH AFRICAN DEFENCE FORCE COMMENDATION (1968)

Instituted: 1968.
Ribbon: None.
Metal: Bronze.
Description: A protea emblem sewn on to the tunic and not worn on medal ribbons.
Comments: *Awarded for mentions in despatches. It was superseded in 1974 by the Chief of the South African Defence Force Commendation Medal (SA21) for which it could be exchanged.*

VALUE:

A	B	C	Miniature
£25	£15	£10	£2

SA21. CHIEF OF THE SA DEFENCE FORCE COMMENDATION MEDAL (1974)

Instituted: 1974.
Ribbon: 32mm orange centre flanked by sky blue stripes and dark blue edges.
Metal: Bronze.
Description: A circular medal with concave curves between twelve points and a plain ring for suspension from a rectangular bar. In the centre, a beaded medallion of the South African Defence Force.
Comments: *Awarded to members of the SA Defence Force (an auxiliary service established to assist the SA Defence Force) who have distinguished themselves by rendering service of a high order which could not be suitably recognised in any other manner. In 1993 this medal was superseded by the Military Merit Medal.*

VALUE:

A	B	C	Miniature
£150	£100	£80	£12

Note: If awarded for downgraded gallantry award with citation: £50

SA22. MILITARY MERIT MEDAL

Instituted: 1993.

Ribbon: As for chief of SA Defence Force Commendation Medal (SA21).

Metal: Bronze plated brass.

Description: As for Chief of SA Defence Force Commendation Medal (SA21) but with fixed suspender.

Comments: *The medal replaced SA21 but with greatly enhanced status. The medal is now awarded to members of the SA Defence Force who have rendered outstanding service of vital importance/permanent significance of the highest order. Because of the anomaly of the previous title of the medal—only the State President and not the Chief of Defence Force could institute the medals, those who had been awarded the Chief of the SA Defence Force Commendation Medal were empowered to change the name of their medal to the new title and like the recipients of the new awards, could enjoy the post-nominal MMM. In 1993 a bar to denote a subsequent award was introduced. The bronze bar carries a centrally placed embossed protea emblem.*

VALUE:

A	A with bar	B	C	Miniature
£175	£200	£100	£80	£15

SA23. DANIE THERON MEDAL

Instituted: 1970

Ribbon: 32mm green with three narrow yellow stripes.

Metal: Silver.

Description: An eagle hovering over mountain peaks, with three stars on either side and DANIE THERON round the top and MEDALJE MEDAL at the foot. Scrolling spurs secure the medal to the plain suspension bar.

Comments: *This medal was named after the most famous Boer scout of the Anglo-Boer War 1899–1902. From 1970 to 1975, this medal was awarded to officers who were members of the commandos of the SA Defence Force, had completed not less than 10 years service in the SA Defence Force and had not yet received any other awards in recognition of outstanding devotion to duty or exceptionally diligent and outstanding service. In 1975, on the abolition of the Jack Hindon Medal, the Danie Theron Medal now covered the provisions of the Jack Hindon Medal. Recipients of the award are entitled to use the post-nominal DTM.*

VALUE:

A	B	C	Miniature
£150	£120	£100	£25

SA24. JACK HINDON MEDAL

Instituted: 1970

Ribbon: 32mm yellow with a narrow central green stripe and broad green stripes at the edges.

Metal: Bronze.

Description: An upright oval medal showing the sun rising over a mountain peak. In the foreground Jack Hindon and two companions unfurling the Vierkleur (Boer flag) during the battle of Spion Kop on January 24, 1900. Inscription JACK HINDON round the top, with MEDALJE MEDAL at the foot. Fitted with scrolled spurs to a plain suspension bar.

Comments: *This medal was named in honour of Captain Oliver John Hindon who fought for the South African Republic (Transvaal) against the British in the Boer war. (He was born in Stirling, Scotland on 20 April 1874 and he deserted from the British Army while serving in Natal in 1888, after severe treatment at the hands of an NCO of his unit. During the early part of the Anglo-Boer war, Hindon, now a citizen of the Transvaal Republic, was a member of Danie Theron's scout corps and was appointed to head a special corps whose function was to disrupt British lines of communication through the derailment of British trains and the cutting of telegraph lines. So successful was he that he became one of the Boer heroes of the war.) The conditions of this award are as the Danie Theron Medal (SA23) but the Jack Hindon medal was awarded to Warrant Officers, NCOs and other ranks. The medal was superseded by the Danie Theron Medal in 1975. Recipients are entitled to the post-nominal JHM.*

VALUE:

A	B	C	Miniature
£150	£120	£100	£20

SA25. COMMANDANT GENERAL'S MEDAL

Instituted: 1956.

Ribbon: 32mm in with, orange with 6.4mm sky blue edges and 6.4mm dark blue central stripe.

Metal: Oxidised silver.

Description: A laurel wreath enclosing a five-sided polygon divided into sectors. In the centre is a circle enclosing crossed rifles above a circular target and bushveld scenery. In the exergue is the inscription KOMMANDANT GENERAALS MEDALJE COMMANDANT GENERALS MEDAL. The top of the polygon has a fluted bar connecting it to the suspension bar decorated with laurel sprays.

Comments: *This medal was awarded for outstanding marksmanship. Subsequent awards of the medal are denoted by bars with a centrally placed silver button inscribed with the year of award. This medal was superseded in 1975 by the SADF Champion Shot Medal (SA26).*

VALUE:

A	B	C	Miniature
£150	£120	£60	£25

SA26. SADF CHAMPION SHOT MEDAL

Instituted: 1975.

Ribbon: As SA25.

Metal: Oxidised silver.

Description: Identical to SA25 except for the inscription in the exergue which now reads SAW KAMPIOENSKUTMEDALJE / SADF CHAMPION SHOT MEDAL.

Comments: *Awarded annually to the champion shot. Subsequent awards of the medal are denoted by bars with centrally placed silver button inscribed with the year of award. The award replaced the Commandant General's Medal (SA25).*

VALUE:

A	B	C	Miniature
£150	£120	£60	£25

SA27. CADET CORPS CHAMPION SHOT MEDAL

Instituted: 1987.
Ribbon: 32mm orange ribbon each side edged with a 6mm green stripe.
Metal: Silver.
Description: Obverse: A prancing springbok facing to the left enclosed on three sides by a wreath of laurels. Reverse: In semicircular format—top: GROOTKAMPIONSKUT, bottom: GRAND CHAMPION SHOT and centrally placed in two lines: KADETKORPS and CADET CORPS.
Comments: *The imaginative concept was that winners' achievements would not be lost on leaving school but they could mount this medal along with their SA Defence Force awards in after years. In 1994 the School Cadet Corps were abolished by the President of South Africa, so the award became obsolete. By that date, 16 awards had been made and these were backdated to 1978.*

VALUE:

A	B	C	Miniature
£100	£80	£50	£15

SA28. UNION MEDAL

Instituted: 1952.
Branch of service: Union of South Africa Permanent Defence Force.
Ribbon: 32mm equal stripes of orange, white and navy blue repeated three times to make a total of 9 stripes.
Metal: Silver.
Description: A scalloped medal with an ornamental suspender of wattle leaves and mimosa flowers. Obverse: Coat of arms of South Africa and the inscription UNION MEDAL—UNIE MEDALJE. Reverse: the Royal Cypher EIIR with crown.
Comments: *This medal was awarded to members of the Union Defence Force Permanent Force, irrespective of rank, for a minimum of 18 years service of an impeccable character. It was superseded in 1961 by the Permanent Force Good Service Medal. This medal replaced no. 253 except its award was extended to include commissioned officers as well. Approximately 1,400 medals were awarded. Those completing an extra 12 years service were eligible for a silver bar with centrally embossed coat of arms of South Africa. When the ribbon alone was worn the bar to the awards was represented by a miniature silver coat of arms.*

VALUE:

	A	B	C	Miniature
	£70	£60	£50	£15
with bar	£80			

Bar for 12 years

Ribbon emblem

SA29. PERMANENT FORCE GOOD SERVICE MEDAL

Instituted: 1961.
Ribbon: As for Union Medal (SA28)
Metal: Silver.
Description: A scalloped medal. Obverse as for SA28 except "UNION MEDAL—UNIE MEDALJE" has been removed. Reverse: carries details over seven lines: VIR LANGDURIGE DIENS EN GOEIE GEDRAG / FOR LONG SERVICE AND GOOD CONDUCT.
Comments: *Awarded for a minimum of 18 years service. A silver bar in the form of the republican arms was added to the ribbon for further periods of 12 years service (as for SA28). About 2,700 of these medals were awarded.*

VALUE:

	A	B	C	Miniature
	£40	£30	£25	£15
With bar	£50			

SA30. SOUTH AFRICAN DEFENCE FORCE GOOD SERVICE MEDAL

1st striking

Instituted: 1975.

Ribbon: 32mm green with different stripes according to the class and branch of service. In 1986 the nine ribbons were reduced to three: gold medal—green with two 7mm yellow stripes 6mm from each edge; silver medal—green edged with 7mm white stripes with a central 6mm white stripe; bronze medal—green edged with two 10mm bronze brown stripes.

Metal: Silver gilt/gilt coated brass for 30 years; silver/silver coated brass for 20 years; bronze/bronze coated brass/bronze sprayed on brass for 10 years. Some of the first issue were struck in 9ct gold.

Description: A scalloped medal bearing (obverse): the coat of arms of the Republic. (Reverse) the inscription VIR TROUE DIENS/FOR GOOD SERVICE. Ornamental suspender of wattle leaves and mimosa flowers.

Comments: *This medal superseded the Permanent Force Good Service Medal of 1961 (see SA29) and was divided into three classes, each having distinctive ribbons as follows:*

Gold Medal:
> *Permanent Force. Three narrow white stripes towards each edge*
> *Citizen Force. Three narrow blue stripes towards each edge*
> *Commandos. Three narrow orange stripes towards each edge*

Silver Medal:
> *Permanent Force. Two narrow white stripes towards each edge*
> *Citizen Force. Two narrow blue stripes towards each edge*
> *Commandos. Two narrow orange stripes towards each edge*

Bronze Medal:
> *Permanent Force. One narrow white stripe 2mm from edge*
> *Citizen Force. One narrow blue stripe 2mm from edge*
> *Commandos. One narrow orange stripe 2mm from edge.*

> *Members of the Citizen Force or Commandos had the option of choosing this series instead of the John Chard series for Citizen Force or the De Wet series for the Commandos. A silver gilt bar identical to the bar mentioned in SA28 and SA29 was awarded for 40 years service and this was sewn on to the ribbon of the 30 year medal. The reverse of the medal bears the title: VIR TROUWE DIENS/ FOR GOOD SERVICE in relief. In the first two strikings of this medal the suspender was decorated with wattle leaves and mimosa flowers on the obverse while the reverse of the suspension was plain.*

There are three strikings to each medal:
1st striking: SA Mint marks.
2nd striking: No Mint marks, no rim to the reverse while the bronze medal is brass coated with bronze and the gauge of the medals is almost 50 per cent thinner.
3rd striking: No Mint marks, reverse rim restored and medal of proper thickness with double faced suspension bar. Brass coated in gold, silver and bronze sprayed-on paint.

VALUE:

	A	B	C	Miniature
First striking:				
Gilt:	£50	£38	£35	£15
Silver:	£35	£30	£25	£12
Bronze:	£30	£25	£20	£5
Second striking:				
Gilt:	£45	£32	£30	£15
Silver:	£35	£27	£25	£10
Bronze:	£30	£22	£20	£5
Third striking:				
Gilt:	£40	£32	£30	£15
Silver:	£35	£27	£25	£10
Bronze:	£30	£23	£20	£5

SA31. SOUTH AFRICAN DEFENCE FORCE MEDAL FOR 40 YEARS DISTINGUISHED CONDUCT AND LOYAL SERVICE

Instituted: 1986.

Ribbon: 32mm green with central portion 1mm white, 3mm black, 3mm white, 3mm orange and 1mm white. In 1994 the ribbon was changed however, reducing the central portion to 10mm, 5x2mm stripes of blue, yellow, black, white and red.

Metal: 9 carat gold.

Description: Obverse: The embellished coat of arms of South Africa. Reverse: The Roman numerals XL within a circular laurel wreath open at the top and the medal suspended from a double faced scrolled suspender.

Comments: *This medal is awarded to all members of the South African Permanent Force, Citizen Force or Commandos for 40 years of meritorious and irreproachable service.*

VALUE:

A	B	C	Miniature
£300	£250	£120	£30

SA32. JOHN CHARD DECORATION

Instituted: 1952.

Ribbon: 32mm dark red with 3mm dark blue (outer) and 2mm white (inner) edges.

Metal: Silver / chromed brass.

Description: An upright oval medal fitted with a ring for suspension. The centre shows a view of Rorke's Drift in 1879. At the top is the inscription JOHN CHARD and at the foot DECORATION: DEKORASIE. See descriptions below for details of the various reverses.

Comments: *This decoration was named in memory of Lieutenant John Chard, VC, who commanded the garrison at the defence of Rorke's Drift during the Zulu War, 1879. The medal ribbon is worn with a silver button embossed with the initials JCD. The measurement from the top to bottom of the upright oval was designed to exactly match the proportions of the Efficiency Decoration (No. 236). A silver bar with crown (as for the Efficiency Medal) was awarded to denote an extra 10 years, i.e. 30 years service up until 1961. In 1962 a bar of silver with centred circle enclosing the initials JCD was awarded for 30 years service. Silver emblems indicate the branch of service: a fouled anchor on the ribbon for the navy, crossed swords for the army and an eagle with outstretched wings for the air force. Holders are entitled to the post-nominals JCD.*

VALUE:

Type	Description	A	B	C	Miniature
I	Royal cypher EIIR above SA coat of arms	£220	£120	£100	£30
II	Royal cypher erased	£100	£80	£60	£20
III	Large coat of arms of SA —voided acorn	£60	£55	£40	£10
IV	Unvoided acorn suspender and no rim on reverse, with coat of arms	£55	£50-	£40	£8
V	As for IV but metal chromed brass, with coat of arms	£45	£40	£30	—
VI	Reverse rim, voided acorn of poor detail and medal stamped silver, with coat of arms	£60	£50	£45	£8

SA33. JOHN CHARD MEDAL

Instituted: 1952.
Ribbon: As for John Chard decoration (SA32).
Metal: Bronze; bronze coated brass; brass sprayed with bronze paint.
Description: Identical to SA32 but with inscription MEDALJE: MEDAL round the foot.
Comments: *This medal replaced the Efficiency Medal and Air Efficiency Award. Silver emblems indicate the branch of service as in SA32.*

VALUE:

Type	Description	A	B	C	Miniature
I	Royal cypher EIIR on SA coat of arms	£170	£60	£40	£20
II	Royal cypher erased	£80	£50	£40	£10
III	Large coat of arms, solid bronze medal	£50	£28	£25	£4
IV	Unvoided acorn and no rim on reverse, bronze coated brass, with coat of arms	£50	£25	£20	£2
V	Poor detailed voided acorn, brass sprayed with bronze paint, with coat of arms	£35	£22	£20	£4

SA34. DE WET DECORATION

Instituted: 1965.
Ribbon: 32mm orange with a broad central blue stripe and 3mm green edges separated from the orange by narrow white stripes.
Metal: Silver.
Description: Two sprays of protea blossom enclose a vignette of General Christiaan De Wet, leader of Boer Forces in 1901–02, on horseback with the inscription DEKORASIE—DE WET—DECORATION round the top of the field, enclosed in a wreath of protea blossom. Foliate spurs link the top of the rim to a plain suspension bar.
Comments: *Awarded to all ranks of Commandos for 20 years service. An additional 10 years service is denoted by a silver bar with centrally placed circle with embossed initials DWD. Holders are entitled to the post nominals DWD.*

VALUE:

A	B	C	Miniature
£175	£100	£70	£15

SA35. DE WET MEDAL

Instituted: 1987.
Ribbon: 32mm central panel (made up of 7mm stripes of navy blue, yellow and navy blue), flanked by 3mm green and 2mm white stripes on either side.
Metal: Brass with lacquered bronze paint.
Description: As for De Wet Decoration (SA34) except inscribed MEDALJE—DE WET—MEDAL on the obverse. Suspender of similar design but double width and uniface.
Comments: *Awarded for 10 years service in the Commandos.*

VALUE:

A	B	C	Miniature
£85	£60	£40	£8

SA36. CADET CORPS MEDAL

Instituted: 1966.
Ribbon: 32mm orange with 5mm blue edges separated from the orange by 1.5mm white stripes.
Metal: Oxidised silver.
Description: A prancing springbok enclosed in a laurel wreath with the inscription CADET CORPS MEDAL and KADETKORPS MEDALJE at the sides.
Comments: *Awarded for 20 years service as an officer in the Cadet Corps. Those who had completed 30 years service were eligible for a silver bar with a prancing springbok embossed in the centre of the bar. It was abolished in August 1976 when the Cadet Corps ceased to exist as a separate force, being absorbed into the Commandos or Citizen Force.*

VALUE:

A	B	C	Miniature
£60	£45	£40	£20

SERVICE MEDALS

SA37. PRO PATRIA MEDAL

Instituted: 1974.
Ribbon: 32mm orange with a broad band of dark blue divided by a thin central orange stripe, with narrow white stripes towards the edges.
Metal: Brass with gilt finish.
Clasp: Cunene clasp awarded for operations into Angola in 1976, sewn on to the ribbon of the Pro Patria Medal.
Description: An eight sided medal with rectangular motifs in each sector with a central dark blue medallion depicting a stylised aloe plant in gold. It has a plain ring attached to a straight suspension bar with a protean emblem flanked by laurel sprays—type I and II have a link suspender whereas type III has a fixed suspender.
Comments: *Awarded for service in the defence of the Republic of South Africa or for suppression or prevention of terrorism with specified conditions of award. There are a number of variations in manufacture for type III.*

VALUE:

Type	Description	A	B	C	Miniature
I	Link suspender. SA Mint striking—serial numbers 1.25mm high	£500	£300	£200	
II	Link suspender	£70	£50	£35	£5
III	Fixed suspender	£50	£40	£30	£5
	With Cunene clasp	£80	£50	£40	£10
	(This value should be added to types I, II and III if there is a Cunene clasp)				

SA38. SOUTHERN AFRICA MEDAL

Instituted: 1989.

Ribbon: 32mm, central black stripe of 12mm centred with 2mm white stripe, flanked on either side with a 5mm red and 5mm yellow stripe.

Metal: Nickel silver.

Description: An eight sided medal with suspender ornamented with protea flower on each scrolled arm. Obverse: A leopard on the prowl beneath an acacia tree to indicate the strike power of the South African Defence Force. Reverse: A laurel wreath open at its uppermost point to embrace a small embellished coat of arms of South Africa, below are the words SUIDER-AFRICA/SOUTHERN AFRICA.

Comments: *The medal was awarded for participation in specified cross-border activities in defence of the Republic of South Africa. The award was to have originally been called the "Trans Jati Medal", the "Jati" being the cut line. The medals were to have been made from the metal of a captured Russian T34 tank but the metal was found to be unsuited for the purpose. Instead a small amount of melted metal from the tank was mixed with nickel silver. There were two strikings of the medal—the first with a uniface suspender struck as an integral part of the medal, the second with a double faced suspender attached to the medal.*

VALUE:	A	B	C	Miniature
Type I uniface suspender	£70	£50	£40	£10
Type II double faced	£150	£100	£60	—

SA39. GENERAL SERVICE MEDAL

Instituted: 1989.

Ribbon: 32mm, 6mm navy blue stripe, 2mm white stripe, 7mm orange stripe, 2mm navy blue stripe, then the first three stripes repeated in reverse.

Metal: Nickel silver.

Description: Obverse: A laurel wreath open at its uppermost point and enclosing the badge of the South African Defence Force which combines the swords, wings and anchor of the Army, Air Force and Navy, on an outline of the Castle of Good Hope. Reverse: The embellished coat of arms of South Africa with GENERAL SERVICE/ALGEMENE DIENS to the right and left of the coat of arms. Suspenders/strikings as for SA38.

Comments: *Originally the medal was awarded for service within the borders of South Africa from 19 August 1983, i.e. all members of the SADF. It was later extended to members of the SANDF who were involved in specific operations. These operations, which had to have a specific name, included service in Lesotho 1998–99 for which a silver bar "Maluti", sewn to the medal ribbon, was issued. Other operations included township duty as well as service in the Democratic Republic of the Congo, Burundi, Algiers, Mozambique, Zimbabwe and the Comorres.*

VALUE:	A	B	C	Miniature
Type I uniface suspender	£10	£7	£5	£10
Type II double faced	£100	£80	£50	—

With Maluti bar: £60 with certification; £40 without certification.
Documentary proof of service in the areas mentioned above would enhance the value of the medal. It is regrettable that no other bars were issued for the operational service mentioned.

COMMEMORATIVE

SA40. UNITAS MEDAL

Instituted: 1994.
Ribbon: 32mm, pale blue with central green stripe of 8mm edged each side by a white stripe of 4mm.
Metal: Lacquered brass.
Description: Obverse: A seven pointed star with central circle enclosing the Greek letter Alpha. Reverse: A small embellished coat of arms of South Africa with date 1994 below. The whole is enclosed by a circle made up of the word "Unity" in all eleven official languages of the new South Africa. Suspender is uniface and struck as one piece with the medal.
Comments: *Awarded to all those who rendered service through being members of a serving force (Permanent Force, Citizen Force, Commandos, members of the armed forces of the former self-governing territories, the armed wing of the ANC (the MK) and APLA) during the period of South Africa's first non-racial elections and inauguration of Mr Mandela as the first black State President in South Africa between 27 April and 10 May 1994. Those medals awarded to members of the British Military Advisory Team in South Africa at the time, for which Her Majesty Queen Elizabeth II granted permission for wear must be considered a rarity.*

VALUE:	A	B	C	Miniature
	£50	£30	£20	£10

MISCELLANEOUS

SA41. MENTION IN DESPATCHES

Instituted: 1967.
Metal: Gilt or bronze.
Description: A miniature replica of the embellished coat of arms of South Africa.
Comments: *Worn either on the ribbon of the Pro Patria Medal or General Service Medal. Prior to the institution of these medals, a bronze version was worn on uniform fabric of the tunic and not affixed to a medal.*

VALUE: A with Citation	A	B	C	Miniature
£40 to £50	£35	£25	£15	£8

SOUTH AFRICAN NATIONAL DEFENCE FORCE INTERIM AWARDS: 1996 TO 2003

In 1994 South Africa entered a new era when the ANC came into power after the Nationalist Government ceased to hold the reins of government. The armed forces underwent a period of transformation where former so called terrorists who had formed part of the armed wing of the African National Congress (MK, Mkhonto Wesizwe), and the Azanian People's Party (APLA, Azanian People's Liberation Army) had to be integrated into the armed forces of South Africa. In keeping with this, the South African Defence Force now became the South African National Defence Force.

Former MK and APLA members entered the SANDF with ribbonless chests. To remedy the situation 18 new medals were instituted for award to members of MK and APLA in 1996—two years after these forces had been disbanded. The awards recognised deeds of bravery or service before 27 April 1994. This decision had a South African precedent. In 1913 members of the armed forces of the old Boer republics of the Orange Free State and Transvaal had been absorbed into the newly formed Union Defence Force. Because of the outbreak of the First World War in 1914, an initiative to recognise the service and meritorious service of former members of the Boer Forces was postponed until 1920. That year the Dekoratie Voor Troue Diens (see MY339) and the Anglo-Boere Oorlog Medalje (MY340) were instituted.

The new awards for former MK and APLA members consisted of three bravery awards in three classes for MK with a corresponding allocation for APLA. Similarly three merit and three long service awards were allocated to MK and APLA. A list of the 18 new awards with post nominal titles is as follows:

• Bravery. MK Star for Bravery in Gold (SBG) Star for Bravery in Silver (SBS) Conspicuous Leadership Star (CLS)	• Bravery. APLA Gilt Star for Bravery (GSB) Bravery Star in Silver (BSS) Star for Conspicuous Leadership (SCL)
• Excellent Service, MK Gold Decoration for Merit in Gold (DMG) Merit Medal in Silver (MMS) Merit Medal in Bronze (MMB)	• Excellent Service, APLA Gold Decoration for Merit (GDM) Silver Medal for Merit (SMM) Bronze Medal for Merit (BMM)
• Long Service, MK Service Medal in Gold (SMG) (30 yrs) Service Medal in Silver (SMS) (20 yrs) Service Medal in Bronze (SMB) (10 yrs)	• Long Service, APLA Gold Service Medal (GSM) (30 yrs) Silver Service Medal (SSM) (20 yrs Bronze Service Medal (BSM) (10 yrs)

COMMENTS

1. Orange and red were used as the basic ribbon colour for the bravery awards; blue for merit and green for long service.
2. The design of the medals and structure of the award system was modelled on that of the SADF instituted in 1975 (see MY SA9 for bravery; MY SA15+16+22 for merit and MY SA30 for long service.)
3. The bravery awards design was a new departure: the MK awards being a five pointed star and the APLA awards a ten pointed star. The centre of the bravery awards has a roundel with the South African Lion.
4. The official coat of arms of the Republic of South African was placed on the reverse of all the new awards
5. The obverse of the merit and long service awards carry the symbols of MK (African shield with wheel of industry plus vertical spear and angled AK47 assault rifle) and APLA (African shield with crossed spear and AK47 assault rifle.)
6. The metal used for the bravery awards and "gold" merit and "gold" long service awards is silver, plated in gold "Enamel" work is in fact not enamel but epoxy covered paint. The obverse of all the medals was poorly struck with a very shallow die so that the design is virtually flat, on a level with the surface of the medal. The medal series gives the over-all impression of hasty preparation which was exactly what had occurred.
7. The medals were issued with a serial number and certificate (see introduction to SA Decorations and Medals regarding the pricing of medals (page 428).
8. In addition to bravery, merit and long service awards already detailed, two other medals were included in this section for service on internal or external active operations (or if you prefer it, campaign service by terrorists or freedom fighters—which ever way you see it). How ironic that the reverse of these medals should carry the coat of arms of South Africa 1910–2003, the country which was responsible for defeating MK/APLA forces in the field. Now that same body—The South African (National) Defence Force became the issuing authority. (In 2004 South Africa received a new computer generated and designed coat of arms.)

SOUTH AFRICAN NATIONAL DEFENCE FORCE NEW AWARDS 2003

The new honours and awards system was instituted on April 27, 2003. All recommendations after that date are to be for the new honours. The new decorations and medals will be issued to all ranks of the SANDF, to any auxiliaries of the SANDF and in certain circumstances to foreign military personnel.

1. Three decorations for bravery are as follows with post nominal titles: Golden Leopard (NG); Silver Leopard (NS); Bronze Leopard (NB). Bars are awarded for subsequent awards of the same decoration.

2. Three decorations for leadership, meritorious conduct or devotion to duty are awarded. Golden Protea (PG); Silver Protea (PS); Bronze Protea (PB) As is the case with the bravery awards, further awards of the same decoration are indicated by bars.

3. A single bronze long service medal replaces the previous awards for 10, 20 and 30 years service, in bronze, silver and gold. The Medal for Loyal Service will be awarded for ten years service, characterised by good conduct. For each additional period of ten years qualifying service, to a maximum of 40 years, extra bars will be awarded to represent each ten year period. For Reserve Force members, a monogram of the letters RD will be attached to the ribbon. These letters stand for "Reserve Distinction" to accord special recognition to part time members of the Reserves.

4. A campaign medal, the General Service Medal, will reward recipients for periods of operational service, minor campaigns and other operations

NOTE: As it will be some years before any of the new awards come onto the market, it has been decided not to illustrate them at this time.

POLICE AWARDS

All the awards listed have the words "SOUTH AFRICAN POLICE in their titles. Those listed here are the medals most commonly encountered by collectors. The information is taken from *Gallantry Awards of the South African Police 1913–1994* by Terence King assisted by Audrey Portman, by courtesy of Rhino Research. The book contains in-depth details of the gallantry medals listed.

SA42. STAR FOR OUTSTANDING SERVICE

Instituted: 1979
Ribbon: 36mm green divided by two stripes of yellow, blue and white.
Metal: Gilded silver
Description: A star composed of the cross of St Cuthbert, each limb notched of four and in each angle, an engrailed ray. (Obverse): in the centre, a white roundel bearing an aloe with three racemes. (Reverse): the unembellished coat of arms of the Republic of South Africa within the legend *STELLA OFFICII ENGREGII* SA POLICE. A bar denoting subsequent awards depicts an aloe with three racemes. A miniature replica of this clasp is attached to the ribbon when the ribbon alone is worn by a recipient who has been awarded a bar. All decorations and bars were issued named to the recipient and stamped with the serial number, rank and name.

Comments: *Awarded to a member of the South African Police or reserve police who: (a) in the execution of his duties in protecting or saving, or endeavouring to protect or save, life or property, has displayed particular gallantry, exceptional ingenuity, skill or perseverance; (b) in the execution of his duties has rendered outstanding services to members of a dynasty or to Heads of State or of Governments; (c) has distinguished himself through outstanding resourcefulness, leadership, and sense of responsibility or by setting a personal example in any branch of the Force. In addition, it could be awarded to any other persons who distinguished themselves through outstanding services rendered to the South African Police. This decoration was also awarded to recognize acts of gallantry as well as acts of outstanding service. In 1989 all references to gallantry were removed where they occurred in the original warrant, and the award was to officers of the general staff. This was in consequence of the institution of the 1989 version of the South African Police Cross for Bravery. Recipients of this decoration are entitled to use the post nominal letters SOE (STELLA OFFICII EGREGII).*

VALUE: Named £120   Unnamed £70   Awards for gallantry £1,000   *Miniature* £40 (add £5 for bar)

SA43. STAR FOR MERIT

Instituted: 1963.
Ribbon: 32mm, orange with white central stripe edged with blue.
Metal: Silver.
Description: (Obverse): two forearms with hands overlaying the letter V resting on the letter M and holding aloft a flame. (Reverse): the badge of the South African Police, with the words VERDIENSTE above and MERIT below. A silver bar with an embossed letter V resting on an M was authorised to denote a subsequent award or completion of 30 years service. When the ribbon alone is worn, the award of a bar is indicated by this circular emblem. All decorations and bars were issued named to the recipient and stamped with the serial number, rank and name.

Comments: *The award is granted to: (a) members of the South African Police or reserve police force who, in the discharge of their duties, have rendered services of a particularly meritorious or exemplary nature; (b) a member who has completed thirty years service (not necessarily continuous), and who has displayed an irreproachable character and exemplary conduct. The medal is also awarded to other persons (civilians) who have rendered services of a particularly meritorious nature to the South African Police. This medal is awarded for long service and good conduct as well as being a decoration for particularly exemplary or meritorious service (gallantry). The majority of awards to members of the police or reserve police were for acts of gallantry.*

VALUE: Named £45   Gallantry award £250–300   *Miniature* £20

SA44. MEDAL FOR FAITHFUL SERVICE

Instituted: 1963.

Ribbon: 32mm, royal blue with 3mm old gold centre stripe.

Metal: Bronze.

Description: (Obverse): the coat of arms of the Republic of South Africa surrounded by a laurel. (Reverse): the official badge of the South African Police with the words TROUE DIENS and FAITHFUL SERVICE in embossed capital letters around.

Comments: *This medal replaced the Police Good Service Medal and was awarded to members of the South African Police who had displayed an irreproachable character and exemplary conduct and served for a qualifying period. A bronze bar embossed with the letters TDFS (Troue Diens/Faithful Service) in ornamental script was awarded for subsequent qualifying periods.*

VALUE	Named	£20	Unnamed	£10	*Miniature*	£10

SA45. STAR FOR FAITHFUL SERVICE

Instituted: 1979.

Ribbon: 36mm, divided into 11 parts: yellow 2mm, green 3mm, yellow 4mm, blue 2mm, yellow 4mm, green 6mm, repeated in reverse.

Metal: Silver.

Description: A circular medal with (obverse): an eight-pointed star, charged in the centre with a medallion, with four aloes in cross, each with three racemes, all in natural colours. (Reverse): the official badge of the South African Police with the words TROUE DIENS and FAITHFUL SERVICE around.

Comments: *This medal was an award to complement the two long service and good conduct awards already in existence.The qualifying period changed over the years and a gold bar bearing the letters TDFS in ornamental script was awarded for further periods of service. Medals were now awarded for 10 years service (Medal for Faithful Service), 20 years service (Star for Faithful Service), 30 years service (Star for Merit) and 40 years service (Bar to Star for Faithful Service).*

VALUE:	Named	£25	Unnamed	£20	*Miniature*	£15

SA46. MEDAL FOR COMBATING TERRORISM

Instituted: 1974.

Ribbon: 31.75mm red, with three wide and two narrow silver stripes.

Metal: Silver.

Description: (Obverse): A six-pointed star, with three long and three short points. Attached to the ribbon by means of a V-shaped silver clevis, which is in turn attached to the medal by means of a rimmed shield depicting a candlestick aloe with four leaves and three candles. (Reverse): The words BEKAMPING VAN TERRORISME—COMBATING TERRORISM around the official badge of the South African Police. A silver bar was authorised to denote a subsequent award. This plain bar bears, in the centre, a silver clasp corresponding to the design on the shield. A maximum of two bars only can be awarded, irrespective of any further qualification period. All medals were issued named to the recipient with the serial number, rank and name stamped on the reverse of the V shaped clevis.

Comments: *Awarded to a member of the South African Police or others who, in support of the police, on or at any time after 26 August 1966 (a) had been involved in combat with terrorists, or in the course of the performance of duties in connection with the prevention and combating of terrorism, sustained injuries arising from terrorist activities; or who, in the execution of such duties, displayed exceptional zeal, ingenuity, skills or leadership; (b) had performed counter insurgency duties for at least six months, which may be cumulative, in an area (operational area) fixed by the Minister; (c) had rendered exceptional and outstanding service to the South African Police in connection with the combating of terrorism. The original qualifying period of six months was later changed to sixty days. Any member of the South African Police who was stationed permanently for a continuous period of at least twelve months in an operational area and behaved in an exemplary manner also qualified for the award of the medal.*

VALUE: Named £70   Unnamed £50   *Miniature* £12

SA47. 75th ANNIVERSARY MEDAL

Instituted: 1988.

Ribbon: Royal blue 32mm edged with light blue and old gold stripes.

Metal: Bronze.

Description: (Obverse): The figures "75", surmounted with an aloe with three racemes and the police motto "SERVAMUS ET SERVIMUS" above and the dates "1913-1988" below. (Reverse): The badge of the South African Police.

Comments: *Instituted to commemorate the 75th anniversary of the founding the South African Police on 1 April 1988. Awarded to permanent and temporary members of the Police Force and Reserve Police Force on 1 April 1988, or people who had rendered service of a particularly meritorious nature to the South African Police. A bar, bearing the figures "75" surmounted by an aloe and three racemes, is to be awarded to those still serving in the Force on 1 April 2013. All awards were issued named and were engraved on the reverse with the serial number, rank and name of the recipient.*

VALUE: Named £10   Unnamed £5   *Miniature* £15

SA47A. RECONCILIATION AND AMALGAMATION MEDAL

Instituted: 2005.

Ribbon: 32mm, stripes as follows: 4mm blue, 2mm yellow, 5mm green, 3mm white with central 4mm red stripe then the first four stripes are repeated in reverse.

Metal: Lightly sprayed matt brass.

Description: (Obverse): A flowering aloe (the central motif of the SAPS cap badge) surrounded by a laurel wreath. (Reverse): Centrally placed embellished coat of Arms (1910–2003) of the Republic of South Africa, below which is the date 15 October 1995, around the perimeter of the reverse is the full title of the medal.

Comments: *Instituted to commemorate the foundation of the South African Police Service which incorporated the South African Police and police forces of the various homeland states. It was awarded to all members of the SAPS (permanent and temporary members) who were serving on 15 October 1995. All awards were issued named with the serial number, rank and name of the recipient, on the reverse*

VALUE: Named £15 Unnamed £10 *Miniature* £3

SA47B. TEN YEAR COMMEMORATION MEDAL

Instituted: 2005.

Ribbon: 32mm, stripes as follows: 5mm blue, 2mm white, 4mm red, 3mm yellow, 4mm green, then the first four stripes are repeated in reverse.

Metal: Lightly sprayed matt brass.

Description: (Obverse): Crossed flags of the Republic of South Africa and SAPS. Above: the new post 2003 Arms of the Republic of South Africa. Below: the dates 1995–2005. (Reverse): Around the perimeter is the name of the medal, a centrally placed SAPS badge below which is an oblong panel with serial number of the medal. The number would correspond with the policeman's service number and name in an issue register/computer print out: a sad departure from the previous practice of naming medals to members of the SAPS.

Comments: *Instituted to commemorate the 10th anniversary of a Democratic South Africa and was awarded to permanent and temporary members of the Police Force and Reserve Police Force who were serving on 27 April 2005.*

VALUE: With certificate £15 without certificate £10 *Miniature* £3

SOUTH AFRICAN PRISONS AWARDS
(Later Department of Correctional Services)

An award system was set up in 1968 but was largely superseded in 1980 when
a new set of insignia was introduced—the medals included here are those most often
encountered by collectors.
All the following medals have the words "SOUTH AFRICAN PRISONS SERVICE" in their
correct title

SA48. DECORATION FOR VALOUR

Instituted: 1968.
Ribbon: Red with green edges divided by thin yellow lines..
Metal: Gold.
Description: A cross in the form of the Castle of Good Hope surmounted
on a star with suspender in form of a lifebuoy. Obverse: DEPARTMENT
VAN GEVANGENISSE / PRISONS DEPARTMENT at edge of medal
with a latin cross with scales of justice above and a lifebuoy on the
lower limb. Reverse: FOR VALOUR (top) and VIR DAPPERHEID
(below) together with the deed engraved below.
Comments: *Awarded to members of the SAPS who had displayed exceptional
bravery or courage in the performance of their duty. A bar with the medal's
obverse was awarded for subsequent acts of valour. Only six awards without
bars were made. Replaced in 1980 by the South African Prisons Service Cross
for Valour (Diamond and Ruby classes).*

VALUE: £750–1000   *Miniature*   £60

SA48A. MEDAL FOR MERIT

Instituted: 1968.
Ribbon: 35mm in width divided into seven parts: blue 6mm; white 5mm;
orange 6mm; white 1mm; then repeated in reverse.
Metal: Silver.
Description: Suspender in form of a lifebuoy. Obverse: DEPARTMENT
VAN GEVANGENISSE / PRISONS DEPARTMENT at edge of medal
with embellished South African coat of arms. Reverse: FOR MERIT
(top) and VIR VERDIENSTELIKHEID (below).
Comments: *Awarded to members of the SAPS who had rendered particularly
meritorious or exemplary service or distinguished himself by his ingenuity,
proficiency or perseverance for a period of not less than 35 years, displaying
irreproachable character and exemplary conduct. Impressed naming on reverse.
A plain bar of silver with the coat of arms of SA embossed in the centre was
awarded for subsequent acts of distinction. Replaced by SA51 (NCOs) in 1979.*

VALUE:

Named with bar	£75
Named	£40
Unnamed	£15
Miniature	£15

SA49. STAR FOR MERIT

Instituted: 1980
Ribbon: 32mm Green with two vertical white stripes each 2mm wide and 12mm from the side.
Metal: Silver.
Description: A 10-point cross with protea flowers in the angles and a plain ring for suspension from a straight bar.
Comments: *Awarded to Commissioned officers for outstanding services rendered on the grounds of ability, efficiency, perseverance or devotion in the discharge of duties. Post nominal title: SPM (Stella Pro Merito). 496 were issued.*

VALUE:
Named with certificate	£70
Named	£40
Unnamed	£20
Miniature (silver)	£20

SA50. CROSS FOR MERIT

Instituted: 1980.
Ribbon: 32mm green with three vertical white stripes each 2mm wide and 2mm from each other with the outer white stripes 11mm from each side.
Metal: Silver with gold plated border to cross.
Description: A cross pattée very similar to the German Iron Cross in appearance, but without any detail on the front. Fitted with a plain ring for suspension from a straight bar.
Comments: *No clasps granted for additional awards. Award conditions as for South Africa Prisons Service Star for Merit (SA49) but awarded to non-commissioned officers. Post nominal title: CPM (Crux Pro Merito). 2655 were issued.*

VALUE:
Named	£60
Unnamed	£30
Miniature	£20

SA51. MEDAL FOR MERIT

Instituted: 1980.
Ribbon: For Commissioned Officers: 32mm divided into seven parts— white 4mm; green 8mm; white 2mm; green 4mm and then repeated in reverse. **For NCOs:** 32mm, divided into nine parts; white 4mm; green 8mm; white 2mm; green 4mm white 2mm and then repeated in reverse.
Metal: Silver.
Description: A radiate star with an open protea floriate centre and an inverted V and ring for suspension from a straight bar.
Comments: *Same conditions of award as SA49 and SA50 except the word "outstanding" is replaced by "special". For the Officer's Medal the eight single rays are gold plated and the eight pairs of narrow rays are silver. The open protea flower in the centre is gold plated. The NCOs Medal is plain silver. 1,248 issued to officers and 5,059 issued to NCO's.*

VALUE:
Officer named	£45
NCO named	£45
Unnamed	£20
Miniature	£10

SA52. FAITHFUL SERVICE MEDAL

Instituted: 1965.
Ribbon: 31mm, divided into five parts: green 6mm; white 5mm; blue 9mm; and then repeated in reverse.
Metal: Silver.
Description: Obverse: coat of arms of the Republic of South Africa with the words DEPARTMENT VAN GEVANGENISSE—PRISONS DEPARTMENT. Reverse: VOOR TROUE DIENS—FOR FAITHFUL SERVICE.
Comments: *Awarded (1) for 18 years service (not necessarily continuous) that displayed exemplary conduct and unimpeachable character or (2) had displayed devotion to duty in a distinguished or gallant manner. This medal superseded No. 291. A bar with the words: VERDIENSTELIK/MERITORIOUS was granted for gallant or distinguished conduct.*

VALUE:

If awarded for (1)	£30
If awarded for (2)	£60
With bar	£75
Unnamed	£25
Miniature	£8

SA53. MEDAL FOR FAITHFUL SERVICE

Instituted: 1968.
Ribbon: 35mm divided into five parts: blue 6mm; white 5mm; green 13mm and then repeated in reverse.
Metal: Bronze.
Description: Obverse: In the form of the official badge of the Prisons Department with the circumscription DEPARTMENT VAN GEVANGINISSE (top) and PRISONS DEPARTMENT (bottom). Reverse: FOR FAITHFUL SERVICE (above) and VIR TROUE DIENS (below). In the central area the space received the engraved name, etc., and date of the award of the recipient.
Comments: *Awarded For: (1) as for (1) in SA52. (2) If the recipient had received SA52 for condition of 2 of SA52 then he would receive this medal on completion of 18 years service, etc. (3) If the recipient was in possession of SA52 after 18 years service he could receive this medal after a completion of a further 12 years. A bar of bronze with the Prisons Department badge in the centre denoted a further 15 years service following the award of the medal.*

VALUE:

Named	£25
Unnamed	£15
Miniature	£10

SA54. MEDAL FOR FAITHFUL SERVICE

Instituted: 1980.
Ribbon: 32mm yellow with two sets of three green stripes each 2mm wide and 2mm apart, the outer stripe set being 2mm from each edge (Gold); two sets of two green stripes each 2mm wide and 2mm apart, the outer stripe set being 2mm from each edge (Silver); or two green stripes each 2mm wide and 2mm from each edge (Bronze).
Metal: Silver-gilt, silver or bronze to denote 30, 20 or 10 years service.
Description: A circular medal with the arms of the Republic in the centre and a garland of protea blossom round the circumference.
Comments: *This replaced SA53. A silver-gilt bar for the gold medal was authorised, embossed with a central circle in the form of the obverse of the medal to indicate a further 10 years service.*

VALUE:

	Named	Unnamed	*Miniature*
With Bar to Gold	£55	£30	£10
Gold (1,130)	£40	£15	£6
Silver (5,594)	£25	£12	£6
Bronze (13,350)	£12	£8	£4

Gold ribbon.

Do you know about the Commemorative Medals available?

Award Productions Ltd has sponsored and issued nineteen* commemorative medals, all at the request of, or in conjunction with, a bona fide veteran group or charity which benefits considerably from the sales. We have been able to raise over £1,000,000 to date.

Each full-size medal is produced and struck in the United Kingdom to the exacting standards for which Award Productions has become internationally renowned and is fitted with a uniquely woven ribbon, complete with a concealed individual brooch bar ready to wear.

Cost approximately £39.50, *send no money now.*

Application forms and details of these and replacement medals are available by contacting:
Award Productions Ltd (Dept. MYB), PO Box 300, Shrewsbury SY5 6WP, U.K.
Tel: 01952 510053 Fax: 01952 510765 E-mail: info@awardmedals.com

Apply online at www.awardmedals.com

AWARD
PROUD TO SERVE

Over £550,000 raised to date for the Poppy Appeal

UNOFFICIAL MEDALS

Interest has been steadily growing in recent years in unofficial medals, a subject on the fringes of medal collecting. The term is deliberately vague and encompasses a very wide range of medals, medalets and medallions of a commercial, private or local nature. Such a generic term would, for example, include regimental medals awarded for marksmanship or good conduct, often associated with official medal groups of the 19th century. This is a very esoteric group, often consisting of medals which were specially engraved for the occasion and therefore exceedingly difficult to quantify.

On the other hand, many of the earlier medals, now highly regarded as forerunners of the general campaign series, were unofficial in origin, and relied upon the enterprise of public-spirited indviduals and prize agents such as Alexander Davison (nos. 78 and 85) or Matthew Boulton (no. 84), generals such as Elliot (no. 74), Earl St Vincent (no. 80) or Gordon of Khartoum (no. 133) or even private bodies such as the Highland Society (no. 83).

Then there is the large and fascinating group of civic or institutional medals which were presented to volunteers returning from the Boer War of 1899–1902. M. G. Hibbard, in his splendid monograph *Boer War Tribute Medals* (1982), recorded no fewer than 78 such medals, 40 from towns and cities in England, 25 from other parts of the United Kingdom and 13 from Commonwealth countries. Some of these were fitted with ribbons and were obviously intended for wear alongside the official medals of the war; others were 'danglers' intended to be fitted to watch-chains; and others still were not fitted with any form of suspension and were thus in the nature of commemorative medals intended purely as a memento of volunteer service.

So far as can be ascertained, such tribute medals were not produced in previous conflicts, which were predominantly fought by regular troops; and such was the scale of the involvement of volunteers and later conscripts in the First World War that the cost of providing civic medals of this nature would have been prohibitive. Instead, returning soldiers had to be content with some form of paper testimonial, at best. A notable exception was the gold medal presented by the Lord Mayor of London to the members of the anti-aircraft gun crews which shot down the first Zeppelin (listed below).

Apart from that, the Boer War group therefore constitutes a unique, but clearly defined group. They are, however, generally outside the scope of this YEARBOOK, although it should be noted that several medals in this category have long been accepted in the regular canon: the Kimberley Star (no. 154), the Kimberley Medals (no. 155), the Yorkshire Imperial Yeomanry Medal (no. 156) and the Medal for the Defence of Ookiep (no. 157). The reason for their acceptance is quite arbitrary, and just why the Yorkshire Imperial Yeomanry medal should be so highly regarded while others are not seems to rest on the fact that this medal is more commonly met with than the others—which is hardly a valid criterion.

For the sake of completing the record we have endeavoured to introduce a number of unofficial medals, particularly as groups including certain of these medals are coming onto the market and inevitably some purchasers are curious to know their origins.

In addition there are a number of other unofficial medals available to veterans such as the "Battle for Britain" medal with its various clasps but it is not the intention to make this a definitive guide, so we have decided to limit this section to those medals that were initially commissioned or supported by the relevant veterans associations and mainly produced in recent years in order to fill the gap left in the official series*.

Credit for reviving such medals must go to the Mayor of Dunkirk on whose initiative the medal awarded to survivors of the 1940 evacuation was instituted in 1965. Subsequently distribution of this medal was taken over by the Dunkirk Veterans' Association, applications being strictly limited to those who could prove that they had taken part in that historic event. This practice continued with the commissioning of the Bomber Command Medal by their Association (following a design competition in MEDAL NEWS) in response to the long-standing grievance of veterans of the Second World War who felt that their contribution to the ultimate victory had been deliberately ignored for political reasons. The success of this medal encouraged the production of similar awards for other categories of servicemen, or for campaigns which many felt should have had a distinctive campaign medal.

It must be stressed that all of these medals are available for purchase only by bona-fide veterans or their proven next of kin with sales also benefitting related charities. The wearing of these medals has always been a contentious issue, with many veterans choosing to wear them below but never alongside their official decorations.

*As many of the modern medals are still being struck, it has been decided not to give valuations for these.

U1. CHERRY MEDAL

Date: 1904.

Campaign: China, 1900–4

Branch of Service: Royal Navy.

Ribbon: Cherry red.

Metal: Silver.

Size: 38mm.

Description: (Obverse) a bare cherry tree with five naval officers in the foreground and a large number of other officers, all in frock coats, moving up in single file, with a scroll across the foot inscribed in Latin SUB HOC CERESO MANEMUS (under this cherry tree we remain); (reverse) a fouled anchor flanked by the Golden Fleece and a Chinese Dragon with the legend ARGONAUT CHINA 1900–1904 round the circumference. The medal is fitted with a plain suspension ring.

Comments: *The name of the medal and the colour of ribbon allude to Captain George Henry Cherry RN, commander of HMS* Argonaut *which served on the China Station in 1900-4. The five officers on one side of the tree represent the only ones remaining of the original number when the ship was paid off: Lieutenant Arthur Vernon Ross, Captain T. H. Hawkins RM, Chief Engineer A. W. Turner, Senior Engineer T. W. Cleave and Chaplain T. A. Dexter. The other line represents those officers who left the ship during the commission. The obverse motto contains a spelling error: CERESO instead of CERASO. This medal started off as a joke. Captain Cherry was a terrible martinet and his disgruntled officers felt that they deserved a medal for having to put up with him. It was designed by Miss Ross, sister of the senior watchkeeper, and struck by Gamage's of London. Only 100 medals were struck. Originally it was intended to be given only to the five officers who had stuck it out to the bitter end, but others complained and thus were awarded the medal with a bar indicating each year of service. Many years later, Admiral Cherry was offered one of the medals and graciously received it.*

VALUE: £175–225

U1A. EMIN RELIEF EXPEDITION STAR

Date: 1889.

Campaign: Sudan.

Ribbon:

Metal: Sterling silver.

Size: 50mm.

Description: A five-pointed star with a plain reverse and a central medallion bearing the monogram of the Royal Geographical Society, surrounded by an incuse inscription EMIN RELIEF EXPEDITION / 1887-9.

Comments: *This medal was awarded mainly to the Zanzibaris forming the bulk of the expedition organised in 1889 to discover the whereabouts of Emin Pasha, Governor of Equatoria, who had retreated south with Egyptian troops, officials and their families in the aftermath of the Mahdist revolt and the fall of Khartoum. The expedition, led by H. M. Stanley, located Emin and his followers in April 1888. Emin, in fact, refused to be relieved and the expedition not only failed in its primary objective but was a disaster, most Europeans and many Zanzibaris perishing before they returned empty-handed. The Royal Geographical Society commissioned the medals from Carrington. Some 200 were produced and of these 178 were issued to surviving members of the expedition. Of these, only nine were named to the recipients.*

VALUE: £450–550

U2. SECOND CRUISER SQUADRON MEDAL

Date: 1908.

Campaign: Goodwill tour of South America and South Africa.

Branch of Service: Royal Navy.

Ribbon: Pale blue.

Metal: Bronze.

Size: 36mm.

Description: (Obverse) a right-facing lady in Edwardian dress waving to distant ships, with the words SOUTH AFRICA and SOUTH AMERICA round the edge on either side of the suspender; (reverse) a seven-line inscription: 2ND CRUISER SQUADRON—GOOD HOPE, DEVONSHIRE, ANTRIM, CARNARVON—1908. The words CLOSER UNION appear at the sides.

Clasps: 14—Buenos Aires, Monte Video, Rio de Janerio, St Helena, Capetown, Simonstown, Port Elizabeth, East London, Ladysmith, Bloemfontein, Johannesburg, Pretoria, Pietermaritzburg, Durban.

Comments: *Privately issued and named to members of the goodwill cruise. It is uncertain how many medals were issued but they can be encountered with various combinations of clasps or none at all. It appears that there were two distinct strikings, the named examples being on a slightly thicker flan. The thinner, unnamed versions are believed to have been restrikes for specimen purposes. It is not known who funded or manufactured these medals.*

VALUE: **£125–350 dependent on number of clasps**

U2A. NATIONAL SERVICE LEAGUE MEDAL

Date: 1912.

Ribbon: White with a narrow central red stripe and narrow blue edges.

Metal: Bronze, silver or gold.

Size: 32mm (bronze) or 26mm (others).

Description: (Obverse) Standing figure of Britannia, helmeted and cloaked, her hands resting on the pommel of an unsheathed broadsword, with the inscription FOR KING AND COUNTRY round the upper part of the circumference. Fitted with a plain ring for suspension, with a brooch bar at the top of the ribbon inscribed NATIONAL SERVICE LEAGUE; (reverse) THE PATH OF DUTY IS THE PATH OF SAFETY and wreath.

Comments: *The National Service League was founded by Field Marshal Lord Roberts in the aftermath of the Boer war. The aim of the League was to warn Britain of the German menace and encourage young men to become proficient marksmen. Its wider aims were "to secure the legislative adoption of universal naval and military training for national defence". Ironically, Lord Roberts was proved right all too soon, and the League was dissolved in 1921.*

VALUE: **£50–75 (bronze), £200–300 (siler) £450–600 (gold)**

U2B. EMDEN MEDAL

Date: 1915.

Campaign: First World War.

Branch of Service: Royal Australian Navy.

Ribbon:

Metal: Silver.

Size: 60mm x 36mm.

Description: Mexican silver dollar surmounted by a crown and two concentric scrolls at the top inscribed NOV. 9. 1914 and HMAS SYDNEY / SMS EMDEN.

Comments: *Shortly after the outbreak of the War the Australian cruiser Sydney located the German light cruiser Emden in the Cocos Islands. After a brief engagement the Emden was boarded and captured. A quantity of Mexican silver dollars were found on board and these were subsequently mounted by the firm of W. Kerr of Sydney and presented to the crew of the Sydney as a memento of the action.*

VALUE: **£450–500**

U3. LORD MAYOR OF LONDON'S MEDAL FOR THE DESTRUCTION OF ZEPPELIN L15

Date: 1916.
Campaign: First World War.
Branch of Service: Royal Artillery.
Ribbon:
Metal: 9 carat gold.
Size: 29mm.
Description: (Obverse) the arms of Sir Charles Wakefield within a double ring inscribed PRESENTED BY THE LORD MAYOR round the top and COLONEL SIR CHARLES WAKEFIELD round the foot; (reverse) An anti-aircraft gun and two scrolls inscribed WELL HIT and MARCH 31st and number L15. It is engraved near the top with the rank and name of the recipient. It was issued unmounted but various ornamental suspensions loops were later fitted privately.
Comments: *The Lord Mayor of London offered a reward of £500 to the first gun crew to shoot down a Zeppelin. On 3 April 1916 Capt. J. Harris submitted a claim on behalf of the Purfleet gun crew that they were responsible for the bringing down of the airship L15, but it later transpired that gun crews from Abbey Wood, Dartford, Erith, North Woolwich, Plumstead and the Royal Arsenal, among others, were also involved. It was decided to use the prize money in procuring these medals, a total of 353 being awarded.*

VALUE: £1000–1500

U3A. HMAS *SYDNEY* MEDAL

Date: 1941.
Campaign: World War II.
Branch of Service: Royal Australian Navy.
Ribbon: none.
Metal: Oxidised silver.
Size: 57mm.
Description: (Obverse) HMAS *Sydney* in action; (reverse) 13-line inscription surmounted by a crowned anchor and flanked by laurel leaves at top and bottom.
Comments: *This medal, struck by Amor of Sydney, was presented by the citizens of Sydney to the officers and crew of HMAS* Sydney *which resulted in the sinking of the Italian cruiser* Bartolomeo Colleoni *on July 19, 1940. Some 640 medals were issued but most of them were lost when the* Sydney *sank in 1941.*

VALUE: £400–450

U4. DUNKIRK MEDAL

Date: 1960.
Campaign: Dunkirk evacuation, 1940
Branch of Service: All British and Allied forces.
Ribbon: Chrome yellow with one thin and one wide red stripe each side with two very thin black lines bisecting both sides.
Metal: Bronze.
Size: 36mm wide.
Description: (Obverse) a shield bearing the arms of Dunkirk (a lion passant above a heraldic dolphin) mounted on an anchor; (reverse) a circle bearing a burning lamp with DUNKERQUE 1940 beneath, surrounded by a laurel wreath and surmounted by crossed swords; the whole mounted on and surrounded by a laurel wreath.
Comments: *This medal was first made available to veterans of the Dunkirk evacuation and later administered by the now disbanded Dunkirk Veterans Association. It was created by the French National Association of Veterans of the Fortified Sector of Flanders and of Dunkirk and awarded in recognition of the sacrifice of 30,000 combatants between 29 May and 3 June 1940.*

VALUE: £60–70   *Miniature*   £10–15

U5. BOMBER COMMAND MEDAL

Date: 1985.
Campaign: Second World War.
Branch of Service: RAF Bomber Command.
Ribbon: Midnight blue with a central flame stripe and blue-grey edges.
Metal: Cupro-nickel.
Size: 36mm.
Description: (Obverse) A Tudor crown surmounting a laurel wreath containing the letters RAF, flanked by smaller wreaths containing the brevet letters of the aircrew signifying courage, team spirit and leadership; (reverse) a Lancaster bomber flanked by the dates 1939 and 1945 with inscription A TRIBUTE TO THE AIRCREW OF BOMBER COMMAND round the circumference.
Comments: *Produced at the behest of Air Vice Marshal Donald Bennett following a design competition in MEDAL NEWS. The competition was the brainchild of author Alan Cooper campaigning on behalf of Bomber Command veterans. The first medal was struck by Lady Harris (widow of the wartime commander of Bomber Command).*

U5A. ARMY CADET FORCE ANNIVERSARY MEDAL

Instituted: 1985.
Branch of Service: Army Cadet Force.
Ribbon: Red and blue separated by a thin yellow stripe.
Metal: Enamelled white metal.
Size: 55 x 85mm.
Description: (Obverse) the insignia of the ACF superimposed by figures of an officer and cadet shaking hands, the dates 1860 and 1985 flanking the motto at the foot. Fitted with a ring above the crown for suspension. (Reverse) plain, apart from the manufacturer's mark of Reu & Company of Heubach, Wurttemberg, Germany. A brooch bar in the form of a scroll 20mm deep is fitted to the top of the ribbon and bears a three-line inscription: ARMY CADET FORCE 125H ANNIVERSARY ONE DAY MARCH 26TH OCTOBER 1985.
Comments: *The medal was awarded to all members of the ACF who took part in the one-day march to celebrate the 125th anniversary of the Force.*

U6. NORMANDY CAMPAIGN MEDAL

Date: 1987.
Campaign: Service in the Normandy campaign between June 6 and August 20, 1944.
Branch of Service: All British and Allied forces.
Ribbon: Dark red with deep navy blue stripes towards the edges and light blue edges, symbolising the three services.
Metal: Cupro-nickel.
Size: 36mm.
Description: (Obverse) insignia of the combined services surrounded by 13 stars (representing the USA) and the inscription BLESSENT MON COEUR D'UNE LANGUEUR MONOTONE ("wounds my heart with monotonous languor"), a quotation from Verlaine broadcast by the BBC at 21.15 on June 5, 1944 to signal the start of the D-Day operations. (Reverse) a tank landing craft with its ramp on the beaches of France symbolised by fleurs-de lys; NORMANDY CAMPAIGN round the top and the date of the campaign inscribed on the ramp. The medal is fitted with a plain suspension bar while the ribbon bears a clasp inscribed NORMANDY between oak leaves.
Comments: *Commissioned by the Normandy Veterans Association whose Welfare and Benevolent Fund benefits from the proceeds of sales.*

U7. ARCTIC CAMPAIGN MEDAL

Date: 1991.
Campaign: Second World War.
Branch of Service: Personnel of the Russian convoys.
Ribbon: 32mm watered weave in equal stripes of blue and white representing ice and sea.
Metal: Cupro-nickel.
Size: 36mm.
Description: (Obverse) a liberty ship framed in the cross-hair of a U-boat periscope, with the inscription FOR SERVICE IN THE ARCTIC ZONE 1939-45 round the top; (reverse) four figures representing merchant seamen, Royal Naval, Army and RAF personnel, with the inscription THE ARCTIC CAMPAIGN round the top.
Comments: *This award was proposed by the Russian Convoy Club in conjunction with the North Russia Club who are the beneficiaries of the project.*

U8. MERCHANT NAVAL SERVICE MEDAL

Date: 1998.
Campaign: —
Branch of Service: Merchant Navy and DEMS Gunners.
Ribbon: Dark blue with a central narrow white stripe flanked by broader green and red stripes, representing the navigation lights of an approaching ship.
Metal: Cupro-nickel.
Size: 36mm.
Description: (Obverse) a stockless anchor encompassed by its heavy cable, surmounted by the initials MN; (reverse) a capstan surmounted by a naval crown and flanked by grotesque sea monsters, the whole encircled by a rope tied at the foot in a reef knot. The outer circumference is inscribed FOR MERCHANT NAVAL SERVICE. The medal is fitted to a plain suspension bar by an ornamental scroll.
Comments: *Veterans were eligible for this medal in respect of at least two years' service in the Merchant Navy. The award was inspired by the fact that although service in the mercantile marine was recognised after World War I and during World War II, it was ignored after World War II. King George's Fund for Sailors' benefits from the sale of this medal.*

U21. CAMERONIANS (SCOTTISH RIFLES) MEDAL

Instituted: 1999.

Branch of Service: Those who served in the regiment either as regulars or on National Service, including wives.

Ribbon: Three stripes of blue, black and dark green taken from the regimental tartan.

Metal: Silver-plated brass.

Size: 36mm.

Description: (Obverse) regimental badge of the Cameronians; (reverse) FOR SERVICE IN THE CAMERONIANS SCOTTISH RIFLES.

Comments: *The regiment was named in memory of the Covenanting leader Richard Cameron and was raised at Douglas, Lanarkshire in 1689. It later merged with the 90th (Perthshire) Regiment, at which point it adopted the Graham tartan.*

U22. BRITISH NUCLEAR WEAPONS TEST MEDAL

Instituted: October 3, 2004.

Branch of Service: Australian and British personnel involved in the testing of nuclear weapons in Australia from 1952 onwards.

Ribbon: White with a narrow central black stripe flanked by two shades of red.

Metal: Cupro-nickel.

Size: 36mm.

Description: (Obverse) depicts the nuclear symbol surrounded by the words "British Nuclear Weapons Test in Australia & Pacific". Fitted with a straight bar for suspension.

Comments: *The medal was produced by Award Productions in conjunction with the Australian and British Nuclear Tests Veterans' Associations.*

U23. ARABIAN SERVICE MEDAL

Instituted: 2005.

Branch of Service: Civil and Military personnel who served in Aden and other parts of Arabia.

Ribbon: Three equal stripes of blue, yellow and green.

Metal: Cupro-nickel.

Size: 36mm.

Description: Crossed daggers within a Saracenic arch border inscribed ARABIAN SERVICE / 1839-1967. A crescent and star attaches the medal to the bar suspension.

Comments: *Instituted by the Aden Veterans Association it commemorates British involvement in South Arabia from 1839 till the withdrawal of British forces in 1967.*

U24. BATTLE FOR MALTA MEDAL

Instituted: September 2005.
Branch of Service: Veterans who served in Malta or supplied the island between 1940 and 1943.
Ribbon: Two equal stripes of white and red.
Metal: Cupro-nickel.
Size: 36mm.
Description: The George Cross with inscription REUNION 7 60TH COMMEMORATION OF VICTORY IN MALTA IN WORLD WAR II.
Comments: *Commissioned by the Battle of Malta International Veterans Committee.*

U25. VIETNAM VETERANS MEDAL

Instituted: 2005.
Branch of Service: Commonwealth forces who served in Vietnam between 1960 and 1972.
Ribbon: Broad central yellow stripe with three thin red stripes superimposed, and green and dark blue stripes at the edges.
Metal: Gold-coloured alloy.
Size: 36mm.
Description: Dragon and soldier in combat gear, with VIETNAM VETERANS MEDAL round the circumference.
Comments: *Produced by Award Productions in association with Tasmedals for the Vietnam Veterans of Australia.*

U26. ACTIVE SERVICE MEDAL

Instituted: 2003.
Branch of Service: British and Commonwealth Forces.
Ribbon: Central white stripe, with red edges surrounded by yellow.
Metal: Gold plated bronze.
Size: 36mm.
Description: (Obverse) A serviceman draws his sword ready for action. Alongside him is the dove of peace. A number of clasps are available for this medal, stating where the recipient has seen his/her active service.
Comments: *This medal is produced for the benefit of SSAFA Forces Help on the initiative of G. E. Harris. It is manufactured by Bigbury Mint Ltd.*

U27. GENERAL SERVICE CROSS

Instituted: 1992.
Branch of Service: British and Commonwealth Forces who have served. in peacetime or during hostilities.
Ribbon: Equal bands of blue, white and red.
Metal: Hallmarked silver.
Size: 36mm.
Description: A Winged Lion carrying a trident is surrounded by the words "For General Service".
Comments: *The War Widows have benefited from the sale of this medal. The medal is manufactured by Bigbury Mint Ltd.*

U28. RAF BOY ENTRANTS COMMEMORATIVE MEDAL

Instituted: 2004.
Branch of Service: Royal Air Force.
Ribbon: Maroon.
Metal: Hallmarked sterling silver.
Size: 36mm.
Description: (Obverse) badge of the Royal Air Force Boy Entrants Association with 1994 10TH ANNIVERSARY RAFBEA 2004 round the circumference; (reverse) a four-bladed propeller with 1934-2004 70th ANNIVERSARY OF FOUNDATION OF BOY ENTRANT SCHEME round the circumference/
Comments: *Medal struck on behalf of the Boy Entrants Association by the Pobjoy Mint.*

U29. BORDER SERVICE MEDAL

Instituted: August 2006.
Branch of Service: British and Commonwealth forces on frontier duty throughout the world (Germany, Hong Kong, Cyprus, Northern Ireland, Malaysia, Borneo, Gibraltar, Belize, etc).
Ribbon: Green with a central red band.
Metal: Antique bronze.
Size: 36mm.
Description: (Obverse) a watch tower with a fortified border in the background; (reverse) the recipient's number, rank and name and place of service. .
Comments: *Produced by Martin Duchemin on behalf of Royal British Legion Industries.*

U30. OPERATION VIBRATTO COMMEMORATIVE MEDAL

Instituted: June 21, 1981.
Branch of Service: Military personnel of Allied Forces Southern Europe who came to the aid of victims of the earthquake of November 23, 1980 in Campania and Baslilicata, Italy.
Ribbon: A narrow blue central stripe, flanked by white stripes, with red, yellow and red, stripes on either side.
Metal: Bronze.
Size: 36mm.
Description: (Obverse) a female, fireman and soldier with arms raised in a supportive gesture towards the earthquake region; (reverse) equestrian statue and public building in Naples with the word BENEMERONZA (Merit) above and COMMISSARIATO STRAORDINARIO DELLA CAMPANIA E DELLA BASILICATA (Office of the Special Commissioner of Campania and Basilicata) round the circumference.
Comments: *About 100 medals were awarded to members of the Tri-Service British contingent based at Naples. Although accepted by the Ministry of Defence it may not be worn on the uniform of serving personnel.*

U31. BLACK WATCH MEDAL

Instituted: 2006.

Branch of Service: Service in the Black Watch (Royal Highland Regiment).

Ribbon: Dark blue, red and green.

Metal: Cupro-nickel.

Size: 37mm.

Description: (Obverse) the regimental badge with inscription THE BLACK WATCH / ROYAL HIGHLAND REGIMENT round the circumference; (reverse) FOR SERVICE TO THE BLACK WATCH x ROYAL HIGHLAND REGIMENT, 1739-2006. The ribbon is fitted with a brooch bar and suspended by a ring attached to the medal.

Comments: *The medal was struck by the Bigbury Mint.*

U32. ROYAL HIGHLAND FUSILIERS MEDAL

Instituted: 2009.

Branch of Service: Service in the Royal Highland Fusiliers.

Ribbon: Dark green and blue bisected by a thin yellow line.

Metal: "Golden" alloy.

Size: 36mm.

Description: (Obverse) the Royal Highland Fusiliers badge with the date 1959; (reverse) the new regimental badge of the Royal Regiment of Scotland with inscription ROYAL HIGHLAND FUSILIERS 50th ANNIVERSARY 1959–2009 round the circumference. The ribbon is fitted with a brooch bar.

Comments: *The medal was produced by ScotMint of Ayr to celebrate the 50th anniversary of the formation of the Royal Highland Fusiliers (after the amalgamation of the Highland Light Infantry and the Royal Scots Fusiliers).*

U33. LOWER SAXONY FIREFIGHTING MEDAL 1975

Instituted: 2009.

Branch of Service: Royal Engineers.

Ribbon: Red with a white stripe at centre.

Metal: Bronze coloured base metal.

Size: 30mm.

Description: (Obverse) a depiction of flames roaring through a forest; (reverse) the words WALDBRAND KATASTROPHE IN NIEDERSACHSEN AUGUST 1975. With ring suspension.

Comments: *This medal was officially presented by the Lower Saxony Land Ministry to members of the team of Royal Engineers who, with their Centurion tanks and bulldozers, helped dig fire breaks to stop a forest fire from spreading on Lunenburg Heath in August 1975.*

U34. ROYAL GREEN JACKETS COMMEMORATIVE MEDAL

Date: 2007.
Branch of Service: Royal Green Jackets.
Ribbon: Green with one red and one black stripe.
Metal: Silver.
Size: 36mm.
Description: (Obverse) Insignia of the Royal Green Jackets; (reverse) RGJ emblem with inscription and date of "coming out of the line" when the new regiment The Rifles were formed.
Comments: *Struck by the Bigbury Mint as an initiative with the RGJRA and available to all past members of the RGJ, RGJ-TA. Eligibility extends to members of the past regiments which made up the RGJ (43 & 52 The Ox & Bucks LI, KRRC and RB).*

U35. RHODESIAN INDEPENDENCE COMMEMORATIVE MEDAL

Date: 2009.
Branch of Service: Available to all those who lived in Rhodesia during its independence from November 11, 1965 until December 11, 1979.
Ribbon: Dark green with a central, wide white stripe.
Metal: Silver.
Size: 36mm.
Description: Roaring lion's head with inscription over.
Comments: *This unofficial medal was commissioned on behalf of the joint committee of the Rhodesian Army, Rhodesian Air Force and British South Africa Police Associations.*

U36. AFPS MEDAL

Date: 2009.
Branch of Service: Members of Parliament.
Ribbon: One stripe of crimson and one of green separated by a thinner yellow stripe, representing the House of Commons, the House of Lords and the Monarch.
Metal: Silver.
Size: 36mm.
Description: The Combined Services emblem surmounted by the Parliamentary portcullis badge.
Comments: *This unofficial medal was instituted by the Armed Forces Parliamentary Scheme to reward MPs who have carried out at least four annual 22-day commitments with the armed forces over a period of ten or more years.*

U37. CADET FORCES COMMEMORATIVE MEDAL

Date: 2010.
Branch of Service: Available to all those who served in the Cadet Forces, their next of kin or direct descendants.
Ribbon: Outer stripes of red, dark blue and light blue representing the Army, Air Force and Navy bounded by equal bands of yellow with a central green stripe.
Metal: Silver.
Size: 36mm.
Description: (Obverse) A fouled anchor, the L98-A1 Cadet GP Rifle and propellor with year dates; (reverse) mottoes of the various Cadet Forces.
Comments: *Produced by Award Productions Ltd to mark the 150th anniversary since the first Cadet Corps formed at Rossall School in 1860 as an army contingent to help the country's defence numbers following heavy losses in the Crimean War.*

U38. COLD WAR COMMEMORATIVE MEDAL

Date: 2010.
Branch of Service: For those who served in the Armed Forces of any country opposing the totalitarian regimes of the Communist Pact between 1945 and 1991 (next of kin or direct descendants also eligible).
Ribbon: Red, white and blue strip on the left representing the Allies and the bright red of the Soviet flag on the right.
Metal: Silver.
Size: 36mm.
Description: (Obverse) Rolled up flags of the three main players in the Cold War—the Soviet Union contained by the UK and US and dates 1945–91; (reverse) The Russian Bear on a wall clutching a missile with the Lion of the UK and the Eagle of the US repelling.
Comments: *Produced by Award Productions Ltd to pay tribute to those who served during this tense period of history. Ten per cent of the net cost of each medal sold will be donated to the National Cold War Exhibition at the RAF Museum Cosford.*

U39. BEVIN BOYS MEDAL

Date: 2009.
Branch of Service: The Bevin Boys Medal was commissioned by the Bevin Boys Association and as such is their official medal.
Ribbon: Black edged on both sides by a pale blue and green stripe.
Metal: Silver.
Size: 36mm.
Description: Colliery gantry with inscription over.
Comments: *The Bevin Boys medal is available to ballotees, optants, volunteers or next of kin called up between 1942 and 1948. There is no minimum length of service to be eligible for this medal but details of the training colliery and name of colliery worked, if known has to be provided. Struck by Bigbury Mint, a donation is made to the Bevin Boys Association from the sale of each medal.*

U40. THE TERRITORIAL ARMY CENTENNIAL MEDAL

Date: April 2008
Campaign: Available to all those who served or are currently serving in the TA or TAVR, their next of kin or direct descendants
Branch of Service: Territorial Army.
Ribbon: Diagonal green and yellow stripes representing the TA and the blue stripe the period 1967-1979 when the TAVR (Territorial Army and Volunteer Reserve) units were formed.
Metal: Gilt nickel.
Size: 36mm.
Description: An antique bronzed oval medal: (obverse) the monogram TA with the year dates 1908 and 2008 in an oak wreath; (reverse) the Army crossed swords symbol with the inscription TERRITORIAL ARMY CENTENNIAL MEDAL.
Comments: *Struck in association with The Resolution Project who are the beneficiary of this project.*

U41. THE COMMEMORATIVE SERVICE MEDAL

Date: September 2008
Campaign: Available to all those who served or are currently serving in any of the 19 Regiments and Services detailed below, their next of kin or direct descendants.
Branch of Service: Royal Navy, Army, Royal Air Force, Royal Marines, Royal Artillery, Royal Army Service Corps, Royal Engineers, REME, Royal Signals, Army Catering Corps, Light Infantry, Parachute Regiment, Royal Army Medical Corps, Royal Army Ordnance Corps, Royal Army Pay Corps, Royal Corps of Transport, Royal Military Police, Royal Tank Regiment and RAF Regiment.
Ribbon: Red for Army and Regiments, Navy Blue for Royal Navy, Green for Royal Marines and Air Force Blue for the RAF and RAF Regiment.
Metal: Silver-plated nickel.
Size: 36mm.
Description: (Obverse) Each medal bears the appropriate Regimental or Service emblem in the nickel silver plated centre framed by a 24 ct gold plated border; (gold plated reverse) a laurel wreath encasing the words FOR CROWN AND COUNTRY.
Comments: *The association of each Service or Regiment are the beneficiary of this project.*

U42. THE CADET FORCES FIRST AID MEDAL

Date: 2010.
Branch of Service: Cadet Forces.
Ribbon: Three stripes of dark blue (RN), red (Army) and light blue (ATC). The central red stripe edged with thin yellow stripes.
Metal: Nickel silver or gilt.
Size: 32mm.
Description: (Obverse) a Maltese cross surrounded by a laurel wreath and an outer legend; (reverse) blank but named to the qualifying participant.
Comments: *The gilt medal was awarded to winning teams in the ACF, ATC, CCF and SCC Cadet 150 2010 national first aid competitions. Nickel silver medals were awarded to qualifying participants in Cadet 150 Festival of First Aid 2010, or trained or supported teams for Cadet 150 Festival of First Aid 2010. Cadet 150 Festival of First Aid signifies any of the events held over the period October 16–17, 2010 including the national first aid competitions of each of the ACF, ATC, CCF and SCC, the Inter Services and St John Ambulance Young Grand Prior events. Nickel silver medals without Cadet 150 reverse engraving may also be issued for qualifying events in 2011 or later years. The medal is unofficial and may not be worn in uniform.*

ABBREVIATIONS AND INITIALS

The medal collector is constantly coming across initials and abbreviations on medals and in documents—many of which are commonplace and easily decipherable. However, there are many more which can cause problems when trying to identify a medal recipient. The following list represents only a small selection of the inexhaustible number of abbreviations encountered, but hopefully it will be of some assistance to the collector. The "Token Book of Militarisms" contains literally hundreds more if you cannot find the abbreviation you are looking for here.

1 E Ang	1st East Anglian Regiment		**AOC**	Army Ordnance Corps
1 R Dgns	1st Royal Dragoons		**APC**	Army Pay Corps
1 QDG	1st Queen's Dragoon Guards		**APL**	Aden Protectorate Levies
11H	11th Royal Hussars		**APTC**	Army Physical Training Corps
12L	12th Royal Lancers		**AQ**	Assistant Quartermaster; Administrative
13/18H	13th/18th Royal Hussars		**Armd**	Armoured
14/20H	14th/20th Royal Hussars		**ASC**	Army Service Corps; Air Service Command
15/19H	15th/19th Royal Hussars		**ATO**	Ammunition Technical Officer
3 E Ang	3rd East Anglian Regiment		**Aux AF**	Auxiliary Air Force
4 QOH	4th Queen's Own Hussars		**B&H**	The Bedfordshire & Hertfordshire Regiment
4H	4th Royal Hussars		**BAAT**	British Army Advisory Team
5 DGds	5th Royal Inniskilling Dragoon Guards		**BATT**	British Army Training Team
7QOH	7th Queen's Own Hussars		**BAO**	British Army of Occupation
7GR	7th Gurkha Rifles		**Bdr**	Bombadier
A/	Acting		**BDU**	Bomb Disposal Unit
A Avn	Army Aviation		**BEM**	British Empire Medal
Abn Inf	Airborne Infantry		**BF**	British Forces
A/CWEM	Acting Chief Weapons Engineering Mechanic		**BGS**	Brigadier, General Staff
			BIY	Bedford Imperial Yeomanry
A/LMEM	Acting Leading Marine Engineering Mechanic		**BM**	Brigade Major
			BORD.R	Border Regiment
A/LRO(G)	Acting Leading Radio Operator (General)		**BR**	British
A/PO	Acting Petty Officer, Acting Pilot Officer		**Brig**	Brigadier
A&SH	The Argyll and Sutherland Highlanders		**Br Coy**	Bearer Company
AAC	Army Air Corps		**BSA Police**	British South Africa Police
AAF, Aux F	Auxiliary Air Force		**Buffs**	The Buffs (Royal East Kent Regiment)
AAU	Air Ambulance Unit		**BW**	Black Watch (Royal Highland Regiment)
AB	Able Seaman; Airborne		**BWM**	British War Medal
ABDS	Army Bomb Disposal Squad		**C&TC**	Commissariat and Transport Corps
AC1	Aircraftman 1st Class		**C/Sgt**	Colour Sergeant
ACC	Army Catering Corps, Armoured Car Company		**C&S**	Command & Staff
			CAC	Canadian Armoured Corps
ACF	Army Cadet Force		**CADAC**	Canadian Army Dental Corps
ADALS	Assistant Director, Army Legal Service		**CAEA**	Chief Air Engineering Artificer
ADC	Aide de Camp		**CAHTC**	Cape Auxiliary Horse Transport Corps
AE	Army Education Officer, Air Efficiency Award		**CAMN HIGH**	Cameron Highlanders
			Capt	Captain
AER	Army Emergency Reserve		**CAR**	Central African Rifles
AFC	Air Force Cross		**CASC**	Canadian Army Service Corps
AFM	Air Force Medal		**CATO**	Commander Ammunition Technical Officers
AGS	Africa General Service Medal		**CB**	Commander of the Order of the Bath
AIF	Australian Imperial Force		**CBE**	Commander of the Order of the British Empire
AIY	Ayrshire Imperial Yeomanry			
ALO	Air Liaison Officer		**CBF**	Commander British Forces
ALS	Army Legal Services		**CC**	Cadet Corps; Coastal Command; Combat
AM	Albert Medal		**CCAEA**	Charge Chief Air Engineering Artificer
AM1	Air Mechanic 1st Class		**CCCC**	Cape Colony Cyclist Corps
AMA	Acting Master at Arms		**CCF**	Combined Cadet Force
AMS	Assistant Military Secretary; Army Medical Staff		**CCMEA**	Charge Chief Marine Engineering Artificer
			CCS	Casualty Clearing Station

C de G	Croix de Guerre	DFM	Distinguished Flying Medal
Cdr	Commander	DG	Dragoon Guards
CE	Canadian Engineers	DI	Defence Intelligence
CEO	Chief Executive Officer; Chief Education Officer	DLI	The Durham Light Infantry
		DMT	District Mounted Troops
CG	Coast Guard; Commanding General; Chaplain General	Dorset	The Dorset Regiment
		DOS	Director of Ordnance Services
CGC	Conspicuous Gallantry Cross	DS	Defence Secretary; Deputy Secretary; Defensive Section
CGM	Conspicuous Gallantry Medal		
Cheshire	The Cheshire Regiment	DSC	Distinguished Service Cross
CI	Crown of India, Imperial Order; Counter Intelligence	DSM	Distinguished Service Medal
		DSO	Distinguished Service Order
CIV	City Imperial Volunteers	DWR	The Duke of Wellington's Regiment
CIE	Companion of the Order of the Indian Empre	EAR	East African Rifles
CLY	County of London Yeomanry	ED	Efficiency Decoration
CMEM	Chief Marine Engineering Mechanic	EF	Expeditionary Force
CMFR	Commonwealth Monitoring Force Rhodesia	EGM	Empire Gallantry Medal
CMG	Companion of the Order of St Michael and St George	EM	Edward Medal; Efficiency Medal
		EOD	Explosive Ordnance Disposal
CMM	Commander of the Order of Military Merit	ERA	Engine Room Artificier
CMO	Chief Medical Officer	ERD	Emergency Reserve Decoration
CMMP	Corps of Military Mounted Police	ERE	Extra Regimentally Employed
CMP	Corps of Military Police	FA	Field Ambulance
CMSC	Cape Medical Staff Corps	FANYC	First Aid Nursing Yeomanry Corps
CMR	Cape Mounted Riflemen	FBRA	Field Battery Royal Artillery
CO	Commanding Officer	FC	Fighter Command
Col	Colonel	Fd	Field
Coldm Gds	Coldstream Guards	FARELF	Far East Land Forces
Comd	Commander	FF	Field Force
COS	Chief of Staff	FFL	French Foreign Legion
CP	Cape Police	FFR	Frontier Force Rifles
Cpl	Corporal	FL, F/L, Flt Lt	Flight Lieutenant
CPO	Chief Petty Officer	FM	Field Marshal
CPOAEA	Chief Petty Officer Air Engineering Artificer	FMR	Frontier Mounted Rifles
CPOWEA	Chief Petty Officer Weapons Engineering Artificer	FO, F/O, Fg Off	Flying Officer
		FS	Fighter Squadron; Field Security
CQMS	Company Quartermaster Sergeant	FS, F/S, Flt/Sgt	Flight Sergeant
CSI	Companion of the Order of the Star of India	Fus	Fusilier
CSM	Company Sergeant Major; Campaign Service Medal	G Howards	Green Howards (Alexandra, Princess of Wales's Own Yorkshire Regiment)
CT, C/T, Ch Tech	Chief Technician	G(OR)	General Staff Operational Requirements
CVO	Commander of the Royal Victorian Order	GBE	Grand Cross, Order of the British Empire
D	Diver	GC	George Cross
D Comd	Deputy Commander	GC, G/C, GpCapt	Group Captain
D&D	The Devon and Dorset Regiment	GCB	Knight Grand Cross Order of the Bath
DAD	Deputy Assistant Director	GCH	Knight Grand Cross Hanoverian Order
DADOS	Deputy Assistant Director of Ordnance Services	GCIE	Knight Grand Commander Order of the Indian Empire
DADVRS	Deputy Assistant Director Veterinary & Remount Services	GCLH	Grand Cross Legion of Honour
		GCM	Good Conduct Medal
DANS	Director of Army Nursing Services	GCMG	Knight Grand Cross Order of St Michael and St George
DAPM	Deputy Assistant Provost Marshall		
DAT	Director of Army Training	GCSI	Knight Grand Commander Order of the Star of India
DBE	Dame Commander, Order of the British Empire		
		GCVO	Knight Grand Cross Royal Victorian Order
DCLI	The Duke of Cornwall's Light Infantry	Gdsmn	Guardsman
DCM	Distinguished Conduct Medal	GLI	Guernsey Light Infantry
DCMG	Dame Commander of the Order of St Michael and St George	Glosters	The Gloucestershire Regiment (28th/61st Foot)
DCO	Duke of Cambridge's Own; Duke of Connaught's Own	GM	George Medal
		Gnr	Gunner
DCOS	Deputy Chief of Staff	GOC	General Officer Commanding
DCVO	Dame Commander of the Royal Victorian Order	Gordons	The Gordon Highlanders (75th/92nd Regiment)
DDSD	Deputy Director Staff Duties	GPR	Glider Pilot Regiment
DEO	Duke of Edinburgh's Own	GR	Gurkha Rifles
DERR	The Duke of Edinburgh's Royal Regiment (Berkshire & Wiltshire)	GS	General Service
		GSC	General Service Corps
Det	Detached; Detachment	GSM	General Service Medal
Devon	The Devonshire Regiment	GSO	General Staff Officer
DFC	Distinguished Flying Cross	HA	Horse Artillery

HAC	Honourable Artillery Company
HBM	Her Britannic Majesty
HCR	Household Cavalry Regiment
HG	Home Guard; Horse Guards
HLI	The Highland Light Infantry
HQ	Headquarters
IAOC	Indian Army Ordnance Corps
IASC	Indian Army Service Corps
IC	In Charge
IDSM	Indian Distinguished Service Medal
IE	Order of the Indian Empire
IG	Irish Guards
Int	Intelligence
Int Corps	Intelligence Corps
Int & Sy Coy	Intelligence and Security Company
IO	Intelligence Officer
IOM	Indian Order of Merit
IRC	Infantry Reserve Corps
ISM	Imperial Service Medal
ISO	Imperial Service Order
IY	Imperial Yeomanry
JSSC	Joint Services Staff College
KAR	King's African Rifles
KB	Knight Bachelor
KBE	Knight Commander, Order of the British Empire
KC	Knight Commander
KCB	Knight Commander Order of the Bath
KCH	Knight Commander of the Royal Hanoverian Guelphic Order
KCIE	Knight Commander Order of the Indian Empire
KCIO	King's Commissioned Indian Officer
KCMG	Knight Commander Order of St Michael and St George
KCSI	Knight Commander Order of the Star of India
KCVO	Knight Commander Royal Victorian Order
KDG	King's Dragoon Guards
KG	Knight of the Order of the Garter
KGL	King's German Legion
Kings	The King's Regiment (Liverpool)
KLH	Knight of the Legion of Honour
KM	King's Medal
KOM	Knight of the Order of Malta
KORB	The King's Own Royal Border Regiment
KOSB	The King's Own Scottish Borderers
KOYLI	The King's Own Yorkshire Light Infantry
KPM	King's Police Medal
KRRC	The King's Royal Rifle Corps
KSG	Knight of the Order of St George
KSLI	The King's Shropshire Light Infantry
KT	Knight of the Order of the Thistle
L/Cpl	Lance Corporal
L/Sgt	Lance Sergeant
LAC	Leading Aircraftman
Lanc Fusiliers	The Lancashire Fusiliers
Lanc R	The Queen's Lancashire Regiment
LC	Labour Corps
Leic	The Royal Leicestershire Regiment
LG	Life Guards; London Gazette
LI	Light Infantry
Linc	The Royal Lincolnshire Regiment
LM	Legion of Merit
LMA	Leading Medical Assistant
LS	Leading Seaman
LS&GC	Long Service and Good Conduct (medal)
Lt	Lieutenant
Lt-Cdr	Lieutenant Commander
Lt-Col	Lieutenant-Colonel
LVO	Lieutenant of the Royal Victorian Order
MA	Military Attache
Maint	Maintenance
Maj	Major
Maj-Gen	Major-General
Mal.LBC	Maltese Labour Corps
MBE	Member of the Order of the British Empire
MC	Military Cross
MEM	Marine Engineering Mechanic
MFA	Mercantile Fleet Auxiliary
MFS	Medical Field Service
MGC	Machine Gun Corps
MGS	Military General Service (medal)
MH	Medal of Honour
MI	Mounted Infantry
MID	Mentioned in Despatches
MKW	Military Knights of Windsor
MM	Military Medal; Medal of Merit
MMGS	Motor Machine Gun Service
MMWM	Mercantile Marine War Medal
Mne	Marine
MMR	Mercantile Marine Reserve
MR	Middlesex Regiment
MRCVS	Member Royal College of Veterinary Surgeons
MSC	Medical Staff Corps
MSM	Meritorious Service Medal
MTO	Motor Transport Office
MVO	Member of the Royal Victorian Order
NACS	Naval Air Commando Squadron
NAS	Naval Air Squadron
NCO	Non-Commissioned Officer
NFA	Natal Field Artillery
NGS	Naval General Service (Medal)
NZEF	New Zealand Expeditionary Force
OBE	Officer of the Order of the British Empire
OBLI	Ox and Bucks Light Infantry
OC	Officer Commanding
OCS	Officer Cadet School
OEO	Ordnance Executive Officer
OHBMS	On Her Britannic Majesty's Service
OM	Order of Merit
OR	Operational Requirements; Other Ranks; Organised Reserve
Ord	Ordnance
OS	Ordinary Seaman; Ordnance Survey
PAOCVA	Prince Albert's Own Cape Volunteer Rifles
PAVG	Prince Albert's Volunteer Guard
Para	The Parachute Regiment
PO	Petty Officer
PO, P/O, Plt Off	Pilot Officer
PO/AC	Petty Officer Aircrewman
POMA	Petty Officer Medical Assistant
POMEM	Petty Officer Marine Engineering Mechanic
PR	Public Relations
PSO	Personal Staff Officer
Pte	Private
PVCP	Permanent Vehicle Check Point
PWO	The Prince of Wales's Own Regiment of Yorkshire
Q Ops	Quartermaster General Branch Operations
QARANC	Queen Alexandra's Royal Army Nursing Corps
QCBA	Queen's Commendation for Bravery in the Air
QCBC	Queen's Commendation for Brave Conduct
QCVS	Queen's Commendation for Valuable Service
QCVSA	Queen's Commendation for Valuable Service in the Air
QFSM	Queen's Fire Service Medal
QDG	The Queen's Dragoon Guards

QGM	Queen's Gallantry Medal	RRC	Royal Red Cross (Medal)
QLR	The Queen's Lancashire Regiment	RRF	Royal Regiment of Fusiliers
QM	Quartermaster	RRW	Royal Regiment of Wales
QMAAC	Queen Mary's Army Auxiliary Corps	RS	The Royal Scots (The Royal Regiment)
QMS	Quartermaster Sergeant	RSDG	Royal Scots Dragoon Guards
QPM	Queen's Police Medal	RSF	Royal Scots Fusiliers
QRIH	Queen's Royal Irish Hussars	R Sig	Royal Signals
QSA	Queen's South Africa (Medal)	RSM	Regimental Sergeant Major
Queens	The Queen's Regiment—Queen's Division	RSO	Regimental Supply Officer
QVRM	Queen's Volunteer Reserves Medal	RTR	Royal Tank Regiment, Royal Armoured Corps
R Anglian	Royal Anglian Regiment	RUC	Royal Ulster Constabulary
R Fus	Royal Fusiliers (City of London Regiment)	RUR	The Royal Ulster Rifles
R Innis	Royal Inniskilling	RVM	Royal Victorian Medal
R Signals	Royal Corps of Signals	RVO	Royal Victorian Order
RA	Royal Artillery	RWF	The Royal Welsh Fusiliers
RAAF	Royal Australian Air Force	RWK	The Queen's Own Royal West Kent Regiment
RAC	Royal Armoured Corps	RW Kent R	Royal West Kent Regiment
RAChD	Royal Army Chaplains Department	S/L, S/Ldr, Sqn Ldr	Squadron Leader
RAEC	Royal Army Educational Corps	S/Sgt	Staff Sergeant
RAF	Royal Air Force	SAAF	South African Air Force
RAFVR	Royal Air Force Volunteer Reserve	SAC	Senior Aircraftman
RAMC	Royal Army Medical Corps	SAS	Special Air Service Regiment
RAOC	Royal Army Ordnance Corps	SC	Staff College; Staff Captain; Second in Command; Signal Corps
RAPC	Royal Army Pay Corps	SF	Special Forces
RARO	Regular Army Reserve of Officers	SG	Scots Guards
RASC	Royal Army Service Corps	SGM	Sea Gallantry Medal
RAVC	Royal Army Veterinary Corps	Sgmn	Signalman
R Aux AF	Royal Auxiliary Air Force	Sgt	Sergeant
RB	The Rifle Brigade	SI	Star of India (Order)
RCAF	Royal Canadian Air Force	SJAB	St John Ambulance Brigade
RCT	Royal Corps of Transport	SMIO	Special Military Intelligence Officer
RE	Corps of Royal Engineers	SMIU	Special Military Intelligence Unit
RECC	Reconnaissance Corps	Smn	Seaman
REME	Corps of Royal Electrical and Mechanical Engineers	SO1	Staff Officer, Grade 1
		Som LI	Somerset Light Infantry
RF	Royal Fusiliers	SWB	The South Wales Borderers
RFA	Royal Field Artillery	TA	Territorial Army
RFC	Royal Flying Corps	T&AVR	Territorial and Army Volunteer Reserve
Rfmn	Rifleman	TD	Territorial Decoration
RFR	Royal Fleet Reserve	TEM	Territorial Efficiency Medal
RGJ	Royal Greenjackets	TF	Territorial Force
RHA	Royal Horse Artillery	TFEM	Territorial Force Efficiency Medal
RHF	The Royal Highland Fusiliers	TFWM	Territorial Force War Medal
RHG	Royal Horse Guards	TG	Town Guard
RHG/D/	The Blues and Royals	Trg Gp	Training Group
RHIGHRS	Royal Highlanders	UKLF	United Kingdom Land Forces
RI	Royal Irish Rangers (27th (Inniskilling), 83rd and 87th)	UNM	United Nations Medal
		UNSM	United Nations Service Medal
RI Regt	Royal Irish Regiment	VA	Victoria and Albert (Order)
RIC	Royal Irish Constabulary	VC	Victoria Cross
RIF	The Royal Irish Fusiliers	VM	Victory Medal
RM	Royal Marines	WAAF	Women's Auxiliary Air Force
RMA	Royal Military Academy	WAFF	West African Frontier Force
RMC	Royal Military College	W/C, W/Cdr, Wg Cdr	Wing Commander
RMLI	Royal Marine Light Infantry	W&S	Worcestershire & Sherwood Foresters
RMP	Corps of Royal Military Police	WEA	Weapons Engineering Artificer
RN	Royal Navy	WG	Welsh Guards
RNAS	Royal Naval Air Services	Wilts	Wiltshire Regiment
RNASBR	Royal Naval Auxiliary Sick Berth Reserve	WO	Warrant Officer
RNF	The Royal Northumberland Fusiliers	WOI	Warrant Officer Class I
RNR	Royal Naval Reserve	WOII	Warrant Officer Class II
RNVR	Royal Naval Volunteer Reserve	WRAC	Women's Royal Army Corps
RNZAF	Royal New Zealand Air Force	WRAF	Women's Royal Air Force
RNWAR	Royal Naval Wireless Auxiliary Reserve		
RO	Radio Operator		
RPC	Royal Pioneer Corps		

CURRENT REGIMENTS

As many British medals carry the names of regiments that no longer exist, we list here all of the regiments of the British Army as published in the current Army List, together with their predecessors, and the dates of amalgamations and redesignations The current regiment title is indicated in bold type with former names underneath in normal type. Old regimental numbers are included in brackets.

Life Guards

1st Life Guards
2nd Life Guards
The Life Guards (1st & 2nd)

Blues and Royals
(Royal Horse Guards and 1st Dragoons)

Royal Horse Guards (The Blues)
Royal Dragoons (1st Dragoons)

1st The Queen's Dragoon Guards

1st The King's Dragoon Guards
Queen's Bays (2nd Dragoon Guards)

Royal Scots Dragoon Guards
(Carabiniers and Greys)

3rd Dragoon Guards (Prince of Wales's)
Carabiniers (6th Dragoons)
3rd/6th Dragoon Guards
3rd Carabiniers (Prince of Wales's Dragoon Guards)
Royal Scots Greys (2nd Dragoons)

Royal Dragoon Guards

4th Royal Irish Dragoon Guards
7th Dragoon Guards (Princess Royal's)
4th/7th Dragoon Guards
4th/7th Royal Dragoon Guards
5th Dragoon Guards (Princess Charlotte of Wales's)
Inniskillings (6th Dragoon Guards)
5th/6th Dragoons
5th Inniskillling Dragoon Guards
5th Royal Inniskilling Dragoon Guards

Queen's Royal Hussars
(The Queen's Own & Royal Irish)

3rd The King's Own Hussars
7th The Queen's Own Hussars
Queen's Own Hussars
4th The Queen's Own Hussars
8th The King's Royal Irish Hussars
Queen's Royal Irish Hussars

9th/12th Royal Lancers (Prince of Wales's)

9th Queen's Royal Lancers
12th Royal Lancers (Prince of Wales's)

King's Royal Hussars

10th Royal Hussars (Prince of Wales's Own)
11th Hussars (Prince Albert's Own)
Royal Hussars (Prince of Wales's Own)
14th King's Hussars
20th Hussars
14th/20th Hussars
14th/20th King's Hussars

Light Dragoons

13th Hussars
18th Royal Hussars (Queen Mary's Own)
13th/18th Hussars
13th/18th Royal Hussars (Queen Mary's Own)
15th The King's Hussars
19th Royal Hussars (Queen Alexandra's Own)
15th/19th Hussars
15th The King's Royal Hussars
15th/19th The King's Royal Hussars

Queen's Royal Lancers

16th The Queen's Lancers
5th Royal Irish Lancers
16th/5th Lancers
16th/5th The Queen's Royal Lancers
17th (Duke of Cambridge's Own Lancers)
21st Lancers (Empress of India's)
17th/21st Lancers

Royal Tank Regiment

Heavy Branch Machine Gun Corps
Tank Corps
Royal Tank Corps

Royal Horse Artillery

Royal Regiment of Artillery

Royal Field Artillery
Royal Garrison Artillery
Royal Malta Artillery

511

Corps of Royal Engineers

Royal Corps of Signals

Grenadier Guards

Coldstream Guards

Scots Guards

Irish Guards

Welsh Guards

Royal Regiment of Scotland / 7 battalions

Royal Scots (The Royal Regiment)(1)
Royal Highland Fusiliers (Princess Margaret's Own Glasgow and Ayrshire Regiment)(21, 71 & 74)
Royal Scots Fusiliers (21)
Highland Light Infantry (City of Glasgow Regiment)(71 & 74)
King's Own Scottish Borderers (25)
Black Watch (Royal Highland Regiment)(42 & 73)
Highlanders (Seaforth, Gordons and Camerons)(72, 75, 78, 79 & 92)
Seaforth Highlanders (Ross-shire Buffs, Duke of Albany's)(72 & 78)
Queen's Own Cameron Highlanders (79)
Queen's Own Highlanders (Seaforth & Camerons)(72, 78 & 79)
Gordon Highlanders
Argyll & Sutherland Highlanders (Princess Louise's)(91 & 93)
52nd Lowland Regiment
51st Highland Regiment

**Princess of Wales's Royal Regiment
(Queen's & Royal Hampshire)
(2, 3, 31, 35, 37, 50, 67, 70, 97 & 107)**

Queen's Royal Regiment (West Surrey)(2)
East Surrey Regiment (31 & 70)
Queen's Royal Surrey Regiment
Buffs (Royal East Kent Regiment)(3)
Queen's Own Royal West Kent Regiment (50 & 97)
Queen's Own Buffs (The Royal Kent Regiment)
Royal Sussex Regiment (35 & 107)
Middlesex Regiment (Duke of Cambridge's Own)(57 & 77)
Queen's Regiment
Royal Hampshire Regiment (37 & 67)

Royal Regiment of Fusiliers (5, 6, 7 & 20)

Royal Northumberland Fusiliers (5)
Royal Warwickshire Regiment (6)
Royal Warwickshire Fusiliers (6)
Royal Fusiliers (City of London Regiment) (7)
Lancashire Fusiliers (20)

**Royal Anglian Regiment
(9, 10, 12, 16, 17, 44, 48, 56 & 58)**

Bedfordshire & Hertfordshire Regiment (16)
Essex Regiment (44 & 56)
3rd East Anglian Regiment (16th/44th Foot)
Royal Norfolk Regiment (9)

Suffolk Regiment (12)
1st East Anglian Regiment (Royal Norfolk & Suffolk)
Royal Lincolnshire Regiment (10)
Northamptonshire Regiment (48 & 58)
2nd East Anglian Regiment (Duchess of Gloucester's Own Royal Lincolnshire & Northamptonshire)
Royal Leicestershire Regiment (17)

**Duke of Lancaster's Regiment
(King's, Lancashire and Border)
3 battalions**

King's Own Royal Border Regiment (4, 34 & 55)
King's Own Royal Regiment (Lancaster)(4)
Queen's Lancashire Regiment (30,40,47,59 81 & 82)
East Lancashire Regiment (30 & 59)
South Lancashire Regiment (The Prince of Wales's Volunteers)(40 & 82)
Lancashire Regiment (Prince of Wales's Volunteers)
Loyal Regiment (North Lancashire)(47 & 48)
Border Regiment (34 & 55)
King's Regiment (8, 63 & 96)
King's Regiment (Liverpool)(8)
Manchester Regiment (63 & 96)
King's Regiment (Manchester & Liverpool)(8, 63 & 96)

Yorkshire Regiment / 4 battalions

Prince of Wales's Own Regiment of Yorkshire (14 & 15)
West Yorkshire (Prince of Wales's Own) (14)
East Yorkshire Regiment (Duke of York's Own) (15)
Green Howards (Alexandra, Princess of Wales's Own Yorkshire Regiment) (19)
Duke of Wellington's Regiment (West Riding) (33 & 76)
Duke of Wellington's Regiment (33)
76th Regiment of Foot
Halifax Regiment

Royal Welsh Regiment / 3 battalions

Royal Welch Fusiliers (23)
Royal Regiment of Wales (24th/41st Foot)
South Wales Borderers (24)
Welch Regiment (41 & 69)
Royal Welsh Regiment TA

Mercian Regiment / 4 Battalions

Cheshire Regiment (22)
Worcestershire & Sherwood Foresters Regiment (29, 36, 45 & 95)
Worcester Regiment (29 & 36)
Sherwood Foresters (Nottingham & Derbyshire Regiment)(45 & 95)
Staffordshire Regiment (Prince of Wales's) (38, 64, 80 & 98)
South Staffordshire Regiment (38 & 80)
North Staffordshire Regiment (Prince of Wales's)(64 & 98)
The Mercian Regiment (Volunteers)

The Rifles / 7 battalions

Devonshire & Dorset Light Infantry (11, 39, & 54)
Devonshire & Dorset Regiment (11, 39, & 54)
Devonshire Regiment (11)

Dorset Regiment (39 & 54)
Royal Gloucestershire, Wiltshire & Berkshire Light Infantry (28, 49, 61, 62, 66 & 99)
Royal Gloucestershire, Wiltshire & Berkshire Regiment (28, 49, 61, 62, 66 & 99)
Wiltshire Regiment (Duke of Edinburgh's) (62 & 99)
Royal Berkshire Regiment (Princess Charlotte of Wales's) (49 & 66)
Duke of Edinburgh's Royal Regiment (Berkshire and Wiltshire)
Gloucestershire Regiment (28 & 61)
Light Infantry (13, 32, 46, 51, 53, 68, 85, 105 & 106)
Somerset Light Infantry (Prince Albert's) (13)
Duke of Cornwall's Light Infantry (32 & 46)
Somerset & Cornwall Light Infantry (13, 32 & 46)
King's Own Yorkshire Light Infantry (51 & 105)
King's Shropshire Light Infantry (53 & 85)
Durham Light Infantry (68 & 106)
Royal Green Jackets (43rd & 52nd, King's Royal Rifle Corps, Rifle Brigade)
Oxfordshire & Buckinghamshire Light Infantry (43 & 52)
1st Green Jackets (43 & 52)
King's Royal Rifle Corps (60)
2nd Green Jackets (The King's Royal Rifle Corps) (60)
Rifle Brigade (Prince Consort's Own)
3rd Green Jackets (The Rifle Brigade)
Royal Rifle Volunteers
Rifle Volunteers
2nd (Volunteer) Battalion The Royal Gloucestershire, Berkshire and Wiltshire Regiment
1st Battalion The Wessex Regiment (Rifle Volunteers)
2nd Battalion The Wessex Regiment (Volunteers)

Royal Irish Regiment (27th (Inniskilling), 83rd, 87th, and Ulster Defence Regiment)

Royal Inniskilling Fusiliers (27 & 108)
Royal Ulster Rifles (83 & 86)
Royal Irish Rifles (83 & 86)
Royal Irish Fusiliers (Princess Victoria's) (87 & 89)
Ulster Defence Regiment
Royal Irish Rangers
4th/5th Battalion The Royal Irish Rangers (Volunteers)

Parachute Regiment / 3 battalions

The Gurkha Brigade

The Royal Gurkha Rifles / 2 battalions

2nd King Edward VII's Own Gurkha Rifles (The Sirmoor Rifles)
6th Queen Elizabeth's Own Gurkha Rifles
7th Duke of Edinburgh's Own Gurkha Rifles
10th Princess Mary's Own Gurkha Rifle

Queen's Gurkha Engineers

Queen's Gurkha Signals

Queen's Own Gurkha Logistic Regiment
Special Air Service Regiment

Army Air Corps

Glider Pilot Regiment

Special Reconnaissance Regiment

Royal Army Chaplains' Department

Royal Logistic Corps

Royal Army Service Corps
Royal Corps of Transport
Royal Army Ordnance Corps
Royal Pioneer Corps
Army Catering Corps

Royal Army Medical Corps

Corps of Royal Electrical & Mechanical Engineers

Adjutant General's Corps

Adjutant General's Corps (Staff and Personnel Support Branch)

Royal Army Pay Corps
Women's Royal Army Corps (less those to Regiments)
Royal Army Ordnance Corps Staff Clerks
Regimental Clerks

Adjutant General's Corps (Provost Branch)

Royal Military Police
Military Provost Staff Corps
Military Provost Guard Service

Adjutant General's Corps (Education & Training Service Branch)

Royal Army Educational Corps

Adjutant General's Corps (Army Legal Branch)

Royal Army Veterinary Corps

Small Arms School Corps

Royal Army Dental Corps

Intelligence Corps

Army Physical Training Corps

Queen Alexandra's Army Nursing Corps

Queen Alexandra's Imperial Military Nursing Service
Queen Alexandra's Military Families Nursing Service

Corps of Army Music

Royal Military Academy Band Corps

TERRITORIAL ARMY
Units with titles different to Regular Units

Royal Monmouth Royal Engineers (Militia)

Honourable Artillery Company

Royal Yeomanry

Royal Wiltshire Yeomanry (Prince of Wales's Own)
Sherwood Rangers Yeomanry
Leicestershire and Derbyshire (Prince Albert's Own) Yeomanry
Kent and County of London Yeomanry (Sharpshooters)
Inns of Court and City Yeomanry
Westminster Dragoons (2nd City of London Yeomanry)

Royal Wessex Yeomanry

Royal Wiltshire Yeomanry (Prince of Wales's Own)
Royal Gloucestershire Hussars.
Royal Devon Yeomanry
Dorset Yeomanry

Royal Mercian and Lancaster Yeomanry

Queen's Own Warwickshire and Worcestershire Yeomanry
Staffordshire Yeomanry (Queen's Own Royal Regiment)
Shropshire Yeomanry
Cheshire Yeomanry (Earl of Chester's)
Duke of Lancaster's Own Yeomanry (Royal Tank Regiment)

Queen's Own Yeomanry

Queen's Own Yorkshire Yeomanry
Ayrshire Yeomanry (Earl of Carrick's Own)
Northumberland Hussars
Fife and Forfar Yeomanry (Scottish Horse)
North Irish Horse
King's Own Yorkshire Yeomanry (Light Infantry)

Engineer and Logistic Staff Corps Royal Engineers (Volunteers)

QUEEN'S DIVISION

3rd (Volunteer) Battalion The Princess of Wales's Royal Regiment (Queen's & Royal Hampshire

London Regiment

East of England Regiment

KING'S DIVISION

Lancaster and Cumbrian Volunteers

Tyne-Tees Regiment

East and West Riding Regiment

PRINCE OF WALES'S DIVISION

West Midlands Regiment

Kings and Cheshire Regiment

4th (Volunteer) Battalion The Parachute Regiment

ARMY AIR CORPS

7th Regiment Army Air Corps (Volunteers)

OTHER CORPS

Officer Training Corps

Royal Gibraltar Regiment

The Bermuda Regiment

SOME DISBANDED REGIMENTS WITH NO LOGICAL SUCCESSOR

22nd Dragoons
23rd Hussars
24th Lancers
25th Dragoons
26th Hussars
27th Lancers
Reconnaissance Regiment
Highland Regiment
Lowland Regiment
Royal Irish Regiment (18)
Cameronians (Scottish Rifles)(26 &90)
York and Lancaster Regiment (65)
Connaught Rangers (88 & 94)
Prince of Wales's Leinster Regiment (Royal Canadians) (100 & 109)
Royal Munster Fusiliers (101 & 104)
Royal Dublin Fusiliers (102 & 103)
Royal Guernsey Light Infantry
Royal Militia of the Island of Jersey
King's Own Malta Regiment of Militia
West India Regiment
Army Cyclist Corps
Machine Gun Corps
Army Remount Service
Cyprus Regiment
Royal Flying Corps
Royal Defence Corps
Queen' Mary's Army Auxiliary Corps
Auxiliary Territorial Service
Women's Royal Army Corps

RESEARCHING YOUR MEDALS

The fact that many British medals are named enables the serious collector to engage in researching both the life and service history of the recipient as well as being able to learn about the history of the regiment/ship/unit or whatever with which he served. There is no easy or definitive guide to the range of research materials that are available, nor to the range of information likely to be found. The sort of information available varies greatly depending on whether the recipient was an officer or other rank, the service and unit with which he served, and the period during which he served. The experience and perseverance of the researcher can also affect the outcome. For those who are new to research, or who live a long way from the original sources, it may be wise to employ a professional researcher, at least initially. The National Archives keep a list of independent researchers who undertake this kind of work.

When researching a medal and its recipient, experienced collectors regularly refer to a mixture of manuscript and printed sources:

Manuscript Sources

The National Archives, previously the Public Record Office (Ruskin Avenue, Kew, Surrey TW9 4DU) and the Oriental & India Office Collections (OIOC, British Library, 96 Euston Road, London NW1 2DB) are the two major depositories of official records of interest to the medal collector. Generally speaking the collector of medals to the British Armed Services will find the National Archive records essential to their enquiries, whilst anyone interest in the Indian Army and Navy (formerly the armed services of the Honourable East India Company), also the participation of British Forces in Indian campaigns, will find the OIOC to be an essential source of information. County Record Offices, Libraries and Museums, and also Regimental Museums can also have important holdings of manuscript records.

A first visit to the National Archive and the OIOC can be daunting. The range of records held by both Record Offices is also awe-inspiring once research has gone beyond consulting medal rolls and service papers.

Whilst there is no substitute for *experience* in learning successfully to branch out from the main stream of records, it is essential to be well prepared. It is important to have some idea of where to start looking and to realise the scope and limitations of the documents—it should be noted that the National Archive is subject to the standard 30 year closure rule for records, with many personal records being closed for longer periods. A great deal of time can be spent in simply locating the relevant references. To help you be more informed and to help eliminate time-wasting there are a number of important guides available that will aid in the location of the most relevant documents.

In addition it is worth noting that:

1. The National Archive produces a range of leaflets which provide useful information about particular classes of records—records relating to military, naval and air services are particularly well-covered. The leaflets are free to visitors.
2. The Mormons have published a wide range of guides to genealogical research which cover subjects of interest

to medal/military researchers.
3. The National Army Museum occasionally holds a study day on the subject of military research.
4. New information is becoming available all the time and in new forms.

Additionally, it is important to be aware that new documents are released periodically to public access. Probably the most important in recent years are those at the National Archive relating to World War I. Also there are a number of important websites of immense help to the researcher. Among these are: www.westernfront. co.uk (Western Front Association), www.crimeanwar. org (Crimean War Research Society), www.cwgc.org (Commonwealth War Graves Commission), www. nationalarchives.gov.uk (National Archives (Downloadable MICs), www.anglozuluwar.com (Anglo Zulu War Society), www.britishmedalforum.com (Medal Forum), www.bl.uk/ collections/orientaloffice.html (India Office).

Medal Entitlement/Verification

Most collectors start their research by checking with the campaign medal roll (if available) that the recipient is indeed entitled to the medal and any clasps. It is a logical point at which to begin. This is often regarded as a simple, routine procedure, but for the unwary there are pitfalls and complications. The following points should always be borne in mind:

1. Printed medal rolls will always contain errors in transcription, thus any discrepancies between a medal and the roll should, whenever possible, be checked back with the original manuscript roll. The more complex the original roll, the more transcription errors are likely to occur (for example, the claimants' lists for the Naval General Service Medal 1793-1840 and even the Military General Service Medal 1793-1814 are good examples of rolls where difficulties are likely to arise).
2. Some rolls have not survived—for example that for the Gwalior Campaign 1843. In such instances prize or bhatta rolls may exist at either the Public Record Office or the India Office. The inclusion of a recipient's name will at least indicate that he was most likely "entitled" to a medal and/or clasp (prize rolls indicate the share of money—realised from the loot captured in an action and then sold—allocated to each participant; bhatta is an extra allowance of pay made for field service).

3. Some medal rolls are incomplete, as with some of the regimental rolls for the Crimea Medal 1854–56.

4. With some campaign medal rolls, supplementary lists and late claimants' documentation have not survived.

5. Some medal rolls are difficult to search and therefore one has to take time in understanding the background to the documents one is looking at—the various lists of recipients for the Military General Service Medal 1794–1814 is a case in point.

It is important to note that the establishment of a recipient's entitlement is not the same thing as verifying a medal. Verification also requires the numismatic knowledge to know that the medal and clasps appear genuine. Where entitlement cannot be confirmed from the medal rolls, some collectors may be happy to rely on their numismatic knowledge to assure themselves that a medal is "genuine".

Published Sources

The published literature on medals is far-reaching and diverse, ranging from simply-produced booklets to detailed studies published in several volumes. A full bibliography of medallic and related works would in itself fill several volumes, particularly if fully cross-referenced.

The references which follow seek to provide a useful list of publications which either relate to orders, decorations and medals in general or to specific items in particular; the list includes medal rolls and casualty lists. No attempt has been made to include journal articles, as this would be an immense task; however a list of useful periodicals, some of which publish regular indexes, appears at the end.

Suggestions for other works that might be considered for inclusion in the next Yearbook are welcomed.

Most collectors seek to build up a solid library which reflects their main interests, but inevitably there are always books that have to be consulted elsewhere. Major libraries and national museums, such as the British Museum Library, the National Army Museum, the Imperial War Museum, the Hendon Royal Air Force Museum, the Greenwich Maritime Museum, and the Portsmouth Naval Musuem have extensive holdings of relevant material which can be consulted on the premises. City and County Reference Libraries are important for collectors who rarely visit London. Some Regimental Museums have libraries attached. Most libraries of any size will have a subject index to their collection of books (and sometimes manuscripts and photographs).

ORDERS, DECORATIONS AND MEDALS

GENERAL WORKS
(listed in alphabetical order by author)

Alexander, E. G. M., Barron, G. K. B. and Bateman, A. J., *South African Orders, Decorations and Medals* (1986).

Blatherwick, Surg. Cmdr. F. J., *Canadian Orders, Decorations and Medals* (4th edition, 1994).

Brine, F., *British Decorations from 1348 to the Present Time, Together with Those Given by Allies* (1880).

Buckman, Richard, *The Royal Sussex Regiment Honours and Awards* (2001).

Burke, J. B., *The Book of Orders of Knighthood and Decorations of Honour of All Nations* (1858).

Campion, Roger, *Police Medals of the World* (2002).

Central Office of Information, *Honours and Titles*. Part of the Aspects of Britain series.

Chapman, Roger, *Beyond Their Duty: Heroes of the Green Howards* (2001).

Coleman, E. C., *Rank & Rate–Royal Naval Officers Insignia Since 1856* (2009).

Downey, M., *The Standard Catalogue of Orders, Decorations and Medals Awarded to Australians* (1971).

Dymond, Steve, *Researching British Military Medals, a Practical Guide* (1999).

Eaton, Col. Hon. H.F. (later Lord Cheylesmore)., *Naval and Military Medals* (1897).

Elvin, C.N., *A Handbook of the Orders of Chivalry, War Medals and Crosses with Their Clasps and Ribbons and Other Decorations* (1892).

Floyd., J. B. (ed), *United States Decorations Awarded to the Armed Forces of the British Empire in World War II, Part I* (1997).

Gibson, J.H., *British War Medals and Other Decorations, Military and Naval* (1866).

Gibson, J.H., *British Military and Naval Medals and Decorations* (1880).

Gordon, Major L.L., *British Orders and Awards* (1959).

Hall, D.C. (in association with Wingate, C.), *British Orders, Decorations and Medals* (1973).

Hastings, Irwin D., *War Medals and Decorations* (1910).

Hieronymussen, Paul, *Orders, Medals and Decorations of Britain and Europe* (1967).

Hayward, J. B. & Son (pub.) *Honours and Awards of the Army, Navy and Air Force 1914-20* (1979).

Irwin, Ross W., *War Medals and Decorations of Canada* (1969).

Jocelyn, A., *Awards of Honour* (1956).

Johnson, Clive., *Australians Awarded* (2008).

Johnson, S. C., *Medals of our Fighting Men* (1916).

Johnson, S. C., *The Medal Collector* (1921).

Johnson, S. C., *Everybodys Medals: Including Medals, Decorations, Honours and Orders* (1914).

Jones, Huw M., *The Boiling Cauldron: Utrecht District and the Anglo-Zulu War* (2008).

Joslin, E., C., *The Observers Book of British Awards and Medals* (1974).

Litherland, A. R. and Simpkin, B. T., *Spink's Standard Catalogue of British Orders, Decorations and Medals* (1990).

McClenaghan, Tony, *Indian Princely Medals: A Record of the Orders, Decorations and Medals of the Indian Princely States* (1997).

Maton, Michael, *Honour the Air Forces (WWII)* (2004).

Maton, Michael, *Honour the Armies (WWII)* (2006).

Maton, Michael, *Honour the Navy (WWII)* (2007).

Maton, Michael, *Honour the Officers (WWI)* (2009).

Maton, Michael, *Honour Those Mentioned* (2010).

Maton, Michael, *The National Honours & Awards of Australia* (1995).

Mayo, J. H., *Medals and Decorations of the British Army and Navy* (1897).

McDonnell, J., & Medal Society of Ireland, *The Insignia of the Officers Training Corps in Ireland 1908-2007* (2009)

Mericka, V., *Book of Orders and Decorations* (1975).

Monick, S., *South African Military Awards 1912-1987* (1988).

Monick, S., *Awards of the South African Uniformed Public Services 1922-1987* (1988).

Morrissey, Paul B. and Westlake, William R., *British Orders, Decorations and Medals Awarded to American Forces for the Korean War* (2003).

Narbeth, Colin, *Collecting Military Medals* (1971).

Nicolas, N.H., *History of the Orders of Knighthood of the British Empire; of the Order of the Guelphs of Hanover, and of the Medals, Clasps and Crosses, Conferred for Naval and Military Services* (1842).

Oldham, G. P. and Delahunt, B., *Orders, Decorations and Medals Awarded to New Zealanders.* (1991).

Pamm, Anthony N., *Honours and Rewards in the British Empire and Commonwealth*, 2 vols. (1995).

Payne, A.A., *A Handbook of British and Foreign Orders, War Medals and Decorations awarded to the Army and Navy* (1911).

Purves, A.A., *Collecting Medals and Decorations* (1968).
Purves, A.A., *The Medals, Decorations and Orders of the Great War 1914-18* (1975).
Purves, A.A., *The Medals, Decorations and Orders of World War II 1939-45* (1986).
Purves, Alec A., *Orders, Decorations and Medals, a Select Bibliography* (1958).
Richardson, Matthew, *Tigers at Dunkirk: The Leicestershire Regiment and the Fall of France* (2010)
Sainty, Guy Stair and Heydel-Mankoo, Rafal , *Burkes Peerage and Gentry: World Orders of Knighthood and Merit* (2007)

Sampson, Geoff, *A Dictionary of the Battle of Britain
Steward, W.A., *War Medals and Their History* (1915).
Stiles, G. M. I., *Mayhem in the Med: A Chronicle of the Cyprus Emergency 1955-1960* (2010)
Tancred, G., *Historical Record of Medals and Honorary Distinctions* (1891).
Taprell-Dorling, Captain H. (ed. Alec A. Purves), *Ribbons and Medals* (1983).
Tinson, Lt-Col. Ashley R., *"Medals Will Be Worn", Wearing Medals Past and Present 1844–1999* (1999).
Tinson, Lt-Col. Ashley R., *Wearing Your Medals in Civilian Clothes* (2003).

ORDERS
(listed by the Order of Precedence)

GENERAL
Burke's Peerage & Gentry (pub.), *World Orders of Knighthood and Merit* (2007).
CB Printers Group (pub)., *Orders of Chivalry and Gallantry Awards* (1963).
De la Bere, Sir I. *The Queen's Orders of Chivalry* (1961).
Harbord, R.E., *Supplement to the Royal Family Orders, Badges of Office, Royal Household Medals and Souvenirs* (1954)
Hunter, John., *A Concise Description of the Insignia of the Orders of British Knighthood*
James, G.P.L., *The Royal Family Orders, Badges of Office, Royal Household Medals and Souvenirs* (1951).
Neville, D.G. *A History of the Early Orders of Knighthood and Chivalry.*
Patterson, Stephen, *Royal Insignia* (1996).
Risk, J.C., *British Orders and Decorations* (1973).

ORDER OF THE GARTER
Anstis, J., *The Register of the Most Noble Order of the Garter* (1724).
Ashmole, E., *The Institution, Laws and Ceremonies of the Most Noble Order of the Garter* (1672).
Ashmole, E., *History of the Most Noble Order of the Garter* (1715).
Begent, P. J. and Chesshyre, H., *The Most Noble Order of the Garter: 650 Years* (1999).
Beltz, G. F., *Memorials of the Most Noble Order of the Garter* (1839).
Buswell, J., *An Historical Account of the Knights of the Most Noble Order of the Garter* (1757).
Dawson, T., *Memoirs of St George The English Patron: And of the Most Noble Order of the Garter* (1714).
Fellowes, Rev. E.H., *The Knights of the Garter 1348-1939* (1939).
Harrison, A.P., *Order of the Garter: Armorial Registry of the Sovereign and the Knights of the Most Noble Order of the Garter—Their Names, Titles, Election, Instalment and Demise* (1845).
Heylyn, P., *The History of that Most Famous Saint and Soldier of Christ Jesus: St George of Cappadocia... The Institution of the Most Noble Order of St George, named The Garter. A Catalogue of all the Knights Thereof Until this Present* (1631).
Holmes, Grace, *The Order of the Garter: Its Knights and Stall Plates, 1384–1984* (1984).
Hope, W.H. St J., *The Stall Plates of the Knights of the Order of the Garter 1348-1485* (1901).
Leake, S.M., *The Statutes of the Most Noble Order of The Garter* (1766).

ORDER OF THE THISTLE
Innes of Learney, Sir T., *The Foundation of the Most Ancient and Most Noble Order of the Thistle* (1959).
Lyon King of Arms, Lord, and Warrack, J., *The Knights of the Most Ancient and Most Noble Order of the Thistle* (1911).

ORDER OF ST PATRICK
Galloway, Peter, *The Order of St Patrick & Its Knights* (1999).
Galloway, Peter, *The Most Illustrious Order* (1996).
Grierson, G.A. & Grierson, J.F., *Statutes and Ordinances of the Most Illustrious Order of St. Patrick* (1831).

ORDER OF THE BATH
Anstis, J., *Observations Introductory to an Historical Essay Upon the Knighthood of the Bath* (1725).
Perkins, Canon J., *The Most Honourable Order of the Bath* (1913).
Risk, J. C., *The History of the Order of the Bath and its Insignia* (1982).

ORDER OF ST MICHAEL AND ST GEORGE
Abela, A. E., *The Order of St Michael and St George in Malta* (1988).
Galloway, Peter, *The Order of St Michael and St George* (2000).

ROYAL VICTORIAN ORDER AND FAMILY ORDERS
Galloway, P., Martin, S., Pownall, H., Risk, J., Stanley, D. and Tamplin, J. *Royal Service, Volumes I–III* (1996, 2001/2).
Malloch, R. J., *The Royal Victorian Chain and Other Honors of the Sovereign,* (The Orders and Medals Society of America 1990).
Royal Victorian Order: Statutes and Lists of Members (1930).

ORDER OF THE BRITISH EMPIRE
Burke, *Handbook to the Order of the British Empire* (1921).
Galloway, Peter, *The Order of the British Empire* (1996).
Thorpe, A. Winton (ed.), *Burke's Handbook to the Most Excellent Order of the British Empire* (1921).

ORDER OF ST JOHN OF JERUSALEM
Bedford, W.K.R., and Holbeche, R., *The Order of the Hospital of St John of Jerusalem* (1902).
Fincham, H.W., *The Order of the Hospital of St John of Jerusalem and its Grand Priory of England* (1915).
The Grand Priory in the British Realm of the Venerable Order of the Hospital of St John of Jerusalem, *Roll of the Order 1931; Centenary Issue* (1936).
King, Col. E. J., *The Knights of St John in England* (1924).
King, Col. E. J., *The Knights of St John in the British Empire, Being the Official History of the British Order of the Hospital of St John of Jerusalem* (1934).
King, Sir Edwin, revised and continued by Sir Harry Luke, *The Knights of St John in the British Realm* (1967).
Luke, Sir H., *An Examination of Certain Claims to be an Order of St John* (1965).
Puddy, E., *A Short History of the Order of the Hospital of St John of Jerusalem in Norfolk* (1961).
Renwick, E.D., *A Short History of the Order of St John* (1959).
Tozer, C.W., *The Insignia and Medals of the Grand Priory of the Most Venerable Order of the Hospital of St John of Jerusalem* (1975).

DECORATIONS
(listed in alphabetical order by name of medal)

GENERAL

Abbott, P.E. and Tamplin, J.M.A., *British Gallantry Awards* (1981).

Abela, A.E., *Maltas George Cross and War Gallantry Awards.*

Bles, G (pub.) *Naval Honours and Awards 1939-1940*(1942).

Brown, G.A., *Commando Gallantry Awards of World War II.*

Campbell, G.L., *Royal Flying Corps (Military Wing)— Honours, Awards and Casualties 1914-17* (1917).

Campion, Roger, *The Call of Duty* (1997).

Chatterton-Dickson,W.W.F., *Seedie's List of Coastal Forces Awards for World War II.*

Chatterton-Dickson, W.W.F., *Seedie's List of Fleet Air Arm Awards 1939-1969.*

Chatterton-Dickson, W.W.F., *Seedie's Roll of Naval Honours & Awards 1939-59* (1990).

Chatterton-Dickson, W.W.F., *Seedie's List of Submarine Awards for World War II.*

Chatterton-Dickson, W.W.F., *Seedie's List of Awards to the Merchant Navy for World War II* (1997).

Clarke, John D., *Gallantry Medals and Decorations of the World* (1993).

Elson, J., *Honours and Awards: the South Staffordshire Regiment 1914-18* (2004).

Elson, J., *Honours and Awards: the Prince of Wales's (North Staffordshire) Regiment 1914-19* (2004).

Escott, Beryl, *20th Century Women of Courage* (1999).

Eyre, Philip, *Those Who Dared—Gallantry Awards to the SAS and Attached SBS Units 1941-46* (2002).

Greenhill (pub.) *South African Honours and Awards 1899-1902.*

Hayward J. B. & Son (pub.) *Honours & Awards to the Indian Army 1914-21* (1992).

Hayward J. B. & Son (pub.) *Honours & Awards of the Old Contemptibles* (1992).

Housley, C., *British Gallantry Awards to Sherwood Foresters* (1999).

Hypher, P.P., *Deeds of Valour Performed by Indian Officers and Soldiers During the Period from 1860 to 1925* (1927).

Jacob, J.R., *Court Jewellers of the World* (1978).

King, Terence, *Gallantry Awards of the South African Police 1913-94 including a Complete Roll of Honour,* (2000).

King, Terence and Portman, Audrey, *South African Police Medal of Honour for Courage and Faithfulness 1963-2001* (2001)

McInness, I. and Webb, J.V., *Contemptible Little Flying Corps* (1991).

Midland (pub.) *Tank Corps Honours & Awards 1916-19* (1982).

O'Shea, P., *An Unknown Few: The Story of Those Holders of the George Cross, the Empire Gallantry Medal, and the Albert Medals Associated with New Zealand.*

Pamm, Anthony N., *Honours and Rewards in the British Empire* (1995) (2 vols.).

Pitchfork, Graham, *Men Behind the Medals* (2004).

Royal Flying Corps: *Casualties and Honours During the War of 1914-17* (1987).

Stanistreet, A. *'Gainst All Disaster: Above and Beyond the Call of Duty* (1986).

Tucker, S/L N. G., *In Adversity—Exploits of Gallantry and Awards to the RAF Regiment and its Associated Forces 1921–1995* (1997).

Wilson, Sir A., and McEwen, Capt. J. H. F., *Gallantry* (1939).

ALBERT MEDAL

Henderson, D.V., *For Heroic Endeavour* (1988).

Oakley, Captain Derek OBE RM, *Albert Medals Awarded to Royal Marines* (2007)

Stanistreet, Allan, *Heroes of the Albert Medal* (2002).

CHIEFS' MEDALS

Jamieson, A.M., *Indian Chief Medals and Medals to African and Other Chiefs* (1936).

CONSPICUOUS GALLANTRY MEDAL

Cooper, A.W., *In Action With The Enemy: The Holders of the Conspicuous Gallantry Medal (Flying).*

Brown, G. and Penhall, R., *Conspicuous Gallantry Medal* (1977).

McDermott, P., *For Conspicuous Gallantry.*

DISTINGUISHED CONDUCT MEDAL

Abbott, P.E., *The Distinguished Conduct Medal 1855-1909* (1987).

Arnold, John *The African DCM* (2004).

Ashton, M., *The Canadian Medal Rolls—Distinguished Conduct and Military Medal (1939-45 & 1950-53).*

Brown, George A., *For Distinguished Conduct in the Field: The Register of the DCM 1939-92* (1993).

Mackinlay, Gordon, *True Courage: The Distinguished Conduct Medal to Australians 1939-1972* (1993).

McDermott, P., *For Distinguished Conduct in the Field: The Register of the DCM 1920-92* (1994).

Polaschek, A.J., *The Complete New Zealand Distinguished Conduct Medal* (1978).

Walker, R.W., *The Distinguished Conduct Medal 1914-20*(1981).

DISTINGUISHED CONDUCT MEDAL (AFRICAN)

Arnold J., *The African DCM to the King's African Rifles and the West African Frontier Force* (1998).

DISTINGUISHED FLYING CROSS

Carter, N. and C., *The Distinguished Flying Cross and How it was Won 1918–1995,* 2 vols. (1998).

Nelson, K. J., *The Royal Air Force Awards. 1918–1919*(2001).

DISTINGUISHED FLYING MEDAL

Ashton, M., *The Canadian Medal Rolls—Distinguished Flying Medal (1939-1945).*

Tavender, Ian, *The Distinguished Flying Medal: A Record of Courage* (1990).

Tavender, Ian, *The DFM Registers for the Second World War* (1999).

DISTINGUISHED SERVICE CROSS

Fevyer, W. H., *Distinguished Service Cross 1901-1938*(1990).

Witte, R. C., *Fringes of the Fleet and the Distinguished Service Cross* (1997).

DISTINGUISHED SERVICE MEDAL

Chhina, Rana, *The Indian Distinguished Service Medal* (2001).

Fevyer, W. H., *The Distinguished Service Medal, 1914–1920* (1982). *1939–1946* (1981).

DISTINGUISHED SERVICE ORDER

Creagh, General Sir O'Moore and Humphris, H.M., *The D.S.O.: A Complete Record of Recipients* (1978).

EDWARD MEDAL

Henderson, D.V., *For Heroic Endeavour* (1988).

EMPIRE GALLANTRY MEDAL

Henderson, D.V., *For Heroic Endeavour* (1988).

GEORGE CROSS

Ashcroft, Michael, *George Cross Heroes* (2010).

Bisset, Lieut. Colonel Ian, *The George Cross* (1961).

Dowling, Dr C., *The Victoria Cross and George Cross* (1970).
Hare-Scott, K., *For Gallantry—The George Cross* (1951).
Smyth, Sir J., *The Story of the George Cross* (1968).
This England (pub.), *The Register of the George Cross* (1990).

GEORGE MEDAL
Fevyer, W.H., *The George Medal*.
Henderson, D.V., *Dragons Can Be Defeated* (1984).
Henderson, D.V., *Fashioned into a Bow* (1995).
Turner, John Frayn, *The Awards of the George Cross 1940-2009* (2010)

INDIAN DISTINGUISHED SERVICE MEDAL
Chhina, Rana, *The Indian Distinguished Service Medal* (2001).

INDIAN ORDER OF MERIT
Hypher, P.P., *Deeds of Valour of the Indian Soldier Which Won the Indian Order of Merit During the Period From 1837 to 1859* (1925).
Parrett, Cliff and Chhina, Rana, *Indian Order of Merit* (2010)
Peterson, C., *Unparalleled Danger Unsurpassed Courage: Recipients of the Indian Order of Merit in the Second World War* (1997).

KING'S POLICE MEDAL
Farmery, J. P., *Police Gallantry: The King's Police Medal, The King's Police and Fire Service Medal and the Queen's Police Medal for Gallantry 1909–1979* (1995).

MILITARY MEDAL
Abbink, H. and C., *The Military Medal: Canadian Recipients 1916-1922*.
Ashton, M., *The Canadian Medal Rolls—Distingushed Conduct and Military Medal (1939-45 & 1950-53)*.
Bate, Chris and Smith, Martin, *For Bravery in the Field: Recipients of the Military Medal 1919-1939, 1939-1945* (1991).

VICTORIA CROSS
Arthur, Max, *Symbol of Courage* (2005).
Biggs, M., *The Story of Gurkha VCs*.
Billiere, Sir Peter de la, *Supreme Courage* (2005).
Chapman., Roger, *Beyond Their Duty, Hores of the Green Howards* (2001).
Clayton, Ann, *Chavasse, Double VC* (1992).
Clayton, Ann, *Liverpool Heroes Book I: The Stories of 16 Liverpool Holders of the Victoria Cross* (2008).

Clayton Ann, *Martin-Leake, Double VC* (1995).
Cooksley, Peter, *The Air VCs* (1998).
Creagh, General Sir O'Moore and Humphris, H.M., *The Victoria Cross 1856-1920* (1993).
Crook, M.J., *The Evolution of the Victoria Cross* (1975).
Dowling, Dr C., *The Victoria Cross and George Cross* (1970).
Gerard, M., *The Victoria Cross* (1892).
Hare-Scott, K., *For Valour—The Victoria Cross* (1949).
Harvey, David, *Monuments to Courage* (1999).
Haydon, A.L., *The Book of the Victoria Cross* (1906).
Hunt, Derek, *Valour Beyond All Praise* (2003).
Johnson, Barry, *Hook of Rorke's Drift* (2005).
Laffin, John, *British VCs of World War 2: A Study in Heroism* (1997).
Lee, P.H., *The Victoria Cross* (1912).
Lennox, Lord W., *The Victoria Cross: The Rewarded and Their Services* (1857).
Leyland, R., *For Valour: The Story of the Victoria Cross*.
Little, M.G., *The Royal Marines Victoria Crosses*.
May, P. R. S., *Beyond Five Points, Masonic Winners of the VC and GC* (2001).
Muddock, J.E., *For Valor—the Victoria Cross 1856-1895* (1895).
Mundell, F., *Stories of the Victoria Cross* (1890).
Mulholland, J. and Jordan, A., *Victoria Cross Bibliography* (1999).
Napier, Gerald, *The Sapper VCs* (1998).
O'Byrne, R.W., *The Victoria Cross* (1865).
Pillinger, D. and Staunton, A., *Victoria Cross Locator* (1991).
Parry, D.H., *Britain's Roll of Glory, or the Victoria Cross, Its Heroes and Their Valour* (1895).
Parry, D.H., *The VC, Its Heroes and Their Valour* (1913).
Perrett, Bryan, *For Valour* (2004).
RAMC Historical Museum, *The Medical Victoria Crosses*.
Sarkar, D., *Guards VC: Blitzkrieg 1940* (1999).
Smyth, Brig. Sir John, *The Story of the Victoria Cross* (1964).
Snelling, Stephen, *VCs of World War I: Gallipoli* (1995).
Stewart, Lt.Col.Rupert., *The Victoria Cross: The Empire's Roll of Valour* (1916).
This England (pub.), *Register of the Victoria Cross* (1988).
Toomey, T.E., *The Victoria Cross and How Won 1854-1889* (1889).
Toomey, T.E., *Heroes of the Victoria Cross* (1895).
Turner, J.F., *VCs of the Air* (1961); *. . . Army 1939-51* (1962); *. . . Royal Navy* (1956).
Uys, Ian., *Victoria Crosses of the Anglo-Boer War* (2000).
Wilkins, P.A., *The History of the Victoria Cross* (1904).
Williams, Alister W. *Heart of a Dragon, The VCs of Wales and the Welsh Regiments 1854-1902* (2008).

CAMPAIGN MEDALS
(listed in chronological order by date of campaign medal)

GENERAL
Carter, T. and Long, W.H., *War Medals of the British Army 1650-1891* (1972).
Douglas-Morris, Captain K.J., *Naval Medals 1793-1856* (1987).
Douglas-Morris, Capt K.J. *Naval Medals Vol. II 1856-1880*.
Hayward, J., Birch, D. and Bishop, R. *British Battles and Medals* (2006).
Johnson, Derek E., *War Medals* (1971).
Joslin, E.C., Litherland, A.R. and Simpkin, B.T., *British Battles and Medals* (1988).
Kerr, Major W.J.W., *Notes on War Medals 1794-1840* (1948).
Laffin, J., *British Campaign Medals*.
Long, W.H., *Medals of the British Navy* (1895).
Poulsom, Major N.W.A., *Catalogue of Campaign and Independence Medals Issued During the Twentieth Century to the British Army* (1969).
Power, J.R., *Identification Data on British War Medals and Their Interpretation* (1962).
Power, J.R., *Addenda and Corrigenda to Identification Data on British War Medals and their Interpretation* (1963).

Purves, A.A., *Some Notes on War Medals for the Collector* (1958).
Steward, W., Augustus, *War Medals and their History* (1915).
Vernon S.B., *Collector's Guide to Orders, Medals and Decorations* (With Valuations) (1990).
Williams, R.D. *Medals to Australians: with Valuations*.

MILITARY GENERAL SERVICE MEDAL 1793-1814
Caldwell, G.J., Cooper, R.B.E., *Rifle Green in the Peninsula, Vol. 1* (1998).
Foster, Col. Kingsley O.N., *The Military General Service Medal Roll 1793-1814* (1947).
Mullen, A.L.T., *The Military General Service Medal 1793-1814*.
Newnham, A.J., *The Peninsula Medal Roll 1793-1814* (privately produced).
Vigors, Lieutenant Colonel D.D. and Macfarlane, Lieutenant Colonel A.M., *The Three Great Retrospective Medals 1793-1840 Awarded to Artillerymen* (1986).
Wilson, B., *Canadian Recipients of the MGS, Egypt (1882-9) and NW Canada Medals*.

NAVAL GENERAL SERVICE MEDAL 1793-1840
Douglas-Morris, Captain K.J., *The Naval General Service Medal Roll, 1793-1840* (1982).
Hailes, Colonel D.A., *Naval General Service Medal Roll 1793-1840* (privately produced).
MacKenzie, Col R.H., *The Trafalgar Roll: The Ships and the Officers* (1989).
Message, C.W., *Alphabetical Naval General Service Medal Roll 1793-1840* (1995).
Newnham A.J., *Naval General Service Medal Roll 1793-1840* (privately produced).
O'Byrne, William, *Naval Biographical Dictionary* (2 vols, 1849).
Roberts, *The Trafalgar Roll* (1995).
Vigors, Lieutenant Colonel D.D. and Macfarlane, Lieutenant Colonel A.M., *The Three Great Retrospective Medals 1793-1840 Awarded to Artillerymen* (1986).

ARMY OF INDIA MEDAL 1799-1826
Gould, R.W. and Douglas-Morris, Captain K.J., *The Army of India Medal Roll 1799-1826* (1974).
Vigors, Lieutenant Colonel D.D. and Macfarlane, Lieutenant Colonel A.M., *The Three Great Retrospective Medals 1793-1840 Awarded to Artillerymen* (1986).

WATERLOO MEDAL
Caldwell, G.J., Cooper, R.B.E., *Rifle Green at Waterloo* (1990).
Dalton, C., *The Waterloo Roll Call* (1904).
Haythornthwaite, P. J., *Waterloo Men* (2000).
Lagden, A. and Sly, J., *The 2/73rd at Waterloo: Including a Roll of All Ranks Present, with Biographical Notes* (1998).

INDIAN CAMPAIGN MEDALS
Biddulph, Major H., *Early Indian Campaigns and the Decorations Awarded for Them* (1913).
Cook, H. C. B., *The Sikh Wars 1845–6, 1848–9* (1975).
Stone, A.G., *The First Afghan War 1839-1842 and Its Medals* (1967).
Punjab Campaign 1848–9 Casualty Roll.
The Army of the Sutlej 1845–6 Casualty Roll

SOUTH AFRICA MEDAL 1835-53
Everson, Gordon R., *The South Africa 1853 Medal Roll* (1978).
Sole, T.E., *The Military Casualties of South Africa: Vol 1 1834-1878.*

NEW ZEALAND MEDAL 1845-66
Cowan, J., *The New Zealand Wars* (2 volumes) (1969).
Gudgeon, T.W., *Heroes of New Zealand and Maori History of the War* (1887).
Longley, H.G., *The New Zealand Wars 1845-1866* (1967).
Stowers, R., *The New Zealand Medal to Colonials: Detailed Medal Rolls for the New Zealand Wars 1845–72* (1999).

INDIA GENERAL SERVICE MEDAL 1854-95
Parritt, Colonel B.A.H., *Red With Two Blue Stripes* (1974).

CRIMEA MEDAL 1854-56
Caldwell, G.J., Cooper, R.B.E., *Rifle Green in the Crimea* (1996).
Cook, F. and Cook, A., *Casualty Roll for the Crimea 1854-55* (1976).
Duckers, P. and Mitchell, N., *The Azoff Campaign 1855* (1997).
Lummis, Canon W.M., *Honour the Light Brigade* (1973).
Mitchell, N. and Duckers, P., *Presented to the Queen: The Crimea Medal Award Ceremony, 18 May 1855* (1996).
Research Publications and Productions (pub.), *Returns Relating to Officers of the Army in the Crimea* (1989).
Savannah Publications (pubs.), *Casualty Roll for the Crimea 1854-55* (1999).

INDIA MUTINY MEDAL 1857-59
Asplin, K. J., *Indian Mutiny Medal Roll (British Forces)* (1999).
Tavender, I.T., *Casualty Roll for the India Mutiny 1857-59* (1983).

CANADA GENERAL SERVICE MEDAL 1866-70
Neale, G. N. and Irwin, R. W., *The Medal Roll of the Red River Campaign in 1870 in Canada* (1982).
Thyen, R., *Canada General Service Medal Roll 1866–70* (1999).

ABYSSINIAN WAR MEDAL 1867–68
Bates, Darrell, *The Abyssinian Difficulty* (1979).

SOUTH AFRICA MEDAL 1877-79
Dutton, R. *Zulu & Basuto Wars, Including complete Medal Roll 1877-8-9.* (2010).
Forsyth, D.R., *South African War Medal 1877-8-9: The Medal Roll.*
Greaves, Adrian and Knight, Ian, *Who's who in the Zulu War 1879: Part 1 The British* (2007)
Holme, N., *The Silver Wreath. The 24th Regiment at Isandhlwana and Rorke's Drift 1879* (1979).
Knight, Ian, *Brave Men's Blood* (1990).
Knight, Ian, *Zulu: Isandlwana and Rorke's Drift 22nd–23rd January 1879* (1997).
Knight, Ian, *Companion to the Anglo Zulu War* (2008)
Mackinnon, J.P. and Shadbolt, S.H., *The South Africa Campaign of 1879* (1882).
Sole, T.E. *The Military Casualties of South Africa: Vol. 1 1834-1878.*
Tavender, I.T., *Casualty Roll for the Zulu and Basuto Wars, South Africa 1877-79* (1985).
Whybra, J., *The Roll Call for Isandhlwana and Rorke's Drift* (1990).
Holme, N., *The Noble 24th, Biographical Records of the 24th Regiment in the Zulu War and the South African Campaigns 1877–1879* (2000).

AFGHANISTAN MEDAL 1878-80
Farrington, A., *The Second Afghan War 1878-80 Casualty Roll* (1986).
Robson, Brian, *The Road to Kabul: The Second Afghan War 1878–1881* (1986).
Shadbolt, S.H., *The Afghanistan Campaigns of 1878-80* (1882).

CAPE OF GOOD HOPE GS MEDAL 1880-97
Forsyth, D.R., *Cape of Good Hope General Service Medal: The Medal Roll.*

EGYPT MEDAL 1882-89
Maurice, Colonel J.F., *The Campaign of 1882 in Egypt.*
Webb, J.V., *Abu Klea Medal Roll.*

KHARTOUM STAR 1884
Fearon, D., *General Gordon's Khartoum Star* (1967).

NORTH WEST CANADA MEDAL 1885
Pacific Publishing Co (pub.), *North-West Canada Medal Roll (The Riel Rebellion 1885)* (1974).

BRITISH SOUTH AFRICA CO. MEDAL 1890-97
Forsyth, D.R., *British South Africa Co. Medal 1890-1897.*
Owen, C.R., *British South African Company Medal Roll 1890-1897.*
Roberts (pub.), *The British South Africa Company Medal Rolls 1890-1897* (1993).

HONG KONG PLAGUE MEDAL
Platt, J. J., Jones, M. E. and Platt, A. K., *The Whitewash Brigade: The Hong Kong Plague 1894* (1999).

INDIA MEDAL 1895–1902
Farrington, A., *India General Service Casualty Roll* (1987).
Barthorp, Michael, *The Frontier Ablaze: The North-West Frontier Rising 1897–98* (1996).

ASHANTI STAR 1896
McInnes, Ian and Fraser, Mark, *The Ashanti Campaign 1896.*

QUEEN'S & KING'S SOUTH AFRICA MEDAL 1899-1902
Biggins, David, *Kimberley, Siege Account & Medal Roll* (2010)
Biggins, David, *Elandslaagte: Account and Medal Roll* (2004).
British Naval Brigades in the South Africa War 1899-1902 (Reprint).
Dooner, M.G., *The Last Post: Roll of All Officers Who Gave Their Lives in the South African War 1899-1902* (1980).
Doogleever, Robin, *Inside Mafeking–The Diary of Captain Herbert Greener*
Fevyer, W.H. and Wilson, J.W., *The Queen's South Africa Medal to the Royal Navy and Royal Marines* (1983).
Gray, S., *The South African War 1899-1902 - Service Records of British and Colonial Women.*
Hayward, J. B. & Son (pub.), *List of Casualties of the South Africa Frontier Force* (Reprint 1972).
Hayward, J. B. & Son (pub.), *South African War Casualty Roll: Natal Field Force* (1980).
Kaplan, Stan, *The Relief of Kimberley Bar for the QSA.*
Kaplan, Stan, *The Wepener Bar for the QSA.*
Kieran, Brian, *Success of a General* (2001).
Lusted, C.A (pub.), *The Queens South Africa Medal 1898-1902* (1974).
Mitchell, Dr F. K., *Roll Of The Bar, Defence of Mafeking, on the Queen's Medal for South Africa, 1899-1902* (1963).
Palmer, A., *The Boer War Casualty List* (1999).
Singlehurst, Peter, *Afloat and Ashore: The Royal Navy in the Boer War* (2006).
Stirling, J., *British Regiments in South Africa 1899-1902* (reprint) (1994).
Stirling, J., *The Colonials in South Africa* (1990).

CAPE COPPER COMPANY'S MEDAL 1902
Forsyth, D.R., *Medal Roll of the Cape Copper Company's Medal.*

CHINA MEDAL 1900
Fevyer, W.H. and Wilson, J.W., *The China War Medal 1900 to the Royal Navy and Royal Marines* (1985).
Narbeth, C., *Taku Forts* (1980).

OOKIEP DEFENCE MEDAL
Kieran, Brian L., *O'okiep* (1996).

AFRICA GENERAL SERVICE MEDAL 1902
Fevyer, W.H. and Wilson, J.W. *African General Service Medal to the RN and RM.*
Magor, R.B., *African General Service Medals.*

TIBET MEDAL 1903–04
Fleming, Peter, *Bayonets to Lhasa* (revised 1985).
Roberts (pub.), *The Tibet Campaign 1904 and the Royal Fusiliers.*

NATAL REBELLION MEDAL 1906
Forsyth, D.R., *Natal Native Rebellion 1906: The Medal Roll.*
Roberts Medals Publications Ltd (pub.), *The Natal Zulu Rebellion 1906.*

INDIA GENERAL SERVICE MEDAL 1908–35
Duckers, Peter, *North West Frontier 1908* (2007)
Stiles, Richard G. M., *The Story of the India General Service Medal 1908–35* (1992).
India General Service Medal 1908–1935 to the Royal Air Force (1994).

FIRST WORLD WAR MEDALS 1914-19
Adler, Revd. M (ed.), *British Jewry Book of Honour 1914-1918* (1922 and reprint 1997).
Bell, E.W., *Soldiers Killed on the First Day of the Somme* (1977).
Christie, N.M. *Officers of the Canadian Expeditionary Force who Died Overseas 1914-1919.*
Fevyer, W. H. and Wilson, J. W., *The 1914 Star to the Royal Navy and the Royal Marines* (1995).
Gooding, Norman, *Honours & Awards to Women—to 1914).* (2008)).
Hayward, J. B. & Son (pub.), *Officers Died in the Great War* (1988).
Hayward, J. B. & Son (pub.), *Soldiers Died in the Great War* (80 parts).
Hobson, C., *Airmen Died in the Great War 1914-18: The Roll of Honour of the British and Commonwealth Air Services of the First World War* (1995)
Imperial War Museum (pub.), *Drake, Hawke, Hood, Howe, Nelson, Royal Naval Division Rolls of Honour.*
Jarvis, S.D. and Jarvis, D.B., *The Cross of Sacrifice* (1990-1994) (several volumes).
Laslo, A.J., *The Interallied Victory Medals of WWI* (1986)
Maton, Michael, *Honour the Officers* (2008).
Merewhether, Lt-Col L. A., CIE and Smith Sir F., Bart., *The Indian Corps in France* (1919).
Mitchell, F.K., *Medals of the Great War Awarded to South Africans* (1983).
New Zealand Expeditionary Force Roll of Honour (Reprint).
Parks, Major Edwin, *The Royal Guernsey Militia* (1993).
Ruvigny, Marquis de, *The Roll of Honour 1916-1919.*
Stuart, Alan, *Services Rendered Volumes I, II, III & IV.*
Walker, R., *To What End Did They Die?—Officers Died At Gallipoli.*
Williams, R. D., *Guide to Collecting and Researching Campaign Medals of the Great War* (1993).
Williamson, H. J., *The Roll of Honour, Royal Flying Corps and Royal Air Force for the Great War 1914-18* (1992).
Williamson, Howard, *The Collector and Researchers Guide to the Great War* (2003).
Williamson, H. J., *The Great War Medal Collectors Companion* (2011).

SECOND WORLD WAR MEDALS
Bisset, M. E, *South African Recipients of the Pacific Star or Clasp* (2010).
Bowman, Martin, *The Immortal Few* (2010)
Dickson, Bill Chatterton, *Seedie's List of Awards to the Merchant Navy for World War II* (1997).
Devereux, J. and Sacker, G., *Roll of Honour, Land Forces World War 2 Volume I* (Cavalry, Yeomanry, RAC, Reconnaissance Corps, RTR and Brigade of Guards—other volumes to follow) (1999).
Eyre, Philip, *Those who Dared: Gallantry Awards to British SAS and Attached SBS Units* (2003).
Hayward, J. B. & Son (pub.), *Prisoners of War (British, Empire and Commonwealth Forces)* (3 vols, reprint).
Maton, Michael, *Honour the Air Forces* (2004).
Maton, Michael, *Honour the Armies* (2006).
Maton, Michael, *Honour the Navies* (2007).
Purves, A. A., *Medals, Decorations & Orders of WWII* (1986).
Savannah Publications (pubs.), *Roll of Honour Land Forces WWII* (2000).

NAVAL GENERAL SERVICE MEDAL 1915
Fevyer, W.H. and Wilson, J.W., *NGS Medal 1915-1962 to the Royal Navy and Royal Marines for the Bars Persian Gulf 1909-1914, Iraq 1919-1920, NW Persia 1920* (1995).

KOREA MEDALS 1950-53
Dyke, P., *Korea 1950-53: Mentions-in-Despatches* (1989).
Gaston, P., *Korea 1950-1953, Prisoners of War, The British Army.*
Harding, Colonel E.D., *The Imjin Roll* (1976).
Ingraham, Kevin R., *The Honors, Medals and Awards of the Korean War 1950-1953* (1993).

MERITORIOUS SERVICE MEDALS

Chamberlain, Howard, *Service Lives Remembered, The MSM in New Zealand and its Recipients 1895–1994* (1995) and *Supplement* (1997).

McInnes, Ian, *The Meritorious Service Medal to Aerial Forces* (1984).

McInnes, Ian, *The Meritorious Service Medal to Naval Forces* (1983).

McInnes, Ian, *Meritorious Service Medal. The Immediate Awards 1916-1928* (1992).

McInnes, Ian, *The Annuity Meritorious Service Medal* (1994).

Sainsbury, Major J.D., *For Gallantry in the Performance of Military Duty* (1980).

LONG SERVICE & GOOD CONDUCT MEDALS

Bolton, R., Howie, L. and Mandry, R., *Badges of the Brigade.* (2000).

Douglas-Morris, Captain K.J., *The Naval Long Service Medals* (1991).

Farmer, G., *Bolton Borough Police Long Service & Good Conduct Medal 1913-1951* (2003).

Lees, J.R., *Recipients of the Long Service & Good Conduct Medal 1833-1916 to the Somerset Light Infantry (Prince Alberts).*

McInnes, I. and Gregson, J. B., *The Army Long Service & Good Conduct Medal 1830–1848* (1996).

Pallas, S.M., *Canadian Recipients of the Colonial Auxiliary Forces Officers Decoration and the Colonial Auxiliary Forces Long Service Medal.*

Tamplin, J.M.A., *The Army Emergency Reserve Decoration and the Efficiency Medal (Army Emergency Reserve)* (1989).

Tamplin, J.M.A., *The Colonial Auxiliary Forces Long Service Medal* (1984.)

Tamplin, J.M.A., *The Colonial Auxiliary Forces Officers' Decoration: the Indian Volunteer Forces Officers' Decoration* (1981).

Tamplin, J.M.A., *The Efficiency Decoration Instituted 1930* (1987).

Tamplin, J.M.A., *The Imperial Yeomanry Long Service and Good Conduct Medal* (1978).

Tamplin, J.M.A., *The Militia Long Service and Good Conduct Medal* (1979).

Tamplin, J.M.A., *The Special Reserve Long Service and Good Conduct Medal* (1979).

Tamplin, J.M.A., *The Territorial Decoration 1908-1930* (1983).

Tamplin, J.M.A., *The Territorial Force Efficiency Medal 1908-1921 and the Territorial Efficiency Medal 1922-1930* (1980).

Tamplin, J.M.A., *The Volunteer Long Service Medal* (1980).

Tamplin, J.M.A., *The Volunteer Officers' Decoration* (1980).

Williams, R.D., *The Victoria Volunteer Long and Efficient Service Medal & the Volunteer Officers' Decoration* (1976).

LIFE SAVING AWARDS

Barclay, C., *Royal Humane Society Medals* (1999).

Besley, Edward, *For Those in Peril* (2004).

Brown, G., *Lloyds War Medal for Bravery at Sea* (1992).

Cox, Barry, *Lifeboat Gallantry: The Complete Record of Royal National Lifeboat Institution Gallantry Medals and How They Were Won 1824–1996* (1998).

Cumming, Sir J., *Literature of the Life-Boat 1785-1947* (1947).

Dibdin, C., *History of the Institution's Gold and Silver Medals* (1909).

Fevyer, William H., *Acts of Gallantry, Vol. 2, 1871–1950* (1997).

Fevyer, William H. and Barclay, Craig, *Acts of Gallantry, Vol. 3, 1951-2000* (2003).

Fevyer, Wilson and Cribb, *The Order of Industrial Heroism* (2004).

Gawler, J., *Lloyds Medals 1836-1989.*

Jeffery, S., *The Liverpool Shipwreck and Humane Society 1839-1939* (1939).

Lamb, Sir J.C., *The Life Boat and Its Work* (1911).

Mundell, F., *Stories of the Royal Humane Society* (1895).

Scarlett, R., *Under Hazardous Circumstances: Lloyds War Medal for Bravery at Sea.*

Scarlett, R., *The Sea Gallantry Medal* (2010).

Young, L., *Acts of Gallantry: . . . Detailed Account of Each Deed of Bravery . . . for which the Gold and Silver Medals and Clasps of the Royal Humane Society Have Been Awarded from 1830-1871.*

OTHER MEDALS

Blatherwick, F. J. *Canadian Orders Decorations and Medals* (1994).

Bolton, R., Howie, L., Mandry, B., *Badges of the Brigade* (2000). (Boy's Brigade Badges and Medals)

Borts, L.H., *UN Medals and Missions* (1998).

Buckman, richard, *The Royal Sussex Regiment Military Honours and Awards* (2002).

Cole, H. N., *Coronation and Royal Commemorative Medals 1887-1977* (1977).

Condon, Major J.P.B., MBE, *The Kings and Queens Medals for Shooting (Regular Army).*

Dalzell, M. and Riches, P., *Mentioned in Despatches 1948-1968* (1999).

Duckers, P., *The Delhi Durbar Medal 1911 to The British Army* (1995).

Fevyer, W. H., Wilson, J. W. and Cribb, J., *The Order of Industrial Heroism* (2000).

Harris, D., *A Guide to Military Temperance Medals,* 2nd edition (2006).

Harris, Trevor, *The Medals and Badges of British Freemasonry* (2008)

Hibbard, M.G., *Boer War Tribute Medals* (1982).

James, G.P.L., *The Royal Family Orders, Badges of Office, Royal Household Medals and Souvenirs* (1951).

Le Chene, Evelyn, *Silent Heroes: The Bravery and Devotion of Animals in War* (1994).

Maloyd, Tony, *South African War 1899-1902 Mentioned in Despatches.*

Oldham, Geoffrey and Delahunt, Brett, *Cambodian Decorations of Honour* (2004).

Owen, D., *The King's and Queen's Medal for Shooting* (1999).

Poulsom, Major N.W., *The White Ribbon: a Medallic Record of British Polar Expeditions* (1968).

Poulsom, Major N.W., *Catalogue of Campaign and Independence Medals Issued During the Twentieth Century to the British Army* (1969).

Rouse, Malcolm, *By Grace of the Lord of the Realm—The Delhi Durbar 1903* (2002).

Saffrey, David, *Rhodesia Medal Roll* (2007).

Scarlett, R.J., *Naval Good Shooting Medal 1903-14* (1990).

Wilson, J. W. and Perkins, R., *Angels in Blue Jackets: The Navy at Messina, 1908.*

Wright, Col. Tim B., *The History of the Northern Rhodesian Police.*

SOCIETIES
FOR MEDAL COLLECTORS

Listed here are some of the many societies around the world that cater for the medal collector or those interested in military history. The details given are mostly the private addresses or telephone numbers of the membership secretaries to whom all correspondence should be sent. We would appreciate any information from other Societies who would like their details included in the next YEARBOOK.

Aldershot Militaria Society (Galpin Hall, Windsor Way, Aldershot, Hants, tel: 0118 987 1937)

Association de Collectionneurs de Décorations et Médailles (MEDEC) (Paasbloemstraat 81, B-2170 Merksem, Belgium).

Austrian Orders Research Society (Salesianergasse 9, A-1037 Wien, Postfach 20, Austria)

Birmingham Medal Society (10 Edward Street, Milverton, Leamington Spa CV32 6AX. Tel: 01926 332884).

Bund Deutscher Ordenssammler e.v. (Postfach 1370, D-95012 Hof, Germany).

The Crimean War Research Society (4 Castle Estate, Ripponden, West Yorkshire HX6 4JY).

Crown Imperial (history, traditions, regalia, insignia) (B. Sutton, The Old Smithy, 35 Liverpool Rd, Buckley, Flintshire CH7 3LH).

Indian Military Historical Society (A. N. McLenaghan, 33 High Street, Tilbrook, Huntingdon, Cambs PE18).

Life Saving Awards Research Society (Jim Lees, PO Box 248 (LSARS), Snettisham, King's Lynn, Norfolk PE31 7TA. Tel: 01485 541279).

London Medal Club (Jim Lees, 020 8560 7648).

Medal Society of Ireland (1 The Hill, Stillorgan, Co. Dublin, Ireland).

Mid-Western Orders & Medals Society (MIDOMS) (5847 Gilbert Avenue, La Grange, IL 60525, USA).

Military Collector's Club of Canada (MCCofC) (PO Box 64009, RPO Morse Place, Winnipeg, MB, R2K 4K2, Canada).

Military Medal Society of South Africa (27 Balvicar Road, Blairgowrie, Johannesburg, SA 2194).

Naval Historical Collectors and Research Association (1 Old Fire Station Court, Nailsea, Bristol BS48 4SE).

Northumbrian Medal Society (Tel: 0191 4217175)

Orders & Medals Society of America (OMSA) (PO Box 198, San Ramon, CA 94583, USA).

Orders & Medals Research Society (OMRS) (PO Box 1233, High Wycombe, HP11 9BW).

ditto, Australia Branch (Sydney) (PO Box 484, Lane Cove, NSW 2066, Australia).

ditto, Canada Branch (Ottawa) (17 Ella Street, Ottawa, Ontario, Canada K1S 2S3).

ditto, Canada Branch (Toronto) (273 Corner Ridge Road, Aurora, Ontario, Canada L4G 6L6).

ditto, Cotswold Branch (Cheltenham) (22 Suffolk Road, Cheltenham, Glos GL50 2AQ).

ditto, Hong Kong Branch (Flat 23, 11/F Mt Nicholson Gap, 103 Mt Nicholson Road, Hong Kong).

ditto, Kent Branch (tel. 01634 725864).

ditto, London Branch (01226 790723).

ditto, New Zealand Branch (Wellington) (470 Te Moana Road, Waikanae, New Zealand. Tel: 64 4 479 1622).

ditto, Northern Branch (Manchester) (7 St Michael's Avenue, Great Lever, Bolton, Lancs BL3 2LP. Tel/Fax: 01204 524011).

ditto, Northumbrian Branch (41 Ashdown Avenue, Durham DH1 1DB).

ditto, Ottawa Branch (+613 231 3036).

ditto, Salisbury Branch (tel. 01722 716605).

ditto, Scottish Branch (21 Hartington Place, Edinburgh EH10 4LF).

ditto, Sussex Branch (9 Merryfield Drive, Horsham, West Sussex RH12 2AA, tel: 01903 879525).

ditto, Medal Ribbon Branch (Rainbows End, 7 Durham Way, Rayleigh, Essex SS6 9RY).

ditto, Miniature Medals Branch (54 Priory Bridge Road, Taunton, Somerset TA1 1QB, tel. 01823 259675).

Ordenshistorik Selskab (Falkoneralle 79, DK 2000 Frederiksberg, Denmark).

Société Suisse de Phaleristique (Case postale 5616, 1211 Geneva 11, Switzerland).

Stockport Militaria Collectors Society, (10 Bradgate Place, Bradgate, Rotherham, South Yorkshire, S61 1LB, tel: 01709 557622).

Studiekring Faleristiek, (Straatakker 2, 8700 Tielt, Belgium).

Studiekring Ridderorden en Ondenscheidingen, (Zamenhoflaan 23, 3706 VA, Zeist, Netherlands. www.vereniging-sro-nl.)

Victorian Military Society (20 Priory Road, Newbury, Berks RG14 7QN).

West of England Medal Club (Exeter) (Otterburn Farm, Halwill, Beaworthy, Devon EX21 5UG).

Zimbabwe Medal Society (Harare) (14 Straker Ave, Gunhill, Harare, Zimbabwe or PO Box GD 470, Greendale, Harare, email: rgill@zol.co.zw)

PROFESSIONAL DIRECTORY

On the following pages are the names and addresses of auctioneers, dealers, booksellers and fair organisers, all of whom will be of assistance to the medal collector. Most are full time and many have retail shops and the collector is usually welcome during normal business hours. Some have extensive stocks of medals whilst others include medals in a more diverse inventory. A number of dealers are part time or work from small premises or from home and appointments are necessary as many keep their stock in the bank for security. Telephone numbers and email addresses have been included where known and it is always sensible to make contact before travelling any distance.

AUCTIONEERS

The following hold regular medal auctions or feature medals in general numismatic or militaria sales.

Baldwin's Auctions
11 Adelphi Terrace, London WC2N 6BJ. Tel: 0207 9309 808 (fax: 02079309450), email: auctions@baldwin.sh, www.baldwin.sh. *Specialist auctioneers of coins and medals.*

Bene Merenti
Emerholzweg 31, 70439 Stuttgart, Germany. Tel: + 49 07 11/76165844. www.benemerenti.de. *Orders, medals and decorations.*

Blythe & Co
Ely Auction Rooms, 7-9 Market Place, Ely CB7 4NP. Tel: 01353 668320. www.blyths.com. *Sales of mlitaria, coins and artefacts.*

Bonhams (Glendining's)
Montpelier Street, London SW7 1HH, 101 New Bond Street, London W1S 1SR. Tel: 020 7393 3900 (fax: 020 7393 3905), www.bonhams. com. *Auctioneers and valuers of medals. Approximately four sales per year.*

Bosleys
Remnantz (The Old Military College), Marlow, Buckinghamshire, SL7 2BS. Tel: 01628 488188 (fax: 01628 488111) www.bosleys.co.uk. *Specialist auctioneers of medals and militaria.*

Brightwells
Antiques and Fine Art Department, Easters Court, Leominster, Herefordshire, HR6 0DE. Tel: 01568 611122. www.brightwells.com. *Occasional auctions of medals and militaria.*

A. F. Brock & Co. Ltd
269 London Road, Hazel Grove, Stockport, Cheshire, SK7 4PL. Tel: 0161 456 5050, tel/fax: 0161 456 5112, email: info@afbrock.co.uk, www. afbrock.co.uk. *Specialist in the sale by auction of coins, medals, banknotes, collectables.*

Charterhouse
The Long Street Salerooms, Sherbourne, Dorset DT9 3BS. Tel: 01935 812277. www.charterhouse-auctions.co.uk. *Auctioneers and valuers.*

City Coins
Tulbagh Square, Cape Town, South Africa. Tel: 0027 21 425 2639 (fax: 0027 21 425 3939), email: auctions@citycoins.co.za, www.citycoins.com. *Postal medal auctions.*

Colonial Coins and Medals
218 Adelaide Street, Brisbane, Australia + 61 7 3221 8460. Email: coinshop@bigpond.net. au. www.coinmedalshop.com.au. *Auctions of medals and coins.*

Corbitts
5 Mosley Street, Newcastle Upon Tyne, NE1 1YE. Tel: 0191 2327268 (fax: 0191 2614130). *Regular sales of coins, medals and stamps.*

Cotswold Auction Co.
Chapel Walk, Cheltenham GL50 3DS. Tel: 01242 256363, email: info@cotswoldauction.co.uk, www.cotswoldauction.co.uk. *Auctioneers and valuers.*

Diss Auction Rooms (Twgaze)
Roydon Road, Diss, Norfok, IP22 4LN. Tel: 01379 650306. www.twgaze.com. *Occasional auctions of medals and militaria.*

Dix Noonan Webb
16 Bolton Street, Piccadilly, London W1J 8BQ. Tel: 020 7016 1700 (fax: 020 7016 1799), email: medals@dnw.co.uk, www.dnw.co.uk. *Auctioneers and valuers. Regular auctions of medals.*

Downie's
11 & 12 Block Arcade, 98–100 Elizabeth Street, Melbourne, Vic 3000, Australia. Tel: 0061 3 9654 4935 (fax: 0061 3 9654 4028), www.downies. com. *Sales with emphasis on Australian and UK medals.*

Dreweatt Neate
St John's Place, Apsley Road, Clifton, Bristol BS8 2ST. Tel: 0117 973 7201. Email bristol@ dnfa.com. *Regular auctions of medals, decorations and militaria.*

Edinburgh Coin Shop
11 West Crosscauseway, Edinburgh EH8 9JW. Tel: 0131 668 2928 or 0131 667 9005 (fax: 0131 668 2926). *Regular postal auctions of medals.*

Gorringes
15 North Street, Lewes, East Sussex BN7 2PD. Tel: 01273 472503, www.gorringes.co.uk. *Sales of medals, militaria and fine art.*

Hermann Historica

Linprunstr. 16, D–80335 Munich. Tel: +49 89 547264999. Email: contact@hermann-historica. com. *Auctions of medals and militaria.*

Jeffrey Hoare Auctions Inc.

319 Springbank Dr., London, Ontario, Canada, N6J 1G6. Tel: (519) 473 7491 (fax: (519) 473 1541), www.jeffreyhoare.on.ca. *Regular sales of medals and militaria.*

Alec Kaplan

PO Box 28913, Sandringham 2131, Johannesburg, South Africa. Fax: 0027 11 640 3427, email: rhodesia@wol.co.za. *Regular sales of medals and militaria.*

George Kidner

The Lymingtoon Saleroom, Emsworth Road, Lymington, Hampshire, SO41 9BL. Tel: 01590 670070. www.georgekidner.co.uk. *Auctions of Arms and Militaria.*

Kunker

Gutenbergstrasse 23, 49076, Osnabruck, Germany. Tel: +49 541962020. Email: service@ kuenker.com, www.kuenker.com. *Coins, medals and decorations.*

Lockdales

37 Upper Orwell Street, Ipswich IP4 1HP. Tel: 01473 218588, www.lockdales.com. *Regular sales of medals, coins, collectables. Call for venue details.*

Mellors & Kirk

Gregory Street, Nottingham NG7 2NL. Tel: 0115 979 0000, email: enquiries@mellorsandkirk. com, www.mellorsandkirk.com. *Medals and collectables.*

Morton & Eden

45 Maddox Street, London W1S 2PE. Tel: 020 7493 5344 (fax: 020 7495 6325), email: info@ mortonandeden.com, www.mortonandeden. com. *Advisory service and auctioneers of medals and coins.*

Noble Numismatics Pty Ltd

169 Macquarie Street, Sydney 2000, Australia. Tel: +61 2 9223 45478 (fax: +61 9 9233 6009), email: info@noble.net.au. *Regular sales of British and Commonwealth medals.*

Spink & Son Ltd

69 Southampton Row, Bloomsbury, London WC1B 4ET. Tel: 020 7563 4049/4053 (fax: 020 7563 4068), email: info@spink.com, www.spink. com. *Auctioneers and valuers. Regular sales of medals. Specialist book publishers.*

Stacks

123, West 57th Street, New York, NY 10019, USA. info@stacks.com, www.stacks.com. *Auctioneers of world orders, decorations and medals. Also USA and world coins.*

Status International Auctions

Tel: +61 292674525. www.statusint.com. Auctions of Medals, militaria, stamps and coins.

Tennants

The Auction Centre, Leyburn, North Yorkshire DL8 5SG. Tel: 01969 623780, www.tennants.co.uk. *Auctions of medals and coins.*

Thomas Del Mar

25 Blythe Road, London W14 0PD. Tel: 020 7602 4805. www.thomasdelmar.com. *Antique arms, armour and militaria.*

Thomson Roddick & Medcalf

Coleridge House, Shaddongate, Carlisle CA2 5TU. Tel: 0151 264 0842, email: auctions@ thomsonroddick.com. *Auctions of orders, medals, militaria and coins.*

Van Stockums

15 Prinsesgract, Netherlands. Tel: 0031 703 649840. www.vanstockums-veilingen.nl. *Auctions of Orders, decorations and medals.*

Wallis & Wallis

West Street Auction Galleries, Lewes, Sussex BN7 2NJ. Tel: 01273 480208 (fax: 01273 476562), email: auctions@wallisandwallis.org, www. wallisandwallis.org. *Regular sales of militaria, arms, armour and medals.*

Warwick & Warwick

Chalon House, Scar Bank, Millers Road, Warwick CV34 5DB. Tel: 01926 499031 (fax: 01926 491906), email: richard.beale@ warwickandwarwick.com, www.warwickandwarwick.com. *Regular sales of Orders, Decorations and other collectables.*

Wellington Auctions

PO Box 5665, London W1A 5EJ. Tel: 0207 495 0115, email: mail@wellingtonauctions.com, www.wellingtonauctions.com. *Bi-monthly postal auctions of orders, decorations and medals.*

Woolley & Wallis

51-61 Castle Street, Salisbury SP1 3SU. Tel: 01722 424530 (fax: 01722 424508). *Medals and silver.*

DEALERS

Aberdeen Medals
PO Box 12086, Aberdeen. 07748 040021. www.
aberdeenmedals.com. Specialists in medals to
Scottish Regeiments, Indian Army and Colonial.

Ackley Unlimited
PO Box 82144, Portland, Oregon, USA 97282-
0144. Tel: (503) 659 4681, email: aunltd@aol.
com. Orders, medals and decorations. Free
quarterly lists on request.

Rod Akeroyd & Son
20 Ribblesdale Place, Preston, Lancs, PR1 3NA.
Tel: 01772 203845, www.firearmscollector.com.
Fine antique arms and armour.

Arctic Medals & Militaria
www.arcticmedals.com. Medals, Military
badges and Insignia.

Michael Autengruber
Orders of the World, Schulthaissstrasse 10,
D-78462 KONSTANZ, Germany. Tel: (0049
7531 284469), email: michael.autengruber@
autengruber.de. World orders, decorations and
medals and reference books.

Award Productions Ltd
PO Box 300, Shrewsbury, Shropshire SY5 6WP.
Tel: 01952 510053 (fax: 01952 510765), www.
awardmedals.com. Suppliers of unofficial
medals for veterans. Medallists to the Royal
British Legion.

Louis Bannon
21 Royal Arcade, Cardiff, CF10 2AE. Tel: 02920
221528. Medals and military antiques, medals to
Welsh regiments.

Val Barley
Tel: 01527 460023. www.valbarley.co.uk. Military
images on canvas.

Bigbury Mint
Bigbury Mint, River Park, Ermington, Ivybridge,
Devon, PL21 9NT. Tel: 01548 830717. Email:
info@bigburymint.com, www.bigburymint.com.
Makers of fine medals, commemorative and
historical products.

Bravo Medals
www.bravomedals.co.uk. Bas Bruntlett
68 Pinfold lane, Methley, Leeds, West Yorkshire,
LS26 9AB. Tel: 01977 515811. Buying and selling
badges.

Bonus Eventus
P/A Willy Dufossez, Cathilleweg 104, 8490
Jabbeke, Belgium. Tel/Fax: (0032 50 812158),
www.bonus-eventus.be, email: bonus.eventus@
telenet.be. Medals and miniature medals.

Bostock Medals
"Pinewoods", 15 Waller Close, Leek Wootton,
Nr Warwick CV35 7QG. (Tel: 01926 856381 / fax:
01926 856 381), email: bostockmilitaria@aol.
com, www.bostockmedals.co.uk. British orders,
medals and decorations. Callers welcome by
appointment.

Britannia Military Antiques
Larch How, Brigsteer Road, Kendal, Cumbria
LA9 5DY. Tel: 01539 724268 mobile 07922
838753. Email: info@britmedals.co.uk, www.
britmedals.co.uk

British Medals (Rennie Alcock)
PO Box 14, Castletown, Isle of Man, IM99 5YY.
Tel: 01624 827664, www.british-medals.co.uk.
British orders, medals and decorations.

David Brookes
31 Fleet Road, Rochester, Kent, ME1 2QB. Tel:
01634 405978. Email: tigerwharf29@talktalk.
net. Dealing in Military Medals, Photos and
Ephemera.

Jim Bullock Militaria
PO Box 217, Romsey, SO51 5XL. Tel/fax: 01794
516455, email: jimbullockmilitaria.com, www.
jimbullockmilitaria.com. Quality medals and
militaria, medal framing and mounting service..

Philip Burman
Blackborough End, Middleton, King's Lynn,
Norfolk PE32 1SE. Tel: 01553 840350 (fax: 01553
841118), www.military-medals.co.uk. Large and
varied stock of orders, medals and decorations.
Send large S.A.E. for lists, issued 5 times a year.

John & Sarah Cant
PO Box 7802, Harlow, Essex, CM20 1WQ. Tel:
07905 331360, Email: jscantmilitaria@hotmail.
com, www.jscantmilitaria.co.uk. Medals
mounted and framed. Militaria bought and sold.

Mark Carter
PO Box 470, Slough, Berkshire, SL3 6RR. Tel:
01753 534777. markgcarter@bulldoghome.com.
Medal dealer and organiser of the Mark Carter
Militaria & Medal Fairs in Aldershot, Stratford
Upon Avon and the West Country.

Cambridge Medal Mounting Services
3 Pepys Road, St Neots, PE19 2EN. Tel: -1480
395827. Email: shelton946@aol.com.

John Cannon
2 Crees Meadow, Windlesham, Surrey, GU20
6QA. Tel: 01276 451126. Medals and militaria.

Castle Galleries
81 Castle Street, Salisbury, Wilts SP1 3SP. Tel:
01722 333734, email: john.lodge1@tesco.net.
Medals, militaria, coins and books.

Cathedral Court Medals
First Floor Office, 30A Market Place, West Ripon,
North Yorks, HG4 1BN. (01765 601400). Coin
and medal sales. Medal mounting and framing.

Chelsea Militaria
7 Whitcomb Street, London WC2 7HA. Tel/fax:
020 7352 0308. Email: richard@chelseamilitaria.
com, www.chelseamilitaria.com. Campaign and
Gallantry Medals. British and Foreign Militaria.

Chester Militaria
Shop 3, Chester Market, 6 Princess Street,
Chester, CH1 2HH. Tel: 01244 350294. Medals,
militaria and mounting service.

Chieftain Medals
Tel: 07882 003678. info@chieftainmedals.com,
www.chieftainmedals.com.

C. J. Medals
Shop 17 Loganholme Shopping Village, 59
Bryants Road, Loganholme, Qld 4129, Australia.
Tel + 07 3806 5980. www.cjmedals.com.

City Coins
PO Box 156, Sea Point, 8060, Cape Town. Tel
+ (0) 21 425 2639. www.citycoins.com. Coins,
banknotes, medals and accessories.

Coinote
74 Elwick Road, Hartlepool TS26 9AP. Tel: 01429
890894. www.coinote.co.uk. Medals, Coins,
Banknotes and accessories.

Norman W. Collett

PO Box 235, London SE23 1NS. Tel/fax: (020) 8291 1435, www.medalsonline.co.uk. British medals and decorations, mainly groups, with an accent on researchable recipients. Medals.

Collectors World

188 Wollaton Road, Wollaton, Nottingham, NG8 1HJ. Tel: 01159 280347. Medals, coins, tokens, banknotes and accessories.

J. Collins Medals Limited

17 Queens Road, Warsash, Hampshire SO31 9JY. Tel/fax: 01489 582222. email: research@ jcollinsmedals.co.uk, www.jcollinsmedals.co.uk. Naval, Miliary, and Airforce Research Service.

Colonial Coins and Medals

218 Adelaide Street, Brisbane, QLD 4001, Australia. Tel: 61 7 3229 3949, email: coinshop@ bigpond.net.au, www.coinmedalshop.com.au. British, Commonwealth orders, decorations and medals. Regular auctions.

Command Post of Militaria

1306 Government Street, Victoria, British Columbia, Canada V8W 1Y8. Tel: (250) 383 4421. Medals, badges and uniforms.

Conglomerate Coins & Medals

GPO Box 2831, Brisbane, Queensland, Australia 4001. Retail: Level 3, 276 Edward Street, Brisbane, QLD. Tel: (07) 3221 1217 (fax: 07 3221 9711, email: alforgan@powerup.com.au. Medals and medallions.

Constantius

Visit our website: www.constantius.co.uk for quality British Victorian campaign medals, WWI groups and plaques. Tel: 015395 32452 or email: constantius@talktalk.net.

Peter R. Cotrel

7 Stanton Road, Bournemouth, Dorset BH10 5DS. Mail order only—callers by appointment. Tel: 01202 388367. British, American, general foreign medals and decorations. Medal albums.

Jamie Cross

PO Box 73, Newmarket, Suffolk CB8 8RY. Specialist in Third Reich medals, badges and decorations.

Cultman Collectables

PO Box 185, Retford, Notts., DN22 1DU. Tel: 01777 703283, or email: info@ cultmancollectables.com, www. cultmancollectables.com. Militaria, medals, badges and police memorabilia.

Death Penny

www.deathpenny.com. The Memorial Plaque and Militaria Listing Service.

De Winters Medals

Tel: 07584 895918. Email: dewintersmedals@ hotmail.com, www.dewintersmedals.co.uk. Specialising in Gurkha, Guards and Royal Marines Campaign medals and decorations.

C. J. & A. J. Dixon Ltd

1st Floor, 23 Prospect Street, Bridlington, East Yorkshire YO15 2AE. Tel: 01262 603348 (fax: 01262 606600), email: chris@dixonsmedals. co.uk, www.dixonsmedals.co.uk. British & world orders, medals and decorations. 4 lists a year £16 (UK), £18 (Europe), £20 (Rest of World).

D.M.D. Services

6 Beehive Way, Reigate, Surrey RH2 8DY. Tel: 01737 240080. Victorian campaign medals and decorations.

Frank Draskovic

PO Box 803, Monterey Park, CA 91754, USA. Email: fdraskovic@ hotmail.com. Tel: 001 626 281 9281. UK and worldwide orders and medals.

M. J. & S. J. Dyas Coins & Medals

Unit 3, 42 Stratford Road, Shirley, Solihull, West Midlands, B90 3LS. Tel: 0121 733 2225 (fax: 0121 733 1533). Email: info@dyasmedals.co.uk. Military medals and books.

Edinburgh Coin Shop (Hiram T. D. Brown)

11 West Crosscauseway, Edinburgh EH8 9JW. Tel: 0131 668 2928 (fax: 0131 668 2926). British medals and decorations. Four lists a year and postal auctions.

Elite-Collections.Com

PO Box 56, Pontypridd CF37 2YL, South Wales. www.elite-collections.com. 30 page catalogue of British medals. Annual Subscription (10 issues) £2 (UK), download free on E-mail.

E. L. M.

57 Medal House, Yishun Industrial Estate, Park A, Singapore 768730. Tel: +65 6487 7777. www. elm.com.sg. Manufacturer of medals. Medal mounting and restoration.

E-Medals.ca

760 Brant Street, Suite 7, Burlington, Ontario, Canada. Tel: + 1 905 634 3848. Bought-Sold-Traded. Email: info@emedals.ca, www. emedals.ca.

FindaMedal.com

www.findamedal.com P.O.Box 2072, Steyning, West Sussex BN5 0BN. Tel: 07710 000964

First Light Militaria

PO Box 4984, Poole, Dorset, BH16 6WA. Email: info@firstlight-militaria.co.uk, www.firstlight-militaria.co.uk. Buying and selling medals and decorations.

Bill Friar Medals

44 Knowsley Drive, Leigh, Lancs, WN7 3LY. Email: sales@billfriarmedals.co.uk, www. billfriarmedals.co.uk. British Medals.

Andrew Fryer Medals

Hazelwood, Osmaston, Ashbourne, Derbyshire, DE6 1LW. Tel: 01335 346720.

Frontier Medals

Unit 4D, Tower 2, 21 Yau On Street, Shatin, New Territories, Hong Kong. Tel: +852 94651496. Email: enquiries@frontiermedals.com, www. frontiermedals.com. Medals and accessories.

Andy Garrett

Unit 9, Brackley Antique Cellar, Draymans Walk, Brackley, Northants NN13 6BE. British and foreign medals, groups, badges and militaria.

G. A. Medal Services

P.O. Box 374, Winchester, SO23 7XQ. Email: peter@gamedals.co.uk. Repairs and restoration.

Gladman & Norman

51–53 Tenby St North, Birmingham B1 3EG. Tel: 0121 236 5752. www.gladman-norman.co.uk. Manufacturer of orders and medals.

Glance Back

17 Upper Church Street, Chepstow, Gwent NP6 5EX. Tel: 01291 626562. Large stock of Medals, badges and military books.

Good Books

PO Box 291 562, Melville, 2109 Johannesburg, South Africa. Tel: +27 82 745 3657. Email: info@ goodbooks.co.za, www.goodbooks.co.za.

Gordons Medals Ltd

Grays Antiques Centre, Davies Mews, Davies Street, London W1K 5AB. Tel: 020 7495 0900 (fax: 020 7495 0115), email: sales@cocollector. co.uk, www.cocollector.co.uk. Monday–Friday, 10.30am–6pm. Campaign medals, militaria, German and Third Reich. Catalogues £6 (UK), £12 (overseas air).

Louis E. Grimshaw

612 Fay Street, R.R. #1 Kingston, Ontario, Canada K7L 4VI. Tel: (613) 549 2500. Military antiques and collectables, including medals. Catalogues of arms, medals and militaria . Single copies $C5 (Canada), $US4 (USA), $US6.

Great War Medals

PO Box 1914, London N14 7XS. 020 8482 1918. Email: info@greatwarmedals.co.uk. Mainly WW1 medals and books. Regular 36 page catalogue of medals and decorations, £7.50 (UK), £11 (overseas).

W. D. Grissom

PO Box 59, Cabot Arkansas, 72023 USA. Email: medalsguy39@yahoo.com. American medals.

Tony Hall

1 Chailey Avenue, Brighton, BN2 7GH. Medals and Militaria.

A. D. Hamilton & Co

7 St. Vincent Place, Glasgow G1 2DW. Tel: 0141 2215423 (fax: 01412486019), email: jefffineman@hotmail.com, www.adhamilton. co.uk. Buying and selling Medals, militaria, badges, coins and banknotes.

Harland Military Antiques

Tel: 01429 232782/07904 349727. www. harlandmilitaryantiques.com. British Medals.

Harpers

P.O Box 7745, Brentwood, CM13 3WZ. Tel: 01277 812 650, email: info@harpershome137@ freeserve.co.uk, www.harpers-online.com. Orders, medals and military antiques.

Intramark Limited

Windsor Lodge, 56 Windsor Street, Burbage, Leic., LE10 2EF. Tel: 01455 612400 (fax: 01455 612483), email: intramark@btclick.com. Manufacturers of miniatures, medal brooch bars & medal ribbon bars, medals ribbons etc.

Jacks Medals and Militaria

7 Lawndale Avenue, North Rocks, New South Wales, Australia, 2151. Tel: 61 2 9871 8015. Email: jacksmedals@bigpond.com. Medals, books and swords.

Jager Medals & Militaria

Tel: 0141 840 2622, Email: enquiries@ jagermedals.com, www.jagermedals.com. British campaign medals bought and sold.

Just-In-Case

PO Box The Workshop, North View, Black Hill, Consett, Co. Durham, DH8 0JN. Tel: 01207 505153, email: sales@just-in-case.biz, www.just-in-case.biz. Display cases for medals.

Alec Kaplan

PO Box 28913, Sandringham 2131, Johannesburg, South Africa. Fax: 0027 11 640 3427, email: medals@wirelessza.co.za. www. aleckaplan.co.za. Contact for free catalogue.

Ian Laidler

No-Where, 17 Wavell Grove, Wakefield, WF2 6JW. Tel: 0781 548 4641, email: ian@ianlaidler. orangehome.co.uk. Medals and militaria.

Liverpool Medal Company

42 Bury Business Centre, Kay Street, Bury Lancs BL9 6BU. Tel: 0161 763 4610 (fax: 0161 763 4963), www.liverpoolmedals.com. World orders, medals, decorations. Plus miniatures & related books.

Lyme Valley Medals Limited

P.O.Box 2404, Stoke on Trent DT7 4WQ. Email: enquiries@Lvmedals.co.uk, www.Lvmedals. co.uk.

John Manning

18 Fengate, Heacham, nr. Kings Lynn, Norfolk, PE31 7BG. Tel: 01485 570153.

M&D Medals

Tel: 07866 717799/012688 730279/07748 940273, email: mdinks1@talktalk.net.

Medal Masters

PO Box 7204, Bundaberg North, Queensland, Australia, 4670. Tel: 61 403 250170, email: info@ medalmasters.com.au, www.medalmasters. com.au. Replica medals and specialist framers

Medals and Collectables

Woodcroft, Brockhills Lane, New Milton, Hampshire BH25 5QL. Tel: 01425 612766/07784 505451, email: medalsandcollectables@hotmail. co.uk, www.medalsandcollectables.co.uk.

Medal-Medaille

www.medal-medaille.com. Selling orders and medals of the world.

Medals, Mementos & More

46 Coromadel Parade, Blackwood, South Australia, 5051. Tel/Fax: (08) 82788530. Medal mounting/framing and refurbishment, replicas and miniatures.

Medals of England

PO Box 258, Lingfield, Surrey, RH7 9AH. Tel: 01342 870926. www.medalsofengland.com. Medals and military items.

www.medalsonline.co.uk

Orders, decorations and medals.

Giuseppe Miceli Coin & Medal Centre

204 Bants Lane, Duston, Northampton NN5 6AH. Tel: 01604 581 533. Medals, militaria etc. Free list.

Peter Morris

PO Box 223, Bromley, Kent BR1 4EQ. Retail premises Bromley North BR Station. Tel: 020 8313 3410 (fax: 020 8466 8502), email: info@ petermorris.co.uk, www.petermorris.co.uk. Medals and decorations, militaria, coins & banknotes.

MSM Awards

8 Price Tce, Matamata, 3400, New Zealand. Tel: (NZ) 647 888 9064, email: mikes@kol.co.nz, www.honours.homestead.com/home.html. Medal remounter for the serving military or Veteran. Supplier of medal ribbons.

Neate Militaria and Antiques

PO Box 3794, Preston St. Mary, Sudbury CO10 9PX. Tel: 01787 248168 (fax: 01787 248363), email: gary@neatemedals.co.uk, www. neatemedals.co.uk. Buyers of all medals.

Detlev Niemann

Ballindamm 9, V Floor, 20095 Hamburg 1, Germany. Tel: 0049 40 3252 5354 (fax: 0049 40 3252 5454), email: Detlev-Niemann@t-online.de, www.Detlev-Niemann.de. Specialist in German orders, decorations, militaria, etc.

Nordheide-Versand

Nordheid-Versand Kai Winkler, Schulstrasse 11a, 21220 Seevetal/Maschen. Tel: (0 41 05) 8 43 84 (fax: (0 41 05) 8 27 88), www. nordheideversand.de. Medals, awards, award-documents, miniatures, pins, uniforms etc.

North West Medal

PO Box 21070, 640 River Street, Thunder Bay, ON, P7A 8A7 Canada, email: nwmedal@shaw. ca, www.northwestmedal.com. Medals and decorations.

Our Heritage War Medals

Tel: 01275 397410. Email: boblynes@hotmail.com, www.ourheritagewarmedals.co.uk. Selling and buying war medals and decorations.

Personalia

Email: enquiries@personalia.co.uk, www. personalia.co.uk. Dealers in historical manuscripts, letters and medals.

Poppy Militaria

Tel: 01691 773142. www.poppymilitaria. co.uk, www.poppymedalframing.co.uk. Medal framing, medals and militaria for sale.

Q & C Militaria

22 Suffolk Road, Cheltenham, Gloucestershire GL50 2AQ. Tel/fax: 01242 519815, www. qcmilitaria.com. British and Commonwealth orders, medals, decorations and miltaria.

R & L Medals

Tel: 00 35 339835933. Email: richard@rlmedals. com. www.rlmedals.com. Specialists in Gallentry and non-Gallentry Groups to Army, Navy and non- Combatants.

R & M International

PO Box 6278, Bellevue, Washington, USA. 98008-0278. Email: surlamer86@prodigy.net. www.randminternational.com. Specialist in British, Canadian. U.S. and Russian orders, medals and decorations.

RBJ Militaria

Parade Antiques Market, 27b New Street, Barbican, Plymouth, Devon, PL1 2NB. Tel: 07714 544777. www.rbjmilitaria.com.

Barbara Radman

Westfield House, 2G Westfield Road, Witney, Oxon OX28 1JG. Tel: 01993 772705. British and Foreign orders, medals and decorations especially Russian.

Royal Insignia

Medal House, 57 Yishun Industrial Park A, Singapore 768730. Tel (65) 6487 7777 (fax: 65 6756 0366), email info@medals.com.sg, www. medals.com.sg. Manufacturers of orders and medals.

ScotMint

68, Sandgate, Ayre, Scotland KA7 1BX. Tel: 01292 268244 (mobile: 07939 345407), email: rob@scotmint.com. British and worldwide medals groups, badges and militaria. Retail premises.

S. E. Sewell

PO Box 149, Stowmarket, IP14 4WD. Tel: 01449 782185, mobile: 07739 071822. Tel/Fax: 01449 782185, email: sewellmedals@hotmail.com, www.sewellmedals.co.uk. A wide variety of medals, mainly British.

Murray Shaw Medals

182 Western Road, Mickleover, Derby DE3 9GT. Tel: 01332 515067. Military medals.

E. C. Snaith & Son Ltd

20 Vale Street, Denbigh, Denbighshire LL16 3BE. Tel: 01745 812218 (fax: 01745 816367). Wholesalers to the Medal Trade.

South African Militaria

Email: andrew@rolynengineering.co.za. www.southafricanmilitaria.com. Medals, badges, militaria.

Southern Medals

PO Box 50, Knebworth, Herts SG3 6UE, www. southernmedals.co.uk. Occasional list of mainly British orders and medals.

Specialist Medals.com

P.O Box 278, Wallingford, Oxon, OX10 1AU. Tel: 01491 825974, email: roger@willoughby.ie, www.specialistmedals.com. Mainly life-saving medals and civil awards.

Spink & Son Ltd

69 Southampton Row, Bloomsbury, London WC1B 4ET. Tel: 020 7563 4049 (fax: 020 7563 4068), email: info@spink.com, www.spink.com. Also at 47, The Shambles, York YO1 7XL. Tel: 01904 654769. Medal dealers and auctioneers.

Strachan Militaria

www.ismilitaria.co.uk. 20th Century German, British, US and international militaria.

Sunset Militaria

Dinedor Cross, Herefordshire HR2 6PF. Tel: 01432 870420 (fax: 01432 870309). Military research and world medal ribbons. Please send SAE for list.

Jeremy Tenniswood

36 St Botolphs Street, Colchester, Essex CO2 7EA. Tel: 01206 368787 (fax: 01206 367836), www.militaria.co.uk. Orders, medals, decorations, militaria and related books.

The Medal Centre

10b Hencoats, Hexham, Northumberland NE46 2EJ. Tel: 01434 609794 mobile: 07950421704 www.themedalcentre.co.uk.

The Mess Dress Ltd

188 Stewart Road, Bournemouth BH8 8NU. Tel: 01202 302846. www.messdress.com.

Toye, Kenning & Spencer Ltd

Regalia House, Newtown Road, Bedworth, Warks CV12 8QR. Tel: 01247 6848800 (fax: 01247 6643018), email: sales@tksmedalsandribbons. co.uk, www.tksmedalsandribbons.co.uk. Manufacturers of medals, ribbons, badges, etc.

Treasure Bunker Militaria Shop

21 King Street, The Trongate, Glasgow G1 5QZ. Tel/fax: 0141 552 8164, email: info@treasure bunker.com, www.treasurebunker.com. Medals, badges, uniforms etc. (Waterloo to WWII)

Matthew Tredwen

PO Box 376, West Malling, Kent, ME6 2DP. Tel: 07795 972452. Email: info: falleneagle.com, www.falleneagle.com. Specialists in Militaria.

Ulric of England

PO Box 55, Chruch Stretton, Shropshire, SY6 6WR. Tel: 01694 781354 (fax: 01694 781372), www.britishmilitarymedals.com. All British military medals, particularly Waterloo medals.

Eugene G. Ursual

PO Box 788, Kemptville, Ontario, Canada, KOG 1JO. Tel: (613) 258 5999 (fax: 613 258 9118), email: egu@magma.ca, www.medalsofwar.com. Medals, orders, decorations, miniatures and militaria. 10 lists a year $17 (Canada), $20 (USA), $25 (overseas).

Vernon

Box 1560MN, Wildomar, California, USA 92595. Canadian-related material.

V. F. M. R. Orders & Medals

Email: victor@vfme-ordersandmedals.com, www.vfmr-ordersandmedals.com. Orders, decorations and Militaria.

V. J. C. Collectables

Email: valbaz@hobs20.fsnet.co.uk. Medals and miltaria.

Fred S. Walland

17 Gyllyngdune Gardens, Seven Kings, Essex IG3 9HH. Tel: 020 8590 4389 (fax: 020 8599 9923). Orders, medals and decorations.

Stephen Wheeler

Retail Outlet: 20 Cecil Court, Leicester Square, London WC2N 4HE. London Military Market, Angel Arcade; Jubilee Antiques Market, Covent Garden, Stand 111, Mondays. Tel: 02072406827 or 07778 848555. British & Foreign Orders and Decorations.

Worcestershire Medal Service Ltd

56 Broad Street, Sidemoor, Bromsgrove B61 8LL. Tel: 01527 835375 (fax: 01527 576798). email: wms@worcmedals.com. www.worcmedals.com. Medals and medal mounting, storage cases, display cases, miniature medals, blazer badges and replacement medals.

Worldwide Militaria

Jeffery Stone, 2000 Bloomingdale Road, Suite, Glendale Heights, IL 60139, USA. Tel + (630) 571 8340. USA Distributor.

I. S. Wright

P.O. Box A1005, Sydney South, 1235, Australia. Tel: 61 2 9264 7555 (fax: 61 2 9264 2656), email: @paddy@iswright.com.au. Military collectables.

Yeovil Collectors Centre

16 Hendford, Yeovil, Somerset BA20 1TE. Tel: 01935 433739. Medals, badges, militiaria.

York Coin & Stamp Centre,

Cavendish Antique & Collectors Centre, 44 Stonegate, York YO1 8AS. (01904 611653.) Medals and decorations.

Carston Zeige

Carsten Zeige, Dammtorstr. 29 D–20354, Hamburg, Germany. Tel:+49 40 3571 3636. Email: info@zeige.com. www.zeige.com. German and Foreign. Catalogue: $35 (5 issues).

BOOKSELLERS/DEALERS

In addition to the names listed below, it should be noted that a number of the medal dealers listed above regularly or occasionally include books on their medal lists.

Ian Allan

4 Watling Drive, Hinckley, Leics LE10 3EY. Tel: 01455 233747 (fax: 01455 233737). Military Titles, email: midlandbooks@compuserve.com, www.ianallansuperstore.com.

Peter Barnes

(www.barnesbooks.co.uk). Pre-owned, out-of-print, rare, old and collectors editions of military, naval and aviation book.

Buffo Books

32, Tadfield Road, Romsey, hants SO51 5AJ. Tel: 01794 517149. Military and aviation only.

Andrew Burroughs

32, St Martins, Stamford, Lincs PE90 2LJ. Tel: 01780 751363. Military and naval, particularly WWII.

Buttercross Books

2 The Paddock, Bingham, Nottingham NG13 8HQ. Tel/fax: 0115 9 837147. Napoleonic era and First World War. Lists available.

Caliver Books

816/818 London Road, Leigh-on-Sea, Essex SS9 3NH. Tel/fax: 01702 73986. Military history up to 1900. Shop and mail order. Lists available.

Chelifer Books

Todd Close, Curthwaite, Wigton, Cumbria CA7 8BE. Military history, including units. Lists available.

The Collector

36 The Colonnade, Piece Hall, Halifax, West Yorks HX1 1RS. Military, naval and aviation history: all periods.

Q. M. Dabney & Company

PO Box 42026-MH, Washington, DC 20015, USA. Military books of all periods. Lists available for $US1 each.

Peter de Lotz

20 Downside Crescent, Hampstead, London NW3 2AP. Tel: 020 7794 5709 (fax: 020 7284 3058). Military, naval and aviation history, with emphasis on regimental and divisional histories.

Tom Donovan Military Books

Flat 4, 22 Florence Road, Brighton, East Sussex BN1 6DJ. Tel: 01273 566230, email: tom@turnerdonovan.com. Printed works and manuscript material relating to the British Military Services. Regular lists.

Francis Edwards

13 Great Newport Street, Charing Cross Road, London WC2H 4JA. Tel: 020 7379 7669 (fax: 020 7836 5977). All aspects of military history. Lists.

Empire Books

61 Broad Lane, Rochdale, Lancs OL16 4PL. Tel: 01706 666678. Military, naval and aviaton. Special interest Australian forces, Vietnam and Colonial wars.

Chris Evans Books

Unit 6, Jervoise Drive, Birmingham B31 2XU. Tel/fax: 0121 477 6700. General military history. Lists available.

Falconwood Transport and Military Bookshop.

5 Falconwood Parade, The Green, Welling, Kent DA16 2PL. Tel: 020 8303 8291. Military, naval and aviation history.

Kenneth Fergusson

The Book Room, The Post Office, Twyning, Tewkesbury, Glos GL20 6DF. Tel: 01684 295855. Military and aviation history.

Ken Ford Military Books

93 Nutshalling Avenue, Rownhams, Southampton SO1 8AY. Tel: 023 8073 9437. British Colonial Wars.

John Gaunt

21 Harvey Road, Bedford MK41 9LF. Tel: 01234 217686. Numismatic books including medal reference.

GM Services

98 Junction Road, Andover, Hampshire SP10 3JA. Tel/fax: 01264 362048. Postal auctions of military books.

Tony Gilbert Antique Books

101 Whipps Cross Road, Leytonstone, London E11 1NW. Tel: 020 8530 7472. Military, naval and aviation history.

G. L. Green.

18 Aldenham Avenue, Radlett, Herts WD7 8HX. Tel: 01923 857077. Naval and maritime history.

George Harris

Heathview, Habberley Road, Bewdley, Worcs DY12 1JH. Tel: 01299 402413. Napoleonic, Victorian campaigns and the First World War.

Hersant's Military Books

17 The Drive, High Barnet, Herts EN5 4JG. Tel/fax: 020 8440 6816. General military history. Lists available by period.

Michael Hicks Beach

99 York Mansions, London SW11 4BN. Tel: 020 7622 2270. British and Imperial military history.

Steven J. Hopkins

Court Farm, Kington, Flyford Flavell, Worc WR7 4DQ. Tel: 01386 793427, email: tokyngton@aol.com. Military books and prints.

Jade Publishing Ltd

5 Leefields Close, Uppermill, Oldham, Lancs OL3 6LA. Tel: 01475 870944. British and imperial military books.

Jerboa-Redcap Books

PO Box 1058, Highstown, N.J. 08520, USA. Tel: (609) 443 3817. British military books (all services), including collectables. Catalogues.

Keegan's Bookshop

Merchant's Place, Reading RG1 1DT. Tel/fax: 01734 587253. Secondhand booksellers with good stock of military titles. Shop in town centre. Parking nearby.

King's Shilling Military History Books

15 Bodiam Avenue, Bexhill-on-Sea, East Sussex TN40 2LS. Tel: 01424 217156. All aspects of military history.

Roger Knowles

26 Church Road, Norton Canes, Cannock, Staffs WS11 3PD. Tel: 01543 279313. Specialising in military history.

John Lewcock

6 Chewells Lane, Haddenham, Ely, Cambs CB6 3SS. Tel: 01353 741152. Naval history.

Liverpool Medal Company Ltd

42 Bury Business Centre, Kay Street, Bury, Lancs BL9 6BU. Tel: 0161 763 4610/4612 (fax: 0161 763 4963). Medal dealers, but also publish an occasional separate book catalogue.

London Pride

14E Fort Lee Road, Bogota, NJ 07603, USA. Tel: 201 525-1828 (fax: 201 525-0815). Military books.

Ian Lynn

258 Upper Fant Road, Maidstone, Kent ME16 8BX. Tel: 01622 728525. Military history.

John . Manning

18, Fengate-Heacham, King's Lynn, Norfolk PE31 7BG, email: jhmanning@tiscali.co.uk. Military medals.

Marcet Books

4a Nelson Road, Greenwich, London SE10 9JB. Tel: 020 8853 5408. Naval history.

G. & D. I. Marrin & Sons

149 Sandgate Road, Folkestone, Kent CT20 2DA. Tel: 01303 253016 (fax: 01303 850956). Specialising in material relating to the First World War.

McLaren Books

91 West Clyde Street, Helensburgh, Dunbartonshire G84 8BB. Tel: 01436 676453. Naval history.

Midland Counties Publications

Unit 3, Maizefield, Hinckley, Leicestershire LE10 1YF. Tel: 01455 233747. Aviation books.

Military Bookman

29 East 93rd Street, New York, NY 10128, USA. Tel: (212) 348 1280. Large stock of military history relating to all services worldwide and all periods.

Military Bookworm

PO Box 235, London SE23 1NS. Tel/fax: (020) 8291 1435. Regimental and divisional histories, campaign histories, biographies, army lists, etc. www.militarybookworm.co.uk.

Military History Bookshop

2 Broadway, London N11 3DU. Tel/fax: 020 8368 8568. Lists, subscription £2.50 (4 issues).

Military Parade Bookshop

The Parade, Marlborough, Wilts SN8 1NE. Tel: 01672 515470 (fax: 01980 630 150). New and secondhand books. Lists available.

Motor Books

St Martins Court, London WC2N 4AL. Tel: 020 7836 5376 (fax: 020 7497 2539). Comprehensive stock of military books in print.

Military & Naval History

54 Regis Road, Tettenhall, Wolverhampton WV6 8RW. Tel: 01902 756402. British military history.

Pen & Sword Books Ltd.

47 Church Street, Barnsley, S. Yorks S70 2AS. Tel: 01226 734555 (fax: 01226 734438). Military titles.

Roberts

PO Box 1, Brimpton, Reading, RG7 4RJ. Tel: 0118 971 4044. New and secondhand military history.

Savannah Publications

90 Dartmouth Road, Forest Hill, London SE23 3HZ. Tel: 020 8244 4350 (fax: 020 8244 2448). Email: savpub@dircon.co.uk. Publisher and distributor of reference works relating to British Army, Navy and RAF history/medals. Biography and service histories/genealogy. Free catalogues. www.savannah-publications.com.

Anthony J. Simmonds

66 Royal Hill, Greenwich, London SE10 8RT. Tel: 020 8692 1794. Naval and maritime history. Occasional catalogues.

Andrew Skinner

42 Earlspark Avenue, Newlands, Glasgow G43 2HW. Tel: 0141 632 4903 (fax: 0141 632 8453). General military history stock with special emphasis on Scotland. Monthly lists.

Southern Medals

PO Box 50, Knebworth, Herts SG3 6UE. Tel: 01438 811657 (fax 01438 813320).

Frank Smith Maritime Aviation Books

98/100 Heaton Road, Newcastle upon Tyne. Tel: 0191 265 6333. Naval, maritime/aviation history.

Spink & Son Ltd (Christie's International)

69 Southampton Row, Bloomsbury, London WC1B 4ET. Tel: 020 7563 4000 (fax: 020 7563 4066). Specialist Book Department. Email: info@spinkandson.com.
www.spink-online.com.

Tasmedals

8 Orana Place, Taroona, Tas 7053, Australia. Tel: 613 6227 8825 (fax: 613 6227 9898).

THCL Books

185 Lammack Road, Blackburn, Lancs BB1 8LH. Military book specialist and publishers of collectors' cards of medal heroes. Lists available.

Stephen Tilston

37 Bennett Park, Blackheath, London SE3 9RA. Tel/fax: 020 8318 9181. General stock, but specialising in the First World War. Lists available.

Token Publishing Ltd.

Orchard House, Duchy Road, Heathpark, Honiton, Devon EX14 1YD. Tel: 01404 46972 (fax: 01404 44788). Email: info@ tokenpublishing.com. www.tokenpublishing. com.

Publishers of *Medal News* and *Coin News* and related titles. Organisers of the Britannia Medal Fair.

Ken Trotman Ltd.

Unit 11, 135 Ditton Walk, Cambridge CB5 8QD. Tel: 01223 211030 (fax: 01223 212317). Large, wide-ranging stock. Lists available: 3 per year.

Brian Turner Military Books

1132 London Road, Leigh-on-Sea, Essex SS9 2AJ. Tel/fax: 01702 78771. Printed works and documentation relating to military, naval and aviation history, specialising in the WWI.

Robin Turner

30 Great Norwood Street, Cheltenham, Glos. GL50 2BH. Tel: 01242 234303. Military, specialising in the Napoleonic period.

Twin Pillars Books

145 Russell St. Kettering, Northamptonshire, NN16 0EW.

Mark Weber

35 Elvaston Place, London SW7 5NW. Tel: 020 7225 2506 (fax: 020 7581 8233). Specialises in official war histories and books by and about Sir Winston Churchill.

Terence Wise

99 Alderson Drive, Doncaster, DN2 6DA. Military history especially regimental and divisional histories. Lists available.

Woodford Books

The Lodge, Well Street, Docking, King's Lynn, Norfolk PE31 8LQ. Tel: 01485 518700. Medal and military books and ephemera. Lists available.

Directory listings in this section are free of charge.

To be included in this section, please email your entry to: abbey@tokenpublishing.com, or write to Token Publishing Limited, Orchard House, Duchy Road, Heathpark, Honiton, Devon EX14 1YD.

FAIRS

Many fairs are held regularly and organised by professionals, in addition a number of societies organise fairs for the public (Victorian Military Society, Aldershot Militaria Society, etc.). The dates are usually well advertised in MEDAL NEWS and other publications, however, times and venues are liable to change so it is advisable in every instance to telephone the organisers beforehand. Listed below are the major fair organisers and the events known to us.

Abergavenny Militaria and Medal Fair

Market Hall, Cross Street, Abergavenny. Tel: 01873 735811.

Aldershot Militaria and Medal Fair

Princes Hall, Princes Way, Aldershot, Hants. Mark Carter. Tel: 01753 534777.

Bolton Militaria Fair

Horwich Leisure Centre, Victoria Road, Bolton. Northern Arms Fairs. Tel: 01423 780759.

Britannia Medal Fair

Carisbrooke Hall, Victory Services Club, 63-79 Seymour Street, Marble Arch, London W2. Two p.a. Token Publishing. Tel: 01404 46972.

Bromley Medal and Militaria Fair

Civic Centre, Kentish Way, Bromley, Kent. Ray Brough. Tel: 07714 094009.

Cardiff Fair

City Hall, Cardiff. M. J. Promotions. Tel: 01792 415293.

Cheltenham Fair

The Regency Hotel, Cheltenham Hotel. Tel: 0117 9623203.

Cheshunt Militaria Fair

Wolsey Hall, Windmill Lane, Cheshunt, Herts. Hands Militaria Fairs. Tel/fax: 01892 730233.

Durham Militaria Fair

County Hall, Aykley Heads, Durham City. Northern Arms Fairs. Tel: 01423 780759.

East Grinstead Fair

Large Parish Hall, De La Warr Road, East Grinsted. Tel: 01342 326317.

Farnham Militaria Fair

The Maltings, Bridge Square, Farnham, Surrey. Hands Militaria Fairs. Tel/fax: 01892 730233.

Guildford Militaria Fair

Guildford Civic, London Road, Guildford. Hands Militaria Fairs. Tel/fax: 01892 730233.

Harwood Military Collectors Fair

The Markland Room, Longsight Methodist Hall, Longsight Lane, Harwood Bolton. Tel: 01204 436501.

Harwood Military Collectors Fair

Houghton Village Hall, Houghton, Carlisle. Tel: 016973 71465.

Liverpool Militaria Fair

The Village Hotel, Whiston, Liverpool. Northern Arms Fairs. Tel: 01423 780759.

London Arms Fairs

The Paragon Hotel, Lillie Road, London SW6. 4 shows per year. Douglas Fryer. Tel: 01273 475 959.

Macclesfield Militaria & Medal Fair

The Senior Citizens Hall, Duke Street Car Park, off Roe Street, Town Centre. Dave Cooper. Tel: 01538 703354 (eves/weekends) or 01538 702738.

Midhurst Militaria Fair

The Grange Leisure Centre, Bepton Road. Hands Militaria Fairs. Tel/fax: 01892 730233.

David Douglas Militaria Fairs

The Original Hotel, Roslin, Edinburgh; Scotch Corner Hotel, Scotch Corner, North Yorkshire and Kingston Park, Newcastle upon Tyne. The Maltings, Easter Wynd, West Street, Berwick Upon Tweed; The Novotel, Kingston Park, Newcastle upon Tyne. David Douglas Militaria Fairs. Tel: 01668 215571.

Preston Arms and Militaria Fair

Nelson Suite, Swallow Hotel, Preston New Road, Samlesbury, Preston. Tel: 01254 362412.

OMRS Annual Convention

NEW VENUE: The British Medical Association, Tavistock Square, London W1. Contact: OMRS Membership Secretary, PO Box 248, Snettisham, King's Lynn, Norfolk PE31 7TA. OMRS members only.

South Coast Coin & Medal Fair

The Pavilion, Southampton University, Wide Lane Sports Grounds, Wide Lane, Eastleigh. Tel: 07890 764452.

Stockport Arms, Medals & MilitariaFair

Britannia Hotel, Dialstone Lane, Offerton. Tel: 0161 624 6211.

Stratford Upon Avon Militaria & Medal Fair

Stratford Leisure & Visitor Centre, Bridgefoot, Stratford upon Avon. Warks. Mark Carter. Tel: 01753 534777.

Victorian Military Fair

Victorian Military Society, 20 Priory Road, Newbury, Berks RG14 7QN. Tel: 01635 48628.

Wakefield Militaria and Medal Fair

Outwood Memorial Hall, Outwood, Wakefield, W. Yorks. The Medal Centre. Tel 01434 609794.

Wakefield Coin & Medal Fair (Eddie Smith)

Cedar Court Hotel, Denby Dale Road, Calder Grove, Wakefield, WF4 3QZ. Eddie Smith. Tel: 01522 684681.

Watford Arms, Militaria and Medal Fair

Bushey Hall School, London Road, Bushey, Herts. Sovereign Fairs. Tel: 01438 811657.

West Country Militaria and Medal Fair

Yate Leisure Centre, Kennedy Way, Yate, near Chipping Sodbury, Bristol. Mark Carter. Tel: 01753 534777.

York Coin & Medal Fair

The Grandstand, York Racecourse, York. Tel: 01793 513431 or 01425 656459.

Military, Aviation & Naval Book Fair, York

The Novotel, Fishergate, York. Northern Arms Fairs. Tel: 01763 248400. Organised by the Provincial Booksellers Fairs Association. Two p.a.

West Midlands Arms Fair

The Village Hall, Walsall. Tel: 01785 663344.

MUSEUMS AND COLLECTIONS

The majority of the museums listed below are the regimental museums of the British Army, Militia, Yeomanry and Territorials, but we have included other museums pertaining to the Royal Navy, the Royal Marines and the Royal Air Force where medals form a significant part of the collections. So, too, the museums of the police forces, fire brigades, Red Cross, Royal National Lifeboat Institution and similar bodies have been included where relevant. Readers should also bear in mind that many general museums in our towns and cities boast fine collections of military medals pertaining to their local regiments. We have included those of which we are aware. The date of foundation is shown in brackets after the name.

Some service museums have been undergoing refits, relocations and amalgamations. We would welcome further information from readers about these changes and about other general museums in their areas with a good coverage of medals to local regiments.

Space prevents us from going into details regarding the scope of individual museum holdings. We give the postal address, telephone number, and the name of the curator wherever possible, also the hours of opening and admission charges (where applicable) at the time of going to press. Where two charges are listed, the first denotes the full adult price and the second the concessionary charge (OAPs, students and children). Where three charges are given the first is the full adult price, the second the OAP concession and the third the children's charge. It is always sensible, particularly before travelling long distances to visit a museum or collection, to telephone and check that the published details are still correct.

Some museums may have libraries holding archival material; this should be checked out and the conditions for use ascertained as such holdings will not have the resources to answer detailed research enquiries.

Where museums are devoted to one particular regimental/service/unit or whatever, they are listed by title in alphabetical order. This may not always accord with the exact official name of the museum which is given on the address line. The well-known national museums are listed alphabetically by name. More general museums which include medal collections are listed by the name of the town. If you cannot see the name of the museum you require at first glance, it may be worth searching through the full list, as some museums escape neat classification and would require extensive cross-referencing to do them full justice.

Aberdeen Maritime Museum (1984)
Provost Ross's House, Shiprow, Aberdeen. (01224 5857888). Monday–Saturday: 10am–5pm. Free.

Airborne Forces Museum (1969)
Browning Barracks, Aldershot, Hants GU11 2BU. (01252 349619). Monday–Friday: 10am-4.30pm (last admission 3.45pm). Saturday, Sunday, Bank Holidays: 10am–4pm. Closed: Christmas and New Year. £3/£1. Tina Pittock and Ann Brown.

Aldershot Military Museum (1984)
Queen's Avenue, Aldershot, Hants GU11 2LG. (01252 314598). Daily 10am–5.00pm. Closed: Christmas and New Year. £2/£1. Sally Day.

Argyll and Sutherland Highlanders Regimental Museum (1945)
Stirling Castle, Stirling FK8 1EH. 01786-475165. Fax: (01786-446038). Daily, Easter–September: 9.30am-5pm, October–Easter: 10am-4.15pm.

Army Medical Services Museum
Keogh Barracks, Ash Vale, Aldershot, GU12 5RQ. (Civilian number: 01252 868612. Fax: 01252 868832. Email: armymedicalmuseum@btinternet.com. www.ams-museum.org.uk). Monday–Friday, 10am–3.30pm (evening and weekend group visits by appointment). Admission free.

Army Physical Training Corps Museum (1949)
Army School of Physical Training, Queen's Avenue, Aldershot, Hants GU11 2LB. (01252 347168, email: aptcmuseum@aspt.mod.uk). Monday–Thursday 9am–4.30pm. Friday 9am–12.30pm. Weekends and Evenings by appointment. Admission free. Major (Retd), R. J. Kelly.

Arundel Toy and Military Museum (1978)
Dolls House, 23 High Street, Arundel, West Sussex. (01903 507446/882908). Daily, June–August: 10.30am–5pm. Otherwise open on Bank Holidays and weekends in winter. £1.25/90p.

Aylmer Military Collection
Nunwell House, Brading, Isle of Wight PO36 0JQ. (01983 407240). July–September: Monday–Wednesday, 1pm–5pm, or by appointment. £5/£4 (children accompanied by adults). J. A. Aylmer.

Ayrshire Yeomanry Museum
Rozelle House, Monument Road, Alloway by Ayr KA7 4NQ. (01292 264091). Monday–Saturday: 10am–5pm. Sundays: April–October, 2–5pm.

Bedfordshire and Hertfordshire Regimental Museum
Wardown Park, Luton LU2 7HA. Tuesday–Saturday: 10am–5pm. Sunday: 1pm–5pm. Free.

Black Watch Museum (1924)
Balhousie Castle, Perth PH1 5HR. (0131 310 8530. Fax: 01738 643245). May–September: Monday–Saturday, 10am–4.30pm. October–April: Monday–Friday, 10am–3.30pm. Free. Maj J. W. Proctor, MBE.

100th Bomb Group Memorial Museum (1978)
Common Road, Dickleburgh, near Diss, Norfolk. (0379 740708). Medals and memorabilia of the Eighth Air Force and 100th Bomb Group. May–September: Saturday, Sunday and Wednesday, 10am–5pm. October–April: weekends only, 10am–4.30pm. Free. S. P. Hurry.

Border Regiment and King's Own Royal Border Regiment Museum (1932)
Queen Mary's Tower, The Castle, Carlisle CA3 8UR. (01228 532774. Fax: 01228 521275. Email: RHQ@kingsownborder.demon.co.uk). Open daily. April–September: 9.30am–6pm, October: 10am–5pm, November–March: 10am–5pm. Closed: 24–26 December & 1 January. Admission included in entry charge to the Castle. £3.50/£1.80/£2.70. Curator: Stuart Eastwood.

British in India Museum (1972)
Hendon Mill, Hallam Road, Nelson BB9 8AD. (01282 613129.) Monday–Friday 10am–4pm. Closed Christmas & Bank Holidays. £2.50/Under 16s £1.

British Red Cross Museum and Archives (1984)
Uk Office, 44 Moorefields, London EC2Y 9AL. (01078 777058. Email: enquiry@redcross.org.uk, www.medicalmuseums.org). Monday–Fridays 10am–1pm and 2pm–4pm. Free, by appt. Jen Young.

Bygones
Fore Street, St Marychurch, Torquay, Devon TQ1 4PR. (01803 326108.) Devonshire Regt., and Royal Marines. Daily (except Christmas Day). Summer: 10am–10pm. Winter: 10am–4pm.

Caernarfon Air Museum
Caernarfon Airport, Dinas Dinlle, Caernarfon, Gwynedd LL54 5TP. March–November: 9.30am–5.30pm. £2.50/£1.50.

Cambridge, Scott Polar Research Institute Museum (1920)
Lensfield Road, Cambridge CB2 1ER. (01223 336540.) Tuesday–Saturday: 2.30pm–4pm (except bank holidays). The Library and archives (by appointment only) are open 9am–1pm and 2pm–5.30pm, Monday–Friday. Free. Robert Headland.

Castle and Regimental Museum
The Castle, Monmouth, NP25 3DG. 01600 772175. Email: curator@monmouthcastlemuseum.org.uk, www.monmouthcastlemuseum.otg.uk April(or March if Easter falls early)–October: 2pm–5pm, daily. Free but donations welcomed. Eric Old.

Cheshire Military Museum (1972)
The Castle, Chester CH1 2DN. 01244 327617. Daily, 10am–5pm. £2/£1. Major Nigel Hine.

Churchill Museum and Cabinet War Rooms (1984)
Clive Steps, King Charles Street, London SW1A 2AQ. 9.30am–6.00pm. £11/£9.

City of London Police Museum (1964)
37 Wood Street, London EC2P 2NQ. 020 7601 2705/2455. Fax: 020 7601 2747 Free, by written appointment only. Roger Appleby.

Coldstream Museum
12 Market Square, Coldstream. TD12 4BD. 01890 882630. Open April to end September: Monday–Saturday, 10am–4pm and Sunday 2–4pm. October: Monday–Saturday 1–4pm.

Dingwall Museum (1975)
Town Hall, High Street, Dingwall, Rossshire IV15 9RY. 01349 865366. May–September: Monday–Saturday, 10am–4:30pm. Otherwise by appt. only. Medals and militaria of the Seaforth Highlanders, and items pertaining to Major General Sir Hector Macdonald ("Fighting Mac") Ian Macleod.

Duke of Cornwall's Light Infantry Regimental Museum (1925)
The Keep, Bodmin PL31 1EG. 01208 72810. Monday–Friday, 9am–5pm. £2.50/50p. Major T. W. Stipling.

Duke of Wellington's Regiment Museum (1960)
Bankfield Museum, Boothtown Road, Halifax HX3 6HQ. 01422 352334/354823. Tues–Sat: 10am–5pm. Sunday: 2.30pm–5pm. Free. John Spencer.

Durham Light Infantry Museum (1969)
Aykley Heads, Durham DH1 5TU. 0191 384 2214. Open every day except Christmas Eve & Christmas Day. Summer: 10am–5pm. Winter: 10am–4pm. £3.25/£2.15/£1.35. Email: dli@durham.gov.uk, www.durham.gov.uk/dli. Stephen D. Shannon.

Essex Regiment Museum (1938)
Oaklands Park, Moulsham Street, Chelmsford, Essex CM2 9AQ. 01245-615100. Fax: 01245-262428. Email: pompadour@chelmsfordbc.gov.uk. Monday–Saturday: 10am–5pm. Sunday: 2pm-5pm (winter, 1pm–4pm). Free. Ian Hook BA.

Fleet Air Arm Museum (1964)
RNAS Yeovilton, Somerset BA22 8HT. 01935 840565. April–October: Open Daily 10am–5.30pm. November–March: Open 10am–4.30pm Closed Mondays, Tuesdays and December 24, 25 & 26. £13.00/£11.00/£9.00. Graham Mottram.

Fusiliers Museum of Northumberland
The Abbot's Tower, Alnwick Castle, Alnwick NE66 1NG. 01665 602152. Easter–October: 11am–5pm, daily. Alnwick Castle admission charges apply. Archive available by appointment.

Glasgow Art Gallery and Museum (1854)
Kelvingrove, Glasgow G3 8AG. 0141 287 2699.
Includes medals of the Glasgow Yeomanry,
Highland Light Infantry and regiments associated
with the city. Monday–Thursday and Saturday
10am–to 5pm, Friday and Sunday 11am–5pm.

Gordon Highlanders' Regimental Museum (1961)
St Lukes, Viewfield Road, Aberdeen AB15
7XH. 01224 311200. Fax: 01224 319323. Email:
museum@gordonhighlanders.com,
www.gordonhighlanders.com. February–
November: Tuesday–Saturday, 10.00am–4/4.30pm
(closed Mondays). Sarah Mackay.

Green Howards Regimental Museum
Trinity Church Square, Richmond, Yorkshire DL10
4QN. 01748 826561. Fax 01748 821924. Contact
museum for opening times. Admission charges
apply.

Guards Museum (1988)
Wellington Barracks, Birdcage Walk, London SW1E
6HQ. 020 7 414 3271. Open every day (Monday–
Sunday) except Bank Holidays and certain
ceremonial days. 10am–4pm. Museum is closed
mid-December–February, 1 each year. £3 adults,
£2 Senior Citizens and under 16's. Curator Andrew
Wallis.

Gurkha Museum (1974)
Peninsular Barracks, Romsey Road, Winchester,
Hants SO23 8TS. 01962 842832. Monday–Saturday:
10am–5pm (last entry 4.30pm). Sunday: 12pm–
4pm (last entry 3.30pm). Adults £2.00, OAP £1.00,
Children under 16 & Servicemen free. Major G.
Davies.

Gwynedd Museum & Art Gallery, Bangor
Ffordd Gwynedd, Bangor, Gwynedd, LL57 1DT.
01248 353368. Tuesday–Friday: 12.30pm–4.30pm,
Saturday: 10.30am–4.30pm. Free. Includes medals
and militaria of the Welsh regiments. Esther
Roberts.

Hawkinge, Kent, Battle of Britain Museum (1969)
Hawkinge, Kent CT18 7AG. 0130 389 3140. Easter-
end of May: 11am–4pm. July–September: 10am-
5pm. £2.50/£2 £1.50. Mike Llewellyn.

Hertford Regiment Museum
At the Hertford Museum at 18 Bull Plain, Hertford.
Tuesday–Saturday: 10am–5pm. Admission Free.
SG14 1DJ. 01992 582686. Fax: 01992 552100.

Hitchin Museum at Hertfordshire Yeomanry
Paynes Park, Hitchin, Herts SG5 1EH. 01462
434476. Monday–Saturday: 10am-5pm. Closed:
Wednesdays, Sundays and Bank holidays. Free.

Honourable Artillery Company Museum
Armoury House, City Road, London EC1 2BQ.
Apply in writing for a visit.

Hornsea Folk Museum (1978)
Burn's Farm, 11 Newbegin, Hornsea, East Yorkshire
HU18 1BP. 01964 533443. Easter weekend, 1
May–30 September: Monday–Saturday, 11am–5pm
and Sunday 2pm–5pm. £1.50/£1. E. Yorkshire Regt,
E. Riding Yeo., Royal Artillery, The Home Front. Dr
J. E. S. Walker.

Household Cavalry Museum
Household Cavalry Museum, Horse Guards,
Whitehall, London SW1A 2AX. 020 7930 3070.
Email: museum@householdcavalry.co.uk. www.
householdcavalrymuseum.co.uk. Monday–Sunday
10am–6pm March–Oct and 10am–5pm Novembe–
February (except 24–26 December and Good
Friday) Last admissions 45 mins before closing.
£6.00/£4.00, groups: 10% discount for 8+, school
parties: On request, family (2+2) £15.00. Martin
Westwood.

Household Cavalry Museum
Combermere Barracks, Windsor, Berkshire SL4
3DN. 01753 755112. Archives open by request for
research and school /group visits. From £27 for
research, £8 per head for groups. John Lloyd

HMS Belfast(1978)
Morgan's Lane, Tooley Street, London SE1 2JH.
1 March–30 October: 10am–6pm. 1 November–28
February: 10.00am–5.00pm. £9.95/£6.15.

Imperial War Museum (1917)
Lambeth Road, London SE1 6HZ. 020 7416 5320.
www.iwm.org.uk. Daily, 10am–6pm. Free.

Imperial War Museum Duxford (1976)
Duxford, Cambridge CB2 4QR. 01223 835000. www.
iwm.org.uk. Daily, March–October: 10am-6pm and
October–March: 10am-4pm. £14.95 (special prices
apply on air shows or event days). Under 16s free.

Imperial War Museum North (2002)
The Quays, Trafford Wharf, Trafford Park,
Manchester M17 1TZ. www.iwm.org.uk. March–
October:10am-6pm. November–February:10am–
5.00pm. Free admission.

Inns of Court and City Yeomanry Museum (1947)
10 Stone Buildings, Lincoln's Inn, London WC2A
3TG. 020 7405 8112. Monday–Friday, 10am–4pm.
By appointment only. Free. Denis Durkin.

Intelligence Corps Museum
Defence Intelligence and Security Centre,
Chicksands, Nr Shefford, Beds SG17 5PR.
01462 752297. Monday–Friday: 10am–3.30pm.
Appointment necessary. Free.
Major A. J. Edwards.

Kent and Sharpshooters Yeomanry Museum
Hever Castle, Tonbridge, Kent TN8 7NG. 1
March–30 November: 12pm–5pm, daily. Winter
(GMT): 11am–4pm. Boris Mollo TD MA FSA.

King's Own Royal Regiment Museum (Lancaster)
Lancaster City Museum, Market Square, Lancaster
LA1 1HT. 01524 64637. Fax: 01524 841692.
Email: kingsownmuseum@iname.com. www.
kingsownmuseum.plus.com. Monday–Saturday,
10am–5pm except between christmas and new
year. Free. Curator: Peter Donnelly BA AMA.

King's Own Scottish Borderers Regimental Museum (1954)
Berwick Barracks, The Parade, Berwick-upon-
Tweed TD15 1DG. 01289 307426. Fax: 01289
331928. Monday–Saturday: 9.30am–4pm. Closed:
Easter, Christmas, New Year and certain other
holidays. £3.30/ £2.50/£1.70. Lieut. Colonel C. G. O.
Hogg OBE , DL.

King's Own Yorkshire Light Infantry Regimental Museum (1932)
Museum and Art Gallery, Chequer Road,
Doncaster, South Yorkshire DN1 2AE. 01302
734293. Email: museum@doncaster.gov.uk.
Monday–Saturday: 10am-5pm. Free. Steve Tagg.

King's Regiment Museum (1930)
Temporarily closed, due to reopen within the new
Museum of Liverpool on the Waterfront (late 2011).
Matthew Buck. 0151 478 4065. Fax: 0151 478 4095.
Email: matthewbuck@liverpoolmuseums.org.uk.

15th/19th King's Royal Hussars (Light Dragoons)/ Northumberland Hussars
Tyne & Wear Museums, Discovery Museum,
Blandford Square, Newcastle-upon-Tyne NE1 4JA.
0191 232 6789. Monday–Saturday: 10am-5pm.
Sunday: 2pm-5pm. Roberta Twinn.

Kohima Museum (1991)
Imphal Barracks, Fulford Road, York YO10 4HD.
01904 635212. Free, by appointment only.

HorsePower: The Museum of The King's Royal Hussars Museum in Winchester (1980)
Home Headquarters (South): Peninsula Barracks,
Romsey Road, Winchester. 01962 828541.
Tuesday–Friday: 10am-4pm. Weekends and Bank
Holidays: 12pm-4pm. Free. Major P. J. C. Beresford,
Regimental Secretary.

Light Infantry Museum (1990)
Peninsular Barracks, Romsey Road, Winchester.
01962 828530. Tuesday–Saturday: 10am-5pm.
Sunday: 12pm-4pm. £1.50/75p. Patrick Kirby.

Liverpool Scottish Regimental Museum
Botanic Road, Wavertree, Liverpool. 0151-645-
5717. By appointment. Mr D. Reeves, Hon. Curator.

London Fire Brigade Museum (1967)
94A Southwark Bridge Road, London SE1 0EG. 020
7587 2894. Fax: 020 7587 2878. Email: museum@
london-fire.gov.uk. Monday–Friday: 9am-4.30pm.
£3 per person or for groups over ten people £2.
Tour by appointment only. Esther Mann.

The London Scottish Regimental Museum
Regimental Headquarters, 95 Horseferry Road,
London SW1P 2DX. 020 7630 1639. Free (by
appointment only).

The Military Museum of Devon and Dorset
The Keep, Bridport Road, Dorchester, Dorset, DT1
1RN. 01305 264066. Email: info@keepmilitary
museum.org. www.keepmilitarymuseum.org. Mon–
Sat 9.30am–5pm, April–September.Tue–Fri, 10am–
4.30pm, October–March. Closed at Christmas.

National Army Museum (1960)
Royal Hospital Road, Chelsea, London SW3 4HT.
020 7730 0717. Fax: 020 7823 6573. Email: info@
chelsea–pensioners.org.uk. (Closed: 1 January,
Good Friday, Early May Bank Holiday and 24–26
December). Daily, 10am–5.30pm. Free. J. Murray.

National Maritime Museum (1934)
Romney Road, Greenwich, London SE10 9NF. 020
8858 4422. Fax: 020 8312 6632. Summer: Monday–
Saturday, 10am-6pm and Sunday, 12pm-5pm.
Winter: Monday–Saturday, 10am-5pm and Sunday,
2pm-5pm. Free. Director: Roy Clare.

National Museum of Ireland (1877)
Collins Barracks, Benburb Street, Dublin 7. 00353
16777 444. www.museum.ie. Free.

National War Museum
The Castle, Edinburgh. 0131 247 4405. Email:
s.allen@nms.ac.uk (enquiries). April–November:
9.45am-5.30pm. December–March: 9.45am-4.30pm.
Free (but entrance fee to the castle). Stuart Allan.

Newark Air Museum (1968)
Winthrop Airfield, Newark-on-Trent NG24 2NY.
01636 707170. Open daily except Christmas Eve/
Day & Boxing Day. April–September: weekdays,
weekends and BH, 10am–5pm. October–March:
10am-5pm, daily. November–February: 10am-4pm,
daily. £5.50/£3.25. Mike Smith.

Northamptonshire Regimental Museum
Abington Park Museum, Abington, Northampton
NN1 5LW. 01604 838110. Tues–Sun/BH: 1pm-5pm
(Nov–Feb: 1pm-4pm). Free. Mrs J.A. Minchinton.

Order of St. John of Jerusalem Museum
St. John's Gate, St. John's Lane, Clerkenwell,
London EC1M 4DA. 0171 253 6644. Tuesday–Friday:
10am–5pm. Saturday: 10am–4pm. P. Willis.

Oxfordshire & Bucks Light Infantry Museum
Currently closed and expected to reopen in 2013.
A research centre manned by volunteers has
been set up at The Old Tannery, Hensington Road,
Woodstock OX20 1JL, email: research@sofo.org.uk.
Open Thursdays 10am–5pm by appointment.

Polish Institute and Sikorski Museum
20 Princes Gate, London SW7 1QA. 0171 589 9249.
Monday–Friday: 2pm-4pm.

Prince of Wales's Own 9th /12th Lancers Regimental Museum (1972)
Derby Museum and Art Gallery, The Strand, Derby DE1 1BS. 01332 716659. Monday: 11am–5pm. Tuesday–Saturday: 10am–5pm. Sunday and Bank Holidays: 1pm–4pm. Free. Vivienne Rudd.

Prince of Wales's Own Regiment of Yorkshire Museum
3A Tower Street, York YO1 9SB. 01904 662790. Email: regsec@pwoyorkshire.army.mod.uk. Mon–Saturday and Bank Holidays: 9.30am-4.30pm. Closed between Christmas and New Year's Day. Includes medals of The West Yorkshire and The East Yorkshire Regiments, and The Prince of Wales's Own Regiment of Yorkshire. £2/£1. Major (Retd) N. Le B. Allbeury MBE.

Princess of Wales's Royal Regiment and Queen's Regiment Museum (1987)
5 Keep Yard, Dover Castle, Kent CT16 1HU. 01304 240121. Email: pwrrqueensmuseum@btconnect. com. Summer: 9.30am-6.30pm, daily. Winter: (closed Tuesday–Wednesday), 10am-4pm. Major J. C. Rogerson.

Queen's Dragoon Guards Regimental Museum
Cardiff Castle, Cardiff, South Glamorgan CF1 2RB. 029 2078 1213. Gareth Gill. For further information and opening times, please visit the website: www. cardiffmuseum.org.uk

Queen's Lancashire Regiment (1929)
Incorporating East Lancashire Regiment, South Lancashire Regiment (Prince of Wales's Volunteers), Loyal Regiment (North Lancashire) Lancashire Regiment.
Fulwood Barracks, Preston, Lancs PR2 8AA. 01772 260 362. Tuesdays–Thursdays or by appointment. 9.30am-4.30pm. Free. Jane Davies MA.

The Queen's Own Highlanders Collection
Fort George, Ardersier, Inverness, IV2 7TD. 01463 224380. Monday–Friday: April–September, 10am-6pm/October–March, 10am-4pm. Free.

Queen's Own Royal West Kent Regimental Museum (1961)
St Faith's Street, Maidstone, Kent ME14 1LH. 01622 602842. Monday–Saturday: 10am-5.15pm. Sunday: 11am-4pm. Free. Colonel H.B.H. Waring, OBE.

Queen's Royal Lancers
Thoresby Courtyard, Thoresby Park, Near Ollerton Nottinghamshire, NG22 9EP. Easter to 31st October: Wednesday to Sunday 10.30-16.30 (Last entry 16.00) incl. Bank Holidays. 1st November to 14th December & 1st March-Easter: Weekends: 10.30-16.30 (Last entry 16.00) By appointment. 15th December-28th February: By appointment. Capt Mick Holtby / Robert Osborn.

Queen's Royal Surrey Regimental Museum (1979)
Clandon Park, Guildford, Surrey GU4 7RQ. 01483 223419. April–October: 12.00–5.00pm. Closed: Monday, Friday and Saturday. Ian E. J. Chatfield.

Redoubt Fortress and Military Museum
Royal Parade, Eastbourne, East Sussex, BN22 7AQ. 01323 410300. www.redoubtmuseum@eastbourne. gov.uk. March–November, Tuesday–Sunday, 10am–5pm. Closed Mondays except Bank Holidays. Adults £4.00, Senior £3.00, Child £2.00.

The Rifles (Berkshire and Wiltshire) Museum
The Wardrobe, 58 The Close, Salisbury, Wilts SP1 2EX. 01722 419419. Royal Berkshire, Wiltshire and Duke of Edinburgh's Royal Regiments. See Gloucestershire Regiments Museum for Gloucestershire Regiment. For charges/opening details: www.thewardrobe.org.uk Simon Cook.

Royal Air Force Museum (1963)
Grahame Park Way, Hendon, London NW9 5LL. 020 8205 2266. Fax: 020 8200 1751. Email: andrew. cormack@rafmuseum.org. Daily, 10am-6pm. Free. Dr M. A. Fopp. Medal queries: A. Cormack FSA.

Royal Air Force Regiment Museum (1965)
Royal Air Force Regiment Depot, Royal Air Force Honington, Bury St Edmunds, Suffolk IP31 1EE. 01359 237824 (Museum Director), or 01359 237472 (Museum Dep. Manager & Visits). Initially by appointment.

Royal Armoured Corps Museum (1939), The Tank Museum (1923)
Bovington, Wareham, Dorset BH20 6JG. 01929 405096 (Library). Email: commerciala@ tankmuseum.co.uk. Website: www.tankmuseum. co.uk. Daily, 10am-5pm. Closed: Christmas. Charges apply: please phone for details. Colonel (Retd) John Woodward.

Royal Armouries Museum (1996)
Armouries Drive, Leeds LS10 1LT. 0113-220-1999. Daily (except Christmas Day). 10am-5pm. Free.

Royal Artillery. Museum—Firepower!
Royal Artillery Museum, Royal Arsenal, Woolwich, London SE18 6ST. 020 8855 7755. November–March: Friday-Sunday; April–October: Wednesday-Sunday (open 7 days a week during the Summer holidays. Closed Christmas Day-New Year's Day). £5.00/£4.50/family ticket £12.00. Library and Archive available via appointment with Librarian on 0208 312 7125, various charges apply.

Royal Devon Yeomanry (1845)
Museum of North Devon, The Square, Barnstaple, Devon EX32 8LN. 01271 346747. Monday–Saturday: 9.30am-5pm. Alison Mills.

Royal Dragoon Guards Museum
The Regimental Museum of the Royal Dragoon Guards, 3a Tower Street, York, YO1 9SB. Tel: 01904 642036. Email: hhq@rdgmuseum.org.uk. Captain (Retired) W. A. Henshall.

Royal East Kent Regiment, Third Foot (The Buffs) Museum (1961)
Closed until mid-2012. All enquiries to the National Army Museum on 0207 730 0717.

Royal Electrical and Mechanical Engineers Museum of Technology. (1958)
Isaac Newton Road, Arborfield, Berkshire, RG2 9NJ. 0118 976 3375. Contact for opening times, charges and events. www.rememuseum.org.uk. Lt Col. I.W.J. Cleasby, MBE.

Royal Engineers Museum
Prince Arthur Road, Gillingham, Kent, ME4 4UG. 01634 822839. All year: Tuesday–Friday, 9am-5pm, (closed Monday). Saturday, Sunday and Bank Holiday Mondays 11.30am-5pm. Closed Christmas week and Good Friday. £5.75/£3.00 for concessions. Angela McLennan.

Royal Fusiliers Museum (1962)
HM Tower of London, EC3N 4AB. 020 7488 5612. Daily, 9.30am-4.30pm. 50p. Maj. C. P. Bowes-Crick.

Royal Green Jackets Museum
Peninsula Barracks, Romsey Road, Winchester. 01962 828549. Monday–Saturday: 10am-5pm. Sunday: 12pm-4pm. £3/£2.

Royal Hampshire Regimental Museum (1933)
Serle's House, Southgate Street, Winchester, Hants SO23 9EG. 01962 863658. All year: Monday–Friday 11am-3.30pm. Weekends/BH: April–October only, 12pm-4pm. Free. Lt–Col. H. D. H. Keatinge.

Royal Highland Fusiliers Regimental Museum (1960)
518 Sauchiehall Street, Glasgow G2 3LW. 0141 332 0961. Mon–Fri: 9am-4pm. Free. Col. R. L. Steele.

Royal Hospital Chelsea
Royal Hospital Road, Chelsea, London SW3 4SR. 020 7881 5203. Email: curator@chelsea-pensioners. org.uk. Monday–Saturday: 10am-12pm and 2pm-4pm. Sundays (April–September only): 2pm-4pm. Closed on Public Holidays. Further details on website: www.chelsea-pensioners.org.uk. Free.

13th/18th Royal Hussars (Queen Mary's Own) Regiment (1957) and The Light Dragoons
Cannon Hall Museum, Cawthorne, Barnsley, South Yorkshire S75 4AT. 01226 790270. April–October: Wednesday–Friday, 10:30am-5pm. Saturday and Sunday: 12-5pm (Last admission at 4:15pm). November, December and March: Sunday only, 12pm-4pm. January and February: Closed. Free.

Royal Inniskilling Fusiliers Regimental Musuem
The Castle, Enniskillen, Co. Fermanagh, N. Ireland BT74 7HL. 028 6632 3142. Email:info@ inniskillingsmuseum.com. Website: www. inniskilling.com. Monday: 2pm-5pm. Tuesday–Friday: 10am–5pm. Saturday: 2pm–5pm (April–October). Sunday: 2pm–5pm (July–August). Open Bank Holidays 10pm–5pm except Christmas, Boxing & New Year's Day. £4/£3. Maj. Jack Dunlop.

Royal Irish Fusiliers
Sovereign's House, The Mall, Armagh BT61 9DL. 028 37 522911. www.rirfus-museum.freeserve. co.uk. Weekdays and Bank Holidays: 10am-12.30pm and 1.30pm-4.00pm. Ms Amanda Moreno.

Royal Irish Regiment Museum (1993)
Regimental Headquarters, Royal Irish Regiment, St Patrick's Barracks, Ballymena, BFPO 808, Northern Ireland. 028 25661 383.
Email: hqrirish@royalirishregiment.co.uk. Website: www.royalirishregiment.co.uk. Wednesday and Saturday: 2pm-5pm. Other days by arrangement. £2/£1. Capt Mark Hegan.

Royal Leicestershire Regiment Museum (1969)
New Walk Museum, New Walk, Leicester, LE1 7EA. April–September: Monday–Saturday, 10am-5pm and Sunday, 1pm-5pm. October–March: close at 4pm. Free.

Royal Lincolnshire Regimental Museum (1985)
Burton Road, Lincoln LN1 3LY. 01522 528448. April–Sept: daily, 10am-5.00pm (last entry 4.00pm). Oct–March: Mon–Sat, 10am-5.30pm. £2.20/£1.50. Family ticket £5.90.

Royal Logistic Corps Museum (1995)
Princess Royal Barracks, Deepcut, near Camberley Surrey GU16 6RW. 01252 8333371. Tues–Fri: 10am-4pm. Sat: 12am-4pm (Easter–end September only). Closed: Suns and BH. Free. Andre Robertshaw.

Royal Marines Museum
Southsea, Hants PO4 9PX. 02392 819385 ext. 242. Whitsun–September: 10am-5pm. Winter: 10am-4.30pm. £5.25/Children £3.25. Website: www. royalmarinesmuseum.co.uk. C. J. Newbery FMA.

Royal Military Police Museum (1979)
Rousillon Barracks, Broyle Road, Chichester, West Sussex PO19 4BN. 01243 534225. April–September: Tuesday–Friday, 10.30am-12.30pm and 1.30pm-4.30pm. Weekends, 2pm-6pm. October–March: Tuesday–Friday, 10.30am-12.30pm and 1.30pm-4.30pm. Closed: January. Free admission. Lt-Col. M. Squier.

Royal National Lifeboat Institution Museum (1937)
Grand Parade, Eastbourne, East Sussex BN21 4BY. 01323 730717. April–Dec: 9.30am-5pm, daily. Jan–March: Mon–Fri, 9.30am-5pm. Free admission. J. M. Shearer.

Royal National Lifeboat Institution Visitor Centre & Gift Shop (1969)
RNLI Boat House, The Promenade, Gwynedd LL42 1NF. Free. Easter–October: 10.30am-4.30pm, daily.

Royal Naval Museum (1911)
HM Naval Base, Portsmouth PO1 3NH. 02392 727562. Daily, 10am-4.30pm. Closed: Christmas day and Boxing day. £4.50. Dr C. S. White FSA FRHistS MA.

Royal Navy Submarine Museum
Haslar Jetty Road, Gosport, Hampshire, PO12 2AS. Mr Bob Mealings. 02392 510354 Ext. 227. Fax: 02392 511349. Email: curator@rnsubmus.co.uk 10am-5.30pm, (April–October), 10.00am-4.30pm (November–March). £4/£2.75. Family entry £11.

Royal Norfolk Regimental Museum (1945)
Shirehall, Market Avenue, Norwich NR1 3JQ.
01603 493625. www.rnrm.org.uk. Email regimental.
museum@norfolk.gov.uk. Tues–Sat: 10am-4.30pm.
School Hols, Mon–Sat: 10am-5pm. Admission: Adults
£3.10, Conc. £2.60, Children £1.70, Family £8.50. Kate
Thaxton.

Royal Observer Corps' Museum
Newhaven Fort, Newhaven, East Sussex. 01273
517622.

**The Royal Regiment of Fusiliers Museum (Royal
Warwickshire)**
St John's House, Warwick CV34 4NF. 01926
491653. Email: rrfhqwark@btconnect.com. www.
warwickfusiliers.co.uk. 10am-5pm: Tues–Sat and
BH. 2.30pm-5pm: Sunday (May–Sept). Free. Maj.
J.N. Turquand.

**The Royal Regiment of Wales (Brecon) Museum
(1934) (Formerly South Wales Borderers and
Monmouthshire Regiment)**
The Barracks, Brecon, Powys LD3 7EB. 01874
6133310. Email: Swb@rrw.org.uk. www.rrw.org.uk,
Open all year Monday–Friday 10am–5pm. Summer
(April–September) Saturdays, Sundays and Bank
Holidays 10am–4pm. £3, under 16s free. Martin
Everett.

Royal Scots Regimental Museum (1951)
The Castle, Edinburgh EH1 2YT. 0131 310 5016.
April–September: Monday–Sunday, 9.30am-
5.30pm. October–March: Monday–Friday, 9.30am-
4pm. Free. Lieutenant Colonel R. P. Mason.

Royal Signals Museum
Blandford Camp, Blandford, Dorset DT11 8RH.
01258 482248. www.info@royalsignalsmuseum.
com. Monday–Friday: 10am-5pm. Weekend:
(February–November only) 10am-4pm. Admission
charged. Nick Kendall-Carpenter.

**Royal Sussex Regimental Museum (1930) also the
4th Queen's Own Hussars; 8th King's Royal Irish
Hussars; Queen's Royal Irish Hussars Museums**
Redoubt Fortress, Royal Parade, Eastbourne, East
Sussex BN22 7AQ. 01323 410300. Open from
April 7–November 11. Closed Mondays (except
bank holidays). Adults £4, OAP £3 Children £2. F.
Stovold.

Royal Ulster Constabulary Museum (1983)
Brooklyn, Knock Road, Belfast BT5 6LE. (028) 90
650222 Ext 22499. Monday–Friday: 9am-5pm. Free.
Hugh Forrester.

Royal Ulster Rifles Museum (1963)
5 Waring Street, Belfast BT1 2EW. 028 9023 2086.
www.rurmuseum.tripod.com. Monday–Friday:
10am-12.30pm and 2pm-4pm. (Friday 3pm). £1
(children, OAPs, current and ex-servicemen free).
Captain J. R. Knox.

Royal Welch Fusiliers Museum (1955)
Caernarfon Castle, Gwynedd LL55 2AY. 01286
673362. Fax: 01286 677042. Open daily (except 1
January and 24–26 December) from 9.30am (11am
Sundays in winter). Closes 6pm (summer), 5pm
(spring/autumn), 4 pm (winter). Peter Crocker.

St Helier, Elizabeth Castle and Militia Museum
St Helier, Jersey, Channel Islands. 01534 23971.
April–October: 10am-5pm, daily. £2/£1.

The Sandhurst Collection, RMAS
The Sandhurst Cadet Through the Years. Old
College, Camberley, Surrey GU15 4NP. 01276
412489. Free admission, by appointment only.
Peter Thwaites.

**School of Infantry and Small Arms School Corps
Weapons Museum (1953)**
School of Infantry, Warminster, BA12 0DJ. 01985
842487. Daily, 9am-4.30pm. Free. Lieut-Colonel Tug
Wilson, MBE.

Scott Polar Research Institute Museum
Cambridge, Lensfield Road, Cambridge, CB2 1ER.
01223 336540. Tuesday–Friday 11am-1pm, 2pm-
4pm, Saturday 12pm-4pm (except BH weekends).
Medals and memorabilia of polar explorers
and scientists. Library and Archives open by
appointment only Monday-Friday, 9pm-5pm. Free.
Heather Lane.

Sherwood Foresters Regimental Museum (1923)
The Castle, Nottingham. 0115 946 5415. Daily:
10am-5pm March–September. 10am-4pm October–
February. Closed: Christmas Day and Boxing Day.

Shropshire Regimental Museum (1985)
The Castle, Shrewsbury, SY1 2AT. 01743 358516.
April–September 30: Every day, 10am-5pm.
Sundays 10am–4pm. Open Tuesday–Saturday,
10am-5pm from October–March. Winter closure:
December–January. £2/Children and students free.
Peter Duckers.

Soldiers of Gloucestershire Museum
Custom House, Gloucester Docks, Gloucester GL1
2HE. 01452 522682. Medals of the Gloucestershire
Regiment Royal Gloucestershire Hussars. Open all
year round. Closed Mondays in winter 10am-5pm. .

Somerset Military Museum (1974)
Somerset County Museum, Taunton Castle,
Taunton, Somerset TA1 1AA. 01823 320201. The
museum is closed until mid-2010 due to a major
refurbishment programme. Lieutenant Colonel
(Ret'd) M. Motum. www.sommiluseum.org.uk.

South Nottinghamshire Hussars Museum (1974)
TA Centre, Hucknall Lane, Bulwell, Nottingham NG6
8AB. 0115 9272251. Free, by appointment only.
Curator Gill Aldridge.

South Wales Police Museum (1950)
Police Headquarters, Cowbridge Road, Bridgend,
CF31 3SU. 01656 303201. Email: ross.mather@
south-wales.pnn.police.uk. Usually open
Wednesday–Friday but please telephone first.

Staffordshire Regimental Museum (1962)
Whittington Barracks, Lichfield, Staffs WS14 9PY.
01534 434395/394/390. All year: Monday–Friday,
10am-4pm. April–October: Saturday, Sunday, Bank
Holidays, 12.30pm-4pm. Closed: Christmas & New
Year. Special events staged. Archives and school
parties by appointment. £3/£2.50, all concessions
£2, family ticket £6. Dr. Eric Blakeley.

Suffolk Regimental Museum (1967)
The Keep, Gibraltar Barracks, Bury St Edmunds, Suffolk IP33 1HF. 01284 752394. Weekdays: 10am-12pm and 2pm-4pm. Free. Major A. G. B. Cobbold.

Sussex & Surrey Yeomanry Museum (1993)
Newhaven Fort, Newhaven, East Sussex. 01273 611055. April–October, other times by appointment. Hon. curator Keith Fuller.

Tangmere, Military Aviation Museum (1992)
Tangmere, near Chichester, West Sussex PO20 6ES. 01243 775223. February–November: 11am-5.30pm, daily. £3/50p. Andy Saunders.

The 11 (Fighter) Group Operations Room
RAF Uxbridge, Middlesex, UB10 0RZ. 01895 815400. Visits are by appointment only and last two hours consisting of a presentation and video on the Battle of Britain and the role of the Ops Room. World War II artefacts. Free entry but donations welcome. Miss Hazel Crozier.

The Fusilier Museum (1933)
Moss Street, Bury, Lanc BL9 0DF. 0161 763 8950. Daily 10.00am–5.00pm (closed 24–27 December and 1 January): 10am-4pm. £1/£2.

The Tank Museum (1923), Royal Armoured Corps Museum (1939)
Bovington, Wareham, Dorset BH20 6JG. 01929 405096 (Library). Email: commerciala@tankmuseum.org. Website: www.tankmuseum.org. Daily, 10am-5pm. Closed at Christmas. Charges apply, please contact for details. David Willey.

Towneley Hall Art Gallery and Museum (1902)
Burnley, Lancs BB11 3RQ. 01282 424213. Monday–Thursday: 12pm-5pm. Email: mtownend@burnley.gov.uk, or towneley@burnley.gov.uk. Small collection including two VCs, other unique items seen by appointment. Free to residents, students and children, others £3.50. Mike Townend.

Warwickshire Yeomanry Museum (1981)
The Court House, Jury Street, Warwick CV34 4EW. 01926 492212. Weekends and Bank Holidays from Good Friday to end of October, 10am–4pm. Entry Free. Archives and Out of Hours Visits by appintment only, pwilson102003@yahoo.co.uk. Bryan Johnson.

Welch Regiment Museum (1927)
The Black and Barbican Towers, Cardiff Castle, Cardiff, South Glamorgan CF1 2RB. 01222 229367. Daily: 10am-6pm (March–October), 10am-4.30pm (November–April). Closed: Saturday–Monday, Christmas, Boxing Day and New Year's Day. Entry to the museum is free after initial entry payment of £3.30 to the castle grounds. John Dart.

Wellington Museum
Apsley House, 149 Piccadilly, Hyde Park Corner, London W1J 7NT. 0207 499 5676. Tuesday–Sunday: 11am-5pm. Free to under 18s/over 60s; otherwise £4.40/£3. Alicia Robinson.

West Midlands Police Museum (1991)
Sparkhill Police Station, 641 Stratford Road, Birmingham B11 6EA. Free, by appointment only.

Woodbridge, 390th Bomb Group Memorial Air Museum (1981)
Parham Airfield, Parham, Woodbridge, Suffolk. 01359 51209. Sundays and Bank Holidays: 11am-6pm. Free.

Worcestershire Regiment Museum (1925)
City Museum and Art Gallery, Foregate Street, Worcester. WR1 1DT.01905 25371. Tuesday to Saturday: 10.30-4.30, closed: Sunday and Monday. Free. Major (Retd) R. S. Prophet. Archives: 01905 354359, by appointment.

York and Lancaster Regimental Museum (1947)
Central Library and Arts Centre, Walker Place, Rotherham, S65 1JH. 01709 336633 ext 3625. Monday–Saturday: 9am-4.30pm. Entry Free: Archive by appointment only. Karl Noble.

York, Yorkshire Air Museum and Allied Air Forces Memorial
Halifax Way, Elvington, York YO41 5AU. 01904 608595. Open Daily, Summer:10am-5pm. Winter: 10am–4pm. Adults £7, Seniors £5, Children £4. Ian Richardson.

As details may change after we have gone to press, please check museum opening times etc. before setting off on your journey

MEDAL RIBBONS

In this section we feature the majority of the ribbons for the medals included in the main sections of the book. Where the same ribbon is used for more than one medal, only one is illustrated here.
(Not all shown to scale, see reference number for actual sizes)

1. The Most Noble Order of the Garter

2. The Most Ancient and Most Noble Order of the Thistle

3. The Most Illustrious Order of St Patrick

4. The Most Honourable Order of the Bath

5. The Royal Guelphic Order

6. The Most Distinguished Order of St Michael & St George

7. The Most Exalted Order of the Star of India

8. The Most Eminent Order of the Indian Empire

9. The Royal Family Order (Edward VII)

9. The Royal Family Order (George V)

9. The Royal Family Order (George VI)

9. The Royal Family Order (Elizabeth II)

11. The Imperial Order of the Crown of India

12. The Royal Victorian Order

13. The Royal Victorian Medal

13. The Royal Victorian Medal (foreign Associates)

15. Order of Merit

16. The Most Excellent Order of the British Empire (Civil 1st type)

16. The Most Excellent Order of the British Empire (Civil 2nd type)

16. The Most Excellent Order of the British Empire (Military 1st type)

16. The Most Excellent Order of the British Empire (Military 2nd type)

17. Medal of the Order of the British Empire (Civil)

17. Medal of the Order of the British Empire (Military)

18. Empire Gallantry Medal (Civil 1922)

18. Empire Gallantry Medal (Military 1922)

18. Empire Gallantry Medal (Civil 1937)

18. Empire Gallantry Medal (Military 1937)

(with smaller miniature emblem when ribbon worn alone)

543

19. British Empire Medal (Civil 1922)	19. British Empire Medal (Military 1922)	19. British Empire Medal (Civil 1937)
19. British Empire Medal (Military 1937)	20. The Order of the Companions of Honour	21. The Baronet's Badge (Nova Scotia)
21. The Baronet's Badge (other Baronets)	22. The Knight Bachelor's Badge	23. Order of St John with miniature emblem when worn alone
24. Victoria Cross (Pre-1918)	24. Victoria Cross (Modern)	25. New Zealand Cross with miniature emblem when worn alone
26. George Cross	27. Distinguished Service Order	28/29. Imperial Service Order/Medal
30. Indian Order of Merit (Military)	30. Indian Order of Merit (Civil)	30A. Conspicuous Gallantry Cross
31. Royal Red Cross	32. Distinguished Service Cross	33. Military Cross
34. Distinguished Flying Cross pre-1919	34. Distinguished Flying Cross post-1919	35. Air Force Cross pre-1919
35. Air Force Cross post-1919	36. Order of British India (Original)	36. Order of British India (1st Class, ii)
36. Order of British India (2nd Class, ii)	36. Order of British India (1st Class, post-1939)	36. Order of British India (2nd class, post-1939)

37. Order of Burma

38. Kaisar-i-Hind

39. Albert Medal, original (1866) and 2nd Class, Sea, 1867-1904

39. Albert Medal, 1st Class, Sea, 1867-1949

39. Albert Medal, 2nd Class, Sea, 1904-71

39. Albert Medal, 1st Class, Land, 1877-1949

39. Albert Medal, 2nd Class, Land, 1877-1904

39. Albert Medal, 2nd Class, Land, 1904-71

40. SA Queen's Medal for Bravery

41. Distinguished Conduct Medal

42. Distinguished Conduct Medal (Dominion & Colonial)

43. DCM (KAR and WAFF)

44. Conspicuous Gallantry, 1st ribbon

44. Conspicuous Gallantry

44. Conspicuous Gallantry, (Flying)

45. George Medal

46. King's Police Medal 1916

46. King's Police Medal (Gallantry)

47. Queen's Police Medal

47. Queen's Police Medal Gallantry

48. Queen's Fire Service Medal

48. Queen's Fire Service Medal (Gallantry)

48A. Queen's Volunteer Reserves Medal

49. King's Police Medal (South Africa)

50/51. Edward Medal

52. Indian Distinguished Service Medal

53. Burma Gallantry Medal

54. Distinguished Service Medal

55. Military Medal

56. Distinguished Flying Medal pre-1919

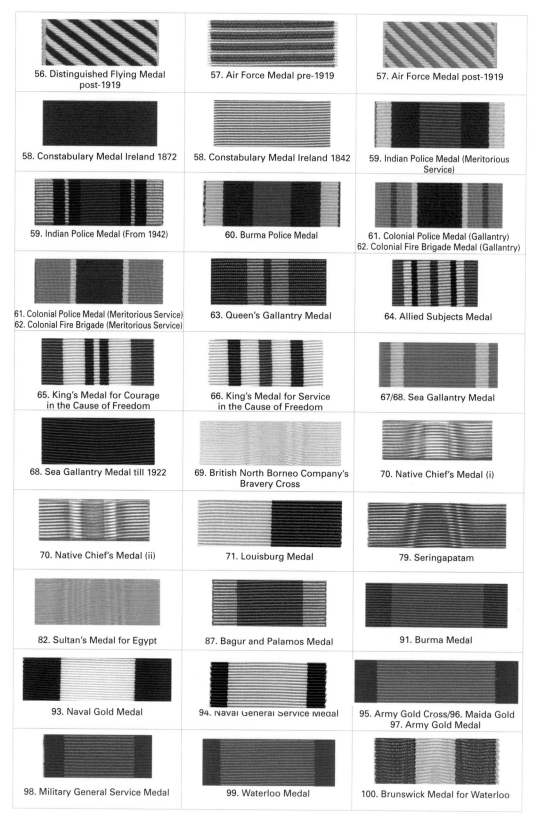

56. Distinguished Flying Medal post-1919

57. Air Force Medal pre-1919

57. Air Force Medal post-1919

58. Constabulary Medal Ireland 1872

58. Constabulary Medal Ireland 1842

59. Indian Police Medal (Meritorious Service)

59. Indian Police Medal (From 1942)

60. Burma Police Medal

61. Colonial Police Medal (Gallantry)
62. Colonial Fire Brigade Medal (Gallantry)

61. Colonial Police Medal (Meritorious Service)
62. Colonial Fire Brigade (Meritorious Service)

63. Queen's Gallantry Medal

64. Allied Subjects Medal

65. King's Medal for Courage in the Cause of Freedom

66. King's Medal for Service in the Cause of Freedom

67/68. Sea Gallantry Medal

68. Sea Gallantry Medal till 1922

69. British North Borneo Company's Bravery Cross

70. Native Chief's Medal (i)

70. Native Chief's Medal (ii)

71. Louisburg Medal

79. Seringapatam

82. Sultan's Medal for Egypt

87. Bagur and Palamos Medal

91. Burma Medal

93. Naval Gold Medal

94. Naval General Service Medal

95. Army Gold Cross/96. Maida Gold 97. Army Gold Medal

98. Military General Service Medal

99. Waterloo Medal

100. Brunswick Medal for Waterloo

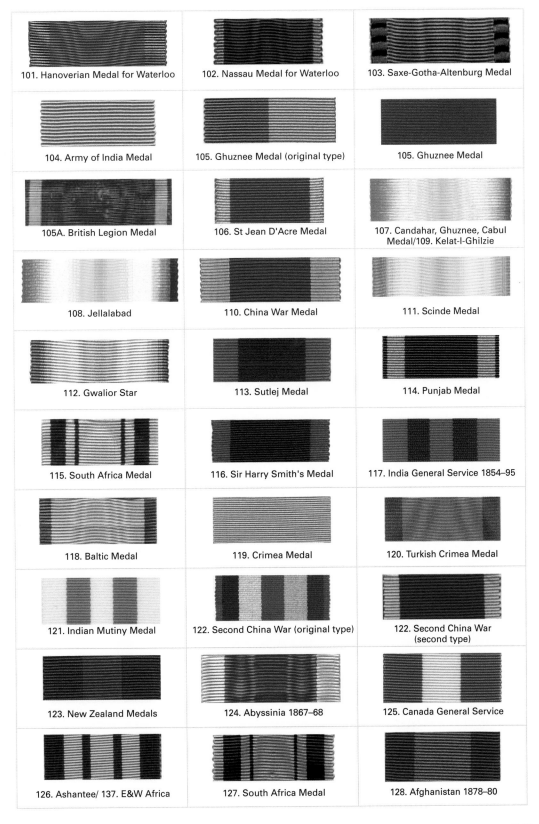

101. Hanoverian Medal for Waterloo

102. Nassau Medal for Waterloo

103. Saxe-Gotha-Altenburg Medal

104. Army of India Medal

105. Ghuznee Medal (original type)

105. Ghuznee Medal

105A. British Legion Medal

106. St Jean D'Acre Medal

107. Candahar, Ghuznee, Cabul Medal/109. Kelat-I-Ghilzie

108. Jellalabad

110. China War Medal

111. Scinde Medal

112. Gwalior Star

113. Sutlej Medal

114. Punjab Medal

115. South Africa Medal

116. Sir Harry Smith's Medal

117. India General Service 1854–95

118. Baltic Medal

119. Crimea Medal

120. Turkish Crimea Medal

121. Indian Mutiny Medal

122. Second China War (original type)

122. Second China War (second type)

123. New Zealand Medals

124. Abyssinia 1867–68

125. Canada General Service

126. Ashantee/ 137. E&W Africa

127. South Africa Medal

128. Afghanistan 1878–80

129. Kabul to Kandahar Star

130. Cape of Good Hope GSM

131. Egypt Medal

132. Khedive's Star
133. Gordon's Khartoum Star

134. North West Canada Medal

135. Royal Niger Company's Medal

136. Imperial BEA Co.s Medal

137. East and West Africa Medal

138. BSA Co.s Medal

139. Hunza Nagar badge

140. Central Africa Medal

141. Hong Kong Plague Medal

142. India Medal 1895–1902

143. Jummoo and Kashmir

144. Ashanti Star

145. Queen's Sudan Medal

146. Khedive's Sudan Medal 1896–1908

147. East and Central Africa Medal

148. BNB Co's Medal (i)

148. BNB Co's Medal (ii)

148A. BNB Co's Medal (iii)

149. Sultan of Zanzibar's Medal

150. Queen's South Africa Medal
151. Queen's Mediterranean Medal

152. King's South Africa Medal

153. St John's Ambulance Brigade
Medal for South Africa

154/155. Kimberley Star/Medal

156. Yorkshire Imperial Yeomanry

157. Medal for the Defence of Ookiep

158. China War Medal

159. Transport Medal

160. Ashanti Medal	161. Africa General Service 1902–56	162. Tibet Medal
163. Natal Medal	163A. Messina Earthquake	164. India General Service 1908–35
165. Khedive's Sudan 1910	166/167. 1914/1914–15 Star	168. British War Medal 1914–20
169. Mercantile Marine	170. Victory Medal	171. Territorial Force War Medal
171A. British Red Cross Society Medal for War Service	173. Naval General Service 1915–62	174. General Service 1918–62
174A. Iraq Active Service Medal	175. India General Service 1936–39	176. North Borneo GSM
176. North Borneo GSM (Bravery)	176A. Sudan Defence Force GSM	177. 1939–1945 Star
178. Atlantic Star	179. Air Crew Europe Star	180. Africa Star
181. Pacific Star	182. Burma Star	183. Italy Star
184. France and Germany Star	185. Defence Medal	186. War Medal 1939–45

187. India Service Medal

188. Canadian Volunteer Service Medal

188A/191A. Canadian & NZ Memorial Cross

189. Africa Service Medal

190. Australia Service Medal

191. New Zealand War Service Medal

192. South African Medal for War Service

193. Southern Rhodesia War Service Medal

194. Newfoundland Volunteer War Service Medal

195. Korea Medal

196. South African Medal for Korea

197. United Nations Korea Medal

198. General Service Medal 1962

198A. Operational Service Medal (Sierra Leone)

198A. Operational Service Medal (Congo)

198A. Operational Service Medal (Afghanistan)

198B. Accumulated Campaign Service

199. UN Emergency Force Medal

200. Vietnam Medal

200A. Vietnam Logistic and Support Medal

201. South Vietnam Campaign Medal

202. Rhodesia Medal

203. South Atlantic Medal

203A. Soviet 40th Anniversary Medal

203B. Pingat Jasa Malaysia Medal

203C. King Hussein Medal

204. Gulf Medal

204A. Brunei General Service Medal

204AA. Sierra Leone General Service Medal

204B. Iraq Medal

204C. IRAQ Reconstruction Service
Medalx

205. Saudi Medal for Liberation
of Kuwait

205A. Multinational Force
and Observers Medal

206. Kuwait Liberation Medals

206A. NATO (i)

206A. NATO (i) Non Article 5

206A. NATO (ii)

206A. NATO (iii)

206A. NATO Service Medal
Eagle Assist

206A. NATO Service Medal
Active Endeavour

206A. NATO
Afghanistan (ISAF)

206A. NATO
(Iraq)

206B. European Community
Monitoring Mission Medal

206C. Western European Union
Mission Service Medal

206D. European Security and Defence
Policy Service Medal

207. United Nations Medal
UNTSO & UNOGIL

207. United Nations Medal
ONUC

207. United Nations Medal
UNTEA

207. United Nations Medal
UNMOGIP & UNIPOM

207. United Nations Medal
UNYOM

207. United Nations Medal
UNFICYP

207. United Nations Medal
UNEF 2

207. United Nations Medal
UNDOF

207. United Nations Medal
UNIFIL

207. United Nations Medal
UNIIMOG

207. United Nations Medal
UNAVEM

207. United Nations Medal
ONUCA

207. United Nations Medal
UNTAG

207. United Nations Medal
ONUSAL

207. United Nations Medal
UNIKOM

207. United Nations Medal MINURSO	207. United Nations Medal UNAMIC	207. United Nations Medal UNTAC
207. United Nations Medal UNOSOM	207. United Nations Medal UNMIH & UNSMIH	207. United Nations Medal UNIMOZ & ONUMOZ
207. United Nations Medal UNPROFOR & UNCRO	207. United Nations Medal UNOMIL	207. United Nations Medal UNOMUR
207. United Nations Medal UNOMIG	207. United Nations Medal UNAMIR	207. United Nations Medal UNHQ
207. United Nations Medal UNPREDEP	207. United Nations Medal UNMOP	207. United Nations Medal UNTAES
207. United Nations Medal UNMOT	207. United Nations Medal UNMIBH	207. United Nations Medal UNMOGUA & MINUGUA
207. United Nations Medal UN Special Service	207. United Nations Medal UNOMSIL	207. United Nations Medal UNPSG
207. United Nations Medal MINURCA	207. United Nations Medal UNMIK	207. United Nations Medal UNAMET
207. United Nations Medal MONUC	207. United Nations Medal UNMEE	207. United Nations Medal UNMINUCI
207. United Nations Medal UNMIL	207. United Nations Medal UNIOCI	207. United Nations Medal UNOB

207. United Nations Medal
MINUSTAH

207. United Nations Medal
UNMIS

207. United Nations Medal
UNMINURCAT

207. United Nations Medal
UNAMID

207. United Nations Medal
UNAMID (alternative)

207A. International Conference
on the Former Yugoslavia

207B. Interfet Medal

207C. Unitas Medal

208/214. Meritorious Service
Medals/212. Colonial MSM (Canada)

209. Royal Marines Meritorious Service
Medal (first type)

209. Royal Marines Meritorious
Service Medal (second type)

210. Army Meritorious Service Medal
(first type)

210. Army Meritorious Service Medal
(second type)

210. Army Meritorious Service Medal
(third type)

211. RAF Meritorious Service
Medal (original)

212. Colonial MSM
(Cape of Good Hope)

212. Colonial MSM
(Natal)

212. Colonial MSM
(Commonwealth of Australia)

212. Colonial MSM
(New South Wales)

212. Colonial MSM
(Queensland)

212. Colonial MSM
(South Australia)

212. Colonial MSM
(Tasmania)

212. Colonial MSM
(New Zealand)

213/214. Indian Army MSM 1848/88

215. African Police Medal
for Meritorious Service

216. Union of South Africa MSM

217. Royal Household FS GVIR

217. Royal Household FS EIIR

218. RN LS & GC (i)

218. RN LS & GC (ii)

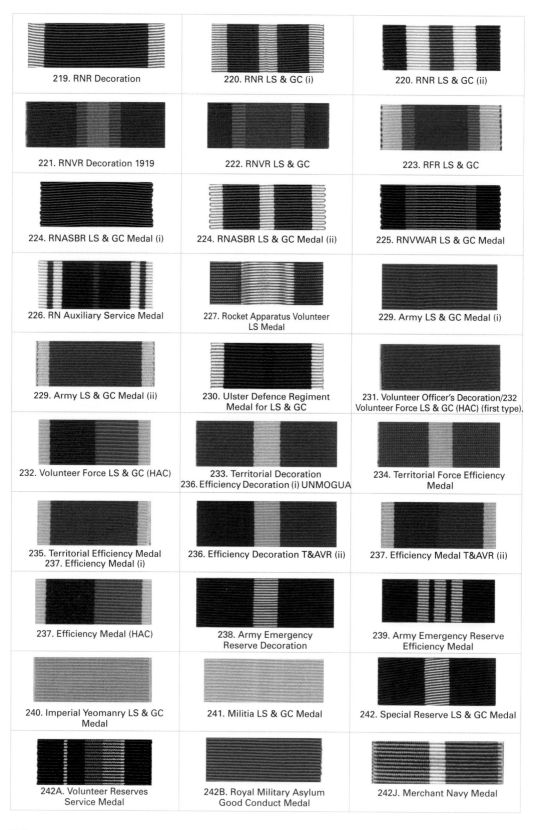

219. RNR Decoration

220. RNR LS & GC (i)

220. RNR LS & GC (ii)

221. RNVR Decoration 1919

222. RNVR LS & GC

223. RFR LS & GC

224. RNASBR LS & GC Medal (i)

224. RNASBR LS & GC Medal (ii)

225. RNVWAR LS & GC Medal

226. RN Auxiliary Service Medal

227. Rocket Apparatus Volunteer LS Medal

229. Army LS & GC Medal (i)

229. Army LS & GC Medal (ii)

230. Ulster Defence Regiment Medal for LS & GC

231. Volunteer Officer's Decoration/232 Volunteer Force LS & GC (HAC) (first type).

232. Volunteer Force LS & GC (HAC)

233. Territorial Decoration 236. Efficiency Decoration (i) UNMOGUA

234. Territorial Force Efficiency Medal

235. Territorial Efficiency Medal 237. Efficiency Medal (i)

236. Efficiency Decoration T&AVR (ii)

237. Efficiency Medal T&AVR (ii)

237. Efficiency Medal (HAC)

238. Army Emergency Reserve Decoration

239. Army Emergency Reserve Efficiency Medal

240. Imperial Yeomanry LS & GC Medal

241. Militia LS & GC Medal

242. Special Reserve LS & GC Medal

242A. Volunteer Reserves Service Medal

242B. Royal Military Asylum Good Conduct Medal

242J. Merchant Navy Medal

243. Indian Army LS & GC (Europeans)

244. Indian Army LS & GC (Indians)

245. Indian Volunteer Forces Officer's Decoration

246/247. Colonial Auxiliary Forces Officer's Decoration/LS Medal

248. Colonial Long Service and Good Conduct Medal

249. Permanent Forces LS & GC

250. RWAFF LS & GC

251. KAR LS & GC Medal

252. Trans-Jordan FF LS & GC Medal

253. SA PF LS & GC Medal

254. Efficiency Medal (SA)

254A. Royal HKR Disbandment Medal

255. Canadian Forces Decoration

256. Victoria Vol. Long & Efficient Service Medal

257. New Zealand Long & Efficient Service Medal

258. NZ Volunteer Service Medal

259. NZ Territorial Service Medal (i)

259. NZ Territorial Service Medal (ii)

261/261A. Ulster Defence Regiment

261B. Northern Ireland Home Service Medal

262. Cadet Forces Medal

263. Royal Observer Corps medal

264. Civil Defence LS

264A. Ambulance Service (Emergency Duties) LS & GC Medal

264B. Assoc. of Chief Ambulance Officer's Service Medal

264C. Royal Fleet Auxiliary Service Medal

265. WVS Long Service Medal

266. Voluntary Medical Service Medal

267. Service Medal of the Order of St John of Jerusalem

268/269. RAF LS & GC Medal

270. Air Efficiency Award

271. Police LS & GC

272. Special Constabulary LS

273. RUC Service Medal (original type)

273. RUC Service Medal (post-2001)

274. Colonial Police LS

275. Colonial Special Constabulary LS

276. Ceylon Police LS & GC Medal (I)

277. Ceylon Police LS & GC Medal (II)

278. Ceylon Police Medal for Merit

278a. Ceylon Police Medal for Gallantry

279. Cyprus MP LS & GC Medal

280. HK Police Medal for Merit (1st Class)

280. HK Police Medal for Merit (2nd Class)

280. HK Police Medal for Merit (3rd Class)

280. HK Police Medal for Merit (4th Class)

280B. Royal Hong Kong Police

280C. Royal HK Aux. Police Commemoration Medal

281A. HK Disciplined Service Medal

281B. Tientsin British Emergency Corps Medal

282. Malta Police LS & GC Medal

282A. Mauritius Police LS & GC

282A. Mauritius Police LS & GC Medal (I) (first type)

282B. Mauritius Police LS & GC Medal (II)

283. NZ Police LS & GC Medal (Second type)

283A. Seychelles Police LS & GC Medal Medal

284. SA Police Good Service Medal

285. SA Railways & Harbour Police LS & GC Medal (& 290)

286. Fire Brigade LS Medal

286A. Assoc. of Professional Fire Brigade Officers LS Medal

286AA. National Fire Bridges Association Long Service Medal

286AB. National Fire Brigades Union Medal

286B. British Fire Services Assoc. Medal

286C. British Fire Service Assoc. Meritorious Service Medal

287. Colonial Fire Brigade LS Medal

288. Ceylon Fire Brigade LS & GC Medal

288A. Northern Ireland Prison Service Medal (i)

289. Colonial Prison Service LS Medal

290. South African Prison Service Faithful Service Medal

291. SA Prisons Dept Faithful Service Medal

291AA. NATO Meritorious Service Medal

292. Empress of India Medal

293/295. Jubilee (VR) 1887/1897

294. Jubilee (Police) 1887

295. Jubilee Medal 1897

296. Jubilee 1897 (Mayors & Provosts)

297. Jubilee (Police) 1897

298. Ceylon Diamond Jubilee 1897

299. HK Diamond Jubilee Medal

299A. Lagos Diamond Jubilee Medal

299B. India Diamond Jubilee Medal

300. Visit to Ireland 1900

301. Coronation 1902

302. Coronation 1902 (Mayors & Provosts)

303. Coronation 1902 (Police)

304. Ceylon Coronation 1902

305. HK Coronation 1902

306. Delhi Durbar 1903

307. Visit to Scotland 1903

308. Visit to Ireland 1903

308A. Visit of the Prince and Princess of Wales to India	308B. George Prince of Wales Medal	309. Coronation 1911 312. Delhi Durbar 1911
309. Guildhall Coronation Medal 1911	310. Coronation 1911 (Police)	311. Visit to Ireland 1911
313. Jubilee 1935	313A. Isle of Man Silver Jubilee 1935	314. Coronation 1937
315. Coronation 1953	315A. Royal Visit to New Zealand Medal 1953–54	316. Jubilee 1977
317. Queen Alex. Children's Banquet Medal 1914	318. Golden Jubilee 2002	318A. Diamond Jubilee
319. King's and Queen's Messenger Badge	320. Arctic Medal (1857)	321. Arctic Medal (1876)
322. Polar Medal	323. EVII Medal for Science, Art & Music	324. Order of the League of Mercy
325. Queen Alex. Imperial Military Nursing Service Cape Badge	325A. Queen Alex. Imperial Military Nursing Service Reserve Cape Badge	326. Territorial Force Nursing Service Cape Badge
326A. Queen Alex. Military Families Nursing Service Cape Badge	326B. Territorial Army Nursing Service Cape Badge	326C. Queen Alex. Royal Army Nursing Corps Cape Badge
327. Indian Title Badge (1st Class)	327. Indian Title Badge (2nd Class)	327. Indian Title Badge (3rd Class)

328. Badge of the Cert. of Honour	329. Badge of Honour (non-African countries)	330. Naval Engineers GC Medal
331. Indian Recruiting Badge (GV)	332. Indian Recruiting Badge (GVI)	333. Naval Good Shooting
334. Army Best Shot Medal	335. Queen's Medal for Champion Shot (RN/RM)	336. Queen's Medal for Champion Shot (RAF)
337. Queen's Medal for Champion Shot NZ Naval Force	338. Union of South Africa Commemoration Medal	339. Loyal Service Decoration (SA)
340. Anglo-Boer War Medal	The various Commonwealth Independence Medals are all included as MYB 341	341. India Independence Medal
341. Pakistan Independence Medal	341. Nigeria Independence Medal	341. Sierra Leone Independence Medal
341. Jamaica Independence Medal	341. Uganda Independence Medal	341. Malawi Independence Medal
341. Guyana Independence Medal	341. Fiji Independence Medal	341. Papua Independence Medal
341. Solomon Islands Independence Medal	341. Gilbert Islands Independence Medal	341. Ellice Islands Independence Medal
341. Zimbabwe Independence Medal	341. Vanuatu Independence Medal	341. Swaziland Independence Medal

341. St. Christopher Independence Medal	341. Ghana Independence Medal	341. Kenya Independence Medal
342. Malta GC Anniversary Commemorative Medal	346. Shanghai Volunteer Fire Brigade Long Service Medal	349. Shanghai Municipal Police LS Medal
351. Shanghai Municipal Council Emergency Medal	352. Automobile Association Service Cross	353. Automobile Association Service Medal
354. Suffragette Medal	355. Florence Nightingale Medal	359. National Canine Defence League Medal
364. Royal Warrant Holders Association Medal	366. Maidstone Typhoid Medal	367. Boys' Life Brigade Medal
367A. Boys' Life Squad Medal	368. Girls' Life Squad Medal	368A. RSPCA Queen Victoria Medal
369. Marine Society Reward of Merit	372. Securicor Medal for Long Service	373. Securicor Medal for Bravery
374. St. Andrew's Association Medal	375. Salvation Army Service Medal	376. Royal Norfolk Veterans Association Medal

LIFESAVING MEDALS:

L1. Royal Humane Society (1921)

L1. Stanhope Gold Medal

L3. Hundred of Salford Humane Society Medals

L4. RNLI Medal

L5. Medals of the Society for the Protection of Life from Fire

L5. SPLF Medal

L6. Lloyd's Medal for Saving Life at sea

L7. Liverpool S&H Society's Marine Medals

L8. SF&MRB Society Medal

L9. Tayleur Fund Medal

L10A. Jersey Humane Society Medal

L12. Lifesaving Medal of the Order of St John (Original)

L12. Lifesaving Medal of the Order of St John (1888 on)

L12. Lifesaving Medal of the Order of St John (1950–1953)

L12. Lifesaving Medal of the Order of St John (1954 on)

L13. Shropshire Society Life Saving Medal

L14. Liverpool Shipwreck and Humane Society's Fire Medal

L15. Liverpool Shipwreck and Humane Society's Swimming Medal

L15a. Ally Sloper's Medall

L16. Answers Medal for Heroism

L17. Lloyd's Medal for Meritorious Service

L18. Liverpool Shipwreck and Humane Society's General Medal

L19. Today Gallantry Fund Medal

L20. Imperial Merchant Service Guild Medal

L21. Pluck Medal for Heroism

L22. Tynemouth Medal

L23. Drummond Castle Medal

L24. New Foundland Silver Star for Bravery

L26. Humane Society of NZ medals	L28. Boys' Brigade Cross for Heroism	L29. Boys' Life Brigade Medal
L29A. Girl's Life Brigade Medal	L31. RSPCA Lifesaving Medal (Silver)	L32. Scout Association Gallantry Medal (bronze)
L32. Scout Association Gallantry Medal (silver)	L32. Scout Association Gallantry Medal (gilt)	L33. CQD Medal
L33A. Bolton & District Humane Society Medal	L34. Carpathia and Titanic Medal	L35. Lloyd's Medal for Services to Lloyds
L36. Order of Industrial Heroism	L37. Corporation of Glasgow Bravery Medal	L37A. Imperial Chemical Industries Bravery Award
L38. RSPCA Margaret Wheatley Cross	L39. Lloyd's Medal for Bravery at Sea	L40. London, Midland and Scottish Railway Medal
L41. Southern Railway Meritorious Service Medal	L42. Dale Medal	L44. London and North Eastern Railway Gallantry Medal
L44A. Dickin Medal	L46/L47. Sea Cadet Gallantry Cross/Medal	L47A. Gallantry Medallists' League Gold Medal for Courage

AUSTRALIAN MEDAL RIBBONS
(Not all shown to scale, see reference number for actual sizes)

A1. Victoria Cross for Australia

A2. Cross of Valour

A3. Order of Australia (General)
A18. Medal of the Order of Australia (Gen.)

A3. Order of Australia (Military)
A18. Medal of the Order of Australia (Mil.)

A4. Star of Gallantry

A5. Star of Courage

A6. Distinguished Service Cross

A8. Conspicuous Service Cross

A9. Nursing Service Cross

A10. Medal for Gallantry

A11. Bravery Medal

A12. Distinguished Service Medal

A13. Public Service Medal

A14. Australian Police Medal

A15. Australian Fire Service Medal

A16. Ambulance Service Medal

A17. Emergency Services Medal

A18. Medal of the Order of Australia

A19. Conspicuous Service Medal

A20. Australian Antarctic Medal

A24. Australian Active Service Medal 1945–1975

A25. Vietnam Medal

A26. Vietnam Logistics & Support Medal

A27. Australian Active Service Medal 1975–

A28. Interfet Medal—
International Force East Timor

A29. Afghanistan Medal

A30. Iraq Medal

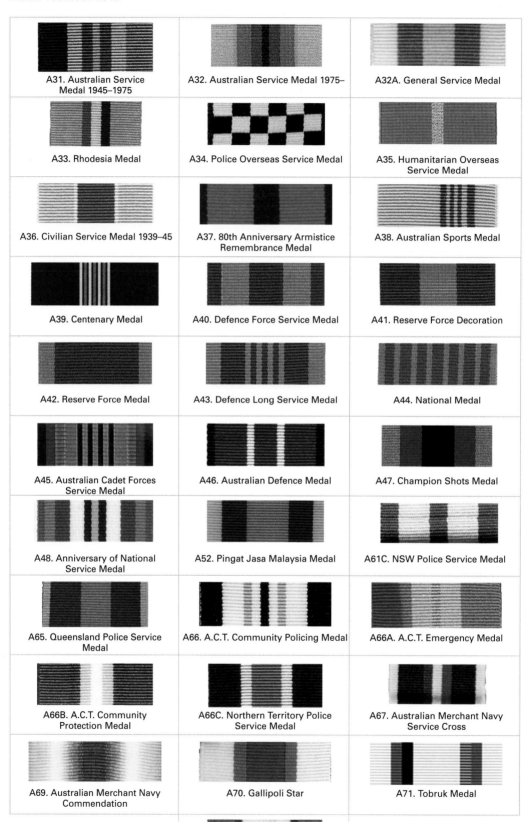

A31. Australian Service Medal 1945–1975	A32. Australian Service Medal 1975–	A32A. General Service Medal
A33. Rhodesia Medal	A34. Police Overseas Service Medal	A35. Humanitarian Overseas Service Medal
A36. Civilian Service Medal 1939–45	A37. 80th Anniversary Armistice Remembrance Medal	A38. Australian Sports Medal
A39. Centenary Medal	A40. Defence Force Service Medal	A41. Reserve Force Decoration
A42. Reserve Force Medal	A43. Defence Long Service Medal	A44. National Medal
A45. Australian Cadet Forces Service Medal	A46. Australian Defence Medal	A47. Champion Shots Medal
A48. Anniversary of National Service Medal	A52. Pingat Jasa Malaysia Medal	A61C. NSW Police Service Medal
A65. Queensland Police Service Medal	A66. A.C.T. Community Policing Medal	A66A. A.C.T. Emergency Medal
A66B. A.C.T. Community Protection Medal	A66C. Northern Territory Police Service Medal	A67. Australian Merchant Navy Service Cross
A69. Australian Merchant Navy Commendation	A70. Gallipoli Star	A71. Tobruk Medal
	A73. British Commonwealth Occupation Forces—BCOF	

CANADIAN NATIONAL MEDAL RIBBONS
(Not all shown to scale, see reference number for actual sizes)

C1. Victoria Cross for Canada

C2. Cross of Valour

C3. Order of Canada

C4. Order of Military Merit

C5. Order of Merit of the Police Forces

C6. L'Ordre National Du Québec

C7. Saskatchewan Order of Merit

C8. Order of Ontario

C9. Order of British Columbia

C10. Alberta Order of Excellence

C11. Order of Prince Edward Island Medal of Merit

C12. Order of Manitoba

C12a. Order of New Brunswick

C12b. Order of Nova Scotia

C12c. Order of Newfoundland and Labrador

C13. Star of Military Valour

C14. Star of Courage

C15. Meritorious Service Cross (Military Division)

C15. Meritorious Service Cross (Civil Division)

C16. Medal of Military Valour

C17. Medal of Bravery

C18. Meritorious Service Medal (Military Division)

C18. Meritorious Service Medal (Civil Division)

C18A. Sacrifice Medal

C19. Canadian Volunteer Service Medal for Korea

C20. Gulf and Kuwait Medal

C21. Somalia Medal

C22. South-West Asia Service Medal

C23. General Campaign Star (Allied Force)

C23. General Campaign Star (South-West Asia)

C23. General Campaign Star (Expedition)

C24. General Service Medal (Allied Force)

C24. General Service Medal (South-West Asia)

C24. General Service Medal (Expedition)

C24A. Operational Service Medal (Expedition)

C24A. Operational Service Medal (Haiti)

C24A. Operational Service Medal (Humanitas)

C24A. Operational Service Medal (Sudan)

C24A. Operational Service Medal (Sierra Leone)

C24A. Operational Service Medal (South West Asia)

C25. Special Service Medal

C26. Canadian Peacekeeping Service Medal

C27. Canadian Centennial Medal

C28. Queen Elizabeth II's Silver Jubilee Medal (Canada)

C29. 125th Anniversary of the Confederation of Canada Medal

C30. Queen Elizabeth II's Golden Jubilee Medal (Canada)

C30A. Queen Elizabeth II's Diamond Jubilee Medal (Canada)

C31. Royal Canadian Mounted Police Long Service Medal

C32. Canadian Forces Decoration

C33. Police Exemplary Service Medal

C34. Fire Services Exemplary Service Medal

C35. Corrections Exemplary Service Medal

C36. Canadian Coast Guard Exemplary Service Medal

C37. Emergency Medical Services Exemplary Service Medal

C37a. Peace Officer Exemplary Service Medal

C38. Queen's Medal for Champion Shot in Canada

C39. Ontario Medal for Good Citizenship

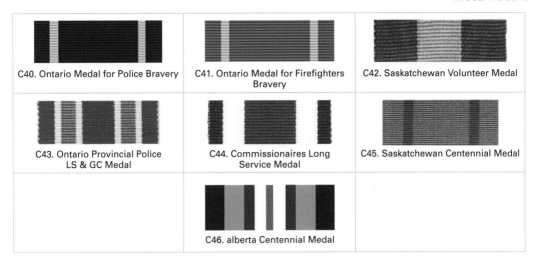

C40. Ontario Medal for Police Bravery	C41. Ontario Medal for Firefighters Bravery	C42. Saskatchewan Volunteer Medal
C43. Ontario Provincial Police LS & GC Medal	C44. Commissionaires Long Service Medal	C45. Saskatchewan Centennial Medal
	C46. alberta Centennial Medal	

NEW ZEALAND
MEDAL RIBBONS
(Not all shown to scale, see reference number for actual sizes)

NZ1. Victoria Cross for New Zealand

NZ2. New Zealand Cross with miniature emblem when worn alone

NZ3. Order of New Zealand

NZ4. NZ Order of Merit

NZ5. NZ Gallantry Star

NZ6. Queen's Service Order

NZ7. Gallantry Decoration

NZ8. Bravery Star

NZ9. Bravery Decoration

NZ10. Gallantry Medal

NZ11. Bravery Medal

NZ12. Queen's Service Medal

NZ12A. NZ Antarctic Medal

NZ12B. Distinguished Service Decoration

NZ13. Operational Service Medal

NZ14A. GSM 2002 (Solomon Islands)

NZ14B. GSM 2002 (Afghanistan) (primary)

NZ14B. GSM 2002 (Afghanistan) (secondary)

NZ14C. GSM 2002 (Iraq)

NZ14D. GSM 2002 (Timor-Leste)

NZ14E. GSM 2002 (Korea)

NZ15. NZ Service Medal 1946-49

NZ16. NZ General Service Medal (Warlike Operations)

NZ17. NZ General Service Medal (Non-Warlike Operations)

NZ18. East Timor Medal

NZ19. Special Service Medal (Nuclear Testing)

NZ19A. New Zealand Special Service Medal (Asian Tsunami)

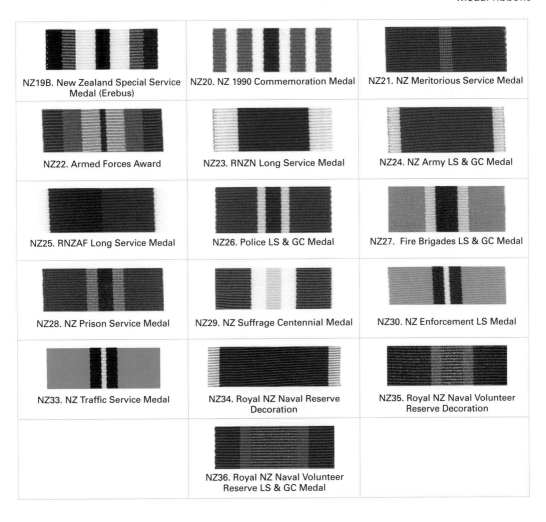

NZ19B. New Zealand Special Service Medal (Erebus)	NZ20. NZ 1990 Commemoration Medal	NZ21. NZ Meritorious Service Medal
NZ22. Armed Forces Award	NZ23. RNZN Long Service Medal	NZ24. NZ Army LS & GC Medal
NZ25. RNZAF Long Service Medal	NZ26. Police LS & GC Medal	NZ27. Fire Brigades LS & GC Medal
NZ28. NZ Prison Service Medal	NZ29. NZ Suffrage Centennial Medal	NZ30. NZ Enforcement LS Medal
NZ33. NZ Traffic Service Medal	NZ34. Royal NZ Naval Reserve Decoration	NZ35. Royal NZ Naval Volunteer Reserve Decoration
	NZ36. Royal NZ Naval Volunteer Reserve LS & GC Medal	

SOUTH AFRICAN MEDAL RIBBONS
(Not all shown to scale, see reference number for actual sizes)

SA1. Star of South Africa

SA2. Order of the Star of South Africa (Military) First Class

SA2. Order of the Star of South Africa Silver (Military) Second Class - *Neck ribbon*

SA2. Order of the Star of South Africa Silver (Military) Second Class - *Breast ribbon*

SA3. Castle of Good Hope

SA4. Louw Wepener Decoration

SA5. Van Riebeeck Decoration

SA6. Van Riebeeck Medal

SA7. Honoris Crux 1952

SA8. Louw Wepener Medal

SA9. Honoris Crux Decoration (Diamond)

SA9. Honoris Crux Decoration (Gold)

SA9. Honoris Crux Decoration (Silver)

SA9. Honoris Crux Decoration

SA10. Pro Virtute Decoration

SA11. Pro Virtute Medal

SA12. Ad Astra Decoration

SA13. The S.A.D.F. Cross (Army)

SA13. The S.A.D.F. Cross (Air Force)

SA13. The S.A.D.F. Cross (Navy)

SA13. The S.A.D.F. Cross (SA Medical Services)

SA14. Southern Cross Medal 1952

SA15. Southern Cross Decoration

SA16. Southern Cross Medal

SA17. Pro Merito Medal (1967)

SA18. Pro Merito Decoration (1975)

SA19. Pro Merito Medal (1975)

SA19. Pro Merito Medal (1986)

SA21. Chief of the SA Defence Force Commendation Medal (1974)

SA22. Military Merit Medal

SA23. Danie Theron Medal

SA24. Jack Hindon Medal

SA25. Commandant General's Medal

SA26. SADF Campion Shots Medal

SA27. Cadet Corps Champion Shot Medal

SA28. Union Medal

SA29. Permanent Force Good Service Medal

SA30. SA Defence Force Good Service Medal (Gold 30yrs)

SA30. SA Defence Force Good Service Medal (Silver 20yrs)

SA30. SA Defence Force Good Service Medal (Bronze 10yrs)

SA30. SA Defence Force Good Service Medal (Bronze/Commandos)

SA30. SA Defence Force Good Service Medal (Silver/Perm. Force)

SA30. SA Defence Force Good Service Medal (Gold/Citizen Force)

SA31. SADF Good Service Medal (40yrs)

SA32. John Chard Decoration

SA33. John Chard Medal

SA34. De Wet Decoration

SA34. De Wet Medal

SA36. Cadet Corps Medal

SA37. Pro Patria Medal

SA38. Southern African Medal

SA39. General Service Medal

SA40. Unitas Medal

SA42. SA Police Star for Outstanding Service (SOE)

SA43. SA Police Star for Merit

SA44. Police Medal for Faithful Service

SA45. SA Police Star for Faithful Service

SA46. SA Police Medal for Combating Terrorism	SA47. SA Police 75th Anniversary Medal	SA47A. SA Police Service Reconciliation and Amalgamation Medal
SA47B. SA Police Service Ten Year Commemoration Medal	SA48. Decoration for Valour	SA48A. Medal for Merit in the SA Prisons Service 1968
SA49. SA Prisons Service Star for Merit	SA50. SA Prisons Service Cross for Merit	SA51. SA Prisons Service Medal for Merit (NCO's)
SA51. SA Prisons Service Medal for Merit (Officers)	SA52. Faithful Service Medal, Prisons Department 1965	SA53. Medal for Faithful Service in the SA Prisons Service
SA54. SA Prisons Service Medal for Faithful Service (Bronze)	SA54. SA Prisons Service Medal for Faithful Service (Silver)	SA54. SA Prisons Service Medal for Faithful Service (Gold)

Index
of medals

Medal No.

Abyssinian War Medal 1867-68 124
Accumulated Campaign Service Medal 198B
Active Service Medal U26
Afghanistan Medal 1878-80 128
AFPS Medal U36
Africa General Service Medal 1902-56 161
Africa Police Medal for Meritorious Service 215
Africa Service Medal 1939-45 189
Africa Star 180
Air Crew Europe Star 179
Air Efficiency Award 270
Air Force Cross 35
Air Force Medal 57
Air Transport Auxiliary Lapel Badge 242H
Albert Medal 39
Allied Subjects Medal 64
Allied Ex-Prisoners of War Medal U9
Ally Sloper Medal L15A
Ambulance Service (Emergency Duties) Long Service
    and Good Conduct Medal 264A
Anglo-Boere Oorlog Medal 340
Answers Medal for Heroism L16
Anzac Commemorative Medal 356
Arabian Service Medal U23
Arctic Medal 1818-55 320
Arctic Medal 1875-76 321
Arctic Campaign Medal U7
Arctic Convoys Veteran Lapel Badge 242E
Armed Forces Veteran Lapel Badge 242C
Army Best Shot Medal 334
Army Cadet Force Anniversary Medal U5A
Army Emergency Reserve Decoration 238
Army Emergency Reserve Medal 239
Army Gold Cross 1806-14 95
Army Gold Medal 1806-14 97
Army Long Service and Good Conduct Medal 229
Army Meritorious Service Medal 210
Army of India Medal 1799-1826 104
Ashantee Medal 1873-74 126
Ashanti Medal 1900 160
Ashanti Star 1896 144
Association of Professional Fire Brigade Officers
    Long Service Medal 286A
Association of Chief Ambulance Officers Service
    Medal 264B
Atlantic Star 178
Australia Service Medal 1939-45 190
Automobile Association Cross 352
Automobile Association Medal 353
Badges of the Certificate of Honour 328/9
Bagur and Palamos Medal 1810 87
Baltic Medal 1854-55 118
Baronet's Badge 21
Bath, Most Honourable Order of the 4
Battle for Malta Medal U24
Belfast Harbour Police Medal 288C
Bevin Boys Lapel Badge 242F
Bevin Boys Medal U39
Binney Memorial Medal L45

Medal No.

Black Watch Medal U31
Bolton & District Humane Society Medal L33A
Board of Trade Rocket Apparatus Volunteer Long
    Service Medal 227
Bomber Command Medal U5
Border Service Medal U29
Boulton's Trafalgar Medal 1805 84
Boys' Brigade Cross for Heroism L28
Boys' Brigade Squad Medal 367A
Boys' Life Brigade Medal 367
British Empire Medal 19
British Empire, Medal of the Order of 17
British Empire, Most Excellent Order of the 16
British Fire Services Association Medal 286B
British Fire Services Association Meritorious Medal ....
    .... 286C
British Forces Germany Medal U15
British India, Order of 36
British Legion Medal 105A
British North Borneo Company's Bravery Cross 69
British North Borneo Company's Medal 1897 148
British North Borneo Company's Medal 1899-1900 ....
    .... 148A
British North Borneo Company's General Service
    Medal 1937–1941 176
British Nuclear Weapons Test Medal U22
British Red Cross Society Medal for War
    Service 171A
British South Africa Company Medal 1890-97 138
British War Medal 1914-20 168
Brunei General Service Medal 204A
Brunswick Medal for Waterloo 1815 100
Burma Gallantry Medal 53
Burma Medal 1824-26 91
Burma, Order of 37
Burma Police Medal 60
Burma Star 1942-45 182
Cadet Forces Commemorative Medal U37
Cadet Forces First Aid Medal U42
Cadet Forces Medal 262
Cameronians Medal U21
Campaign Service Medal 1962 (GSM) 198
Canada General Service Medal 1866-70 125
Canadian Forces Decoration 255
Canadian Memorial Cross 188A
Canadian Volunteer Service Medal 1939-47 188
Candahar-Ghuznee-Cabul Medal 1841-42 107
Cape Copper Company's Medal 1902 157
Cape of Good Hope GSM 1880-97 130
Capture of Ceylon Medal 1795–96 77
Capture of Louisburg Medal 1758 71
Capture of Rodrigues, Isle of Bourbon and Isle
    of France Medal 86
Carib War Medal 1773 72
Carnegie Hero Fund Medal L30
Carpathia and *Titanic* Medal L34
Central Africa Medal 1891-98 140
Ceylon, Capture of, 1795–96 Medal 77
Ceylon Coronation Medal 1902 304

Ceylon Diamond Jubilee Medal 1897........................ 298
Ceylon Fire Brigade Long Service and Good Conduct
    Medal.. 288
Ceylon Medal 1818.. 90
Ceylon Police Long Service and Good Conduct
    Medal 1925-34.. 276
Ceylon Police Long Service and Good Conduct
    Medal 1950-72.. 277
Ceylon Police Medal for Gallantry 278A
Ceylon Police Medal for Merit 278
Ceylon Volunteer Service Medal.............................. 172B
Cherry Medal.. U1
China War Medal 1840-42 110
China War Medal 1857-63 122
China War Medal 1900 158
Chinese Maritime Customs Service Medals..... 351A/B
Civil Defence Long Service Medal 264
Civilian Service Medal (Afghanistan).................... 204D
Coastguard Auxiliary Service Long Service
    Medal 227
Coastguard Commendation 228
Cold War Commemorative Medal U38
Colonial Auxiliary Forces Long Service Medal 247
Colonial Auxiliary Forces Decoration...................... 246
Colonial Fire Brigade Long Service Medal.............. 287
Colonial Fire Brigade Medal.. 62
Colonial Long Service and Good Conduct
    Medals... 248
Colonial Meritorious Service Medals...................... 212
Colonial Police Long Service Medal.......................... 274
Colonial Police Medal for Gallantry.......................... 61
Colonial Police Medal for Meritorious Service.......... 61
Colonial Prison Service Long Service Medal 289
Colonial Special Constabulary Long Service
    Medal 275
Commemorative Service Medal.............................. U41
Commonwealth Independence Medals.................... 341
Companion of Honour, Order of the.......................... 20
Conspicuous Gallantry Cross.................................... 30A
Conspicuous Gallantry Medal 44
Constabulary Medal for Ireland 58
Coorg Medal 1837 92
Cornwell Scout Badge L32A
Coronation Medals 1603–1838.......................291A–N
Coronation Medal 1902 301
Coronation Medal (Mayors and Provosts) 1902...... 302
Coronation Medal (Police) 1902................................ 303
Coronation Medal 1911 309
Coronation Medal (Police) 1911 310
Coronation Medal 1937 314
Coronation Medal 1953 315
Corporation of Glasgow Bravery Medal L37
Corps of Commissionaires Medal 362
CQD Medal L33
Crimea Medal 1854-56 119
Crown of India, Imperial Order of the...................... 11
Cyprus Military Police Long Service and Good
    Conduct Medal... 279
Dale Award L42
Davison's Nile Medal 1798.. 78
Davison's Trafalgar Medal 1805................................. 85
Deccan Medal 1778-84.. 73
Defence Medal 1939-45... 185
Defence of Gibraltar Medal 1783 74
Defence of Kelat-i-Ghilzie Medal 1842.................... 109
Defence of Ookiep... 157
Dekoratie voor Trouwe Dienst 339

Delhi Durbar Medal 1903.. 306
Delhi Durbar Medal 1911.. 312
Delhi Durbar Military Tournament Medal......... 312AA
Diamond Jubilee Medal 2012 .... 318A
Dickin Medal L44A
Distinguished Conduct Medal 41
Distinguished Conduct Medal (Colonial and
    Dominion) 42
Distinguished Conduct Medal (KAR and WAFF).... 43
Distinguished Flying Cross 34
Distinguished Flying Medal 56
Distinguished Service Cross 32
Distinguished Service Medal 54
Distinguished Service Order 27
Drummond Castle Medal L23
Dunkirk Medal U4
Earl St Vincent's Medal 1800 80
East and Central Africa Medal 1897-99.................... 147
East and West Africa Medal 1887-1900 137
East Indian Railway Medal......................................311A
Edward Medal (Industry).. 51
Edward Medal (Mines)... 50
Edward VII Medal for Science, Art and Music........ 323
Efficiency Decoration.. 236
Efficiency Medal 237
Efficiency Medal (South Africa) 254
Efficiency Medal (Army Emergency Reserve)......... 239
Egypt Medal 1801... 81
Egypt Medal 1882-89 131
Eliott's Defence of Gibraltar Medal 1779-83.............. 74
The Elizabeth Cross 194A
Ellice Islands Independence Medal........................... 341
Emden Medal...U2B
Emin Relief Expedition Star....................................... U1A
Empire Gallantry Medal 18
Empress of India Medal 1877 292
Erinpura and *Topaze* Medal..............................L35A
European Community Monitoring Mission
    Medal 206B
European Security & Defence Policy Service Medal.....
    ....206D
Fiji Independence Medal.. 341
Fire Brigade Long Service Medal.............................. 286
Florence Nightingale Medal 355
France and Germany Star 184
Gallantry Medallists' League Gold Medal for Bravery
    ....L47A
Garter, Most Noble Order of the............................... 1
GC & OS Lapel Badge ....242 I
General Gordon's Star for the Siege of
    Khartoum 133
General Service Cross.. U27
General Service Medal 1918-62 174
General Service Medal 1962 (CSM) 198
George Cross 26
George Medal 45
George Prince of Wales Medal 308B
Ghuznee Medal 1839 105
Gibraltar Defence Medals 1779-83............................ 74
Gilbert Islands Independence Medal 341
Girls' Life Brigade Medal.. 368
Glasgow Humane Society Medal L2
Golden Jubilee Medal 2002.. 318
Granton Medal for Zeal.. 371
Guelphic Order, Royal... 5
Guildhall Jubilee Medal 1935 ....313B
Guildhall Coronation Reception Medal 1911........ 309A

Guildhall Coronation Medal 1937 .... 314A
Gulf Medal 1990-91 204
Guyana Independence Medal 341
Gwalior Star 1843 112
Hanoverian Medal for Waterloo 1815 101
Hartley Colliery Medal L10
Highland Society's Medal for Egypt 1801 83
HMAS *Sydney* Medal U3A
Hong Kong Coronation Medal 1902 305
Hong Kong Diamond Jubilee Medal 1897 299
Hong Kong Disciplined Services Medal 281A
Hong Kong District Watch Force Merit Medal 280A
Hong Kond Military Service Corps Medal 280D
Hong Kong Plague Medal 1894 141
Hong Kong Police Medal for Merit 280
Hong Kong Royal Naval Dockyard Police Long
    Service Medal 281
Hong Kong Service Medal U14
Hors of Combat Medal U17
Humane Society of New Zealand Medals L26
Hundred of Salford Humane Society Medal L3
Hundred of Salford Humane Society Swimming
    Proficiency Medal L48
Hunza Nagar Badge 1891 139
Hyderabad Medal 1843 111
Imperial British East Africa Company's Medal 136
Imperial Chemical Industries Bravery Award L37A
Imperial Merchant Service Guild Medal L20
Imperial Service Medal 29
Imperial Service Order 28
Imperial Yeomanry Long Service & Good Conduct
    Medal 240
Indian Army Long Service & Good Conduct
    Medal 1888 244
Indian Army Long Service & Good Conduct
    Medal for Europeans 1848 243
Indian Army Meritorious Service Medal 1848 213
Indian Army Meritorious Service Medal 1888 214
Indian Distinguished Service Medal 52
Indian Empire, Most Eminent Order of the 8
Indian Mutiny Medal 1857-59 121
Indian Order of Merit 30
Indian Police Medal 59
Indian Recruiting Badge (George V) 331
Indian Recruiting Badge (George VI) 332
Indian Title Badge 327
Indian Volunteer Forces Officers' Decoration 245
Industrial Heroism, Order of L36
Interfet Medal 207B
International Conference on the Former Yoguslavia
    Medal 207A
International Submarine Service Medal U18
Iraq Active Service Medal 174A
Iraq Medal 204B
Iraq Reconstruction Service Medal 204C
Isle of Man Silver Jubilee Medal 313A
Italy Star 1943-45 183
Jamaica Independence Medal 341
Java Medal 1811 88

Jellalabad Medals 1841-43 108
Jersey Humane Society Medal L10A
Jordan Service Medal U13
Jubilee Medal 1887 293
Jubilee Medal (Police) 1887 294
Jubilee Medal 1897 295
Jubilee Medal (Mayors' and Provosts') 1897 296
Jubilee Medal (Police) 1897 297
Jubilee Medal 1935 313
Jubilee Medal 1977 316
Jubilee, Golden, Medal 2002 318
Jummoo and Kashmir Medal 1895 143
Kabul to Kandahar Star 1880 129
Kaisar-i-Hind Medal 38
Kelat-i-Ghilzie Medal 1842 109
Khartoum Star 133
Khedive's Star 1882-91 132
Khedive's Sudan Medal 1896-1908 146
Khedive's Sudan Medal 1910 165
Kimberley Medal 1899-1900 155
Kimberley Star 1899-1900 154
King Hussein Medal 203C
King's African Rifles Distinguished Conduct
    Medal 43
King's African Rifles Long Service and Good
    Conduct Medal 251
King's Badge for War Service 186A
King's and Queen's Messenger Badge 319
King's Medal for Courage in the Cause of
    Freedom 65
King's Medal for Native Chiefs 70
King's Medal for Service in the Cause of Freedom ... 66
King's Police Medal 1909 46
King's Police Medal (South Africa) 49
King's Police and Fire Service Medal 1940 46
King's South Africa Medal 152
Knight Bachelor's Badge 22
Korea Medal 1950-53 195
Kuwait Liberation Medals 1991 206
Lagos Diamond Jubilee Medal 299A
League of Mercy, Order of the 324
Liverpool Shipwreck & Humane Society Fire
    Medal L14
Liverpool Shipwreck & Humane Society General
    Medal L18
Liverpool Shipwreck & Humane Society Marine
    Medals L7
Liverpool Shipwreck & Humane Society Swimming
    Medal L15
Lloyd's Medal for Meritorious Services L17
Lloyd's Medal for Saving Life at Sea L6
Lloyd's Medal for Services to Lloyd's L35
Lloyd's War Medal for Bravery at Sea L39
London Passenger Transport Medal L43
London, Midland and Scottish Railway Medal L40
London & North Eastern Railway Gallantry
    Medal L44
Lord Mayor of London's Gold Medal for the
    Destruction of Zeppelin L15 .... U3
Louisburg Medal 1758 71
Lower Saxony Fire Fighting Medal 1975 .... U33
Maharajpoor Star 1843 112
Maharajah of Burdwan's Medal L12A
Maida Gold Medal 1806 96
Maidstone Typhoid Medal 366
Malawi Independence Medal 341
Malta George Cross Fiftieth Anniversary Medal 342

Malta Police Long Service and Good Conduct Medal 282
Marine Society Reward of Merit 369
Mauritius Police Long Service and Good Conduct Medals 282A/B
Meeanee Medal 1843 111
Memorial Plaque 172
Mercantile Marine War Medal 1914-18 169
Mercantile Marine Service Association Medal L11
Merchant Navy Medal ....
                        242JMerchant Naval Service Medal U8
Merchant Seafarers Veteran Lapel Badge 242D
Merit, Order of 15
Meritorious Service Medal (Army) 210
Meritorious Service Medal (Royal Air Force) 211
Meritorious Service Medal (Royal Navy) 208
Meritorious Service Medal of South Africa 216
Messina Earthquake Commemorative Medal 163A
Military Cross 33
Military General Service Medal 1793-1814 98
Military Medal 55
Militia Long Service and Good Conduct Medal 241
Mons Star 1914 166
Multinational Force & Observers Medal 205A
Mysore Medal 1790-92 75
Nassau Medal for Waterloo 1815 102
Natal Coronation Medal 1902 .... 305A
Natal Rebellion Medal 163
Native Chief's Medal 70
NATO Service Medals 206A
NATO Meritorious Service Medal 291AA
National Canine Defence League Medal L31A
National Emergency Medal 363
National Fire Brigades Union Medal 286AB
National Fire Brigade's Union Medal for South Africa 153A
National Fire Brigade's Association Long Service Medal 286AA
National Service League Medal U2A
National Service Medal U12
Naval Engineers' Good Conduct Medal 330
Naval General Service Medal 1793-1840 94
Naval General Service Medal 1915-62 173
Naval Gold Medal 1795-1815 93
Naval Good Shooting Medal 333
Nepaul Medal 1814-16 89
New Zealand Cadet District Medal 357
New Zealand Cross 25
New Zealand Long and Efficient Service Medal 257
New Zealand Medal 1845-47 123
New Zealand Medal 1860-66 123
New Zealand Memorial Cross 191A
New Zealand Police Long Service and Good Conduct Medal 283
New Zealand Territorial Service Medal 259
New Zealand Volunteer Service Medal 258
New Zealand War Service Medal 1939-45 191
Newfoundland Silver Star for Bravery L24
Newfoundland Volunteer War Service Medal 1939-45 194
Nigeria Independence Medal 341
Normandy Campaign Medal U6
North Africa Service Medal U20
Northern Ireland Home Service Medal 261B
Northern Ireland Prison Service Service Medal ... 288A
North West Canada Medal 1885 134
Ookiep, Defence of 157

Operation Vibratto Medal U30
Operational Service Medal 198A
Our Dumb Friends League Medal L31C
Pacific Star 1941-45 181
Pakistan Independence Medal 341
Papua New Guinea Independence Medal 341
PDSA Cross L31B
Permanent Forces of the Empire Beyond the Seas Long Service Medal 249
Picton's Defence of Gibralter Medal 74
Pingat Jasa Malaysia Medal 203B
Pluck Award for Heroism L21
Plym, Tamar, Lynher and Tavy Humane Society Medal L4A
Polar Medal 1904 322
Police Long Service and Good Conduct Medal 271
Port of Plymouth Swimming Association and Humane Society Medal L4B
Port Sunlight Order of Conspicuous Merit L26A
Prison Service Medal 288B
Punjab Medal 1848-49 114
Punniar Star 1843 112
Queen Alexandra's Children's Medal 312AB
Queen Alexandra's Imperial Military Nursing Service Cape Badge 325
Queen Alexandra's Imperial Military Nursing Service Reserve Cape Badge 325A
Queen Alexandra's Military Families Nursing Service Cape Badge 326A
Queen Alexandra's Royal Army Nursing Corps Cape Badge 326C
Queen's Fire Service Medal 1954 48
Queen's Gallantry Medal 63
Queen's Golden Jubilee Commemorative Medal U19
Queen's Medal for Champion Shots of the Royal Air Force 336
Queen's Medal for Champion Shots of the New Zealand Forces 337
Queen's Medal for Champion Shots of the Royal Navy and Royal Marines 335
Queen's Mediterranean Medal 1899-1902 151
Queen's Police Medal 1954 47
Queen's South Africa Medal 1899-1902 150
Queen's Sudan Medal 1896-98 145
Queen's Volunteer Reserves Medal 48A
Quiver Medal L25
Restoration of Peace Medal U10
Rhodesia Medal 1980 202
Rhodesian Independence Commemorative Medal .. U35
Rocket Apparatus Volunteer Long Service Medal . 227
Rodrigues, Capture of 86
Royal Air Force Boy Entrants Commemorative Medal U28
Royal Air Force Levies Long Service and Good Conduct Medal 269
Royal Air Force Long Service and Good Conduct Medal 268
Royal Air Force Meritorious Service Medal 211
Royal Bristol Volunteers Medal 1814 370
Royal Falkland Islands Police Jubilee Medal 279A
Royal Family Order 9
Royal Fleet Auxiliary Service Medal 264C
Royal Fleet Reserve Long Service and Good Conduct Medal 223
Royal Green Jackets Commemorative Medal U34
Royal Highland Fusiliers Medal U32

Royal Hong Kong Auxiliary Police Medal 280C
Royal Hong Kong Police Commemoration
    Medal 280B
Royal Hong Kong Regiment Disbandment
    Medal 254A
Royal Household Faithful Service Medals 217
Royal Humane Society Medals L1
Royal Humane Society Swimming Proficiency
    Medal L49
Royal Life Saving Society—Mountbatten Medal L50
Royal Marines Meritorious Service Medal 209
Royal Military Asylum Gold Conduct Medal 242B
Royal National Lifeboat Institution Decoration 365
Royal National Lifeboat Institution Medals.............L4
Royal Naval Auxiliary Service Medal 226
Royal Naval Auxiliary Sick Berth Reserve Long
    Service and Good Conduct Medal 224
Royal Naval Long Service and Good Conduct
    Medal 218
Royal Naval Meritorious Service Medal.................. 208
Royal Naval Reserve Decoration 219
Royal Naval Patrol Service Medal U16
Royal Naval Reserve Long Service and Good Conduct
    Medal 220
Royal Naval Volunteer Reserve Decoration............. 221
Royal Naval Volunteer Reserve Long Service and
    Good Conduct Medal.. 222
Royal Naval Volunteer (Wireless) Reserve Long
    Service and Good Conduct Medal 225
Royal Niger Company's Medal 135
Royal Norfolk Veterans Association Medal 376
Royal Observer Corps Medal 263
Royal Order of Victoria and Albert 10
Royal Red Cross 31
Royal Society for the Prevention of Cruelty to
    Animals Life Saving Medal L31
RSPCA Queen Victoria Medal................................ 368A
Royal Society for the Prevention of Cruelty to
    Animals Margaret Wheatley Cross L38
Royal Ulster Constabulary Service Medal................ 273
Royal Victorian Chain 14
Royal Victorian Medal 13
Royal Victorian Order.. 12
Royal Visit to the Colonies Medal 1901 .... 300A
Royal Visit to India Medal 1875 .... 292A
Royal Visit to India Medal 1905 .... 308A
Royal Visit to India Medals 1911-21 .... 312A-E
Royal Visit to Ireland Medal 1900........................... 300
Royal Visit to Ireland Medal 1903........................... 308
Royal Visit to Ireland Medal 1911 311
Royal Visit to Malta 1954..315B
Royal Visit to New Zealand Medal 315A
Royal Visit to Nigeria Medal 315C
Royal Visit to Scotland Medal 1903 307
Royal Visit to South Africa Medal 1947 ....314B
Royal Warrant Holders Association Medal.............. 364
Royal West Africa Frontier Force Long Service and
    Good Conduct Medal.. 250
St Andrews' Association Medal 374
St Christopher Nevis and Anguilla Independence
    Medal 341
St Jean d'Acre Medal 1840 106
St John Ambulance Brigade Medal for South Africa
    1899-1902 153
St John, Order of.. 23
St John Life Saving Medal.......................................L12
St John Service Medal 267
St Michael and St George, Most Distinguished
    Order of 6
St Patrick, Most Illustrious Order of 3

St Vincent Black Corps Medal 1795 76
St Vincent's Medal 1800... 80
Salford Humane Society Medals................................L3
Salvation Army Service Medal 375
Saudi Arabian Medal for the Liberation of Kuwait
    1991... 205
Saxe-Gotha-Altenburg Medal for Waterloo 1815 103
Scinde Medals 1843...111
Scout Association Gallantry Medals L32
Sea Cadet Gallantry Cross L46
Sea Cadet Gallantry Medal L47
Sea Gallantry Medal 67
Sea Gallantry Medal (Foreign Services).................... 68
Second China War Medal 1857-60 122
Second Cruiser Squadron Medal U2
Securicor Medal for Bravery 373
Securicor Medal for Long Service............................ 372
Seringapatam Medal 1799... 79
Service Medal of the Order of St John of
    Jerusalem 267
Seychelles Police Long Service and Good Conduct
    Medal 283A
Shanghai Fire Brigade Long Service Medal 345
Shanghai Jubilee Medal.. 344
Shanghai Municipal Council Emergency Medal..... 351
Shanghai Municipal Police Distinguished Conduct
    Medal 348
Shanghai Municipal Police Long Service Medal 349
Shanghai Municipal Special Constabulary Long
    Service Medal 350
Shanghai Volunteer Corps Long Service Medal...... 347
Shanghai Volunteer Corps Medal............................ 343
Shanghai Volunteer Fire Brigade Long Service
    Medal 346
Sheffield Society for the Recognition of Bravery
    Medal L27
Shipping Federation Medal for Meritorious
    Service 377
Shipwrecked Fishermen and Mariners Royal
    Benevolent Society Medals...................................L8
Shropshire Society Life Saving Medal.....................L13
Sierra Leone General Service Medal 204AA
Sierra Leone Independence Medal 341
Silver War Badge 172A
Sir Harry Smith's Medal for Gallantry 1851............ 116
Society for the Protection of Life from Fire
    Medals..L5
Solomon Islands Independence Medal.................... 341
South Africa Medal 1834-53.................................... 115
South Africa Medal 1877-79.................................... 127
South Africa Medal for War Service 1939-45........... 192
South Africa Permanent Force Long Service and Good
    Conduct Medal.. 253
South African Efficiency Medal 254
South African Medal For Korea 1950-53.................. 196
South African Memorial Plaque............................. 192A
South African Police Good Service Medal................ 284
South African Prison Service Long Service
    Medals...290/291
South African Railways & Harbour Police
    Long Service & Good Conduct Medal 285
South Atlantic Medal 1982....................................... 203
South Vietnam Campaign Medal 1964..................... 201
Southern Railway Meritorious Service Medal.........L41
Southern Rhodesia War Service Medal 1939-45 193
Soviet 40th Anniversary Medal............................. 203A
Special Constabulary Long Service Medal.............. 272
Special Reserve Long Service & Good Conduct
    Medal 242
Stanhope Medals..L1

Star of India, Most Exalted Order of the....................... 7
Suez Canal Zone Medal U11
Sudan Defence Force GSM 176A
Suffragette Medal 354
Sultan of Zanzibar's Medal 1896 149
Sultan's Medal for Egypt 1801 82
Sutlej Medal 1845-46 113
Tayleur Fund Medal L9
Territorial Army Centennial Medal............................ U40
Territorial Army Nursing Service Cape Badge......326B
Territorial Decoration 1908-30.................................... 233
Territorial Efficiency Medal 1921 235
Territorial Force Efficiency Medal 1908.................... 234
Territorial Force Imperial Service Badge 234A
Territorial Force War Medal 1914-18 171
Territorial Force Nursing Service Cape Badge........ 326
Thistle, Most Ancient and Most Noble Order of the 2
Tibet Medal 1903-04 162
Tientsin British Emergency Corps Medal...............281B
Today Gallantry Fund Medal L19
Trans-Jordan Frontier Force Long Service and Good
    Conduct Medal.. 252
Transport Medal 1899-1902....................................... 159
Turkish Crimea Medal 1854-56 120
Tynemouth Medal... L22
Uganda Independence Medal 341
Uganda Star 147A
Ulster Defence Regiment Long Service and Good
    Conduct Medal.. 230
Ulster Defence Regiment Medal 261
Ulster Defence Regiment Medallion 261A

Union of South Africa Commemoration Medal 338
Union of South Africa Meritorious Service Medal.. 216
United Nations Emergency Force Medal 199
United Nations Korea Medal 1950-53 197
United Nations Medals 207
Vanuatu Independence Medal 341
Victoria Cross... 24
Victoria Volunteer Long & Efficient Service Medal 256
Victory Medal 1914-19.. 170
Vietnam Medal 1964 200
Vietnam Logistic & Support Medal........................ 200A
Vietnam Veterans Medal U25
Voluntary Medical Service Medal............................. 266
Volunteer Officers Decoration.................................. 231
Volunteer Long Service and Good Conduct
    Medal... 232
Volunteer Reserves Service Medal 242A
War Medal 1939-45.. 186
Waterloo Medal 1815 99
West Africa Frontier Force Distinguished
    Conduct Medal.. 43
Western European Union Mission Service
    Medal 206C
Woltemade Medal 40
Womens Land Army & Timber Corps Lapel Badge. 242G
WRVS Long Service Medal.. 265
Yorkshire Imperial Yeomanry Medal 156
Zimbabwe Independence Medal 341
1914 Star.. 166
1914–15 Star... 167
1939–45 Star... 177

IRELAND

1916 Medal E1
1916–1966 "Survivors" Medal................................... E12
1921–71 "Survivors" Medal....................................... E13
Civil Medal for Bravery.. E4
Civil Defence Long Service Medal E20
Civil Defence Millenniium Medal E21
Distinguished Service Medal..................................... E3
The Emergency Service Medal 1939–46.................... E6
Garda Síochána Long Service Medal E16
Garda Síochána Golden Jubilee Medal E17

Garda Síochána Millennium Medal E18
Garda Síochána United Nations Service Medal E19
General Service Medal 1917–21.................................. E5
Merchant Service Medal 1939–46.............................. E7
Military Medal for Gallantry E2
Permanent Defence Forces Service Medal............... E8
Reserve Defence Forces Long Service Medal.......... E14
Scott Medal for Valor... E15
St John Ambulance Brigade of Ireland Service Medal E10
The United Nations Peacekeepers Medal................ E11

AUSTRALIA

ACT Community Policing Medal............................. A66
ACT Emergency Medal... A66A
ACT Community Protection Medal A66B
Active Service Medal 1945–1975............................... A24
Active Service Medal 1975–...................................... A27
Afghanistan Campaign Medal.................................. A29
Ambulance Service Medal A16
Anniversary of National Service Medal A48
Antarctic Medal... A20
Armistice Remembrance Medal................................ A37
Australian Cadet Forces Service Medal A45
Australian Defence Medal.. A46
Australian Sports Medal A38
Bravery Medal A11
British Commonwealth Occupation Forces A73

Canine Service Medal.. A76
Centenary Medal.. A39
Champion Shots Medal.. A47
Civilian Service Medal 1939–45 .... A36
Commendation For Brave Conduct A22
Commendation For Distinguished Service A23
Commendation For Gallantry A21
Commissioner's Unit Citation A61
Commissioner's Commendation for Bravery,
    QLD... A58
Commissioner's Commendation for Courage,
    NSW A59
Commissioner's Commendation for Service,
    NSW A60
Conspicuous Service Cross.. A8

Conspicuous Service Medal A19
Corrective Service Bravery Medal, NSW A54
Corrective Service Exemplary Conduct Cross, NSW A55
Corrective Service Long Service Medal, NSW A57
Corrective Service Meritorious Service Medal,
    NSW A56
Defence Long Service Medal A43
Defence Force Service Medal A40
Distinguished Service Cross A6
Distinguished Service Medal A12
Emergency Services Medal A17
Fire Service Medal A15
Front Line Service Medal A72
Gallantry, Medal For A10
Gallipoli Star A70
General Service Medals A32A
Group Citation For Bravery A51
Humanitarian Overseas Service Medal A35
Interfet Medal A28
Iraq Medal A30
Merchant Navy Commendation A69
Merchant Navy Service Cross A67
Merchant Navy Meritorious Medal A68
Meritorious Unit Citation A50
National Medal A44
Northern Territory Police Service Medal A66C
Nursing Service Cross A9
Order of Australia A3
Order of Australia, Medal of A18

Order of Australia, Member A7
Pingat Jasa Malaysia Medal A52
Police Bravery Medal, NSW A58
Police Medal A14
Police Overseas Service Medal A34
Police Valour Award, VA A65a
Police Valour Award, Queensland A64
Prison Service Officers Long Service Medal,
    Queensland A63
Prison Service Superintendent's Long Service Medal,
    Queensland A62
Public Service Medal A13
Queensland Police Service Medal A65
Queensland Flood & Cyclone Citation 2010–11 .. A65B
    Reserve Force Decoration A41
Reserve Force Medal A42
Rhodesia Medal A33
RSPCA Australia Purple Cross Award A74
Service Medal 1945–75 .... A31
Service Medal 1975– A32
Star of Courage A5
Star of Gallantry A4
Tobruk T Medal A71
Unit Citation for Gallantry A49
Valour, Cross of A2
Victoria Cross (Australia) A1
Vietnam Logistics & Support Medal A26
Vietnam Medal A25
War Dog Operational Medal A75

CANADA

125th Anniversary of the Confederation of Canada
    Medal C29
Alberta Centennial Medal C46
Alberta Emergency Service Medal C58
Alberta Law Enforcement Long Service Medal C59
Alberta Municipal Enforcement Long Service
    Medal C57
Alberta Order of Excellence C10
Canadian Banks Law Enforcement Award C64
Canadian Centennial Medal C27
Canadian Coastguard Exemplary Service
    Medal C36
Canadian Forces Decoration C32
Canadian Lifeboat Institution Medal C62
Canadian Peacekeeping Medal C26
Canadian Red Cross Society Order of the Red
    Cross C63
Canadian Volunteer Service Medal for Korea C19
Commissionaires Long Service Medal C44
Corrections Exemplary Service Medal C34
Cross of Valour C2
Edmonton Police Medal of Honour C61
Edmonton Police Service Medal of Valour C60
Emergency Medical Services Exemplary Service
    Medal C37
Fire Services Exemplary Service Medal C35
General Campaign Star C23
General Service Medal C24
Gulf and Kuwait Medal C20
Medal of Bravery C17
Medal of Military Valour C16
Meritorious Service Cross (Military and Civil
    Divisions) C15
Meritorious Service Medal (Military and Civil
    Divisions) C18
Moose Jaw Medal of Merit C65
L'Ordre National Du Quebec C6
Ontario Medal for Firefighters Bravery C41

Ontario Medal for Good Citizenship C39
Ontario Medal for Police Bravery C40
Ontario Provincial Police Long Service and Good
    Conduct Medal C43
Operational Service Medal C24A
Order of British Columbia C9
Order of Canada C3
Order of Manitoba C12
Order of New Brunswick C12A
Order of Newfoundland and Labrador C12C
Order of Nova Scotia C12B
Order of Merit of the Police Forces C5
Order of Military Merit C4
Order of Ontario C8
Order of Prince Edward Island Medal of Merit C11
Peace Officer Exemplary Service Medal C37A
Police Exemplary Service Medal C33
Queen Elizabeth II's Diamond Jubilee Medal
    (Canada) C30A
Queen Elizabeth II's Golden Jubilee Medal
    (Canada) ... C30
Queen Elizabeth II's Silver Jubilee Medal
    (Canada) C28
Queen's Ambulance Service Medal for Distinguished
    Service 264BB
Queen's Medal for Champion Shot in Canada C38
Royal Canadian Mounted Police Long Service
    Medal C31
Sacrifice Medal C18A
Saskatchewan Centennial Medal C45
Saskatchewan Order of Merit C7
Saskatchewan Volunteer Medal C42
Somalia Medal C21
South-West Asia Service Medal C22
Special Service Medal C25
Star of Courage C14
Star of Military Valour C13
Victoria Cross (Canada) C1

NEW ZEALAND

Air Force Long Service Medal NZ25
Antarctic Medal NZ12A
Armed Forces Award NZ22
Army Long Service & Good Conduct Medal NZ24
Bravery Decoration NZ9
Bravery Medal NZ11
Bravery Star NZ8
Commemoration Medal 1990 .... NZ20
Commendations NZ37–40
Customs Service Medal NZ32
Defence Service Medal NZ41
Distinguished Service Decoration NZ12B
East Timor Medal NZ18
Enforcement Long Service Medal NZ30
Fire Brigades LS & GC NZ27
Gallantry Decoration NZ7
Gallantry Medal NZ10
Gallantry Star NZ5
General Service Medals NZ14
General Service Medal (Peacekeeping Operations). NZ17
General Service Medal (Warlike Operations) NZ16

Meritorious Service Medal NZ21
Navy Long Service Medal NZ23
Naval Reserve Decoration NZ34
Naval Volunteer Reserve Decoration NZ35
Naval Volunteer Reserve LS & GC Medal NZ36
New Zealand Cross NZ2
Order of Merit NZ4
Order of New Zealand NZ3
Operational Service Medal NZ13
Police LS & GC Medal NZ26
Prison Service Medal NZ28
Queen's Service Medal NZ12
Queen's Service Order NZ6
Service Medal 1946–1949 .... NZ15
Special Service Medals NZ19
Suffrage Centennial Medal NZ29
Territorial Service Medal NZ22
Traffic Service Medal NZ31
Traffic Enforcement Long Service Medal NZ30
Victoria Cross (New Zealand) NZ1

SOUTH AFRICA

Ad Astra Decoration SA12
Cadet Corps Medal SA36
Cadet Corps Champion Shot Medal SA27
Castle of Good Hope Decoration SA3
Chief of the South African Defence Force
    Commendation Medal SA21
Commandant General's Medal SA25
Commandant General of the South African Defence
    Force Commendation SA20
Danie Theron Medal SA23
Decoration for Valour in the SA Prisons Service .. SA48
De Wet Decoration SA34
De Wet Medal SA35
Faithful Service Medal, Prisons Department SA52
General Service Medal SA39
Honoris Crux SA7
Honoris Crux Decoration SA9
Jack Hindon Medal SA24
John Chard Decoration SA32
John Chard Medal SA33
Louw Wepener Decoration SA4
Louw Wepener Medal SA8
Medal for Merit in the SA Prisons Service SA48a
Medal for Faithful Service in the SA Prisons
    Service SA53
Mention in Despatches SA41
Military Merit Medal SA22
Order of the Star of South Africa, Military SA2
Permanent Force Good Service Medal SA29
Police Medal For Combating Terrorism SA46
Police Medal For Faithful Service SA44
Police 75th Anniversary Medal SA47

Police Service Reconciliation and Amalgamation
    Medal SA47a
Police Service Ten Year Commemoration Medal SA47b
Police Star For Faithful Service SA45
Police Star For Merit SA43
Police Star For Outstanding Service SA42
Prisons Service Cross For Merit SA50
Prisons Service Medal For Merit 1980 .... SA51
Prisons Service Star For Merit SA49
Pro Merito Medal 1967 .... SA17
Pro Merito Medal 1975 .... SA19
Pro Merito Decoration SA18
Pro Patria Medal SA37
Pro Virtute Decoration SA10
Pro Virtute Medal SA11
SADF Champion Shots Medal SA26
SADF Crosses SA13
South Africa Prisons Service Medal For Faithful
    Service SA54
South African Defence Force Good Service Medal. SA30
South African Defence Force Medal for 40 Years
    Distinguished Conduct and Loyal 10Service SA31
Southern Africa Medal SA38
Southern Cross Decoration 1975 .... SA15
Southern Cross Medal 1952 .... SA14
Southern Cross Medal 1975 .... SA16
Star of South Africa SA1
Union Medal SA28
Unitas Medal SA40
Van Riebeeck Decoration SA5
Van Riebeeck Medal SA6